Hungary

THE ROUGH GUIDE

There are more than sixty Rough ~~~~~~~~~ ~~vering
destinations from Amsterd~~~~~

Forthcoming travel ~~~~~
Bali • Costa Rica • Goa • ~~~~~
Rhodes • Singapore • Vietnam

Rough Guide Reference Series
Classical Music • World Music

Rough Guide Phrasebooks
Czech • French • German • Greek • Italian • Spanish

D1353832

Rough Guide credits

Text editor:	Tanya Colbourne
Series editor:	Mark Ellingham
Editorial:	Martin Dunford, Jonathan Buckley, Graham Parker, Jo Mead, Samantha Cook, Alison Cowan, Amanda Tomlin, Annie Shaw, Lemisse al-Hafidh, Catherine McHale
Production:	Susanne Hillen, Andy Hilliard, Melissa Flack, Alan Spicer, Judy Pang, Link Hall, Nicola Williamson
Finance:	John Fisher, Celia Crowley, Simon Carloss
Publicity:	Richard Trillo (UK), Jean-Marie Kelly (US)
Administration:	Tania Hummel

Acknowledgements

Continuing **thanks** are due on this edition to Dan L Andin and Jill Denton for invaluable original research. Many thanks also to friends in *Magyarország*, especially Elisabeth (x 2), Előd, Emma, Gyöngyvér, Julie and Tourinform staff everywhere. On the production front, thanks to Link Hall for cool and patient typesetting, Matt Welton for his excellent maps, Pat Yale for typically precise proofreading, Jules for holding things together, and finally Tanya Colbourne, whose enlightened editing left no stone unturned.

We'd also like to thank the many **readers** of the guide who took time to annotate our errors, omissions and lapses of taste. The roll of honour (in alphabetical order) reads: John Allen; Martin Armstrong; Ruth Barber and Andrew Willis; Alan Bell, Paul Bethell; Gary M Bilkus; Mike Billington; John Braidwood; Norman Brooke; Martina Chamberlain; Kathryn J Chinn; Nate Clement; Judy Colin; Keith Crane; Rosemary Creeser; Gareth Davies, Attila Domby; T C Dunn; Julian Duplain; Kester J Eddy; Peter Foersom; R E Fricke; Danny Gallagher; Simon Gill; Susan Greenberg; Rebecca Grinter; Raoul Gunning, Martyn Harris; E. Huxter; Somló Katalin; Pat Kelly; Martin Kender; Julia Kerr; Sophia Lambert; Andrew Lawler; Margaret Levene; Richard Levy; Bill Lomax; Josphine Lönngren and Anders Gustafsson, Alastair Macaulay; Rose Marie and Herb Taylor; Maureen (who missed the fair at Kecskemét); John McClelland; Dave Major; Fred Nederhoed, Michael O'Hare & Sally Manders; Nicholas Parsons; Pamela Peters; Henry Race; Ed Raw; Dr L J Ray; Rodney Read & Jill Turner; Adam Roch; Keneth Ross; Byron Russell; Rosemary E Silva; Helen Sim; Martin Stafford; Karin Steininger; Krisztina Szendi-Horvath; Anne Tillyer; Rebecca Tracey, Hazel Walmsley; Dick Wash; Lorraine Weber. Apologies to anyone whose name we missed or whose signature we couldn't quite decipher.

This third edition published 1995 by Rough Guides Ltd, 1 Mercer St, London WC2H 9QJ.
Distributed by the Penguin Group:

Penguin Books Ltd, 27 Wrights Lane, London W8 5TZ
Penguin Books USA Inc., 375 Hudson Street, New York 10014, USA
Penguin Books Australia Ltd, 487 Maroondah Highway, PO Box 257, Ringwood, Victoria 3134, Australia
Penguin Books Canada Ltd, 10 Alcorn Avenue, Toronto, Ontario, Canada M4V 1E4
Penguin Books (NZ) Ltd, 182–190 Wairau Road, Auckland 10, New Zealand

Previous edition published in the US and Canada as *The Real Guide Hungary*.

Typeset in Linotron Univers and Century Old Style to an original design by Andrew Oliver.
Printed in the United Kingdom by Cox and Wyman Ltd (Reading).
Illustrations in Part One and Part Three by Edward Briant.
Basics illustration by Hilary McManus; Contexts illustration by Tommy Yamaha.

400p. Includes index.

A catalogue record for this book is available from the British Library.

ISBN 1-85828-123-7

Hungary

THE ROUGH GUIDE

Written and researched by
**Dan Richardson
and Charles Hebbert**

With additional research by
Helen Teitelbaum and Karen Davies

THE ROUGH GUIDES

CONTENTS

Introduction viii

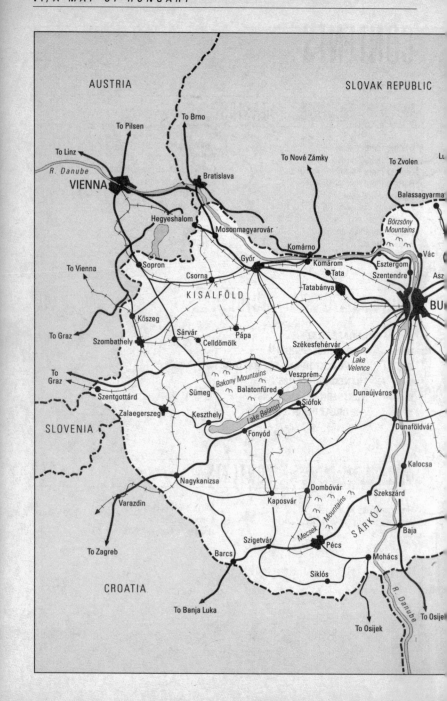

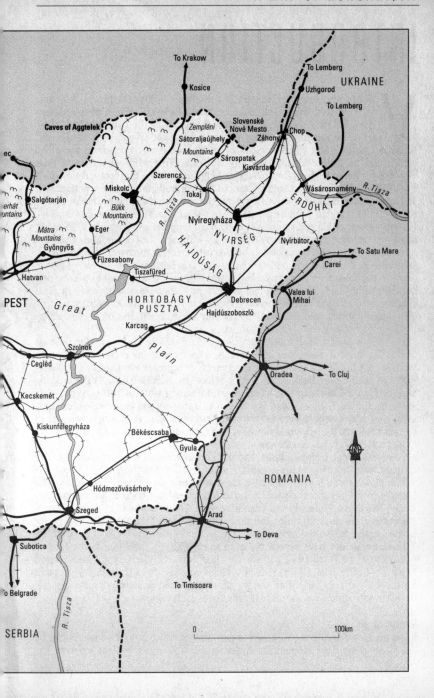

INTRODUCTION

Visitors who refer to **Hungary** as a Balkan country risk getting a lecture on how this small, landlocked nation of eleven million people differs from "all those Slavs". Hungary was likened by the poet Ady to a "river ferry, continually travelling between East and West, with always the sensation of not going anywhere but of being on the way back from the other bank"; and its people identify strongly with the West while at the same time displaying a fierce pride in themselves as Magyars – a race that transplanted itself from Central Asia into the heart of Europe. Any contradiction between nationalism and cosmopolitanism is resolved by what the Scottish expatriate Charlie Coutts called the Hungarian "genius for not taking things to their logical conclusion". Having embarked on reforming state socialism long before Gorbachev, Hungary made the transition to multi-party democracy without a shot being fired, while the removal of the iron curtain along its border set in motion the events leading to the fall of the Berlin Wall. The end of communism has hastened the spread of glossy western capitalism, and on arrival in Budapest your first impressions will be of a fast-developing and prosperous nation. However, there is another side to post-communist Hungary, and beyond the capital and Lake Balaton living standards have fallen sharply amongst many people, for whom the transition to democracy has brought very mixed blessings indeed.

Hungary's capital, **Budapest**, inspires a feeling of déjà vu. It's not just the vast Gothic parliament and other monuments of a bygone imperial era that seem familiar, but the latest fashions on the streets, or a poster advertising something that was all the rage back home a year before. In coffee houses, Turkish baths, and the fad for Habsburg bric-à-brac, there's a strong whiff of *Mitteleuropa* – that ambient culture that welcomed Beethoven in Budapest and Hungarian-born Liszt in Vienna. Meanwhile a wave of new clubs and restaurants and a burgeoning sex industry reflects the advent of nouveau riche entrepreneurs, and a massive influx of tourists and foreign investment.

After Budapest, **Lake Balaton** and the **Danube Bend** vie for popularity. The Balaton, with its string of brash resorts, styles itself as the "Nation's Playground," and enjoys a fortuitous proximity to the Badacsony wine-producing region. The Danube Bend has more to offer in terms of scenery and historic architecture, as do the **Northern Uplands** and **Transdanubia**. The beautiful old parts of Sopron, Győr and Pécs are, rightfully, the main attractions in Transdanubia, though for castle enthusiasts the Zempléni range and the lowlands of southern Transdanubia also have several treats in store; while in the Uplands the famous wine centres of Tokaj and Eger are the chief draw. On the **Great Plain** Szeged hosts a major festival, and its rival city, Debrecen, serves as the jumping-off point for the archaic Erdőhát region and the mirage-haunted Hortobágy *puszta*. See the **chapter introductions** for more details about each region.

When to go

Most visitors come in the summer, when nine or ten hours of sunshine can be relied on most days, sometimes interspersed with short, violent storms. The humidity that causes these is really only uncomfortable in Budapest, where the crowds don't help; elsewhere the **climate** is agreeable. Budapest, with its spring and autumn festivals, sights and culinary delights, is a standing invitation to come out of season. But other parts of Hungary have little to offer during the winter, and the weather doesn't become appealing until late spring. May, warm but showery, is the time to see the Danube Bend, Tihany or Sopron before everyone else arrives; June is hotter and drier, a pattern reinforced throughout July, August and September. There's little variation in **temperatures** across the country: the Great Plain is drier, and the highlands are wetter, during summer, but that's about as far as climatic changes go. The number of **tourists** varies more – the popular areas can be mobbed in summer, but rural areas receive few visitors, even during the high season.

AVERAGE DAYTIME TEMPERATURES											
	Jan	Feb	May	Apr	May	June	July	Aug	Sept	Oct	Nov	Dec
Budapest												
°F	29	32	42	53	61	68	72	70	63	52	42	34
°C	-2	0	6	12	16	20	22	21	17	11	6	1
Debrecen												
°F	27	31	41	51	60	66	70	68	61	51	41	32
°C	-3	-1	5	10	16	19	21	20	16	11	5	0

PART ONE

THE

BASICS

GETTING THERE FROM BRITAIN

Hungary is easily accessible from Britain by air, rail or road. Flying is the easiest option, with direct access from London and connections from most other British airports. Going by land involves rather a long haul, and you'll save little if anything by taking the train, although with an *InterRail* or *Eurail* pass you are able to make Hungary part of a wider European trip. Buses, on the other hand, can cost less than half the price of the plane. Other possible options include picking up discounted flights to Frankfurt or Vienna and continuing by land; or driving, a journey of over 1700 kilometres, best covered over a couple of days or more.

BY PLANE

Both *British Airways* and the Hungarian national airline, *Malév*, run daily **direct scheduled flights from London (Heathrow) to Budapest**, taking around 2hr 20min. While the full economy return fare costs in the region of £650, both airlines offer APEX fares of around £160–200: *Malév* is usually cheaper, but *BA* operates special offers out of season. APEX tickets must be booked and paid for at least 14 days in advance, you are required to stay at least one Saturday night, and confirmed bookings can't be changed. **Indirect flights** with other airlines (including *Air France*, *Austrian Airlines*, *CSA*, *KLM*, *LOT*, *Lufthansa*, *Sabena*, *Swissair* and *Sabena*) are also possibilities, but hardly worth the effort since apart from taking longer, they will

almost certainly work out quite a bit more expensive.

There are no direct scheduled services from any **other British airports**, but most offer connecting flights to Heathrow. BA has add-on fares of £110–160 on top of the return fare from London; while from Edinburgh, Glasgow, Leeds and Teesside, you can buy a through ticket with *British Midland* and *Malév* for an add-on fare of just over £100, though this is not available from the airlines and must be bought from an agent such as *Danube Travel* or *Intra Travel* (see below). From regional airports served by *Air France*, *Air UK*, *KLM*, *Lufthansa* or *Sabena*, you can avoid London completely, changing planes in Europe instead (indeed, from Birmingham, which has no flights to London, this is your only option). Tickets to Budapest bought from these airlines themselves will cost upwards of £400 return, but can be obtained at more reasonable prices from *Bridgwater Travel* and *Regent Holidays* (see below).

A number of **specialist tour operators** also handle flights from the UK to Hungary, and you can save a lot of time, effort and money by calling these first. *Hungarian Air Tours* sometimes has winter special offers at around £150 return, in addition to selling regular *Malév* tickets; they also sell one-way tickets, should you want them, from £130. *Danube Travel* has APEX returns with *Malév* at £155–210, depending on season, and add-on fares of around £100 with *British Midland* from some regional airports. *Bridgwater Travel* sometimes operates charters from Gatwick and also offers good-value tickets with European airlines from regional UK airports, as do *Regent Holidays*; *Intra Travel* and *Canterbury Travel* are also worth trying. For addresses, phone numbers and more details of all these companies, see the box on p.5.

For the very cheapest deals, *STA Travel* and *Campus Travel*, both with branches around the country, are highly reliable, and offer special discount deals for **students and under-26-year-olds**. Although **charter flights** to Hungary are not common, *STA*, *Bridgwater Travel* and *Attila Tours* do occasionally offer them, usually in summer, out of London Gatwick, at prices of around £150 return.

Another possibility is to buy a bargain **flight to Frankfurt or Vienna** and continue from there, but of course you'll still have the expense of travelling to and from Hungary. In London, check the ads in the *Evening Standard* and *Time Out*; in Manchester try *City Life*, and elsewhere look in local listings magazines or the classified sections of the Sunday newspapers. The *German Travel Centre*, 403–409 Rayners Lane, Harrow, Middlesex HA5 5ER (☎0181/429 2900) has round-trips from London to Frankfurt starting at £85 in winter, and, while flights to Vienna are likely to be pricier, you may find a special offer or last-minute deal. There are also direct flights to either city from other UK airports.

Finally, note that you will have to add **airport departure tax** to all these prices, currently £10 in the UK, and around £5.50 in Hungary.

PACKAGE HOLIDAYS

The list of addresses and sample **package holidays** given below is merely a small selection of what's available. Send off for brochures if you're interested, and compare the various deals carefully, since there are variations in seasonal prices and accommodation amongst the various companies. Unless stated otherwise, prices detailed below are per person sharing the cheapest available double room during the high season, and include return flights and airport tax. Expect add-ons of around £95 if flying from UK airports other than London.

BY TRAIN

Travelling **by train**, the shortest journey from London's Victoria Station takes about 25 hours, including the ferry crossing, and fares are generally more expensive than flights. However, stopovers on the way are possible – in the Netherlands, Germany, the Czech Republic or Slovakia – and prices are more attractive if you're

AIRLINES

Air France, 177 Piccadilly, London W1Z 0LX (☎0181/742 6600).

Air UK, Stansted Airport (☎0345/666777).

Austrian Airlines, 10 Wardour St, London W1V 4BJ (☎0171/434 7300).

British Airways, 156 Regent St, London W1R 5TA (☎0171/434 4700).

British Midland Airways, Donington Hall, Castle Donington, Derby DE74 2SB (☎0345/554554).

ČSA, 72 Margaret St, London W1 (☎0171/255 1898).

KLM, Plesman House, 190 Great South West Rd, Feltham, Middlesex (☎0181/750 9000). TW14 9RL

LOT, 313 Regent St, London W1R 7PE (☎0171/580 5037).

Lufthansa, 10 Old Bond St, London W1X 4EN (☎0181/750 3500).

Malév, 10 Vigo St, London W1X 1AJ (☎0171/439 0577).

Sabena, 10/18 Putney Hill, London SW15 6AA (☎0181/780 1444).

Swissair, Swiss Centre, 10 Wardour St, London W1V 4BJ (☎0171/434 7300).

INDEPENDENT TRAVEL SPECIALISTS

Campus Travel, 52 Grosvenor Gardens, London SW1W 0AG (☎0171/730 3402); 541 Bristol Rd, Selly Oak, Birmingham B29 6AU (☎0121/414 1848); 39 Queen's Rd, Bristol B58 1QE (☎0117/929 2494); 5 Emmanuel St, Cambridge CB1 1NE (☎01223/324283); 53 Forest Rd, Edinburgh EH1 2QP (☎0131/225 6111); 166 Deansgate, Manchester M3 3FE (☎0161/833 2046); 105–106 St Aldates, Oxford OX1 1DD (☎01865/258000). *Student/youth travel specialists, with branches also in YHA shops and on university campuses all over Britain.*

Council Travel, 28a Poland St, London W1 (☎0171/437 7767). *Flights and student discounts.*

South Coast Student Travel, 61 Ditchling Rd, Brighton BN1 4SP (☎01273/570226). *Student experts but plenty to offer non-students as well.*

STA Travel, 74 Old Brompton Rd, London SW7 3LH (☎0171/581 4132); 25 Queen's Rd, Bristol B58 1QE (☎0117/929 4399); 38 Sidney St, Cambridge CB2 3HX (☎01223/66966); 75 Deansgate, Manchester M3 2BW (☎0161/834 0668); 36 George St, Oxford OX1 2AQ (☎01865/792800); and personal callers at 117 Euston Rd, London NW1 2SX (☎0171/937 9921); 88 Vicar Lane, Leeds LS1 7HJ (☎0113/244 9212); and offices at the universities of Birmingham, London, Kent and Loughborough. *Discount fares, with particularly good deals for students and young people.*

Travel Bug, 597 Cheetham Hill Rd, Manchester M8 5EJ (☎0161/721 4000). *Large range of discounted tickets.*

SPECIALIST TOUR OPERATORS

Attila Tours, 36a Kilburn High Rd, London NW6 5UA (☎0171/372 0470). Bargain holidays: a week's accommodation on a Budapest campsite and bus travel to and from Hungary for around £125 (May–Sept). Buses also run during winter (£80–100 return), and charter flights are sometimes available, too.

Bike Tours, PO Box 75, Bath BA1 1BX (☎01225/480130). Well-run cycling tours, sometimes covering Hungary.

Bridgwater Travel, 217 Monton St, Manchester M30 9PN (☎0161/707 8547). Packages (city breaks, bus tours) plus flight-only deals from London, Manchester and other UK airports.

Canterbury Travel, 42 High St, Northwood Middlesex HA6 1BL (☎01923/822388). Pricey Budapest city breaks (around £380–460 for 3–7 nights) and combinations of Budapest with Vienna, Prague or Warsaw from £700 and upwards.

Crystal Holidays, Crystal House, The Courtyard, Arlington Rd, Surbiton, Surrey KT6 6BW (☎0181/390 9900). City breaks (£349–555) and twin-centre (with Budapest or Vienna) deals.

Danube Travel, 6 Conduit St, London W1R 9TG (☎0171/493 0263). Budapest city breaks from £300–400, with the option of staying in a pension (£320–420) or with a Hungarian family (£275–320); plus 7-night spa holidays or 9-day bus tours (for under £800) and city breaks combining Budapest with Vienna or Prague.

Hungarian Air Tours, 3 Heddon St, London W1R 7LE (☎0171/437 9405). Offers 3- to 7-night Budapest city breaks (£299–376); week-long spa holidays from around £1200–1350; the Budapest Spring Festival (3 nights, £349); sailing packages (from around £600); and golf weekends (£439).

Intra Travel, 44 Maple St, London W1P 5GD (☎0171/323 3305). Full range of holidays, including 3- to 7-night Budapest city breaks (under £400); 3-night two-centre holidays (Budapest with Pécs, Sopron, Eger or Lake Balaton) from under £450; 12-day tours (around £650 by train, £820 with car rental); and 7-night combinations of Budapest with Vienna (£599), Prague (£549), or both (£795).

Martin Randall Travel, 10 Barley Mow Passage, London W4 4PH (☎0181/742 3355). Art and architecture tours on specific summer dates with expert guides: 4 nights in Budapest from £695, 8-day tour around £900.

New Millennium Holidays, 20 High St, Solihull, West Midlands B91 3TB (☎0121/711 2232). Week-long holidays near Hévíz in the Balaton region for as little as £129, Budapest from £149, or two-centre holidays from £164. Return transport is by bus.

Prospect Music and Art Tours, 454 Chiswick High St, London W4 5TT (☎0181/995 2151). Fourteen-day spring tours for the music festival.

Regent Holidays, 15 John St, Bristol BS1 2HR (☎0117/921 1711). Eastern European specialists offering tailor-made touring itineraries.

Thermalia Travel, 12 New College Parade, Finchley Rd, London NW3 5EP (☎0171/483 1898). Spa holiday specialists offering holidays at thermal resorts in Budapest and around the country from about £650 for 7 nights; plus beauty, fitness and slimming courses, tennis for beginners, golf, or sailing.

a student, under 26 or over 60. If you have an *InterRail* (see below) or *Eurail* (p.11) train pass, you can take in Hungary as part of a wider rail trip around Europe.

Canadian, Australian and New Zealand passport-holders considering this journey should be aware that they will need **transit visas** in order to get through the Czech Republic and Slovakia, which are best obtained in advance

TICKETS AND PASSES

A standard second-class London to Budapest **return ticket** costs £271–287 (depending on whether you go via Ostend or Paris), on top of which you'll probably want to reserve a couchette (£12). If you are **under 26**, a *BIJ* ticket to Budapest, available through *Eurotrain* or *Wasteels* (see box below), costs £212–219, depending on your route. *Wasteels* also offers reduced tickets for over-26-year-olds starting at £222 return. Both regular and *BIJ* tickets have two months' return validity; stopovers are allowed as long as you stick to the prescribed route. Through fares are not currently available for travel via the Channel Tunnel, though they should soon become so: until then, the only option is to take the *Eurostar* service to Brussels (standard return, £155; £95 if booked in advance), and buy an onward ticket from there.

Better value by far is to buy an **InterRail pass**, available to anyone resident in participating European countries for six months (the North American equivalent is called *Eurail*, for details of which see p.11). You can buy *InterRail* passes from *British Rail* (or some travel agents) and the pass offers unlimited travel on a zonal basis on up to 25 European rail networks. The only extras you pay are supplements on certain express trains, plus half-price fares in Britain (or the country of issue) and on the cross-Channel ferries. To reach Hungary from the UK you'll need a pass valid for at least three zones; Hungary is zoned with Poland, the Czech Republic, Slovakia, Croatia, Romania and Bulgaria. Prices are currently £229 for a three-zone one-month pass if you're under 26 (£249 for all zones) and £269 for the over-26 version which, due to restrictions, is only valid in certain countries (the Netherlands, Germany and points east). For under-26s, an alternative is *Eurotrain's* **Eastern Explorer** ticket (£240), valid for a two-month circuit of cities such as Berlin, Prague and Budapest.

Finally, anyone over 60 and holding a British Rail Senior Citizen Railcard, can buy a **Rail Europe Senior Card**, which grants reductions of approximately 30 percent on European rail fares and sea crossings. Ask at any *British Rail* station or some travel agents for details.

BY BUS

Buses are an economical alternative to taking the train from **London to Budapest**, particularly if you're over 26. The cheapest deals are offered by *Attila Travel* (see also "Specialist Tour Operators" above) which charges £100 for a return ticket; journey time is around 26 hours. The only other company plying the route is *Eurolines*, which runs a weekly service from Victoria Coach Station direct to Györ and Budapest (around 31hr), and a twice-weekly service (up to five times weekly in summer) to Frankfurt, for a connection to Györ, Budapest and Siófok (total journey time to Budapest, 35hr). A return ticket costs £119 or £109 for under-25s.

BY CAR: THE FERRIES AND LE SHUTTLE

If you have the time and inclination, **driving to Hungary** can be a pleasant proposition. Realistically, though, it's only worth considering

if you are going to travel in Hungary for an extended period, or want to take advantage of various stopovers en route. If Budapest is your main goal, you'd be better off flying and renting a car once you're there.

It's important to plan ahead. The *Automobile Association* (AA) provides a comprehensive service offering general advice on all facets of driving to Hungary; their European Route Service (☎01256/20123) can provide a detailed printout of a route to follow. Driving licence, vehicle registration documents and insurance are essential; a Green Card is recommended.

CROSSING THE CHANNEL

The *Le Shuttle* service through the **Channel Tunnel** doesn't significantly affect travel times for drivers to Hungary, though it does of course speed up the cross-Channel section of the journey. There are trains 24 hours a day, carrying cars, motorcycles, buses and their passengers, and taking 35 minutes between Folkestone and Calais. The Channel Tunnel entrance is off the M20 at junction 11A, just outside Folkestone, and *Le Shuttle* has 21 services daily, including one every hour or so throughout the night. Tickets are available through *Le Shuttle's* Customer Services Centre or from your local travel agent, but because of the frequency of the service, you don't have to buy a ticket in advance. Fares are calculated per car, regardless of the number of passengers: the standard one-way fare is currently £107–154, depending on season (peak period is July and August).

The alternative cross-Channel options for most travellers are the conventional **ferry or**

CROSS-CHANNEL/NORTH SEA INFORMATION

Hoverspeed, Dover (☎01304/240202). *Dover and Folkestone to Boulogne and Calais by hovercraft or catamaran.*

Le Shuttle, Customer Services Centre, PO Box 300, Folkestone, Kent (☎0990/353535). *Information and ticket sales.*

North Sea Ferries, Hull (☎01482/377177). *Hull–Zeebrugge/Rotterdam.*

P&O European Ferries, Dover (☎01304/203388); Portsmouth (☎01705/772244); London (☎0181/575 8555). *Dover–Calais , Portsmouth–Le Havre, Felixstowe–Zeebrugge.*

Sally Line, Ramsgate (☎01843/595522); London (☎0171/409 2240). *Ramsgate–Ostend/Dunkerque.*

Stena Sealink Line, Ashford (☎01233/647047). *Dover–Calais, Newhaven–Dieppe, Harwich–Hoek van Holland.*

---

hovercraft links between Ramsgate and Ostend (the most direct route); or from Dover, Folkestone, Ramsgate, Newhaven and Portsmouth to France; Felixtowe to Zeebrugge; Harwich and Sheerness to Holland; or Hull to Zeebrugge and Rotterdam. Ferry prices vary according to the time of year and, for motorists, the size of your car. The Ramsgate–Ostend run, for example, starts at about £133 standard return low season, £196 high season (more on the busiest weekends of the year) for a car carrying three to five passengers. Foot passengers should be able to cross the Channel for about £22 each way year round (£6–9 more by jetfoil); taking a motorbike costs from £40–80 return.

THE DRIVING ROUTE

The most direct **route** from Ostend to Budapest runs via Brussels, Aachen, Cologne, Frankfurt, Nürnberg, Linz and Vienna. It's a distance of 1500km, and you shouldn't bank on driving it in under 36 hours. To avoid the long queues at Hegyeshalom and other main border crossings over summer, consider entering Hungary instead from Deutsch-Kreutz, just south of Eisenstadt. See under "Driving", in the *Getting Around* section below, for information about licences, insurance and driving inside Hungary. **Hitching** along the same route can take up to three days, so you'd be wise to pack rainwear, a tent, a good road map, some Deutschmarks and/or food. Rather than risk the lifts, you may instead want to contact *Freewheelers*, 25 Low Friar St,

---

CONNECTIONS FROM CONTINENTAL EUROPE

Flights
The cost of direct **flights from other European cities** to Budapest isn't always proportionate to their proximity to Hungary. However, it's certainly worthwhile checking out flight prices with *Malév, Air France, KLM, Alitalia* or *Lufthansa* in any country.

Trains
There are two daily trains **from Paris** (Gare de l'Est), both taking roughly 21 hours to reach Keleti Station in Budapest. Munich, Frankfurt and Berlin are the main points of departure **from Germany**; Frankfurt to Budapest (two trains a day) takes around 11 hours. Travellers coming **from the Czech Republic** have a choice of half a dozen trains from Prague via Bratislava (Canadians, Australians and New Zealanders are among those requiring transit visas for Slovakia), while Warsaw, Kraków and Czestochowa are the points of departure **from Poland**. Most of the dozen or so services **from Vienna** leave from the Westbahnhof, arriving at Keleti Station three to four hours later. If you're coming back the same way, it's worth buying a return ticket in Vienna, as one-way tickets cost more in Hungary. On some trains from Austria you can exchange money or travellers' cheques after crossing the Hungarian border, saving you from queuing at an exchange desk in one of the main Budapest stations.

Hydrofoils
Although the frequency of **hydrofoils from Vienna** varies seasonally, the journey to Budapest always takes around four and a half hours. Departures are at 9am daily during the low season (April & mid-Sept to Oct), 8am and 2.30pm daily from May to mid-September, but check in Vienna, as schedules may change. In Vienna, tickets are available from *Ibusz* (I. Krugerstrasse 26; ☎43 1/515-55) or the office of the Austrian company *DDSG* (Praterkai, II. Mexiko Platz 8), where the hydrofoils depart. A one-way ticket costs about 750 schillings/£45/US$68; it's 1100 schillings return. Make bookings at least 24 hours in advance.

Newcastle-upon-Tyne NE1 5UE (☎0191/222 0090), which matches passengers and drivers for lifts across the UK and to Europe.

Passengers pay a small annual fee to join and then a recommended fuel contribution direct to the driver.

GETTING THERE FROM IRELAND

There are no direct flights from Ireland to Hungary, and consequently all air journeys involve changing planes, normally in London.

From Dublin to Budapest, you can take *Aer Lingus* to Heathrow and then a *BA* flight from there or, alternatively, *British Midland* and then *Malév*. Standard APEX return fares start at around IR£373 from Dublin, IR£413 from Shannon.

From Belfast, flights are also via London, either with *BA* all the way, or *British Midland* to Heathrow, then *Malév*. A through ticket to Budapest, bought from *BA*, costs £277–317, but lower prices are generally available fron *USIT* in Belfast, *STA Travel* or *Danube Travel* in London, or possibly (flying via Europe) with *Bridgwater Travel* in Manchester. British-based package tour operators also usually offer the option of flying from Belfast, with an add-on fare of around £95.

For **youth and student discount fares** in both the Republic and the North, the best first stop is *USIT* (see below for address). From Dublin, you can expect to pay IR£235–260, depending on the season, around IR£15 more from Shannon. From Belfast, prices are around £265–305 with *BA*, with occasional special winter offers for around £240 return.

Travelling to London by land and sea may save you a little money, but on the whole it's rarely worth the time and effort. Buying a *Eurotrain* boat-and-train ticket to London will slightly undercut the plane fares, but by this time you're starting to talk about a journey of days not hours to reach Budapest.

FLIGHTS, PACKAGES AND TOURS FROM IRELAND

Delta Travel, 10 Malahide Rd, Artana, Dublin 5 (☎01/874 7666). *Occasional one-off packages.*

Go Holidays, 12 Upper O'Connell St, Dublin 1 (☎01/874 4126). *City breaks in Budapest and other holidays.*

Terry Flynn Travel, 47 The Quay, Waterford (☎051/72126). *Packages and flights.*

Thomas Cook, 118 Grafton St, Dublin (☎01/677 1721). *Mainstream package holiday and flight agent, with occasional discount offers.*

USIT. Branches at: Aston Quay, O'Connell Bridge, Dublin 2 (☎01/679 8833); 10–11 Market Parade, Cork (☎021/270 900); Fountain Centre, College St, Belfast (☎01232/324073). *Student and youth travel specialist.*

AIRLINES

Aer Lingus, 41 Upper O'Connell St, Dublin 1 (☎01/844 4777); 46–48 Castle St, Belfast (☎01232/245151); 2 Academy St, Cork (☎021/274331).

British Airways, 60 Dawson St, Dublin (☎0800/626747); Fountain Centre, College St, Belfast (☎0345/222111).

GETTING THERE FROM NORTH AMERICA

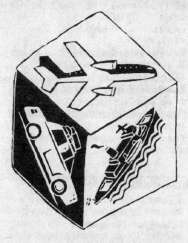

The quickest way to reach Hungary from the US or Canada is to fly to Budapest, on a one- or two-stop direct flight via another European city; there are no non-stop flights. Direct flights are comparatively expensive, however, so you might be better off flying to London (or Paris, Frankfurt or Vienna) and making your way overland from there (see "Getting There from Britain", above, for details). If you're planning to see Hungary as part of a wider European rail tour, then consider also buying a *Eurail* pass before you leave home.

SHOPPING FOR TICKETS

Barring special offers, the cheapest fare is usually an **Apex** ticket, although with these you have to book – and pay – at least 21 days before departure, spend at least seven days abroad (maximum stay three months), and you tend to get penalized if you change your schedule. There are also winter **Super Apex** tickets, sometimes known as "Eurosavers" – slightly cheaper than an ordinary Apex, but limiting your stay to between 7 and 21 days. Some airlines also issue **Special Apex** tickets to people younger than 24, often extending the maximum stay to a year; and many airlines offer youth or student fares to **under 25s**. It's worth remembering that most cheap return fares involve spending at least one Saturday night away and

that many will only give a percentage refund if you need to cancel or alter your journey; check the restrictions carefully before buying a ticket.

You can normally cut costs further by going through a **specialist flight agent** – either a **consolidator**, who buys up blocks of tickets from the airlines and sells them at a discount, or a **discount agent**, who wheels and deals in blocks of tickets offloaded by the airlines, and often offers special student and youth fares and a range of other travel-related services such as travel insurance, rail passes, car rentals, tours and the like. Bear in mind, though, that penalties for changing your plans can be stiff. Some agents specialize in **charter flights**, which may be cheaper than anything available on a scheduled flight, but again departure dates are fixed and withdrawal penalties are high (check the refund policy). If you travel a lot, **discount travel clubs** are another option – the annual membership fee may be worth it for benefits such as cut-price air tickets and car rental.

Don't automatically assume that tickets purchased through a travel specialist will be cheapest – once you get a quote, check with the airlines and you may turn up an even better deal. Be advised also that the pool of travel companies is swimming with sharks – exercise caution and *never* deal with a company that demands cash up front or refuses to accept payment by credit card.

Regardless of where you buy your ticket, the **fare** will depend on the season, and will be highest from around June to September. Note also that flying on weekends ordinarily adds $50 to the round-trip fare; **prices quoted below assume midweek travel**.

FROM THE US

If saving time is more important than finding the cheapest fare, you can get to Budapest from most US cities in around fifteen hours. Services are on a variety of airlines, including *Malév*, the Hungarian national airline, which flies via Frankfurt. Schedules and routings are subject to change, but the last leg of the journey is likely to be on *Malév* no matter which airline you buy your ticket from.

APEX fares are virtually identical on all carriers. Low-season midweek return fares to

AIRLINES IN NORTH AMERICA

Air France (in US, ☎1-800/237-2747; in Canada, ☎1-800/667-2747).

American Airlines (☎1-800/433-7300).

British Airways (in US, ☎1-800/247-9297; in Canada ☎1-800/668-1059).

ČSA Czechoslovak Airlines (☎1-800/223-2365 or ☎1-800/628-6107).

Delta Airlines (domestic, ☎1-800/221-1212; international, ☎1-800/241-4141; in Canada, call directory inquiries, ☎1-800/555-1212, for local toll-free number).

KLM (in US, ☎1-800/374-7747; in Canada, ☎1-800/361-5073).

LOT Polish Airlines (in US, ☎1-800/223-0593; in Canada, ☎1-800/361-1017).

Lufthansa (in US, ☎1-800/645-3880; in Canada, ☎1-800/563-5954).

Malév Hungarian Airlines (East Coast: ☎1-800/223-6884; West Coast ☎1-800/262-5380).

SAS (☎1-800/221-2350).

Swissair (in US, ☎1-800/221-4750; in Canada, ☎1-800/267-9477).

TWA (domestic, ☎1-800/221-2000; international, ☎1-800/892-4141).

United Airlines (domestic, ☎1-800/241-6522; international, ☎1-800/538-2929).

DISCOUNT TRAVEL COMPANIES IN NORTH AMERICA

Air Brokers International
323 Geary St, Suite 411, San Francisco, CA 94102 (☎1-800/883-3273).
Consolidator.

Air Courier Association
191 University Boulevard, Suite 300, Denver, CO 80206 (☎303/278-8810).
Courier flight broker.

Council Travel
Head Office: 205 E 42nd St, New York, NY 10017 (☎1-800/743-1823).
Student travel organization with branches in many US cities. A sister company, Council Charter (☎1-800/223-7402), specializes in charter flights. Both

are subsidiaries of the Council for International Educational Exchange (see "Work and Study").

Discount Travel International
Ives Bldg, 114 Forrest Ave, Suite 205, Narberth, PA 19072 (☎1-800/334-9294).
Discount travel club.

Educational Travel Center
438 N Frances St, Madison, WI 53703 (☎1-800/747-5551).
Student/youth discount agent.

Encore Travel Club
4501 Forbes Blvd, Lanham, MD 20706 (☎1-800/444-9800).
Discount travel club.

Budapest start at around $600 from New York and $820 from West Coast cities, rising to $860 and $1100 respectively during high season. If you want to stay longer, you'll have to upgrade your ticket to a much more expensive, one-year return. You can sometimes cut the cost of high-season travel by buying a ticket from **travel agencies specializing in Eastern Europe**, such as *Hungaria Travel* and *Lotus Travel* (see box below). Both agencies are excellent sources of advice on travelling in Hungary, and your best bet for finding out about any bargains that might be available.

Full-time students and anyone under 26 can take advantage of the excellent deals offered by **student/youth travel agencies** such as *Council Travel*, *STA Travel* and *Nouvelles Frontières*. Their flights go for around $800 from the East Coast, $1000 from the West Coast, even in high season, and an added advantage is their flexibil-

ity: there are low penalties for changes or cancellations, and the tickets are valid for six months to a year. Those who don't meet the student/youth requirements can still save some money by buying tickets through **discount agencies** like those listed in the box above.

PACKAGE TOURS

Package tours can save you time and effort, and the hassle of finding your way around an unfamiliar country. Fully fledged guided tours are offered by *Fugazy International*, and the Hungarian tourist organisation *Ibusz* (see p.21), which has a range of packages focusing on various aspects of Hungarian culture, plus horse-riding, walking and cycling tours. Tours (including escorted and independent bicycling tours) are also available from *Forum Travel* (see box below for addresses). Expect to pay from $2,000–2,900

Interworld Travel
800 Douglass Rd, Miami, FL 33134 (☎305/443-4929).
Consolidator.

Last Minute Travel Club
132 Brookline Ave, Boston, MA 02215 (☎1-800/LAST MIN).
Travel club specializing in standby deals.

Moment's Notice
425 Madison Ave, New York, NY 10017 (☎212/486-0503).
Discount travel club.

New Frontiers/Nouvelles Frontières
Head offices: 12 E 33rd St, New York, NY 10016 (☎1-800/366-6387); 1001 Sherbrook East, Suite 720, Montréal, H2L 1L3 (☎514/526-8444).
French discount travel firm. Other branches in LA, San Francisco and Québec City.

Now Voyager
74 Varick St, Suite 307, New York, NY 10013 (☎212/431-1616).
Courier flight broker.

STA Travel
Head office: 48 East 11th St, New York, NY 10003 (☎1-800/777-0112; nationwide).
Worldwide specialist in independent travel with branches in the Los Angeles, San Francisco and Boston areas.

TFI Tours International
Head office: 34 W 32nd St, New York, NY 10001 (☎1-800/745-8000).
Consolidator; other offices in Las Vegas, San Francisco and Los Angeles.

Travac
Head office: 989 6th Ave, New York NY 10018 (☎1-800/872-8800).
Consolidator and charter broker; has another branch in Orlando.

Travel Avenue
10 S Riverside, Suite 1404, Chicago, IL 60606 (☎1-800/333-3335).
Discount travel agent.

Travel Cuts
Head office: 187 College St, Toronto, ON M5T 1P7 (☎416/979-2406).
Canadian student travel organization with branches all over the country.

Travelers Advantage
3033 S Parker Rd, Suite 900, Aurora, CO 80014 (☎1-800/548-1116).
Discount travel club.

UniTravel
1177 N Warson Rd, St Louis, MO 63132 (☎1-800/325-2222).
Consolidator.

Worldtek Travel
111 Water St, New Haven, CT 06511 (☎1-800/243-1723).
Discount travel agency.

Worldwide Discount Travel Club
1674 Meridian Ave, Miami Beach, FL 33139 (☎305/534-2082).
Discount travel club.

per person for a ten- to fourteen-day holiday, including return flights, accommodation and most meals. *Forum Travel's* escorted bicycle tours operate from May to September and start at $945 per person for a seven-night holiday out of Vienna (excluding flights from the US).

If you're simply interested in **booking accommodation** and transport within Hungary, contact *Lotus Travel* or *Hungaria Travel*. Information on accommodation can also be obtained through *Tradsesco Tours and Hungarian Hotels* (6033 W. Century Blvd, Suite 670, Los Angeles, CA; ☎1-800/448-4321), but bookings must be made through one of the agencies mentioned above.

FROM CANADA

The only airlines to fly **from Canada to Budapest** are *Lufthansa* (via Frankfurt) and *KLM* (via Amsterdam). APEX fares start at CDN$1100 from Toronto (with *Lufthansa* or *KLM*) and CDN$1500 from Vancouver (*Lufthansa* only) during the low season, rising to CDN$1500 and CDN$1800 over summer. The alternatives are to travel to the US and then fly from there (see above), or fly to a European city and then carry on to Hungary by air or overland. Although London is the cheapest "gateway" city, a bargain flight to Frankfurt or Vienna might prove less expensive in the long run.

TRAIN PASSES

If you're planning to do much train travel in Europe, then consider buying a **Eurail pass**, which comes in various forms and must be bought before you leave home. Although it's not likely to pay for itself if you're planning to stick to Hungary, the pass also allows unlimited free train travel in sixteen other countries. The **Eurail**

HUNGARIAN TRAVEL SPECIALISTS

ETT Tours, 198 Boston Post Rd, Mamaroneck, NY 10543 (☎1-800/551-2085).

Forum Travel, 91 Gregory Lane, Pleasant Hill, CA (☎510/671-2900).

Fugazy International, 770 US-1, North Brunswick, NJ (☎1-800/828-4488).

Hungaria Travel, 1603 Second Ave, New York, NY (☎212/249-9342).

Lotus Travel, 5455 Garden Grove Rd, Suite 100, Westminster, CA (☎1-800/675-0559).

Youthpass (for under-26s) costs US$398 for 15 days, $578 for one month or $768 for two months; if you're 26 or over you'll have to buy a first-class pass, available in 15-day ($498), 21-day ($648), one-month ($798), two-month ($1098) and three-month ($1398) increments. You stand a better chance of getting your money's worth out of a **Eurail Flexipass**, which is good for a certain number of travel days in a two-month period. This, too, comes in under-26/first-class versions: 5 days cost $255/$348; 10 days, $398/$560; and 15 days, $540/$740. A further alternative is to attempt to buy an *InterRail* Pass in Europe (see "Getting There From Britain", above) – most

agents don't check residential qualifications, but once you're in Europe it'll be too late to buy a *Eurail Pass* if you have problems. You can purchase *Eurail* passes from one of the agents listed below.

North Americans are also eligible to purchase a more specific pass valid for travel in Hungary only, for details of which see "Getting Around", p.22.

RAIL CONTACTS IN NORTH AMERICA

CIT Tours, 342 Madison Ave, Suite 207, New York, NY 10173 (☎1-800/223-7987).
Eurail passes.

DER Tours/GermanRail, 9501 W Divon Ave, Suite 400, Rosemont, IL 60018 (☎1-800/421-2929).
Eurail passes.

Orbis Polish Travel Bureau, 342 Madison Ave, New York, NY 10173 (☎1-800/223-6037).
Passes for Hungary.

Rail Europe, 226 Westchester Ave, White Plains, NY 10604 (☎1-800/438 7245).
Official Eurail pass agent in North America.

ScanTours, 1535 6th St, Suite 205, Santa Monica, CA 90401 (☎1-800/223-7226).
Eurail passes.

GETTING THERE FROM AUSTRALASIA

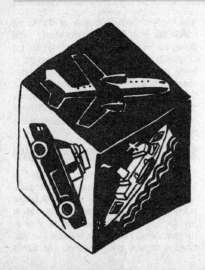

Hungary is not a cheap place to reach from either Australia or New Zealand, and you may want to think about including the country as part of a longer European tour.

From **Australia**, the cheapest method is to aim for Vienna or Frankfurt with *MAS* ($1620) or *Garuda* ($1760), and continue from there by road or rail. Alternatively, *Finnair*, *Balkan*, *CSA* or *Polish-LOT* have deals with the likes of *Qantas* or *British Airways* to fly you to Bangkok, Singapore or Tokyo, where you catch a connection to the airline's capital (Helsinki, Sofia, Prague or Warsaw respectively), and thence to Budapest, for around $2000 or less. More directly, *KLM* is good value to Budapest at around $2100, while *Lufthansa/Lauda Air* charge around $2499. Other major carriers, such as *Qantas*, *British Airways*, *Air New Zealand* or *Alitalia*, charge $2600 or more for the same flight, so you may want to make use of *BA*'s $2500 **Round the World** fare, allowing five stopovers worldwide.

There are no really cheap flights from **New Zealand**; *Lufthansa/Lauda Air* or *Air New Zealand* charge around NZ$2799 to Vienna or Frankfurt, and you'll possibly be better off buying a discounted fare to Australia (NZ$650 or less) and proceeding from there.

Discount flight agents, and specialist operators like *Danube Travel* (see below for contact numbers), should be able to get ten percent off the mid-season fares quoted above.

AIRLINES

Aeroflot, 388 George St, Sydney (☎02/233 7911). No NZ office.

Air France 12 Castlereagh St, Sydney (02 321 1030); 57 Fort St, Auckland (09 303 1229).

Air New Zealand 5 Elizabeth St, Sydney (02 223 4666); Cnr. Customs and Queen streets, Auckland (09 366 2424).

British Airways, 64 Castlereagh St, Sydney (☎02/258 3300); Dilworth Building, Cnr. Queen and Customs streets, Auckland (☎09/367 7500).

Garuda, 175 Clarence Street, Sydney (☎02/334 9900); 120 Albert St, Auckland (☎09/366 1855).

KLM, 5 Elizabeth St, Sydney (☎02/231 6333/008 222 747). No NZ office.

Lufthansa/Air Lauda, 143 Macquarie St, Sydney (☎02/367 3800); 109 Queen St, Auckland (☎09/303 1529).

MAS, 388 George St, Sydney (☎02/231 5066 or ☎008/269 998); Floor 12, Swanson Centre, 12–26 Swanson St, Auckland (☎09/373 2741).

Qantas, International Square, Jamison St, Sydney (☎02/957 0111/236 3636); Qantas House, 154 Queen St, Auckland (☎09/303 2506).

United 10 Barrack St, Sydney (☎02/237 8888); 7 City Road, Auckland (☎09/307 9500).

NOTE: ☎*008 numbers are toll free, but only apply if dialled outside the city in the address.*

DISCOUNT FLIGHT AGENTS

Budget Travel, PO Box 505, Auckland (☎09/309 4313).

Contal Travel, 446 George St, Brisbane (☎07/236 2929).

Danube Travel, 106 Chapel St, St Kilda, Melbourne (☎03/525 4733).

Discount Travel Specialists, Shop 53, Forrest Chase, Perth (☎09/221 1400).

Flight Centres Australia: Circular Quay, Sydney (☎02/241 2422); Bourke St, Melbourne (☎03/650 2899); plus other branches nationwide. New Zealand: National Bank Towers, 205-225 Queen St, Auckland (☎09/309 6171); Shop 1M, National Mutual Arcade, 152 Hereford St, Christchurch (☎09/379 7145); 50-52 Willis St, Wellington (☎04/472 8101); plus other branches nationwide.

Metro Travel, 379 Kent Street, Sydney (☎02/290 3866).

STA Travel Australia: 732 Harris St, Ultimo, Sydney (☎02/212 1255); 256 Flinders St, Melbourne (☎03/347 4711); other offices in Townsville and state capitals. New Zealand: Traveller's Centre, 10 High St, Auckland (☎09/309 9995); 233 Cuba St, Wellington (☎04/385 0561); 223 High St, Christchurch (☎03/379 9098); other offices in Dunedin, Palmerston North and Hamilton.

Topdeck Travel, 45 Grenfell St, Adelaide (☎08/410 1110).

Tymtro Travel, 314 Victorian Ave, Chatswood, Sydney (☎02/411 1000).

Note that all Australian phone numbers are due to have extra digits added to them in the next two years.

VISAS AND RED TAPE

Citizens of the United States, Canada and EU countries no longer require visas, and simply receive a stamp in their passport at the border, which allows a stay of up to six months. Australians, New Zealanders and other nationalities, however, must still obtain a visa – either from a Hungarian consulate abroad, or on arrival at Budapest airport or any road crossing along the border. Visas are not issued at rail cross-ings or the passenger dock for hydrofoils from Vienna.

Assuming that you require a visa, applications can be made to any Hungarian consulate abroad in person or by post. **Tourist visas** are valid for thirty days' stay, with the option of single, double or multiple entries, while **transit visas** entitle you to 48 hours' stay. Besides two passport photos, you will need to submit your passport and the requisite fee (currently £12 for a single-entry visa obtained in Britain; consulates in Eastern Europe require payment in US$).

Applications in person are generally processed within 24 hours, though some consulates will issue visas the same day for a surcharge. To apply by post, obtain an application form from the consulate; then send the completed form and your passport by registered post, including a postal order (in Britain) or certi-fied check (in the US), plus a stamped addressed envelope for return. Applications can also be made through *Ibusz* (1 Parker Plaza, Suite 1004, Fort Lee NJ 07024; ☎1-800/367-7878) in the US, or *Danube Travel* (6 Conduit St, London W1R 9TG; ☎0171/493 0263) in Britain, which levy a surcharge.

HUNGARIAN EMBASSIES AND CONSULATES ABROAD

AUSTRALIA: Embassy: 17 Beale Crescent, Deakin ACT 2600, Canberra (☎06/282 3226 or ☎06/285 3484); Consulate: Suite 405 Edgecliffe Centre 203-233, New South Head Rd, Edgecliffe SW 2027, Sydney (☎02/328 7859 or ☎02/328 7860).

AUSTRIA: 1, Bank Gasse 4-6, A-1010, Vienna (☎0222/533-26-31 or ☎0222/535-47-47).

BRITAIN: 35b Eaton Place, London SW1X 8BY (☎0171/235 2664; open Mon-Fri 10am-noon).

CANADA: Embassy: 299 Waverley St, Ottawa, Ontario, K2P OV9 (☎613/230-2717); Consulates: 1200 McGill College St, Suite 2030, Montréal, Québec H3B 4G7 (☎514/393-1555); and 102 Bloor St West, Suite 1005, Toronto, (☎416/923-3596 or ☎416/923-35-97).

DENMARK: Strandvejen 170, 2920 Charlottenlund, Copenhagen (☎31-63-16-88 or ☎31-63-19-29).

FRANCE Embassy: 5 Bis, Square de l'Avenue Foch, 75116 Paris (☎1/45-00-00-29 or ☎1/45-00-41-59); Consulate: 92, Rue Bonaparte, 75006 Paris (☎1/43-54-66-96).

GERMANY: Embassy: Turmstrasse 30 (Plittersdorf), 53175 Bonn 2 (☎228/37-11-12); Unter den Linden 76, 10177 Berlin (☎30/220-25-61).

NETHERLANDS: Hogeweg 14, 2585 JD, Den Haag (☎070/350-0404 or ☎070/350-0954).

NEW ZEALAND: 151 Orangi Taupapa Rd, Wellington 6000Z (☎04/475 8574).

NORWAY: Sophus Lies gt. 3, Oslo 2 (☎255-24-18 or ☎255-24-19).

SWEDEN: Strandvägen 74, 115.27 Stockholm (☎661-67-62 or ☎662-56-75).

USA: Embassy: 3910 Shoemaker St. NW, Washington DC 20008 (☎202/362-6730; visa enquiries ☎202/362-6795); 223 E 52nd St, New York NY 10022 (☎212/752-0661); Consulate: 11766 Wilshire Blvd, Suite 410, Los Angeles, CA 90025 (☎213/473-9344); 223 E 52nd St., New York, NY 10022 (☎212/752-0661).

VISA EXTENSIONS AND REGISTRATION

In theory, visitors can stay up to six months, although after three months they are required to register with the police. **Applications for extensions** must be made 48 hours before the visa expires, and you may be asked to show evidence of funds or proof of having exchanged money. In Budapest, go to the district police station (*kerületi rendőrség*) nearest to your place of residence; in provincial towns, apply to police headquarters (*főkapitányság*). The process usually takes about fifteen minutes. A simpler method of extending your stay, whether you need a visa or not, is to leave the country, either by taking the bus to Vienna and spending the day there, or taking the train to Komarom, walking across the bridge to Slovakia, and then back again. This saves all the hassle of dealing with officials and showing how much money you have.

After three months' stay, all visitors are required to register their address (and any subsequent changes of address) with the local police. In practice, however, **registration** need only concern those staying in "unofficial" accommodation (for example, with friends), since residents in hotels, hostels, pensions, guesthouses and campsites are automatically registered. Should you need to register, get an Alien's Registration form (*Lakcímbejelentő lap küföldiek részére*) from any post office and have it countersigned by your host before taking it to the police station.

Lost passports must be reported to the local police station (who'll issue a visa, if necessary) and your own consulate. If found, they will be forwarded to *KEO* (the Aliens' Registration Office) in Budapest (Izabella utca 61, ☎131-7376, 111-5889 or 111-8669; Mon, Wed & Fri 8am–noon, Tues 1–6pm, Thurs 8am–6pm).

CUSTOMS

Customs formalities are normally painless, though visitors arriving from Austria or Romania by road may get stuck in long queues at the border crossings. Duty-free allowances for visitors over the age of sixteen are 250 cigarettes (or 250g of tobacco or 50 cigars), 2 litres or wine and 1 litre of spirits. Food is allowed up to five kilogrammes, but may not contain raw meat. There is no **import duty** on personal effects such as bicycles, cameras, portable cassette recorders and TV sets, but items with a high resale value (like laptop computers and video cameras) are liable to customs duty and 25 percent VAT unless you can prove that they are for personal use.

These customs regulations change fairly frequently, so it's worth checking the latest rules at a Hungarian consulate or tourist office before leaving home. You can **export** five kilos of foodstuffs which may include two kilos of processed meat products (for example, salami and canned meats). Duty-free export limits for tobacco and alcohol are the same as the import limits.

HEALTH AND INSURANCE

No inoculations are required for Hungary, and standards of public health are good. Tap water is safe everywhere, while potable springs (*forrás*) and streams are designated on maps, and with signs, as *ivóvíz*. The national health service (*OTBF*) will provide free emergency treatment in any hospital or doctor's office for citizens of Britain, Finland, Norway, Sweden, the countries of the former Soviet Union, and former Eastern Bloc countries - but there is a charge for drugs and non-emergency care.

Even so, it's a very good idea to have some kind of **travel insurance**, since with this you're covered for loss of possessions and money, as well as the cost of all medical and dental treatment. Insurance is often included if you pay for your trip by credit card. Remember that certain activities classified as hazardous sports are unlikely to be covered by most policies, although by paying an extra premium you can usually get added cover for the period in which these activities are taking place.

With all policies you have to pay up front and **reclaim the money** when you get home, producing hospital receipts or a police report to verify your claim.

UK INSURANCE

UK citizens can ask about policies at any bank or travel agent, or use a policy issued by a specialist travel company like *Campus Travel* or *STA Travel* (see p.4 for address), or by the low-cost **insurers** *Endsleigh Insurance* (97–107 Southampton Row, London WC1; ☎0171/436 4451) or *Columbus Travel Insurance* (17 Devonshire Square, London EC2; ☎0171/375 0011). Two weeks' cover starts at around £18; a month costs from £24.

INSURANCE FOR NORTH AMERICAN TRAVELLERS

Before buying an insurance policy, check that you're not already covered. **Canadians** are usually covered for medical mishaps overseas by their provincial health plans. Holders of official **student/teacher/youth cards** are entitled to accident coverage and hospital in-patient benefits. **Students** will often find that their student health coverage extends during the vacations and for one term beyond the date of last enrolment. Bank and credit cards (particularly *American Express*) often have certain levels of medical or other insurance included, and travel insurance may also be included if you use a major credit or charge card to pay for your trip. **Homeowners' or renters'** insurance often covers theft or loss of documents, money and valuables while overseas, though conditions and maximum amounts vary from company to company.

After exhausting the possibilities above, you might want to contact a specialist **travel insurance** company; your travel agent can usually recommend one, or see the box opposite. Policies are comprehensive (accidents, illnesses, delayed or lost luggage, cancelled flights, etc.), but maximum payouts tend to be meagre. Premiums vary,

---

TRAVEL INSURANCE COMPANIES IN NORTH AMERICA

Access America, PO Box 90310, Richmond, VA 23230 (☎1-800/284-8300).

Carefree Travel Insurance, PO Box 310, 120 Mineola Blvd, Mineola, NY 11501 (☎1-800/323-3149).

International Student Insurance Service (ISIS) – sold by *STA Travel*, which has several branches in the US (head office is 48 E 11th St, New York, NY 10003; ☎1-800/777-0112).

Travel Assistance International, 1133 15th St NW, Suite 400, Washington, DC 20005 (☎1-800/821-2828).

Travel Guard, 1145 Clark St, Stevens Point, WI 54481 (☎1-800/826-1300).

Travel Insurance Services, 2930 Camino Diablo, Suite 300, Walnut Creek, CA 94596 (☎1-800/937-1387).

---

so shop around. The best deals are usually to be had through student/youth travel agencies – *ISIS* policies, for example, cost $48–69 for fifteen days (depending on coverage), $80–105 for a month, $149–207 for two months, on up to $510–700 for a year.

Most North American travel policies apply only to items lost, stolen or damaged while in the custody of an identifiable, responsible third party – hotel porter, airline, luggage consignment, etc. Even in these cases you will have to contact the local police within a certain time limit to have a complete report made out so that your insurer can process the claim.

AUSTRALIAN TRAVEL INSURANCE

In **Australia**, *CIC Insurance*, offered by *Cover-More Insurance Services* (Level 9, 32 Walker St, North Sydney; ☎02/202 8000; branches in Victoria and Queensland), has some of the widest cover available and can be arranged through most travel agents. It costs from A$140 for 31 days.

HEALTH CARE, PHARMACIES AND HOSPITALS

Sunburn (*napszúrás*) and insect bites (*rovarcsípés*) are the most common **minor complaints**: suntan lotion is sold in supermarkets and pharmacists stock *Vietnámi balzsam* (Vietnamese-made "Tiger Balm" - the best bug repellent going) and bite ointment. Mosquitoes are pesky, but the bug to beware of in forests is the *kullancs*, which bites and then burrows into human skin, causing inflammation of the brain. The risk seems fairly small, but if you get a bite which seems particularly painful, or are suffering from a high temperature and stiff neck following a bite, it's worth having it inspected as quickly as possible.

All towns and some villages have a **pharmacy** (*gyógyszertár* or *patika*), with staff (most likely to understand German) authorized to issue a wide range of drugs, including painkillers. However, pharmaceutical products are mainly of East European origin, so anyone requiring specific medication should bring a supply with them. Opening hours are normally Monday-Friday 9am–6pm, Saturday 9am–noon or 1pm; signs in the window give the location or telephone number of the nearest all-night (*éjjeli* or *ügyeleti szolgálat*) pharmacy.

In more serious cases, provincial tourist offices can direct you to local **medical centres**

or doctors' offices (*orvosi rendelő*), while your embassy in Budapest will have the addresses of foreign-language-speaking **doctors** and **dentists**, who will probably be in private (*magán*) practice. Private medicine is much cheaper than in the West, as attested to by the thousands of Austrians who come here for treatment. For muscular, skin or gynaecological complaints, doctors often prescribe a soak at one of Hungary's numerous **medicinal baths** (*gyógyfürdő*).

In **emergencies**, dial ☎**04** for the *Mentők* ambulance service, or catch a taxi to the nearest *Kórház*. The standard of **hospitals** varies enormously, but low morale and shortages of beds testify to poor wages and the general underfunding of the health service. Depending on local conditions, Westerners might get the best available treatment, or be cold-shouldered; in the event of the latter, it's worth trying to bribe the staff as a last resort.

COSTS, MONEY AND BANKS

Hungary was one of the first former Eastern Bloc countries to begin moving towards a market economy, enabling the post-Communist government to avoid imposing the shock therapy currently being applied in Russia and elsewhere. Even so, most Hungarians complain of "paying Swedish taxes on an Ethiopian wage" and of the rising cost of living, which is now approaching Western levels.

With **inflation** running at 20 percent, Hungarian *forint* prices quoted in this guide will

inevitably become outdated, but unless your own currency slips badly, real costs should remain fairly stable. For this reason, many **prices given in this guide** are either expressed in US dollars or Deutschmarks (DM).

AVERAGE COSTS

Although foreigners no longer find Hungary a really cheap place to visit, it's still good value on the whole. Depending on the exchange rate (see below) and where you go, most **costs** are two-thirds to three-quarters of what you'd pay at home, except in Budapest and the Lake Balaton resorts, which are more expensive than other parts of Hungary. Wherever you are, the biggest item of expenditure will be **accommodation**. Outside Budapest and the Balaton, the average three-star hotel charges £35–40 (US$53–60) for a double room with bath, while the same in a private guesthouse costs about £10/$15. Although you can get stung for more in some **restaurants**, a three-course meal with wine can generally be had for £5–10/$8–15. With flat fares (roughly 15p/25¢) in urban areas, and cheap inter-city trains and buses (averaging under £2–3/$3–5), **transport** will be the least of your expenses.

If you're keeping to a tight budget, remember that some campsites and hostels give discounts to holders of IUS (student) cards (see "Directory", below). Further **savings** can be made by hitching, making or buying your own food, or eating in public canteens.

CURRENCY AND EXCHANGE RATE

The Hungarian unit of currency is the **forint** (Ft or HUF), with the **exchange rate** currently 175Ft to the £ sterling, 115Ft to the US$.

The forint comes in **notes** of 50, 100, 500, 1000 and 5000Ft, with 1, 2, 5, 10 and 20Ft coins; the little *fillér* (100 fillér = 1Ft) **coins** are practically useless though still in circulation. Forints can't be exchanged outside the country; and while they can be bought at a favourable rate in Vienna, importing or exporting banknotes of denominations higher than 1000Ft, and totalling over 5000Ft is illegal. There's no restriction on bringing in or taking out convertible currency - although if all your cash is in small denominations, declare this on entry (or a zealous customs person might suspect you of smuggling them on the way out).

TRAVELLERS' CHEQUES AND CREDIT CARDS

Although a modest amount of low-denomination US dollar bills or Deutschmarks can be useful, it's safest to carry the bulk of your money in **travellers' cheques**. Travellers' cheques issued by American, Australian, British, Dutch, Norwegian and German banks are all accepted; but for speedy refunds in case of loss, *American Express* (represented in Budapest at Deák Ferenc utca 10; ☎267-8680) is much the most reliable brand. You can cash **Eurocheques** up to the value of 18,000Ft at places displaying the Eurocheque logo. *Amex, Visa, Mastercard, Diners' Club, Carte Blanche* and *Eurocard* **credit and charge cards** can be used to rent cars, buy airline tickets or pay your bills directly in hotels and restaurants and

many shops. Outside the main tourist centres their usefulness is more restricted.

BANKS AND CHANGING MONEY

Exchange rates vary somewhat and it's best to use the main tourist offices and banks when you want to change money - in Budapest, avoid the exchange offices on and around Vörösmarty tér, where the good rate offered is for exchanges of large sums and a high commission is charged, or *American Express*, where rates are low.

Providing you produce your passport, **changing money or travellers' cheques** is a painless operation at any *Ibusz* or regional tourist office, or at the majority of large hotels and campsites; *valuta* desks in **banks** take longer over transactions, and work shorter hours (Mon-Fri 8.30am-3.30pm) than tourist offices. Keep the **receipts**, as these are required both to pay for international tickets in forints and to re-exchange forints back into hard currency when you leave Hungary. At road checkpoints, fifty percent of any remaining forints can be re-exchanged up to the value of US$50. The advantages of changing money on the illegal **black market** are minimal (ten percent above the official rate), and scalpers are skilled at cheating.

If you want to open a **foreign currency bank account** (*devizaszamla*) ask around to find the best conditions - some require a high minimum deposit (from zero at the *Postabank* to $2,500 at the *Hungarian Foreign Trade Bank, MKB*), but money transferred from abroad takes days to come through here rather than weeks. Inter-bank money transfers are fastest through the SWIFT system, to which most Hungarian banks and some British banks (*Barclays* and *Midland*) are linked. However, funds can still take a long time to reach your Hungarian branch - especially if your account is not with the bank's main branch. You can also use the *American Express* office in central Budapest (V, Deák Ferenc utca 10) for **money transfers**, which might prove quicker and cheaper.

INFORMATION AND MAPS

A large number of photo-packed brochures, maps and special-interest leaflets are available free from the Hungarian Tourist Board (HTB), and distributed by their offices abroad and, sometimes, by the offices of the travel organization *Ibusz*.

The most useful things to pick up are the large road map (which is perfectly adequate for travelling around Hungary); a pamphlet detailing the year's festivals and events; and the *Hotels* and *Camping* booklets, which list accommodation on a town-by-town basis, together with the tourist offices that handle bookings. Unfortunately, neither is fully comprehensive, omitting many of the pensions featured in the privately published *Tourism Almanac* (available in Budapest), which only lists places that have paid to be included. There is also a rather dated map designed for campers, and a useful booklet on cycling tours.

TOURIST AGENCIES IN HUNGARY

In Hungary itself you'll find **local tourist agencies** in most larger towns (called, variously, *Savaria Tourist*, *Komturist*, etc) and a growing network of **Tourinform** offices, set up by the Hungarian Tourist Board, which have excellent information on accommodation and activities, although they do not book rooms. Generally, *Tourinform* office staff are friendly, and hand out a free monthly magazine, *Programme*, which details tourist **events** throughout Hungary.

There are also four other agencies operating nationwide: *Ibusz*, *Volántourist* – linked to the *Volán* bus company – which specializes in travel bookings and tour groups; *Cooptourist* which deals with car and apartment rental for relatively upmarket travellers; and the "youth travel" agency *Express*, which no longer confines itself to the under-35s and will now book anyone into its stable of hotels and campsites, or college hostels that are vacant at weekends and during school holidays.

Addresses, opening hours and phone numbers for the local agencies are given wherever possible in the guide section of this book.

MAPS

You may want to supplement the maps in this book with Hungarian *városi-térkép*, which also detail accents and tram and bus routes. These maps cost between 40Ft and 130Ft and are available from local tourist offices or, failing that, from bookshops (*könyvesbolt*). Better value is the ***Magyar Auto Atlasz***, which contains plans of most towns (some of the street names may be out of date) plus road maps, and can be bought from bookshops for 120Ft. Bookshops also stock **hiking maps** or *turistatérkép* covering the Mátra, Bükk and other highland regions (50-100Ft), which should be purchased in advance wherever possible, as they may not be available on the spot. They are not totally reliable, however, so hikers should always carry a

MAP OUTLETS IN THE UK

London

National Map Centre, 22–24 Caxton St, SW1
(☎0171/222 4945).

Stanfords, 12–14 Long Acre, WC2
(☎0171/836 1321).

The Travellers Bookshop, 25 Cecil Court, WC2
(☎0171/836 9132).

Edinburgh

Thomas Nelson and Sons Ltd, 51 York Place, EH1
3JD (☎0131/557 3011).

Glasgow

John Smith and Sons, 57–61 St Vincent St G2 5TB
(☎0141/221 7472).

Maps by **mail or phone order** are available from *Stanfords* (☎0171/836 1321).

MAP OUTLETS IN NORTH AMERICA

Chicago

Rand McNally, 444 N Michigan Ave, IL 60611
(☎312/321-1751).

Montréal

Ulysses Travel Bookshop, 4176 St-Denis
(☎514/289-0993).

New York

British Travel Bookshop, 551 5th Ave, NY 10176
(☎1-800/448-3039 or ☎212/490-6688).

The Complete Traveler Bookstore, 199 Madison
Ave, NY 10016 (☎212/685-9007).

Rand McNally, 150 E 52nd St, NY 10022 (☎212/
758-7488).

Traveler's Bookstore, 22 W 52nd St, NY 10019
(☎212/664-0995).

San Francisco

The Complete Traveler Bookstore, 3207 Fillmore
St, CA 92123 (☎415/923-1511).

Rand McNally, 595 Market St, CA 94105 (☎415/
777-3131).

Santa Barbara

Pacific Traveler Supply, 25 E Mason St, 93101
(☎805/963-4438; phone orders: ☎805/968-
4402).

Seattle

Elliot Bay Book Company, 101 South Main St,
WA 98104 (☎206/624-6600).

Toronto

Open Air Books and Maps, 25 Toronto St, M5R
2C1 (☎416/363-0719).

Vancouver

World Wide Books and Maps, 736A Granville St.
V6Z 1G3 (☎604/687-3320).

Washington DC

Rand McNally, 1201 Connecticut Ave NW,
Washington DC 20036 (☎202/223-6751).

Note that *Rand McNally* now have 20 stores across the US; phone ☎1-800/333-0136 (ext 2111) for the
address of your nearest store, or for **direct mail** maps.

MAP OUTLETS IN AUSTRALIA

Adelaide

The Map Shop, 16a Peel St, Adelaide, SA 5000
(☎08/231 2033).

Brisbane

Hema, 239 George St, Brisbane, QLD 4000 (☎07/
221 4330).

Melbourne

Bowyangs, 372 Little Bourke St, Melbourne, VIC
3000 (☎03/670 4383).

Sydney

Travel Bookshop, 20 Bridge St, Sydney, NSW 2000
(☎02/241 3554).

Perth

Perth Map Centre, 891 Hay St, Perth, WA 6000
(☎09/322 5733).

compass. *Tourinform* issues a variety of useful, free **road maps**, including one showing Budapest's one-way streets and bypasses.

If you want to buy Hungarian maps in advance of your trip, try one of the specialist map suppliers listed in the box below.

IBUSZ AGENTS ABROAD

Australia: Suite 401, 115 Pitt St, Sydney NSW (☎61 2/223-41-97).

Britain: *Danube Travel Ltd*, 6 Conduit St, London W1R 9TG (☎071/493 0263).

Germany: 6000 Frankfurt am Main, Schaftergasse 17 (☎49 69/299-88-70); 2000 Hamburg, Holzdamm 53 (☎49 40/24-59-62); 8000 München, Dachauer Str. 5 (☎49 89/557-217); 5000 Köln, Mauritiussteinweg 114–116 (☎49 221/20-64-50); 7000 Stuttgart, Kronprinz Str. 6 (☎49 711/296-233).

Holland: Strawinskylaan 1425, 1077 Amsterdam (☎31 20/644-98-51).

Sweden: 10326 Stockholm, Beridarebanan 1 (☎46 8/23-20-30).

USA: 1 Parker Plaza, Suite 1104, Fort Lee, NJ 07024 (☎201/592-8585 or ☎1-800/367-7878); M/C79/50 5000 Airport Plaza Drive, Long Beach, Los Angeles CA (☎213/593-2952).

GETTING AROUND

Although it doesn't break any speed records, public transport reaches most parts of Hungary and, despite recent price increases, remains remarkably cheap. Regional transport schedules are summarized under "Travel Details" at the end of each chapter.

BY TRAIN

The centralization of the **MÁV** rail network means that many cross-country journeys are easier if you travel via Budapest rather than on branch lines where services are slower and less frequent. Timetables are in yellow (for departures) or white (for arrivals), with the different types of fast **trains** picked out in red. The fastest are the *Intercity* ("*IC*" on the timetable) trains, which run express services between Budapest and Miskolc, Szeged and other larger towns; and

Express trains (marked "*Ex*" on timetables), stopping at major centres only, and costing ten percent more than *gyorsvonat* and *sebesvonat* services, which stop more regularly. The slowest trains (*személyvonat*) halt at every hamlet along the way, and since the fare is the same as on a *gyorsvonat*, you might as well opt for the latter. Do not use international trains for journeys within Hungary, as this can prove expensive.

All trains have first- and second-class (*osztály*) sections, and many also feature a buffet car (indicated on timetables). International services routed through Budapest have **sleeping cars** and **couchettes** (*hálókocsi* and *kusett*), for which tickets can be bought at *MÁV* offices in advance, or sometimes on the train itself. There's also a **car train** on the Budapest-Dresden line in the summer, which travellers to Germany might find useful, although it doesn't carry camper vans or minibuses. **Bicycles** can be carried on all passenger trains, except Intercity, Expresses and international trains. However, there are restrictions on the number of bikes allowed on trains during rush hour (before 8am and from 2–3.30pm on weekdays), and if you're departing from mainline stations in Budapest it's tricky getting hold of the right paperwork, so allow plenty of time.

If you're planning to travel a lot by rail, it's worth investing in the **timetables** available from the *MÁV* office in Budapest (VI, Andrássy út 35;

TRAVEL INFORMATION

Finding out travel information (*információ*) can be your biggest problem, since transport staff rarely speak anything but Hungarian, which is the only language used for notices and announcements (except around Lake Balaton, where German is widely spoken). You'll find some pertinent phrases in the "Language" section of this guide (p.366–367), while the following should be useful for **deciphering timetables**.

Érkező járatok (or *érkezés*) means "**arrivals**", and *induló járatok* (or *indulás*) "**departures**". Trains or buses **to** (*hova*) a particular destination leave from a designated **platform** (for example *vágány 1*) or **bus-stand** (*kocsiállás*); and the point of arrival for services **from** (*honnan*) a place may also be indicated.

Some services run (*közlekedik, köz.* for short) *munkaszüneti napok kivételével naponta köz - **daily, except on rest days**, meaning Sunday and public holidays; *munkanapokon (hetfőtől-péntekig) köz - **weekdays, Monday to Friday***; *munkaszüneti napokon köz - **on rest days***; or *09.30-tól 12-ig vasárnap köz - **on Sunday 9.30am-midnight***. *Atszállás* means "**change**"; *át* "**via**"; and *kivételével* "**except**".

☎122-8049) or large train stations. Train (domestic and international) services are covered by the chunky *Hivatalos Menetrend* (300Ft; note that the larger format 500Ft version has no extra information), which also details boat and ferry services on the Danube and the Balaton as well as all internal trains; an English-language section at the front explains the symbols used.

TICKETS AND PASSES

Tickets (*jegy*) for domestic train services can be bought at the station (*pályaudvar* or *vasútállomás*) on the day of departure, although it's possible to reserve them up to sixty days in advance. You can break your journey once between the point of departure and the final destination, but must get your ticket validated within an hour of arrival at the interim station. Most Hungarians purchase one-way tickets (*egy útra*), so specify a *retur* or *oda-vissza* if you want a **return ticket**. If you're found travelling without a ticket you have to buy one at many times the normal price.

Seat bookings (*helyjegy*), in the form of a separate numbered bit of card, are obligatory for services marked ☐R☐ on timetables (mostly international or express trains), and optional on those designated by an ⓇR. They cost 30Ft on most domestic routes, 100Ft on express trains and 260Ft on international services, and can be made up to two months in advance at any *MÁV* or *Volántourist* office.

It's best to buy tickets for **international trains** (*nemzetközi gyorsvonat*) at least 36 hours in advance, since demand is heavy. The "Hungarian stage" of the journey can be paid for in forints, but the "international" section usually has to be paid for in hard currency, unless you can produce an exchange receipt for the sum concerned. However, if you buy your ticket at one of the train stations in Budapest, you can often pay in forints. The central *MÁV* ticket office in Budapest, which handles bookings, gets very crowded during summer; and staff and customers won't thank anybody who tries to pay by cheque or credit card. Note that holders of student cards are entitled to fifty percent reductions on services to Poland, forty percent for Russia, thirty percent to Bulgaria and twenty-five percent to the Ukraine.

Concessionary fares on domestic services are also available: there's a 33 percent discount for groups of 10-19, and 50 percent for groups of over 20 people; *BIJ/Eurotrain* ticket holders get 50 percent off (if the *BIJ* ticket was bought outside Hungary); and pensioners (women over 55 and men over 60) get a 20 percent reduction if they show a passport - no special permit required. *InterRail/Eurail* passes also allow **free travel**. Children under four travel free if they don't occupy a separate seat, while children up to the age of fourteen pay fifty percent of the fare.

MÁV itself issues various **train passes**, valid on domestic lines nationwide (but not on the international trains within Hungary) for a week or ten days, but you'd need to travel fairly extensively to make savings. A seven-day pass costs 6138Ft first class, 4092Ft second class; a ten-day pass 9207Ft/6138Ft. There's also a short-term **Hungarian Flexipass**, which you must buy in your own country before departure (available from any agent selling *InterRail/Eurail* passes): a pass valid for any 5 days in 15 costs around £35/ $55 (1st class); any 10 days in 1 month, £45/$69.

BY BUS

Regional **Volán** ("Wheel") companies run the bulk of Hungary's **buses**, which are called *busz* (pronounced "boose" as in "loose", *not* "bus", which means "fuck" in Hungarian). Buses are often the quickest way to travel between towns, and while fares are higher than on the railways they're still good value (roughly 4Ft per km). Schedules are clearly displayed in bus stations (*autóbuszállomás* or *autóbusz pályaudvar*) in every Hungarian town. Arrive early to confirm the departure bay (*kocsiállás*) and to be sure of getting a seat. For long-distance services originating in Budapest or major towns, you can buy tickets with a seat booking up to half an hour before departure; after that you get them from the driver, and risk standing throughout the journey. Services **in rural areas** may be limited to one or two a day, and tickets are only available on board the bus. As on trains, children under four travel free unless they occupy a separate seat, and at half-fare up to the age of ten; otherwise there are no concessions.

Volán also operates **international services** to neighbouring countries and a few points further west. The main depot for these is Erzsébet tér in Budapest (see p.51), but services also run from provincial towns like Siófok, Szombathely, Győr, Miskolc, Szeged, Baja, Mohács and Debrecen. It's fractionally cheaper to travel from Budapest to Vienna by bus, but other destinations may cost less by train.

URBAN PUBLIC TRANSPORT

Public transport **within towns** is generally excellent, with buses, trolleybuses (*trolibusz*) and trams (*villamos*) running from dawn until around 10.30 or 11pm. Express buses (numbered in red) halt only at main stops, while express buses whose number is accompanied by an "E" run almost non-stop between termini, so be careful about boarding these.

Tickets for all services are sold in strips at tobacconists and street stands, and should be punched on board the vehicle. Municipalities set their own flat rates, causing some variation in prices nationwide. Generally, the local fare for all transport is identical, so the same kind of ticket can be used on all services. Tickets from one town aren't supposed to be used in another. In Budapest, various types of **passes** are available (see p.55).

DRIVING

To drive in Hungary you'll need an **international driving permit** (issued by national motoring organizations for a small fee; contact the AA in Britain, AAA in the US) and **third-party insurance**. If you're taking your own car, check with your insurance company to see if you're covered; you'll probably need a **Green Card**. You can also purchase insurance at the border, but this only covers damage to third parties in Hungary and pays out in forints, so it's wiser to fix it up before leaving home.

Autostop or **hitchhiking** is widely practised by young Magyars, and only forbidden on motorways. Although a fair number of drivers seem willing to give lifts, we do not recommend hitching as a means of getting around the country, especially for solo women travellers.

ROADS AND SERVICES

Hungary's roads fall into four categories. Hungary's small **motorway** network consists of the M1 to Győr (to be extended to the border at Hegyeshalom), the M3 towards Miskolc (it stops halfway at present), the M7 to Balaton, and the M5 towards Kecskemét, the latter the most dangerous road in the country – on a forty-kilometre stretch the motorway is reduced to three lanes, with high speed traffic competing for the middle lane. The M0 is the ring motorway around the capital, of which the stretch between the M5 and the M1 is complete.

Lesser **highways** (numbered with a single digit from 1 to 8) radiate from Budapest like spokes in a wheel, linked by **secondary roads** identified by two or three digits (the first one indicates the highway which the road joins; for example roads 82 and 811 both meet route 8 at some point). Lastly, there are unnumbered, bumpy **back-country roads**, which tourists seldom use. **Pedestrian zones** (found in many towns and shaded light blue on maps) are indicated by "Restricted Access" signs - *kivéve célforgalom*. Information on nationwide **driving conditions** can be obtained from *ÚTINFORM* (☎322-7643); conditions in Budapest are monitored by *FŐVINFORM* (☎117-1173).

Most **service stations** (*benzinkút*) stock 98 octane *extra*; 92 octane *szuper*, 86 octane *normál*, and diesel. **Lead-free** fuel (*olómmentes benzin*) is available at stations in big cities and along major routes, although the countryside can have blank spots. If you are travelling in the country, you're best advised to get an *AFOR* (the state petrol company) map of country service stations from the *Hungarian Automobile Association* (see below), or buy a map of *Shell* outlets at one of their stations. Service stations usually function daily from 6am to 10pm, except on highways and in the capital, where many operate around the clock.

RULES AND REGULATIONS

Speed limits for vehicles are 120kph on motorways, 100kph on highways, 80kph on other roads and 50kph in built-up areas. Offenders can expect to be heavily fined on the spot. In rural areas, wagons, cyclists, livestock and pedestrians are potential **traffic hazards**, so you should drive slowly - especially at night. Besides driving on the right, the most important **rules** are the prohibitions against repeatedly switching from lane to lane on highways; overtaking near pedestrian crossings; and sounding the horn in built-up areas unless to avert accidents. At crossroads, vehicles coming from the right have right of way, unless otherwise indicated by signs, and pedestrians have priority over cars turning onto the road. Remember that trams *always* have right of way, and that some traffic islands serve as bus or tram stops. On highways and secondary roads it's illegal to reverse, make U-turns, or stop at islands.

Drinking and driving is totally prohibited, and offenders with in excess of eight milligrams of alcohol are liable to felony charges. The state requires cars to be roadworthy (steering, brakes and all lights must work); and carry certain **mandatory equipment** - a triangular breakdown sign; spare bulbs for the indicators, head-, rear- and brake-lights; a first-aid box; and a supplementary mud-guard made of a non-rigid material, attached to rear bumpers. Passengers must wear three-point safety belts in the front seats, where children are forbidden to travel.

A note for **pedestrians**: never assume that a car will stop for you on a pedestrian crossing. Drivers in Hungary will often do anything to avoid having to slow down and make way for pedestrians, instead swerving around them or screeching to a sudden halt.

ACCIDENTS AND EMERGENCIES

Accidents should be reported to the *Hungaria Biztositó* insurance department in Budapest (XIV, Gvadányi út 69; ☎252-6333; Mon-Fri 7.30am-12.30pm in person, Mon-Thurs 12.30am-4pm by telephone) within 24 hours; if someone is injured the police must also be notified (☎07).

In Budapest you can summon the "Yellow Angels" **24-hour breakdown service** (☎252-8000), which is free if the repairs take no longer than one hour to complete and your own motoring organization belongs to the *FIA* or *AIT* federations, to which the **Hungarian Automobile Club** - *MAK* - is also affiliated. The *MAK*'s national headquarters is at Rómer Flóris utca 4A in Budapest's II district (Mon-Thurs 8am-4pm, Fri 8am-3pm; ☎212-2938); but their depot for **technical assistance** in the capital is at Boldizsár utca 2 in the XI district (☎185-0722). **Spare parts** for foreign cars are easiest to find in Budapest (see "Listings" at the end of *Budapest*).

CAR RENTAL

Renting a car is easy provided you're 21 or older, and hold a valid national driving licence that's at least one year old. You can order a car through rental agencies in your own country (see box below), and from hotel reception desks or certain travel agencies within Hungary, using cash or credit cards. In Budapest these agencies are *Cooptourist* (IX, Ferenc körút 43; ☎113-1466); *Ibusz* (V, Szervita tér 8; ☎118-4158); and *Fötaxi* (☎122-1471); *Ibusz*, *Volántourist* and *Cooptourist* offices offer the same service in the provinces.

Rental **costs** vary from £7/$11 per day for a *Lada Nova* to £15-25/$23-38 per day for an *Opel Corsa* and £30-40/$45-60 for a *Ford Transit* – not to mention the cost of fuel. Note that the savings you make renting a *Lada* can be outweighed by the lack of reliability. You might find you get a better deal if you arrange a package **fly-drive** holiday in your own country. Credit cards are usually accepted for a deposit, and there are charges of 30–50p/45–75¢ per km and £9–11/

CAR RENTAL AGENCIES

Britain
Avis ☎0181/848 8733.
Europcar/InterRent ☎0345/222 525.
Budget ☎0800/181 181.
Hertz ☎0181/679 1799.
Holiday Autos ☎0171/491 1111.

North America
Avis ☎1-800/331-1084.
Hertz ☎1-800/654-3001; in Canada ☎1-800/263-0600.
Holiday Autos ☎1-800/422-7737.

$13–16 insurance per day. These prices include 25 percent VAT (ÁFA in Hungarian).

BY PLANE AND BOAT

Malév doesn't operate any **domestic flights**, but many of their **flights abroad** (departing from Budapest's Ferihegy airport) are a good deal. If you're heading on to Greece or Turkey, they may prove an attractive alternative to travelling by train - especially for holders of student cards, who sometimes qualify for substantial discounts. *Vista Travel* (Budapest VII, Károly körút 21; ☎142 1534) sells discounted flights; or try *Malév Air Tours* (Roosevelt tér 2; ☎266 6614), which sometimes has special offers. You can also make bookings through hotel desks, at *Malév* offices in Vörösmarty tér in central Budapest, or by telephone (☎118-4333).

The *Mahart* company operates **passenger boats** in Hungary, with services on Lake Balaton, between Budapest and Esztergom, and on the section of the Danube running through the capital. Between April and October, *Mahart* also operates a daily **hydrofoil service between Budapest and Vienna**, a five-and-a-half-hour journey (one hour longer than the downriver journey). Tickets to Vienna are sold at the International Boat Station on the Belgrád rakpart (the Pest embankment), where the hydrofoil departs; at *DDSG* (V, Régiposta utca 19, 2nd floor, no. 1; ☎118 3585); or at *Ibusz* (V, Károly körút 3C). For details of the service from Vienna to Budapest, see p.52 and p.117.

BY BIKE

The only potential drawback to **motorcycling** is that spare parts may be problematic should you have a breakdown. Motorcyclists must be over 18, wear a helmet, and have a log book or other registration document, plus a Green Card for insurance. Aside from being required to use dimmed headlights by day, the rules of the road (and speed limits) are the same as for cars.

Given the generally flat terrain, and the light winds and low rainfall from July until the end of September, **cycling** should also be a good way to see Hungary. In practice, however, there are several caveats. Cyclists are not allowed on main roads (with single-digit numbers), and on some secondary roads between "peak hours" (7–9.30am and 4–6pm); bikes can be carried on all passenger trains except Intercity Expresses and international trains, though in practice railway officials are not always that helpful. In towns, there are sunken tramlines and slippery cobbled streets to contend with. The *Cycling Tours in Hungary* booklet produced by *Ibusz* describes over three dozen routes, graded according to effort. The most scenic areas are the Northern Uplands, the Danube Bend and parts of Transdanubia and the Bakony, where you'll find a few stiff climbs and lots of rolling hills. Conversely, the easiest cycling terrain - the Great Plain – tends to be visually monotonous.

It is possible **to rent bikes** (by the day or week) in most large towns and the Balaton resorts, from *MÁV*, private operators or certain campsites (details are given where appropriate in the guide). Unfortunately, most machines are low-slung and heavy, with limited gears, although superior models are increasingly available. Bike shops are much more frequent than they used to be, with repair shops in most larger towns, including several in Budapest.

ACCOMMODATION

The move towards a fully capitalist econ-omy has meant a steep rise in hotel prices and the closure of many provincial tourist hostels. On the other hand, competitively priced pensions and guesthouses are springing up everywhere, and tourists can now stay in holiday complexes formerly reserved for trade unionists, or in hostels attached to colleges. All in all, it shouldn't prove difficult to find somewhere that suits your tastes and budget.

Most towns have several hotels and pensions, and private lodgings, and quite often a campsite or hostel within easy reach of the centre. Even so, the cheapest places tend to fill up quickly during high season (June-Sept), so it's wise to make **reservations** if you're on a tight budget or bound for somewhere with limited possibilities. This can be done **from abroad** either through specialist travel agents (*Danube Travel* in Britain charges £10 for any number of bookings) or by telexing places yourself. The telex numbers for hotels, campsites and pensions appear in the *Hotel* and *Camping* booklets and the *Tourism Almanac* (see below).

Inside Hungary, bookings for the three nationwide upmarket hotel chains are handled through their respective head offices in Budapest: *HungarHotels* (V, Petőfi utca 16; ☎118-3018), *Pannonia* (VIII, Rákóczi út 9; ☎266-8281) and *Danubius* (V, Szervita tér 8; ☎117-3652). Less expensive hotels and private lodgings in the prov-inces can be reserved through regional tourist offices or local branches of *Ibusz*, while beds in

college dormitories can usually be booked through the local *Express* agency or regional tour-ist office.

The chain of *Tourinform* offices in Budapest and the provinces is the best source of up-to-date information on accommodation of all kinds, although you cannot book beds through them. In the absence of any single, comprehensive **guide to accommodation** in Hungary, you'll have to make do with the free *Camping* and *Hotels* book-lets stocked by most tourist offices, or invest in the *Tourism Almanac* – a trilingual volume (500Ft) known to Hungarians as the *Idegenforgalmi Almanach Magyarország* (available in Budapest bookstores like the *Muszaki Konyvaruhaz*, VI, Liszt Ferenc tér 6, near the Oktogon). This lists numerous pensions and campsites not mentioned in the booklets, but omits others that are.

HOTELS

Although natives call **hotels** *szálló* or *szállóda*, everyone understands the English term. Aside from smaller places in the provinces and a number of "international" hotels in Budapest, most belong to the *HungarHotels*, *Pannonia* or *Danubius* chains (though these are currently in the process of being privatized). For the moment, all hotels still have an official three- or four-star rating (five-star estab-lishments are restricted to Budapest and the Balaton), although this gives only a vague idea of **prices**, which vary according to the locality and the time of year; **high season** is June to September. The star-ratings are also a poor guide to standards, as some places officially meet the basic criteria in terms of facilities, but are in fact awful. This is especially the case in rural areas. As an indication of the way pricing policy is going, many places now simply post current room rates in Deutschmarks (although you pay in forints). More predictably, prices in Budapest and the Balaton region are 15-35 percent higher than in other areas, though rates can drop by as much as 30 percent over **winter**. Breakfast is invariably included in the price.

As with prices, **standards** vary. While four- and five-star establishments are reliably comfort-able, with private bathrooms, TV and central heating, three-star places can be soulless in gone-to-seed Seventies fashion, or redolent of

ACCOMMODATION PRICE CODES

All accommodation listed in the guide is given a price category which refers to the cost of the cheapest available double room in high season, unless otherwise stated. The categories are:

① Under 650Ft (under £4/$6/DM10)
② 650–1500FT (£4–8/$6–13/DM10–20)
③ 1500–3000Ft (£8–17/$13–27/DM20–40)
④ 3000–4500Ft (£17–25/$27–40/DM40–60)

⑤ 4500–6500Ft (£25–36/$40–57/DM60–85)
⑥ 6500–10,000Ft (£36–56/$57–88/DM85–130)
⑦ Over 10,000Ft (over £56/$88/DM130)

"old" Central Europe (a few are ensconced in former stately homes or castles). One- and two-star hotels probably won't have private bathrooms, but might have a sink in the room. Single rooms are rare and **solo travellers** will generally have to pay for a double.

PENSIONS, INNS AND MOTELS

Other types of accommodation are also categorized, with one to three stars. Private (often family owned) **pensions** are appearing in all the towns and villages frequented by tourists, where they often undercut hotels with the same star rating. While some are purpose-built, with a restaurant on the premises, others are simply someone's house with a TV in the living room and a few rooms upstairs. There's no correlation between their appearance and title – some style themselves *panzió* (or *penzió*), others as *fogadó*. The latter designation is also used for **inns**, which can be a pension under another name or more of a motel. Places that actually describe themselves as **motels** are usually on the edge of town, or further out along the highway. Some coexist with bungalows and a campsite to form a tourist complex; quite a few are near a thermal bath or swimming pool, with restaurants and sports facilities, too.

Although the rating system bears some relation to **prices**, local circumstances – and the trade-off between cost and convenience – are more relevant. In some towns, a centrally located pension might cost more than an older one- or two-star hotel; elsewhere they could be the best alternative to a pricey three-star establishment. Similarly, some motels are really cheap, and others on a par with equivalently rated hotels in a better location. Even the rule of thumb that places get cheaper the further you are from Austria or Budapest doesn't always hold, since a pension in a remote village might exploit its monopoly to the hilt.

PRIVATE ROOMS AND FARMSREAD ACCOMMODATION

In Budapest and many towns, **private rooms** in households are often the cheapest options in the centre. This type of accommodation (termed *Fiz*, short for *fizetővendégszolgálat*) can be arranged by local tourist offices for a fee, or by knocking on the door of places with *szoba kiadó* or *Zimmer frei* signs advertising vacant rooms – which abound along the west bank of the Danube Bend, both shores of Lake Balaton, and in thermal spas throughout Hungary. In Budapest and the Balaton region, the **price** of a private double room is well below hotel and pension rates, although places accustomed to an influx of Germans and Austrians sometimes charge premium prices. Unfortunately, many landlords also charge thirty percent extra if you stay fewer than three nights, and a general lack of single rooms means that solo travellers have to pay for a double.

Although tourist offices rent sight unseen, you can still exercise judgement when **choosing a room** by rejecting dubious-sounding locations. As a rule of thumb, a town's *Belváros* (inner sector) is likely to consist of spacious apartments with parquet floors, high ceilings and a balcony overlooking a courtyard, whereas the outlying zones are probably charmless, high-rise modern developments. Either way, your hostess (widows and divorcees are the biggest renters) will probably be helpful and then self-effacing, but a few words of Hungarian will make you seem less of a stranger. Use of the washing machine comes free, and some landladies will provide breakfast for a fee, although most leave early for work. For this reason, it's usually impossible to take possession of the room before 5pm; after that you can come and go with a key.

It's possible to rent whole **apartments** in some towns and resorts, while in western and southern Hungary many tourist offices can arrange rural **farmstead accommodation** in old buildings converted into holiday homes with kitchen facilities. Both come more expensive than private rooms, but if there's a group of you, or you're travelling with children, they could prove to be just the thing.

HOSTELS AND DORMITORIES

Although many are due to close or become private pensions in the future, hostels are currently the cheapest available lodgings in Hungary. There are two kinds of official **tourist hostels**: *Túristaszálló* - generally found in provincial towns - and *Túristaház*, located in highland areas favoured by hikers. Both are graded "A" or "B" depending on the availability of hot water and the number of beds per room. *Túristaszálló* rates range from £2–8/$3-12: the former for a bed, the latter for a double or triple room. In *Túristaház*, which rarely have separate rooms, a dormitory bed goes for £2-3/$3-5. It's generally advisable to make bookings through the regional tourist office. Some hostels are official IYHF hostels, for which you'll need a membership card issued by the national hostel organization in your own country – though, in practice, many hostels in Hungary don't insist you have the card.

In many towns, you can also stay in vacant **college dormitories** for about £3/$5 a night. Generally, these accept tourists at weekends throughout the year, and over the whole of the summer vacation (roughly July to mid-Aug). It is usually possible to make bookings through the local *Express* agency or the regional tourist office, but otherwise you can just turn up at the designated college (*kollégium*) and ask if there are any beds available.

BUNGALOWS AND CAMPSITES

Throughout Hungary, bungalows and campsites come together in complexes where tourists of the world unite. **Bungalows** (*üdölőház*) proliferate around resorts, where many were previously reserved for trade union members but now take anyone to balance their books. Rates for renting bungalows (aka *faház*, literally "wooden houses") go for £4–15/$6-23, depending on amenities and size (usually 2-4 persons). The first-class bungalows – with well-equipped kitchens, hot water and a sitting room or terrace – are excellent, while the most primitive at least have clean bedding and don't leak.

Campsites – usually signposted *Kemping* – similarly range across the spectrum from "deluxe" to third class. The more elaborate places boast a restaurant and shops (sometimes even a disco) and tend to be overcrowded; second- or third-class sites often have a nicer ambience, with lots of old trees rather than a manicured lawn ineffectually shaded by saplings, and acres of campers and trailers. Expect to pay at least £2/$3, or twice that around Lake Balaton, which has the most expensive sites in Hungary. Fees are calculated on a basic ground rent, plus a charge per head and for any vehicle, plus, for non-students, an obligatory local tax (*kurtaxe*). There are **reductions** of 25–30 percent during "low" season (Oct–May) when fewer sites are open, and during the high season for members of the *FICC* (International Camping and Caravanning Club). Children up to the age of 14 also qualify for fifty percent reductions off the cost of camping. While a few resorts and towns have semi-official **free campsites** (*szabad kemping*), **camping rough** is illegal, although young Hungarians sometimes do it in highland areas where there are "rain shelters" (*esőház*).

EATING AND DRINKING

Even under Communism, Hungary was renowned for its abundance of food: material proof of the "goulash socialism" that amazed visitors from Romania and the Soviet Union. Nowadays, there is more choice than ever, particularly in Budapest, where almost every cuisine in the world is available.

For foreigners the archetypal Magyar dish is "goulash" - historically the basis of much **Hungarian cooking**. The ancient Magyars relished cauldrons of *gulyás* (pronounced "gou-yash") - a soup made of potatoes and whatever meat was available, which was later flavoured with paprika and beefed up into a variety of stews, modified over the centuries by various foreign influences. Hungary's Slav neighbours probably introduced native cooks to yogurt and sour cream (vital ingredients in many dishes); while the influence of the Turks, Austrians and Germans is apparent in a variety of sticky pastries and strudels, plus recipes featuring sauerkraut or dumplings. Another influence was that of France, which revolutionized Hungarian cooking in the Middle Ages and again in the nineteenth century. Today, the influences are "international", with fast food such as pizzas, hamburgers and kebabs spreading from the capital to provincial towns, and even signs of vegetarian and *nouvelle cuisine*.

BREAKFAST, SNACKS AND TAKEAWAY FOOD

As a nation of early risers, Hungarians like to have a calorific **breakfast** (*reggeli*). Commonly,

this includes cheese, eggs or salami together with bread and jam, and in rural areas is often accompanied by a shot of *pálinka* (brandy) to "clear the palate" or "aid digestion". By 8am, cafés and snack bars are already functioning, and the rush hour is prime time for *Tej-bár* or *Tejivó*. These stand-up milk bars serve mugs of hot milk (*meleg tej*) and sugary cocoa (*kakaó*), cheese-filled pastry cones (*sajtos pogácsa*) and rolls (*sajtos-rolló*), envelopes of dough filled with curds (*túrós táska*), spongy milk-bread with raisins (*mazsolás kalács*), and other dunkable pastries.

Everyone is addicted to **coffee**. At intervals throughout the day, people consume tiny glasses of *kávé* - super-strong, served black and sweetened to taste - a brew that can double your heart beat. **Coffee houses** were once the centres of Budapest's cultural and political life, hotbeds of gossip where penurious writers got credit and the clientele dawdled for hours over the free newspapers. Sadly this is no longer the case, but you'll find plenty of unpretentious *kávéház* serving the beverage with milk (*tejeskávé*) or whipped cream (*tejszínhabbal*) should you request it. Most coffee houses have some pastries on offer, although you'll find much more choice in the patisseries (see "Cakes and ice cream", below) which, of course, also serve coffee. **Tea**-drinkers are a minority here, perhaps because Hungarian tea with milk (*tejes tea*) is so insipid - although *tea citrommal* (with lemon) is fine.

A whole range of places purvey **snacks**, notably *Csemege* or **delicatessens**, which display a tempting spread of salads, open sandwiches, pickles and cold meats; in a few, you can eat on the premises. Unfortunately, many delis (like *Tej-bár*) use the system whereby customers order and pay at the cash desk (*kassza*) in return for a receipt to be exchanged at the food counter. If your Hungarian is minimal, this can throw up a few misunderstandings.

For sit-down nibbles, people patronize either **bisztró**, which tend to offer a couple of hot dishes besides the inevitable salami rolls; *snackbár*, which are superior versions of the same, with leanings in the direction of being a patisserie; or *büfé*. These last are found in department stores and stations, and are sometimes open around the clock. The food on offer,

DISHES AND TERMS

What follows is by no means a comprehensive list of Hungarian dishes, but by combining names and terms it should be possible to decipher anything that you're likely to see on a menu. Alcoholic and soft drinks are covered in the text, as are desserts and pastries, which are best sampled in the ubiquitous *cukrászda*.

Basics, and how to order

bors	pepper	*kenyér*	bread
cukor	sugar	*kifli*	croissant
ecet	vinegar	*méz*	honey
egészségedre!	Cheers!	*mustár*	mustard
jó étvágyat!	Bon appetit!	*rizs*	rice

só	salt
vaj	butter
zsemle or	bread rolls
péksütemeny	

Legyen szives ("Would you be so kind . . ".) is the polite way of attracting a waiter's attention; while you can say *Kérnék . . .* or *Szeretnék . . .* ("I'd like . . ".), or *Kaphatnék . . .* ("Can I have . . . ?") **to order**. Using these grammatical forms, Hungarians add a suffix (*-t, -et, -ot* or *-at*) to the item being requested, so that *vaj* becomes *vajat, kávé, kávét*, and so on.

Appetizers (*előételek*), soups (*levesek*) and salads (*saláták*)

bécsi hering-saláta	Viennese-style herring with vinegar	*gulyásleves*	meat, vegetable and paprika soup
halmajonéz	fish with mayonnaise	*kunsági pandúrleves*	chicken or pigeon soup
majonézes kukorica	sweetcorn with mayonnaise		seasoned with nutmeg, paprika, ginger and
bakonyi betyárleves	"Outlaw soup" of chicken, beef, noodles and vegetables, richly spiced		garlic
		lencseleves	lentil soup
csirke-aprólék leves	mixed vegetable and giblet soup	*meggyleves*	delicious chilled sour cherry soup
csontleves	bland bone and noodle consommé	*palócleves*	mutton, bean and sour cream soup
bajai halászlé	fish and tomato soup	*paradicsomleves*	tomato soup
bableves	beans and meat soup – a meal in itself	*szegedi halászlé*	Szeged-style mixed-fish soup
		zöldségleves	vegetable soup
burgonyaleves	potato, onion and paprika soup	*alföldi saláta*	"Puszta salad" – sliced sausages in a vinaigrette dressing
gombaleves	mushroom soup		
(kalocsai) halászleves	spicy fish soup (with red wine)	*almás cékla*	dressed apple and beetroot slices

The names of other **salads** are easy to work out if you refer to the section on vegetables. **Cream** and **sour cream** feature in dishes whose name includes the words *tejszín, krém*, and *tejföl*.

Fish dishes (*halételek*)

csuka tejfölben sütve	fried pike with sour cream	*paprikás ponty*	carp in paprika sauce
fogas	a local fish of the pike-perch family	*ponty filé gombával*	carp fillet in mushroom sauce
fogasszeletek Gundel modra	breaded fillet of fogas	*pisztráng tejszínes mártásban*	trout baked in cream
kecsege	sterlet (small sturgeon)	*rostélyos töltött ponty*	carp stuffed with bread, egg, herbs and fish liver or roe
. . tejszínes paprikás mártásban	. . . in a cream and paprika sauce	*sült hal*	fried fish
nyelvhal	sole	*tőkehal*	cod
		tonhal	tuna

Meat (*húsételek*) and poultry (*baromfi*) dishes

alföldi marha-rostélyos	steak with a rich sauce and stewed vegetables	*paprikás-csirke*	chicken in paprika sauce
bográcsgulyás	what foreigners mean by "Goulash"	*rablóhús nyárson*	kebab of pork, veal and bacon
borjúpörkölt	veal stew seasoned with garlic	*sertésborda*	pork chop
csabai szarvascomb	venison stuffed with spicy sausage	*sonka*	ham
		töltött-káposzta	cabbage stuffed with meat and rice, in a tomato sauce
cigányrostélyos	"Gypsy-style" steak with brown sauce	*töltött-paprika*	peppers stuffed with meat and rice, in a tomato sauce
csikós tokány	strips of beef braised in bacon, onion rings, sour cream and tomato sauce	*vaddisznó borókamártással*	wild boar in juniper sauce
csirke	chicken	*virsli*	frankfurter
erdélyi rakott-káposzta	layers of cabbage, rice and ground pork baked in sour cream – a Transylvanian speciality	**Terms**	
		comb	leg
fasírozott	meatballs	*angolosan (Englishly)*	underdone/rare
hortobágyi rostélyos	steak "Hortobágy style"; braised in stock, with a large dumpling	*főve*	boiled
		jól megsütve	well done (fried)
kacsa	duck	*jól megfőzve*	well done (boiled)
kolbász	spicy sausage	*pörkölt*	stewed slowly
liba	goose	*rántott*	in breadcrumbs
máj	liver	*roston sütve*	grilled
marhahús	beef	*sülve*	roasted
nyúl	rabbit	*sült/sütve*	fried

Sauces (*mártásban*)

Many restaurants serve meat or fish dishes in rich **sauces** – a legacy of French culinary influence.

almamártásban	in an apple sauce	*kapormártásban*	in a dill sauce
bormártásban	in a wine sauce	*meggymártásban*	in a morello cherry sauce
gombamártásban	in a mushroom sauce	*paprikás mártásban*	in a paprika sauce
ecetes torma	with horseradish	*tárkonyos mártásban*	in a tarragon sauce
fehérhagyma mártásban	in an onion sauce	*vadasmártásban*	in a brown sauce (made of mushrooms, almonds, herbs and brandy)
fokhagymás mártásban	in a garlic sauce		

Vegetables (*zöldség*)

bab	beans	*fokhagyma*	garlic	*paprika – édes* or *erős*	peppers – sweet or hot
borsó	peas	*gomba*	mushrooms	*paradicsom*	tomatoes
burgonya (krumpli)	potatoes ("spuds")	*hagyma*	onions	*sárgarepa*	carrots
		káposzta	cabbage	*spárga*	asparagus
ecetes uborka	gherkin	*karfiol*	cauliflower	*uborka*	cucumber
fejes saláta	lettuce	*kukorica*	sweet corn	*zöldbab*	green beans

Fruit (*gyümölcs*) and cheese (*sajt*)

alma	apples	*málna*	raspberries	*füstölt sajt*	smoked cheese
barack	apricots	*mandula*	almonds	*karaván*	tasty smoked cheese
citrancs	grapefruit	*meggy*	morello cherries	*márvány*	Stilton-like blue cheese
citrom	lemon				
dió	walnuts	*mogyoró*	hazelnuts	*trappista*	rubbery, Edam-type cheese
eper	strawberries	*narancs*	oranges		
füge	figs	*őszibarack*	peaches		
(görög) dinnye	(water) melon	*szilva*	plums		
körte	pears	*szőlő*	grapes		

though, is often limited to tired sandwiches and greasy sausages filled with rice (called *hurka* and *kolbász*).

On the streets, according to season, vendors preside over vats of *kukorica* (corn on the cob) or trays of *gesztenye* (roasted chestnuts); while fried fish (*sült hal*) shops are common in towns near rivers or lakes. *Szendvics*, *hamburger* and *gofri* (waffle) stands are mushrooming in the larger towns, while *McDonald's* and *Burger King* are spreading across the country. **Around resorts**, another popular munch is *lángos*: the native, mega-size equivalent of doughnuts, often sold with a sprinkling of cheese or a dash of syrup. Fruit, too, is sold by street vendors and **in markets**, where you'll also find various greasy spoon cafés forking out *hurka* and the like. Outdoor markets (*piac*) are colourful affairs, sometimes with the bizarre sight of rows of poultry sheltered beneath sunshades; in market halls (*vásárcsarnok*) people select their fish fresh from glass tanks, and their mushrooms from a staggering array of *gomba*, which are displayed alongside toxic fungi in a "mushroom parade" to enable shoppers to recognize the difference.

No list of snacks is complete without mentioning **bread** (*kenyér*), which is so popular, as the old saying has it, that "Hungarians will even eat bread with bread". White bread remains the staple of the nation, but in many supermarkets, especially in Budapest, you can usually get a range of brown (*barna*) and rye (*rozs*) breads.

MAIN MEALS

Traditionally, Hungarians take their main meal at **midday**; although the old tendency for restaurants to have fewer dishes available in the evenings has now disappeared. However, it is worth remembering that many places still close early, around 10pm, although this is changing, particularly in Budapest. There's some compensation, though, in the bands of musicians that play in many restaurants at lunchtime and in the evening, their violin airs and melodic plonkings of the cimbalom (see "Gypsy and Folk Music", p.37) an essential element of the "Hungarian scene".

Places used to tourists often have **menus** in German (and sometimes English), a language of which most waiters and waitresses have a smattering. Particularly in Budapest, tourist-oriented establishments may give you a menu without

prices - a sure sign that they're expensive, or plan to rip you off. Unfortunately, **overcharging** is on the increase, and even fluent Hungarian speakers can get burned if they don't check the bill carefully. While some restaurants offer a bargain menu (*napi menü*) of basic dishes, the majority of places are strictly *à la carte*. For a three-course meal with wine, expect to pay £5–10/$8–15 in an average restaurant, twice that in downtown Budapest. A service charge isn't usually included in the bill and the staff depend on customers **tipping** (ten percent of the total is customary). If you say "thank you" as you hand the money over, this implies that they can keep the change, so be warned.

Hungarians have a variety of words implying fine distinctions among **restaurants**. In theory an **étterem** is a proper restaurant, while a **vendéglő** approximates to the Western notion of a bistro, but in practice the terms are often used interchangeably. The old word for an inn, **csárda**, applies to posh places specializing in certain dishes (for example, a "Fishermen's inn" or **halászcsárda**), restaurants alongside roads or with rustic pretensions, as well as to the humbler rural establishments that the name originally signified.

When they can afford to be, Hungarians are enthusiastic eaters, so as a (presumably rich) Westerner you'll be asked if you want **starters** (*előételek*) - generally a soup or salad. Nobody will mind, however, if you just have one of the dishes offered as the **main course** (*főételek*) or, alternatively, order just a soup and a starter. Bread is supplied almost automatically, on the grounds that "a meal without bread is no meal". **Drinks** are normally listed on the menu under the heading *italok*.

VEGETARIANS

Despite the emergence of *vegetarianus* restaurants in Budapest, and a growing understanding of the concept, the outlook for **vegetarians** remains poor: most Hungarians are amazed that anyone might forgo meat willingly. Aside from cooked vegetables (notably *rántott gomba*, mushrooms in breadcrumbs), the only meatless dish that's widely available is **eggs** - fried (literally "mirror" - *tükörtojás*), soft-boiled (*lágy tojás*), scrambled (*tojásrántotta*), or in mayonnaise (*kaszinótojás*). Even innocuous vegetable soups may contain meat stock, and the pervasive use of sour cream and animal fat in cooking means that avoiding animal products or by-products is difficult. However, greengrocers (*zöldségbolt*) and markets sell excellent produce which, combined with judicious shopping in supermarkets (for pulses, grains, etc), should see you through.

CAKES AND ICE CREAM

Numerous **patisseries** (*cukrászda*) pander to the Magyar fondness for sweet things. **Pancakes** (*palacsinta*) **with fillings** - *almás* (apple), *diós* (walnuts), *fahéjas* (cinnamon), *mákos* (poppy seeds), *mandula* (almonds) or *Gundel*-style, with nuts, chocolate sauce, cream and raisins - are very popular, as are **strudels** (*rétes*) made with curds and dill (*kapros túrós rétes*), poppy seeds (*mákosrétes*) or plums (*szilvás rétes*). Even the humble dumpling is transformed into a *somlói galuska*, flavoured with vanilla, nuts and chocolate. But the frontrunners in the rich 'n' sticky stakes have to be chestnut pureé with whipped cream (*gesztenyepüré*); coffee soufflé (*kapucineres felfújt*); baked apple with vanilla, raisins and cream (*töltött alma*); and the staggering array of **cakes**. *Dobostorta* (chocolate cream cake topped with caramel) and the pineapple-laden *ananásztorta* are just two; the average *cukrászda* displays a dozen or more types.

If you're still not satiated, there's **ice cream** (*fagylalt*), the opium of the masses, sold by the scoop (*gombóc*) and priced low enough so that anyone can afford a cone. The most common flavours are *vanília*, *csokoládé*, *puncs* (fruit punch), *citrom* and *kávé*; but mango, pistachio, and various nutty flavours can be found - see the fruit section of the food glossary for the Magyar names. And finally there's *metélt or tészta* - a rather unlikely sounding but quite tasty dessert of chopped sweet noodles, served cold with poppy seeds or some other topping.

DRINKING: WINES, BEERS, SPIRITS AND SOFT DRINKS

Hungary's mild climate and diversity of soils is perfect for **wine** (*bor*), which is perennially cheap, whether you buy it by the bottle (*üveg*) or the glass (*pohár*). The main wine-growing regions surround Pécs, Eger, Kecskemét, Sopron and Tokaj, and cover large areas of the Balaton and Mátra highlands. Standards are constantly rising as more vineyards try to win the right to label their bottles *minöségi bor* (quality wine), the equivalent of *appelation contrôlée*. In recent years, Hungary's wines have improved dramatically, as private vineyards are now able to make and sell their own wine without handing it in to the local cooperative. They are also reviving the old skills, and taking better care of their grapes - in the old days the main concern was to supply the bottomless Soviet market, and to this end poor-quality grapes were grown. That market has now gone, restricting sales dramatically, but improving quality. Prices have also risen sharply, though there are still cheaper varieties available on shop shelves.

Hungarian **red wines** (*Vörös bor*) can be divided into light-bodied and full-bodied varieties. Examples of the former are *Villányi burgundi*, *Vaskúti kadarka* and *Egri pinot noir*; in the full-bodied category are *Villányi medoc noir*, *Tihanyi merlot*, *Soproni kékfrankos* and the famous *Egri bikavér*, or "Bulls' Blood of Eger". **White wines** (*fehér bor*) are classified as sweet (*édes*) or dry (*száraz or furmint*). *Olasz riszling* wines tend to be sweet, with the exception of the "Sand Wines" produced on the sandy soil between the Tisza and the Danube. Other sweet whites include *Balatonfüredi szemelt*, *Akali zöldszilváni* and the richest of the Tokaj wines, *Tokaji aszú*. In the dry category are two wines from the Badacsony vineyards, *szürkebarát* and *zöldszilváni*; *Egri Leányka* from the Gyöngyös region; and two varieties of Tokaj, *furmint* and *szamorodni*. *Tököly* and *Pannonia* are sparkling wines.

Wine bars (*borozó*) are ubiquitous and generally far less pretentious than in the West; true devotees of the grape make pilgrimages to the extensive **wine cellars** (*borpince*) that honeycomb towns like Tokaj and Eger. By day, people often drink wine with water or soda water, specifying a *fröccs* or a yet more diluted *hosszú lépés* (literally, a "long step"). Hungarians enjoy the ritual of **toasting**, so the first word to get your tongue around is *egészségedre* ("EGG-aish-shaig-edreh") - cheers! When toasting more than one other person, it's grammatically correct to change this to *egészségünkre* (Cheers to us!). Hungarians only consider it appropriate to toast with wine or spirits.

SPIRITS

As long as you stick to native brands, **spirits** are also cheap. The best-known type of *pálinka* - brandy - is distilled from apricots (*barack*), and is a speciality of the Kecskemét region, but spirits are also produced from peaches (*öszibarack*), pears (*körte*), and any other fruits available. This is particularly true of *szilva* - a lethal spirit produced on cottage stills in rural areas, allegedly based on plums. Hungarians with money to burn order whisky (*viszki*) to impress, but most people find its cost prohibitive. Vodka isn't popular, despite the availability of excellent Russian *Stolichnaya* in *ABC*s.

BEER

Bottled **beer** (*sör*) of the lager type (*világos*) predominates, although you might come across brown ale (*barna sör*) and draught beer (*csapolt sör*). Western brands like *Tuborg, Wernesgrünner* and *Gold Fassel* are imported or brewed under licence at Nagykanizsa, and the famous old Austro-Hungarian beer *Dreher* has made a comeback, displacing cheaper Magyar brands such as

Kőbányai, or imported Czech *Urquell* Pilsen. Other brands to try are *Arany Ászok*, a very cheap light beer, and *Pannonia Sör*, a pleasant hoppy beer from Pécs.

Beer halls (*söröző*) range from plush establishments sponsored by foreign breweries to humble stand-up joints where you order either a small glass (*pohár*) or a half-litre mug (*korsó*).

SOFT DRINKS

Pepsi and Coke and various sugary, fruit-flavoured **soft drinks** are sold everywhere. A few (mostly German) brands of unsweetened fruit juices can be found in supermarkets and *Vitamin Porta* shops. Most *ABC*s also stock bottled *limonádé*, mineral water (*ásvány víz*), soda water (*szóda víz*) and a range of fruit juice.

COMMUNICATIONS: POST, PHONES AND MEDIA

POST OFFICES

Post offices (*posta*) are usually open Monday to Friday 8am-6pm and until noon on Saturday, although in Budapest you'll find several offices functioning around the clock. Mail from abroad should be addressed "*poste restante, posta*" followed by the name of the town; tell your friends to write your surname first, Hungarian-style, and underline it; even this may not prevent your mail being misfiled, so ask them to check under all your names. To collect mail, show your passport and ask "*Van posta a részemre?*" It's

probably safer to send mail to the *American Express* office in Budapest (V, Deák Ferenc utca 10), or their former office, the 24-hour *Ibusz* bureau (V, Petőfi tér 3) - where letters marked "c/o American Express" are lovingly guarded until collection and the staff speak English.

It's quicker to buy **stamps** (*bélyeg*) at tobacconists; post offices are often full of people making complicated transactions or sending telegrams (*távirat*), which can also be dictated by dialling ☎02.

TELEPHONES

Hungary's **telephone network** is being improved and expanded, but remains patchy and inefficient at the time of writing. In towns and cities, **local calls** can be made from public phones with 5, 10 or 20Ft coins. **Long-distance calls** are more problematic, for while lines between Budapest and provincial centres are fine, communications between smaller towns are poor and all incoming or outgoing calls must be placed by the post office or the operator (☎01). This goes for all numbers prefixed by the locality's name rather than an area code. Elsewhere, it should be possible to make direct calls by dialling ☎06 (which gives a strange tone), followed by the area code and the subscriber's number. Even so, you might still achieve better results by

---

TELEPHONE CODES

Phoning abroad from Hungary
Dial the following numbers + area code +
subscriber number
Australia ☎00 61
Ireland ☎00 353
New Zealand ☎00 64
UK ☎00 44
USA and Canada ☎00 1

Phoning Hungary from abroad
Dial the following numbers + Hungarian area code
+ subscriber number
Australia ☎0011 36
Ireland ☎00 36
New Zealand ☎00 36
UK ☎00 36
USA and Canada ☎011 36

Area codes for Hungarian towns and cities appear throughout the guide.

---

getting the post office or operator to place the call.

In downtown Budapest and the Balaton resorts there are now booths taking **phonecards**, which can be bought from main post offices for 250Ft or 600Ft – an innovation that is fast spreading throughout the country. You can use the cards in the special red or grey booths (also taking 10Ft and 20Ft coins) that allow you to make **international calls**. Dial ☎00, then the country code (see box above), the area code and finally the number – and keep your fingers crossed. Alternatively, you can place calls through the **international operator** (☎09), the Central Telephone Bureau in Budapest, or fancy hotels in the provinces (which levy a hefty surcharge).

THE MEDIA

Without a knowledge of Hungarian you can only appreciate certain aspects of the **media**. Foreign cable and satellite television have made huge inroads, and there is a rash of tabloids and magazines devoted to soft porn and celebrity trivia.

Western programmes are much in evidence on the two national **television** stations, TV1 and TV2, which many Hungarians augment by subscribing to satellite channels like *Sky*, *MTV* or *Super Channel*, with whole apartment blocks sharing the cost of installation. Television has been the scene of political battles in recent years as the newly elected democratic governments try to retain control of the medium. With the failure of parliament to pass a law on commercial broadcasting,

the only local rivals to state-controlled television are a few, small, local television stations.

The serious **press** is strictly partisan, with *Uj Magyarország* supporting the conservatives, while *Népszabadság* (formerly Communist, but now avowedly socialist) and *Magyar Hirlap* adopt a stance that is less critical of the incumbent socialist coalition government. Having made a big splash as Hungary's first "independent" paper in 1988, the tabloid weekly *Reform* no longer attracts much attention with its mix of scandal and scantily clad pin-ups.

In Budapest you can buy papers and magazines **in English** and other languages, notably *The Times, Guardian, Herald Tribune, Newsweek* and *Time*; German publications are also sold around Lake Balaton. There is a wealth of English-language weeklies: *Budapest Week* and *Budapest Sun* both have entertainment and events listings as well as news coverage that is occasionally informative, while the *Budapest Business Journal* covers business and some politics only.

If these don't appeal, drop into the British or American cultural centres in Budapest, or try the **radio**. A new German-language station, *Radio Danubius*, lets rip with pop, rap and ads, broadcasting on a daily basis from 6.30am to 10pm throughout the summer until October 31 (100.5, 103.3, or 102 MHz VHF); while *Radio Petőfi* broadcasts news in English once daily from June to August. Alternatively, you can tune into the *BBC World Service*.

OPENING HOURS AND HOLIDAYS

During the week, most public buildings are open from 8.30am to 5pm, but it's worth remembering that the staff at lesser institutions usually take an hour off around noon for lunch. Aside from shops (see below) and tourist offices, the most obvious exceptions are museums, which almost always close on Monday. Otherwise, opening times are affected by public holidays, when most things shut down; there's a list in the box below. For the opening hours of pharmacies (see p.17) and banks (p.18), see the relevant sections of *Basics*, above

SHOPS

Shops are open Mon-Fri 10am-6pm, with supermarkets and grocery stores open 8am-6pm or until 7pm in larger towns. On Saturday most places close at 1pm, and you cannot rely on finding shops open after that. There are exceptions: one or two shops have extended their Saturday opening hours, and in Budapest and other larger centres there are numerous 24-hour shops - the

---

PUBLIC HOLIDAYS

On the following days, most things in Hungary shut down; and note that **should any of these holidays fall on a Tuesday or Thursday, the day between it and the weekend also becomes a holiday.**

January 1
March 15
Easter Monday
May 1
August 20
October 23
December 25
December 26

For the dates of other major festivals and celebrations, not all of which are public holidays, see "Festivals", p.39.

---

signs to look for are *Non-Stop, 0-24* or *Ejjel-Nappali*. Generally, supermarkets are called *ABC* and department stores *Aruház*, while shops are usually named after their wares, for example *húsbolt* (butchers), *italbolt* (drink), *papírirószerbolt* (stationery shop) and *ciposbolt* (shoe shop).

MUSEUMS

Museums are generally open Tuesday to Sunday 10am-6pm (winter 9am-5pm, or earlier), but there are many exceptions; current hours are detailed in the guide. As public subsidies are withdrawn, many of the smaller museums may close down altogether over winter. For details of admission charges, see "Directory", p.43.

CHURCHES AND SYNAGOGUES

Hungary's few remaining mosques (*djami*) now qualify as museums rather than places of worship, but getting into **churches** (*templom*) may pose problems. The really important ones charge a small fee to see their crypts and treasures, and may prohibit sightseeing during services (*szertartás*, or *Gottdienst* in German). In small towns and villages, however, churches are usually kept locked except for worship in the early morning and/or the evening (between around 6 and 9pm). A small tip is in order if you rouse the verger to unlock the building during the day; he normally lives nearby in a house with a doorbell marked *plébánia csengője*. Visitors are expected to wear "decorous" dress - that is, no shorts or sleeveless tops.

Most of Hungary's **synagogues** were ransacked during World War II and subsequently left derelict or given over to other functions. Although a fair number have been reopened and restored since the late 1980s, only Budapest retains a sizeable Jewish community.

The Hungarian terms for the main **religious denominations** are: *Katolikus* (Catholic), *Református* (Reformed or Calvinist), *Evangélikus* (Lutheran), *Görög* (Greek Orthodox), *Görög-Katolikus* (Uniate) and *Zsidó* (Jewish).

POLICE, TROUBLE AND SEXUAL HARASSMENT

The Hungarian police (*Rendőrség*) always had a milder reputation than their counterparts in other Eastern Bloc states, and are keen to present a favourable image. Foreign tourists are generally handled with kid gloves unless suspected of black-marketeering, drug-smuggling, driving under the influence of alcohol, or of being illegal immigrants (who, like Hungary's Gypsy minority, are roughly treated).

PAPERWORK, EMERGENCIES AND TROUBLE

Since police in towns occasionally ask to inspect **passports and visas**, you should make sure that everything's in order. In border regions, solo travellers may be (politely and briefly) questioned by plain-clothes officers; but here too, if your stamps are in order, there shouldn't be any problem. Most police officers have at least a smattering of German, but rarely any other foreign language. If you need the police, dial ☎07 in **emergencies**; should you be arrested or need legal advice, ask to contact your embassy or consulate (see "Listings" in *Budapest* for the addresses).

Although **theft** and violent crime are rare, their incidence is growing, not least because of the widening gap between rich and poor.

Budapest in particular is no longer utterly safe at night, though still far less risky than any Western capital. There has also been a worrying upsurge in **racist attacks** on Africans, Asians and Arabs, in some cases encouraged by foreign neo-Nazis. That said, most **trouble** can be avoided: don't sunbathe nude or topless unless everyone else is, or deal on the black market, and you've eliminated the likeliest causes.

SEXUAL HARASSMENT

The exception is **sexual harassment**, which is mainly a problem for women travelling alone, and more likely in certain situations than in others. "Provocative" clothing may encourage unwelcome male attention if you visit rural or working-class *italbolt* (bars); hitchhiking alone is not recommended. It is also advisable to avoid travelling on the "black train" (see p.290), and walking around Budapest's VIII district or in Miskolc after dark.

Mostly, harassment is of the annoying rather than the frightening variety, and it's probably not worth responding with "*ne fogdoss!*" (keep your hands to yourself!) or "*menj a fenébe!*" (go to hell!). The important word to remember is *segítség!* - help! - although it's unlikely that you'll need to use it.

ENTERTAINMENT AND FESTIVALS

Music and dance are probably the easiest paths through the thicket of language that surrounds Hungarian culture, but they're not the only accessible forms of entertainment. During the summer in particular, you'll find plays or films in foreign languages - or festivals where language is a minor obstacle - in many of the main towns and resorts.

GYPSY AND FOLK MUSIC

No visitor to Hungary should fail to experience **Gypsy music** or *cigányzene*, which is widely performed in restaurants during the evening, usually by one or two violinists, a bass player and a guy on the **cimbalom** - a stringed instrument played with little hammers. *Mulatni* means "to be possessed by music", and the Gypsies have always venerated the range of sounds and emotions produced by the violin, the playing of which - *bashavav* - has traditionally had magical associations. The sense of awe that great violinists used to inspire, and their bohemian lifestyles, are well captured in Walter Starkie's book *Raggle Taggle* (see "Books" in *Contexts*).

Hungarians are keen to make requests or sing along when the *Prímás* (band leader) comes to the table, soliciting tips. If approached yourself, it is acceptable (though rather awkward) to decline with a *nem, köszönöm*. Nowadays, most musicians are townspeople and graduates of the *Rajkó* music school, rather than wandering, self-taught artists like János Bihari, Czinka Panna and Czermak (a nobleman turned vagabond) - who were legendary figures during the nineteenth century. However, it's still common for sons to follow their fathers into the profession.

Confusingly, this archetypal "Hungarian" music is neither Hungarian nor Gypsy in its origins. The music performed by Gypsies among their own communities (in Szabolcs-Szatmár county, for example) is actually far closer to the music of India and Central Asia. Look out for groups such as *Kalyi Jag* (Black Fire), *Lindri* or *Andro Drom*, or keep an eye out for Gypsy evenings at the Almássy tér Centre in Budapest.

Hungarian folk music (*Magyar népzene*) is different again, having originated around the Urals and the Turkic steppes over a millennium ago. The haunting rhythms and pentatonic scale of this "Old Style" music (to use Bartók's terminology) were subsequently overlaid by "New Style" European influences - which have been discarded by twentieth-century enthusiasts in the folk revival centred around **Táncház**. These "Dance Houses" encourage people to build and learn to play archaic instruments, besides providing the site for **dances** which are usually fast and furious - particularly the wild, foot-stamping *csárdás*, or "tavern dance". Aside from Dance Houses, you can hear folk music at various festivals (see below), and at concerts by **groups** like *Muzsikás* and Téka ensembles.

POPULAR MUSIC AND JAZZ

At Budapest clubs and Balaton discos, the most **popular music** is whatever was the rage in the West six months earlier. Depending on the venue, this is likely to be Eurorock, house or rap music - either imported straight from New York or Berlin, or cooked up by a sound-alike group in Budapest. Live music - at least outside the capital - is pretty much limited to the obligatory summer concerts by native pop stars (advertised in *Programme* magazine), or appearances by bands in smoky local clubs (look for flyposters carrying the word *zene*, music). Budapest itself, since it became established on the international concert circuit in the mid-1980s, has been visited by such diverse foreign acts as Talking Heads, Bob Dylan, Bruce Springsteen, Public Enemy and Tina Turner. Concerts usually take place in one of the city's football stadiums over summer.

At the time of writing the **contemporary music scene** is derivative and uninspiring. The charts are dominated by Kylie Minogue clones such as *Dora* and *Szandi*, or heavy metal/thrash groups like *Ossian, V. Moto-rock* and *Bikini*. The punky female duo *Pa-dö-dö* is also popular at the moment, as is *Bonanza Banzai*. The local club circuit also throws up skinhead bands like *Akció, Egység* (Action, Unity) and *Egészéges Fejbőr* (Healthy Headskin), whose neo-Nazi fans are best avoided.

Though nowhere near as popular, **jazz** is currently undergoing a revival. The Budapest club scene offers the widest choice, but aficionados should check *Programme* magazine for advance notice of jazz **festivals** at Debrecen, Tatabánya, Székesfehérvár, Nagykanizsa or Zalaegerszeg - usually over summer. *Aladár Pege* and the *Benkó Dixieland Band* have both achieved success outside Hungary, but foreign jazz fans have yet to cotton on to pianist György Szabados, who works on the interface between jazz and classical music.

CLASSICAL MUSIC, OPERA AND DANCE

Bartók, Kodály and Liszt still enjoy pride of place in the field of **classical music**, but modern composers can be heard at the *Interforum* festival, staged at Keszthely every three years (scheduled next for 1996) and the contemporary music festival in Budapest in the autumn. The **Budapest Spring Festival** has become a major event, with classical music, contemporary dance, film and other arts represented. Smaller Spring festivals take place at the same time in Szeged, Debrecen, Szombathely, Kecskemet and other towns; there are also similar "seasons" over **summer** (in Szeged) and **autumn** (in Budapest and Nyíregyháza).

Aside from these landmarks, the concert year features Haydn's and Beethoven's works (performed in the palatial surroundings of the Esterházy and Brunswick mansions); orchestral concerts at Veszprém and Diósgyőr castles; organ recitals in the main churches of Pécs, Buda, Debrecen, Eger, Miskolc, Szeged and Tihany; and chorales in the Gothic churches at Kőröshegy and Nyírbátor (mainly over summer). Performers to watch out for are pianists András Schiff, Dezsö Ránki and Zoltán Kocsis, and cellist Miklôs Perényi. The best of the country's orchestras is the youthful Budapest Festival Orchestra, under its leading conductor Iván Fischer.

The state **opera** produces some good performances, but suffers from a lack of money and a rather wooden approach to stage performance, and from the fact that its best talents are drawn abroad. Smaller ensembles such as the Chamber Opera (*Kamaraopera*) are worth watching out for, featuring notable talents like singer Adrienne Csengery, who has won rapturous acclaim abroad. The Budapest Opera's **ballet** company is classically oriented, and most of the impetus for **modern dance** comes from the Pécs and Győr companies, whose reputations make it difficult to get tickets when they visit the capital.

CINEMA

Hungarian cinema is going through an identity crisis, its former role as licensed social critic no longer relevant in a post-Communist Hungary, where people would rather watch Hollywood blockbusters. Directors seem at a loss now that censorship has been abolished: ideological subtleties count for nothing, and they are expected to cater for lowbrow tastes. Their uncertainty is compounded by the reduction of subsidies and the need to find commercial support. For this reason, the annual **Hungarian Film Festival** in Budapest (*Magyar Filmszemle*) has survived precariously over recent years, though at least it now seems to be back as a regular event, held every February, when films (including a huge number of documentary films) made in the past year are given a showing. You can usually find some films simultaneously translated into English during the festival - check at the Film Institute (V, Báthory utca 10).

The shortage of funds afflicting the industry has sharply reduced the number of **Hungarian films** made. Some directors work abroad (István Szabó, Miklós Jancsó, Márta Mészáros), while others have entered into co-productions with foreign teams, changing the whole character of Hungarian films - though given the films that were being turned out by the early 1990s, some would say that was no bad thing. **Directors** to watch out for are the dynamic Ildikó Enyedi (*My Twentieth Century*, *The Magic Hunter*), András Szőke's zany films, Peter Gothár (*Time Stands Still*) and Júlia Szederkényi. Understandably, their compatriots prefer to watch foreign films, the majority of them dubbed into Hungarian (indicated by *m.b.* or *Magyarul bészelő* on posters); the Hungarian for cinema is *filmszínház* or *mozi*.

FESTIVALS

The **festival year** kicks off with the **Mohács Carnival** of masked revellers re-enacting ancient spring rites and ritual abomination of the Turks on March 1, followed later in the month by the **Spring Festivals** (*Taraszi Fesztival*) of music and drama in Budapest, Szeged, Kecskemét, Debrecen and other towns. On **March 15**, wreaths are laid at monuments to commemorate the anniversary of the 1848 Revolution against the Habsburgs. Nowadays, **May 1** is just a public holiday, shorn of the Soviet-style parades that characterized it during the Communist period.

With the onset of tourists and fine weather, the summer months soon get crowded with events. With the exception of the week-long *Téka Tábor* **festival of folk arts** at Nagykálló (in late July), most of them are listed in *Programme* magazine, or you can get information at *Tourinform* offices in Budapest.

You can see **historical pageants** at Veszprém, Tihany, Visegrád, Gyula or Esztergom; and **equestrian shows** with a "rodeo" atmosphere and amazing displays of horsemanship at Nagyvázsony, Apajpuszta, Tamási, Kisbér, Szántódpuszta and Hortobágy. The two-day Hortobágy Bridge Fair and the **Szeged Weeks** of music and drama reach their climax on **St Stephen's Day** (Aug 20), which honours the death of Hungary's patron saint and "founding father" with parades and fireworks in Budapest, a Flower Carnival in Debrecen and lesser displays in provincial towns.

Budapest's **Autumn Music Weeks** (late Sept to late Nov) more or less round off the year. **October 23**, the anniversary of the 1956 Uprising, has lost the emotional potency it had as a "forbidden anniversary" under Communism, since its belated commemoration with patriotic pageantry and cathartic reburials in 1990.

Although Saint Stephen's relics attract multitudes of worshippers to the great Basilica in Pest, **religious festivals** aren't widely observed in contemporary Hungary. The most obvious exception is Easter, when the churches and cathedrals are packed - particularly in Esztergom, the seat of Hungarian Catholicism. Another, more remote focus for religious fervour is the village of

Máriapócs in eastern Hungary, which draws thousands of pilgrims on August 15 and September 8 (see p.333).

It is also worth knowing about the tradition of **name-day celebrations**, which are as important to Hungarians as birthdays are in other countries. Customarily, the celebrant invites relatives and friends to a party, and receives gifts and salutations. Lest you forget someone's name-day, tradition allows congratulations to be rendered up to a week afterwards.

SPORTS

Since hosting the 1988 World Ice Skating Championships, Hungary has been angling for other major sporting events to supplement its annual Budapest Marathon and Hungarian Grand Prix. Full details of these, and national championships in everything from parachuting to canoeing are available from *Ibusz*, regional tourist offices and *Programme* magazine.

PARTICIPATORY SPORTS

Several pages of the weekly paper *Népsport* are devoted to **football** (*labdarúgás*), Hungary's most popular sport. Current First Division contenders include the Budapest teams *Kispest Honvéd*, *Ferencváros* (aka "*Fradi*") and *Ujpesti TE*; and *Győri ETO*, *DVTK* and *Váci Izzó MTE* from the provinces. Tickets for matches are cheap, as are facilities at local **sports halls** (*Sportcsarnok*).

Windsurfing (*szörf*) and **sailing** equipment can be rented from the *kölcsönzo* at the main Balaton boat stations and Lake Velence, and **tennis** (*tenisz*) courts are often attached to more upmarket hotels in Budapest and main resorts. Hungary's topography rules out any dramatic or lengthy slopes, but that doesn't stop enthusiasts from **skiing** in the Mátra Mountains and the Buda Hills. Visitors into **hiking** can avail themselves of detailed maps of the highland regions (see box below).

HORSE RIDING

Hungarians profess a lingering attachment to the horse - their equestrian ally since the time of the great migration and the Magyar conquest - and the horse herds or *csikós* of the Plain are romantic figures of national folklore. Most native **horses** are mixed breeds descended from Arab and English thoroughbreds, crossed in recent years with Hanoverian and Holstein stock. The adjective most commonly used to describe their character is "spirited" or "mettlesome".

Horse-riding tours come in various forms. There are several itineraries around the Balaton, the northern uplands and the Great Plain, lasting from a week to ten days, with meals, lodgings and guide included; and somewhat bizarre expeditions by **covered wagons**, which tourists drive and navigate across the *puszta*. To give you an idea of prices, an eight-day tour starts at around 1,200DM; ask for details at travel agencies in Budapest.

Regional tourist offices and local enterprises offer equestrian programmes and instruction at **riding schools** (*Lovarda*), namely: Alag, Dunakeszi, Isaszeg, Üllő-Tornyoslöb and Ady-liget **near Budapest**; Taliándorog, Nagyvázsony, Nagyberek, Szentbékkálla, Szántódpuszta, Siófok and Keszthely **around the Balaton**; Tata, Szombathely, Sárvár, Radiháza, Nagycenk and

---

HIKING SYMBOLS

Mountain trails are generally marked with multi-coloured symbols (painted on tree trunks or boulders) which correspond with routes marked by the following initial letters on maps:

K - *kék* (blue)

R - *piros* (red)

S - *sárga* (yellow)

F - *zöld* (green)

Dunakiliti **in Transdanubia**; Visegrád on the **Danube Bend**; Szilvásvárad in the **Northern Uplands**; and Hortobágy, Bugac, Tiszafüred, Makó and Szatymaz on the **Great Plain**. *Tourinform* in Budapest (V, Sütő utca 2, ☎117- 9800) has the most comprehensive file on riding schools in Hungary and a map indicating where accommodation is also provided by the school. The schools provide saddlery, but you'll need your own riding clothes.

WORK AND STUDY

Teaching English is the main opportunity for work in Hungary, where a command of the language is now required for university entrance examinations (replacing Russian, which was compulsory until 1989). Native speakers are in great demand and language teaching is a big business, particularly in Budapest. As most teaching is at an intermediate or advanced level, you are seldom required to speak much (if any) Hungarian.

TEACHING

Assuming you can get enough clients, the most profitable option is **giving private lessons**. Qualified teachers can charge up to around 2000Ft an hour, but as few Hungarians can afford this, it's more realistic to settle for 800-1000Ft per hour. This is roughly twice what you'd get **working in a language school**, where monthly salaries average 30,000-40,000Ft for around 24 lessons (45min) a week (minus 30-40 percent tax and health insurance).

Naturally, language schools are good business and consequently attract their share of cowboys,

and you hear plenty of stories of schools employing students and then not paying them. The most reputable schools in Budapest are *IHLS* (II Bimbó utca 7; ☎212-4010) and the *Bells* School (II, Tulipán utca 8; ☎115-6259); both requiring TEFL certificates. Some employers will arrange **work permits**, but others leave it up to you. The process involves a lot of paperwork and medical reports.

Although **teaching in primary or secondary schools** pays much less (around 15,000-20,000Ft per month), the deal usually includes subsidized or free accommodation. Expect to work fifteen hours a week, mostly in the morning. Primary school work is not exam oriented and largely involves playing games with pupils aged 6-14. Secondary school classes are smaller, but teachers will need at least basic Hungarian, since the exam is based on translation. The former may take anyone who seems capable and enthusiastic; the latter are likely to require at least a TEFL and/or a PGCE certificate.

Recruitment for state schools is handled by several agencies abroad (see below) and three clearing houses inside Hungary. The *Budapest Pedagogical Institute* (VIII, Horváth Mihály tér 8) recruits for schools in the capital; the *English Teacher's Association of the National Pedagogical Institute* (II, Bolyai utca 14), also in Budapest, recruits for the provinces; while *IATEFL* in the southern town of Kecskemét (Academia körút 20), does likewise.

Better still you can make arrangements abroad. Qualified teachers (with a degree or TEFL certificate) are currently being recruited **in Britain** by the *Eastern European Partnership*, 15 Princeton Court, 53–55 Felsham Road, London SW15 1AZ (☎0181/780 2841). The two-year contract includes travel, accommodation and medical expenses. Other agencies such as the British Council may also advertise for teachers (usually in the *TES* or *Guardian* between April and June).

Native-speaking sixth-formers, students or teachers (up to the age of 45) can apply for jobs at English-language **summer camps** (generally three weeks during July/Aug). Besides giving Hungarian 15- to 17-year-olds the chance to practice their English, you're expected to organize sports and/or drama and musical activities - so previous experience in these areas is desirable. Board and accommodation is provided but applicants must pay for their own travel to Hungary; applications should be made to the *Youth Exchange Centre*, Seymour Mews House, Seymour Mews, London W1H 9PE (☎0171/486 5101, ext 24) by the end of March.

In the **United States** volunteer teachers can apply to the Peace Corps (1990 K St NW, Washington DC 20526) for two-year assignments; the Fulbright Program (which offers a round-trip fare, salary and housing); or George Washington University (PO Box 2798, Washington DC 20057).

SUMMER COURSES

Eager to publicize their cultural achievements and earn foreign exchange, the Hungarians also organize **summer courses** in everything from folk art to environmental studies. Full details are contained in a booklet published in the spring,

which can be obtained by writing to *TIT* (the Society for the Dissemination of Scientific Knowledge), H-1088 Budapest, VIII, Bródy Sándor utca 16. The deadline for most applications is May 1, so it's advisable to write months in advance. Students are of all ages and come from countries as diverse as Switzerland and Venezuela, so the chance to meet people can be as much an attraction as the subject to be studied. These include photography (at Vác), Hungarian language and culture (Debrecen), fine arts (Zebegény), Esperanto (Gyula), Baroque recorder music (Sopron), jazz (Tatabánya), orchestral music (Pécs and Kecskemét), music-teaching by the Kodály method (Esztergom and Kecskemét), folk art (Zalaegerszeg) and nature studies (Keszthely). Fees include room and board and various excursions and entertainments.

Finally, **Volunteers for Peace**, 43 Tiffany Rd, Belmont, VT 05730 (☎802/259-2759), is a non-profit organization with links to a huge international network of "workcamps," including some in Hungary, two- to four-week programmes that bring volunteers together from many countries to carry out needed community projects. Most workcamps are in summer, with registration in April-May.

DIRECTORY

körút (ring boulevard). You may also encounter *rakpart* (embankment), *sétány* (promenade), *híd* (bridge), *köz* (lane), *hegy* (hill) or *liget* (park). Town centres are signposted *Belváros*, *Városközpont* or *Centrum*. A *lakótelep* is a high-rise housing estate.

BRING Any specific medication or contact lens sundries that you might need. Western fashion and pop magazines are much appreciated in trendy (*divatos*) circles. Passport-sized photos come in handy for season tickets, student cards, etc.

CAMPERS should bring a primus stove, which takes local *spiritusz*, since camping gas canisters are hard to find. Candles - *gyertya* - are sold in supermarkets; buy lots if you're going on to Romania or Bulgaria, since they're hard to find there, and may be so poor that they won't burn.

CHILDREN (*gyerek*) qualify for reductions on most forms of public transport (see "Getting Around"), and fifty percent off the cost of camping up to the age of 14. Separate visas aren't

ADDRESSES usually begin with the postcode, which indicates the town or city and locality. The most common terms are *utca* (street, abbreviated to *u.*), *út* (or *útja*, avenue), *tér* (or *tere*, square) and

required for children under 14 who are included on their parent's passport (assuming they need one at all). The best facilities and entertainments for kids are in Budapest and the Balaton resorts. Children are forbidden to ride in the front seat of a car. Most supermarkets stock baby food and *Libero* disposable nappies.

CIGARETTES are sold in tobacconists (*dohánybolt*), supermarkets, bars and restaurants. *Marlboro* and *Camel* made under licence are cheaper than imports, but still more expensive than "native" brands like charcoal-filtered *Helikon* and *Sopianae*, or throat-rasping *Symphonia* and *Munkás*. Matches are *gyufa*. *Tilos a dohányzás* means "no smoking", and applies to cinemas, the metro, all buses, trams and trolleybuses.

CONTRACEPTIVES Hungarian or German-made condoms (*óvszer*, *gumi* or *kondom*) are available at the cash tills in chemists, and in food stores. Reliable, locally manufactured contraceptive pills are available on prescription, although it's always more sensible to bring your own.

ELECTRIC POWER 220 volts. Round, two-pin plugs are used. A standard continental adaptor allows the use of 13 amp, square-pin plugs.

FILM *Kodak*, *Fuji*, *Agfa* and *Konica* film is readily available, and most towns offer colour processing services. Mini-labs in Budapest and major towns can process and print films in a couple of hours.

GAY AND LESBIAN LIFE Although the age of consent for lesbians and gay men is 18, they remain liable to police harassment and public disapproval. The organization *HOMEROS-Lambda*, founded in 1988, maintains a low profile, fearful of antagonizing the newly powerful Catholic Church, which allegedly pressured the government into halting advertisments for condoms and safer sex. A law passed under the Communists permits the compulsory blood-testing of "suspected" HIV-carriers. Given this, and public homophobia, it's hardly surprising that visible manifestations of gay life are limited to Budapest (see p.109).

LAUNDRY Self-service launderettes (*mosoda*) are rare, and *Patyolat* (local cleaning services) are unlikely to have your washing or dry-cleaning back in less than 48 hours. Staying in private lodgings, you may be allowed to use your host's washing machine. All supermarkets sell detergent.

LEFT LUGGAGE Most train stations have a left-luggage office (*ruhatár*), which charges 60Ft a day, or 120Ft for larger and heavier goods, for each item deposited - sometimes including "each item" strapped to your backpack. Beware of huge queues for baggage at Budapest's main stations (and some Balaton termini) during the summer, and keep *all* of the scrappy little receipts, or you'll never get your gear back. A few main stations have automatic luggage lockers, which take three 20Ft coins and store your baggage for up to 24 hours.

LOST PROPERTY is kept for one to three weeks at the destination of the train it was found on, or where it was handed in, and then stored at Váci út 3 by Budapest's Nyugati Station (Mon-Fri 8am-3pm). Passports are first sent to the police and then forwarded to embassies.

MUSEUMS Almost none of Hungary's museums have captions in any language but Hungarian, although important museums in provincial centres and the capital might sell catalogues in German, French or English. For surmounting the language barrier, Skanzens or Village Museums are probably the most effective - fascinating ensembles of buildings and domestic objects culled from old settlements around the country, assembled on the outskirts of Szentendre, Nyíregyháza, Zalaegerszeg and Szombathely, or preserved in situ at Szalafő and Hollókő. Museum admission charges vary from 10Ft to 100Ft, while student cards (see below) secure reductions, or free entry in many cases. Some places have free admission on Saturdays or Wednesdays.

NAMES Surnames precede forenames in Hungary, to the confusion of foreigners. In this book, the names of historical personages are rendered in the Western fashion - for instance, Lajos Kossuth rather than Kossuth Lajos (Hungarian-style) - except when referring to buildings, streets, etc.

NUDISM Often known by the German initials *FKK*, nudism is gaining ground - with nudist camps outside Budapest, Szeged, Mohács and Balatonberény, and nude sunbathing on segregated terraces at some pools - but you can't assume that it's permitted. For more information, contact the *Naturisták Egyesülete* (Naturist Union) in Budapest (XIII, Kárpát utca 8).

STUDENT CARDS These entitle you to small reductions at some hostels and campsites, free or reduced admission to museums, and significant discounts on certain international railway tickets and *Malév* flights. The East European student organization, IUS, produces its own card, which in the past has been the only one to give discounts; it may, however, be superseded by the ISIC card in the future. It's best to bring an ISIC card with you and then get an IUS card in Hungary from an *Express* office or railway station.

TAXES Prices often include a consumer tax (ÁFA), which ranges from 10 to 25 percent, so that any prices quoted - for purchases or car rentals - are likely to jump sharply when it comes to paying. Check on whether ÁFA is included

(*Árak nem tartalmaznak ÁFA-t* is Hungarian for "Prices do not include tax").

TIME Hungary is one hour ahead of GMT, six hours ahead of Eastern Standard Time and nine ahead of Pacific Standard Time in North America. During summertime (from the end of March to the end of Sept) these differences increase by one hour. A word of caution: Hungarians express time in a way that might confuse the anglophone traveller. For example, 10.30am is expressed as "half eleven" (written $1/_2 11$), 10.45am is three-quarter-eleven ($3/_4 11$), and 10.15am is "a quarter of the next hour" ($1/_4 11$).

PART TWO

THE

GUIDE

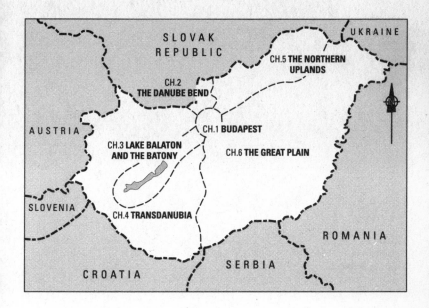

CHAPTER ONE

BUDAPEST

The importance of **BUDAPEST** to Hungary is difficult to overestimate. Over two million people live here – one fifth of the population – and everything converges on the capital: roads and rail lines; air travel (Ferihegy is the only civilian airport); industry, commerce and culture; opportunities, wealth and power. Like Paris, it has a tradition of revolutions – in 1849, 1918 and 1956 – buildings, parks and avenues on a monumental scale, and a reputation for hedonism, style and parochial pride. In short, it's a city worthy of comparison with other great European capitals.

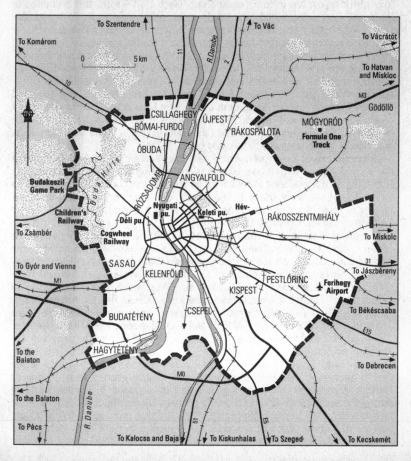

Surveying Budapest from the embankments or the bastions of Castle Hill, it's obvious why the city was dubbed the "Pearl of the Danube". Its grand buildings and sweeping bridges look magnificent, especially when floodlit or illuminated by the barrage of fireworks launched from Gellért Hill on St Stephen's Day. The eclectic inner-city and radial boulevards combine brash commercialism with a *fin-de-siècle* sophistication, while a distinctively Hungarian character is highlighted by the sounds and appearance of the Magyar language at every turn.

Long known as the liveliest city in the Eastern Bloc, Budapest has experienced a new surge of energy since the end of Communism. The choice of restaurants, bars and entertainment has never been greater – and there's also a sleazy side to the city that accounts for its reputation as the "Bangkok of Europe". While some Hungarians fear the corruption and ultimate erosion of their culture by foreign influences, others herald the start of a new golden age with Budapest as the foremost city in *Mitteleuropa*.

Some history

Though Budapest has formally existed only since 1873 – when the twin cities of Buda and Pest were united in a single municipality together with the smaller Óbuda – the history of settlement here goes back to the second millennium BC, or even earlier. During the first Age of Migrations, the area was settled by waves of peoples, notably Scythians from the Caucasus and Celts from what is now France.

During the first century BC, the Celtic Eravisci tribe was absorbed into the Roman Empire as part of the vast province of Pannonia. Pannonia was subsequently divided into two regions. One of them, Pannonia Inferior, was governed from the garrison town of **Aquincum** on the west bank of the Danube. Ruins of a camp, villas, baths and an amphitheatre can still be seen today. In the fifth century AD the Romans pulled out and the Huns moved in, Attila's brother, Buda, purportedly giving his name to the west bank.

Germanic tribes, Lombards, Avars and Slavs succeeded one another during the second Age of Migrations, until finally the **Magyars** arrived in about 896. According to the medieval chronicler Anonymous, the clan of Árpád settled on Csepel Island, the other tribes spreading out across the Carpathian basin. It was under the Árpád dynasty that Hungary became a Christian state, ruled first from Esztergom and then from Székesfehérvár.

The **development of Buda and Pest** did not really begin until the twelfth century, and was largely thanks to French, Walloon and German settlers who worked and traded here under royal protection. Both towns were devastated by the Mongols in 1241, but rebuilt by colonists from Germany, who named Buda *Ofen*, after its numerous lime-kilns (the name Pest, which is of Slav origin, also means "oven"). Building a succession of palaces on Castle Hill, the Angevin kings established Buda as a **royal seat**. It reached its apogee in Renaissance times under the reign of "Good King" Mátyás and his Italian-born wife, Queen Beatrice.

Hungary's catastrophic defeat at Mohács in 1526 paved the way for the **Turkish occupation** of Buda and Pest, which lasted 160 years before a pan-European army finally recaptured Buda Castle – after a six-week siege – at the twelfth attempt. Under **Habsburg rule**, with control exerted from Vienna or Pozsony (Bratislava), recovery was followed by a period of intensive growth during the second half of the eighteenth century. During the first decades of the next century, Pest became the centre of the **Reform movement** led by Count Széchenyi – whose vision of progress was embodied in the **Chain Bridge**, the first permanent link between Buda and Pest (which had hitherto relied on pontoon bridges or barges).

When the Habsburg empire was shaken by revolutions across Europe in **March 1848**, local reformists and radicals seized the moment. While Kossuth dominated Parliament, Petőfi and his fellow revolutionaries from the *Café Pilvax* mobilized crowds on the streets of Pest. After the War of Independence ended in defeat for the Hungarians, Habsburg repression was epitomized by the hilltop Citadella, built to cow the citizenry with its guns.

Following the Compromise of 1867, which established the Dual Monarchy familiarly known to its subjects as the *K & K* (from the German for "Emperor and King"), the twin cities underwent rapid **expansion** and formally merged. Pest was extensively remodelled, acquiring the Great Boulevard and the grand thoroughfare that runs from the Belváros to the Városliget, where Hősök tere (Heroes' Square) and Vajdhunyad Castle were constructed for Hungary's **millennial anniversary celebrations** in 1896. New suburbs were created to house the burgeoning population, which was by now predominantly Magyar, although there were still large German and Jewish communities. Early this century Budapest's **cultural efflorescence** rivalled that of Vienna, its café society that of Paris – a Belle Époque doomed by World War I.

In the aftermath of defeat, Budapest experienced the tumultuous **Republic of Councils** under Béla Kun, and occupation by the Romanian army. The *status quo ante* was restored by **Admiral Horthy**, self-appointed Regent for the exiled Karl IV (the "Admiral without a fleet, for the king without a kingdom"). His regency was characterized by gala balls and hunger marches, bombastic nationalism and anti-Semitism. Yet Horthy was a moderate compared to the Arrow Cross fascists, whose power grew as **World War II** raged.

Anticipating Horthy's defection from the Axis in 1944, Nazi Germany staged a coup, installing an Arrow Cross government, which helped them begin to massacre the **Jews** of Budapest; and blew up the Danube bridges to hamper the advancing Red Army. The six-month-long **siege of Budapest** reduced Castle Hill to rubble and severely damaged much of the rest of the city, making **reconstruction** the first priority for the post-war coalition government.

As the **Communists** gained ascendancy, the former Arrow Cross torture chambers filled up again. A huge statue of the Soviet dictator (whose name was bestowed upon Budapest's premier boulevard) symbolized the reign of terror carried out by **Mátyás Rákosi**, Hungary's "Little Stalin". However, his liberally inclined successor, Imre Nagy, gave hope to the people, who refused to tolerate a comeback by the hardliners in **1956**. In Budapest, peaceful protests turned into a city-wide **uprising** literally overnight: men, women and children defying Soviet tanks on the streets.

After Soviet power had been bloodily restored, **János Kádár** – initially reviled as a quisling – gradually normalized conditions, embarking on cautious reforms to create a **"goulash socialism"** that made Hungary the envy of its Warsaw Pact neighbours and the West's favourite Communist state during the late Seventies. A decade later, the regime saw the writing on the wall and anticipated Gorbachev by promising **free elections**, hoping to reap public gratitude. Instead – as Communism was toppled in Berlin and Prague – the Party was simply voted out of power in Hungary.

The removal of the red star from Budapest's Parliament building and the restoration of old street names throughout the city are symbolic of a desire to go back to **the future**. Many of the changes unfolding bring with them new uncertainties – what fate awaits the venerated institutions taken over by foreign capital, for example, or the refugees interned to discourage others from hustling on Váci utca? And so people pass time, arguing over a flow of *kávé* and cigarettes, or wallowing in Turkish baths that remind them that troubles pass, but Budapest is enduring.

Orientation, arrival and information

The River Danube – which is never blue – determines basic **orientation**, with Buda on the hilly west bank and Pest covering the plain across the river. More precisely, you can refer to Budapest's 22 districts (*kerület*), designated on maps and street signs by Roman numerals; or use the historic names of quarters (some only recently restored after decades of official disfavour). In **Buda**, the focus of attention is the I district, comprising Castle Hill and the Watertown; the XI, XII, II and III districts are worth visiting for the Gellért and Buda hills, Óbuda and Római-Fürdő. **Pest** revolves around the downtown Belváros (V district) within the Small Boulevard, beyond which lie the VI, VII, VIII and IX districts, respectively known as the Terézváros, Erzsébetváros, Józsefváros and Ferencváros.

It's easier to make sense of this in practice than the welter of names might suggest. Districts and streets are well signposted, and those in Pest conform to an overall plan based on radial avenues and semicircular boulevards. The finer points of addresses are covered in the box below.

Arrival

Other than the airport, all points of **arrival** are fairly central, most within walking distance or just a few stops by metro from downtown Pest. Depending on when and where you arrive, consider either arranging somewhere to stay before leav-

---

BUDAPEST ADDRESSES

For everyday purposes, **Budapest addresses** begin with the number of the district – for example, V, Petőfi tér 3 – a system used throughout this chapter. When addressing letters, however, a four-digit postal code is used instead, the middle digits indicating the district (so that 1054 refers to a place in the V district). Far more relevant to visitors is the wholesale **renaming of streets** on a district-by-district basis. To help people adjust, the new signs show the old names, too, but crossed out in red.

As a rule of thumb, **street numbers** ascend away from the Danube, or the Kossuth utca/Rákóczi út axis in Pest. Even numbers are generally on the left-hand side, odd numbers on the right. One number may refer to several premises or an entire apartment building, while an additional combination of numerals denotes the floor and number of individual **apartments** (eg III/24). Confusingly, some old buildings in Pest are designated as having a half-floor (*félemelet*) or upper ground floor (*magas földszint*) between the ground (*földszint*) and first floor (*első emelet*) proper – so that what a Briton would call the second floor, an American the third, Hungarians describe as the first. This stems from a nineteenth-century taxation fiddle, whereby landlords avoided the higher tax on buildings with more than three floors.

ing the terminal (there are reservation services at all of them), or stashing your luggage before setting out to look on your own. For all **departure** information, see the relevant sections of "Listings", pp.115–16.

By air

Ferihegy Airport has two terminals: Ferihegy 1, which is used by most airlines, and Ferihegy 2, serving *Malév, Alitalia, Air France* and *Lufthansa*. A shuttle bus runs every 30 minutes to Erzsebet tér in downtown Pest (buy tickets on the bus). There is also an *Airport Minibus* service which takes you directly to your destination. Tickets (600Ft) can be purchased while waiting for your luggage or in the main concourse – you'll be asked for your address, then between five and fifteen minutes later a driver will announce his ports of call. (You can also return to the airport on the minibus – ring a day in advance if you're on an early flight, and allow a couple of hours get there. See "Listings", p.114, for details.) A slower but cheaper way into the city centre is to take the red #93 bus to Kőbánya-Kispest, and then switch to metro line 3, alighting ten stops later at Deák tér (about a 40-min journey). Airport taxis are mafia controlled and charge way above the odds – expect to pay a variable fixed rate of around 2000–2700Ft, depending on your destination. Alternatively, go to the *Hertz* car rental desk, and ask for a *Főtaxi* – the two companies work together, so they should be able to help you. Any of the tourist offices at Ferihegy can reserve accommodation in Budapest.

By train

The Hungarian word *pályaudvar* (abbreviated to *pu.* in writing only) is used to designate seven of Budapest's **train stations**, only three of which are on the metro and useful to tourists. Translated into English, their names refer to the direction of services handled rather than location, so that the Western Station (*Nyugati pu.*) is actually north of downtown Pest, and the Southern Station (*Déli pu.*) further north than the Eastern Station (*Keleti pu.*).

On the northern edge of Pest's Great Boulevard, **Nyugati Station** has a left-luggage office inside the waiting room beside platform 13 and an *Ibusz* office on platform 10. With pickpockets working the crowd, it's safer to change money at *Cooptourist* or *Budapest Tourist* in the metro arcade outside the station, where you can also book rooms. To reach Deák tér, ride the metro two stops in the direction of Kőbánya-Kispest.

Trains from Vienna's Westbahnhof terminate at Pest's **Keleti Station**, on Baross tér in the VIII district. This station is even worse for thieves and hustlers – especially at night, when it's taken over by prostitutes and the homeless. In summer there are long line-ups at the left-luggage, *Ibusz* and *Express* offices, making it better to do business with *Budapest Tourist* at Baross tér 3 (beyond the overpass on the other side of the square) or Erzsébet körút 41. Keleti is three stops from Deák tér by Déli pu.-bound metro.

Déli Station itself is 500m behind Castle Hill in Buda. Rooms and exchange are handled by *Ibusz* and *Budapest Tourist* in the mall by the metro entrance (left-luggage is around the corner), or you can cross the park towards Castle Hill to deal with *Cooptourist* at Attila út 107. Déli Station is four stops from Deák tér by metro.

By bus

International bus services invariably wind up at the **Erzsébet tér bus station**, just by Deák tér on the edge of downtown Pest (one exception being *Attila Tours* from

Britain, which deposits you at the Déli train station in Buda). The bus station's left-luggage office is small but rarely busy, and there are several tourist offices in the vicinity – you'll find *Dunatours* and *Cooptourist* at Bajcsy-Zsilinszky út 17, 150m north of the bus station; and *Ibusz* at Károly körút 21, slightly further in the other direction. *Tourinform* (see below) is just around the corner and the 24-hour *Ibusz* bureau on the Pest embankment is less than ten minutes' walk away.

Coming from another part of Hungary, you might arrive instead at **Népstadion bus station** in the XIV district, or the **Árpád híd bus station** in the XIII. Neither has any tourist facilities, but they're both just four or five metro stops from the centre of Pest.

By hydrofoil

Hydrofoils from Vienna dock at the **international landing stage** on the Belgrád rakpart (embankment), near downtown Pest. *Volántourist* is just outside the terminal and there are two *Ibusz* offices five minutes' walk north, on Ferenciek tere inland of the Erzsébet Bridge, and on Petőfi tér, on the road leading up to the *Marriott Hotel*.

Information and maps

Leaving aside the business of finding accommodation, the best source of **information** is *Tourinform* at V, Sütő utca 2 (summer daily 8am–8pm; winter Mon–Fri 8am–8pm & Sat–Sun 8am–3pm; ☎117-9800), just around the corner from Deák tér metro. Their friendly polyglot staff can answer just about any question on Budapest, or travel elsewhere in Hungary.

Get hold of a proper **map** of the city at the earliest opportunity. The small freebies supplied by tourist offices give an idea of Budapest's layout and principal monuments, but lack the detail of the larger, folding maps sold all over the place. The *Inner City of Budapest* map covers just that, in excellent detail, but for total coverage you can't beat the light-blue *Budapest Atlasz* (600Ft), showing every street, bus and tram route; the location of restaurants, museums and suchlike; and even marking the numbers on many streets. It also contains enlarged maps of Castle Hill, central Pest, Margit Island and the Városliget, plus a comprehensive index.

Details of **what's on** can be found in the hotel magazines *Where Budapest* and *Panoráma* (both of which are free), the weeklies *Budapest Week* and *Budapest Sun* (around 100Ft), and the Hungarian-language listings weekly, *Program Magazin*. For more on this, see "Entertainment" at the end of the chapter.

Tours

Although Budapest can easily be explored without a guide, visitors hard-pressed for time might appreciate a **city tour** (2–3hr). These range in price from 1500Ft to 1700Ft and can be arranged through *Tourinform*, *Budapest Tourist* (leaving from their office at V, Roosevelt tér 5; ☎117-3555) or *Buda Tours* (leaving from Szent György tér by Buda Palace). *Ibusz* and *Budapest Tourist* also organize **guided tours of the Parliament building**, combined with visits to the Ethnographical Museum or the National Gallery (see p.90 for details).

The telephone code for Budapest is ☎1

Getting around

Budapest's excellent **public transport** system ensures that few parts of the city are more than thirty minutes' journey from the centre, and much of it can be reached in half that time. The language and local geography may be unfamiliar, but it doesn't take long to pick up the basics and start using the system to full effect. It's also extremely cheap – unlike **taxis** (which may take advantage of tourists) – and preferable to **driving** or **cycling** amidst the traffic jams and exhaust fumes that afflict the main thoroughfares. Budapest's outer suburbs are well served by overground **HÉV trains**, while Danube **ferries** and the **Children's Railway** in the Buda Hills offer fun excursions.

Walking

Most of Budapest's backstreets and historic quarters are eminently suited to **walking** – and this is much the best way to appreciate their character. Traffic is restricted in downtown Pest and around Castle Hill in Buda, and fairly light in the residential backstreets off the main boulevards, which are the nicest areas to wander around. Be careful on main roads, though, as drivers are careless of pedestrians – even at crossings. Personal security can also be an issue **at night**, particularly on Gellért Hill, in the VIII (red-light) district and around main-line train stations. Though rarer than in most Western cities, muggings do occur, and their frequency is on the increase.

The metro, buses, trams and trolleybuses

Running at two- to five-minute intervals between 4.30am and 11.10pm, Budapest's **metro** reaches most areas of interest to tourists, its three lines intersecting at Deák tér in downtown Pest (see map). From nearby Vörösmarty tér, **line 1** (coded yellow) runs out beneath Andrássy út to Mexikoi út, beyond the Városliget. The red **line 2** connects Déli Station in Buda with Keleti Station and Örs vezér tere in Pest; and the blue **line 3** describes an arc from Kőbánya-Kispest to Újpest-Központ, via Ferenciek tere and Nyugati Station. There's little risk of going astray once you've learned to recognize the signs *bejárat* (entrance), *kijárat* (exit), *vonal* (line) and *felé* (towards). Drivers announce the next stop between stations and the train's direction is indicated by the name of the station at the end of the line – eg for a southbound train on the blue line you look for the platform marked "Kőbánya-Kispest felé".

Tickets must be punched aboard the trains on line 1, and at the entrance barriers on lines 2 and 3. Sticking to one line you can travel for up to an hour and break your journey as often as you like using a single ticket; however each change of line requires a new ticket. A word of warning: be aware that there's an active **pickpocket battalion** both in the metro (especially on yellow line 1) and on city buses.

Buses (*autóbusz*) are useful for journeys that can't be made by metro – especially around Buda, where Moszkva tér (on metro line 2) and Móricz Zsigmond körtér (southwest of Gellért Hill) are the main bus depots. Most buses run every ten to twenty minutes from 5am to 11pm. Regular services are numbered in black; buses with red numbers make fewer stops en route; and those with an "E"

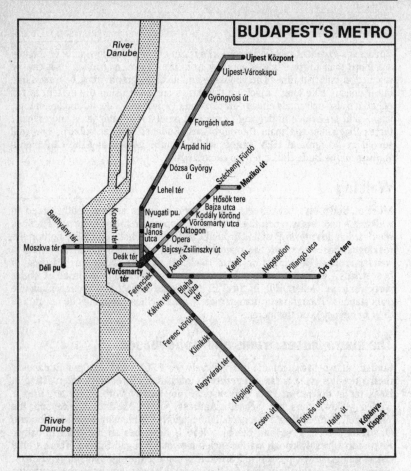

BUDAPEST'S METRO

suffix run non-stop between terminals. You should cancel your own ticket on board using the orange punch-machines; to get the bus to stop push the button above the door. Busy routes are also served by **night buses** (one to four an hour) with black numbers and an "É" suffix. After 8pm, you are required to show your ticket or pass to the driver as you board.

Yellow **trams** (*villamos*) are chiefly good for travelling around the Great Boulevard or along the embankments. Services run from early in the morning to 10 or 11pm (*Utolsó kocsi indul . . .* means "the last one leaves . . ."), with **night trams** (from one to four an hour) along a limited number of routes. From May to September, special 1920s **"nostalgia trams"** (60Ft) run along the Pest embankment on Saturdays and the Buda embankment on Sundays for sightseeing.

Tourists have little need to use **trolleybuses** (*trolibusz*), since none of the thirteen routes are especially notable. The reason the route numbers start at 70 is allegedly because the first trolleybus line was inaugurated on Stalin's seventieth birthday in 1949.

Tickets and passes

Tickets valid for the metro, buses, trams, trolleybuses and suburban HÉV lines (see below) are sold at metro stations, newspaper kiosks and tobacconists, and currently cost 35Ft. You can also buy **day passes** (*Napijegy*) costing 280Ft, which are valid for unlimited travel until midnight, or three-day passes for 560Ft. **Season tickets** are available from metro stations: the cheaper one covers trams, trolleybuses, the metro, HÉV and cogwheel trains; the other more expensive one can be used on buses too. They cost around 600Ft for a week; 800Ft for two weeks; and 1200Ft for a month. Bring a picture of yourself along as you'll also need to buy a photocard.

There is a 400Ft **fine** for travelling without a ticket. If you have a season ticket but were not carrying it the fine is 825Ft, of which 725Ft is refunded upon presentation of the ticket at the *BKV* office within three days (VII, Akácfa utca 15, near Blaha Lujza tér metro). **Children** up to the age of six travel free.

USEFUL BUS AND TRAM ROUTES

BUSES

#1 Kelenföld Station–Deák tér–Hősök tere–Mexikoi út (for the Gellért Baths, National Museum and Széchenyi Baths).

#7 Bosnyák tér–Keleti Station–Móricz Zsigmond körtér (via Rákóczi út, Ferenciek tere, the *Hotel Gellért*, Rác and Rudas Baths). Red #7s continue on to Kelenföld Station.

#16 Erzsébet tér–Dísz tér (Castle Hill).

#22 Moszkva tér–Budakeszi.

#26 Nyugati tér–Szent István körút–Margit Island–Árpád híd metro station.

#27 Móricz Zsigmond körtér–Gellért Hill.

#56 Moszkva tér–Szilyági E. fasor–Hűvösvölgy.

#65 Kolosy tér–Pál-völgyi Cave–Hármasmatár-hegy.

#86 Southern Buda–Gellért tér–the Watertown–Flórián tér (Óbuda).

#105 Lékai J. tér–Chain Bridge–Deák tér–Hősök tere.

NIGHT BUSES

#6É Moszkva tér–Margit Island–Nyugati Station–Great Boulevard–Móricz Zsigmond körtér.

#78É Örs vezér tere–Keleti Station–Buda side of the Erzsébet Bridge, following the route of metro line 2 most of the way.

#182É Kőbánya-Kispest–Újpest along the route of metro line 3.

TRAMS

#2 Along the Pest embankment.

#4 Moszkva tér–Margit Island–Nyugati Station–Great Boulevard–Boráros tér–Schönherz Zoltán utca.

#6 Moszkva tér–Margit Island–Nyugati Station–Great Boulevard–Boráros tér–Móricz Zsigmond körtér.

#19 Batthyány tér–the Watertown–Kelenföld Station.

#56 Moszkva tér–Szilyági E. fasor–Hűvösvölgy.

Taxis

Budapest has over 15,000 registered **taxis**, though the drivers have gained themselves a reputation for ripping off foreigners – the best advice is to use one of the following established companies: *Főtaxi*, which is the cheapest and most reliable (☎222-2222); *Tele-5-taxi* (☎155-5555); *Citytaxi* (☎211-1111); *Volántaxi* (☎166-6666); and *Rádió Taxi* (☎177-7777). Be sure your taxi has a meter that is visible, and that it is switched on when you get in; rates should also be clearly displayed. Fares begin at 30–50Ft, and the price per kilometre is 70–90Ft (though this is bound to go up as the price of fuel increases). The taxis to avoid are the unmarked private cars and those hanging around the stations and airport – be warned that the latter often charge six times the official fare from the airport into town.

Taxis can be flagged down on the street or ordered by phone. *Tele-5-taxi* is the easiest to deal with – you give them your name and number and they read back your address. There are ranks throughout the city and you can hop into whichever cab you choose – don't feel you have to opt for the one at the front of the line if it looks at all dodgy.

Driving, car rental and cycling

All things considered, **driving** in Budapest can't be recommended. Road manners are non-existent, parking space is scarce and traffic jams are frequent. The Pest side of the Chain Bridge and the roundabout before the tunnel under Castle Hill are notorious for collisions. Careering trams, smoke-belching Trabants and unexpected one-way systems make things worse. If you do have a car, you might be better off parking it somewhere outside the centre and using public transport to get in and out.

If you're going **to rent a car**, eschew cheaper, unreliable Ladas (from £6/$9 a day rental charge, plus £2.50/$4 a day insurance and mileage surcharge) in favour of Western models (upwards of £12/$20 a day). Most agencies also rent minivans. Most places will take a credit card as a deposit; if they don't or you don't have one, you can expect to pay up to £600/$1000. See "Listings", p.114, for agency addresses.

Cyclists must contend with the same hazards as drivers, plus sunken tramlines and slippery cobbles. They are also banned from major thoroughfares (with one or two exceptions – for example the main road out to Szentendre now has something resembling a cycle route). Although biking under these conditions is hardly ideal, Budapest is the best place in Hungary **to get repairs or buy a bike** for use elsewhere. Given that state retailers sell bikes unassembled and it takes ten days for them to be put together at a depot (XIV, Egressy út 17–21), it's not surprising that private bike stores are mushrooming. Try *Nella Bikes* off Bajcsy-Zsilinszky út at V, Kálmán Imre utca 23 (Mon–Fri 10am–6pm & Sat 9am–1pm; ☎131-3184) or *Tura Mobil* at Nagymező utca 43 (☎112-5219).

HÉV trains

Overground **HÉV trains** provide easy access to Budapest's suburbs, running at least four times an hour between 6.30am and 11pm. As far as tourists are concerned, the most useful line is the one from **Batthyány tér** (on metro line 2) out to **Szentendre**, north of Budapest, which passes through Óbuda, Aquincum and Római-Fürdő. The other lines originate in Pest, with one running northeast from **Örs vezér tere** (also on metro line 2) to **Gödöllő** via the Formula 1 racing track at Mogyoród; the other southwards from **Soroksári út** (bus #23 or #54 from Boráros tér) to **Ráckeve**, on Csepel Island. Szentendre, Gödöllő and Ráckeve are attractions in their own right, and are covered in chapters Two, Five and Six respectively. On all these routes, a yellow ticket will take you to the city limits, beyond which you must punch additional tickets according to the distance travelled. Alternatively you can purchase a ticket that covers the whole journey.

Ferries and other rides

Although **ferries** play little useful part in the transport system, they do offer an enjoyable ride. From May to September there are regular excursion boats from the Vigadó tér dock on the Pest embankment, south to Boráros tér and north to Jászi Mari tér – both brief, scenic routes (7am–7pm; every 15–30min). From May to August there is also a boat from the Jászi Mari tér dock to Pünkösfürdő in northern Buda (1hr), though you might prefer to disembark at Margit Island, before the boat reaches dismal Békásmegyer. Ferry tickets can be obtained from kiosks (where timetables are posted) or machines at the docks.

Other pleasure rides can be found in the Buda Hills, on the **Cogwheel Railway**, the **Children's Railway** (largely staffed by kids) and the **chairlift** between Zugliget and János-hegy. Details are given in the "Buda Hills" section (see p.82).

Accommodation

The **accommodation** situation in Budapest, which used to be fairly dire, has improved markedly in recent years. Predictably, the heaviest demand and highest prices occur over summer, when the city feels like it's bursting at the seams. Christmas and New Year, the Grand Prix and the Autumn Music Weeks are also busy periods, with higher rates in most hotels. Even so it should always be possible to find somewhere that's reasonably priced, if not well sited.

ACCOMMODATION PRICE CODES

All accommodation in this guide is graded according to the price bands given below. Note that all prices refer to the cheapest available double room in high season except where otherwise indicated. For more details, see p.26.

① Under 650Ft (under £4/$6/DM10)

② 650–1500Ft (£4–8/$6–13/DM10–20)

③ 1500–3000Ft (£8–17/$13–27/DM20–40)

④ 3000–4500Ft (£17–25/$27–40/DM40–60)

⑤ 4500–6500Ft (£25–36/$40–57/DM60–85)

⑥ 6500–10,000Ft (£36–56/$57–88/DM85–130)

⑦ Over 10,000Ft (over £56/$88/DM130)

ACCOMMODATION BOOKING AGENCIES

Budapest Tourist
Private rooms, apartments and bungalows
Ferihegy airport (daily 8am–8pm; ☎157-8670).

Nyugati Station, in the metro arcade outside (Mon–Fri 9am–5.30pm & Sun 9am–12.30pm; ☎132-4911).

VIII, Baross tér 3, across from Keleti Station (Mon–Fri 9am–5pm, plus summer Sat 9am–noon; ☎133-6587).

Déli Station, in the mall by the metro entrance (Mon–Fri 9am–5pm & Sat 9am–1pm; ☎115-7167).

VII, Erzsébet körút 41 (Mon–Sat 8am–8pm; ☎142-6521).

V, Roosevelt tér 5 (Mon–Thurs 9am–5.30pm & Fri 9am–3pm ☎117-3555).

Cooptourist
Private rooms and apartments
Ferihegy (☎147-7328).

Skála Metro department store opposite Nyugati Station (Mon–Fri 9am–4.30pm; ☎112-3621).

V, Bajcsy-Zsilinszky út 17 (Mon–Fri 9am–5pm; ☎121-0992).

V, Kossuth tér 13 (Mon, Tues, Thurs & Fri 8am–4pm, Wed 8am–6pm; ☎112-1017).

I, Attila út 107 (Mon–Fri 8.30am–5pm; ☎175-2937).

Danubius
V, Szervita tér 8 (Mon–Fri 8.30am–5pm; ☎117-3652).

Express
Hostels and student accommodation
VIII, Baross tér, Keleti Station (24hr).

V, Semmelweiss utca 4 (Mon–Wed 8.30am–noon & 12.45–4.30pm, Thurs 8.30am–noon & 12.45–5pm, Fri 8.30am–noon & 12.45–3pm; ☎117-6634 or ☎117-8600).

V, Szabadság tér 16 (Mon–Thurs 8am–4.30pm, Fri 8am–2.30pm; ☎131-7777). Group bookings only.

HungarHotels
V, Petőfi utca 16 (Mon–Fri 9am–5pm; ☎118-3018).

V, Magyar utca 3 (Mon–Fri 8am–5pm; ☎117-6227).

Ibusz
Private rooms, apartments and hotels
Ferihegy airport.

Nyugati Station, platform 10 (Mon–Fri 8am–8pm & Sat 8am–3pm; ☎149-1715).

Keleti Station (daily 8am–8pm; ☎322-8210).

Déli Station, in the mall by the metro entrance (Mon–Fri 8.15am–6pm & Sat 9am–noon; ☎156-3767).

Ferenciek tere 5, by the metro stop (Mon–Fri 8.15am–5pm; ☎118-1120).

V, Petőfi tér 3, on the embankment (24hr; ☎118-5707).

VII, Károly körút 17–19 (Mon–Fri 8am–6pm & Sat–Sun 8am–4pm; ☎122-5429).

Pannonia Service
V, Kigyó utca 4–6 (Mon–Fri 9am–5pm & Sat 9am–1pm; ☎118-3910).

VIII, Rákóczi út 9 (Mon–Fri 9am–5pm; ☎266-8281).

Budget travellers will find most **hotels** affordable only during low season (Nov–March, excluding the New Year period), though a few remain viable options year-round. **Pensions** are cheaper, but tend to fill up quickly as most are quite small. Your safest bet is a **private room**, arranged through a tourist agency. Though its location might not be perfect, the price should be reasonable and you can be sure of finding one at any time of year, day or night. The cheapest options are **hostels** – which fill rapidly but can be unbeatable bargains – and **campsites**, where tent space can usually be found, even if all the **bungalows** are taken. The listings below are divided according to the type of accommodation, then arranged by area.

Hotels

To get the pick of the hotels you must **book** before leaving home (see also "Accommodation" in *Basics*) or, failing that, through an agency (*HungarHotels, Pannonia* or *Danubius*) or any airport tourist office on arrival. Many hotels still belong to the *HungarHotels* or *Pannonia* chains, both of which are in the process of being privatized. The information given below is thus subject to widespread change.

Hotel star ratings give a fair idea of **standards**, though facilities at some of the older three-star places don't compare with their Western equivalents. Air conditioning is comparatively rare, for example. Most hotels vary their **prices** according to season – the price codes given below are what you'd expect to pay in high season.

Buda

Buda has fewer hotels than Pest, with less choice in the mid-range in particular, though there are some cheaper places in the northern suburbs (if the best locations seem beyond your means, check out the section on hostels, a few of which enjoy superb settings). Broadly speaking, Buda hotels are in four main areas:

CASTLE HILL AND THE WATERTOWN

The charm and cachet of this historic locality is reflected in the hotel prices.

Alba Hotel, I, Apor Péter utca 3 (☎175-9244). Brand new four-star hotel in the Watertown below Castle Hill. ⑦.

Budapest Hilton, I, Hess András tér 1–3 (☎175-1000). By the Mátyás Church on Castle Hill, with superb views across the river. Luxurious to a fault. ⑦.

Dunapart Hotel, I, Szilágyi Dezső tér 33 (☎155-9244). A floating hotel moored upriver from the Chain Bridge, open year-round unless ice endangers the boat. ⑦.

Victoria Hotel, I, Bem rakpart 11 (☎201-8644). On the embankment overlooking the Chain Bridge. The manager is in dispute with the council after adding an extra floor without permission. ⑦.

AROUND TABÁN AND GELLÉRT HILL

Another pricey area – also far less scenic if you're behind Castle Hill and away from the river.

Buda Penta Hotel, I, Krisztina körút 41–43 (☎156-6333). Comfortable establishment on the far side of Castle Hill, near Déli Station. ⑦.

Flamenco Occidental, XI, Tas vezér utca 7 (☎161-2250). Behind Gellért Hill, with quiet grounds and indoor tennis facilities. ⑦

Hotel Gellért, XI, Gellért tér 1 (☎185-2200). The facade and thermal pool are magnificent, but the rooms are nothing special. Rates rise by twenty percent during events such as the Formula 1 race. ⑦.

Novotel, XII, Alkotás utca 63–67 (☎186-9588), off Hegyalja út, 1km from the Erzsébet Bridge. Eighties complex with air-conditioning, indoor pool and bowling alley. Children under 16 share their parents' room for free. ⑦.

Orion Hotel, I, Döbrentei utca 13 (☎175–5418). Small, modern place in the Tabán district, just south of Castle Hill. ⑦.

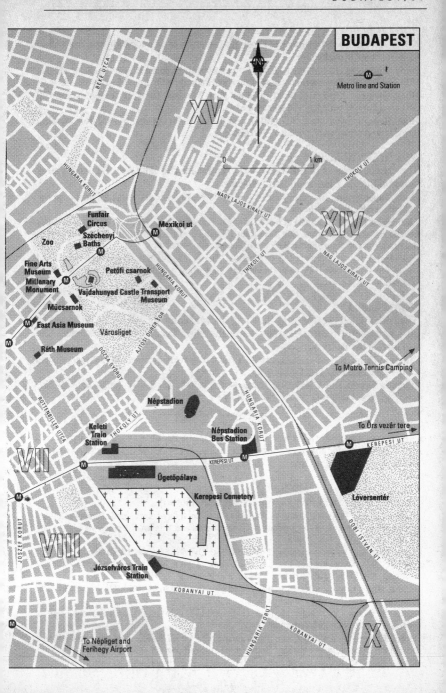

BUDAPEST

Metro line and Station

XV

XIV

Funfair
Circus

Mexikoi ut

Zoo

Széchenyi
Baths

Fine Arts
Museum

Petöfi csarnok

Millenary
Monument

Vajdahunyad Castle Transport
Museum

Mücsarnok

East Asia Museum

Városliget

Ráth Museum

To Metro Tennis Camping

Népstadion

Keleti
Train
Station

Népstadion
Bus Station

To Örs vezér tere

VII

KEREPESI UT

Ügetöpálaya

KEREPESI UT

Kerepesi Cemetery

Löversentér

JOSZEF KORUT

VIII

Józsefváros Train
Station

KOBANYAI UT

X

To Népliget and
Ferihegy Airport

KOBANYAI UT

BUDA HILLS

Not much cheaper, but most of these places enjoy a nice location and are within easy reach of Moszkva tér.

Hotel Budapest, II, Szilágyi E. fasor 47 (☎202-0044). Cylindrical tower facing the Buda Hills, opposite the lower terminal of the Cogwheel Railway, 500m from Moszkva tér. ⑦.

Hotel Olympia, XII, Eötvös út 40 (☎156-8011), at Normafa (bus #21E from Moszkva tér). Seventies low-rise with pool and tennis courts. ⑦.

Hotel Rege, II, Pálos utca 2 (☎176-7311), near the foot of Janos-hegy (bus #22 from Moszkva tér). Three-star place with pool, gym and disco. ⑥.

NORTHERN SUBURBS

The cheapest places in Buda are out in Aquincum and Római-Fürdő, mostly near stops on the HÉV line from Batthyány tér.

Hotel Tusculanum, III, Záhony utca 10 (☎188-7673). Another new establishment, near the Aquincum HÉV stop and Roman ruins. ⑥.

Lido Sport Hotel, III, Nánási út 67 (☎250-4549). An older place near the Danube with tennis courts, sauna and solarium. Bus #134 from Flórián tér stops nearby, or you can walk from the Aquincum or Római-Fürdő HÉV stop. Shared bathrooms. ③.

Polo Hotel, III, Mozaik utca 1–3 (☎250-0192). One-star establishment between Óbuda and Aquincum (Filatorigát HÉV stop), behind the long white building to the east of the tracks. Shared bathrooms. ③.

Margit Island

The island's hotels cater to wealthy tourists who come for the seclusion and fresh air – and for the thermal springs that made this a fashionable spa resort around the turn of the century.

Thermal Hotel, XIII, Margit-sziget (☎111-1000). Modern luxury hotel with thermal bath and pool, sauna, gym and other facilities. ⑦.

Ramada Grand Hotel, XIII, Margit-sziget (☎132-1100). The island's original, *fin-de-siècle* spa hotel, now totally refurbished with the full range of facilities. ⑦.

Pest

Staying in **Pest** offers greater choice, and more in the way of restaurants and nightlife, but traffic noise and fumes are worse. Most of the outlying locations are easily accessible by metro.

DOWNTOWN

These hotels are all within (or on) the Small Boulevard.

Astoria Hotel, V, Kossuth utca 19 (☎117-3411). Completely refurbished, famous old hotel which lends its name to the junction of Kossuth utca and the Small Boulevard (metro line 2). ⑦.

Atrium Hyatt, V, Roosevelt tér 2 (☎266-1234). Overlooking the Chain Bridge and the Danube, this five-star hotel has air-conditioning, a pool, sauna and landscaped atrium. Doubles from £125/$220; apartments also available. ⑦.

Grand Hotel Corvinus Kempinski, V, Erzsébet tér 7–8 (☎266-1000). Flashy new five-star establishment in the centre of town. ⑦.

Hotel Erzsébet, V, Károlyi M. utca 11–15 (☎138-2111). On the unfashionable side of Ferenciek tere. Soundproofed rooms. ⑦.

Hotel Forum, V, Apáczai Csere János utca 12–14 (☎117-8088). Four-star establishment beside the Danube, where Richard Burton used to stay incognito. ⑦.

K&K Opera, VI, Révay utca 24 (☎269-0222). New four-star hotel by the Opera. ⑦.

Korona Hotel, V, Kecskeméti utca 14 (☎117-4111). Post-modernist edifice beside Kálvin tér (metro line 3), a short walk from the National Museum. Every facility, including a pool and sauna. ⑦.

Marriott Budapest, V, Apáczai Csere János utca 4 (☎266-7000). All rooms in this five-star air-conditioned hotel overlook the Danube. Apartment suites also available. ⑦.

Taverna Hotel, V, Váci utca 20 (☎138-4999). Shoehorned into place on the trendy thorough-fare where everyone promenades. ⑦.

AROUND THE GREAT BOULEVARD

While most of the following places are on (or just off) the Great Boulevard, a couple are further out near Keleti Station.

Emke Hotel, VII, Akácfa utca 1–3 (☎122-9230). Sixties construction near the junction of Rákóczi út and the Great Boulevard, off Blaha Lujza tér (metro line 2). ⑦.

Grand Hotel Hungária, VII, Rákóczi út 90 (☎122-9050). Sited opposite Keleti Station, this classic railway hotel was totally refurbished in 1985. ⑦.

Hotel Park, VIII, Baross tér 10 (☎113-1420). Also near Keleti Station, but rather noisy. ⑤.

Hotel Radisson Béke, VI, Teréz körút 43 (☎132-3300). Refurbished vintage hotel on the Great Boulevard, 200m south of Nyugati Station. Sauna and pool. ⑦.

Medosz Hotel, VI, Jókai tér 9 (☎153-1700). Next to the Puppet Theatre, just off Andrássy út near the Oktogon (metro line 1). ⑤.

Metropol Hotel, VIII, Rákóczi út 58 (☎142-1175). Near Keleti Station and a stone's throw from Blaha Lujza tér. ⑥.

Nemzeti Hotel, VIII, József körút 4 (☎269-9310). Small Art Nouveau-style place overlooking Blaha Lujza tér (metro line 2). ⑦. ✳

FURTHER OUT

These are all within fifteen minutes of the centre by metro. The first four are near big parks: the Városliget (City Park) and Népliget.

Benczúr Hotel, VI, Benczúr utca 35 (☎142-7970). Quietly situated two blocks from Andrássy út and Hősök tere, near Bajza utca (metro line 1). ⑥.

Hotel Délibab, VI, Délibab utca 35 (☎122-8763). A former Esterházy mansion across from Hősök tere, now noisy and a bit run-down. ⑤.

Hotel Liget, VI, Aréna út (formerly Dózsa György út) 106 7☎269-5300). Stylish new hotel opposite the Fine Arts Museum on Hősök tere, bordering the Városliget. Noisy but great location. ⑥.

Hotel Platánus, X, Könyves Kálmán körút 44 (☎113-5086). On a major thoroughfare opposite the Népliget (metro line 3). ⑤.

Hotel Volga, XIII, Dózsa György út 65 (☎129-0200). Another three-star place, by the line 3 Dózsa György út metro stop, 1km beyond Nyugati Station. ⑦.

Stadion Hotel, XIV, Ifjúság útja 1–3 (☎252-9333). In the sports complex near Népstadion bus station (metro line 2). ⑦.

Thermal Hotel Helia, XIII, Kárpát utca 62–64 (☎270-3277). Finnish-owned modern four-star hotel with thermal baths. Located in north Pest. ⑥.

Pensions

Pensions are likely to fill up fast during summer, so reservations are pretty much essential. In most cases, you need to phone them direct. The following places are all **in Buda** and listed according to location, from south to north.

Jäger–Trió Panzió, XI, Ördögorom út 20D (☎185-1880). In the Sasad district in the hills; bus #8 from Március 15. tér to the end of the line, then a 10-minute walk. Open March 15–Nov 15. ④.

Bara Panzió, I, Hegyalja út 34–36 (☎185-3445). On the main road to Vienna, below Gellért Hill. ⑥.

Molnár Panzió, XII, Fodor utca 143 (☎209-2973). In the Orbánhegy district of the Buda Hills; bus #102 from Déli Station runs nearby. Some triple rooms. ⑥.

Beatrix Panzió, II, Szehér út 3 (☎176-3730). Near *Hárshegy Camping* in the Buda Hills; bus #56 from Moszkva tér. ⑥.

San Marcó Panzió, III, San Marcó utca 6 (☎188-9997); bus #60 from Batthyány tér. Small, friendly pension in Óbuda, run by Mrs Steininger. Shared bathrooms. ④.

Pál Vendégház Panzió, III, Pálvölgyi köz 15 (☎188-7099), near the Pál-völgyi Stalactite Cave; bus #65 from Kolosy tér in Óbuda. Eight double rooms. ④.

Aquincum Panzió, III, Szentendrei út 105 (☎168-7868). Near the Köles utca HÉV stop, one stop before Aquincum. Some triple rooms. ③.

Private rooms and apartments

There are **private rooms** throughout the city, many in the sort of locations where a hotel would be unaffordable. Depending on location and amenities, **prices** for a double room range from 800Ft to 1500Ft a night. On the downside, solo travellers will almost certainly have to pay for a double, and rates are thirty percent higher if you stay fewer than four nights (making pensions or hostels more economical for short-staying visitors). **Apartments**, from 3000Ft a night, are not as common as rooms, but you should be able to find an agency with one on its books.

It's easy enough to get a room from one of the **touts** at the train stations, but it's safer to go through a tourist agency, where you book and pay at the counter signposted *fizetővendég*. The four main **agencies** – *Budapest Tourist*, *Ibusz*, *Cooptourist* and *Volántourist* – have offices all over the city (see box on p.58 for addresses), but the ones in the stations and central Pest are obviously the most convenient for new arrivals.

Since rooms are rented sight unseen, it pays to take some trouble over your choice. Your host and the premises should give no cause for complaint (both are checked out), but the **location** or ambience might. For atmosphere and comfort, you can't beat those nineteenth-century blocks where spacious, high-ceilinged apartments surround a courtyard with wrought-iron balconies – most common in Pest's V, VI and VII districts, and the parts of Buda nearest Castle Hill. Elsewhere – particularly in Újpest (IV district), Csepel (XXI) or Óbuda (III) – you're likely to end up in a box on the twelfth floor of a *lakótelep*. The *Budapest Atlasz* is invaluable for checking the location of sites and access by public transport.

Because many proprietors go out to work, you might not be able to take possession of the room until 5pm – if so, the tourist office will say. Some knowledge of Hungarian facilitates **settling in**; guests normally receive an explanation of the boiler system and multiple door keys (*kulcs*), and may have use of the washing machine (which requires another demonstration).

Hostels

If you don't have a tent, a dormitory bed in a **hostel** is the cheapest alternative – most also have rooms at much the same price as private accommodation (and with no surcharge for staying fewer than four nights). In summer, you can't always be sure of getting a bed in the hostel of your choice without **booking** in advance through *Express* (see box on p.58 for addresses). Out of season, there are five hostels that remain open, though even then it doesn't hurt to book ahead. An IYHF card can be obtained from *Express* if needed, though in practice there don't seem to be any age or membership requirements.

The first five hostels listed below are open year-round; the last five are **college hostels** which function only in the summer. For information about other hostels in the city, contact *Express* or *More Than Ways* at Dózsa György út 152 (☎129-8644 or ☎140-8585).

Ananda, XIV, Kőszeg utca 21 (☎220-2413). Located out in Pest near Örs vezér tér (last stop on the red metro). 2-, 6-, 8-, and 10-bed rooms; 650–750Ft per bed.

Back Pack, XI, Takács Menyhért utca 33 (☎185-5089). Tram #49 to "Tétényi út" stop out in Buda. 5- and 8-bed dorms; 650–750Ft per bed.

Citadella, I, Citadella sétány (☎166-5794). Bus #27 from Móricz Zsigmond körtér. Romantically sited atop Gellért Hill with breathtaking views, the citadel offers doubles with showers and Budapest's cheapest dorms. Reservations can be made direct or through *Budapest Tourist* (not *Express*). 10- and 14-bed rooms; 550Ft per bed.

Diáksport Hotel, XIII, Dózsa György út 152 (☎140-8585). Near Dózsa György út metro on the blue line. Singles, doubles and triples, plus dorms with 4, 6, 9 and 12 beds. 740–980Ft per bed.

Hotel Express, XII, Beethoven utca 7–9 (☎175-2528). In the backstreets south of Déli Station – two stops by tram #59. Curiously, *Express* claims that its "youth hotel" is always full, even when it's not, so ring direct or just turn up. Open year-round; 10 percent discount for IYHF and ISIC card holders. Doubles ③; rooms with 4 beds ④.

Felvinci Kollégium, II, Felvinci út 8 (☎135-4989). A no-frills college hostel with dormitory beds below the exclusive Rózsadomb quarter, close to Moszkva tér (metro line 2). Open mid-July to mid-Aug. 800Ft per bed.

KÉK Somogyi Kollégium, XI, Szüret utca 2–18 (☎185-2369). Around the back of Gellért Hill, two stops from Móricz Zsigmond körtér on bus #27. Open July–Aug. Doubles ②; dormitory beds ①.

Rózsa, XI, Bercsényi utca 28 (☎156-8726). One of the hostels run by Universum, near Móricz Zsigmond körtér in southern Buda.

Universitas, XI, Irinyi József utca 9–11 (☎181-2313 or ☎181-1122). At the Buda end of the Petöfi Bridge. Doubles ② and dormitory rooms (480Ft per bed).

Campsites

Budapest's campsites, which are mostly located in the Buda Hills or the outer suburbs of Pest, generally offer good facilities, though they can become unpleasantly crowded between June and September and the smaller ones might run out of space. It is illegal to camp anywhere else, and the parks are patrolled to enforce this. The police tolerate people **sleeping rough** in train stations, but there's a high risk of theft (or worse) – especially at Keleti.

Buda

Buda's sites are the more pleasant, with trees and grass and maybe even a pool. The first three listed below are in the Buda Hills, twenty minutes' bus ride from Moszkva tér; the last is in the northern suburbs, accessible by HÉV train from Batthyány tér.

Hárshegy Camping, II, Hárshegyi út 5–7 (☎115-1482). Bus #22 from Moszkva tér stops at nearby Denes utca. Pleasant, shady hillside site run by *Budapest Tourist*. Open mid-April to mid-Oct. Bungalows range from doubles without showers ② to four-bed rooms with bathroom ③.

Zugligeti Niche Camping, XII, Zugligeti út 101 (☎156-8641). At the end of the #158 bus route, opposite the chairlift up to János-hegy. Small, terraced ravine site in the woods with space for 260 campers and good facilities including a pleasant little restaurant occupying the former tram station at the far end. Open March–Oct. 280Ft per person plus 200–300Ft tent fee.

Tündérhegyi-Feeburg Camping, XII, Szillássy út 8 (no phone). At the end of the #28 bus route, near the János-hegy chairlift and close to a nature reserve. Nice, very small site accommodating 95 campers. Open March–Oct. 300Ft per person plus 260–360Ft tent fee; two-person bungalows with no bathroom ② and 9-person bungalows with bathroom ⑤ also available.

Római-Fürdő Camping, III, Szentrendrei út 189 (☎168-6260). Huge site with space for 2500 campers beside the road to Szentendre in Római-Fürdő (25min by HÉV). Open May to mid-Oct. Higher than average rates (500Ft per person plus 430Ft tent fee) include use of the nearby swimming pool. Also has bungalows (from ② per person) bookable through *Budapest Tourist*.

Pest

Located in the dusty outer suburbs, these are all accessible by bus from Örs vezér tere, at the end of metro line 2.

Expo AutoCamp, X, Dobi István út 10 (☎147-0990); bus #100. Shadeless, gravelled expanse near gate IV of the International Fairground, used by trailers. Open July & Aug only. 320Ft per person plus 350Ft tent fee and 300Ft for vehicle.

Metro Tennis Camping, XVI, Csömöri út 158 (☎163-5584); three stops by #31 bus. Larger site with tennis courts. Open April–Oct. 280Ft per person plus 250Ft tent fee and 200Ft for car.

Rózsakert Camping, X, Pilisi utca 7 (no phone); off Kerepesi út, three stops by bus #45 or #4. Small, privately owned site with space for 50 campers. Open year-round. 250–350Ft per person plus 300Ft tent fee; bungalows for 1000–1200Ft.

Bungalows

Budapest Tourist (see p.58 for addresses) can arrange detached **bungalows** of various sizes at Hárshegy and Római-Fürdő campsites (see above), and the following locations:

Csillaghegyi Strand, III, Pusztakúti út 3 (☎167-1999); one HÉV stop past Római-Fürdő. Set in a wooded area with bathing. Cheaper second- and third-class bungalows. Open mid-April to mid-Oct. ②.

Haladás Motel, IV, Üdülősor 8 (☎189-1114); bus #104 from the Árpad híd (metro line 3). Second-class bungalows beside the Danube in Újpest. Open April–Oct. ③.

Panoráma Bungalows, XII, Rege út 21 (☎175-0522). Upmarket complex by the *Panoráma Hotel*. Bungalows with baths, sleeping four or five. Open year-round. ⑦.

Buda

Seen from the embankments of the Danube, **BUDA** forms a collage of palatial buildings, archaic spires and outsize statues, crowning craggy massifs. This glamorous image conceals more mundane aspects, but at times, in the right place, the city can really live up to it. To experience **Castle Hill** at its best, come early in the morning before the crowds arrive. Then you can beat them to the **museums**, wander off for lunch or a soak in one of the Turkish baths, and return to catch street life in full swing during the afternoon. The outlying **Buda Hills** – accessible by chairlift and the Children's Railway – are obviously less visited during the week, while **Gellért Hill**, the **Rózsadomb** and **Roman ruins** can be seen any time the weather's fine.

Castle Hill

Castle Hill (*Várhegy*) is Buda's most prominent feature, a long plateau laden with bastions, mansions and a huge palace, commanding the Watertown below. Its grandiosity and strategic utility have long gone hand in hand: Hungarian kings built their palaces here because it was easy to defend, a fact appreciated by the Turks, Habsburgs and other occupiers. Its buildings, a legacy of bygone Magyar glories, have been almost wholly reconstructed from the rubble of 1945, when the Wehrmacht and the Red Army battled over the Hill while Buda's inhabitants cowered underground.

Though the Hill's appearance has changed much since building began in the thirteenth century, its main **streets** still follow their medieval courses, with Gothic arches and stone carvings half-concealed in the courtyards and passages of eighteenth- and nineteenth-century Baroque **houses**, whose facades are embellished with fancy ironwork grilles. Practically every building displays a *Müemlék* plaque giving details of its history.

There are several **approaches** to Castle Hill, mostly starting from the Watertown (described on p.174). The simplest is to ascend to the palace by **Sikló** – a renovated nineteenth-century **funicular** that runs from Clark Ádám tér near the Chain Bridge (daily 7.30am–10pm, closed every other Mon; 80Ft for adults & 60Ft for children). Alternatively you can start from Moszkva tér (on metro line 2) and walk up to the Vienna Gate or take the Várbusz – a minibus that terminates on Dísz tér. Finally from Batthány tér (metro line 2), you can proceed along Fő utca **on foot** until you see the spires. From this point in the Watertown, various flights of steps (*lepcső*) climb up to the Fishermen's Bastion and the Mátyás Church, where most people begin their tour of Castle Hill. **From Pest**, the easiest journey is by bus #16 from Erzsébet tér, but it's probably more enjoyable to head for the Watertown and approach from there.

The Fishermen's Bastion

The **Fishermen's Bastion** (*Halászbástya*) could have been dreamed up by the illusionist artist Escher: an undulating white rampart of cloisters and flights of steps, intersecting at turrets, like one of his Endless Stairways. Although fishermen from the Watertown reputedly defended this stretch of the Hill during the Middle Ages, the existing structure is purely decorative, providing a perfect frame for the Mátyás Church and the view of Parliament across the river. The seven tent-like turrets, designed by Frigyes Schulek at the turn of the century, allude to the seven Magyar tribes that gave rise to the nation a thousand years earlier. By day the bastion is besieged by tourists, buskers and vendors, its cloisters awash with countrywomen selling embroidery from Transylvania.

THE MÁTYÁS CHURCH

Occupying centre stage right in the middle of Castle Hill, the **Mátyás Church** is an example of neo-Gothic run riot, with diamond-patterned roof tiles and a multi-

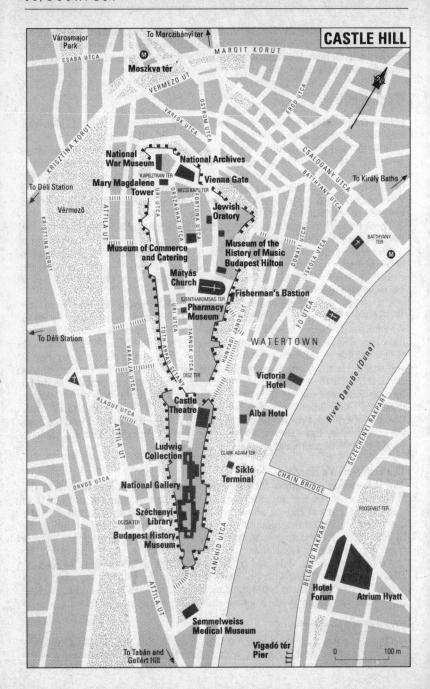

CASTLE HILL

Városmajor Park

CSABA UTCA

To Marczibányi ter

MARGIT KORUT

Moszkva tér

VERMEZO UT

VARFOK UTCA

OSTROM UTCA

EROD UTCA

CSALOGANY UTCA

BATTHYANY UTCA

To Király Baths

National War Museum

National Archives

KRISZTINA KORUT

KAPISZTRAN TER

Vienna Gate

To Déli Station

Mary Magdalene Tower

BECSI KAPU TER

URI UTCA

ORSZAGHAZ UTCA

FORTUNA UTCA

Vérmező

ATTILA UT

Jewish Oratory

Museum of the History of Music
Budapest Hilton

Museum of Commerce and Catering

KRISZTINA KORUT

Mátyás Church

Fisherman's Bastion

SZENTHAROMSAG TER

DONATI UTCA

ISKOLA UTCA

BATTHYANY TER

FO UTCA

To Déli Station

URI UTCA

Pharmacy Museum

TOTH ARPAD SETANY

TARNOK UTCA

HUNYADI JANOS UT

WATERTOWN

VARALJA UTCA

DISZ TER

ALAGUT UTCA

Victoria Hotel

River Danube (Duna)

SZÉCHENYI RAKPART

Castle Theatre

ATTILA UT

Alba Hotel

Ludwig Collection

CLARK ADAM TER

CHAIN BRIDGE

Sikló Terminal

ORVOS UTCA

National Gallery

ROOSEVELT TER

Széchenyi Library

DOZSA TER

Budapest History Museum

LANCHID UTCA

BELGRAD RAKPART

Hotel Forum

Atrium Hyatt

ATTILA UT

Semmelweiss Medical Museum

To Tabán and Gellért Hill

Vigadó tér Pier

0   100 m

tude of toothy spires, wildly asymmetrical but nevertheless coherent in form. Officially dedicated to Our Lady but popularly named after "Good King Mátyás", the building is a superb nineteenth-century recreation by Frigyes Schulek, grafted onto those portions of the original thirteenth-century church that survived the siege of 1686. Prior to that date it had served as a mosque, the Büyük Dzjami, whose Turkish occupants whitewashed over the medieval murals and removed the furnishings. In the spring of 1994 the church and its windows were damaged by a bomb, one of several blasts in the city. No one claimed responsibility for it, though Serbian groups were suspected.

Entering the church through its **Mary Portal**, visitors gape at the richness of the interior. Painted leaves and geometric motifs run up columns and under vaulting, while shafts of light fall through rose windows onto gilded altars and statues with stunning effect. Most of the **frescoes** were executed by Károly Lotz or Bertalan Székely, the foremost historical painters of the late nineteenth century. The **coat of arms of King Mátyás** can be seen on the wall to your left, inside the entrance; his family name, Corvinus, comes from the raven (*corvus* in Latin) that appeared on his heraldry and every volume in the famous *Biblioteca Corvinus*.

Around the corner beneath the south tower is the **Loreto Chapel**, containing a Baroque Madonna. Across the way, two medieval capitals, carved with monsters and a bearded figure with a book, lurk below the Béla Tower, so-called after the fourth king of that name. His predecessor lies in the second chapel along, sharing a double sarcophagus with Anne of Chatillon. Originally located in Székesfehérvár, the **tomb of Béla III** and his queen was moved here after its discovery in 1848. Although Hungary's medieval kings were crowned at Székesfehérvár, it was customary to make a prior appearance in Buda – hence yet another sobriquet, the "Coronation Church".

The church's **crypt** and collection of **ecclesiastical treasures** (April–Sept daily 8.30am–8pm; Oct–March daily 9am–7pm) are reached by a portal to the right of the chancel. From here, stairs ascend to **Saint Stephen's Chapel**, decorated with scenes from the king's life, whence another staircase leads to the **Royal Oratory**, exhibiting the coronation robes and thrones of emperors Franz Josef and Karl IV, and a **replica of the Hungarian Crown Jewels** (the originals are in the National Museum).

Mass is still celebrated here every morning, with several services on Sunday including a sung Mass at 10am and 7pm. **Organ recitals** are held in the church on Friday evenings, and **concerts** during the Spring Festival and summer season.

SZENTHÁROMSÁG TÉR

Beyond the Mátyás Church lies **Szentháromság tér** (Holy Trinity Square), which derives its name from a Trinity Column erected in 1713, in thanks for the abatement of a plague – there are many such monuments in Central Europe. The copper and glass facade of the **Budapest Hilton**, which incorporates chunks of a medieval Dominican church and monastery, reflects the image of the church and the Fishermen's Bastion. Around the back is a fine equestrian **statue of King Stephen**. On Szentháromság utca, running off by the Old Town Hall building, **Ruszwurm's patisserie** has thrived at no. 7 since 1827 on a site where a ginger-bread shop stood in the Middle Ages. It's invariably too crowded to get a table, but worth a look before you strike out towards Buda Palace or the Vienna Gate, and you can buy cakes to munch on the way.

KING STEPHEN

If you commit only one figure from Hungarian history to memory, make it **King Stephen**, for it was *István* (as Hungarians know him) who welded the tribal Magyar fiefdoms into a state and won recognition from Christendom. Like his father, Prince Géza, Stephen strove to Christianize the pagan Magyars and to develop Hungary with the help of foreign preachers, craftsmen and merchants. By marrying Gizella of Bavaria in 996, he was able to use her father's knights to crush a pagan revolt after Géza's death, and subsequently received an apostolic cross and crown from Pope Sylvester II for his coronation on Christmas Day in 1000 AD.

Though noted for his enlightened admonitions (such as the need for tolerance and the desirability of multi-racial nations), he could act ruthlessly when necessary. After his only son Imre died in an accident and a suspected pagan seemed likely to inherit, Stephen had the man blinded and poured molten lead into his ears, before choosing another successor. Posthumously canonized, **Saint Stephen** became a national talisman; his mummified right hand a sacred relic; and his Coronation regalia the symbol of statehood. Despite downplaying his cult for decades, even the Communists eventually embraced it in a bid for some legitimacy.

To the Vienna Gate and back

The following circuit covers the sector up to the Vienna Gate, at the northern end of Castle Hill. Depending on where you begin, places can be seen more or less in the order described here by cutting back and forth through the side streets. Otherwise, drop in on your way back from the gate. Almost immediately you set off in this direction you'll pass a couple of fine examples of the Hill's ancient buildings on Hess András tér: the *Fortuna* restaurant at no. 4 occupies the site of Hungary's first printing press, while the medieval *Red Hedgehog* inn (no. 3) is now a private residence.

Head up Fortuna utca and you'll find the intriguing **Museum of Commerce and Catering** (Tues–Sun 10am–6pm) at no. 4, where the *Fortuna Inn* was located between 1784 and 1868. Three rooms smelling of vanilla relate the history of confectionery – a serious art in a country that heralded the creator of the *dobostorta* as a hero – while across the corridor is a fine collection of posters, shop windows and illuminated signs from before and after World War I.

By returning to Hess András tér and following Táncsics Mihály utca to the former Erdödy Palace at no. 7, you can visit the **Museum of the History of Music** (Mon 4–9pm & Wed–Sun 10am–6pm). Beethoven once stayed here and Bartók had his workshop in the building. Its Baroque decor is as much an attraction as the antique instruments within. Concerts are regularly held here – for information consult one of the English-language weeklies or monthlies.

Next door to the museum is the former prison where the writer Mihály Táncsics was held for nationalist agitation, until freed during the 1848 Revolution. During the Middle Ages this street was chiefly inhabited by Jews (Italians, Germans and French congregated in neighbouring quarters), hence the **Jewish Oratory** at no. 26, displaying artefacts and gravestones from that era (May–Oct Tues–Fri 10am–2pm & Sat– Sun 10am–6pm).

AROUND THE VIENNA GATE AND KAPISZTRÁN TÉR

At the end of the road lies **Bécsi Kapu tér**, known as the "Saturday" (market) square before its devastation in 1686. Given a new and sombre cast when it was rebuilt in the eighteenth century, it was subsequently renamed after the chunky **Vienna Gate** (*Bécsi Kapu*) that was erected on the 250th anniversary of the recapture of Buda from the Turks. To the west loom the neo-Romanesque **National Archives** (closed to the public) and the **National War Museum** (Tues–Sun 10am–6pm). The latter is entered from the Tóth Árpád sétány, a promenade overlooking Buda's western districts. Inside are weapons and uniforms galore, and a courtyard full of armoured vehicles.

The museum flanks one corner of **Kapisztrán tér**, named after Friar John Capistranus, who exhorted the Hungarians to victory over the Turks at the siege of Belgrade in 1456. On the south side of the square rises the **Mary Magdalene Tower** (whose accompanying church had to be pulled down after World War II), which now serves as a private picture gallery. From here, you can head back along one of two historic streets, Országház utca or Úri utca.

ORSZÁGHÁZ UTCA AND ÚRI UTCA

During the 145 years of Turkish occupation the Hill's main thoroughfare was known as the "street of the baths" (*Hamam Yolu*), and the Castle district contained 34 mosques, three Dervish monasteries and over 100 tanneries – all of which have long vanished. However, many curious architectural features have survived along what is now **Országház utca** (Parliament Street), so-called after the parliamentary sessions held in a building here during the 1780s.

Heading south you'll pass the *Régi Orsághá* restaurant, whose gate's keystone bears a relief of a croissant; the gateway of no. 9 contains a set of niches with lily-ended traceries (thought by some to have served as stalls for merchants). Across the street, no. 22 retains some Renaissance graffiti on the bottom of its bay window, while no. 20 has a trefoil-arched cornice dating back to the fourteenth century.

Historic architecture also dignifies **Úri utca** (Gentlemanly Street), where the Hungarian Jacobins were imprisoned at no. 52 prior to being executed below the Hill in 1795. Allegorical statues of the four seasons decorate the first-floor niches at nos. 54–56, while Gothic sedilia embellish the gateway of nos. 48–50. The facade of no. 31 is almost entirely Gothic, and medieval gateways are incorporated in the houses across the street. The main attraction, however, lies underground, a couple of blocks beyond the equestrian statue at the junction with Szentháromság utca.

Here, at Úri utca 9, you'll find the entrance to the **labyrinth of caves** beneath Castle Hill (Tues–Sun 10am–6pm; 250Ft or 200Ft for students). During the Middle Ages, ten kilometres of galleries were tunnelled between cavities in the bedrock, and wells were dug to make them habitable in case of siege. The cellars of many houses connected directly to the labyrinth, which served as air-raid shelter and field hospital in the winter of 1944–45. Nowadays part is given over to a dank **waxworks**, with tableaux of the goriest events in Magyar history; a guide ensures that visitors don't stray and get lost in the tunnels.

South towards the Palace

Heading south from Szentháromság tér or continuing down Úri utca, you can easily reach Tárnok utca (named after the royal treasurers who once lived here), whose nineteenth-century inhabitants impressed John Paget with their "sedateness of air" and "pompous vacancy of expression". At the top of the street stands the seventeenth-century *Golden Eagle* apothecary, now a **Pharmacy Museum** of

Hussars were a Hungarian innovation later adopted by armies throughout Europe. The first such unit of light cavalry was organized by King Mátyás in 1480; armed with sabres, pikes and daggers, it excelled in surprise attacks and rapid manoeuvres. By the time of the Napoleonic Wars every national army fielded hussars and most infantry wore hussar-style cylindrical felt or leather hats (called *shako*, from the Magyar word for a peaked hat) instead of metal helmets. Although Hussar is one of the few Hungarian words to have entered the English language, it is thought to derive from the Latin *cursor* (runner) rather than the Magyar *húsz* (meaning twenty). In Hungary their romantic image endures, and costumed riders sometimes appear on the Hill in summer, to popular approval.

dubious nostrums and wicked-looking instruments (Tues–Sun 10.30am–5.30pm). The *Arany Hordó* restaurant, 20m south, occupies one of the few buildings on the Hill to have kept its original *sgraffiti* – a red and orange chequerboard pattern covering the facade.

Both Tárnok utca and Úri utca end in **Dísz tér** (Parade Square), whose cobbled expanses are guarded by a statue of a hussar. From here on ramparts and gateways buttress the hillside and control access to the palace grounds. Straight ahead lies the scarred hulk of the old Premier's residence, the last outbuilding of the palace complex still to be restored, while to your left stands the **Castle Theatre**. A Carmelite church until the order was dissolved by Emperor Josef II, its conversion was supervised by Farkas Kempelen, inventor of a chess-playing automaton. Here, the first ever play in Hungarian was staged in 1790, and Beethoven performed in 1808.

Around the corner of the theatre is the upper terminal of the Sikló funicular, overlooked from the terrace of Buda Palace by a bronze **Turul statue**, honouring the mythical bird that begat Álmos, father of Árpád, who led the Magyar tribes into Europe. In recent years the bird has become a symbol of Hungary's active skinhead population.

Buda Palace

As befits a former royal residence, the lineage of **Buda Palace**, the *Budavári Palota*, can be traced back to medieval times, and the rise and fall of various palaces on the Hill is symbolic of the changing fortunes of the Hungarian state. The first fortifications and dwellings here, hastily erected by Béla III after the thirteenth-century Mongol invasion, were replaced by ever more luxurious palaces by the Angevin kings, who ruled in more prosperous and stable times. The zenith was attained in the reign of Mátyás Corvinus (1458–90), whose palace was a Renaissance extravaganza to which artists and scholars from all over Europe were drawn by the blandishments of Queen Beatrice and the prospect of lavish hospitality. After the Turkish occupation, and the long siege that ended it, only ruins were left – these the Austrian Habsburgs, Hungary's new rulers, levelled to build a palace of their own.

From Maria Theresa's modest beginnings (a mere 203 rooms, which she never saw completed), the **Royal Palace** expanded inexorably throughout the nineteenth century, though no monarch ever dwelt here, only the Habsburg Palatine (viceroy). After the collapse of the empire, Admiral Horthy inhabited the building with all the pomp of monarchy until he was deposed by a German coup in October 1944. The palace was left unoccupied, and it wasn't long before the siege of Buda once again resulted in total devastation: since then Pest has been the seat of all decision making. Reconstruction work began in the 1950s, and the sombre wings of the Palace now contain a clutch of museums and medieval structures discovered in the course of excavation.

THE LUDWIG COLLECTION
The northern (A) wing of the palace formerly housed the Museum of the Working Class Movement, giving the Communist Party's view of history. In 1990, the museum's staff made amends for decades of misinformation by organizing a huge exhibition on the Stalinist era called *RÁ-KO-SI STA-LIN* (the chant, naming the leaders of Hungary and the former USSR, that was obligatory at rallies of the time). Sadly, this fascinating display has since been replaced in turn by the **Ludwig Collection** (Tues–Sun 10am–6pm), a privately assembled hoard of modern art that includes the odd Lichtenstein and Picasso, accompanied by temporary exhibitions. Find out what's showing before forking out the 100Ft admission (students/pensioners half price; free on Tues).

THE NATIONAL GALLERY
The central and southern wings of the palace contain the **National Gallery** (April–Nov daily 10am–6pm; Dec–March daily 10am–4pm; free on Sat), devoted to Hungarian art since the Middle Ages. Few visitors see every section, which have separate entrances (though one ticket suffices for all of them); the main entrance is on the eastern side of Building C, in the courtyard with the stone lions.

To follow it chronologically, start with the ground floor of **Building D**, displaying **Romanesque** and **Gothic stone carvings** from Ják, Esztergom and Veszprém. On the floor above, in what used to be the throne room, are **Renaissance altarpieces** from churches in what is now Slovakia, and **Baroque ecclesiastical art**, much of it confiscated from private owners in the Fifties. The ground floors of **Buildings B and C** are used for temporary exhibits, while those above are devoted to **Hungarian painting since the nineteenth century**, from genre painting to Impressionism, historicism to avant garde. Don't miss the vast painting by Csontváry on the landing between the second and third floors, which cover twentieth-century art. The Nagybánya and Szentendre artists' colonies are well represented, as is József Rippl-Rónai, the chief Hungarian exponent of Art Nouveau. **Contemporary art** is displayed on the third floor of Building D.

THE MÁTYÁS FOUNTAIN AND SZÉCHENYI LIBRARY
In the outer courtyard of the palace, flanked by A, B and C wings, stands the **Mátyás Fountain**, whose bronze figures recall the legend of Szép Ilonka. This beautiful peasant girl supposedly met the king while he was hunting incognito, fell in love with him, and died of a broken heart after discovering his identity and realizing the futility of her hopes. The figure on the king's right is his Italian chronicler, who recorded the story for posterity (it is also enshrined in a folk song).

To the west of the inner **Lion Courtyard** stands the **Széchenyi Library**, a repository for publications in Hungarian, and material relating to the country from around the world. By law, the Library receives a copy of every book, newspaper and magazine that is published in Hungary. Like the Hungarian Academy, it was founded by Count Széchenyi during the Reform era. Its central reading room is open to the public, and there are exhibitions on diverse themes (Mon 1–9pm, Tues–Sat 10am–6pm).

THE BUDAPEST HISTORY MUSEUM AND SOUTHERN BASTIONS

The palace's E wing, on the far side of the Lion Courtyard, contains the **Budapest History Museum** (daily except Tues 10am–6pm; 50Ft admission, free on Wed), which incorporates marbled and flagstoned halls from the Renaissance palace, unearthed during post-war excavations. These are far below the current street level, giving visitors "the sensation of burrowing into the history of the city". In the Renaissance Room are portraits of Mátyás and Beatrice (whose coat of arms decorates the Beatrice Courtyard outside). Upstairs are old prints, ceramics and other artefacts tracing the evolution of Óbuda, Buda and Pest over the centuries.

The southern end of the Hill, once terraced with vineyards, now supports a maze of paths and promenades leading into the **Round Bastion** and guarded by the **Mace Tower** and Lihegő Gate. From 1961 to 1984, the **Youth Park** *(Ifjúsági Park)* on the hillside overlooking the embankment played a vital role in Hungarian pop culture, since practically every band either played here or aspired to do so, until it was closed down as unsafe. Down at the bottom, you can either backtrack through the Watertown or head south towards Gellért Hill.

The Watertown

The **Watertown** *(Víziváros)*, between Castle Hill and the Danube, was originally a poor quarter housing fishermen, craftsmen and their families, which became depopulated during the seventeenth century save for a few "Turkified Hungarians selling fruit". Today it's a reclusive neighbourhood of mansions and old buildings meeting at odd angles on the hillside, reached by alleys which mostly consist of steps rising from the main street – **Fő utca**. Some are still lit by gas lamps, looking quite Dickensian on misty evenings. The following account progresses southwards from Batthyány tér; see p.79 for details of the northern sector where the Király Baths are located.

Batthyány tér

The Watertown's main square, named **Batthyány tér** after the nineteenth-century prime minister, was originally called Bomba (bomb) tér after an ammunition depot sited here. Now home to a long-established market and the underground interchange between metro line 2 and the HÉV rail line to Szentendre, it's always busy with shoppers and commuters. To the right of the market is a sunken, two-storey building that used to be the *White Horse Inn*, where Casanova reputedly once stayed – this is now a nightclub, predictably named after him. The twin-towered **Watertown Parish Church** on the southern corner of the square sports the Buda coat of arms on its tympanum.

Heading south along Fő utca, you'll see a spiky polychrome-tiled church on **Szilágyi Desző tér**, and a floating hotel moored alongside the embankment. It was here that the Arrow Cross massacred hundreds of Jews and dumped their bodies in the river in the bitterly cold January of 1945, when Eichmann and the

SS had already fled the city, which was by then encircled by the Red Army. An inconspicuous plaque commemorates the victims. Further on, you can see the old Capuchin Church featuring Turkish window arches, at no. 30 on the left-hand side. A couple of blocks later you emerge on to Clark Ádám tér, facing the Chain Bridge.

The Chain Bridge

The majestic **Chain Bridge** (*lánchíd*) has a special place in the hearts of locals as the first permanent link between Buda and Pest, and as a symbol of civic endurance. Austrian troops tried and failed to destroy it in 1849, but in 1945 it fell victim to the Wehrmacht, who dynamited all of Budapest's bridges in a bid to check the Red Army. Their reconstruction was one of the first tasks of the post-war era, the Chain Bridge being reopened on November 21, 1949, the exact centenary of its inauguration.

The bridge was instigated by **Count István Széchenyi**, a horse-fancying Anglophile with a passion for innovation, who founded the National Library and brought steam engines to Hungary, amongst other achievements. Designed by **William Tierney Clark**, it was constructed under the supervision of a Scottish engineer, **Adam Clark** (no relation), who personally thwarted the Austrian attempts to destroy it by flooding the chain-lockers. While Széchenyi died in an asylum having witnessed the triumph (and subsequent defeat) of Kossuth and the 1848 Revolution (see *Contexts*) – Adam Clark settled happily in Budapest with his Hungarian wife. Clark also built the **tunnel** (*alagút*) under Castle Hill which, Budapesters joked, could be used to store the new bridge when it rained.

The Sikló and Kilometre Zero

Near the tunnel entrance is the lower terminal of the **Sikló**, a lovingly restored nineteenth-century **funicular** running up to the palace (daily 7.30am–10pm; closed every other Mon). Constructed on the initiative of Ödön, Széchenyi's son, it was only the second funicular in the world when it was inaugurated in 1870, and functioned without a hitch until wrecked by a shell in 1945. The yellow carriages are exact replicas of the originals, but are now lifted by an electric winch rather than a steam engine as before. In the small park further south stands "Kilometre Zero", a zero-shaped monument whence all distances from Budapest are measured.

Tabán, Gellért Hill and beyond

South of Castle Hill lies the **Tabán** district, once Buda's artisan quarter, largely inhabited by Serbs (known as *Rác* in Hungarian), but almost totally destroyed by redevelopment in the 1930s. Nowadays it seems to consist mostly of parks and highways, but there are a few survivors worth seeking out. The **Semmelweiss Medical Museum** at Apród utca 1–3 (Tues–Sun 10am–6pm) honours the "saviour of mothers", Ignác Semmelweiss (1815–65). He discovered the cause of puerperal fever (a form of blood poisoning contracted in childbirth) and a simple method for preventing the disease, which until then was usually fatal. Inside are displayed medical instruments and mementoes of Semmelweiss. The real reason to come to Tabán, though, is the Turkish baths – the place to immerse yourself in history.

BATHING MATTERS

Most bathhouses are divided into a **swimming** area and a separate section for **thermal baths** (*gyógyfürdő*), sauna, steamrooms and sometimes even mud baths. To enter this latter section, you must exchange your swimsuit for an apron (for women) or loincloth (for men). A basic ticket covers three hours in the pools, *szauna* and steamrooms (*gőzfürdő*); and supplementary tickets will buy you a massage *(masszázs)*, tub (*kadfürdő*) or mud bath (*iszapfürdő*). Swimmers are required to wear a bathing cap, which can be rented if necessary (as can swimsuits and towels).

The Rác and Rudas Baths

The relaxing and curative effects of Buda's **mineral springs** have been appreciated for 2000 years. The Romans built splendid bathhouses at Aquincum and, while these declined with the empire, interest revived after the Knights of Saint John built a hospice on the site of the present Rudas baths, near where Saint Elizabeth cured lepers in the springs below Gellért Hill. However, it was the Turks who consolidated the habit of bathing (as Muslims, they were obliged to wash five times daily in preparation for prayer) and created proper bathhouses which function to this day.

The **Rác Baths** (Mon–Sat 7.30am–6pm), on Hadnagy utca below the Hegyalja út flyover, have an octagonal stone pool from Turkish times, but were otherwise rebuilt in the last century. The sulphurous water (40°C) is good for skin complaints and conditions affecting the joints. There are separate admission days for men (Mon, Wed & Fri) and women (Tues, Thurs & Sat). Heading on towards the Rudas Baths, you pass the Ivocsarnok (Water Hall) below the road to the Erzsébet Bridge – drinking water from three nearby springs is sold here (Mon, Wed & Fri 11am–6pm, Tues & Thurs 7am–2pm).

The **Rudas Baths** (Mon–Fri 6.30am–6pm & Sat 6am–1pm), south of the Erzsébet bridge, are outwardly nondescript, but the interior has hardly changed since it was constructed in 1556 on the orders of Pasha Sokoli Mustapha. Tselebi called this place the "bath with green pillars", and these columns can still be seen today. Bathers wallow in an octagonal stone pool with steam billowing around the shadowy recesses and shafts of light pouring in from the star-shaped apertures in the domed ceiling. To the left of the entrance is a swimming pool, open to both sexes. Like all steam baths in Budapest, the Rudas also has a thriving gay scene.

Gellért Hill

Gellért Hill (*Gellérthegy*) is as much a feature of the waterfront panorama as Castle Hill and the Parliament building: a craggy dolomite cliff rearing 130m above the embankment, surmounted by the Liberation Monument and the Citadella. The hill is named after Bishop Ghirardus (Gellért in Hungarian), who converted pagan Magyars to Christianity at the behest of King Stephen. After his royal protector's demise vengeful heathens strapped Gellért to a barrow and toppled him off the cliff, where a **statue of Saint Gellért** now stands astride a waterfall facing the Erzsébet Bridge.

To reach the **summit** you can either travel to Móricz Zsigmond körtér and catch bus #27 to the top; or you can climb one of the paths from the statue or the *Hotel Gellért* (10–15min). Set in a cave on the river side of the hill, you pass a small **chapel** which was blocked up during the Communist regime and only recently restored to the Paulites, a small Hungarian religious order. The **panoramic view** from the top of the hill is stunning, drawing one's eye slowly along the curving river, past bridges and monumental landmarks, and then on to the Buda Hills and Pest's suburbs, merging hazily with the distant plain.

THE GELLÉRT HOTEL AND BATHS

Before ascending the hill, take a look at the **Gellért Hotel**, a famous Art Nouveau establishment opened in 1918, which Admiral Horthy commandeered after his triumphal entry into "sinful Budapest" in 1920. During the Thirties and Forties, its balls were the highlight of Budapest's social calendar, debutantes dancing on a glass floor laid over its pool. The **Gellért Baths** are magnificently appointed with majolica tiles and columns, and lion-headed spouts gushing into its thermal pool (Mon–Sat 6am–7pm & Sun 6.30am–1pm; mixed sex). At the far end of the pool, stairs lead down to the Turkish baths, with ornate plunge pools at different levels and separate areas for men and women. There's also an outdoor summer pool with a wave-machine and terraces for nude sunbathing.

Sadly the staff are unhelpful and prices double over summer (bring a cap and towel to save money), but even if you don't plan on taking a dip you should at least take a peek into the foyer, entered via the portal carved with writhing figures.

THE CITADELLA AND LIBERATION MONUMENT

The hilltop **Citadella** was built by the Habsburgs in the aftermath of the 1848–49 Revolution to dominate the city with its cannons. When the historic "Compromise" was reached in 1867, citizens breached the walls to affirm that it no longer posed a threat to them. Since World War II, when an SS regiment holed up in the fortress, nothing more sinister than fireworks has been launched from the citadel. Today, it contains a casino and a tourist hostel, plus a "museum" comprising a few display cabinets; to gain free admission enter through the gate marked "hotel", which is always open.

From the ramparts you get a fine view of the towering **Liberation Monument** beside the citadel – a female figure brandishing the palm of victory over 100 feet aloft – which is too large to be properly appreciated when you stand directly below it. The monument's history is ironic, since it was originally commissioned by Admiral Horthy in memory of his son – killed in the "Crusade against Bolshevism" – but was ultimately dedicated to the Soviet soldiers who died liberating Budapest from the Nazis*. Its sculptor, Zsigmond Kisfaludi-Strobl, simply added smaller figures of Soviet armymen around the base to gain approval as a "Proletarian Artist". Having previously specialized in busts of the aristocracy, he was henceforth known by his compatriots as "Kisfaludi-Strébel" (*strébel* means "to climb" or "step from side to side"). Despite calls for its removal, the statue

---

*In reality, joy at being rid of the Nazis was rapidly dispelled as the Red Army raped and looted its way across Hungary. Once Communist rule became entrenched, mention of the very word rape was forbidden in the media; and a protest delegation of writers received a chilling rebuff from the Communist leader, Rákosi. "What is there to write about? In Hungary there are, say, 3000 villages. Supposing the Russians violated, say, three women in every village. Nine thousand in all. Is that so much? You writers have no idea of the law of large numbers."

survived the recent changes, though the Soviet soldier-figures that used to surround it have been taken away.

Further afield

South of the hill, along the embankment, Budapest's **Technological University** (*Műszaki Egyetem*) sometimes opens its halls of residence to tourists in the summer, while in term time there are concerts and discos in the *E*- and *R-klubs* (see "Entertainment"). Unless you venture further afield into the XI or XXII districts, however, there are no real "sights" here.

Way over to the northwest, the Wolf's Meadow or **Farkasréti Cemetery** (tram #59 from Moszkva tér to the end of the line) contains the **tomb of Béla Bartók**, whose remains were ceremonially reinterred here in July 1988 following their return from America, where the composer died in exile in 1945. His will forbade reburial in Hungary so long as there were any streets named after Hitler or Mussolini – but his return was delayed for decades to prevent the Communists from capitalizing on the event. More impressive than his tomb is the amazing **crypt** in the cemetery chapel, whose wooden vault resembles the oesophagus or belly of a beast – a typically striking design by **Imre Makovecz**.

If you're willing to make a ten-kilometre journey south by bus #3 from Móricz Zsigmond körtér, you can get a feel for how the old nobility lived at the **Nagytétény Castle Museum**, XXII, Kastélymúzeum utca 9 (Tues–Sun 10am– 6pm). Built for the Rudnyánszky family in the mid-eighteenth century, this Baroque mansion contains a collection of antique furniture from Hungary and other countries (some dating from the fifteenth century), and huge tiled stoves. Heading out on the main Vienna road you pass the **Gazdagrét housing estate** in the Budaörs district, where *Szomszédok* – the Hungarian equivalent of *Neighbours* – is set and filmed. If you're curious to watch the programme, it's broadcast every second Thursday at 8.35pm.

A new attraction out on the southwest edge of the city is the **Statue Park**, which brings together many of the monuments that were toppled when the Communist regime fell (summer daily 10am–6pm; Nov–March weekends only 9am–4pm). Here you'll find Lenin standing proud, countless proud proletarians, and the interesting work commemorating the 1919 Hungarian Soviet of Béla Kun, in which umbrella-bearing figures bring up the rear of the revolutionary crowd.

Around Moszkva tér and the Rózsadomb

The area immediately north of Castle Hill is largely defined by the transport hub of **Moszkva tér** and the reclusive residential quarter covering the **Rózsadomb** (Rose Hill). The interest here lies in the ambience of the latter, a couple of minor sights in the backstreets, and easy access to the Buda Hills. For practical purposes, this section also includes the initial stretch of Szilágyi Erzsébet fasor and the Király Baths at the northern end of Fő utca.

Moszkva tér and Szilágyi Erzsébet fasor

Once a quarry, and subsequently an ice rink and tennis courts, the busy transport nexus of Moszkva tér (Moscow Square) has succeeded in keeping its name despite the recent political changes. Among the useful services that run from here are the red metro line; bus #22 to Budakeszi; bus or tram #56 to

Hüvösvölgy; and trams #4 and #6 to Margit Island and Pest's Great Boulevard. Aside from **transport**, Moszkva tér is only notable for the flower and vegetable **markets** in the sidestreets to the north, and **Varosmajor Park**, where chess fans play beneath the elms.

Alongside the park, **Szilágyi Erzsébet fasor** runs past the cylindrical **Hotel Budapest** – nicknamed "the dustbin" for its shape – and the terminal of the **Cogwheel Railway** (see p.82), across the road. One kilometre on, you can glimpse on the right a red marble **monument to Raoul Wallenberg**, the "Righteous Gentile", who gave up a playboy life in neutral Sweden to help the Jews of Hungary in 1944. Armed with diplomatic status and money for bribing officials, Wallenberg and his assistants plucked thousands from the cattle trucks and lodged them in "safe houses", manoeuvring to buy time until the Russians arrived. Shortly after they did, Wallenberg was arrested as a spy and vanished into the Gulag, where he probably died in 1953. The monument was unveiled just before Budapest hosted the World Jewish Congress in 1987.

Around the Király Baths and Bem tér

The area **north of Batthyány tér** (strictly speaking part of the Watertown) can be reached by heading up Fő utca to the Király Baths– alternatively catch a bus #86 or #60 along the embankment to Bem tér and walk west from there. On the former route you'll pass the gloomy premises of the **Military Court of Justice** (nos. 70–72), where Imre Nagy and other leaders of the 1956 Uprising were tried and executed in 1958. The square outside has recently been renamed after Nagy, whose body lay in an unmarked grave for over thirty years. The brand-new brick building at the far side of the square is the new Foreign Ministry.

You can identify the **Király Baths** at Fő utca 82–86 by the four copper cupolas, shaped like tortoise shells, poking from its eighteenth-century facade. The octagonal pool – lit by star-shaped apertures in the dome – was built by the Turks in 1570 for the Buda garrison. The bath's name, meaning "king", comes from that of the König family who owned it in the eighteenth century. Perhaps because there are separate days for men (Mon, Wed & Fri) and women (Tues, Thurs & Sat), the baths have become a major centre of Budapest's **gay life** (Mon–Fri 6.30am–6pm & Sat 6.30am–noon).

A little further north, **Bem tér** was named after the Polish general Joseph Bem, who fought for the Hungarians in the 1849 War of Independence. Traditionally a site for demonstrations, it was here that crowds assembled on October 23, 1956, prior to marching on Parliament bearing Hungarian flags with the hammer and sickle cut out, hours before the Uprising. The square was also the focus for peace demonstrations and protests against the Nagymaros Dam during the Eighties.

At Bem utca 20, 200m in the direction of the Rózsadomb, the **Foundry Museum** (Tues–Sun 10am–5pm) is housed in the ironworks founded by Abrahám Ganz in 1844, which grew into a massive industrial complex. The huge ladles and jib-cranes are still in their original setting, while the museum's collection includes some fine cast-iron stoves.

By continuing northwards past the Margit Bridge instead, you can find the Neoclassical **Lukács Baths**, where there's both a thermal pool (daily 6.30am–8pm: men Tues, Thurs, Sat & Sun; women Mon, Wed & Fri) and a mixed swimming pool (Mon–Sat 6am–8pm & Sun 6am–7pm). The adjacent **Császár Baths** have a Turkish bath-hall dating from the sixteenth century, still in use. The entrances to both are on Üstökös utca, around the back, rather than on the embankment side of the building.

The Rózsadomb

Budapest's most exclusive neighbourhood lies beyond smog-ridden **Margit körút** and the backstreets off Moszkva tér. If you're coming from Bem tér, consider a preliminary detour to the **tomb of Gül Baba** on Mecset utca, just above Mártirok útja. This small octagonal building is a shrine to the "Father of the Roses", a Sufi Dervish who participated in the Turkish capture of Buda but died during the thanksgiving service afterwards: ever since, Muslim pilgrims have come here for *baraka* (blessings). Carpets, examples of calligraphy and Gül Baba's personal effects line the walls of the shrine, which fittingly stands in a rose garden (May–Oct Tues–Sun 10am–6pm).

The **Rózsadomb** itself is as much a social category as a neighbourhood, for a list of residents would read like a Hungarian Who's Who. During the Communist era this included the top Party *funcionárusok*, whose homes featured secret exits that enabled several ÁVO chiefs to escape lynching during the Uprising. Nowadays, wealthy film directors and entrepreneurs predominate, and the sloping streets are lined with spacious villas and flashy cars.

Óbuda and Római-Fürdő

The district of **Óbuda**, north of the Rózsadomb, is the oldest part of Budapest, though that's hardly the impression given by the factories and high-rises that dominate the area today, hiding such ancient ruins as remain. Nonetheless it was here that the Romans built a legionary camp and a civilian town, later taken over by the Huns and named Buda, supposedly in honour of Attila's brother. This developed into an important town under the Hungarian Árpád dynasty, but after the fourteenth century it was eclipsed by the Castle district. The original settlement became known as Óbuda (Old Buda) and was incorporated into the newly formed Budapest in 1874. The best preserved ruins lie further north, in the **Római-Fürdő** district, accessible by HÉV train from Batthyány tér or the Margit Bridge.

The old quarter

The section of Óbuda **around Fő tér** blends gaudy Baroque with modern art and overpriced gastronomy, all within a minute's walk of the Árpád híd HÉV stop. At Szentlélek tér 1, the former Zichy mansion has been coverted into the **Vásárhely Museum** (Tues–Sun 10am–6pm), displaying eyeball-throbbing Op-Art paintings by Viktor Vásárhely, one of the founders of the genre. On cobbled Fő tér, just around the corner, you'll find the *Sipos Halászkert* and *Postakocsi* restaurants (see "Eating and Drinking"). Whatever the weather there are always several figures sheltering beneath umbrellas here: life-sized sculptures by Imre Varga, whose *oeuvre* is the subject of the nearby **Varga Museum** at Laktanya utca 7 (Tues–Sun 10am–6pm). A sense of humour pervades his sheet-metal, iron and bronze effigies of famous personages.

Roman ruins in Óbuda

Although the largest site lies further out in the Római-Fürdő district, Óbuda does have several excavated ruins to show for its past. The finest of them is the weed-choked, crumbling **amphitheatre** at the junction of Nagyszombat and Pacsirtamező utca: this once covered a greater area than the Colosseum in Rome, seating up to 16,000 spectators. The *amfiteátrum* can be reached by bus #86 (from Batthyány tér or anywhere along the embankment), or by walking 400m north from the Kolósy tér (near the Szépvölgyi út HÉV stop). Having seen it, you can continue to the next batch of ruins by bus #6 or #84.

The **Camp Museum**, a modern edifice at Pacsirtamező utca 63, displays sarcophagi, the ruins of a bathhouse, fragmented murals and other relics of the legionary camp (May–Oct Tues–Fri 10am–2pm & Sat–Sun 10am–6pm). This was situated near modern-day Flórián tér, where graceful columns now stand incongruously amid a shopping plaza, while the old **military baths** and other finds are huddled beneath the Szentendrei út flyover.

Ten minutes' walk to the northwest, behind apartment building 19–21 on Meggyfa utca, three blue canopies shelter the remains of the **Hercules Villa** (May–Oct Tues–Fri 10am–2pm & Sat–Sun 10am–6pm), whose name derives from the third-century AD **mosaic floor** beneath the largest canopy. This mosaic, originally composed of 60,000 stones carefully selected and arranged in Alexandria, depicts Hercules about to vomit at a wine festival. Another mosaic portrays the centaur Nessus abducting Deianeira, whom Hercules had to rescue as one of his twelve labours.

Aquincum

The legionary garrison of 6000 spawned a settlement of camp followers – Aquincum – which, over time, became a *Municipum* and later a *Colonia*, the provincial capital of Pannonia Inferior. The **ruins of Aquincum** (May–Oct Tues–Fri 10am–2pm & Sat–Sun 10am–6pm), easily visible from the Aquincum HÉV stop, lie along the Szentendre road a couple of kilometres north of Flórián tér: further up are the remains of an **aqueduct** and another **amphitheatre** near the next HÉV stop, Római-Fürdő (Roman Bath).

Enough foundation walls and underground piping survive to give a fair idea of the **layout** of Aquincum, although you'll need to pay a visit to the museum and use considerable imagination to envisage the town during its heyday in the second to third century AD. A great concourse of people would have filled the main street, doing business in the Forum and law courts (near the site entrance), and steaming in the public baths. Herbs and wine were burned before altars in sanctuaries holy to the goddesses Epona and Fortuna Augusta, while fraternal societies met in the Collegiums and bath houses further east. The **museum** contains oddments of the imperium – cake moulds, a bronze military diploma, buttons used as admission tickets to the theatre – and statues of gods and goddesses.

The Buda Hills

Thirty minutes' journey from Moszkva tér, the **Buda Hills** provide a welcome respite from Budapest's summertime heat. While particular hills are often busy with people at the weekend, it's possible to ramble through the woods for hours and see hardly a soul during the week. If your time is limited, the most rewarding options are the "railway circuit" or a visit to **Budakeszi Game Park** (daily 9am–5pm), reached by taking bus #22 from Moskva tér to the Korányi Sanatorium stop, and then following the *Vadaspark* signs for a couple of kilometres. Beyond the park's exhibition centre lie woods and fields inhabited by red, roe and shovel-antlered fallow deer, wild boar, mallards, pheasants and other birds – unrepentant carnivores have the opportunity of savouring these delicacies at the *Vadaspark* restaurant by the entrance.

The "railway circuit"

The railway circuit begins with a short ride on tram #18 or #56 or bus #56 from Moskva tér out along Szilágyi Erzsébet fasor, to the lower terminal of the **Cogwheel Railway**. From here, every ten minutes or so, a small train clicks up through the **Svábhegy** suburb, past the world-famous **Pető Institute** for conductive therapy, to the summit of Széchenyi-hegy.

The terminal of the **Children's Railway**, a narrow-gauge line that's almost entirely run by 13- to 17-year-olds, is a short walk across the park. Built by youth brigades in 1948, this enables kids who fancy a career with MÁV to get hands-on experience. Watching them wave flags, collect tickets and salute departures with solemnity, you can see why it appealed to the Communists. Until a few years ago, it was known as the Pioneers' Railway after the organization that replaced the disbanded Scouts and Guides movements (now reformed). Currently struggling with financial difficulties, the train runs at weekends only (9am–5pm), stopping at various points en route to Hűvösvölgy. The eleven-kilometre journey takes about 45 minutes.

The first stop, **Normafa**, is a popular excursion centre with a modest **ski-run**. Its name comes from a performance of the aria from Bellini's *Norma*, given here by the actress Rozália Klein in 1840. Just nearby in a wooden hut is *Rétes büfé*, where you can get delicious strudel and coffee every day of the year including holidays. János-hegy, three stops on, is the highest point in Budapest. On the 527-metre-high summit, fifteen minutes' climb from the station, the **Erzsébet lookout tower** offers a panoramic view of Budapest and the Buda Hills. By the buffet below the summit is the upper terminal of the **chairlift** (9am–5pm; off-season 9.30am–4pm; 80Ft one-way & 140Ft return) down to Zugliget, whence #158 buses return to Moszkva tér.

From the main road by the next stop, **Szépjuhászné**, you can catch bus #22 to Budakeszi Game Park. **Wild boars** (which prefer to roam during the evening and sleep by day) are occasionally sighted in the forests above **Hárshegy**, one stop before Hűvösvölgy. Also linked directly to Moskva tér by #56 and #56E (non-stop) buses, **Hűvösvölgy** is the site of the popular *Náncsi Néni* restaurant (see "Eating and Drinking").

Stalactite caves and other sights

The hills further to the northwest harbour a second clutch of attractions, best reached in a separate excursion from Kolósy tér in Óbuda (by Szépvölgyi út HÉV stop). From here, ride bus #65 five stops out to Szépvölgyi út 162 to find the **Pál-völgyi Stalactite Caves** (April–Oct Tues–Sat 10am–6pm). Hourly guided tours of this spectacular labyrinth start on the lowest level, boasting rock formations like the "Organ Pipes" and "Beehive". From "John's Lookout" in the largest chamber, you ascend a crevice onto the upper level, there to enter "Fairyland" and finally "Paradise", overlooking the hellish "Radium Hall" 50m below.

From the Pál-völgyi cave another stalactite labyrinth and the Kiscelli Museum are each just twenty minutes' walk away – in opposite directions. Buses also run to both from Kolósy tér. The **Szemlőhegy Cave** at Pusztaszeri út 35 (9am–4pm;

closed Tues) abounds in pea-shaped formations and aragonite crystals resembling bunches of grapes. Coming from Kolósy tér by bus #29, alight at the fourth stop near the Pusztaszeri út turn-off. The **Kiscelli Museum** (April–Oct Tues–Sun 10am–6pm; Nov–March Tues–Sun 10am–4pm) occupies a former Trinitarian monastery and church at Kiscelli utca 108. Its collection includes antique printing presses and the furnishings of the *Golden Lion* apothecary. Bus #165 from Kolósy tér turns around to begin its return journey near the museum, or you can take bus #60 from Batthyány tér to the stop by the Margit korház (hospital) and walk up the steep Kiscelli utca.

A pleasant alternative is to ride bus #65 from Pál-völgyi to the end of the line at **Hármashatár-hegy**. This hill provides a fabulous **view** of Budapest from a different perspective, while **hang-gliders** launch themselves off from the western side. It is also the best spot in the hills for **mushroom hunting**, a pastime that's almost as popular amongst Budapesters as it is with city folk in Russia and Poland. People can take their fungi to special *gomba* stalls (there's one on Lövőház utca just by the market near Moszkva tér), where experts distinguish the edible from the poisonous.

Margit Island

A saying has it that "love begins and ends on **Margit Island**" (*Margit-sziget*), for this verdant expanse has been a favourite spot for lovers since the nineteenth century, although a stiff admission charge deterred the poor before 1945. Today, it is one of the most popular recreation grounds in the city, its thermal springs feeding outdoor pools and ritzy spa-hotels. The easiest way of **getting there** is to catch bus #26 (which runs all the way along the island) from either the Nyugati pu. or Árpád híd metro stations in Pest. Alternatively, you can take tram #4 or #6 from Moszkva tér or the Great Boulevard, and walk from the stop in the middle of Margit Bridge. Motorists can only approach from the north, via the Árpád Bridge, at which point they must abandon their vehicles at a paying car park.

The southern part of the island features a **Casino** and the **Hajós Alfréd Swimming Pool**, named after the winner of the 100m and 1200m swimming races at the 1896 Olympics. Hajós was also an architect, who designed the indoor pool. Further north, before the rose garden on the right, are the **ruins of a Franciscan church** from the late thirteenth century. On the other side of the road, the **Palatinus Strand** (daily May–Sept) can hold as many as 10,000 people at a time in seven open-air thermal pools, complete with a water chute, wave machine and segregated terraces for nude sunbathing.

The **outdoor theatre** (*Szabadtéri Színpad*) hosts plays and operas during summer, and together with the nearby Water Tower provides a convenient landmark to help you locate the **ruined Dominican church and convent**. Legend has it that Béla IV vowed to bring his daughter up as a nun if Hungary survived the Mongol invasion, and duly confined nine-year-old Princess **Margit** (Margaret) when it did. She apparently made the best of it, acquiring a reputation for curing lepers and other saintly deeds. Beatification came after her death in 1271, and a belated canonization in 1943. The convent itself fell into ruin during the Turkish occupation, when the island was turned into a harem.

Northeast of the Water Tower is a **Premonstratensian Chapel** whose Romanesque tower dates back to the twelfth century, when the order first established a monastery on the island. The tower's fifteenth-century bell is one of the oldest in Hungary. Beyond lie the *fin-de-siècle* **Ramada Grand Hotel** and the modern **Thermal Hotel**, both catering to wealthy invalids. Warm springs in the rock garden beside the latter sustain tropical fish and giant water lilies.

Csepel Island

In the south of the city, the far greater expanse of **Csepel Island** is the polar opposite to its northern counterpart. An industrial zone that's had its heart ripped out by the closure of its loss-making plants, Csepel is the XXI district of the city, and the bit that tourists rarely visit. Traditionally known as "Red Csepel" for its militant workforce, the complex bore the name of Rákosi during the Stalinist era, when the dictator chose this as his own parliamentary constituency. Ironically, its arms factories and workers played a major role in the 1956 Uprising, their factory councils holding out for weeks after the Soviets had crushed resistance elsewhere. In recent years the complex was broken down into smaller units, many of which then went bankrupt or were taken over by foreign companies, leaving swaths of derelict land. The site was earmarked as the venue of Budapest Expo 1996 which, had it gone ahead, would have brought some financial relief to the area.

Further south, beyond the belt of high-rise *lakótelep*, are tumbledown cottages surrounded by market gardens, and the now abandoned Soviet base at Tököl, whose tanks engaged insurgents during the first days of the Uprising. The remainder of the island is mostly lush semi-wilderness, except near Ráckeve, 50km south of Budapest.

Not a great deal of history attaches to Csepel: according to the scribe Anonymous, Prince Árpád was so impressed by the island's fertility that he built a palace here; and the name is said to have been borrowed from a Cumanian master-of-horse called Shepel. If you're interested in **visiting**, the northern end of the island is easily reached by HÉV train from Boráros tér, near the Petőfi Bridge. It is not a good idea to look rich or foreign, or hang around after dark, however.

Pest

PEST is busier, more populous and vital than Buda: the place where things are decided, made and sold. While Buda grew up around Castle Hill's forts and palaces, the east bank was settled by merchants and artisans, and commerce has always been its lifeblood. Much of the architecture and layout dates from the late nineteenth-century, giving Pest a homogenous appearance compared to other European capitals. Boulevards, public buildings and apartment houses were built on a scale appropriate to the Habsburg empire's second city, and the capital of a nation which celebrated its millennial anniversary in 1896. Now bullet-scarred and grimy – or in the throes of restoration – these grand edifices form the backdrop to life in the **Belváros** (inner city) and the residential districts, hulking gloomily above the cafés, wine cellars and courtyards where people socialize. While there's plenty to see and do, it's the less tangible ambience that sticks in one's memory.

Away from the waterfront, you'll find that two semicircular boulevards are fundamental to **orientation**. The inner city lies within the **Small Boulevard**

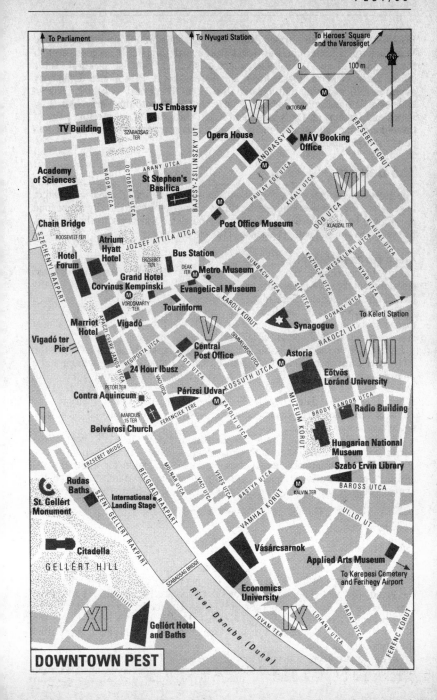

To Parliament

To Nyugati Station

To Heroes' Square
and the Varosliget

0   100 m

US Embassy

TV Building

SZABADSAG
TER

VI

OKTOGON

M

Opera House

MÁV Booking
Office

ERZSEBET KORUT

ANDRASSY UT

Academy
of Sciences

ARANY UTCA

St Stephen's
Basilica

VII

PAULAY EDE UTCA

KIRALY UTCA

BAJCSY-ZSILINSZKY UT

OKTOBER 6 UTCA

NADOR UTCA

DOB UTCA

KLAUZAL TER

Chain Bridge

ROOSEVELT TER

M

Post Office Museum

KAZINCZY UTCA

WESSELENYI UTCA

NYAR UTCA

KLAUZAL UTCA

Atrium
Hyatt
Hotel

JOZSEF ATTILA UTCA

Bus Station

Hotel
Forum

SZECHENYI RAKPART

ERZSEBET
TER

DEAK
TER

Metro Museum

RUMBACH UTCA

SIP UTCA

DOHANY UTCA

To Keleti Station

Grand Hotel
Corvinus Kempinski

VOROSMARTY
TER

Evangelical Museum

KAROLY KORUT

Synagogue

RAKOCZI UT

Tourinform

V

Marriot
Hotel

APACZAI CSERE JANOS UTCA

Vigadó

VIII

Central
Post Office

SZAMMELWEISS UTCA

Astoria

M

Vigadó ter
Pier

REGIPOSTA UTCA

PETOFI UTCA

KOSSUTH UTCA

Eötvös
Loránd University

24 Hour Ibusz

VACI UTCA

MUZEUM KORUT

I

PETOFI TER

BRODY SANDOR UTCA

Radio Building

Contra Aquincum

Párizsi Udvar

KAROLYI UTCA

MARCIUS
15 TER

FERENCIEK TERE

M

Belvárosi Church

Hungarian National
Museum

VERES UTCA

Szabó Ervin Library

BASTYA UTCA

BAROSS UTCA

Rudas
Baths

M

KALVIN TER

St. Gellért
Monument

ERZSEBET BRIDGE

SZENT GELLERT RAKPART

International
Landing Stage

BELGRAD RAKPART

MOLNAR UTCA

VAMHAZ KORUT

UI LOI UT

Citadella

GELLÉRT HILL

XI

SZABADSAG BRIDGE

Vásárcsarnok

Applied Arts Museum

To Kerepesi Cemetery
and Ferihegy Airport

RADAY UTCA

LOHANY UTCA

FERENC KORUT

Gellért Hotel
and Baths

River Danube (Duna)

Economics
University

FOVAM TER

IX

DOWNTOWN PEST

(*Kiskörút*), made up of József Attila utca, Károly körút, Múzeum körút and Vámház körút. Farther out, the **Great Boulevard** (*Nagykörút*) sweeps through the VI, VII, VIII and IX districts, where it is called Szent István körút, Teréz körút, Erzsébet körút, József körút and Ferenc körút. Pest is also defined by **avenues** (*út*) radiating out beyond the Great Boulevard – notably Bajcsy-Zsilinszky út (for Nyugati Station); Andrássy út, leading to the **Városliget** (City Park); and Rakóczi út, for Nyugati and Keleti **stations**. As the meeting point of three metro lines and several main avenues, Deák tér makes a good jumping-off point for explorations.

The Belváros

The **Belváros**, or inner city, corresponds closely to the walled, medieval town of Pest before the massive nineteenth-century expansion swept the city far beyond its original boundaries. Particularly in the quieter backstreets to the south of Kossuth utca you can still get a sense of the old atmosphere.

Along the embankment

Luxury hotels occupy most of the prime sites along the **Belgrád rakpart** embankment, but the occasional views of Castle Hill amply compensate for the lack of obvious "sights". Such historic architecture as remains can easily be seen during a fifteen-minute stroll between the Erzsébet and Chain bridges. The following account starts near the former: should you tire of the waterfront, almost any sidestreet will lead you to Váci utca within a few minutes.

Immediately to the north of the Erzsébet Bridge ramp, the grimy facade of the **Belvárosi Church** conceals Renaissance niches, Baroque barrel-vaulting and a *mihrab* from the time of the Turkish occupation, indicating the direction of Mecca. The name of the square on which it stands, **Március 15. tér**, refers to March 15, 1848, the date when the Revolution began. Also on the square are the **ruins of a Roman fort** – Contra-Aquincum – which served as an outpost of their settlement across the river.

An adjacent square and statue honour Sándor Petőfi (1823–49), poet of the *puszta* and revolutionary firebrand, whose *National Song* – the anthem of 1848 – and romantic death in battle made him a patriotic icon. **Petőfi tér** is a traditional site for **demonstrations** against authority – usually on March 15, when the statue is decked out with flags and flowers. There is a **24-hour Ibusz bureau** at Petőfi tér 3.

VIGADÓ TÉR

North of Petőfi tér, the **Marriott Hotel** interposes itself between the embankment and the street running parallel, Apáczai Csere János utca, as far north as Vigadó tér. Here stands the **Vigadó**, a splendidly romantic concert hall, the name of which translates as "having a ball" or "making merry". Since it opened in 1865, the Vigadó has hosted performances by Liszt (who was Hungarian), Mahler (who also directed the Budapest Opera) and Wagner. The modern construction on the right occupies the site of the *Angol királynő* (English Queen) hotel, where the likes of the Shah of Persia and Emperor Dom Pedro of Brazil used to stay during the city's Belle Époque.

On the square itself, notice the maritime reliefs and ships' hulls decorating the headquarters of *Mahart*, the state shipping company, which is responsible for the pleasure cruisers and ferries to the Danube Bend that leave from the **Vigadó tér pier** (see p.117). A little further upriver the **Kossuth Museum Ship**, a 1913-vintage steamer, contains an exhibition on the history of the Danube (April–Oct Tues–Sun 10am–6pm) and an expensive restaurant.

ROOSEVELT TÉR

At the Pest end of the Chain Bridge, **Roosevelt tér** is overlooked by the **Atrium Hyatt** and **Forum** hotels. Emperor Franz Josef was crowned King of Hungary here in 1867, and soil from across the nation was piled up to form a Coronation Hill, whence he flourished the sword of Saint Stephen and pledged to defend Hungary against any foe. Eighty years later, the square was renamed in honour of the late US president.

Dominating the eastern side of the square is the **Gresham Palace**, a grimy but splendid example of Art Nouveau, commissioned by a British insurance company in 1904. Its entrance passage leads into a T-shaped, glass-roofed arcade off which three staircases lead to different parts of the building. On the ground floor, below a warren of offices, are a pleasant bar and a casino.

The **Hungarian Academy** at the northern end of the square is another bequest from Count Széchenyi, who donated a year's income from his estates towards its foundation in 1825 (as depicted on the wall facing Akadémia utca). Unlike the Széchenyi Library, however, the public are not admitted to the building. The Nobel Prize winning scientist György Hevesy (1885–1966) – discoverer of the element hafnium – was born at Akadémia utca 1, behind the academy.

From here you can continue northwards to the Parliament building on Kossuth tér, or head back towards the Vigadó and then cut inland to Vörösmarty tér.

From Erzsébet Bridge to Astoria

The inner city is more or less bisected by the thoroughfare – whose name changes with bewildering frequency – that crosses the river at the Erzsébet Bridge. Near the bridge it is called Szabadsajtó út and flanked by the two imposing **Klothild Palaces** – beneath the fancy title, essentially ornate nineteenth-century office buildings. The wider section further inland, known in the Communist era as Feldszabadulás tér (Liberation Square), is currently named **Ferenciek tere** (Franciscans' Square) after the church on the corner.

Flanking Ferenciek tere to the north is the **Párizsi udvar** (Parisian Arcade), a slab of gilt and gingerbread architecture. There's a big *Ibusz* office on the corner and an ice-cream parlour facing the square, but it's the stained-glass Art Nouveau passageway that draws you into the arcade. On Kigyó utca, around the corner, it's also worth looking into the *Apostolok* restaurant, whose salons are decorated with paintings of the apostles and towns that were lost to Hungary after World War I. At the far end of this street is Váci utca (see below).

Meanwhile, the main road becomes **Kossuth utca** as it runs to meet the Small Boulevard at **Astoria** – site of a famous hotel and a metro station beneath the intersection. Once a haunt of spies and journalists, the **Astoria Hotel** was badly damaged in the 1956 Uprising and served as a Soviet *Komandantura* in the aftermath, but has now been restored to its former elegance. Across the road, on the corner of Semmelweiss utca, you can peek into the foyer of what is still (but unlikely to remain) the **Soviet House of Culture** at Semmelweiss utca 1–3, occupying the premises of the pre-war National Casino club. Until a few years ago, jackbooted officers could be seen swaggering in and out, attended by their lackeys.

From Váci utca to Vörösmarty tér

Visitors inevitably gravitate towards **Váci utca**, the fashionable *korzó* running north from the Párizsi udvar. Lined with boutiques and street cafés, this bustling promenade has been likened to Bond Street in London or the Ramblas in Barcelona. Though neither is a very accurate comparison, you can see what they're getting at, as Váci utca combines hauteur and flirtatiousness in equal measure. During the Eighties, its vivid **streetlife** became a symbol of the "consumer socialism" that distinguished Hungary from other Eastern Bloc states, and invariably featured in documentaries about the country. Shops proliferate in the courtyards behind Váci utca, some of them delightful places with spiralling stairs.

Heading north up Váci utca you'll pass the **Pest Theatre** (no. 9), where the twelve-year-old Liszt made his concert debut and lines of women sell embroidered quilts and tablecloths – those in traditional dress from the ethnic Hungarian regions of Transylvania. While the police tolerate some dire one-man-bands, other **hustlers** are fair game for harassment, especially the Africans on roller-skates who hawk *Budapest Week* and the *Budapest Sun*. Within a few blocks you can hear every language from Arabic to German, Italian to Yoruba.

VÖRÖSMARTY TÉR

The crowd flows on from here to **Vörösmarty tér**, breaking on a reef of portraitists to eddy about conjurers, violinists and other street performers. While children play in the fountains, youths congregate around the statue of Mihály Vörösmarty (1800–50), a poet and translator whose hymn to Magyar identity, *Szózat* (Appeal), is publicly declaimed at moments of national crisis. Its opening line – "Be faithful to your land forever, O Hungarians" – is carved upon the pedestal.

On the far side of the square, the famous **Gerbeaud patisserie** has been a haunt of Budapest high society since 1884, when the coffee house was bought by the Swiss confectioner Emile Gerbeaud. Though its gilded ceilings and china recall the Belle Époque, the waitresses no longer have time to discuss the customers in their private code language, and the octogenarian "Gerbeaud ladies" with their furs and lace gloves have been driven away by the tourists.

Beside Gerbeaud's terrace is the entrance to the **Millennial Railway** (metro line l), the first underground on the European continent when it was inaugurated in 1896, following the construction of London's Metropolitan line. Coincidentally the **British Embassy** is just a stone's throw away on Harmincad utca: the street's name – meaning "one thirtieth" – recalls an old tax.

PETŐFI UTCA AND SZERVITA TÉR

Petőfi utca, running parallel to the *korzó*, has none of the glamour of Váci utca and all the traffic, but it still manages a couple of places worth noting. At no. 13 is the **Central Post Office** with its *poste restante* department, followed by the **Central Telephone and Telegraph Bureau** at nos. 17–19. Just north of here the street opens on to **Szervita tér**. Look out for the **Rózsavölgyi House** (no. 5), which blends the National Romantic and Modernist styles (and houses the excellent *Rózsavölgyi* record store), and also the erstwhile **Turkish Banking House** (no. 3), its gable aglow with a mosaic of Hungaria – the Magyar equivalent of Britain's Britannia – flanked by shepherds and angels. From here, you can head past a multi-storey car park to reach Deák tér.

Deák tér and Erzsébet tér

Three metro lines, two segments of the Small Boulevard and several important avenues meet at **Deák tér** and Erzsébet tér (two squares which merge into one another, making local addresses extremely confusing), but for all its importance as a transport hub there's little reason to hang around. You'll recognize the area by two landmarks: the yellow Lutheran church on one side, and the huge mustard-coloured, mansard-roofed Anker Palace on the other. Beneath this, next to the metro entrance in the pedestrian underpass, is the **Metro Museum** (*FAV Múzeum*), where rail buffs can grow maudlin over yellow trams dating from the 1890s, ornate fixtures, tiling and the like (Tues–Sun 10am–6pm; admission by metro ticket).

Behind the Lutheran church, next to one of the metro exits, the **National Lutheran Museum** (Tues–Sun 10am–6pm) contains relics pertaining to the Lutheran or *Evangélikus* faith, including a facsimile of Luther's last will and testament. Across the way is a Porsche/VW showroom, occupying what used to be a propaganda bureau for the old German Democratic Republic – one of those jokes played by history that Marx was keen on. On Sütő utca, running off between the two, you'll find *Tourinform*, the capital's best source of **tourist information** (summer daily 8am–8pm; Nov–March 8am–3pm; ☎117-9800).

In the other direction lies **Erzsébet tér bus station**, the place to board international services or embark on tours of the city in an open-topped bus.

The Lipótváros

This section and the ones that follow cover the areas immediately beyond the Belváros, moving in a clockwise direction starting with the Lipótváros north of Vörösmarty tér. The **Lipótváros** (Leopold Town) started to develop in the late eighteenth century, first as a financial centre and later as the seat of government and bureaucracy. Though much of its architecture is ponderously Neoclassical, the main squares are enlivened by touches of Eclectic and Art Nouveau style. The following account assumes Vörösmarty tér as the starting point: coming from Erzsébet tér, it's logical to visit the Basilica first, then Szabadság tér and Parliament.

Szabadság tér

Immediately north of the Small Boulevard (József Attila utca), narrow streets lined with administrative buildings lead towards the government district, only to have their gloomy progress interrupted by Szabadság tér (Liberty Square). Here, opposite the vast Hungarian **Television Building** (originally the Stock Exchange) is the **National Bank** with its bas-reliefs symbolizing honest toil and profit, and a small **Museum of Banknotes and Coins** inside (Thurs 9am–2pm only). Just north of here is the **US Embassy** (no. 12), where Cardinal Mindszenty spent fifteen years of "internal exile" after the 1956 Uprising. A nearby statue commemorates General Harry Bandholtz of the US Army, who intervened with a dogwhip to prevent Romanian forces from looting the National Museum in 1920. In the centre of the square is one of the few remaining Soviet war memorials, which has allegedly survived – despite threats from right-wing groups to blow it up – thanks to the logistical problems of transporting the remains of the soldiers buried there. The fascist Arrow Cross had its headquarters at no. 15, behind and to the left.

In the interwar years, the square boasted several **statues** loaded with symbolism, which the Communists removed and some groups still hope to restore. The Monument to Hungarian Grief – featuring a flag at half mast and a quotation from Mussolini – commemorated the loss of Hungarian territory to the Successor States (Romania and the then Yugoslavia and Czechoslavakia), as did four statues called North, South, East and West. For a few years, the square even had a statue titled "Gratitude", which was erected in 1949 on the occasion of Stalin's seventieth birthday – but nobody has proposed restoring that.

Parliament and Kossuth tér

Continue northwards and the **Parliament building** *(Országház)* suddenly appears. Variously described as "Eclectic" or "neo-Gothic" in style, it sprawls for 268 metres between the embankment and Kossuth tér, dominating the vicinity with a spiky facade embellished by 88 statues of Hungarian rulers. The symmetrical wings housing the Assemblies meet beneath a gigantic cupola 96 metres high, which can accommodate both chambers when they meet in ceremonial conclave. A vital force during the Reform Era, Parliament had grown sluggish by the time its grandiose seat was built (in 1884–1902). Under Fascism, opposition MPs learned to fear for their lives; after the Communist takeover in 1948, parliamentary politics became a mere echo of decisions taken by the Politburo and Secretariat of the Communist Party, at MSzMP headquarters on Akadémia utca. In the late Eighties it began to recover authority, and now functions as a parliament should. When it's not in session, there are **guided tours** of the splendid interior, arranged by *Budapest Tourist* and *Ibusz*. The price (950–1700Ft) includes a visit to the Ethnographical Museum or National Gallery. A far cheaper way of seeing the Parliament building is to join a tour on the spot (Wed–Sun 10am (English) and 11am (German); twice daily in summer). Tickets (400Ft) can be purchased at Gate X, and tours commence from Gate XII.

Kossuth tér itself, named after the leader of the 1848 Revolution, contains statues of Lajos Kossuth and Prince Ferenc Rákóczi II, an earlier hero of the struggle for Hungarian independence. The quote inscribed on the latter's plinth – "The wounds of the noble Hungarian nation burst open!" – refers to the anti-Habsburg war of 1703–11. It also perfectly describes the evening of October 23, 1956, when crowds filled the square chanting anti-Stalinist slogans at Parliament and called for the appearance of the popular reformist Imre Nagy – the prelude to the Uprising that night.

Thirty-three years later, the wheel turned full circle as the Republic of Hungary was proclaimed to an enthusiastic crowd from the same balcony that Nagy had spoken from, and the People's Republic of Hungary was officially consigned to the dustbin of history. This watershed was also symbolized by the removal of the red star from Parliament's dome, and the replacement of Communist emblems by the traditional coat of arms, featuring the double cross of King Stephen. Another step in Hungary's transition came in October 1992, when the mild-mannered president of the republic, Árpád Göncz, was prevented from making his commemorative speech by a jeering crowd led by skinheads, some in fascist uniforms.

A neo-Renaissance pile at Kossuth tér 12 houses the **Ethnographic Museum** (Tues–Sun 10am–6pm), whose richly frescoed foyer is as much an attraction as the diverse collection of Inuit furs and kayaks, African instruments and barkcloth and wonderfully carved Melanesian masks. Though often overlooked, this is one of the finest museums in Budapest.

St Stephen's Basilica and Bajcsy-Zsilinszky út

The restoration of **Saint Stephen's Basilica** is proceeding almost as slowly as its construction, lack of funds being a problem now as then. Building originally began in 1851 under the supervision of József Hild, continued after his death under Miklós Ybl, and was finally completed by Joseph Krauser in 1905. At the inaugural ceremony Emperor Franz Josef was seen to glance anxiously at the dome, whose collapse during a storm in 1868 had naturally set progress back. At 96 metres it is exactly the same height as the dome of Parliament – both allude to the date of the Magyars' arrival in Hungary.

The cavernous interior is poorly lit and undergoing restoration, but it's worth going inside to view the **mummified hand of Saint Stephen**, in a chapel behind the altar. Drop 20Ft into the cabinet and it will light up to reveal the *Szent Jobb* (literally, "sacred right"), which is paraded around the church on August 20, the anniversary of his death. There is also a one-room **treasury** of chalices and monstrances (May–Sept daily 9am–5pm; Oct–April daily 10am–6pm), as well as a superb view of the city from the basilica's tower (open in summer only).

While Stephen is revered as the founder and patron saint of Hungary, the pantheon of national heroes includes a niche for Endre Bajcsy-Zsilinszky (1866–1944). Originally a right-winger, he ended up an outspoken critic of fascism, was arrested in Parliament (a statue on Deák tér captures the moment) and shot as the Russians neared Sopron. **Bajcsy-Zsilinszky út** runs northwards to terminate at **Nyugati tér**, where the *Skála-Metró* department store (a proto-capitalist competitor to the state-run *Centrum* chain in the mid-Eighties) faces **Nyugati Station**, an elegant, iron-beamed terminal built (1874–77) by the Eiffel Company of Paris, which now contains probably the ritziest *McDonald's* in the world.

The VI district: Terézváros

The VI district, or **Terézváros** (Theresa Town), was laid out in the late nineteenth century, under the influence of Haussman's redevelopment of Paris. At that time it was one of the smartest districts in the city – especially around the Városliget – but much of it is now run down and getting poorer. Hopes for its revival are pinned on the "Hungarian Broadway", which cuts across the main thoroughfare, Andrássy út, just below the Oktogon intersection.

Andrássy út

Running for two and a half kilometres up to Hősök tere on the edge of the Városliget, this is Budapest's longest – and most renamed – avenue. Inaugurated as the Sugár (Radial) út in 1884, it later became **Andrássy út** (after a statesman of the era) – a name that stayed in popular use throughout the years when this was officially Stalin Avenue (1949–56) or the Avenue of the People's Republic (1957–89). The last name was always a jawbreaker for foreigners, being rendered as Népköztársaság útja in Hungarian.

With its parade of grand buildings laden with stone dryads and colonnades, its Opera House and coffee houses, the avenue retains something of the style that made it fashionable in the 1890s, when "Bertie", the Prince of Wales, drove its length in a landau offering flowers to women passing by. Early this century it was also famous for a luxurious brothel – the House of Nations – and sleazier versions in the backstreets to the east.

The initial stretch up to the Oktogon is within walking distance of Erzsébet tér, but if you're going any further it's best to travel from sight to sight by metro line 1 (running beneath the avenue) or bus #1 or #4. At Andrássy út 3 the **Post Office Museum** (Tues–Sun 10am–6pm) occupies a fabulous old apartment building complete with parquet floors, marble fireplaces, Venetian mirrors and frescoes by Károly Lotz. Exhibits include a compressed-air mail tube, push-button displays of *Magyar Posta* in the telecommunications age, blunderbusses and thigh-high boots (attesting to the hazards of a postman's life in Habsburg times), and a display on the inventor Tivadar Puskás, a colleague of Thomas Edison.

The Opera House and "Broadway"
Founded by Ferenc Erkel (1810–93), composer of Hungary's national anthem, the **State Opera House** is a magnificent neo-Renaissance pile built (1875–84) by Miklós Ybl. The opera can boast of being directed by Mahler, hosting performances conducted by Otto Klemper and Antal Doráti, and sheltering hundreds of local residents in its huge cellars during the siege of Budapest. Tours of the building's grand interior take place daily at 3 and 4pm, leaving from the side entrances (performance schedules permitting). Also worth seeing is the interior of the **Arany János Theatre** in the backstreets across the road, a stunning Art Nouveau building, recently restored – ask at the door.

One block north of the Opera House, Andrássy út is crossed by **Nagymező utca** – nicknamed "Broadway" after the clubs and theatres that cluster here, either side of the avenue. A little further up on the right-hand side, the *MÁV Bookings Office* at no. 35 is the place to buy **international rail tickets**. Shortly afterwards, Andrássy út meets the Great Boulevard at the **Oktogon**, so-called after the octagonal configuration of the junction. During the Horthy period it rejoiced in the name Mussolini tér, changing to November 7 tér during the Communist era. Today it boasts a *Burger King* and a *Wendy's* on two of its eight sides, making it a fast-food paradise.

To the Kodály köröñd and beyond
Andrássy út 60 was once the most terrifying address in Budapest – the **headquarters of the secret police**. Jews and other victims of the Arrow Cross were tortured here during World War II, and the ÁVO (see box) subsequently used the building for the same purpose. Prisoners were brought in by the side entrance on Csengery utca. When the building was captured by insurgents in 1956, no trace was found of the giant meat-grinder rumoured to have been used to dispose of corpses. On the exterior of the building (now the offices of a chemical trading company) are recently affixed memorial plaques.

On the opposite side of the road a little further on, the building on the corner of Vörösmarty utca contains the **Liszt Memorial Museum** (Mon–Fri noon–6pm & Sat 9am–5pm), where the composer lived from 1879. His glass piano and travelling keyboard are the highlights of an extensive collection of memorabilia and scores. Concerts are performed by young pianists every Sunday at 11am and at other times during the week (free with admission to museum). Another great Hungarian composer lends his name to the **Kodály köröñd** junction, where Kodály spent the last years of his life at no. 1. Across the way stands a magnificent neo-Renaissance mansion with gold *sgraffiti* on its facade. Before and during World War II, the köröñd suffered the indignity of being called Hitler tér.

> ### THE AVO
>
> The **Communist secret police** began as the Party's private security section during the Horthy era, when its chief, **Gábor Péter**, betrayed Trotskyites to the police to take the heat off their Stalinist comrades. After World War II it became the *Allamvédelmi Osztály* or **ÁVO** (State Security Department), its growing power implicit in a change of name in 1948 – to the State Security *Authority* or **ÁVH** (though the old title stuck). Ex-Nazi torturers were easily persuaded to apply their skills on its behalf, and its network of spies permeated society. So hated was the ÁVO that any members caught during the Uprising were summarily killed, and their mouths stuffed with banknotes (secret policemen earned more than anyone else).

By detouring a few blocks off the körönd, you can find the **Ráth György Museum** at Városligeti fasor 12 (Tues–Sun 10am–6pm). Housed in a beautifully preserved Art Nouveau villa, this features a private collection of Chinese and Japanese art, worth a look if you're in the mood. The collection is complemented by the **Museum of Eastern Asiatic Art** at Andrássy út 103 (Tues–Sun 10am–6pm), a choice selection of Japanese and Indian silks, puppets, ivory and the like, trawled by Ferenc Hopp on his many voyages east.

The final stretch of the avenue, **up to Hősök tere**, is lined with plane trees and embassies. It was at the Yugoslav Embassy that Imre Nagy took refuge after the Uprising, but was tricked into emerging, arrested by the Soviets, spirited away to Romania, and finally returned home to be executed in 1958.

Hősök tere

Laid out in in 1896 to mark the thousandth anniversary of the Magyar conquest, **Hősök tere** (Heroes' Square) is appropriately grand. The **Millenary Monument** in the centre of the square consists of a 36-metres-high column topped by the figure of Archangel Gabriel who, according to legend, appeared to Stephen in a dream and offered him the crown of Hungary. Around the base are Prince Arpád and his chieftains, who led the Magyar tribes into the Carpathian Basin. As a backdrop to this, a semicircular colonnade displays statues of Hungary's most illustrious leaders, from King Stephen to Kossuth. During the brief Republic of Councils, when the country was governed by revolutionary soviets, the square was decked out in red banners and the column enclosed in a huge red obelisk. More recently, it was the setting for the ceremonial reburial of Nagy and other murdered leaders of the Uprising (including an empty coffin to represent the "unknown insurgent") on June 16, 1989 – an event which symbolized the dawning of a new era in Hungary.

The Fine Arts Museum and Műcsarnok

To the left of Hősök tere stands the **Museum of Fine Arts** (*Szépművészeti Múzeum*), whose diverse collection embraces everything from Egyptian funerary relics to Impressionist paintings (Tues–Sun 10am–6pm). Ongoing reorganization makes it difficult to predict what will be on show, and staff shortages also mean that some rooms are closed during the lunch break. Amongst the drawings, look out for Leonardo's *Head of a Warrior* and Raphael's *Esterházy Madonna*. Most of the Italian, Dutch and German Old Masters are represented, and there's also one of the best collections of El Grecos and Spanish painting outside Spain, as well as works by Rodin, Renoir, Toulouse-Lautrec, Chagall and Picasso and other important modern artists. Across the square, the **Műcsarnok** (same hours) has just reopened in all its magnificence after a lengthy restoration, hosting foreign exhibitions on tour, as well as thematic, avant-garde shows.

The Stalin and Lenin statues

Before venturing into the Városliget behind Hősök tere, spare a thought for the statues that once stood on Aréna út, the main road running alongside the park. Here, 200m south of the square, the Communist leaders used to review parades from a grandstand like their bigger brothers on Red Square. During the Uprising, the 70-tonne **statue of Stalin** was torn down and dragged to the Great Boulevard. There it suffered decapitation and incineration at the hands of a constantly changing crowd, who hammered away at it for souvenirs – one ear being donated to the Rákosi-Stalin exhibition of 1990.

After the Uprising had been crushed, a **Lenin statue** was erected in its place, remaining until 1989, when it was carted away "for structural repairs". It can now be admired in all its glory at the Statue Park on the southwest edge of the city (see. p.78).

The Városliget

The leafy **VÁROSLIGET** (City Park) starts just behind Hősök tere, where the fairy-tale towers of **Vajdahunyad Castle** rear above an island girdled by an artificial lake used for boating or skating. Like the park, the castle was created for the Millenary Anniversary celebrations, so dramatic effects were the order of the day. This "stone catalogue" of architectural styles incorporates a **replica of the Chapel at Ják** in western Hungary and two Transylvanian castles (one of the originals, the Hunyadi Castle in Romania, gives its name to the building).

The main wing houses an **Agricultural Museum** (Tues–Sat 10am–5pm & Sun 10am–6pm) which is guaranteed to make vegetarians blanch and everybody else yawn, but children are delighted by the hooded **statue of "Anonymous"** outside. This nameless chronicler to King Béla is the prime source of information about early medieval Hungary, but the existence of several monarchs of that name during the twelfth and thirteenth centuries makes it hard to date him with any exactitude.

Leaving the island by the causeway at the rear, you're on course for the **Petőfi csarnok**, a "Metropolitan Youth Centre" that regularly hosts concerts, films, discos and other events (☎142-4327 for information in English). On the first floor is an **Aviation Museum** (April–Nov Tues–Sun 10am–6pm) whose vintage planes and genuine space capsule appeal to kids. In a similar vein, there is the **Transport Museum** at the back of the park, which includes antique cars, models galore, and mothballed steam trains (Tues–Sun 10am–6pm).

On the other side of the park's central promenade lie the **Széchenyi Baths**, fronted by a statue of the geologist Zsigmondy Vilmos, discoverer of the thermal spring that feeds its outdoor pool (Mon–Sat 6am–7pm; Sun till 7pm in summer, 4pm in winter) and Turkish baths (Mon–Sat 6am–8pm, Sun till 1pm). Here you can enjoy the surreal spectacle of people playing chess whilst immersed up to their chests in steaming water – bring you own set if you wish to join in.

The Zoo, Circus and Vidám Park

The northwestern side of the park beyond Állatkerti körút harbours Budapest's **Zoo** (April–Sept daily 9am–6pm; Oct–March daily 9am–4pm). When opened in 1866, its Art Nouveau pavilions by Károly Kós seemed the last word in zoological architecture, but by modern standards few of them look fit for bird or beast. A refit is underway, however, which also aims to restore the botanical strengths of the zoo. The hippos, meanwhile, seem to thrive, apparently because they can wallow in hot water whenever they like. The children's corner is signposted *Állatóvoda*.

Just down the road is the municipal **Circus**, which traces its origins back to 1783, when the Hetz Theatre played to spectators around what is now Deák tér (performances mid-April to end of Aug: Wed at 7.30pm; Thurs–Fri at 3.30pm & 7.30pm; Sat at 10am, 3.30pm & 7.30pm; Sun 10am & 3.30pm; ☎142-8300 for details). Next door lies **Vidám Park**, an old-fashioned, rather shabby amusement park (summer daily 8am–8pm; winter daily 10am–6pm), known as the "English Park" before the war. It has all the usual rides, only a few of which operate over winter.

The VII district: Erzsébetváros

The VII district or **Erzsébetváros** (Elizabeth Town), between Andrássy út and Rákóczi út, is mainly residential, composed of nineteenth-century buildings whose bullet-scarred facades, adorned with fancy wrought ironwork, conceal a warren of dwellings and leafy courtyards. It is also traditionally the **Jewish quarter** of the city, which was transformed into a ghetto during the Nazi occupation and almost wiped out in 1944–45, but miraculously retained its cultural identity. Though specific things to see are few, there is no better part of Pest to wander around, soaking up the atmosphere and discovering things for yourself.

Before Andrássy út was built in the 1890s, the quarter's boundary was defined by **Király utca**, a congested thoroughfare noted for its brothels where – as Patrick Leigh Fermor was told in 1934 – "any man could be a cavalier for five pengöes". The street retains many buildings from the mid-nineteenth century (mostly at the Erzsébet tér end) and at least one dating from 1810. Many house second-hand *(bizományi)* stores, though in recent years a number of new shops have opened, reviving the street's former atmosphere. Approaching the area from the south, as most people do, the first landmark is the Central Synagogue just off Károly körút.

The Central Synagogue

Budapest's **Central Synagogue** is the largest in Europe. Capable of holding 3000 worshippers, it is part of a complex of buildings on the site of the birthplace of Theodor Herzl, founder of the Zionist movement. It is also a spectacular example of the Byzantine Moorish style of synagogue architecture favoured in the 1850s, sporting onion domes, crenellations and geometric friezes. After decades of neglect, restoration is underway, largely funded from abroad by the Hungarian-Jewish diaspora, with Tony Curtis (born of Twenties emigrants) spearheading the drive.

Depending on its progress, you'll be able to see at least part of the *zsinagóga* complex (summer Mon–Thurs 10am–3pm & Fri–Sun 10am–1pm; closed winter). On the first floor, the **National Jewish Museum** (May–Oct Mon & Thurs 2–6pm;

Tues, Wed, Fri & Sun 10am–lpm) displays torahs and other Judaica dating back to the Middle Ages, along with examples of the Jewish cultural florescence of the nineteenth century. A harrowing Holocaust exhibit casts something of a chill over the third section, which portrays Jewish cultural life today. This current resurgence owes much to the increased contacts with international Jewry, and a revival of interest in religion and roots amongst the 80,000-strong Jewish community of Budapest, which had previously tended towards assimilation and been reluctant to proclaim itself in a country where anti-Semitic prejudices linger. In August 1994 eighty percent of the museum's treasures were stolen while the guards on duty were dozing in their car outside. These were recovered in Romania later in the year, and duly returned to the museum where they are now back on display.

In the courtyard stands a weeping willow-shaped **memorial** by sculptor Imre Varga, each leaf bearing the names of families massacred by the Nazis.

Around the backstreets

Fanning out behind the synagogue are backstreets where many apartment buildings contain run-down yet beautiful courtyards with stained-glass panels inscribed in Hebrew characters, and sad memorial plaques naming those who perished during the "autumn that bled" in 1944. Rampaging through the ghetto, Nazi squads left Jewish corpses piled in the streets while gentiles averted their eyes. As the Zionist underground prepared for escape or last-ditch insurrection, the Wallenberg group (see p.79) manoeuvred and bribed to gain time. Though unable to thwart the murderous Arrow Cross, they nevertheless succeeded in forestalling a final SS assault on the ghetto even as Soviet troops were encircling the city.

At the lower end of Dob utca stands a recently erected **monument to Carl Lutz**, a Swiss emigré who saved Jews by issuing them with foreign identity passes – the tactic adopted by Wallenberg. Lutz, however, was a more ambiguous figure (ironically regarded as pro-Nazi by the British), who ceased issuing passes and tried to stop others from faking them after being threatened by the Gestapo. After the war he was criticized in his homeland for abusing Swiss law. Feeling unjustly slighted, he proposed himself for the Nobel Peace Prize. His monument – a golden angel stooping to help a prostrate victim – is locally known as "the figure jumping out of a window".

Further north and to the left, **Rumbach utca** harbours a twin-towered, Romantic-style synagogue started in 1872 for the so-called Status Quo or middling-conservative Jews. Behind the synagogue, running between Dob and Király utca, is an atmospheric series of courtyards known as the Gozsdu udvar. Little of the life that thrived here before the war remains, just a few theatre workshops and a kindly old barber (*fodrász*).

The VIII district: Józsefváros

The **VIII district** – otherwise known as Józsefváros (Joseph Town) – is separated from the VII district by Rákóczi út, which runs out to Keleti Station, and from the Belváros by Múzeum körút, part of the Small Boulevard. This quarter has a mixed reputation – the site of prestigious institutions but also something of a red-light district and thieves' hang-out, nicknamed "Chicago" during the Twenties and Thirties.

Múzeum körút resembles Andrássy út in miniature, with trees, shops and grandiose piles curving round to meet Kálvin tér. Immediately below the Astoria junction stands the natural sciences faculty of **Eötvös Loránd University**, whence many of the scientists who worked on the US atomic bombs graduated before World War II, including Edward Teller, the "Father of the Hydrogen Bomb". Further on and across the street, remnants of the **medieval walls of Pest** can be seen in the courtyards of nos. 17 and 21. The walls gradually disappeared as the city was built up on either side, but fragments remain here and there.

The Hungarian National Museum

The **Hungarian National Museum**, like so many other institutions in Budapest, was the brainchild of Count Széchenyi, who donated thousands of prints and manuscripts to form the basis of its collection in 1802. Shortly after it opened, the Neoclassical edifice (designed by Mihály Pollack) became the stage for a famous event in the 1848 Revolution, when Sándor Petőfi first declaimed the *National Song* with its rousing refrain – "Choose! Now is the time! Shall we be slaves or shall we be free?" – from its steps. Since then, March 15 has always been commemorated here with flags and patriotic speeches.

The museum (Tues–Sun 10am–6pm) is divided into two main sections – before and after the Magyar conquest – of which the latter, on the first floor, is the more interesting. As most captions are in Hungarian only, a catalogue may be a worthwhile investment. Highlights include the captured tent of a Turkish general, Renaissance pews from Nyírbátor, and the **Coronation Regalia** – reputedly the very crown, orb and sceptre used by King Stephen. The Hungarian coat of arms faithfully reproduces the distinctive bent cross that surmounts the crown. As the symbol of Hungarian statehood for over a millennium, the regalia has been buried in Transylvania to hide it from the Habsburgs, and taken by Hungarian fascists to Germany in 1945, and thence to the US, where it reposed in Fort Knox until its return home in 1978.

Bródy Sándor utca and Kálvin tér

Bródy Sándor utca, flanking the museum grounds, seems an unlikely place for a revolution to start – yet one did outside the nondescript **Radio Building** (no. 7), when ÁVO guards fired upon students demanding access to the airwaves, an act which turned the hitherto peaceful protests of October 23, 1956 into an uprising against the secret police and other manifestations of Stalinism.

Street fighting was especially fierce around **Kálvin tér**, at the junction of Üllői út and the Small Boulevard, where insurgents battled tanks rumbling in from the Soviet base on Csepel Island. It seems almost miraculous that the ornate reading room of the **Szabó Ervin Library** (Mon, Tues & Thurs 9am–9pm & Sat–Sun 9am–1pm), on the corner of Baross utca, survived unscathed. Until recently a famous illustrator had lived all her life in an apartment over the square, where she witnessed three revolutions and two world wars from her window.

Beyond the Great Boulevard

The József körút section of the Great Boulevard marks the beginning of the **red-light district**, where topless bars vie with streetwalkers for custom around **Rákóczi tér** (see box below). Women would do well to avoid the area after nightfall (or even by day), although there's less risk if you stick to the northwest corner of **Köztársaság tér**, where the **Erkel Theatre** draws crowds of respectable folk most evenings. Some way northeast of here are **Keleti Station** and **Baross tér**, whence you can reach a couple of places of mild interest, further out.

PROSTITUTION IN BUDAPEST

During the Habsburg and Horthy eras, **prostitution** was licensed much as it still is in Vienna, with fixed prices for each quarter of the city. In 1950, the Communists shut down the licensed brothels and compelled many of the prostitutes to undergo "re-education through labour" at Dunaújváros, but they gradually drifted back into Budapest in the Sixties, just as a wave of *digozok* or "amateurs" was emerging to cater for tourists. Today, with the sex industry booming, there is still a great divide between the highly-paid hookers of the Belváros nightclubs and the streetwalkers of the VIII district, who service Hungarians.

KEREPESI CEMETERY
Kerepesi Cemetery, between the Ügetopálya racing track and Mező Imre út, is the Père Lachaise of Budapest, where the famous, great and not-so-good are buried. From the main entrance (one stop from Baross tér by tram #23 or #24), it's a ten-minute walk to the **Pantheon of the Working Class Movement**, where former Party leader János Kádár and other Communists are interred. This used to include the tomb of László Rajk – Kádár's predecessor as Minister of the Interior in 1949. Following a so-called "confession" extracted from him by Kádár, Rajk was executed. Though subsequently "rehabilitated" with full honours, his body was recently removed from the Pantheon by his son László (a famous dissident of the Eighties).

Further south lie the florid **nineteenth-century mausoleums** of Kossuth, leader of the 1848 Revolution against the Habsburgs; Count Batthyány, whom they executed for rebellion; and Ferenc Deák, who engineered the "Compromise" between Hungary and the Empire. The great *diva* Lujza Blaha, the "Nation's Nightingale", is also buried in Kerepesi.

NÉPSTADION
The **Népstadion** district, north across Kerepesi út, is chiefly notable for the 76,000-seat **People's Stadium**, where league championship and international **football** matches and **concerts** by foreign rock stars occur. Stalinist statues of healthy proletarian youth line the court that separates it from the smaller **Kistadion** and the indoor **Sportscsarnok**, which also hosts occasional concerts. The **Népstadion bus station**, for services to most parts of the country east of the Danube, completes this concrete ensemble. All are best reached by metro line 2 (from Keleti Station or downtown) or by bus #30 along Dózsa György út (from the edge of the Városliget).

The IX district: Ferencváros and beyond

The IX district, **Ferencváros** (Francis Town), was developed to house workers in the latter half of the nineteenth century, and remains the most working class of Budapest's inner suburbs. During the Thirties and Forties, its population confounded Marxist orthodoxy by voting for the extreme right. In recent times, the local football team (*FTC* or *Fradi* as it's popularly known) has once again become the focus for the extreme right wing, with skinhead groups congregating at its matches.

Ferencváros begins at **Vámház körút**, the section of the Great Boulevard running from Kálvin tér to the Szabadság Bridge, where the largest section of the **medieval walls** of Pest can be found in the courtyard of no. 16. Nearer the bridge stands the recently restored **Vásárcsarnok**, Budapest's main **market hall**, noted for its ambience as much as for its produce, with tanks of live fish and stalls festooned with strings of paprika at the back (Mon 6am–4pm, Tues–Fri 6am–6pm & Sat 6am–2pm). Mrs Thatcher endeared herself to locals here by haggling during a visit in 1984. The embankment area is dominated by the **Economics University** (which shed the name of Karl Marx in 1989), another grandly restored old building and a delightful sight at night reflected in the river.

Along Üllői út

Don't bother with **Üllői út** unless you have a particular destination in mind, since this grimy thoroughfare of ponderous Neoclassical constructions runs for miles out to the Airport and Debrecen highways. Fortunately, its principal attraction lies only one block back from the Ferenc körút metro stop at the junction with the Great Boulevard.

The **Applied Arts Museum** (*Iparművészet Múzeum*) at Üllői út 33–37 (Tues–Sun 10am–6pm) occupies a grandiose pile designed by Ödön Lechner in a mixture of Art Nouveau and Turkic folk styles. Although layers of soot obscure the rich Zsolnay porcelain and yolk-coloured tiles cover the portico and facade, the interior is marvellous, modelled on the Alhambra in Granada. Since many of the exhibits are displayed only on a temporary basis, you could find anything from Transylvanian enamelware to Finnish glass – or scrolls and prayer rugs collected by Sándor Kőrosi Csoma (1784–1842), who tramped on foot to Tibet and compiled the first Tibetan-English dictionary.

Just beyond the Great Boulevard, the massive pile on the right is the former **Kilián Barracks**, whose garrison was the first to join the 1956 insurgents. As the Uprising spread, this became the headquarters of Colonel Pál Maleter and teams of teenage guerrillas who sallied forth from the passages surrounding the nearby Corvin Cinema to lob Molotov cocktails at Soviet tanks. Maleter himself was arrested by the KGB whilst negotiating for an armistice, and executed along with Nagy (see below). Further out near the Nagyvárad tér metro stop, the high-rise **Semmelweiss Medical University** (*SOTE*) hosts one of the largest discos in town (see "Entertainment").

Further out

To the north of Üllői út beyond smoggy Könyves Kálmán körút (the continuation of Hungaria körút, named after King Kálmán the Booklover) lies the leafy **Népliget** or People's Park, at the entrance of which stands Budapest's **Planetarium**. There are separate shows for children and adults (☎265-0725 for details), including a **Laser Show**. The Planetarium is about 100m from the Népliget metro stop.

Further still, out in the X district, is the **Új köztemető Cemetery**, where Nagy, Maleter and other leaders of the 1956 Uprising were secretly buried in unmarked graves in 1958. The police removed any floral tributes left at **Plot 301** until 1989, when they were accorded a ceremonial funeral in Hősök tere before being returned to their graves, which were subsequently dignified by the erection of 301 crosses. The plot lies in the farthest corner of the cemetery, a thirty-minute walk from the main entrance on Kozma utca (accessible by bus #95 from Zalka Máté tér in the Kőbánya district).

Finally, you might enjoy the **Ecseri flea market**, some way to the south along Nagykörösi út in the XX district (bus #54 from Boráros tér, and ask when to get off). There are stalls selling everything from bike parts and jackboots to nineteenth-century peasant clothing and hand-carved pipes – with a few genuine antiques in amongst all the junk. Bargain hard and avoid being taken for an Austrian or German – they're always overcharged. Opening hours are a bit irregular, but when last heard the *Ecseri piac* operated Mon–Fri 8am–4pm.

Eating and Drinking

Hungarians relish **eating and drinking**, and Budapest is great for both. Though Magyar cuisine naturally predominates, you can find everything from Middle Eastern to Japanese food, bagels to Big Macs. The diversity of cuisine is matched by the range of outlets and prices – from deluxe restaurants where a meal costs an average citizen's monthly wage, to backstreet diners that anyone can afford. Many restaurants and bars have live music in the evenings; places where music and dancing are paramount are covered under "Entertainment".

Coffee houses and patisseries

Daily life in Budapest is punctuated by the consumption of black coffee drunk from little glasses, and for anyone who can afford it, a pastry or ice cream. Together they make a quintessentially Central European interlude, although nowadays less prolonged than before the war, when Budapest's **coffee houses** *(kávéház)* were social club, home and haven for their respective clientele. Free newspapers were available to the regulars – writers, journalists and lawyers (for whom the cafés were effectively "offices") or posing revolutionaries – with sympathy drinks or credit to those down on their luck. Today's coffee houses and **patisseries** *(cukrászda)* are less romantic but still full of character; whether fabulously opulent, with silver service, or homely and idiosyncratic.

With the exception of the *Ruszwurm* and the *Angelika*, all of the following are in Pest.

Angelika, 1, Batthyány tér 7. Old-fashioned and quiet, next to the Watertown Parish Church. Also does cocktails. Daily 10am–8pm.

Astoria Kávéház, V, Kossuth utca 19. Another famous turn-of-the-century coffee-house-cum-cocktail-bar, in the *Astoria Hotel*.

Bécsi Kávéház, V, Apáczai Csere János utca 12. Exquisite cakes and smooth service, on the first floor of the *Forum Hotel*.

Café Mozart, VII, Erzsébet körút 36. Popular new place offering delectable cakes in modern surroundings. Daily 9am–10pm.

Fröhlich Cukiszda, VII, Dob utca 22. A kosher patisserie whose speciality is *Flodni*, an apple, walnut and poppy-seed cake. Closed Fri afternoon and weekends.

Gerbeaud, V, Vörösmarty tér 7 (hence its other name, Vörösmarty's). A Budapest institution with a gilded salon (daily 9am–10pm) and terrace. Costly, and full of tourists. The *Kis Gerbeaud* round the corner is a cheaper, stand-up version of the same.

Kaffee Károlyi, V, Károly Mihály utca. Popular place among the younger generation, with music from the Seventies. Open 9am–9pm.

Lukács Cukrászda, VI, Andrássy út 70. Vintage patisserie with Baroque and Thirties decor, confiscated from the Lukács family by the Communist authorities to serve as the secret police cafeteria. Open Mon–Fri 9am–8pm.

Művész Cukrászda, VI, Andrássy út 29. The best of the old coffee houses, frequented by writers and fur-hatted old ladies. Open 8am–midnight.

New York, VII, Teréz körut 9–11. Wonderful Art Nouveau decor, worth the price of a cappuccino or a cocktail. There is also a restaurant downstairs. Daily 9am–10pm.

Ruszwurm, 1, Szentháromság tér 7. Diminutive Baroque coffee house near the Mátyás Church; almost impossible to get a seat. Delicious cakes and ices. Daily 10am–8pm.

Fast food, self-service and snack bars

Budapest has taken to **fast food** in a big way, and new outlets and **snack bars** are opening all the time. Another innovation are the **Étkezde** – small, lunch-time diners with shared tables and a rapid turnover, serving hearty home cooking.

Arany Paprika A new fast-food chain serving Hungarian fare. Branches in Pest at Szent István körút 3, near the Margit Bridge; and Harmincad utca 4, beside the British Embassy (upstairs – downstairs is a costly restaurant).

City Grill, V, Váci utca 20. A fast-food joint with longer hours and more varied menu than *McDonald's*.

Falafel, V, Paulay E. utca 53. Budapest's best *falafel* joint, with rooms upstairs (Mon–Fri 10am–8pm & Sat 10am–6pm).

Izes Sarok, V, Bajcsy-Zsilinszky út 1 (on the edge of Erzsébet tér). Good for open sandwiches, coffee and juices. Open Mon–Thurs 8am–7pm, Fri 8am–5pm.

Kádár Étkezde, VII, Klauzál utca 10. The best cheap diner in Pest with delicious home cooking (traditional non-kosher Budapest Jewish food on Fri). Open lunchtimes only Mon–Sat 11.30am–3.30pm; closed mid-July to mid-Aug.

Marquis de Salade, VI, Hajós utca 4 (Arany János utca metro, just off Bajcsy Zsilinszky út). Good salad bar in a land where such things are a rarity. Open daily 11am–midnight.

McDonald's, V, Régiposta utca 2, just off Váci utca; in Nyugati Station's magnificently decorated erstwhile restaurant (both daily 8am–9pm); and at many other outlets across the city.

New York Bagels, Bajcsy Zsilinszky út 21 (by the Arany János metro); and inside the Wizards entertainment arcade by Ferenciek tere. A chain restaurant with outlets around the city serving New York-style bagels and fillings – almost as good as the real thing.

Minerva, V, Kossuth Lajos tér. Self-service eatery open to office workers and the public on the 7th floor of the Hungarian Chamber of Commerce (entrance next door to the metro station). Offers cheap food and good views.

Mini Étkezde, Dob utca. A similar set-up to the *Kádár* just around the corner. Open Mon–Fri 11.30am–3pm; closed mid-July to mid-Aug.

Saláta Bar, VII, Asboth utca (just off Mádach tér and Károly körút); and on the corner of the *Grand Hotel Hungária* (across from Keleti Station) – both offer a range of salads.

Szezám, V, Papnövelde utca 1. Good *falafes* and *doner kebabs* from friendly staff. Open Mon–Fri 10am–7pm.

Restaurants

The city's **culinary scene** has diversified enormously in recent years, with many new places offering Chinese and Japanese food to wealthy tourists and nouveau riche natives. While you can still eat well and cheaply if you know where to look, **rip-offs** abound. Favoured tactics include issuing menus without prices (sometimes just to women, on the grounds that only men need to know*), exaggerating

*A more amusing example of Hungarian chauvinism is the old convention that men precede women through the door of a bar or restaurant, in case there's a brawl inside!

the bill or charging exorbitant amounts for the wine. Insist on a proper menu (including prices for drinks) and don't be shy about querying the total. It is also wise to reserve a table at the restaurant of your choice, though you can usually find an alternative within a couple of blocks.

As forint **prices** rise continuously, we have classified restaurants in comparative terms. Expect to pay no more than £7/$11 per head for a full meal with drinks in a **cheap** place; around £10/$16 in an **inexpensive** one; £18/$28 in a **moderately priced** restaurant; £25–35/$40–55 in an expensive one; and upwards of £35/$55 in a **very expensive** establishment. Some of the places listed below are rough and ready, others glittering citadels of *haute cuisine* – it's worth checking out both ends of the spectrum. Should you find yourself being serenaded by Hungarian Gypsy bands, be aware that you do have to pay for the pleasure.

For places not on the list, you can generally reckon that the further from the Belváros or Castle Hill the cheaper they are likely to be. If they don't have a menu (*étlap*) in German (which most waiters understand) or English, the food and drink vocabulary in *Basics* should suffice for **ordering meals**. Simply pointing to dishes on the menu or neighbouring tables might result in some surprises.

Buda

Despite the plethora of tourist traps on Castle Hill, **Buda** offers some excellent possibilities if you don't mind a bit of a journey. Of the following places – grouped according to locality – the best value for money are the *Marcello* and the *Náncsi Néni;* while the *Kisbuda* and *Hársfa* are recommended to those who are more solvent.

CASTLE HILL AND THE WATERTOWN
All the **"historic" restaurants on Castle Hill** charge exorbitant prices for mediocre food, though the *Alabárdos* deserves a mention for its medieval furnishings and roaring fire. Some cheaper options include:

Horgásztanya, I, Fő utca 27 (☎115-4664). Enjoyable fish restaurant on the Watertown's main street. Daily noon–midnight. Inexpensive.

Mama Rosa, I, Ostrom utca 31; farther down towards Moszkva ter. Excellent pizzas and spaghetti, including vegetarian options. Daily noon–9pm. Inexpensive.

Tabáni kakas, I, Attila út 27 (☎175-7165). The "Tabán Rooster", on the other side of Castle Hill, specializes in game dishes. Open daily noon–midnight. Moderately priced.

RÓZSADOMB, HŰVÖSVÖLGY AND SASAD
Ezüst Ponty, XII, Németvölgyi út 96 (☎209-1715). Agreeable fish restaurant with summer garden; catch tram #59 from Moszkva tér. Reservations essential. Daily noon–midnight. Expensive.

Gusto's, II, Frankel Leo utca (☎115-3970). Near the Buda side of Margit Bridge, a tiny little bar serving the best *tiramisu* in town. Open Mon–Sat 10am–11pm; booking essential.

Il Treno, XII, Alkotás utca 15 (☎156-4251). Good big pizzas across the road from the Déli Station. Open daily 11am–2am. Inexpensive.

Kikelet Vendéglő, II, Fillér utca 85 (☎135-5331). Moderately priced restaurant situated up on a hill above Moszkva tér with a view over the city and a lovely shaded garden. Limited menu, but ask what else they have on offer. Bus #49 from Moszkva tér.

Krisztina Söröző, XII, Krisztina Körút 25 (☎155-7383). Ordinary-looking restaurant near Moszkva tér serving surprisingly good food. Moderately priced.

Makkhetes, XII, Németvölgyi út 56 (☎155-7330). Typical Hungarian restaurant with a typically early closing time of 10pm (opens 11am). Inexpensive.

Marcello, XI, Bartók Béla út 40 (☎166-6231). Inconspicuous basement place serving good pizzas, near Móricz Zsigmond körtér. Inexpensive.

Markus Vendéglő, II, Lövőház utca 17 (☎115-1024). Friendly Hungarian restaurant. Inexpensive.

Náncsi Néni, II, Ördögárok út 80 (☎l76-5809). Popular garden restaurant in the leafy Hűvösvölgy, 10 minutes' walk from the end stop of the #56 bus. Live music and excellent food. Bookings essential. Mon–Sat noon–9pm, Sun noon–5pm. Inexpensive.

Söröző a Szent Jupáthoz, II, Retek utca 16 (☎115-1898). Cheap Hungarian dishes served 24 hours a day, with the emphasis on quantity not quality.

Udvarház, 111, Harmashatárhegy (bus #65 from Kolosy tér in Óbuda). At the top of Harmashatár hill, a cool place to dine on hot summer days with the city shimmering in the distance. Expensive.

ÓBUDA

Kehli, III, Mókus utca 22 (☎250-4241). Drawing on traditions of gourmet Gyula Krúdy who frequented the place earlier this century, this restaurant has a good lively atmosphere with excellent Gypsy music and alfresco dining in the summer. Open daily 6pm–midnight. Expensive.

Kisbuda Gyöngye, III, Kenyeres utca 34 (☎168-6402). Good food in finely decorated turn-of-the-century-style surroundings. Booking essential. Open daily noon–midnight. Expensive.

Sipos Halászkert, III, Fő ter 6 (☎188-8745). Touristy fish restaurant with Hungarian Gypsy music on the old main square of Óbuda. The *Postakocsi* across the square and the *Vasmacska* on nearby Laktanya utca are similar tourist traps. Expensive.

Pest

The number and variety of places is greater in **Pest**, particularly within the Great Boulevard, where rip-offs await the unwary. It's also possible to find some excellent restaurants, especially if you're prepared to do a bit of exploring: the *Bohémtanya, Tüköry, Csarnok* and *Finom Falatok* are the best options if you're on a tight budget, while the *Kiskakukk* is worth trading up for. If money isn't an issue, go for the *Cyrano*, the *Museum* or *Robinson's* – or the *Japan* for oriental cooking. Non-carnivores will find the *Vegetárium* restaurant a welcome relief. Finally, if it's Hungarian Gypsy music you're after, try the *Százéves* on Pesti Barnabás utca, or the less touristy *Kiskakukk* near Margit Bridge.

WITHIN THE GREAT BOULEVARD

Of the dozens of places around the centre (as far out as the Great Boulevard), the ones to **avoid** are the *Napoletana* on Apáczai Csere János utca; the *Mátyás Pince* on Március 15. tér; the *Kárpátia* in the backstreets nearby; and the *Berlin-Alex* on Szent István körút. All of the following are **recommended**.

Berlini Sörkatakomba ("Beer Catacombs"), IX, Ráday utca 9 (☎217-6757). Smoky cellar restaurant by the Kálvin tér metro. Genial atmosphere; popular among the younger generation. Inexpensive.

Bohémtanya, VI, Paulay E. utca 6, just off Erzsébet tér (☎l22-1453). Popular, cheap place serving huge portions of Magyar cooking. Bookings essential. Open daily 11am–10pm. Cheap.

Carmel, VII, Kazinczy utca 31 (☎142-4585). Non-kosher Jewish cooking. Family atmosphere on Sundays, when cheap lunches are served. Open noon–11pm. Moderately priced.

Chan-Chan, V, Váci utca 69 (☎118-0452). The only Thai restaurant in the city. Entrance opposite the *Fatál* restaurant in Pintér utca. Moderately priced.

Csarnok, V, Hold utca 11, one block east of Szabadság tér (☎112-2016). Good, down-to-earth Hungarian eatery specializing in mutton, lamb and bone-marrow dishes. Open Mon–Fri 9am–11pm. Inexpensive.

Cyrano, V, Kristóf tér 7–8 (☎266-3096). Popular new place with a good menu though rather leisurely service. The name derives from the chandelier, a prop in the *Cyrano de Bergerac* film which was partly shot in Hungary. Open daily 11am–midnight. Expensive.

Fatál ("Wooden Dish"), V, Váci utca 67 (☎266-2607). Gargantuan servings, but avoid the "vegetable feast" which is mostly batter. Entrance is on Pintér utca, which runs between Váci utca and the *Fregatt* pub on Molnár utca. Open daily 11.30pm–2am. Inexpensive.

Fészek Klub, on the corner of Dob and Akácfa utca (☎322-6043). A lovely summer court-yard and stunning decor, though the food and service can be a letdown. As a club, it charges 50Ft at the door – beware of waiters trying to add this to your bill. Moderately priced.

Finom Falatok Vendéglő ("Tasty Bites"), VII, Dob utca 50 (☎268-0382). Big plates full of wholesome Hungarian food. Inexpensive.

Góbé, VIII, József körút 28. Frequented by whores and pimps of the red-light quarter, the "Rascal" is only recommended to those seeking genuine lowlife – though it must be said its lamb dishes are surprisingly good. Almost always open, though not necessarily for eating. Cheap.

Hanna, VII, Dob utca 35 (☎142-1072). An unpretentious kosher diner, secreted in a court-yard. Open daily except Fri 11.30am–4pm. Inexpensive.

Japan, VIII, Luther utca 4–6 (☎114-3427). Authentic Japanese restaurant between Rákóczi út and Köztársaság tér. Open daily noon–midnight. Expensive. (There's a cheaper Chinese place, the *Tian Ma*, on the same street.)

Kispipa, VII, Akácfa utca 38 (☎142-2587). The "Little Pipe" excels in the cuisine of Budapest's assimilated Jewish middle class. Open daily noon–midnight. Moderately priced.

Marco Polo, V, Vigadó tér 3 (☎138-3925). Wonderful Italian food and stylish decor. Open daily noon–2pm & 7.30–11pm. Expensive.

Múzeum Kávéház, VIII, Múzeum körút 12 (☎267-0375). Excellent food in grand setting with piano music in the background. Near Astoria metro. Open daily 10am–1am. Expensive.

Shalom, VII, Klauzál tér 2 (☎122-1464). Only kosher restaurant open in the evening. Open daily except Sat noon–11pm & Sat noon–3pm. Moderately priced.

Szindbád, V, Markó utca 33 (☎132-2966). An epicurean's paradise north of Parliament, named after the character invented by writer and gourmet Gyula Krúdy. Superb food and service. Very expensive (especially the wine).

Taverna Dionysos, V, Belgrád rakpart 16 (☎118-1222). Greek restaurant done up to resem-ble a Greek village square. Good atmosphere and live music on Fri and Sat evenings. Terrace in summer looking out towards Buda. Open daily noon–midnight. Moderately priced.

Tüköry, V, Hold utca 15 (☎131-1931). Another good place for those on a budget, a few doors along from the *Csarnok*. Open Mon–Fri noon–11pm. Inexpensive.

Vegetárium, V, Cukor utca 3, near Ferenciek tere. Budapest's only eating place serving vegetarian and macrobiotic food. Agreeable service and ambience. Open noon–10pm daily. Moderately priced.

FURTHER OUT

Most of the following are easily accessible from downtown Pest, though you should reserve a table to avoid a wasted journey.

Bagolyvár, XIV, Állatkerti körút 20 (☎121-3550). Sister to the *Gundel*, but offering traditional Hungarian family-style cooking at far lower prices. Open daily noon–11pm. Moderate.

Becketts, V, Bajcsy Zsilinszky út 72 (☎111-1035). Irish-run Italian restaurant, popular with the local ex-pats. Open daily 11.30am–2.30pm & 5.30–11pm. Moderately priced.

Bombay Palace, VI, Andrássy út 44 (☎132-8363). Part of an international chain of Indian restaurants. Expensive.

Great Wall, VII, Ajtósi Durer Utca 1. Moderately priced Chinese restaurant near the south-eastern corner of the Városliget.

Gundel, XIV, Állatkerti körút 2, near the zoo in the Városliget (☎122-1002). Budapest's most famous restaurant offers plush surroundings and a fantastically expensive menu. Bookings and smart dress required. Open daily noon–4pm & 7pm–midnight.

Kiskakukk, XIII, Pozsonyi út 12 (☎132-1732). The "Little Cuckoo" near the Margit Bridge offers Gypsy music and wonderful game dishes such as wild boar in juniper sauce. Open Mon–Sat noon–11pm & Sun noon–4pm (closed over summer). Moderately priced.

Okay Italia, XIII, Szent István körút 20 (☎131-6991); and Nyugati tér 6 (☎132-6960). Excellent and very popular Italian eatery. No reservations at the first address, which means you often have to wait for a table. Inexpensive.

Robinson, in the park behind the Fine Arts Museum, beside the lake (☎142-0955). Top-flight international restaurant with superb food and service. Open daily noon–midnight on the terrace; noon–3pm & 7pm–midnight indoors. Very expensive.

Sport Étterem, XVI, Csömöri út 198 (☎183-3364). Next to the *Metro* campsite in Rákosszentmihály; four stops by bus #130 from Örs vezér tere metro terminal. Offers a huge range of dishes, including cock's balls. Good cooking, worth the forty-minute journey. Moderately priced.

Thököly, XIV, Thököly út 80 (☎122-5444). Delicious Transylvanian food, served outdoors or indoors, where the band can be a nuisance. Catch bus #7 or tram #67 from Baross tér, by Keleti Station. Open daily noon–midnight. Moderately priced.

Bars, wine bars and beer halls

It's hard to draw a firm line between places to eat and places to **drink** in Budapest, since some patisseries double as cocktail bars, and restaurants as beer halls (or vice versa), while the provision of live music or pool tables blurs the distinction between drinking-spots and clubs. The scene is constantly changing as places open or close, revamp their image, become trendy or the pits.

Insofar as you can generalize, most places that style themselves **bars** (or "drink") are chiefly into cocktails. The majority of *borozó* or **wine bars** are less pretentious than in the West, offering such humble snacks as *zsíros kenyér* (bread and pork dripping with onion and paprika). Conversely, **beer halls** *(söröző)* are often quite upmarket, striving to resemble an English pub or a German *bierkeller*, and serving full meals. The addition of *pince* to the name of an outlet for wine *(bor)* or beer *(sör)* signifies that it is in a cellar; many of the new places stink of mould until the crowds arrive.

The following list is hardly exhaustive, excluding as it does various **club-ish places** (covered under "Entertainment") and **strip bars** (at the Margit and Erzsébet bridge ends of the Pest embankment and around Rákóczi tér).

Buda

Teázó, I, Attila út 27. Quiet, spacious place specializing in tea. Closes 1am.

Ászok Söröző, I, Győző utca 5. A rowdy joint northwest of Déli Station, offering videos, Ászok and Alpesi beers.

Café Pierrot, I, Fortuna utca 14. Stylish cocktail bar on Castle Hill, where you can ask the pianist to *Play It Again Sam* after 8pm. Open Mon–Sat 5pm–1am & Sun 10am–11pm.

Hattyú, I, Hattyú utca 1. Typical cheap and cheerful neighbourhood wine bar, in the back-streets north of Castle Hill.

Kecskeméti Borozó Another such place, just off Moskva tér on the corner of Retek utca and Széna tér. Closes 9pm.

Marxim's, II, Kis Rókus utca 23, off Mártírok útja near Moskva tér. A "socialist nostalgia" theme bar serving pizza and other fare, with busts of Lenin, red flags, and other symbols of the People's Republic and its fraternal allies (RIP).

Miniatűr Espresszó, II, Rózsahegy utca 1. Small bohemian bar run by a mother and daughter since the Sixties. If they like you, you get to sit in the inner room (pianist after 9pm); if they don't, you'll be politely frozen out. Open daily except Sun 7pm–3am.

Te meg Én, II, Bem rakpart 30. Café-bar north of Batthyány tér, with cocktails and a pool table.

Vinceller Borozó, I, Fő utca 71. Agreeable wine cellar near the Király Baths. Open daily 8am–10pm.

Pest

Art Café, V, Veres Pálné utca 18. Good atmosphere and open 24 hours a day. Near Ferenciek tere metro.

Broadway Drink, VI, Nagymező utca 49. Pleasant cocktail bar on the other side of "Broadway" – try the *Zöld özvegy* (Green Widow).

Café Incognito, VI, Liszt Ferenc tér 3. Small intimate place that gets very crowded – a good start to an evening.

Dóm Sörbár, V, Szent István tér. A small place facing the basilica, offering draught Wernesgrüner and a big selection of bottled beers. Open daily 9am–5am.

Fregatt, V, Molnár utca 26. An earlier attempt at a pub in the backstreets south of Ferenciek tere, packed out by resident foreigners most nights. Offers Holsten beer and tasty chicken liver snacks. A bell is rung when someone gives a tip. Open till midnight.

Gösser Sörpatika, V, Régiposta utca 4. The "beer pharmacy" prescribes Gösser beer and sandwiches, just off Váci utca. Open daily 10am–11pm.

Gresham Borozó, V, Merlég utca 4. In the atmospheric old Gresham Palace on Roosevelt tér (entrance around the corner from the *Szecsuán* restaurant). Inexpensive for its location.

Irish Cat Pub, V, Múzeum körút 41 (☎266-4085). Popular bar with pub-like atmosphere specializing in Irish drinks. Near Kálvin tér metro. Open daily 11am–2am; live music Sun, Mon and Tues.

John Bull Pub, V, Apáczai Csere János utca 17. One of a chain of John Bulls in the city – like the others, a lifeless imitation of an English pub serving John Bull bitter and Skol lager at nigh-on London prices, with receipts for its business-type clients. Open till midnight.

Kaltenberger, IX, Kinizsi utca 30–32 (☎118-4792). A liveried doorman sets the tone for this smartly appointed beer cellar, near the Applied Arts Museum on Üllői út. Kaltenberger beer brewed on the premises, hearty roasts and attentive service; reservations essential in the evening. Open daily till 11pm.

Paris-Texas, IX, Ráday utca 22. Stylish café with good atmosphere near Kalvin tér. Open 9am–dawn.

Pragai Svejk Vendéglő, VII, Király utca 59B. Located in a sidestreet off "Broadway", this imitates the favourite Prague beer hall of the fictional Good Soldier Svejk, with great Czech beer and food, and a portrait of Emperor Franz Joseph.

Sörcsárda, X, Jászberenyi út 7. Attached to the Kőbányai Brewery, so heaving with workers enjoying the fruits of their labours. Rowdy but fun. Open Mon–Fri 9am–8pm & Sat–Sun 9am–3pm. Bus #168 from Örs vezér tere.

Talk-Talk Café, V, Magyar utca 12–14. Excellent cappuccino bar just behind the Astoria Hotel. Open 24 hours.

Trojka Söröző, VI, Andrássy út 28. An all-night hang-out for oddballs, with videos upstairs. Does Ratskeller, Egger and other beers. Open daily 10am–6am.

Winstons, VI, Jókai tér 3 (☎131-1955). Ever-so-English-style pub; also serves expensive pub food.

Entertainment

The range of **entertainment** available in Budapest includes everything from nightclubbing to opera-going, jazz to folk dancing and Formula One racing to football. To find out **what's on**, check out *Where Budapest* or *Programme*, both free magazines distributed in the hotels; the listings in *Budapest Week* and *Budapest Sun*; or the Hungarian-language weekly *Program Magazin*. The latter's review columns are headed: *szinház* (theatre), *zene* (music), *pop*, *film*, *képzőművészet* (fine arts) and *TIT* (lectures). Another source is the monthly *Koncert Kalendárium* (free from *Tourinform* and the *National Philharmonic Ticket office* on Vörösmarty tér) which lists classical music performances, plus **booking agencies**.

Festivals and events: the Budapest year

The highlights of Budapest's cultural calendar are the **Spring Festival** in late March and the **Autumn Arts Weeks**, from late September to late October. Both offer a wealth of music, ballet and drama (including star acts from abroad). The ten-day **Film Festival** is another fixture (in Feb), though its future is not at present certain. For the last couple of years the **BudaFest** opera festival has been held in the opera house during the summer recess.

On **March 15** Budapest decks itself out in flags and cockades in honour of the 1848 Revolution, and there are patriotic gatherings at the Petőfi statue and the National Museum. **Easter** is marked by church services and outbreaks of *locsolkodás* (splashing) – when men and boys visit their female friends to spray them with cologne and receive a painted egg or pocket money in return. The fall of Communism has put paid to grandiose parades on April 4 and May 1, but **May Day** remains a workers' holiday, with beer tents and music in the Városliget and the Népliget, sponsored by rival trade unions.

While many theatres close down for the season, there are plenty of concerts and two major sporting events (see below) over **summer**. **Saint Stephen's Day** (August 20), honouring the founder of the Hungarian state, occasions day-long celebrations at the Basilica (see p.191) and a spectacular display of **fireworks** at 9pm. Over a million people line the embankments to watch them fired off from Gellért Hill, so prime vantage points like the Erszébet and Szabadság bridges are taken by 8pm, and the traffic jam that follows the display is equally mind-blowing.

As the Autumn Arts Weeks wind down and trees in the parks turn russet and gold, it is nowadays permitted to honour the anniversary of the 1956 Uprising. **October 23** was a taboo anniversary for decades, then suddenly accorded cathartic, televised, recognition: interest now seems to be waning among the majority of Hungarians who are too young to have experienced the Uprising. On December 6, children hang up Christmas boots for "little Jesus" to fill, and people prepare for the **Christmas Eve feast** of jellied carp or turkey. Festivities build up towards **New Year's Eve**, when revellers gather on the Great Boulevard, engaging in trumpet battles at the junction with Rákóczi út.

Concerts, clubs and discos

Budapest attracts every Hungarian band worth its amplifiers and a growing roll-call of international stars, making it the best place for **rock concerts** in Hungary. Major foreign acts appear at the vast *Népstadion* or the nearby *Budapest Sportscsarnok*, and their appearances are well publicized in the media. Don't get too excited by flyposters advertising Michael Jackson or the Cure, however, as these refer to light shows or DJs at clubs and discos. Posters around town –

particularly around Deák tér, Ferenciek tere and the Astoria underpass – also publicize concerts by **Hungarian bands**.

For an authentically Magyar **rock-opera**, you can't beat *István a király* (*Stephen the King*) or the new *Attila Sword of God*, both of which are about the early heroes of the Hungarian nation. If, on the other hand, **laser shows** are your thing, there's an hour-long extravaganza to music by Pink Floyd, Queen, Jean Michael Jarre and Vangelis at the Planetarium in the Népliget (☎265-0725). Schedules vary, but you can ring to enquire about the *Lézerszinház*, or ask *Tourinform*. Tickets cost 400Ft.

Concert venues

Local bands most often perform at the *Petőfi Csarnok*, a huge youth centre near the Városliget (see p.94). The following cultural centres are also popular venues, as are many of the clubs and discos listed in the next section.

Almássy téri szabadidő központ, VII, Almássy tér 6 (☎142-0387). One of the city's main district cultural centres, located in downtown Pest.

Fővárosi művelődési ház, XI, Fehérvári út 47 (☎181-1360). Cultural centre in Buda where several rock concerts are staged each month.

I Kerületi Művelődesi Ház, I, Bem rakpart 6 (☎201-0324). The I district community centre, between the Chain Bridge and the Hotel Victoria.

Clubs and discos

Some clubs and discos in the city are still run under the aegis of universities, though there are an increasing number of private ventures, some of which have a fairly strict entrance policy. Clubbers are fickle, so places open and close, lose their credibility or acquire cachet – something to bear in mind as you check out the following venues, most of which are located in Pest. The gay and jazz scenes are covered separately (see p.109).

Crazy Café, VI, Jókai utca 30 (☎269-5484). Part of an underground complex comprising restaurants, cafés and live music bars (karaoke on Mon). A range of beers on offer and good, moderately priced food (though note that the menu also includes horse meat).

E-Klub, X, Népliget (at the Planetarium). Formerly in block E of the Technical University, this once-wild cattle market for engineering students was exiled to outer Pest. Today a more mixed crowd packs in for live rock music on Fridays, plus two discos and beer galore. Open Fri & Sat 8pm–5am. Bring ID.

Franklin Trocadero Café, V, Szent István körút 15. Excellent Latin music and dancing just up from Nyugati Station. Open 9pm–5am.

Közgáz DC, IX, Fővám tér 8 (☎215-4373). Massive, sweaty party scene at the Economics University with a live rock band and non-stop disco, two films and a karaoke show, plus a "tea house", ice-cream bar and lots of beer. Bring ID. Open Fri 8.30pm–3am.

Made Inn, VI, Andrássy út 112 (☎111-3437). Ultra-trendy disco and hang-out for jetsetters dressed (or barely dressed) in the flashiest MTV fashions. Look out for the gleaming sports cars out front. Outdoor patio packed in summer; live bands most Fridays and a Greek band most Sundays. Good Greek food. Open daily noon–3am. 200–300Ft cover charge.

Petőfi Csarnok, XIV, Zichy M. út 14 (☎142-4327). Huge purpose-built youth centre near the back of the Városliget, hosting concerts by local and big-name foreign bands, contemporary dance performances, Greek folk dancing (Sun in summer), the *Madonna Club*, the *Pet Shop Boys Club* and other band-specific DJ nights. Exhibitions are also held here, and there's a flea market on Saturday and Sunday mornings. Ring the above number for more details in English.

Piaf, VI, Nagymező utca 20 (☎112-3823). This fashionable bar on "Broadway" has a selective entry policy in the evening – it helps to know a regular. Basically a room and a cellar graced by the odd film star and lots of wannabes, with occasional jazz or rock sets. Open daily from 10pm until well after dawn.

Picasso Point, VI, Hajós utca 31 (☎132-4750). Popular, trendy spot for locals and tourists alike. Disco downstairs and live jazz or rock about once a week. Open Mon–Thurs noon–4am, Fri–Sat noon–5am & Sun noon–4am.

SOTE Club, IX, Nagyvárad tér 4 (in the Semmelweiss Medical University near Nagyvárad tér metro stop). A heaving disco plus sideshows including jazz gigs, rock concerts and movies. Bring ID.

Tilos az Á, VIII, Mikszáth Kálmán ter 2, near Kálvin tér (☎118-0684). A meeting place for *FIDESZ* supporters, entrepreneurs and social climbers, but not at all flash. Though its name (from the "Trespassers W" sign in Winnie the Pooh, which is cult reading in Budapest) means "no entry", in fact anyone can get in (100–200Ft). Head-bangers gravitate to the cellar. Closes between 3am & 5am.

Titanic, VII, Akácfa utca 56 (☎142-7569). Large, mellow subterranean hang-out with local rock and blues bands Thurs–Sat. Low-priced food and beer. Open daily 10am–4pm.

Total Car, VI, Teréz körút 55, next to Nyugati station. Rock club with live bands during the week and a sweaty disco at weekends. Popular among the teenyboppers.

Vén Diák, V, Egyetem tér 5 (☎267-0226). A jam-packed disco opposite the Law Faculty of Eötvös University, playing current hits and classic oldies. Its name – meaning "former student" – is abbreviated to *VD* on posters. Open daily 10pm–5am.

Gay life

Budapest's **gay scene** has taken wings in recent years, with new, overtly gay clubs replacing the old, covert hang-outs, and the appearance of a trilingual monthly listings magazine, *Mások* ("Outsiders"). However, gays must still tread warily and lesbians are several steps behind. (The Magyar euphemisms for gay and lesbian are *meleg* and *hideg*, "warm" and "cold".) Aside from places listed below, gays frequent the Király, the Rudas and the Gellert baths, as well as the Palatinus pool on Margit Island.

Art 44, XI, Halmi utca 44. Out beyond Móricz Zsigmond körtér, this new in place goes gay after midnight, when the door is locked and you have to ring to get in.

Angyal Bár, VII, Rákóczi út 51. Budapest's premier gay club, with a nightly disco and drag shows at midnight on Sun and Thurs. Lesbian night on Sun. Open Thurs–Sun 10pm–5am.

Darling, V, Szép utca 1. A beer-house and gallery that gets "warmer" after 9pm and stays open late.

Lokál, VII, Kertész utca 31. Now eclipsed by the *Angyal*, so less crowded. Nightly show, with discos on Fri and Sat. Open 9pm–4am.

Mystery Bar-klub, V, Nagysándor József utca 3 (☎112-1436). Very small bar near the Arany József metro stop, for talking rather than dancing (no disco). If the door's locked you might have to wait to be let in. Open Mon–Sat 9pm–4am.

Jazz

Although jazz is currently fashionable in Budapest, regular venues are few in number. Some bands appear at local cultural centres, others in some of the places listed above under "Clubs and discos".

Black & White Pizzeria, VII, Akácfa utca 13 (☎122-7645). Pizza, beer and jazz bands every night. Open daily till 2am.

Jazz Café, V, Balassi B. utca 25 (☎132-4377). Small underground club with blue neon lighting. One of the few places in town with live jazz every night (starting 8pm). Open Mon–Fri 3pm–3am & Sat–Sun 6pm–3am.

Kosztolányi Művelődesi Ház, IX, Török Pál utca 3 (☎118-0193). The world famous Benkó Dixieland Band plays here every Wed evening when not abroad.

Közgáz Jazz Klub, IX, Kinizsi utca 2–4 (☎217-5110). Belongs to the Economics University and favours progressive jazz. Local ethno-jazz wizard Mihály Dresch and his quartet play here to a packed crowd of loyal fans most Fridays from 8pm. Ring before going, though, as opening dates and times tend to vary.

Óbudai Jazz Klub, III, Hídfo utca 13 (☎250-3647). Cellar *söröző* (bar) up in Óbuda with superb New Orleans dixie from the Hot Jazz Band on Tues and top-notch standards from singer Bontovics Kati and the Vukán György Trio on Wed, both from 9pm. No live music on other nights.

Folk music and Táncház

Hungarian **folk music and dancing** underwent a revival in the Seventies, drawing inspiration from communities in Transylvania, regarded as pure wellsprings of Magyar culture. Enthusiasts formed "Dance Houses" or **Táncház** to revive traditional instruments and dances, and get people *involved* in the process. Visitors are welcome to attend the weekly gatherings at selected clubs or community centres, where the 60–100Ft admission charge contributes to new instruments and costumes. Muzsikás and the Téka and Kalamajka ensembles play sounds from Transylvania, while other groups are inspired by South Slav music from Serbia, Croatia and Bulgaria.

Besides the following venues, folk music might also feature at some of the clubs, discos and jazz clubs listed above. Details of events are available from the information service of the *Petőfi csarnok* (☎142-4327), or in *Program Magazin*, *Where Budapest*, *Budapest Sun* and *Budapest Week*. Bear in mind that many cultural centres close for summer, so check before you go.

Almássy téri Szabadidő Központ, VII, Almássy tér 6, north of Blaha Lujza tér (☎267-8709). The Rece Fice ensemble plays southern Slavic, Bulgarian and Greek music every Mon at 6pm.

Belvárosi Művelődési Ház, V, Molnár utca 9 (☎117-5928). The Kalamajka ensemble plays to a packed dance floor Sat nights at this downtown Pest cultural centre. Instruction 7–8pm.

Fővárosi Művelődési Ház, XI, Fehérvári út 47 (☎181-1360). Márta Sebestyén and Muzsikás play for kids every Tues from 5.30–6.30pm; the Falkafolk Balkan band play on Wed at 7pm; and from April to Oct the Budapest Dance Ensemble appears most nights at 8.30pm. The latter is more of a show than a *táncház*, but still fun. Tram #18 from Szent Gellért tér or bus #3 from Móricz Zsigmond körtér.

Gyökér Club, VI, Eötvös utca 46, near Nyugati Station (entrance round the corner in Szob utca). Dancing on Mon and Fri; pleasant atmosphere and good restaurant.

I Kerületi Művelődési Ház (see concert venues above) hosts the Téka ensemble dance house every Fri. Kids 5–6pm, teenagers 6–7pm and adults from 7pm.

Opera, ballet and classical music

Opera is highly esteemed in Hungary, whose composers and writers have created such works as *Bánk Bán*, *László Hunyadi*, *The Queen of Sheba* and *Blood Wedding*. Most productions are in Hungarian, and fans prefer their opera "old style", with lavish sets and costumes and histrionic performances which they interrupt with ovations after particularly bravura passages. Operas by Mozart, Verdi, Puccini, Wagner and national composers are staged throughout the year, while several new productions are premiered during the Spring and Autumn festivals, when you can also catch performances by the State Opera **ballet** and visiting foreign companies.

The city excels in its choice of **classical music**, with several concerts every night of the year, especially during the two festivals. Look out for performances by the Liszt Ferenc Chamber Orchestra and the Budapest Festival Orchestra; pianists Zoltán Kócsis and Desző Ránki, and cellist Miklós Perényi. The State Symphony Orchestra is conducted by Kobayashi Ken-Ichiro of Japan. Over summer, smaller concerts occur outdoors on Margit Island, and in historic buildings such as the Mátyás Church. It's also worth knowing about the season of concerts **at Vácrátót** (p.138) and **Martonvásár** (p.151) – both within commuting distance of Budapest. Again, bear in mind that many places close for the summer.

Weekly and monthly listings magazines cover the events, and **information** can also be obtained from *Tourinform* and the main ticket offices. **Tickets** for the Opera, Operetta and Erkel theatres are available from the *Central Box Office* at VI, Andrássy út 18 (☎112-0000); from II, Moszkva tér 3 (☎135-9136) in Buda; and from the *National Philharmonic Ticket Office* at V, Vörösmarty tér 1 (☎117-6222) – the latter also supplies tickets for concerts elsewhere. Tickets for outdoor performances are sold at the *Szabad Tér Ticket Office* at XIII, Hollán E. utca 10 (☎111-4823) and at the *Central Box Office* on Andrássy út. *Music Mix* at V, Váci utca 33 (☎138-2237) and *Publika* at V, Ferenciek tere (118-2430) also sell tickets to most classical and other events in town.

Academy of Music, VI, Liszt Ferenc tér 8 (☎142-0179). Nightly concerts and recitals in the magnificent *Nagyterem* (Great Hall) or the smaller *Kisterem*. The former is usually shut during summer, as it gets too hot.

Erkel Theatre, VIII, Köztársaság tér 30 (☎133-0540). A modernized venue for operas, ballet and musicals, on the edge of the red-light district near Keleti Station.

Mátyás Church, Choral or organ recitals, usually on Fri and sometimes on Sat at 8pm (June–Sept), and less frequently the rest of the year.

Operetta Theatre, VI, Nagymező utca 17 (☎132-0535). Stages classical Hungarian operettas and modern musicals; located on "Broadway", a few blocks from the opera house.

Saint Stephen's Basilica, Occasional concerts – consult *Tourinform* for details.

State Opera House, VI, Andrássy út 22 (☎153-0170). Budapest's grandest venue, with gilded frescos and three-ton chandeliers – a place to dress up for. Box office (Tues–Sat 11am–7pm, Sun 10am–1pm & 4–7pm) on Dalszínház utca, round the corner; **returns** also sold at Andrássy út 18. Higher prices for performances on Fri and Sat.

Vigadó, V, Vigadó tér 1 (☎117-6222). Another fabulously decorated hall, but the acoustics are inferior and concerts tend to be formal affairs attended by diplomats. Box office opens 1pm.

Theatre

If you're undeterred by the language barrier, **theatre** can also be a rewarding experience. The **Kátona József Company** won plaudits at the Old Vic in London and the Odéon in Paris, and remains the most exciting company in town. Their permanent repertory includes *The Government Inspector*, *Ubu Roi* and *Twelfth Night*. The Kátona Theatre is at Petőfi Sándor utca 6, next to the Párizsi Udvar. Its box office opens at 2pm, while tickets "for any unoccupied seat" are sold just before the show starts at 7pm.

During summer there are easy-to-understand performances at the outdoor theatre on Margit Island and occasional English-language productions at the

Merlin International Theatre at V, Gerlóczy utca 4 (☎117-9338) – all of them advertised in the usual publications. Puppet theatres are covered under "Children's Budapest" below.

Films and cinemas

Hollywood blockbusters and Euro soft-porn films currently dominate Budapest's **cinemas**, as evinced by the billboards along Rákóczi út and the Great Boulevard. *Budapest Week* and *Budapest Sun* both run listings of all movies playing in English, with the latter covering films in other languages as well. If you can deal with Hungarian, the fullest **listings** appear in *Program Magazin*, under the heading *Budapesti mozik műsora*. Here, the times of shows are cryptically abbreviated to *n8* or *1/4 8* for 7.15pm; *f8* or *1/2 8* for 7.30pm; and *h8* or *3/4 8* for 7.45pm. *"Mb."* indicates the film is dubbed, and *"fel."* or *"feliratos"* means that it has Hungarian subtitles. Serious film buffs should investigate **Art Cinemas**, which specialize in the latest releases and obscure films from Eastern and Western Europe. Their provenance is indicated thus: *Angol* (British), *Lengyel* (Polish), *Német* (German), *Olasz* (Italian), and *Orusz* (Russian). Cinemas belonging to the *Art Kino* network include the *Blue Box* at IX, Kinizsi utca 28 (☎118-0983); *Toldi* at V, Bajcsy-Zsilinszky út 36–38 (☎131-8129); the *Művesz* at VI, Teréz körút 88 (☎132-6726); and the *Hunnia* at VII, Erzsébet körút 26 (☎122-3471).

Sports

Most of this section is about **spectator sports** – soccer, horse-racing, the Grand Prix and the Budapest marathon – but the city also offers a range of **participatory sports** facilities. There's a **swimming pool** in the southern part of Margit Island, the Hajós Alfréd (see p.83), as well as pools in many of the thermal baths, for example the Rudas, the Lukács and the Gellért. **Tennis** courts can be hired at the *Thermal Hotel Helia* in north Pest, XIII, Kárpát utca 62 (☎270-3277) and at the *Club-sziget* on Margit Island (☎112-9472). You can go **horseriding** year-round at the Petneházy school at II, Feketefej utca 2–4 (Tues–Fri 9am–noon & 2–4pm, Sat–Sun 9am–1pm; ☎176-5937), or alternatively head out for the Great Plain where there are many small riding schools. In winter, it's possible to **ski** at Normafa and Jánoshegy in the Buda Hills – rental equipment is available from *Suli Sí* in the Komjádi swimming complex at II, Árpád Fejedelem utca 8 (☎212-2750). Skates can also be rented at the **ice rink** in the Városliget (City Park).

Soccer

While **international matches** are held at the 76,000-seater Népstadion, national football revolves around the turf of two **premier league teams**. *Ferencvárosi Torna Club* (aka *FTC* or *Fradi*) are based at IX, Üllői út 129 (☎113-6025), near the Népliget metro stop. Their colours are green and white and their fans are keen to fight with supporters of *Újpesti Torna Egylet*, whose ground is at IV, Megyeri út 13 (three stops on bus #30 from Újpest Központ metro station). Honvéd-Kispest is another big rival based at XIX, Új temető út 1–3 (tram #42 from Határ út metro stop to the end of the line). Matches are played on Saturday afternoons and Monday evenings; see *Programme* or any Hungarian newspaper for details.

A day at the races

Horse-racing was introduced from England by Count Széchenyi in 1827 and flourished until 1949, when flat-racing (*galopp*) was banned by the Communists. In the mid-Eighties it resumed at the **Lóversenyter** (☎252-0888), north of the International Fair grounds at X, Albertirsai út 2 (Pillangó utca metro stop). Punters gather here every Sunday afternoon during the racing season, and the **Hungarian Derby** is held on the second or third Sunday in July. Devoted fans also attend **trotting races** at the **Ügetőpalya** at Kerepesi út 11 (bus #95 or trolleybus #80 from either Népstadion or Keleti Station), starting at 2pm on Saturday and 4pm on Wednesday. The atmosphere at both tracks is informal, but photographing the race-goers is frowned upon, since many attend unbeknownst to their spouses or employers. Races are advertised in *Fortuna* magazine and *Programme*.

The Hungarian Grand Prix

The **Hungarian Grand Prix**, first held in 1986, occurs every summer at the purpose-built **Formula 1 Racing** track at Mogyoród, 20km northeast of Budapest. It is usually but not always scheduled for early August; details are available from *Ibusz, Tourinform* or any listings magazine. You can reach the track by special buses from the Árpád Bridge; trains from Keleti Station to Fót, and then a bus from there; or by HÉV train from Örs vezér tere to the Szilasliget stop, which is 1800m northeast of Gate C. Tickets, available from *Ibusz* or *Budapest Tourist*, range from £5/$8 to £32/$50 for the first two days, from £8/$13 to £120/$190 for the final day, and from £10/$15 to £130/$200 for a three-day pass – the price being partly determined by the location, and whether you book in advance or risk disappointment on the day.

The Budapest Marathon

An increasingly popular event held in late April or early May, the 42-km–long **Mars Marathon** (formerly called the Budapest Marathon) runs from Visegrád, north of the city, down the Danube and into the Tabán Parl in Buda. Further information is available from the Magyar Marathon Club (☎155-6583 or ☎175-4369). **Jogging** is also becoming popular, particulary on Margit Island, where a circuit equals about 5km.

Children's Budapest

From Klauzál tér's scaled-down assault course to the folksy wooden see-saws and swings erected on Széchenyi-hegy, there are **children's playgrounds** all over Budapest. Adults could combine a visit to Jubilemi Park on Gellért Hill with some sightseeing, or extract a series of childish diversions from the Városliget (see p.94) with its mock castle and old trains, its **amusement park, circus** and **zoo**. The "railway circuit" of the Buda Hills (p.82) should also appeal to all ages, while the **Waxworks** on Castle Hill (p.71) could be just the thing for kids going through a gory phase.

If the *Petőfi Csarnok* has nothing suitable for children you could take them to a dance club at one of the local cultural centres, or alternatively one of Budapest's **puppet theatres**. Morning and matinée performances are for kids, while the evening's occasional masked grotesqueries or renditions of Bartók's *The Wooden*

Prince and *The Miraculous Mandarin* are intended for adults. Tickets are available from the *Central Box Office* or the *Bábszinház* themselves, at VI, Andrássy út 69 (☎142-2702) and VI, Jókai tér 10 (☎112-0622). Children's films are advertised in *Program Magazin* under the heading *Gyermeknek ajánlott.*

Last but not least, there is "Kidstown" (*Kölyökvár*), a play and activity centre open every Sunday (10am–1pm) at VII, Almássy tér 6. This organizes everything from face-painting to model-building – plus films, music and drama from mid-October to April (☎267-8709 for details).

Listings

Airlines *Aeroflot*, V, Váci utca 4 (☎118-5955); *Air France*, V, Kristóf tér 6 (☎118-0411); *Alitalia*, V, Ferenciek tere 1 (☎118-6882); *Balkan*, V, Párizsi utca 7 (☎117-1818); *British Airways*, V, Apáczai Csere János utca 5 (☎118-3299); *CSA*, V, Vörösmarty tér 2 (☎118-3045); *JAT*, V, Párizsi utca 9 (☎117-1595); *KLM*, VIII, Rákóczi út 1–3 (☎117-4522); *Lufthansa*, V, Váci utca 19–21 (☎266-4511); *Malév*, V, Roosevelt tér 2 (☎266-9033); *SABENA*, V, Váci utca 1–3 (☎118-4111); *SAS*, V, Váci utca 1–3 (☎266-2633); *Swissair*, V, Kristóf ter 7–8 (☎267-2500); *TAROM*, Ferihegy airport terminal (☎157-9123).

Airport The journey to Ferihegy airport takes about an hour if all goes well, but for safety you should probably allow two, especially if travelling by public transport or during rush hour. Taxis out to the airport are less extortionate than those into the city, but you can still get stung. The alternatives are to take the metro to Kobánya-Kispest and then a bus (red bus #95 – not the black one – to Terminal 1 and then on to Terminal 2); the LRI minivan from the Erzsébet tér bus station (operates daily 5.30am–9pm, leaving every half hour and taking just over an hour); or the private minibus shuttle which will pick you up anywhere in the city (☎157-8555 to book a seat; 600Ft). Terminal 1 (☎157-2122) serves all airlines except *Malév, Alitalia, Lufthansa* and *Air France*, which use Terminal 2 (☎157-8768 for departures; ☎157-8406 for arrivals).

Banks Most *OTP* branches are open Mon–Thurs 9am–4pm & Fri 9am–1pm, but changing money and traveller's cheques is easier at almost any tourist office (24-hour service at V, Petőfi tér 3). You can transfer money from abroad through the *Magyar Külkereskedelmí Bank*, V, Szent István tér 11; through *Western Union* at *Budapest Bank*, V, Hercegprímás utca 5 (☎266-3222); and through the *American Express* Moneygram service (minimum $100), V, Deák F. utca 10 (☎267-8680). Money transfers allegedly take only a few minutes.

Books in English from: *Bestsellers* at V, Október 6 utca 11 (☎112-1295); *Libri* at V, Váci 32–33 (☎118-2718); *The Foreign Language Bookshop* at V, Petőfi Sándor utca 2 (☎118-3136); *Fókusz* at VII, Rákóczi út 14–16 (☎121-5205), *Litea* at I, Hess András tér 4 (☎175-6987); and Vörösmarty tér 4. Second-hand (*Antikvárium*) bookstores: Váci utca 28 & 75; Múzeum körút 15; and on the corner of Deák tér and Bajcsy-Zsilinszky út. All in the Belváros.

British Council, VI, Benczúr utca 26 (☎121-4039). Library, newspapers and a noticeboard. Mon–Thurs 11am–6pm & Fri 11am–5pm.

Bus stations The most useful are: *Népstadion* (metro line 2; ☎252-0696) serving areas east of the Danube; *Erzsébet tér*, in the Belváros, for Transdanubia and abroad (☎118-2122); and *Árpád híd* (metro line 3; ☎120-9229), covering both banks of the Danube Bend. Destinations and schedules are given in "Travel Details" on p.116.

Camping and Caravanning Club, IX, Kálvin tér 9 (Mon–Fri 9am–5pm; ☎217-7248). Can supply canoeing maps of the Danube, advise on equipment and arrange reductions for *FICC* members.

Car rental *Budget* at the Hotel Buda-Penta, I, Krisztina körút 41–43 (☎156-6333); *Főtaxi* at VII, Kertész utca 24–28 (☎111-6116); *Europcar* at VIII, Üllői út 62 (☎113-1492); *Hertz* at V,

---

The telephone code for Budapest is ☎1

Aranykéz utca 4–8 (☎117-7533); *American Rent-A-Car* at the Hotel Volga, XIII, Dozsa György út 65 (☎129-0200); and *Inka* (for Ladas) at V, Bajcsy-Zsilinszky út 16 (☎117-2150).

Car repairs American cars at *Americar Service Kft*, XIX, Méta utca 31 (☎157-2503 or ☎280-4859); *Fiat* models at XII, Boldizsár út 1–3 (☎162-1608 or ☎181-2909); *Mercedes* at XIII, Kárpat utca 21 (☎129-9990); *Ford, Opel, Toyota, Mazda* and *Suzuki* on the corner of Mexikói út and Besnyői utca (☎283-5975); *Peugeot, Renault* and *Citroen* at XXI, Jókai utca 25 (☎147-8533); *VW* and *Audi* at III, Mozaik utca 1–3 (☎250-0222); and most makes and models at *Euro-Auto*, XXII, Bartók Béla út 21 (☎226-1415). The *Magyar Autó Klub* runs a 24-hour breakdown service (☎252-8000).

Department stores *Centrum*, VIII, Blaha Lujza tér 1–2; *Luxus*, V, Vörösmarty tér 3; *Made In World Center*, V, Váci utca 30; *Divatcsarnok*, VI, Andrássy út 39; *Lottó*, VIII, Rákóczi út 36.

Embassies/consulates *Australia*, XII, Királyhágo tér 8–9 (☎201-8899); *Austria*, VI, Benczúr utca 16 (☎269-6700); *Bulgaria*, VI, Andrássy út 115 (☎122-0836); *Canada*, XII, Budakeszi út 32 (☎176-7711); *China*, VI, Benczúr utca 17 (☎122-4872); *CIS*, Andrássy út 104 (☎131-8985); *Czech Republic*, VI, Rózsa utca 61 (☎132-5589); *Denmark*, XII, Határőr út 37 (☎155-7320); *Germany*, XIV, Stéfania út 101–3 (☎251-8999); *Israel*, II, Fullánk utca 8 (☎176-7896); *Netherlands*, XIV, Abonyi utca 31 (☎122-8432); *Norway*, XII, Határőr út 35 (☎155-1811); *Romania*, XIV, Thököly út 72 (☎142-6941); *Slovakia*, XIV, Stefánia út 22 (☎251-1700); *Slovenia*, VI, Lendvay utca 23 (☎112-6896); *Sweden*, XIV, Ajtósi sor 27A (☎268-0804); *UK*, V, Harmincad utca 6 (☎266-2888); *USA*, V, Szabadság tér 12 (☎112-6450).

Emergencies Ambulance: ☎04; Police: ☎07; Fire service: ☎05.

Hospitals and dentistry There are 24-hour casualty departments at V, Hold Utca 19, behind the US embassy (☎111-6816), and at the *Szent János Hospital* at XII, Diosárok 1, off Szilágyi E. fasor in Buda (☎156-1122). The *Országos Traumatológiai Korház*, VIII, Fiumei út 17 (☎133-7599), specializes in broken limbs; the *Szájsebészeti Klinika, Stomatológiai Intézet*, VIII, Szentkirályi utca 40 (☎133-0970) in dentistry. SOS, VIII, Kerpesi út 15 (☎118-8212 or ☎118-8288) is a private ambulance service with English-speaking staff operating round the clock. Private clinics with English-speaking personnel include the *IMS* (International Medical Services), open 24 hours a day at XIII, Váci út 202 (☎129-8423); and the *R-Klinika* at II, Zöldalmádi út 13 (☎250-3488 or ☎250-3489). Embassies can also recommend private, foreign-language-speaking doctors and dentists.

Lost property For items left on public transport, VII, Akácfa utca 18 (Mon, Tues & Thurs 7.30am–3pm, Wed 7.30am–7pm, Fri 7.30am–2pm; ☎122-6613). Lost/stolen passports should be reported to the police station in the district where they were lost. Any found are handed into the *KEOKH* office at VI, Izabella utca 61, by Andrássy út (Mon, Wed & Fri 8am–noon, Tues 1–6pm, Thurs 8am–6pm; ☎118-0800).

Motoring information *Magyar Autó Klub*, II, Rórner Floris utca 4A (☎115-2040); *Fővinforn* for traffic conditions in Budapest (☎117-1173); *Útinform* (☎122-2238) for national conditions.

Naturism There is a nudist camp (☎155-4691) at the Délegyháza Lakes, 40km southeast of Budapest (by route 51 or train from Józsefváros Station) or, closer at hand, nude sunbathing is permitted on the single-sex terraces of the Gellért and Palatinus baths, and the *strand* at Csillaghegyi in the III district.

Pharmacies The following are all open 24 hours: II, Frankel Leó út 22 (☎115-8290); VI, Teréz körút 95 (☎111-4439); VII, Rákóczi út 86, at Baross tér (☎l22-9613); XI, Kosztolányi Dezső tér 11 (☎166-6494); XII, Alkotás utca lB, at Déli Station (☎155-4691); XIV, Bosnyák utca lA (☎183-0391). For herbal remedies try *Herbária*, VIII, Rákóczi út 49 and V, Bajcsy-Zsilinszky út 58.

Photomats Passport-sized photos are available from automatic booths in Deák tér, Kálvin tér and Moszkva tér metro stations (300Ft for 4 colour photos); *Sooter's* at V, Deák F. utca 22 (399Ft for 4 colour shots); and the third floor of the *Centrum* department store on Blaha Lujza tér.

Post Offices Main office/poste restante at V, Petőfi utca 13 (Mon–Fri 8am–8pm & Sat 8am–2pm); 24-hour *postas* at VI, Teréz körút 51 and VII, Baross tér 11C (near Nyugati and Keleti stations, respectively).

Radio *Radio Bridge* (102.1 FM) broadcasts a regional news and business bulletin called *Central Europe Today* (weekdays 8– 8.30am), while *Budapest Day and Night* has local news (Wed 8–8.30pm). The *Voice of America* can be heard in English daily, every hour on the hour (except 8pm Mon, Tues, Thurs & Fri), while the *BBC World Service* is available on short-wave (11,780 kHz in the morning and 12,095 kHz or 15,070 kHz during the day). *Radio Danubius* (100.5 & 103.3 FM) is another commercial channel, broadcasting in German. *Calypso 873* plays rock oldies (873 KHz); *Radio Bartók* classical music and jazz (69.38 MHz).

Record stores Rock, pop and jazz (including bootlegs) from *DOB Records*, VII, Dob utca 71; *Lemezkucko*, VI, Király utca 67; and *WAVE Records*, V, Bajcsy-Zsilinszky út 15. For classical music, try *Hungaroton* at *V*, Vörösmarty tér 1 or the *Amadeus* CD shop by the Danube behind the *Forum Hotel*. The friendly *Rózsavölgyi* at V, Szervita tér 5, has an excellent selection of pop and folk downstairs, plus sheet music. *CD Bar* at VI, Székely M. utca 10 allows you to listen to any CD they have in stock, and drinks and refreshments are also sold. *Fotex Records* at V, Szervita tér 2 is a large new store with a wide selection.

Taxis Volántaxi (☎166-6666), Főtaxi (☎222-2222), Citytaxi (☎211-1111), Rádió Taxi (☎177-7777), Tele-5-taxi (☎155-5555).

Telephones International calls can be made from the *Telephone and Telegram Bureau*, V, Petőfi utca 17–19 (Mon–Fri 8am–8pm & Sat 10am–4pm) or from direct-dial phone booths in the downtown area; the international operator can be reached on ☎09.

Television The *BBC World Service* broadcasts news on Channel 1 at around midnight on weekdays, and there's a daily English news bulletin on *Nap TV* (5–5.15pm). The main *Hungarian News* programme is at 7.30pm on Channel 1.

Trains International rail tickets should be purchased 24 to 36 hours in advance, preferably at the *MÁV* booking office, VI, Andrássy út 35 (Mon–Fri 9am–5pm; ☎122-8049) where lines are shorter than at *Nemzetközi-jegy* (international tickets) counters in stations, and where they are less likely to insist that foreigners pay for international tickets with hard currency.

travel details

Trains

Déli Station to Balatonfüred (every 1–2hr; 2hr–2hr 30min); Balatonszentgyörgy (every 1–2hr; 3–4hr); Dombóvár (4 daily; 2hr 15min); Pécs (4 daily; 3hr); Siófok (7 daily; 2hr 30min); Székesfehérvár (every 60–90min; 1hr); Szekszárd (3 daily; 3hr); Szombathely (5 daily; 3hr 30min); Veszprém (5 daily; 2hr 15min–3hr); Zalaegerszeg (2 daily; 4hr).

Keleti Station to Békéscsaba (4 daily; 2hr 30min); Eger (3 daily; 2hr); Győr (10 daily; 2hr 30min); Miskolc (11 daily; 1hr 45min–2hr 15min); Sopron (5 daily; 3hr 30min); Tata (4 daily; 1hr 15min).

Nyugati Station to Debrecen (11 daily; 2hr 30min–3hr 30min); Kecskemét (8 daily; 1hr 30min); Nyíregyháza (11 daily; 3hr–3hr 30 min); Szeged (8 daily; 2hr 30min).

Intercity buses

Árpád híd to the Danube Bend: Dobogókő (1–3 daily; 2hr 30min); Esztergom via the Bend (every 90min; 3hr) or Dorog (every 30min; 2hr); Pomáz (hourly; 45min); Szentendre (hourly; 1hr); Vác (every 30min; 30min); Visegrád (hourly; 2hr).

Erzsébet tér to Lake Balaton and Transdanubia: Balatonfüred (2 daily; 2hr 15min); Dunaújváros (4 daily; 1hr 30min); Győr (every 40–60min; 1hr 15min–2hr); Harkány (1 daily; 4hr 30min); Herend (2 daily; 2hr 40min); Hévíz (2 daily; 4hr); Keszthely (2 daily; 3hr 45min); Mohács (2 daily; 4hr); Nagyvázsony (2 daily except Sun; 3hr); Pécs (5 daily; 4hr); Siklós (1 daily; 5hr); Siófok (2 daily; 1hr 45min–2hr 15min); Sopron (2 daily; 3hr 45min); Sümeg (2 daily; 4hr 30min); Szekszárd (8 daily; 3hr 15min); Székesfehérvár (every 40–60min; 1hr 15min); Szombathely (2 daily; 4hr 15min); Veszprém (every 60–90min; 2hr 15min); Zalaegerszeg (1 daily; 4hr 45min); Zirc (4 daily; 2hr 30min).

Népstadion to Northern Hungary and the Great Plain: Aggtelek (1 daily; 5hr); Baja (every 1–2hr; 3hr 15min); Balassagyarmat (every 1–2hr; 2hr 30min);

Békéscsaba (3 daily; 4hr); Eger (every 90min; 3hr); Gyöngyös (hourly; 2hr); Kalocsa (every 1–2hr; 2hr); Kecskemét (15–20 daily; 1hr 45min); Kiskunfélegyháza (8–10 daily; 2hr); Lillafüred (1 daily; 3hr 30min); Mátraháza (4 daily; 2hr); Szeged (1 daily; 3hr 45min); Vác (hourly; 30min).

International trains

Bookings are required on all international routes, but it may not be possible to obtain them on trains leaving from Kőbánya-Kispest. This also applies to services from Zugló Station, which sometimes handles international traffic. The Vienna-bound *Wiener Waltzer* often runs late, so reserve sleepers on from Austria in Budapest. Also bring drinks, as the buffet staff overcharge shamelessly.

Déli Station to Vienna (1 daily; 3hr 30min); Zagreb (1 daily; 6hr).

Keleti Station to Athens (1 daily; 30hr); Arad (4 daily; 5hr 30min); Basel (1 daily; 14hr 30min); Belgrade (5 daily; 6hr); Berlin (2 daily; 14hr); Braşov (3 daily; 11hr); Bratislava (3 daily; 3hr); Bucharest (4 daily; 14hr); Cologne (2 daily; 14hr); Dresden (2 daily; 12hr); Frankfurt (2 daily; 11hr); Gdansk (2 daily; 16); Istanbul (1 daily; 29hr); Katowice (2 daily; 10hr); Kiev (2–3 daily; 25hr); Kraków (1 daily; 12hr); Leipzig (1 daily; 13hr); Moscow (1 daily; 42hr); Munich (3 daily; 9hr); Novi Sad (5 daily; 5hr); Nürnberg (2 daily; 9hr); Paris (1 daily; 18hr); Plovdiv (1 daily; 19hr); Poprad Tatry (1 daily; 6hr); Poznan (1 daily; 14hr 30min); Prague (3 daily; 8hr); Sibiu (2 daily; 10hr 45min); Sighişoara (2 daily; 10hr 30min); Skopje (1 daily; 16hr); Sofia (1 daily; 16hr); Szczecin (1 daily; 17hr 30min); Thessaloniki (1 daily; 21hr); Venice (2 daily; 13hr); Vienna (6 daily; 3hr 30min); Warsaw (2 daily; 12hr); Wroclaw (1 daily; 12hr); Zagreb (1 daily; 6hr).

Kőbánya-Kispest Station to Arad (June–Sept Thurs–Sat 1 daily; 6hr 15min); Bratislava (June–Sept 3 weekly; 3hr 45min); Burgas (June–Sept 1 daily; 28hr); Katowice (June–Sept 1 daily; 10hr); Prague (June–Sept 3 weekly; 10hr); Ruse (June–Sept 1–2 daily; 20hr); Timişoara (June–Sept 2 weekly; 9hr); Varna (June–Sept 2 weekly; 21hr); Warsaw (June–Sept daily; 17hr).

Nyugati Station to Baia Mare (1 daily; 9hr); Braşov (1 daily; 15hr); Bratislava (3 daily; 3hr);

Berlin (3 daily; 16hr 30min); Bucharest (2 daily; 18hr 30min); Burgas (June–Sept 1 daily; 27hr); Chop (1 daily; 7hr); Cluj (2 daily; 8hr); Dresden (1 daily; 12hr); Oradea (2 daily; 6hr); Prague (1 daily; 8hr); Satu Mare (1 daily; 7hr); Sighişoara (2 daily; 13hr); Sofia (1 daily; 26hr); Timişoara (1 daily; 7hr).

International buses

Tickets must be purchased at the bus station in hard currency, and should be booked 24 hours in advance.

Erzsébet tér to Amsterdam (June–Sept 1 daily; 20hr); Arad (1 daily; 7hr); Athens (June–Sept 2 daily; 28hr); Banská Bystrica (2 daily; 4hr); Berlin (1 daily; 16hr); Bratislava (3 daily; 3hr); Brussels (June–Sept 1 daily; 22hr); Cluj (2 daily; 9hr 30min); Dresden (1–2 daily; 13hr); Florence (June–Sept 1 daily; 21hr); Friedberg (1 daily; 5hr 30min); Galanta (1–2 daily; 4hr); Gdansk (June–Aug 1 daily; 21hr); Gheorgeni (1 daily; 16hr 30min); Graz (1 daily; 7hr); Hamburg (1 daily; 20hr); Helsinki (June–Aug 1 daily; 55hr); Istanbul (1 daily; 25hr); Komarnó (1–2 daily; 3hr 30min); Kraków (1 daily; 15hr); Levice (1 daily; 3hr); Lučenec (June–Oct 1 daily; 3hr); Miercurea Ciuc (2 daily; 15hr); Milan (1 daily; 17hr); Munich (2 daily; 9hr); Nitra (1 daily; 4hr); Nürnberg (3 daily; 13hr); Oradea (2 daily; 6hr); Paris (1 daily; 23hr); Prague (2 daily; 8hr); Propad-Tatry (1 daily; 5hr); Rome (June–Sept 1 daily; 22hr); Rožňava (1 daily; 4hr 30min); Sfîntu Gheorghe (1 daily; 16hr 30min); Sighişoara (1 daily; 13hr 30min); Stockholm (June–Aug 1 daily; 40hr); Stuttgart (1 daily; 11hr 30min); Subotica (1 daily; 5hr); Tatranská Lomnica (2 daily; 7hr 30min); Timişoara (1 daily; 8hr 30min); Tîrgu Mureş (2 daily; 11hr 45min); Velké Kapušany (1 daily; 7hr); Venice (April–Oct 2–3 daily; 14hr); Vienna (3–4 daily; 4hr); Warsaw (1 daily; 14hr); Zakopane (1 daily; 8hr).

Hydrofoils and Ferries

Belgrád rakpart international landing stage to Vienna (April–Oct 1–2 daily; 5hr).

Vigadó tér pier to Esztergom (1–2 daily; 5hr); Szentendre (May–Sept 1 daily; 90min); Vác (1 daily; 2hr 45min); Visegrád (1–2 daily; 3hr).

CHAPTER TWO

THE DANUBE BEND

To escape Budapest's humid summers, people flock north of the city to the **Danube Bend** (*Dunakanyar*), one of the grandest stretches of the river, outdone only by the Kazan Gorge in Romania. Entering the Carpathian Basin, the Danube widens dramatically, only to be forced by hills and mountains through a narrow, twisting valley, almost a U-turn – the "Bend" – before dividing for the length of Szentendrei Island and flowing into Budapest. The **historic towns and ruins** of Szentendre, Esztergom and Visegrád can be seen on a long day trip from Budapest to the west bank, but with the chance of **hiking** or **horseriding** in the neighbouring Pilis and Börzsöny highlands, it would be a shame not to linger.

The **Danube** is the second longest river in Europe after the Volga, flowing 2857km from the Black Forest to the Black Sea. Between the confluence of the Bereg and Briach streams at Donauschingen and its shifting Delta on the Black Sea, the Danube is fed by over 300 tributaries from a catchment area of 816,000 square kilometres, with ten nations along its banks. Known as the Donau in Germany and Austria, it becomes the Duna from the Czech Republic down through Slovakia, Slovenia, Croatia, Serbia, Bulgaria, Romania and Moldova, forming the frontier for much of the way.

Used by armies and tribes since antiquity, this "dustless highway" deeply impressed the German poet Hölderlein who saw it as an allegory for the mythical voyage of the ancient German forefathers to the Black Sea, and Hercules' journey from Greece to the land of the Hyperboreans. Attila Jószef described it as "cloudy, wise and great", its waters from many lands as intermingled as the peoples of the Carpathian Basin. While the Danube's strategic value ended after World War II, economic and environmental concerns became live issues

---

ACCOMMODATION PRICE CODES

All accommodation in this guide is graded according to the price bands given below. Note that all prices refer to the cheapest available double room in high season except where otherwise indicated. For more details, see p.26.

① Under 650Ft (under £4/$6/ DM10)

② 650–1500Ft (£4–8/$6–13/DM10– 20)

③ 1500–3000Ft (£8–17/$13–27/ DM20–40)

④ 3000–4500Ft (£17–25/$27–40/ DM40–60)

⑤ 4500–6500Ft (£25–36/$40–57/ DM60–85)

⑥ 6500–10,000Ft (£36–56/$57–88/ DM85–130)

⑦ Over 10,000Ft (over £56/$88/ DM130)

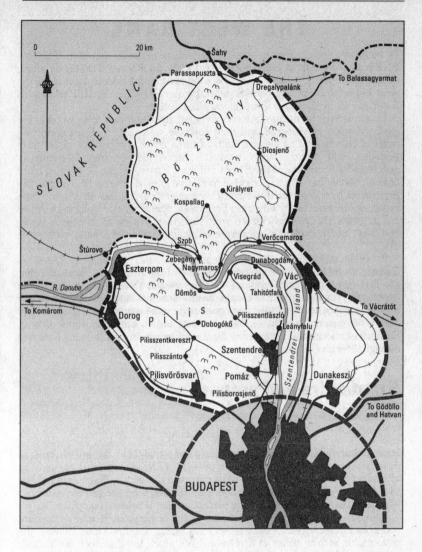

in the 1980s, when the governments of Hungary, Austria and the then Czechoslovakia agreed to dam the river between Gabčikovo and Nagymaros. The public opposition that compelled Hungary to abandon the project was a milestone along the road to democracy, mobilizing society in a way no overtly political cause could ever have done. The dam's ability to stir up trouble has survived the 1989 changes, as it has now become a source of deep friction between Hungary and Slovakia, which has pressed ahead and diverted the Danube on its own.

THE WEST BANK

By building a line of *castra* to keep the barbarians on the far side of the Danube, the Romans unwittingly staked out the sites of the future castles of Magyar kings, who had to repel the Mongols. These are the most tourist-ridden places along the **west bank** today, and Baroque **Szentendre** (around 40min by HÉV train from Batthyány tér in Budapest) is the logical place to start.

Buses on from Szentendre are very frequent, making it easy to move on to the medieval ruins of **Visegrád** and then continue westwards to **Esztergom**, the heart of Hungarian Catholicism. Both of these are also accessible direct from Budapest, with hourly buses from the Árpád híd terminus following an anticlockwise route around the Bend – although Esztergom can be reached more directly by the less scenic clockwise route that goes via Dorog (this is also the route taken by trains from the capital's Nyugati station). Various sites in the **Pilis range** can be reached by bus from Esztergom, Szentendre or Budapest's Árpád híd terminus, though services are pretty irregular. In view of its hairpin bends and heavy traffic, **cycling** is not permitted along the main west bank road (route 11).

Between mid-May and mid–September, it's also possible to travel to **Esztergom by boat**. There are two ferries daily from Budapest's Vigadó tér pier; the first (leaving at 8am) sails via Vác; the second (leaving at 2pm) sails via Szentendre, where you have to change boats – note that in winter only the former service is operational. Another ferry goes as far as **Visegrád**, leaving twice daily during the summer months (7.30am & 10am) and once daily in winter (10am). For further information, contact any *Ibusz* office or the *Mahart* shipping company by Vigadó tér pier.

Szentendre and around

Szentendre is the Montmartre of the Danube

Claudio Magris

Having cleared the bus and HÉV terminals and found their way into its Baroque heart, visitors are seldom disappointed by **SZENTENDRE**. Ignoring the outlying apartment buildings and the rash of boutiques in the centre, "Saint Andrew" is a friendly maze of houses painted in autumnal colours, secretive gardens and lanes winding up to hilltop churches – the perfect spot for an **artists' colony**.

Before the artists moved in at the turn of the century, Szentendre's character had been formed by waves of refugees from Serbia. The first influx followed the catastrophic Serbian defeat at Kosovo in 1389, which foreshadowed the Turkish occupation of Hungary in the sixteenth century, when Szentendre itself fell into ruin. In 1690, after the Turks had been expelled by the Habsburgs, eight hundred families of Serbians, Albanians, Bosnians and Greeks arrived here under Patriarch Crnojevič, who made Szentendre the seat of the exiled Serbian Orthodox Church. Prospering through trade, the immigrants replaced their wooden churches with stone ones, and built handsome town houses. Most returned to Serbia after the 1880s, however, and only about seventy families of Serbian descent still live here today.

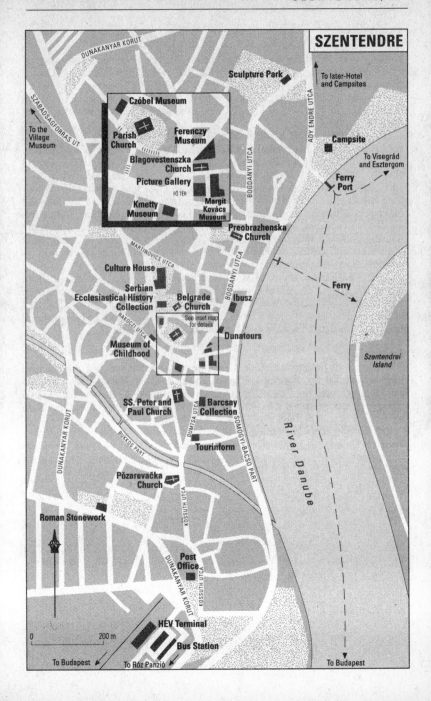

SZENTENDRE

DUNAKANYAR KORUT

Sculpture Park

To Ister-Hotel
and Campsites

ADY ENDRE UTCA

SZABADSAGFORRAS UT

To the
Village
Museum

Czóbel Museum

Parish
Church

Ferenczy
Museum

BOGDANYI UTCA

Campsite

To Visegrád
and Esztergom

Ferry
Port

Blagovestenszka
Church

Picture Gallery

FŐ TÉR

Kmetty
Museum

Margit
Kovács
Museum

Preobrazhenska
Church

MARTINOVICS UTCA

Culture House

Serbian
Ecclesiastical History
Collection

BOGDANYI UTCA

Belgrade
Church

Ibusz

Ferry

RAKOCZI UTCA

See inset map
for details

Dunatours

Museum of
Childhood

Szentendrei
Island

SS. Peter and
Paul Church

DUMTSA UTCA

Barcsay
Collection

SOMOGYI-BACSO PART

River Danube

Tourinform

DUNAKANYAR KORUT

BÜKKOS PART

Pozarevacka
Church

KOSSUTH UTCA

Roman Stonework

Post
Office

DUNAKANYAR KORUT

KOSSUTH UTCA

0   200 m

HÉV Terminal

Bus Station

To Budapest

To Róz Panzió

To Budapest

The Town

Walking from either the train or bus station into the town centre takes ten or fifteen minutes, unless you choose to detour off Kossuth utca to examine a hoard of **Roman stonework** at Dunakanyar körút 1 (May–Oct Tues–Sun 10am–6pm). The eroded lintels and sarcophagi belonged to *Ulcisia Castra*, a military town named after the Eravisci, an Illyrian-Celtic tribe subdued by the Romans during the first century.

Further north along Kossuth utca, just before the Bükkös stream, you'll encounter the first evidence of a Serbian presence – the **Požarevačka Church**. Typically, this was built in the late eighteenth century to replace an older wooden church, although its Byzantine-style iconostasis was inherited rather than specially commissioned. Beyond the stream, Dumtsa Jenő utca continues past the birthplace of Serbian novelist Jakov Ignjatovic (1822–49) and the adjacent **Marzipan Museum and Pastry Shop**. Opposite is the **Barcsay Collection** (April–Oct Tues–Sun 10am–4pm; Nov–March Fri–Sun 10am–4pm), a museum housing drawings and paintings by Jenő Barcsay, who was born in Transylvania but worked in Szentendre after 1928. The courtyard of the museum is used for concerts during the summer festival.

A little further on, the road is crossed by Péter-Pál utca, where a left turn brings you to the **Peter-Paul Church**, built in 1708. Its original furnishings were taken back to Serbia after World War I. From here, or from the last uphill stretch of Dumtsa Jenő utca, it's just a block to the main square, which in 1989 reverted to its traditional name after several decades of being "Marx tér".

Around Fő tér

Swarming with buskers and tourists during the summer months, Szentendre's main square, **Fő tér**, is a place either to savour or avoid. Horse-drawn carriages can be rented near the Plague Cross, which was erected by the merchants' guild after Szentendre escaped infection in 1763. From here diverging alleys lead to an assortment of galleries and museums around the square.

If your appetite for such things is limited, don't waste time on the **Szentendre Picture Gallery** of contemporary work by local artists (April–Oct Tues–Sun 10am–6pm; Nov–March Tues–Sun 9am–5pm), occupying three Baroque houses united under a single roof. As in the **workshop** (*Műhely*) opposite, the bulk of the exhibits are touristy dross (same hours). An alley beside the *Műhely* leads to the **Kmetty Museum** (April–Oct Tues–Sun 10am–6pm; Nov–March Tues–Sun 9am–5pm), containing sombre daubs by János Kmetty (1889–1955).

Far more appealing is the **Margit Kovács Museum** (daily 9am–5.30pm) at Vastagh György utca 1, behind the Szentendre Picture Gallery. This wonderful museum never fails to delight visitors with its graceful sculptures and reliefs, for the artist's themes are legends, dreams, love and motherhood. Given its universal appeal, it's a shame that her work isn't better known abroad. In Hungary, however, Kovács (1907–77) is duly honoured as the nation's greatest ceramicist. The museum is small and very popular, but the inevitable wait at the entrance is well worthwhile.

Almost as striking, but utterly different in spirit, are the icons within the Annunciation or **Blagoveštenska Church**. Painted by Mikhail Zivković of Buda early last century, they evoke all the richness and tragedy of Serbian history. The building itself is thought to have been designed by András Mayerhoffer in the

1750s. Look out for the tomb of a Greek merchant of Macedonian origin to the left of the entrance, and the Rococo windows and gate facing Görög utca (Greek Street). Next door, a portal carved with emblems of science and learning is the entrance to the former Serbian school, now the **Ferenczy Museum** (Tues–Sun 10am–4pm). Károly Ferenczy (1862–1917) pioneered Impressionism and *plein air* painting in Hungary, while his eldest son Valér (1885–1954) swung towards Expressionism. The younger twins Nóemi (1890–1957) and Béni (1890–67) branched out into textiles and bronzeware, with diminishing returns.

Several of the houses on the square (nos. 8, 17, 19 and 22) are old Baroque trading houses with their dates and trades written above the gates. The former Pálffy House (no. 17) bears the sign of the merchants' guild, combining the patriarchal cross of Orthodoxy with an anchor and a number four to symbolize Danube trade and the percentage of profit deemed appropriate. At Rákóczi utca 1, 50m further up, is the **Folk Art Museum** (Tues–Sun 10am–4pm) housed in the old bellhouse of the Catholic church, from where covered wooden stairs lead up the hill behind.

Templom tér and beyond

From Fő tér or Rákóczi utca you can ascend an alley of steps to gain a lovely view of Szentendre's rooftops and gardens from **Templom tér**, where **crafts fairs** are frequently held to help finance the restoration of the Catholic **parish church**. Of medieval origin, with Romanesque and Gothic features, it was rebuilt in the Baroque style after falling derelict in Turkish times; the frescoes in its sanctuary were collectively painted by the artists' colony. Across the square, the **Czóbel Museum** (Tues–Sun 10am–5pm) exhibits paintings by Béla Czóbel (1883–1976) and his wife Mária Modok (1896–1971), whose fierce brush strokes challenged the Neoclassicism of the Horthy era.

Beyond Templom tér, the burgundy spire of the Orthodox episcopal cathedral or **Belgrade Church** (1756–64) pokes above a walled garden dark with trees. Its sexton (who lives in a nearby house marked *plebánia csengője*) is reluctant to open its doors to tourists, but the finest of the icons and *objets d'art* are displayed in the adjacent **Serbian Ecclesiastical History Collection** (Wed–Sun 10am–5.30pm). The museum's entrance is at no. 5 Patriarka utca.

From the Belgrade Church you can follow a lane down to Bogdányi utca, where another painterly couple are commemorated by the **Imre Ámos–Margit Anna Collection** at no. 12 (April–Oct Tues–Sun 10am–5pm; Nov–March Tues–Sun 9am–5pm). Just next door is the **Bor Múzeum** (Wine Museum), which claims to be the only wine museum in the country that covers every region. Further along, Bogdányi utca opens on to a square flanked by the **Lazar Cross** honouring King Lazar of Serbia, whom the Turks beheaded in revenge for the death of Sultan Murad at Kosovo.

The **Preobraženska Church**, 400m on, was erected by the tanners' guild in 1741–76, and its *embonpoint* enhanced by a Louis XVI gate the following century. Though its lavish iconostasis merits a look, the church is chiefly notable for its role in the Serbian festival on August 19, when it hosts the Blessing of the Grapes ceremony (recalling Szentendre's former role as a wine-producing centre). This is followed by a traditional procession round the church and further celebrations in the town square and elsewhere. At the end of Bogdányi utca, the **Vinegrowers' Cross** was raised by another local guild and is fittingly wreathed in grapevines.

Across the road at no. 49 is the **Szentendre Artists' Colony** itself, which has temporary exhibitions by current and past members in its gallery (mid-March–late October). Having come this far, you might as well check out the hulking creations of Jenő Kerényi (1908–75) in the **sculpture park** at Ady utca 5 (April–Oct Tues–Sun 10am–6pm; Nov–March Tues–Sun 9am–5pm).

Szentendre Village Museum

The **Szentendre Village Museum** (April–Oct Tues–Sun 9am–5pm), 4km out of town, is by a long way the most enjoyable local attraction – so visit it before your energy flags. It is Hungary's largest open-air museum of rural architecture (termed a *Skanzen*, after the first such museum, founded in a Stockholm suburb in 1891), and will eventually include "samples" from ten different regions of the country. The museum lies along Szabadságforrás út, west of town, and is accessible by bus from stand 8 of the bus terminal near the HÉV station. Get off when you see the spires in a field to the right.

Downhill from the entrance is a composite village from **Szabolcs-Szatmár** county, culled from isolated settlements in the Erdőhát region (see *The Great Plain*). The brochure on sale at the entrance points out the finer distinctions between the various humble peasant dwellings scattered among the barns and woven pigsties – like the house from Kispalad and the cottage from Uszka, formerly occupied by squires. Rural carpenters produced highly skilled work, examples of which are the circular "dry mill", the wooden belltower from Nemesborzova, and the carving inside the church from Mand (on a hilltop).

The second village "unit" seems far more regimented, originating from the ethnic **German** communities of the *Kisalföld* (Little Plain) in Transdanubia. Neatly aligned and whitewashed, the houses are filled with knick-knacks and embroidered samplers bearing homilies like "When the Hausfrau is capable, the clocks keep good time". Beyond lies the Western Transdanubia unit.

Demonstrations of traditional crafts such as weaving, pottery and basket-making take place at the museum on the first and third Sunday of each month. Local festivals are also celebrated; for instance the grape harvest is celebrated in October with folkloric programmes and grape-pressing (☎312-304 for details, or enquire at the *Tourinform* office in town). A stand outside the museum's entrance sells good pancakes. From here walk 100m up the main road and you'll find the stop for buses back into town.

Practicalities

Szentendre's **bus and train (HÉV) stations** are next door to one another, ten to fifteen minutes' walk from the town centre. The best place to go for **tourist information** is *Tourinform* on Dumsta Jenő utca 22 (Mon–Fri 9am–5pm & Sat–Sun 10am–4pm; ☎317-965) – the staff are friendly and speak English. *Dunatours* at Bogdányi utca 1 (Mon–Fri 9am–4pm; ☎311-311) and *Ibusz* at no. 15 are similar setups. Szentendre's main **post office** is at Rákóczi út 4, with another branch at Kossuth 23–25, which you pass walking in from the HÉV terminal. The **police station** can be found at Martinovics utca 11.

The Szentendre telephone code is ☎ 26

Accommodation

All three tourist offices can arrange **private rooms** (②), or alternatively look out for *Zimmer frei* signs advertising vacant rooms. Some could well be located in outlying suburbs such as Tyukos-Dűlő or Leányfalu, off route 11. Aside from the options listed below, there are two **campsites** north of the centre. *Aquatours Camping* (May–Sept; ☎311-106) at Ady utca 9–11 is 200m past the sculpture park. On Pap-Sziget ("Priest's Island"), opposite the *Hotel Ister*, the larger, noisier *Pap-Sziget* site (May–Sept; ☎310-697) has two- to four-person bungalows (②–③), a motel (②) and restaurant. The camping fee includes use of the swimming pool on the island.

HOTELS AND PENSIONS

Aradi Panzió, Aradi utca 4 (☎314-274). Convenient location near the HÉV station. ③.

Bükkös Panzió, Bükköspart 16 (☎312-021). Nice location by a small canal 200m west of the Požarevačka Church and a 5-minute walk from the town centre. ④.

Coca Cola Panzió, Dunakanyar körút 50 (☎310-410). Further out and less attractively sited, but run by a friendly and helpful proprietor. ④.

Ilona Panzió, Rakocsi F. utca 11 (☎313-599). Pleasant location in the centre of town. ③.

Panzió No. 100, Ady Endre utca 100 (☎312-881). Situated to the north of the town centre. ④.

Piroska Panzió, A'chim A. utca 2 (☎312-425). Seven-room pension 10 minutes' walk from the town centre, just off Dunakanyar körút. ④.

Róz Panzió, Pannónia út 6B (☎311-737). Small pension to the south of the bus station. ④.

Eating and drinking

Like everything in Szentendre, **restaurants** are pricey by Hungarian standards, and crowded during the summer. Tour groups tend to make for the ones on Fő tér, but just yards further up the hill is the small *Aranysarkany* ("Golden Dragon") at Alkotmány utca 1A, which serves excellent Hungarian food – nothing Chinese despite its name. Down by the river is the *Görög Kancsó Vendéglő* ("Greek Jug") at Görög utca 1 – again, nothing Greek about it except its name. More expensive but stylish is the *Rab Ráby Vendéglő* at Péter-Pál utca 1A (daily noon–midnight). Near the boat pier at Ady Endre utca 3 (15min north of the town centre) is *La Paella*, a boat restaurant serving Spanish-style food. The *Surányi Cukrászda* at Görög utca 4 (closed Mon & Tues) sells the best ice cream in town, and an excellent *somlói galuska* (walnut and raisin sponge covered with thick chocolate sauce and whipped cream). If you fancy a tasty snack, look out for a yellow sign in the main square pointing up a small alleyway for "*lángos*" (deep-fried batter topped with cheese or sour cream). The *Szigetgyöngye Étterem* on Pap-Sziget is recommended for campers.

Entertainment and nightlife

All three tourist offices will furnish you with information on the diverse events of the *Szentendrei Nyár* **summer festival** (late June to late Aug), which culminates in a pop concert and fireworks on August 20. On the preceding day, a **Serbian festival** with *kolo* dancing takes place at the Preobraženska Church. **Discos** are the main form of nightlife the rest of the year – most venues are transitory (look for flyposters in the centre), but there's usually something going on at the *Szigetgyöngye Étterem* (8pm–2am).

Moving on

Szentendre has two docks for **Danube ferries**: one for boats across to Szentendrei Island; the other – 500m further north – for services between

Budapest and Esztergom. However, it's quicker to travel north using the hourly **buses** to Visegrád and Esztergom, or the more frequent local services (*Helyvonat*) to Leányfalu and Dunabogdány. Nothwithstanding the construction of a highland road via Pilisszentlászló – intended to relieve congestion between Szentendre and Visegrád – most buses stick to the embankment route.

Szentendrei Island, Leányfalu and Dunabogdány

Szentendre's northern suburbs merge into **LEÁNYFALU**, a leafy resort first popularized in the late nineteenth century by writers like Zsigmond Móricz. There are numerous **rooms** and villas to rent here, as well as a *strand* where you can swim or luxuriate in the thermal pool (May–Sept 6am–6pm; 120Ft for a day's admission). Right next to the pool is the *Hableány* restaurant, with good fish soup and alfresco dining in the summer; it's cheaper and more charming than the touristy *Huszárcsarda* nearby. Another moderately priced eating place is the *Hársfa Vendéglő*, on the main road next to the post office. Also signposted along the main road are the *Duna Panzió* (☎26/323-161; ③) and the *Dunakanyar* **campsite** (mid-April–mid-Oct; ☎26/323-154), which has chalets (②) and tennis courts.

Between Budapest and Visegrád the Danube splits in two by **Szentendrei Island**, an attenuated slab of mud and vegetation, whose villages are linked to the east or west bank by small ferries. From the wharf between Szentendre and Leányfalu you can cross over to **Szigetmonostor**, where the *Horány Gyöngye Panzió* (☎26/323-544; ③) supervises a **campsite** (mid-April–mid-Oct) that caters to nudists from June to August. Tahitófalu, 4km further north, has one foot on the island (where architect Mihály Pollack once resided) and the other on the west bank (where there are two campsites and numerous rooms for rent), connected by a bridge. From Tahitófalu a road runs to the eastern side of the island, where you can catch a boat across to Vác (see p.139). There is a **golf course** at **Kisoroszi** at the northern end of the island, accessible by ferry from Verőcemaros on the east bank (see p.142), as well as campsites offering great views of Visegrád.

Sticking to the west bank, the land starts to rise and orchards and vineyards flourish around **DUNABOGDÁNY**, a picturesque village where many Budapesters have weekend cottages. Its Germanic traditions are commemorated by a **Local History Collection** at Kossuth utca 93 (Mon–Fri 9am–noon & Sat 2–4pm), and help attract many German tourists to the village **campsite** (May–Sept). A few kilometres further on, the Danube Bend and Visegrád heave into sight.

Visegrád and around

When the hillsides start to plunge and the river twists, keep your eyes fixed on the mountains to the west for a first glimpse of the citadel and ramparts of **VISEGRÁD**. The city is still almost as it appeared to János Thuroczy in 1488, who described its "upper walls stretching to the clouds floating in the sky, and the lower bastions reaching down as far as the river". At that time, courtly life in Visegrád – the royal seat – was nearing its apogee, and the palace of King Mátyás and Queen Beatrice was famed throughout Europe. The papal legate Cardinal Castelli described it as a *"paradiso terrestri"*, seemingly unperturbed by the presence of Vlad the Impaler, who resided here under duress between 1462 and 1475.

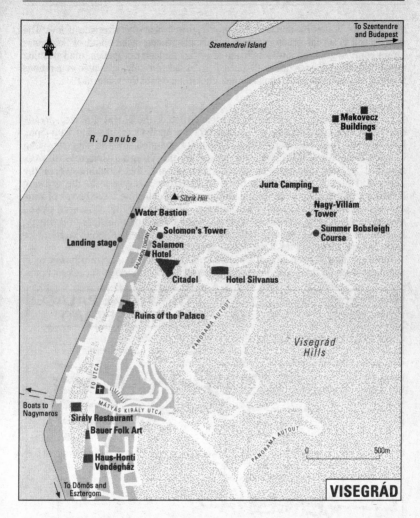

Today, visitors come to the village to admire the ruins of the palace and the gorgeous view from the surrounding Visegrád Hills, an unexpected but appropriate setting for several works by the visionary architect Imre Makovecz (see below). While the ruins can be seen on a flying visit, the hills require a full day and a fair amount of walking, with the option of longer hikes or pony-trekking.

The Ruins of Visegrád

The layout of the **ruins of Visegrád** (whose Slavic name means "High Castle") dates back to the thirteenth century, when Béla IV began fortifying the north against a recurrence of the Mongol invasion. Its most prominent features are the citadel on the hill, and the Water Bastion and Solomon's Tower near the riverside below. The palace itself is inconspicuously sited, further inland and 500m south of Solomon's Tower. As Visegrád fell into dereliction after the Turkish occupation, mud washing down from the hillsides gradually buried the palace entirely, and later generations doubted its existence until János Schulek unearthed one of the vaults in 1934.

The palace

Now largely excavated and partially reconstructed, the **Royal Palace** spreads over four levels or terraces at Fő utca 27–29 (April–Oct Tues–Sun 9am–5pm; Nov–March Tues–Sun 8am–4pm). Originally founded by the Angevin king Charles Robert in 1323, it was the setting for the Visegrád Congress of 1335, attended by the monarchs of Central Europe and the Grandmaster of the Teutonic Knights. Though they failed to agree on a response to the growing Habsburg threat, they nevertheless did manage to consume 10,000 litres of wine and vast amounts of victuals in the process. In February 1991, Visegrád played host to another less extravagant summit, when the prime ministers of Hungary, Poland and the then Czechoslovakia met here to put together a joint strategy for trade and EC membership in the post-Communist era.

Although nothing remains of Charles Robert's palace, the **cour d'honneur** is still to be seen on the second terrace. Constructed for Charles's successor Louis,

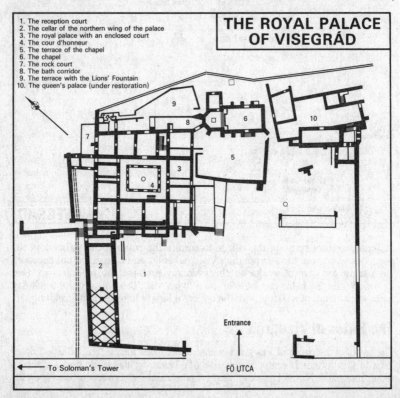

1. The reception court
2. The cellar of the northern wing of the palace
3. The royal palace with an enclosed court
4. The cour d'honneur
5. The terrace of the chapel
6. The chapel
7. The rock court
8. The bath corridor
9. The terrace with the Lions' Fountain
10. The queen's palace (under restoration)

THE ROYAL PALACE OF VISEGRÁD

Entrance

To Soloman's Tower

FŐ UTCA

it provided the basis for subsequent building by Sigismund and, later, Mátyás Corvinu. Its chief features are the pillastered **Renaissance loggia** and two panels from the **Hercules Fountain**. The upper storey, which was made of heavily carved and gilded wood, disappeared long ago.

Legend has it that Mátyás was eventually poisened by his wife Beatrice, who desired to rule alone. The chalice containing the fatal potion may well have passed between the **royal suites** that once stood beneath an overhang on the third terrace, separated by a magnificent **chapel**. Reportedly, the finest sight was the garden above the bath corridor, embellished by the **Lion Fountain**. A perfect copy of the original (carved by Ernő Szakál) bears Mátyás's raven crest and dozens of sleepy-looking lions although, unlike the original, it's not fed by the gutters and pipes that channelled water down from the citadel. Visegrád fell into disuse after the Turkish invasion in the sixteenth century, and excavation work didn't get underway until 1935.

In July each year the ruins provide the setting for **medieval pageants** and/or films intended to recreate the splendour of Visegrád's Renaissance heyday.

The Water Bastion and Solomon's Tower

North along Fő utca past the Mátyás statue, you can follow the embankment highway to the decrepit **Water Bastion** near the ferry landing stage. Alternatively, head up Salamon torony utca to reach **Solomon's Tower**, a mighty hexagonal keep buttressed by concrete slabs. The **Mátyás Museum** (May–early Nov Tues–Sun 9am–5pm) inside the tower exhibits finds from the palace, including the white Anjou Fountain of the Angevins and the red marble "Visegrád Madonna" carved by Tomaso Fiamberti – the probable sculptor of the Lion and Hercules fountains.

Rather than walking on to the **ruined Roman fort** atop Sibrik Hill, save your energy for the climb to Visegrád's citadel.

The Citadel

Dramatically sited on a crag, Visegrád's triangular **Citadel** (Oct–April weekends only) served as a repository for the Hungarian crown jewels until they were stolen by a treacherous maid of honour in the sixteenth century. Though only partly restored, the citadel is still mightily impressive, commanding a superb view of Nagymaros and the Börzsöny Mountains on the east bank. Within the citadel is the Museum of Hunting, depicting the lives of local hunters and fishermen during the Middle Ages.

You can reach the citadel via the "Calvary" footpath (signposted *Fellegvár)* starting on Salamon torony utca and heading towards Solomon's Tower (40min). Stairs next to the Vár Étterem across from the landing stage (*Hajóállomás)* lead up to Salamon torony utca. Alternatively, catch a bus (June–Aug only) from the Mátyás statue, which follows the scenic Panorama autóút into the hills.

The Visegrád Hills

Thickly wooded and crisscrossed with paths, the **Visegrád Hills** are a popular rambling spot. From the car park near the citadel, you can follow the autóút and then a signposted path to the **Nagy-Villám observation tower**, or *Kilátó* as it's called in Hungarian (March–Oct daily 9am–7pm; winter Sat–Sun when there's no snow). Sited at the highest point on the Danube Bend, it offers a view that stretches as far as Slovakia. The *Nagy-Villám Vendéglő* on the way up offers a pricey meal with fine views. By the *Kilátó* is the **Summer Bobsleigh Course** (*Nyári Bob*), where for 100Ft you can race down a one-kilometre run (April–Oct, except on rainy days when the brakes are rendered ineffective; ☎397-397). If you feel like **hiking**, there's a twelve-kilometre trail marked with blue stripes running from the tower, via Paprét (Priest's Meadow), to Pilisszentlászló, which takes two to three hours. **Horse riding** can be arranged through the *Dunatours* office in Visegrád (see below).

Imre Makovecz at Visegrád

A kilometre north of the observation tower lies Mogyoró-hegy (Hazelnut Hill) and its amazing wooden **buildings by Imre Makovecz**. As a promising architect in the Kádár years, Makovecz was branded a troublemaker for his outspoken nationalism, banned from teaching, and "exiled" to the Visegrád forestry department in 1977. Over the next decade he refined his ideas, acquiring a following of students for whom he held summer schools. Employing cheap, low-technology methods in a specifically Magyar way, he taught his students how to construct temporary buildings using raw materials such as branches and twigs.

Now one of the most influential architects in Hungary, Makovecz holds classes on trains as he shuttles from one building site to another, in provincial towns and villages. What you see here is mainly the result of Makovecz's forestry department commissions, along with a few of the smaller structures that are designed to decay. The shingled Community Centre is the focal point, a cluster of helmet-shaped domes around a central plumed dome with elaborate arched entrances, the whole appearing to rise organically out of the earth. Other notable examples of work by the architect's *Mákona* company include the community centres in Sárospatak, Zalaszentlászló and Szigetvár, and the oesophagus-like crypt of the Farkasréti cemetery in Budapest. Makovecz also designed the much admired Hungarian Pavilion at the 1992 Expo in Seville. However, his passionately felt nationalism, once a righteous tool against the old regime, now seems somewhat passé as he continues to advocate a return to the "real" Hungarian style of building.

> The Visegrád telephone code is ☎ 26

Practicalities

Visegrád has no bus or train station – just a few bus stops. *Bauer Folk Art* at Fő utca 46 (summer daily 9am–6pm) provides tourist **information** and can also help with accommodation. If it's closed, try *Visegrád Tours* in the *Sirály* restaurant down by the landing stage (☎398-160) or the *Haus-Honti Vendégház* just down the road at Fő utca 66 (☎398-120).

Accommodation

The nearest place to pitch a tent is at *Visegrád Camping* (May–Sept), which is well placed by the Danube about 2km from the town centre along the main road to Esztergom. Not so easy to reach, but with a nice view once you're there, is the well-equipped *Jurta Camping* (May–Sept; ☎398-227) near Mogyoró-hegy. The latter also rents chalets (②–③).

Walking along Fő utca you'll see plenty of *Zimmer frei* signs advertising vacant rooms. Otherwise try one of the establishments listed below.

ELTE Guest House, Fő utca 117 (☎398-165). Moderately priced but a bit run down. ②.

Haus-Honti Vendégház, Fő utca 66 (☎398-120). Clean, quiet with a charming atmosphere. Can also arrange private rooms elsewhere. ③.

Hotel Magiszter, Salamon torony utca 3 (☎398-321). Just up the stairs from the landing stage, a cheap and pleasant option. ② doubles; ① dormitory beds.

Hotel Silvanus, Fekete-hegy (☎398-311). Luxury hotel up in the hills with tennis courts, bowling green and sauna. ⑤.

Salamon Hotel, Salamon torony utca 1 (☎398-278). Recently restored and with a good view but not much in the way of charm. ③.

Eating and drinking

Fried-fish and sausage stalls along the promenade are augmented by several **restaurants**. The *Sirály* at Rév utca 7 is touristy and quite pricey but the best available option. If you're on a lower budget you might try the *Gulás Csarda* in Rév utca (just across from the temple), which serves good Hungarian food at reasonable prices. Another inexpensive restaurant on the same road is the *Fekete Holló*. The *Skandinávia* at Fő utca 48 offers Swedish and Hungarian specialities, but it's not cheap.

Entertainment

In summer there are **discos** at the *Sirály*, and sporadic disco **cruises** between Visegrád and Esztergom (which leave from the main landing stage as advertised). Although Visegrád itself has nowhere to swim, there is a salubrious terraced *strand* and natural warm-water **pool** 4km away at Lepence (May–Sept 9am–6pm; ☎398-208), at the Pilisszentlászló turn-off towards Dömös (see below).

Moving on

Buses and thrice-daily **ferries** travel from Visegrád (from the main landing stage) to Esztergom, and there's a small car ferry that sails to Nagymaros every forty minutes from the jetty near Rév utca.

Dömös and Pilismarót

Seven kilometres round the Bend, **DÖMÖS** is a verdant straggle of overgrown houses and holiday homes. If you have a tent, look out for a sign on the main road to *Dömös Camping* (not to be confused with the large "CAMP" sign just before it), a nice campsite by the river with a beautiful view of the Börzsöny Hills (May–mid-Sept). Less conspicuous signposts indicate the start of **trails into the Pilis range**, abounding in raspberries during early summer. Follow the Malom tributary 2.5km upstream and you'll reach a path that forks right for the Rám precipice (3hr) and Dobogókő (4–5hr), and left for the Vadallo Rocks (3hr) beneath the towering "Pulpit Seat" – a 641-metre crag that only the experienced should attempt to climb.

PILISMARÓT, 4km on, has two **ferry crossings** for the east bank. Ferries run to Zebegény from the village itself, and to Szob from another landing stage at Basaharc, 2km beyond Pilismarót.

Esztergom

Beautifully situated in a crook of the Danube facing Slovakia, **ESZTERGOM** is dominated by its basilica, whose dome is visible for miles around. The sight is richly symbolic, since it was here that the locally born St Stephen, king of Hungary, converted his subjects to Catholicism in 1000 AD – the city has remained a centre for Catholicism ever since. It also served as the royal seat from the tenth to the thirteenth century, when the Mongol invasion forced the royal court to move to Buda. The capture of the town by the Turks in the sixteenth century curtailed the Church's influence until the nineteenth century, when a

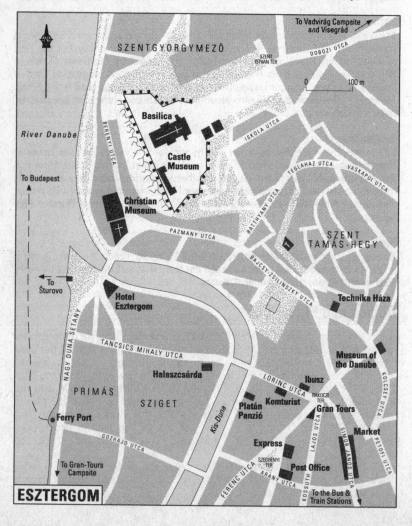

To Vadvirág Campsite
and Visegrád

SZENTGYÖRGYMEZŐ

SZENT
ISTVÁN TÉR

DOBOZI UTCA

0   100 m

Basilica

River Danube

BERÉNYI UTCA

ISKOLA UTCA

**Castle
Museum**

TÉGLAHÁZ UTCA

VASKAPUI UTCA

To Budapest

**Christian
Museum**

PÁZMÁNY UTCA

BATTHYÁNY UTCA

SZENT
TAMÁS-HEGY

BAJCSY-ZSILINSZKY UTCA

To
Šturovo

**Hotel
Esztergom**

Technika Háza

NAGY DUNA SÉTÁNY

TÁNCSICS MIHÁLY UTCA

**Museum of
the Danube**

Halászcsárda

LŐRINC UTCA

Ibusz

KÖLCSEY UTCA

PRIMÁS

SZIGET

Kis-Duna

**Platán
Panzió**

Komturist

RÁKÓCZI
TÉR

Gran Tours

LAJOS UTCA

SIMOR JÁNOS UTCA

PETŐFI UTCA

Market

• **Ferry Port**

GŐZHAJÓ UTCA

Express

SZÉCHENYI
TÉR

Post Office

To Gran-Tours
Campsite

FERENC UTCA

ARANY UTCA

KOSSUTH UTCA

To the Bus &
Train Stations

ESZTERGOM

concerted campaign was started by the Catholic Church to restore Esztergom as its centre. As a pillar of the *ancien régime*, the Church was ruthlessly attacked during the Rákosi era, when hundreds of priests were tortured and jailed. It is claimed that Esztergom's basilica was well maintained because Khruschev's wife was particularly fond of it. However in its change of approach the regime settled for a *modus vivendi* from the Sixties onwards, hoping to enlist the Church's help with social problems and to harness the patriotic spirit of the faithful. The avowedly Christian government elected in 1990 did its best to restore prestige and property to the Church, while the return of the reform communists in 1994 has sparked off new worries about anti-Church policies. One change in the local landscape has been the arrival of the Suzuki car plant which you pass as you enter town by train.

The Town

Esztergom's craggy **Basilica Hill** is the natural focus of attention. It was here that Prince Géza established the royal seat. Subsequently it was chosen as the site of Hungary's first cathedral by his son Stephen. His coronation by a papal envoy on Christmas Day 1000 AD signified the country's recognition by Christendom. In 1991, the hill was the setting for two events symbolizing the Church's triumph over Communism: the reburial of the exiled Cardinal Mindszenty and the first papal visit to Hungary.

The Basilica

Esztergom's **Basilica** (March–Sept daily 7am–6pm; Oct–Feb Tues–Sun 7am–5pm) is the largest in Hungary, measuring 118m in length and 40m in width, capped by a dome 100m high. Built on the site of the medieval basilica ruined by the Turks, it was begun by Pál Kühneland and János Packh in 1822, and finally completed by József Hild in 1869. It was consecrated thirteen year earlier in 1856 (as soon as the dome was in place), and Liszt's *Gran Mass* was composed for the occasion – *Gran* being the German name for Esztergom.

As befits what is claimed to be the fifth largest church in the world, its nave is on a massive scale, clad in marble, gilding and mosaics. To the left of the entrance is the lavish red marble **Bakócz Chapel**. Its Florentine altar was salvaged by Archbishop Tamás Bakócz from the original basilica for which it was commissioned. It was this prelate whose papal ambitions were dashed when "his" crusade turned into the great peasants' revolt of 1514. The basilica's main altarpiece was painted by the Venetian Michelangelo Grigoletti, based on Titian's *Assumption* in the Frari Church in Venice.

Don't miss the **crypt**, which resembles a set from a Dracula film with giant stone women flanking the stairway down to gloomy vaults full of entombed prelates. Though several other mausolea look more arresting, it is the **tomb of Cardinal Mindszenty** that transfixes Hungarians (see box below). The walls of the crypt are 17m thick, to support the weight of the basilica.

Having seen the overpowering collection of bejewelled crooks and chalices and kitsch papal souvenirs in the **treasury** (May–Oct daily 9am–5pm; Nov–Dec & Feb–April daily 10am–4pm; closed Jan), it is almost a relief to climb the seemingly endless stairway to the **belltower** (May–Oct daily 9am–5pm). The stifling heat inside the cupola and the pigeon droppings within the bellroom are forgotten the moment you step outside and see the magnificent view of Esztergom,

THE RETURN OF CARDINAL MINDSZENTY

When the much-travelled body of **Cardinal József Mindszenty** was finally laid to rest with state honours in May 1991, it was a vindication of his uncompromising heroism – and the Vatican *realpolitik* that Mindszenty despised.

As a conservative and monarchist, he had stubbornly opposed the Communist takeover, warning that "cruel hands are reaching out to seize hold of our children, claws belonging to people who have nothing but evil to teach them". Arrested in 1948, tortured for 39 days and nights, and sentenced to life imprisonment for "treason", Mindszenty was freed during the Uprising and took refuge in the US Embassy in Budapest. He remained there for fifteen years, appalled by the miniskirts and pop music that he witnessed from a window overlooking Szabadság tér.

When the Vatican struck a deal with the Kádár regime in 1971, Mindszenty had to be pushed into resigning his position and going into exile, where he died in 1975. Although his will stated that his body should not return home until "the red star of Moscow had fallen from Hungarian skies", his reburial occurred some weeks before the last Soviet soldier left, in preparation for the pope's visit in August. Nowadays the Vatican proclaims his greatness, without any hint of apology for its past actions.

with Slovak Štúrovo across the water. Tickets for the treasury (*kincstar*) and belltower (*harangtorony*) are sold at the entrance to the crypt.

Palace ruins: the Castle Museum

South of the basilica are the ruins of the palace founded by Géza, now known as the **Castle Museum** (April–Oct Tues–Sun 9am–5pm; Nov–March Tues–Sun 10am–4pm). In its former life the royal palace entertained Louis VII and Frederick Barbarossa on their way to the Crusades and, after Buda became the capital in 1249, the widowed Queen Beatrice and sundry archbishops lived here. According to the chronicler Djelalzade, the Turks "knocked down idols in the churches and destroyed the symbols of infidelity and error" when they sacked Esztergom in 1543, but left intact the wheel and "narrow copper tube" which piped water up to the castle from the Danube.

Excavations in the 1930s uncovered a twelfth-century **chapel** with a beautiful rose window and Byzantine-style frescoes. You can also visit Beatrice's suite, and the study of Archbishop Vítez – known as the **Hall of Virtues** after its allegorical murals depicting Intelligence, Moderation, Strength and Justice. During June and July, **plays and dances** are staged at the open-air theatre nearby (look out for advertisements).

Coming back down the hill, look out for the monumental **Dark Gate** beneath it. Constructed to facilitate access between church buildings on either side of the hill, this tunnel was later exploited by the Red Army, who maintained a base below "Peace Square" until 1989.

Watertown and Prímás-Sziget

Below the hill, the sound of choirs seems to float through the Baroque streets of the **Watertown** district (*Viziváros*). Turning into Pázmány utca, you pass the **Cathedral Library** at no. 21, and the **Bálint Balassi Museum** at no. 63. The latter, a small art gallery, is named after the poet Bálint Balassi (1554–94), who perished in the battle to recapture Esztergom from the Turks – a campaign in which the Italian composer Monteverdi also fought.

Further west stands the Italianate Baroque **Watertown Parish Church**, fronted by an equestrian statue of King Stephen. A few doors along, the old Primate's Palace at Berényi utca 2 makes a worthy setting for the **Christian Museum** (Tues–Sun 10am–5.30pm), Hungary's richest hoard of religious art. This includes the largest collection of Italian prints outside Italy; Renaissance paintings and wood carvings by German and Austrian masters; and the *Lord's Coffin of Garamszentbenedek*, a wheeled and gilded structure originally used in Easter Week processions.

From the parish church cross Archbishop Mindszenty Square and the Kossuth Bridge onto **Prímás-Sziget** (Primate's Island). A popular tourist spot with two campsites and an outdoor *Halászcsárda* (fish restaurant), it faces the Slovak city of Štúrovo across the river. The towns were linked by a wrought-iron **bridge** until it was blown up in World War II. Its elegant stump – decorated with a freshly painted Hungarian coat of arms – rises between the ferry landing stages. Having admired the scene, head east along Táncsics utca and over the Bottyán Bridge into the lower town.

Szent Tamás-hegy and the lower town

Should you come directly from Watertown instead, it's worth a detour up to **Szent Tamás-hegy** (St Thomas's Hill), if only for the view. The hill is named after the English martyr Thomas à Becket. A chapel was built here in his honour by Margaret Capet, whose father-in-law, Henry II of England, prompted the assassination of Thomas by raging "Who will rid me of this turbulent priest?" In the way of medieval royalty, Margaret later married Béla III of Hungary, but her conscience would not let her forget the saint. The existing chapel was built after the Turkish occupation.

Walking down Bajcsy-Zsilinszky utca, you might consider another detour to Esztergom's former synagogue, a flamboyant, Moorish-style edifice on Imház utca that now serves as a science club or **Technika Háza**. From here you can cut across Vörösmarty utca to the **Museum of the Danube** (March–Oct Tues–Sun 10am–5.30pm) at Kölcsey utca 2, containing exhibits on the history and ecology of this great river. Unfortunately there is little information in English, but the photos and models are interesting. Among the latter is a replica of the *Vidra*, the first steam dredger in Hungary, introduced from England by Count Széchenyi.

Otherwise, carry on to Rákóczi tér and the older **lower town** beyond. By following the pavement cafés, you should emerge on to **Széchenyi tér** – a pleasant square culminating in a town hall with Rococo windows. A couple of blocks further south stands the eighteenth-century **City Parish Church**, built on the site of a medieval monastery where Béla IV and Queen Mária were buried. The marble plaque to the right of the gate shows the level of the flood of 1832. More exciting and only slightly further from the square is the outdoor **market** halfway along Simor János utca.

The Esztergom telephone code is ☎ 33

Practicalities

Arriving by bus from Visegrád, alight near the Basilica Hill or down in the centre, rather than staying on to the bus terminal on Simor utca in the south of town. Should you arrive at the train station, 1km farther south, buses #1 and #5 run into the centre. Ferries from Budapest tie up alongside the island to the west of the lower town, fifteen minutes' walk from the centre.

All the **tourist offices** are near Rákóczi or Széchenyi tér. While *Komtourist* at Lőrinc utca 6 (☎312-082) is useless, *Ibusz* on the corner of Rákóczi tér wins first prize for being the least friendly. The staff are helpful and speak English at *Gran Tours* at Széchenyi tér 25 (May–Sept Mon–Fri 8am–4pm & Sat 8am–noon; Oct–April Mon–Fri 8am–4pm; ☎313-756); you can also change money and book rooms here, or at the *Express* office at Széchenyi tér 7 (Mon–Fri 8am–4pm; ☎313-113).

Accommodation

The cheapest accommodation in July and August is college **dormitory beds** (①) – contact *Express* or *Gran Tours* for bookings. The next best deal are **private rooms** (①–②), available year-round from *Ibusz* or *Gran Tours*; the latter also has apartments sleeping four to five (④).

Alabardos Panzió, Bajcsy-Zsilinszky utca 49 (☎312-640). Centrally located hotel with 12 rooms. ⑤.

Hotel Esztergom, Nagy Duna sétány, Prímás-Sziget (☎312-883). Modern and stylish, with a restaurant, roof terrace and sports facilities. ⑥.

Mátra Panzió, Bocskoroskuti út 1 (☎311-983). Twenty minutes from town on the Visegrád road. ③.

Platán Panzió, Kis-Duna sétány 11 (☎311-355). Nice place opposite the Prímás-Sziget. ③.

Ria Panzió, Batthány utca 11 (☎313-115). A small, comfortable pension with a good location below the Basilica Hill. ④.

Rózsa Panzió, Török Ignác utca 11 (☎317-355). Cheap place by the path to Szent Tamás-hegy.

St Kristóf Panzió, Dobozi Mihály utca 11 (☎316-255). Attractive new pension with an excellent restaurant – one of the best in town. ④.

CAMPSITES

Gran-Tours Camping, Nagy Duna sétány, Prímás-Sziget (☎311-327). Noisy but well-equipped campsite with bungalows 300m south of the ruined bridge on Prímás-Sziget. Open May–mid-Oct (bungalows until late Sept). ②–③.

Vadvirág Camping, Banomi dűlő (☎312-234). Rather noisy campsite 3km along the road to Visegrád, near the tail-end of the #6 bus route. Rents grassy tent-space and two-person bungalows. Open mid-April–mid-Sept. ①.

Eating and drinking

Most of the **restaurants** around the centre are pretty touristy, but none the worse for that. The best one in Watertown is the *Anonym Étterem* at Berényi utca 6; another place near Basilica Hill is the *Csülök Csárda*, at Batthyány utca 9. In the lower town you'll find the *Kispipa Étterem* (which has pool tables) at Kossuth utca 19 (daily 8am–10pm). The *Prímás Pince* at Béke tér 4 serves wholesome Hungarian food, while the *Arany Elefánt* ("Golden Elephant") on Petőfi utca is good and not too touristy. On Prímás-Sziget, there's an excellent but expensive restaurant in the *Hotel Esztergom*, and violinists serenade diners at the outdoor *Halászcsárda* on Táncsics Mihály utca (8am–10pm).

Entertainment

Should you happen to visit during the first half of August in an odd-numbered year, look out for posters advertising the **Guitar Festival**. Summer is also the time for **concerts** of choral or organ music in the basilica and the Watertown parish church (details from *Ibusz* or *Gran Tours*), and Saturday and Sunday night **disco cruises** to Visegrád (advertised around the centre). To boogie on terra firma, check out the *Galeria Disco* (Fri & Sat 9pm–4am), near the cinema on Rákóczi tér. By day, you might care to soak in the **thermal bath** (May–Sept daily 9am–5pm) behind the *Hotel Fürdő*.

Moving on

Buses from the depot on Simor utca serve most parts of the west bank and the Pilis range, with a couple of long-distance services to Veszprém (5am & 2.40pm), Győr and Sopron (5am & 1.40pm) in western Hungary. Most services to Budapest go via Dorog rather than the west bank.

As the hourly **car ferry** between Esztergom and Štúrovo only carries Hungarians and Slovaks, the nearest points for **crossing into Slovakia** are Komárom, 60km to the west, or Parassapuszta, in the Börzsöny range on the east bank.

The Pilis Range

Whether you describe it as mountains or hills, the **Pilis range** (*Pilis hegység*) offers scope for **hiking** amidst lovely scenery. The beech and oak woods on these limestone slopes are most beautiful in the autumn, but always hold the possibility of encounters with red deer or wild boars. Ruined lodges and monasteries attest to the hermits of the Order of St Paul and royal hunting parties who frequented the hills in medieval times.

The Pilis is directly accessible by bus from Esztergom, Szentendre or the Árpád híd terminus in Budapest, or you can hike up by various routes – from the Nagy-Villám Tower, or from Dömös to Dobogókő. If you're planning any walking, get hold of a **map** that marks the paths (*turistaút/foldút*), caves (*barlang*), and rain shelters (*esőház*) throughout the highlands.

Dobogókő

Standing in the shadow of 756-metre-high Pilis-tető, **DOBOGÓKŐ** has been a hiking centre since the late nineteenth century, when one of Hungary's first hostels was established here. It is still the best base for walking in the Pilis. The most popular way to see the area is to take the bus up (buses leave hourly from just by the HÉV terminal at Pomáz, and twice daily from the Budapest's Árpád híd terminal), and then to walk down the Rám precipice – a muddy or icy 4- to 5-hour hike – to Dömös, which offers fabulous views down to the river.

The hostel building at Dobogókő is now home to the **Museum of Rambling and Nature Tourism** (Thurs–Sun 10am–4pm). For those wishing to stay overnight, local accommodation consists of the *Hotel Dobogókő* (☎26/327-059; ③), the *Hotel Nimród* (☎26/327-644; ⑤), and the cheap but basic *Eötvös Lóránd Tourist House* (reservations on ☎26/327-534; ①). Tents can be pitched further down from the latter, whose toilet facilities are available to campers. If there's nothing else available in Dobogókő, try the *Platán Panzió*, 1km down the road. From June to August, accommodation in isolated hunting lodges (②–④) can be booked through *Natours Travel* in Budapest (XII, Győri út 2B).

Pilisborosjenő and Pomáz

The southern foothills of the Pilis are good for **pony-trekking**, which can be arranged either through *Natours Travel* or on the spot. In **PILISBOROSJENŐ**, off the Dorog–Budapest road, contact the *Zsíros Panzió* at Var utca 14 (☎26/334-059), which also does rooms (③). From Pilisborosjenő there's a nice hike to the top of Nagy-Kevély, the rocky hill north of the village, from where there are fabulous views of Budapest. This is also a popular spot among paragliders.

POMÁZ, on the HÉV line between Budapest and Szentendre, has a **riding school** (9am–6pm) at Mártírok útja 1, and a couple of **pensions**: the *Rákos Panzió* at Beniczky utca 63 (☎26/325-355; ③) and the *Tutti Panzió* at Lévai út 14 (②).

Many residents of Pomáz are of Serbian or Croatian extraction, giving a different flavour to the local *Táncház* (Dance House). This is the meeting place of the **Vujicsics Ensemble** (named after its founder, Tihamer Vujicsics, who died in 1975), which plays **South Slav music**. Concerts are usually advertised in Szentendre or Budapest.

THE EAST BANK

The **east bank** has fewer monuments than its western counterpart, so tourists are thinner on the ground. As the only sizeable town, with a monopoly on historic architecture, **Vác** styles itself the "city of churches". More or less en route to Vác are the **Dunakeszi** riding school and the beautiful botanical garden at **Vácrátót**. Farther north are **Zebegény** and **Nagymaros**, which have the finest scenery in the Danube Bend and, like other settlements beneath the **Börzsöny range**, mark the start of trails into the highlands.

Starting **from Budapest**, you can reach anywhere along the east bank within an hour or two by train from Nyugati Station, or bus from the Árpád híd terminus. The slower alternative is to sail from Budapest's Vigadó tér pier to Vác (2hr 30min), or on to Nagymaros and Zebegény. Approaching **from the west bank**, there are regular ferries across from Visegrád to Nagymaros; Pilismarót to Zebegény; and from Basaharc, north of Pilismarót, to Szob. Vác is accessible by ferry from the far side of Szentendrei Island, 4km from Tahitófalu.

Dunakeszi, Göd and Vácrátót

DUNAKESZI, 18km north of the capital, is the home of the **Alag Riding School**, patronized by Budapest's diplomatic corps. Less illustrious mortals may join the cross-country rides (held weekly Sept–Nov) providing they have some equestrian experience and book in advance – for details, contact *Pegazus Tours* in Budapest (Ferenciek tere; ☎1/117-1644) or Dunakeszi's *Magyar Loverseny Vallalat* (☎27/341-656).

Holidaymakers here for the fishing, swimming and sunbathing are catered for with a variety of **accommodation**. The *Hotel Dunakeszi* at Tábor utca 2 (☎27/341-611; ⑤) has sports facilities and all mod cons. Cheaper options include the *Fészek Panzió* on Malomárok (☎27/341-653; ③), which has a **campsite** next door (May–Sept), and the *Kikelet Panzió* at Kikelet utca 1 (☎27/342-554; ④). The larger *Dunakeszi* campsite (mid-May–mid-Sept; ☎27/342-358) is on Liget utca beside the Danube, north of *Dunatours*, which can book private rooms (②).

Heading north the next settlement is **GÖD** – today a mass of holiday homes – where workers' sports camps provided a cover for underground activism during the Horthy era. Five kilometres up the road to Vác you'll find good bathing at **SZŐDLIGET**, plus the *Liget Panzió* on Határ út (☎27/353-320; ③) with horse riding facilities.

The Botanical Garden at Vácrátót

VÁCRÁTÓT is famous for its **Botanical Garden** (April–Sept daily 7am–6pm; Oct–March daily 8am–4pm), founded in the 1870s by Count Vigyázó and subsequently bequeathed by him to the Academy of Sciences. Complete with waterfalls and mock ruins, the garden contains thousands of different trees and shrubs from around the world, providing a wonderful setting for **concerts** of classical music on summer evenings. Concert tickets (from Vörösmarty tér in Budapest or *Dunatours* in Vác) allow free admission to the park after midday, encouraging you to make a day of it. As bad weather can disrupt concert schedules, look out for *rossz idő esetén*, signifying an alternative date.

Motorists can reach Vácrátót by turning east off the main road a few kilometres north of Sződliget. The village is otherwise accessible in ninety minutes by train from Nyugati Station, or by bus or rail from Vác. It also has **connections** with the Northern Uplands (see *The Great Plain*), namely a branch line to Aszód where one can board trains for Balassagyarmat, and regular buses to Gödöllő. The nearest **accommodation** is the *Kastély Panzió* at Veres utca 3 (☎27/366-048) in **VÁCHARTYÁN** (midway between Vácrátót and Vác), where you'll also find horse riding facilities.

Vác

The small town of **VÁC** has a worldlier past than its present sleepy atmosphere suggests. Its bishops traditionally showed a flair for self-promotion, endowing monuments and colleges like the cardinals of Esztergom. Under Turkish occupation (1544–1686) Vác assumed an oriental character, with seven mosques and a public *hammam*, while during the Reform Era it was linked to Budapest by Hungary's first rail line (the second carried on to Bratislava). In modern times, Vác became notorious for its (now defunct) prison, used to incarcerate leftists under Admiral Horthy and "counter-revolutionaries" under Communism. Though its legacy of sights justifies a visit, it's not worth staying unless you're planning to visit Vácrátót or Zebegény as well, or are coming specially for the annual **Baroque Music Festival** at the end of July (see "Practicalities" below).

The Town

Arriving by bus, train or ferry, you can walk into the centre in around ten minutes. From the train station, head 400m along Széchenyi utca to reach Március 15 tér, passing a couple of tourist offices en route. Coming from the bus station, cross over Dr Csányi László körút to get onto Széchenyi utca. Disembarking at the landing stage for ferries from Budapest, you can see the prison and triumphal arch before following Köztársaság út or the riverside promenade into the centre. Ferries from Szentendrei Island dock only two blocks from Március 15 tér.

Around Március 15 tér

The triangular square at the heart of Vác rivals Szentendre for its handsome melange of Baroque and Rococo. The latter style was developed to a fine art locally, as evinced by the gorgeous decor of the **Dominican church**. At no. 6 stands the original Bishop's Palace, converted into Hungary's first Institute for the Deaf and Dumb in 1802. It was Bishop Kristóf Migazzi who erected the Baroque **Town Hall** across the square, its gable adorned with two prostrate females bearing the coats of arms of Hungary and Migazzi himself. This ambitious prelate was the moving force behind Vác's eighteenth-century revival, which impressed Empress Maria Theresa sufficiently to make him Archbishop of Vienna.

Aside from Migazzi's triumphal arch and Vác prison, all the sights are south of here. There's a small but lively **market** in the side street behind the Dominican church, and an **art gallery** (Tues–Sun 10am–6pm) of local artists' work on Kaptalan utca, nearby. Heading south along Köztársaság út you'll pass the Baroque Piarist Church and Trinity Statue on Szentháromság tér, before emerging on to Konstantin tér, dominated by Vác Cathedral.

Vác's Cathedral and Museum

Chiefly impressive for its gigantic Corinthian columns, Migazzi's **Cathedral** is a temple to self-esteem more than anything else. Its Neoclassical design by Isidore Canevale was considered revolutionary in the 1770s, the style not becoming generally accepted in Hungary until the following century. Migazzi himself took umbrage at one of the frescoes by Franz Anton Maulbertsch, and ordered the *Meeting of Mary and Elizabeth*, above the altar, to be bricked over. Plans are afoot to display the riches of the cathedral's **Treasury** – ask *Tourinform* for details.

From here you can walk along Múzeum utca to the **Vak-Bottyán Museum** (Tues–Sun 10am–noon & 1–5pm), named after the blind general of the Rákóczi War of Independence. The pre-Turkish era is reduced to a sorry collection of broken masonry, silver coins from Vác's fourteenth-century royal mint, and some lovely, though fragmented, mosaics. There are also some fine paintings of nineteenth-century markets, and unintelligible exhibits on the development of craft guilds. Múzeum utca continues round to Géza király tér, the centre of Vác in medieval times, where there's a Baroque **Franciscan church** with magnificent pulpits, altars and organ.

Along the waterfront

For a break from churches or a pleasant stroll towards the prison, follow one of the side streets off the main squares down to the **riverside promenade** (*sétány*) that runs the length of town. On Ady Endre sétány, level with Március 15 tér, is the wharf for **ferries to Szentendrei Island**, where townsfolk go to dine at the *Pokol Csárda* (Hell's Inn). From here you can walk across the island to Tahitófalu (4km), or perhaps thumb a lift.

The northern stretch of promenade – named after Liszt – runs past the **Round Tower**, the only remnant of Vác's medieval fortifications. There are rooms for rent in the side streets past here, while beyond the dock for ferries to Budapest and Esztergom rises the forbidding hulk of Vác prison.

The Prison and Triumphal Arch

Ironically, the building that became **Vác Prison** was originally an academy for noble youths, founded by Maria Theresa. Turned into a barracks in 1784, it began its penal career a century later, achieving infamy during the Horthy era, when two Communists died of beatings after going on hunger strike to protest against maltreatment. Today, their memorial plaque is set to be joined by one honouring the victims of the Stalinist period and their mass escape in October 1956. Thrown into panic by reports from Budapest, where their colleagues were being "hunted down like animals, hung on trees, or just beaten to death by passers-by", the ÁVO guards donned civilian clothing and mounted guns on the rooftop, fomenting rumours among prisoners whose hopes had been raised by snatches of patriotic songs overheard from the streets. A glimpse of national flags with the Soviet emblem cut from the centre provided the spark: a guard was overpowered, locks were shot off, and the prisoners burst free*.

The **Triumphal Arch** flanking the prison was another venture by Migazzi and his architect Canevale, occasioned by Maria Theresa's visit in 1764. Migazzi initially planned theatrical facades to hide the town's dismal housing (perhaps inspired by Potemkin's fake villages in Russia, created around the same time), but settled for the Neoclassical arch, from which Habsburg heads grimace a stony welcome.

> The Vác telephone code is ☎ 27

Practicalities

Vác has three tourist information offices: *Tourinform*, at Dr Csányi körút 545 (Mon–Fri 9am–5pm; ☎316-160), which is, as usual, the best; *Dunatours* at Széchenyi utca 14 (Mon–Fri 8am–4pm & Sat 8am–noon; ☎310-950); and *Ibusz* at no. 4–6 (Mon–Fri 8am–3.30pm; ☎317-640). All three offices can help with accommodation and can fill you in on local events such as Vác's annual three-day **Baroque Music Festival** at the end of July.

Accommodation
Private rooms can be rented through *Dunatours* or *Ibusz*, or directly at Liszt sétány 13 (☎312-683; ①) and Molnár utca 1 (①), near the Round Tower; otherwise there's the *Tabán Panzió* at Corvin lépcső 3 (☎315-607; ③) and a handful of other pensions for which *Tourinform* can supply details. Staying at Váchartyán or Verőcemaros is another option (see above and below).

Eating and drinking
Whereas the medieval traveller Nicolaus Kleeman found Vác's innkeepers "the quintessence of innkeeperish incivility", modern visitors should enjoy two outdoor **restaurants**: the *Halászkert* at Liszt sétány 9 and the dearer *Pokol Csárda* on Szentendrei Island (closed Tues). Other places include the *Kőkapu Étterem* at Dózsa utca 5, near the triumphal arch, and, for snacks, the *Széchenyi Ételbár* on the corner of Széchenyi utca and Galcsek utca, near the train station.

---

*One who didn't was the Englishwoman Dr Edith Bone, who came to Budapest as correspondent for the Daily Worker at the age of 68, and was arrested in 1949 on Rákosi's personal orders. Happily, she was released by insurgents from a prison in the capital in 1956, emerging frail but self-educated in Greek after many years of solitary confinement at Vác.

Moving on

From Vác you can either carry on up the east bank of the Danube by boat or rail, or catch a bus or train (5–7 daily) northwards through the Börzsöny towards Balassagyarmat, which allows for a night in Diósjenő (see p.144). Buses to other Börzsöny villages follow such roundabout routes that hitching or walking might be a quicker way of getting there.

Verőcemaros

Not content with his work in Vác, Migazzi plumped for another Baroque church and a summer mansion at **VERŐCEMAROS**, 10km further round the Bend. However, the only "sight" that's accessible is a **memorial museum** (April–Oct Tues–Sun 10am–6pm; Nov–March Tues–Sun 9am–5pm) in the home of the ceramicist **Géza Gorka** (1894–1971) at Szamos utca 22. The settlement sprawls along the Danube, merging into **KISMAROS**, a resort with a more youthful profile. It is here that you'll find the terminal of the *Kis-vasút*, a **miniature rail line** leading up to Királyrét in the Börzsöny (see p.144). From Verőcemaros itself there are ferries to Kisoroszi on Szentendrei Island (see p.126).

Should you care to stay for the swimming, riding or fishing, both places offer **accommodation**. Verőcemaros proper has the *Orgona Tourist Hostel* on Magyarkúti utca (☎27/350-045; ①), the *Ezüstfenyő* at Magyarkuti utca 5 (☎27/350-110; ②), and the *Treff* or *Salon Panzió* at Árpád utca 67 (②). In Kismaros, the youth travel agency *Express* maintains the *Hotel Touring* (mid-April–mid-Oct; ④), *Express Motel* (mid-April–mid-Oct; ③), a **campsite** (June–Sept) and bungalow complex (May–Sept; ②), all located near the Kis-vasút terminal, and sharing the same phone number (☎27/350-166).

Nagymaros and the Dam

A quietly prosperous village with an air of faded grandeur (nobles lived here in the age of royal Visegrád), **NAGYMAROS** seems an unlikely focus for years of environmental protest. The cause is not Nagymaros itself, where a drunk's ejection from an *italbolt* still counts as a major disturbance, but a short way upriver, where the aborted **dam** languishes amid the detritus of its construction (see box).

The village lies across the river from Visegrád, with a superb view of the latter's citadel ("Visegrád has the castle, but Nagymaros has the view", locals have always boasted). From the Gothic church by the train station, whitewashed houses straggle up the hillside; and social life centres around the patisseries and leafy squares. From the station, duck under the bridge to reach the main road and head up the principal backstreet towards the hills above. One kilometre uphill, the path divides at a car park – one fork heads south to Hegyes-tető, where you can enjoy a **panoramic view of the Bend**, the other heads up **into the Börzsöny**, towards Törökmező (see below).

Private **accommodation** in Nagymaros is best found on the spot by wandering the streets in search of *Zimmer frei* signs. Alternatively, you can stay among the beech woods at the *Törökmező Hostel* (☎27/350-063; ①), which is 5km by footpath (marked with blue signs) from the car park, or slightly further if you follow the Panorama út road. Beds here can be reserved through *Ibusz*.

THE GABČIKOVO-NAGYMAROS DAM

Controversy concerning the building of a dam at Nagymaros became a focus of opposition to the Communist regime in the 1980s and hastened its demise. The dam was part of the Gabčikovo-Nagymaros Hydroelectric Barrage, a grandiose project dreamt up by Hungarian and Czechoslovak planners in 1978, and supported and partly financed by the Austrians who hoped to have access to a cheap source of electricity. The barrage was intended to make use of 200km of the River Danube, diverting it for 25km and tapping its energy with two dams. While work on the dam at Nagymaros was abandoned in 1989 after five years of opposition by *Duna Kör* (the Danube Circle), the dam at Gabčikovo was almost completed at the time of the Velvet Revolution. Having invested heavily in the project, the newly constituted Slovak government pressed ahead and diverted the Danube away from Hungary onto the Gabčikovo turbines, wreaking environmental havoc for comparatively little energy gains, as an operating dam at Nagymaros had been an essential part of the project as originally conceived.

In 1994 the Hungarian government began demolishing the unused dam at Nagymaros, and both Hungary and Slovakia now have cases pending at the International Court at The Hague concerning the project. The issues are whether Hungary has failed to meet its obligation in discontinuing the work, or whether Slovakia is legally entitled to divert the waters of the Danube for its own use.

Zebegény and Szob

At **ZEBEGÉNY** the Danube turns south before taking the Bend, and the magnificent scenery has lured painters ever since István Szőnyi (1894–1960) first put brush to canvas here, and his **memorial house** at Bartók utca 7 (March–Nov Tues–Sun 9am–5pm; Dec–Feb Tues–Sun 10am–6pm) began hosting an international **art school** every summer. Another sign of Zebegény's bold horizons is the **Navigation Museum** (April–Oct Tues–Sun 9am–5pm) at Szőnyi utca 9, housing the private collection of Captain Vince Farkas, who has sailed the world and amassed some nifty carved figureheads in the process. The local **Catholic church** was designed by Károly Kós, and deserves a mention for being the only one in Hungary to be built in the National Romantic style (an amalgam of Art Nouveau and folk art). Its frescoes, by Aladár Körösfői Kreisch, depict the vision of Emperor Constantine and Saint Helena finding the Holy Cross in Jerusalem.

Accommodation consists of the *Almáskert Pension* on Almáskert utca 13 (②) per person) and the *Feiszl* at Malom utca 21–23 (① per person); the *Törökmező Hostel* (see above) is a two- to three-hour trek from Zebegény. From mid-April to mid-October you might also find lodgings at the summer art camp (*Szőnyi István Nyári Képzőművészeti Szabadiskola Tábora*) at Bartók utca 7 (☎27/370-104; ②). Nagymaros and Szob are the nearest alternatives, or you could take the **ferry** across to Pilismarót on the west bank to stay at Dömös, Esztergom or Visegrád. As for **restaurants**, the *Mátyás Vendéglő* at Magyar utca 24 and the *Maros Vendéglő* at Kossuth tér 2 are both equally recommended.

Szob

Depots, dust and *ennui* sum up most frontier posts, and **SZOB** is no exception. As trains merely pass through, and motorists can't drive across, few tourists come here. For chance visitors, however, the **Börzsöny Museum** at Hámán utca 14 (Tues–Sun 10am–5pm) is ready with peasant costumes, carved tombstones, and a piece of the petrified primeval tree found at Ipolytarnoc and now distributed among several provincial museums. **Accommodation** boils down to camping at the *Sportcentrum* beside the ferry landing stage or staying at the agreeable *Malomkert Fogadó*, Malomkert utca 5 (☎27/370-233; ③).

The nearest road crossing **into Slovakia** is 30km north at **PARASSAPUSZTA**, on the Ipoly River which demarcates the frontier. The neighbouring village of Drégelypalánk is on the Vác–Diósjenő–Balassagyarmat line (trains roughly every 2hr).

Walking in the Börzsöny

The **Börzsöny Range** sees few visitors despite its scattering of hostels and forest footpaths, and the abundance of rabbits, pheasants and deer watched only by circling eagles. It's feasible to camp rough here, though most of the following sites offer some form of accommodation. Would-be walkers should buy Cartographia's *Börzsöny-hegység* map (available at the *Tourinform* office in Vác), which shows paths and the location of hostels (*túristáház*).

Mount Csóványos (939m) is the highest peak in the Börzsöny, and also the most challenging. Hikers usually approach it from the direction of **DIÓSJENŐ**, a sleepy mountain village that's accessible by bus or train from Vác. Unfortunately, Diósjenő's **campsite** (May–Sept; ☎35/310-660) lies 1km from the village and 2km from the rail halt, and its small stock of rooms (②) can only be reserved through *Nógrád Tourist* in Salgótarján (☎32/310-660).

An alternative route into the mountains begins at Kismaros beside the Danube, whence narrow-gauge trains trundle every couple of hours up to **Királyrét** between 8.40am and 5.30pm (weekends only in winter). Supposedly once the hunting ground of Beatrice and Mátyás, this "Royal Meadow" is now the site of a forking path; one trail (marked in red) leads 3km to the *Magas-Tax Hostel*, the other to the "Big Cold" peak, **Nagy Hideg**. The latter has excellent views and its own **hostel**, and is the starting point for walks to Mount Csóványos and the villages of Nagybörzsöny (5–6hr) and Kospallag – use the *Börzsöny-hegység* map to guide you.

Nagybörzsöny

From Nagy Hideg, a trail marked by blue squares leads westwards to **NAGYBÖRZSÖNY**, 20km from Szob; motorists can get there by turning off the Parassapuszta road beyond Ipolytölgyes. A wealthy town during the Middle Ages, Nagybörzsöny declined with the depletion of its copper, gold and iron mines, and is now a mere logging village. Visitors can see the thirteenth-century Romanesque **Church of St Stephen** and the fifteenth-century Gothic **Miners' Church**; plus an exhibition of folk costumes and gems in the **Mining Museum** at Petőfi utca 19 (Sat & Sun 10am–5pm) and the village's still-working water mill. **Horse riding** can be arranged through the *Nagybörzsöny Körség Vendégháza* (☎27/378-025; ①) – which, incidentally, is the only **accommodation** available.

Kospallag

The other trail from Nagy Hideg (marked in red) runs south down to **KOSPALLAG**, another prosaic village, redeemed only by a **hostel** (①) with a **restaurant**, and **buses** to Vác until 9pm. However, things improve beyond the Vác–Szob road junction below the village, where the path wanders through beech woods to a lovely open meadow graced with a solitary tree and the first view of the Danube. Cutting southwest across the meadow puts you back on the path to the *Törökmező Hostel*, or you can head west towards Zebegény when the path divides by the exercise camp in the woods. This leads eventually to a car park at the junction of paths to Hegyes-tető and Nagymaros.

If you take the road from Kopallag to Szob, you come to **MÁRIANOSTRA**, a place of pilgrimage whose church, decorated with folk carvings, is always open. There are buses here from Vác and Szob. An hour's walk north from the village takes you to **Kopasz hegy** (Bald Hill) which affords some of the best views in the region.

travel details

Trains

Budapest to Esztergom (every 40–90min; 1hr 15min); Szentendre (every 15–30min; 45min); Vác (every 30min; 45min); Váctrátót (7 daily; 1hr 20min).

Esztergom to Budapest (every 40–90min; 1hr 30min); Komárom (4 daily; 45min).

Kismaros to Királyrét (5 daily; 45min).

Vác to Balassagyarmat (7–9 daily; 2hr); Budapest (every 30min; 45min); Diósjenő (7–9 daily; 45min).

Vácrátót to Aszód (3 daily; 1hr 30min); Vác and Budapest (10 daily; 15min/1hr 20min).

Buses

Budapest *Árpád híd* terminus to Esztergom via the Bend (every 1hr 30min; 3hr) or Dorog (every 30min; 2hr); Dobogókő (1–3 daily; 2hr 30min); Vác (every 30min; 30min); Visegrád (hourly; 2hr). From *Népstadion* terminus to Vác (hourly; 30min).

Esztergom to Budapest (every 30min; 2hr); Győr (2 daily; 2hr); Komárom (hourly; 90min); Sopron (2 daily; 4hr); Szentendre (hourly; 1hr 45min); Visegrád (every 20–40min; 1hr).

Szentendre to Dobogókő (3–4 daily; 1hr 30min); Esztergom (hourly; 1hr 45min); Visegrád (hourly; 30min).

Vác to Budapest (hourly; 30min); Diósjenő (5–7 daily; 1hr); Kospallag (every 90min; 90min); Szob (every 20–40min; 30min); Vácrátót (hourly; 45min).

Visegrád to Budapest (hourly; 2hr); Dömös (every 20–40min; 15min); Esztergom (every 20–40min; 1hr).

Ferries

Most ferries between Budapest, Esztergom, Szentrendre, Vác and Visegrád operate only from May to mid-September, though services marked below with an asterisk also run at weekends and on public holidays at other times of the year. All other ferry services operate year-round.

Budapest (Vigadó tér) to Esztergom (3 daily; 5hr); Szentendre (3–5 daily; 1hr 30min); Vác (1 daily; 2hr 45min); Visegrád (4 daily; 3hr); Zebegény (3 daily; 3hr 45min).

Esztergom to Budapest (1–2 daily; 4hr); Szentendre (May to mid-Sept 3 daily; mid-Sept to April 2 weekly; 2hr 40min); Vác (1–2 daily; 2hr 15min); Visegrád (1–2 daily; 1hr 30min).

Kisoroszi to Kismaros (every 30–90min).

Kismaros to Kisoroszi (every 30–90min).

Leányfalu to Pócsmegyer (every 20–60min).

Nagymaros to Visegrád (every 45–60min).

Pilismarót to Szob (hourly); Zebegény (hourly).

Szob to Pilismarót (hourly).

Tahitófalu to Vác (hourly).

Vác to Budapest (1 daily; 1hr 45min); Tahitófalu (hourly); Esztergom (mid-May to mid-Sept 1 daily; winter 2 weekly; 3hr); Nagymaros (mid-May to mid-Sept 1 daily; winter 2 weekly; 1hr 10min).

Visegrád to Budapest (1–3 daily; 2hr 30min); Esztergom (3 daily; 1hr 45min); Esztergom (1–2 daily); Kisoroszi (every 45–90min); Nagymaros (1–2 daily; 20min); Vác (1–3 daily; 45min); Zebegény (3 daily; 45min).

Hydrofoil

Hydrofoils between the Danube Bend and Budapest run from late May to early September on Saturdays, Sundays and holidays, with an additional Friday service from late June onwards. Esztergom to Budapest takes around an hour.

CHAPTER THREE

LAKE BALATON AND THE BAKONY

F ew Magyars would still subscribe to the old romantic view of **Lake Balaton** as the "Hungarian sea" but, despite rising prices pushing out natives in favour of Austrians and Germans, it is still very much the "nation's playground". Holiday resorts line the lake's **southern shore**, almost wholly given over to the pleasures of guzzling, swimming and sunbathing. With **Siófok** as the archetype, one place here is much like another. Nature only reasserts itself at the western end of the lake, where the River Zala flows through the reeds to **Kis-Balaton**, a bird reserve. The **northern shore** is equally crowded, but waterfront development has been limited by reed banks and cooler, deeper water, giving tourism a different slant. Historic **Tihany** and the wine-producing **Badacsony Hills** offer fine sightseeing, while anyone whose social life doesn't take off in **Keszthely** can go soak themselves in the thermal lake at **Hévíz**.

Another centre for bathing and boozing is **Lake Velence**, midway between the Balaton and Budapest. Close by is **Martonvásár**, where Beethoven concerts are held in the grounds of the Brunswick Mansion during summer. And while you're visiting the Balaton area, it would be a shame not to see the romantic-looking Belváros and "Bory Castle" at **Székesfehérvár**, or something of the hills that roll picturesquely into **the Bakony**. A wine-producing region dotted with small villages and ruined castles, the Bakony is dominated by the historic towns of **Veszprém** and **Sümeg** and exploited for its mineral wealth at **Tapolca**.

The telephone code for Lake Velence, Martonvásár and Székesfehérvár is ☎22

Approaches

There are several possible approaches from Budapest, and your choice depends largely on which shore of Lake Balaton you're aiming for. Most **trains** from Déli station to Siófok call at Lake Velence, Székesfehérvár, and the main settlements along the southern shore, before veering off towards Nagykanizsa at Balatonszentgyörgy. From mid-July to late August *MÁV* even runs **steam trains** to Siófok – though you have to be a real enthusiast to last the ten-hour journey (over twice as long as the regular train). Regular services to Balatonfüred are likewise routed through Székesfehérvár, and continue along the northern shore to the Badacsony Hills, where they head off towards Tapolca. All of these towns – plus Keszthely, Veszprém and Sümeg – are also accessible by **bus** from the capital's Erzsébet tér depot.

Since the M7 bypasses everywhere en route to Siófok, **drivers** wishing to keep their options open should use route 70 instead, which permits you to switch to

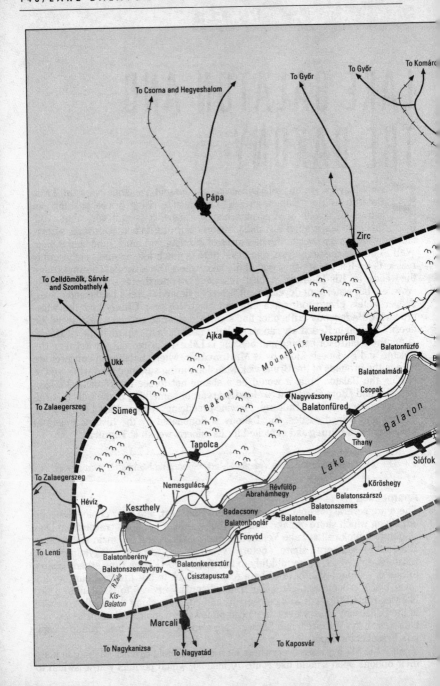

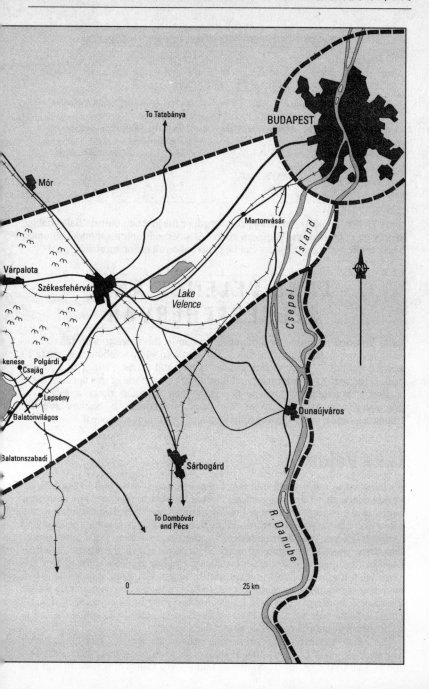

ACCOMMODATION PRICE CODES

All accommodation in this guide is graded according to the price bands given below. Note that all prices refer to the cheapest available double room in high season except where otherwise indicated. For more details, see p.26.

① Under 650Ft (under £4/$6/ DM10)

② 650–1500Ft (£4–8/$6–13/DM10–20)

③ 1500–3000Ft (£8–17/$13–27/ DM20–40)

④ 3000–4500Ft (£17–25/$27–40/ DM40–60)

⑤ 4500–6500Ft (£25–36/$40–57/ DM60–85)

⑥ 6500–10,000Ft (£36–56/$57–88/ DM85–130)

⑦ Over 10,000Ft (over £56/$88/ DM130)

---

route 71 (for the northern shore) at Polgárdi or the junction outside Balatonaliga, or stay on course for the southern shore. At weekends and throughout summer, heavy traffic and long tailbacks can be expected on all major approaches.

LAKE VELENCE AND SZÉKESFEHÉRVÁR

Lake Velence resembles a diminutive version of the Balaton, with hills to the north and two contrasting shorelines. The southern shore – followed by route 70 and the rail line – is awash with holiday homes and tourists, while the opposite bank is too reedy for swimming, but ideal for birds. If none of this appeals, there is always **Martonvásár**, where the Brunswick Mansion hosts a season of Beethoven concerts. Otherwise the focus of attention is **Székesfehérvár**, Hungary's capital in the days of King Stephen – with ruins to prove it.

Lake Velence

It's hard not to smile when told that **Lake Velence** (*Velencei-tó*) is named after Venice, since anywhere less romantic would be hard to imagine. The **southern shore** is one continuous strip of holiday homes, campsites, and enclosed *strand* where you have to pay for a swim and the dubious privilege of using the changing rooms. If it weren't for their individually named train stations, you'd never realize that there used to be three separate settlements along the shore: **Velence**, **Gárdony** and **Agárd**. Watersports facilities are widely available along this stretch of the lake. It's an ideal spot to learn windsurfing as the water is only one to two metres deep, warming up to an acceptable 22°C or more over summer. In winter the water often freezes solid and ice-skating becomes the favoured sport. If none of this appeals, you can always head for the thermal baths in Agárd, at the end of Határ utca (summer 10am–7pm; winter 10am–5pm).

The reedy **western end** is a nesting ground for some 30,000 birds, which migrate here in spring. According to legend, three sisters who turned themselves into herons to escape the Turks return home every year. Permission to visit this nature reserve (*Madárrezervátum*) must be obtained in Budapest (XII, Költő utca 21; ☎156-2133); the entrance is 2km north of the Dinnye train halt, beyond Agárd.

The less built-up **northern shore** is accessible by ferry from Velence or Agárd to a small peninsula near the village of **Pákozd**. From the landing stage, it's a short walk up to **Mészeg Hill**, where an obelisk commemorates the first Hungarian victory in the 1848–49 revolution, and you can gaze across the lake or the Velence Hills. Geologically speaking, these are the oldest hills in Hungary, formed from magma and granite. Atop the 351-metre-high **Meleg Hill** are several colossal "rocking stones" (*ingókővek*) that sway perceptibly in the wind.

Arrival and information
Wherever you get off the train, simply head for the lake – it would be hard to lose your way round here. **Information** is available from *Albatours* at Szabadság utca 24 (daily 9am–5pm); *Cooptourist* (Mon–Sat 10am–6pm) next to *Albatours*; and the friendly *Villa Tours* (May–Sept daily 9am–7pm; ☎22/356-018) – all three of which are across from or near the Gárdony train station.

Accommodation
Private rooms are bookable through all three tourist offices, and there's also an office at the *Panorama* campsite in Velence (see below) that can arrange rooms (③–④). Many householders also rent them directly (look for *Zimmer frei* signs), but these are just as expensive as the rest of the accommodation on offer here.

Places to try include:

Agárd Hotel, Akácfa utca (☎355-016). Next to *Nemeskócsag Camping* 100m east and inland of Agárd station. ④–⑤.

Fortuna Panzió, Vörösmarty utca 53 (☎368-125). A tiny pension in Kápolnásnyek, 1km east of Velence. ④.

Helios Hotel, Tópart utca 34 (☎368-159). Not far from the *Juventus Hotel*, but smaller, with fewer facilities. ④–⑤.

Juventus Hotel, Tópart utca 25A (☎368-159). Near the lake and Velence station, with a sauna, tennis and watersports. ⑤.

Touring Hotel, Tópart utca 1 (☎355-019). Another place with sports facilities, beside the lake in Agárd. Open May–Oct. ④–⑥.

Viking Hotel, Gallér utca 2 (☎355-287). Similar setup to the *Touring Hotel*, but open year-round. ⑤.

CAMPSITES
Nemeskócsag Camping, Akácfa utca (☎355-016). Sandwiched between the rail tracks and the main road in Agárd – noisy and grossly overcrowded. Open mid-April to mid-Oct.

Panorama Camping, Kemping utca (☎368-043). 2km from Velence station, a huge site on the northeastern shore of the lake with watersports facilities and bungalows (③) for rent. Open April–Oct.

Termál Camping, Határ utca (☎355-294). By the thermal baths on the southern edge of Agárd; also has a pension. Open May–Sept.

Martonvásár

Visiting **MARTONVÁSÁR** – on the rail line roughly halfway between Budapest and Velence and just fifteen minutes from the lake – you are transported into another era. The road opposite the station leads to the neo-Gothic **Brunswick**

Mansion (daily 10am–dusk), set in a lovely 64-acre park, where **Teréz Brunswick** founded Hungary's first nursery school in 1828. Her sister **Josephine** may have been the "immortal beloved" of **Beethoven**'s love letters, and the inspiration for his *Moonlight* and *Appassionata* sonatas. Certainly the composer was a regular visitor, though others reckon that his muse was **Giulietta Guiccardi**, the "beautiful devil" whom he also met here between 1800 and 1806.

Whatever the truth, the small **Beethoven Museum** (Tues–Thurs 10am–noon & 2–4pm; Sat–Sun 10am–noon & 2–6pm) exhibits manuscripts and personal belongings, and on summer evenings performances of Beethoven's symphonies are held on an island in the middle of the park, beneath a great bower of beech and sycamore. Armed with mosquito repellent and a couple of bottles (there's a bar-buffet), you can watch the sun set and hear the soaring music. Tickets are available from the *Central Box Office* in Budapest (V, Vörösmarty tér 1) or *Albatours* in Székesfehérvár.

Practicalities

Should you miss the last train back to the capital (around 11pm on Sat), **accommodation** is available at the *Hotel Kukorica* at Szent László utca 9, down Dozsa Gyorgy utca from the mansion (☎22/379-067); or the *Macska Pension* at Budai út 21, on the main road to Budapest (☎22/379-127). Both places have **restaurants**, or there is the *Postakocsi* eatery at Fehérvári utca 1.

Székesfehérvár

Reputedly the site where Árpád pitched camp and founded his dynasty, **SZÉKESFEHÉRVÁR** was probably the earliest Hungarian town. Its name (pronounced "SAIKesh-fehair-var") comes from the white castle (*fehérvár*) founded by Prince Géza, whose son Stephen made it his royal seat (*szék*). As the centre of his efforts to civilize the Magyars, it was named in Latin *Alba Civitas* or *Alba Regia*. Since this medieval town was utterly destroyed by the Turks, Székesfehérvár as it exists today owes its Belváros to the Habsburgs, and its high-rise suburbs to the final German counterattack in 1945, which levelled everywhere else.

The Town

Székesfehérvár's **Belváros** occupies approximately the same area as the great castle once did, as evinced by a section of the medieval walls alongside the **Romkert** (April–Oct Tues–Sun 9am–6pm). Amongst the stonework in this "Garden of Ruins" is a richly carved Roman sarcophagus, found in 1803 and believed to hold the remains of King Stephen. Directly across the road are the excavated **foundations of the cathedral** where Stephen was buried – it was designed for him by Italian architects, in an attempt to rival Saint Mark's in Venice. Thirty-eight Hungarian kings were crowned here, hence its name of the Coronation Church. After the town fell to the Turks in 1543, the cathedral was plundered of its gold and jewels, and blown up.

Városház tér recalls Székesfehérvár's revival under Maria Theresa, with its Baroque town hall, Franciscan church and Zopf-style **Bishop's Palace**, built with

stones from the ruined cathedral by Bishop Milassin, whose coat of arms appears on the gable. Fő utca, running off to the north, is so perfectly preserved that you expect to see crinolined ladies emerging from the **Fekete Sas Pharmacy Museum** at no. 9 (Tues–Sun 10am–6pm). This eighteenth-century apothecary, the *Black Eagle*, was open right up to 1971: today you can still see the original fittings and fixtures, along with displays on traditional remedies. Like the Baroque Church of Saint John across the street, it was founded by the Jesuits.

On Bartok tér, around the back of the church, the **Csók Museum** (Tues–Fri 10am–7pm & Sat–Sun 10am–6pm) displays paintings by István Csók (1865–1961). Initially associated with the Nagybánya School, he fell under the influence of Vuillard and Bonnard in Paris and returned to Hungary to practice *plein air* painting. More interesting, though, is the **István Király Museum** on Országzászló tér (Tues–Sun 10am–6pm). Its archeological finds and domestic treasures are laid out to form a vivid exhibition on local history; especially notable are the eastern Celtic pottery and nineteenth-century court dress.

More historic architecture clusters south of Városház tér. Walking south down Arany Janos utca you'll pass **Saint Stephen's Cathedral**. Essentially now Baroque, this much-rebuilt edifice actually dates back to the thirteenth century. Next to the cathedral is the **Chapel of Saint Anna**, the only remainder of medieval Székesfehérvár spared by the Turks for use as a mosque – note the Koranic inscriptions and arabesque murals. By continuing south along Arany utca, you'll come to the fanciful Zopf-style **Budenz House** at no. 12 (Tues–Sun 10am–6pm) and a **Carmelite church** with Rococo carvings and frescoes by the Austrian painter Maulbertsch.

Bory's Castle

The town's best sight is **Bory's Castle** (*Bory Vár*), situated out in the eastern suburbs beyond the microchip and TV factories (March–Sept daily 9am–5pm & Sat–Sun 10am–noon & 3–5pm; ring first as opening times can vary; ☎22/305-570). An eclectic structure combining features of Scottish, Romanesque and Gothic architecture, it was built of reinforced concrete, ceramics and stone by a group of students directed by the artist Jenő Bory (1879–1959). Its rooms and courtyards are filled with statues and paintings of Ilona Komocsin, Bory's wife and model, whose memory the castle enshrines. Although the overall effect of Ilona's multiple images is slightly morbid, this is a marvellous place to wander around. Situated at Máriavölgy utca 54, the castle is accessible by bus #26 from Piac tér; bus #32 from the train station; or bus #26A from the bus station.

Practicalities

Arriving at the train station, 1km south of the centre, catch any bus heading up Prahószka út – which subsequently becomes Vár körút – and get off near the *Hotel Alba Regia*. The intercity bus station, on Piac tér just by the old city walls, is more convenient being only a few minutes' walk from the Belváros. **Information** is available from the helpful *Albatours* at Városház tér 1 (Mon–Fri 8am–4pm; ☎312-494); *Ibusz*, in a beautiful building at Ady Endre utca 2 (Mon–Fri 8am–4pm; ☎329-393); or *Express* at Rákoczi utca 4 (Mon–Fri 8am–4pm ☎329-010). Ask *Albatours* about plays at the **Vörösmarty Theatre** near the *Hotel Magyar Király*, or recitals at the **Bartók Concert Hall**. The main **post office** is on the corner of Kossuth utca and Petőfi utca, and the **police** are at Dózsa tér 12.

Accommodation

Private **rooms** (③) can be booked for a minimum of two nights through *Albatours*, *Ibusz* (addresses above) or *Cooptourist*, at Rákóczi utca 3 (☎314-391). *Express* may be able to arrange beds in college dorms (①) over summer, and there's also *Székesfehérvári Camping* open from May to September at Bergyó köz 1 (☎313-433). Other options include:

Hotel Alba Regia, Rákóczi utca 1 (☎313-484). Three-star Seventies establishment with a central location near the Garden of Ruins. ④.

Két Góbé Panzió, Gugásvölgyi út 4 (☎327-578). A noisy 28-room pension just off the outer ring road, 2km east of the centre. ③.

Magyar Király ("Hungarian king") Hotel, Fő utca 10 (☎311-262). A grand hotel built in the 1870s, but with disappointingly ordinary rooms. ⑤.

Renzó Panzió, Krasznai utca 46 (☎310-624). Another pension, in the Öreg-hegy district off the Budapest highway. ③.

Rév Hotel, József utca 42 (☎314-441). This high-rise workers' hostel 500m east of the centre also takes tourists. Rooms with sinks and shared bathrooms. ②.

Törökudvar Tourist Hostel, Jókai utca 2 (☎324-975). Beds in rooms sleeping 8–12. Booking advisable. ①.

Eating and drinking

Hearty **meals** at moderate prices can be had at the *Ősfehérvár Étterem* opposite the Romkert, while the *Kaiser Söröző* at Távírda utca 14 has a good lunch menu and pool tables. There's also the *Fehérvár* at Kégl György utca 25; the dining room (and casino) of the *Hotel Magyar Király*, and the *Rex* at Petöfi utca 14 – the latter serving scrumptious cakes. **Drinking holes** abound along Fő utca, including the *Korzó Söröző* which has Czech beer and outdoor seating. *Royal Darts* is a student hang-out near the *Rév Hotel* at Budai út 18.

On from Székesfehérvár

Moving on from Székesfehérvár you have a choice of destinations and routes. Aside from international trains to Vienna or Leipzig, and long-haul buses to Szekszárd in Transdanubia and Kecskemét or Szeged on the Great Plain, there are basically three options:

North through the Vértes

Komárom-bound trains and buses heading for Győr (both covered in the *Transdanubia* chapter) take a scenic route through the **Vértes Hills**. Most trains call at **BODAJK**, where the *Galyavölgye Hostel* at Petőfi utca 93 has rooms (②), bookable through *Albatours* in Székesfehérvár. From here it's a six-kilometre hike to **CSÓKAKŐ**, overlooked by a **ruined castle**. Buses and trains also usually stop at **MÓR**, another starting point for **walks**, and the centre of a wine-producing region. You can enjoy a tipple in the **Wine Museum** opposite the run-down *Vértes Tourist Hostel* at Ezerjó utca 2 (②).

West towards Veszprém

Travelling **towards Veszprém** in the Bakony by bus or train (a convenient bus leaves Székesfehérvár daily at 3pm, heading for Zalaegerszeg via Veszprém, Balatonfüred, Badacsony and Hévíz), **VÁRPALOTA** appears through a haze of lignite smoke. Even though emissions from its power plant and aluminium foundry are quietly falling as acid rain upon the Bakony's forests, ecological concerns are ignored in the **Museum of the Chemical Industry** (April–Oct Tues–Sun 11am–5pm). You're unlikely to be tempted to stop either by this or the **Roman weir** constructed of gigantic stones, whose remains stretch for almost 1km near the suburban swimming resort of **PÉTFÜRDŐ**. Motorists, however, might consider a stopover at **ÖSKÜ**, 9km further west, which boasts an extraordinary **circular chapel** with a mushroom-shaped cupola, dating from the eleventh century.

Towards the Balaton

Heading for the southern shore of Lake Balaton, people with transport (or those willing to get off at Szabadbattyán train station and hope for a local bus) can make a detour to **TÁC**, 5km off route 70, where signs point towards the **Roman ruins of Gorsium**. This began life as a military camp at the junction of two roads, but by the beginning of the second century had become the religious centre of Lower Pannonia. The site (daily 8am–dusk) covers two square kilometres, and includes the walls of a palace, a temple, forum and houses. Carved stonework and other finds are displayed in a **museum** (May–Oct Tues–Sun 9am–6pm; Nov–April Tues–Sun 10am–5pm).

LAKE BALATON

With 197km of shoreline to exploit, **Lake Balaton** is a huge money-spinner, generating over a third of Hungary's income from tourism. Since 1987, massive sums have been invested to create five new harbours and belatedly clean up the lake's water and beaches. In truth, little of the shoreline has escaped being embanked in concrete and turned into *strand* (the generic term for any bathing place but rarely what you'd call a beach), and holiday homes have virtually filled the spaces between once separate settlements. The result isn't to everyone's taste, but it certainly tries hard to be. While the southern shore is unabashedly hedonistic, the northern shore can boast of historic monuments, cultural events and scenic landscapes. Tennis, horse riding and watersports are easily arranged, and most resorts offer some form of nightlife.

The lake itself is the largest in Europe, stretching for almost 80km and varying in width from 14km to 1.5km (at the point where it's almost cut in two by the Tihany peninsula). With an average depth of only three metres, it warms up quickly and maintains a pleasant temperature from May to October. In winter the lake often freezes over (the ice growing as thick as 25cm) and horse-drawn carts can be seen driving across.

Though its **history** is hardly writ large, the region was first settled in the Iron Age, and has been a wine-growing centre since Roman times. During the sixteenth century, it formed the front line between Turkish and Habsburg-ruled Hungary, with an Ottoman fleet based at Siófok and an Austrian one at Balatonfüred. Spas and villas appeared from 1765 onwards, but catered largely to the wealthy until the Communists began promoting holidays for the masses after World War II. During the Sixties, footloose youths started flocking to the *Balcsi* (Balaton's familiar nickname), while the Seventies and Eighties witnessed a boom in private holiday homes and room-letting, fuelled by an influx of tourists from Germany and Austria.

Accommodation around the Balaton

The Balaton has more tourist **accommodation** than anywhere else in Hungary, but there can still be a shortage during the summer. Especially at the main resorts and scenic spots (Siófok, Balatonfüred, Tihany, Badacsony and Keszthely), you'll be lucky to find a room in any of the cheaper hotels or pensions. Unless you have a reservation, your best option is a **private room** from one of the **tourist agencies** – foremost amongst which are *Siótour* (on the southern shore) and *Balatontourist* (on the northern shore). However, it's often cheaper to rent directly from householders: the signs to look for are *Zimmer frei* or *Szoba kiádo*. Balaton's **campsites** are among the dearest in Hungary: most of the large ones operate from May to September, whilst in many resorts auxiliary sites open from June to August to handle the overflow.

STORM WARNINGS

From May to September the Balaton is prone to occasional **storms**. Storm **warnings** are given by flashing lights: 30 flashes per minute indicates winds of 40–60km per hour; 60 flashes per minute winds over 60km per hour. Windsurfers or sailors should head for land at once.

Transport

Though all the main resorts are accessible by rail from Budapest or Székesfehérvár, it's worth knowing that the so-called *Balaton Express* is actually a slow train, stopping everywhere as it circles the lake. Such **trains** are the easiest way of travelling along the southern shore, and between Balatonalmádi and Badacsony on the opposite bank, whereas **buses** are better for journeys between Balatonfüred and Tihany, Badacsony and Keszthely, and Veszprém and Siófok.

From mid-April to late September or mid-October, fairly regular **passenger ferries** zigzag from Siófok to Balatonfüred on the other bank, then west to Tihany-rév and back across the lake to Balatonföldvár. During July and August, another service runs the length of the lake from Balatonkenese to Keszthely (5hr), making regular stops on both banks en route. Additionally, **car ferries** ply between Tihany-rév and Szántódrév (April–Nov), Révfülop and Balatonboglár, and Badacsony and Fonyód (both mid-April to mid-Oct). See "Travel Details" at the end of this chapter for more information.

The southern shore from Siófok to the Kis-Balaton

Approaching **the southern shore** from the direction of Budapest by train, you'll catch your first glimpse of the Balaton at **BALATONVILÁGOS**. As one of the lushest, least commercialized resorts, built on wooded cliffs and along the shore, it was formerly reserved for Party officials, while boats – even those seeking refuge from storms – were forbidden to dock in the harbour. Unlike other resorts, Balatonvilágos has something that could properly be called a beach. The whole place is currently undergoing a face-lift, with the result that the *Volán Hotel* at Zrínyi utca 135 (☎88/380-095; ⑤) and the *Kék Balaton Hotel* at no. 3 (☎88/380-827; ③) are among the few establishments ready for business.

Siófok

SIÓFOK is the largest port on the southern shore: a plebeian, open-armed place that was the first resort to introduce video-discos in the Eighties, and strip bars in more recent years. Its vitality and tackiness might appeal for a while, but you're unlikely to want to stay for long – and the accommodation situation is dire. A string of high-rise hotels – their communal beach always crammed with bodies – typifies the modern resort, belying its pre-war reputation as a centre of quiet elegance. A token reminder of this past can be found in the **Petőfi sétány**, a leafy promenade lined with sedate villas that terminates by a rose garden in **Jókai Park**.

You can trace some of the history of Siófok and the lake at the **Beszédes József Museum** (Tues–Sun 9am–1pm & 2–6pm) at Sió út 2 by the Sió canal, just south of the obvious landmark of the meteorological tower on Szabadság tér. Among the items covered are the first canal and locks – initiated by Emperor Galerius in 292 AD; the Turkish occupation, when an Ottoman fleet of 10,000 men was stationed in Siófok; and an assortment of old boats. As is obvious from some of the vessels exhibited, crossing the lake was a hazardous business before steam boats were introduced by Count Széchenyi in the 1840s.

Siófok's other museums include the **Imre Kálmán Museum** at Kálmán Imre sétány 5 (Tues–Sun 9am–1pm & 2–6pm), named after the Hungarian operetta composer born here and featuring exhibits on his life and times; the **Mineral Museum** further along the same street, with displays of various minerals from the region; and the **Wine Museum** at Fő utca 212 (April–Sept daily 10am–10pm), where you can test the local tipple. East of Fő utca is the **Lutheran church**, designed by the visionary architect Imre Makovecz.

> The Siófok telephone code is ☎84

Arrival and information
The bus and train **stations** are next to each other on **Fő utca**, the town's main axis. **Ferries** dock to the west of the park, at the mouth of the Sió canal. The main sources of **information** (easily located by heading for the meteorological tower) are *Tourinform*, housed in the water tower on Fő utca (May–Sept Mon–Sat 9am–6pm & Sun 10am–noon; ☎310-117); *Siótour* at Szabadság tér 6 (summer Mon–Sat 8am–8pm, Sun 9am–6pm; winter Mon–Fri 8am–4.30pm, Sat 8am–noon; ☎310-900); and *Ibusz* at Fő utca 174 (summer Mon–Fri 8am–6pm & Sat 8am–4pm; winter Mon–Fri 8am–4pm; ☎311-066).

Accommodation
All three tourist agencies listed above can get completely swamped in summer, so if you simply want to book a **private room** (②) try *MÁV Tours* in the train station; *Cooptourist* at Indóház utca 10 (same hours as *Ibusz*; ☎310-279); or *Safeta Tours* at Fő utca 216 – you might have to settle for something in a distant suburb, but at least it will be a roof over your head. Solo travellers or people wishing to stay less than three nights are likely to be disappointed. The alternatives are to reserve ahead (or hope for a vacancy) at a **pension**, pay through the nose at a lakeside **hotel**, resign yourself to a **campsite** far from the centre, or head one town west to Zamardi.

HOTELS AND PENSIONS
The first four places listed below can be reserved through *Pannonia Tourist* (VIII, Rákóczi út 9; ☎1/138-4225) in Budapest.

Hotel Balaton, Petőfi sétány 9 (☎310-655). Reasonably smart three-star hotel along the promenade. Half-board in summer; closed in winter. ⑥.

Hotel Európa, Petőfi sétány 15 (☎313-411). Modern three-star structure along the promenade. ⑦

Hotel Hungária, Petőfi sétány 13 (☎310-677). Another modern three-star pile along the promenade. ⑥.

Hotel Lídó, Petőfi sétány 11 (☎310-633). Seventies low-rise next door to the *Balaton*; also three-star and with similar arrangements. ⑥.

Hotel Napfény, Mártirok útja 8 (☎311-408). Nondescript Seventies low-rise between the park and the promenade. Summer rates include half-board; closed over winter. ⑤.

Azur Hotel, Vitorlás utca 11 (☎312-033). Large, reasonably priced place west of the canal. ③–④.

Diana Panzió, Szent László utca 41 (☎313-360). A couple of blocks inland from the *Magistern*, with only 15 beds. ⑤.

Magistern Hotel, Beszédes sétány 72 (☎312-544). On Aranypart *strand*, 200m east of the *Európa*. ④–⑤.

Oázis Panzió, Szigliget utca 5 (☎313-650). Relatively quiet place with single, double and triple rooms, 500m west of the Sió canal and one block in from the lake. ④.

Tengerszem Panzió, Karinthy Frigyes utca 4 (☎310-146). Quaint old establishment near the lakefront.

HOSTELS AND CAMPSITES

Siófok has only one hostel to its name, though there are at least twenty campsites along Balaton's southern shore.

Aranypart Camping, Szent László utca 183–185, 5km east of town centre (where Siófok merges into Balatonszabadi). Beachfront campsite – no shade, but a great waterchute. Open mid-May to mid-Aug.

Ezústpart Camping, November 7 tér. Fairly large, shadeless site, 4km west of the centre (bus #1 from the Baross Bridge).

Trade School Holiday Home, Erkel Ferenc utca 46 (☎310-131). Hostel with large dorms – enquire at *Tourinform*. Open June–Sept.

Activities and nightlife

Although the stretch of waterfront in the centre consists of paying **beaches** (daily 8am–7pm), there are free *strand* 1km out at Aranypart and Ezüsztpart, to the east and west respectively. On most of the beaches and at many campsites you can rent windsurfing boards and small sailing boats. *Siótour* can arrange **horse riding** and various **excursions** and **pleasure cruises**. The latter should not be confused with cruises on the *Love Boat*, a sex emporium moored on the canal, which together with the *Intim Kiss Kiss*, *Hawaii Bar* and *Tengerszem Disco*, leads the field in sleazy **nightlife**. More salubrious forms of nightlife can be found along the lakefront and on Fő utca/tér.

Between Siófok and Fonyód

Blink as you pass through **ZAMÁRDI**, the next settlement, and you'll miss it – which isn't a great shame. Red signs lead from the station to **Szamárkő** (Donkey Rock), thought by archeologists to have been a sacrificial site of the ancient Magyars, and claimed by some Christians to bear the hoof-print of Christ's donkey. Nearer to the main street is a **Tájház** displaying peasant pottery, tiled ovens and old agricultural equipment. Otherwise Zamárdi offers the standard beach'n'bars setup. The *Siótour* **information** office is at Petofi S. utca 1 (March–Nov daily 9am–6pm; ☎84/348-772). *Auto-camping I* (mid-May to mid-Sept) and *II* (June–Aug) are both on the shore road, and the *Touring Hotel* is at Petőfi utca 146 (☎84/331-008; ④–⑤).

Neighbouring **SZÁNTÓD** has the expensive *Rév Camping* (April–Aug; ☎84/331-159) and *Touring Hotel* (☎84/331-096; ⑤–⑥), both sited near the docks for **car ferries** to Tihany on the northern shore. By the *Shell* filling station is another *Siótour* office (May–Sept Mon–Sat 9am–6pm). Further inland by the main road a collection of eighteenth- and nineteenth-century farm buildings, known as the **Szántódpuszta**, houses exhibitions of crafts and local history, a blacksmith's, aquarium and two *csárdas* or traditional inns (summer daily 9am–5pm; winter Tues–Sat 8am–4.30pm & Sun 8am–noon).

BALATONFÖLDVÁR is in a similar vein but on a larger scale. Swimming began here at the turn of the century, and now thousands come to amble from snack bar to snack bar through carefully laid out parks and holiday complexes. The cheapest places **to stay** are the pleasant *Magyar Tenger* campsite (☎84/340-

240) down by the *Hotel Neptun* (☎84/376-038; ⑥); and the *Hotel Juventus* (☎84/340-379; ④) and bungalows (May–Sept; ☎84/340-371; ②–③) on József utca – both owned by *Express*. *Siótour*, at Szécheny utca 9–11, can also help with accommodation (mid-Jan to June & Sept to mid-Nov Mon–Fri 8am–4.30pm plus July–Aug Sat–Sun 3–7pm; ☎84/340-099). Three kilometres inland, **KŐRŐSHEGY** boasts a fifteenth-century **church** where chamber-music concerts are held on summer evenings. If you're in the mood for **walking**, the villages further south are pretty, and the hills beyond resound with the choruses of mating deer.

Balatonszárszó and Balatonszemes

The boundary of **BALATONSZÁRSZÓ** is marked by a cemetery containing the **grave of Attila József**, the tragic proletarian poet. Dismissed by his literary peers and rejected by his lover and the Communist Party, he threw himself beneath a local freight train on December 3, 1937. Every year, a few desperate souls emulate his suicide. Attila spent his last days in a pension that's now a **memorial museum** (April–Oct Tues–Sun 10am–6pm; Nov–March Tues–Sun 10am–2pm). You'll find it at József utca 7, 100m from *Tura Camping*, by the rail tracks (mid-June to Aug). There is a *Tourist Hostel* at Fő utca 37 (☎84/340-492; ①), and *Siótour*, by the train station, can also help with accommodation (May–Sept Mon–Fri 9am–6pm; ☎84/362-956).

BALATONSZEMES, 5km west, has an old coaching inn converted into a **Postal Museum** (June–Sept Tues–Sun 10am–6pm), with antique stage coaches in the courtyard. Besides **rooms** in the *Lídó Fogadó* at Ady utca 53 (May–Sept; ☎84/345-112; ②), there are several **campsites**: *Lídó Camping* at Ady utca 8 (April–Sept; ☎384/345-112); *Hullám Camping* at Kaza utca (☎84/345-116); and the *Bagódomb* site (July–Aug; ☎84/345-117), uphill towards the ruined Bagolyvár Castle. *Siótour* is the place to go for information (mid-April to Sept Mon–Fri 9am–6pm & Sat 9am–1pm; ☎84/360-149).

Balatonlelle and Balatonboglár

Merged during the Kádár era and renamed Boglárlelle, the two settlements of **BALATONLELLE** and **BALATONBOGLÁR** have recently re-established their separate identities. The former, nearer Balatonszemes, offers **folk dancing** in July and August in an old mansion at Kossuth utca 2, while the latter is known for its **wine harvest festival** (*Boglári Szüret*) from August 18 to 20, and exhibitions by artists in the two chapels atop Cemetery Hill (*Temetődomb*) further inland. On neighbouring Castle Hill, a spherical **lookout tower** commands a sweeping view from Keszthely to Tihany.

There are *Siótour* **information** offices at Dózsa György utca 1 in Boglár (mid-May to mid-Sept daily 8am–noon & 3–7pm; mid-Sept to mid-May Mon–Fri 8am–4.30pm & Sat 8am–noon; ☎84/350-665), and Szent István utca 1 in Lelle (Feb–Nov Mon–Fri 9am–6pm & Sat 9am–1pm; ☎84/351-086). Both can book private **rooms** (②–③), and the Boglár branch handles college beds (①) over summer. Boglár also features *Sellő Camping* (June–Sept; ☎85/350-800) near the landing stage, and more **bungalows** at the *Guiseppe Hotel*, Köztársaság út 36–38 (June–Sept; ☎85/350-074). Lelle has three bungalow complexes: *Hullám* at Köztársaság utca 14 (mid-May to mid-Sept; ☎84/350-440), *Liget* at Kikötősétány 3 (same dates; ☎84/350-687) and at Hunyadi utca 32 (open year-round; ☎84/351-118). They all charge about the same (③).

The *Albatross Étterem* on the main road between Lelle and Boglár is a good place to **eat**, while draught Holsten can be quaffed at the *Zöld Lugas* on Honvéd utca in Lelle.

Fonyód, Nagyberek and the Kis-Balaton

Between the resorts of Fonyód and Keszthely the Balaton shore quietens down markedly, attracting a more Hungarian crowd. Instead of high-rise hotels and discos, you now find narrow-gauge trains, horse riding, birdlife, and one of the few nudist beaches along the lake shore.

Fonyód

FONYÓD grew up between the Sipos and Sándor hills and subsequently spread itself along the lakeside; the symmetry of its setting is best appreciated from the far shore. A built-up *strand* and bleak modern architecture make this an unlikely setting for the grand passion that inspired Fonyód's "**Crypt Villa**". Raised above a red marble crypt with room for two, this was built by a grieving widower who lived there in seclusion for many years, waiting to join his wife below. It is now undergoing restoration as a "sight" in a place otherwise bereft of curiosities. Most people, however, come here only for the **ferries to Badacsony** on the northern shore.

Should you need **information**, *Siótour* (Mon–Fri 9am–6pm, plus Sat–Sun 9am–6pm in summer; ☎85/361-214) is located in the station, and *Ibusz* (summer Mon–Sat 8am–6pm & Sun 9am–noon; winter Mon–Fri 8am–4pm; ☎85/361-816) at Szent István utca 4. During summer, they might be able to find beds (①) in a local *kollégium*. Otherwise, **accommodation** boils down to private rooms (through the same agencies; ③), camping or a bungalow (②–③) at the *Napsugár* complex Komjáth utca 5 in Fonyód-Bélatelep (☎84/361-211) 2km east of the centre; or the *Korona Panzió* at Szent István utca 3 (☎85/361-608; ⑤).

Nagyberek and Csisztapuszta

Behind the lakeside sprawl of Balatonfenyves and Balatonmáriafürdő (see below) lies an extensive swampland that was partially drained in the Sixties, under the auspices of the **NAGYBEREK** state farm. This produced fewer benefits than expected and spoiled a rich breeding ground for fish, so the emphasis has now switched to conservation. The primal swamp of **Fehérvíz** (*Fehérvízi őslap*) is a nesting ground for little and white egrets, spoonbills, purple and night herons and other **birdlife**. The area can be visited on a **narrow-gauge train** running from Balatonfenyves to Csisztapuszta. Trains run every day except Monday – three times a day over winter and every couple of hours during summer, when there's a *nosztálgia* **steam train** in the morning. At CSISZTAPUSZTA, where drilling for oil unexpectedly yielded warm springs instead of "black gold", you can wallow in the baths or go horse riding in the surrounding countryside (*Siótour* has details).

From Balatonkeresztúr to the Kis-Balaton

The final stretch of the southern shore is reedy in places and very shallow. Whole tribes of swimmers decamp to rafts anchored offshore, armed with crates of beer and piles of *lángos*. **BALATONMÁRIAFÜRDŐ** has private **rooms** (② – look for the signs); a **hostel** (☎84/346-383; ①–②) and a basic **campsite**; plus **ferries to Balatongyörok** on the northern shore.

Consider a brief stopover at **BALATONKERESZTÚR** to see the **Baroque church** at the main crossroads, entirely decorated with gorgeous frescoes in the style of Maulbertsch. These include portraits of the Festetics family, who owned most of the land around Keszthely. Count Kristóf appears at the rear of the church and to the left of the altar, accompanied by his wife Judit Szegedi. A former Festetics mansion at Ady utca 26 now serves as a **hostel** (mid-May to late Aug; ☎85/376-779; ①–②); beds can be booked through *Siótour* at Ady Endre út 26 (May–Sept 9am–6pm & Sat 9am–1pm; ☎85/376-180).

BALATONSZENTGYÖRGY, several kilometres inland, has nothing to recommend it but the *Csillagvár* restaurant at Berzsenyi utca 50–58 (daily 7am–10pm); and buses to Keszthely and trains to Nagykanizsa in southern Transdanubia. Lakeside **BALATONBERÉNY**, however, features the only **nudist beach** on the southern shore, the agreeable *Kócsag* **campsite** (June–Aug; ☎85/377-154), as well as two agencies letting **rooms** (②–③): *Halló Ungarn* at Botond utca 2 (open year-round; ☎84/377-408) and *Fortuna Kft* at Kossuth utca 14 (June & July; ☎84/377-163). There's also a *Siótour* office on the strand for local information (May–Sept 9am–6pm & Sat 9am–1pm; ☎85/377-701).

The Kis-Balaton

At the far end of the lake, reeds obscure the mouth of the River Zala and stretch for miles upstream to the **Kis-Balaton** (Little Balaton). This lake once covered forty square kilometres, but was half-drained in the Fifties to provide irrigation for new cropland, while the dumping of pollutants into the Zala nearly killed it during the Eighties. Its regeneration is currently top priority for the Office of Environmental Protection, which has declared it a **nature reserve** for over eighty breeds of bird, including spoonbills, egrets and cormorants. Visits require permission from the *National Office for Nature Conservation* in Budapest (V, Arany utca 25; ☎1/132-7371). Keszthely, at the western end of Lake Balaton, is covered on p.172.

The northern shore to Balatonfüred

To reach Lake Balaton's **northern shore** by road from Budapest, turn off route 70 just outside Balatonaliga and follow the shoreline round through **BALATONKARATTYA**. This elegant place is distinguished by the dead trunk of the *Rákóczi fa* (the tree to which the famous freedom fighter Rákóczi is reputed to have tied his horse), and the **nudist campsite** *FKK Piroska* at Aligai út 15 (mid-May to late Sept; ☎88/381-084; 1200Ft per tent).

From neighbouring **BALATONKENESE** you can get a view extending the entire length of the lake, while a Baroque church and peasant houses still stand along Bajcsy-Zsilinszky, Kossuth and Fő utca. Until the end of the last century people continued to live in caves dug into the clay banks above the settlement by refugees fleeing from the Turks. Those seeking **accommodation** will discover plenty of *Zimmer frei* signs dotted around, and there's also the *Fortuna Hotel/ Camping* at Bacsó Béla utca 136 (April–Oct; ☎88/381-242), a quiet and relatively cheap outfit (600Ft per tent; ② for a double room) with an excellent location – follow signs to Honvéd Üdülő. *Romantic Camping* at Gesztenyefaso (mid-May to

Sept; ☎88/381-335) is a cheaper option, though it's not on the waterfront. Further along the lake in **BALATONFÜZFŐ** there's a tourist information office near the train station at Balaton körút 50 (☎88/351-714), and a large swimming pool for those who deem the lake too polluted.

Balatonalmádi

Beyond the smelly nitro-chemicals plant that disfigures Balatonfüző, the main road approaches the first town on the northern shore, **BALATONALMÁDI** (also accessible by ferry from June to August).

A resort since 1877, Balatonalmádi's only sight that engenders any historical interest is the now modern-looking medieval **Chapel of Saint Jobb**. Originally part of Buda Castle, it was transplanted here towards the end of the nineteenth century and incorporated into the Catholic church. The murals are the work of Károly Lotz, the nineteenth-century historicist painter. Cultural **entertainment** in the form of the **Almádi Days** takes place every year at the end of July and includes a series of concerts.

Should the paying *strand* induce you to stay, **accommodation** in Balatonalmádi ranges from the expensive *Hotel Auróra* at Bajcsy-Zsilinszky utca 14 (☎88/338-810; ⑥) and the *Tulipán Hotel* at Városház tér 1 (☎88/338-317; ⑤–⑥); to relatively inexpensive **private rooms**, bookable through *Balatontourist* at Petőfi utca 6 (June–Aug Mon–Sat 8.30am–6pm & Sun 8.30am–noon; ☎88/338-707; ②–③) or *Ibusz*, just across from the train station at Petőfi utca 21 (June–Aug daily 8am–6pm; ☎88/338-149). *Yacht Camping* (mid-May to mid-Sept; ☎88/338-906) rents out boats and bungalows by the lake (②); *Kristóf Camping* next door is also on the waterfront and has its own private beach (mid-April to mid-Oct; ☎88/338-902); and *Bikini Camping* at Óvari utca 70 (June to mid-Sept; ☎88/338-302) is cheaper but away from the lake.

Alsóörs, Csopak and Felsőörs

Ferries and trains continue around to **ALSÓÖRS**, formerly a mining village where the rock was used to make millstones. In the centre of the village at Petőfi köz 7 stands an odd remnant of the Ottoman occupation – a **Gothic manor house** once inhabited by the local Turkish tax collector, distinguished by a turban-topped chimney (a sign of wealth in the days when smoke left most houses through a hole in the roof). Although there's no particular reason to linger in Alsóörs (aside from the fact that it's quiet and relatively cheap), there are a few **places in which to stay**: the *Pelikán Hotel* at Füredi út 62 (☎87/347-149; ④); the *Szivárvány Panzió* at Szegfű utca 13 (mid-April to mid-Sept; ☎87/347-124; ③); and *Riviera Camping* on the *strand*.

Neighbouring **CSOPAK** – with a reputation for its *Olaszrizling* and *Furmint* **wines** – also offers **accommodation** in the form of bungalows on Sport utca (May–Sept; ☎86/346-035); the charming *Rozmaring Panzió*, by the *strand* at Rozmaring utca 10 (May–Oct; ☎86/346-583); and the *Youth Hostel* at Sport utca 9 (May–Sept; ☎86/346-505). Further along Sport utca is the *Orient Express Étterem*, an old rail carriage-turned-restaurant set in a garden. About a kilometre inland, **FELSŐÖRS** has a **Baroque church** built from purple-red sandstone, whose tower is carved with the "Knots of Hercules", ancient ornamental reliefs designed to ward off demons. Otherwise, there's nothing to stop you from pushing on to Balatonfüred.

Balatonfüred

Seventeenth-century chronicles tell of pilgrims descending on **BALATONFÜRED** to "camp in scattered tents" and benefit from the mineral springs. Nowadays some 30,000 people come every year for treatment, mingling with hordes of tourists to make this one of the busiest and liveliest of the Balaton resorts. **Arriving** at the bus or train station, northwest of the centre, walk to Jókai utca and down to the waterfront (15min), or catch bus #1, which takes a roundabout route to the embankment before heading west along Széchenyi út. Ferries dock near the start of the Tagore sétány promenade, named after the Bengali poet who came here in 1926 and planted a tree in gratitude for his cure. Other celebrities followed his example – the origin of the memorial grove which opens on to the main square.

The Town

Gyógy tér (Health Square) is aptly named. Its columned, pagoda-like **Kossuth Well** gushes carbonated water, while other springs feed the trade union sanatorium and cardiac hospital – whose **mineral baths** are reserved for patients – which flank the northern and eastern sides of the square. Excavated villas suggest that the Romans were the first to exploit the springs, using the waters to treat stomach ailments and, when mixed with goats' milk whey, as a cure for lung diseases.

Across the square stands the eighteenth-century **Horváth House**, one of the first inns in a land where inn-keeping developed late. Magyars tended to consider such work beneath them: Petőfi complained that his landlord wouldn't utter a word of welcome until he had been paid, and served food "as if by the special grace of God"; another traveller reported that his host was "capable of giving his guests a good hammering or throwing them out" on impulse. The inn was patronized by writers and politicians during the Reform era, and is now a sanatorium for uranium miners – it has recently started taking tourists.

Beyond this lies Blaha Lujza utca, named after the "Nation's Nightingale", Lujza Blaha (1850–1926), who spent her summers in a **villa** at no. 4 (now a hotel) and had her tea at the *Kedves Cukrászda* across the road. Opposite the mid-nineteenth-century **Round Church**, at the junction with Jókai utca, stands the **Jókai Memorial House** (April–Oct Tues–Sun 10am–6pm). The novelist Jókai came to Balatonfüred at the age of 37, half-expecting to die from a serious lung infection. He built this villa as a refuge to return to each year, and lived to the ripe old age of 84. The museum shares the building with the *Jókai kávézó*, an excellent coffee house.

Heading northeast, Jókai utca becomes Ady utca once it crosses the rail tracks; an ironic juxtaposition of names, since the poet Ady died of syphilis at the age of 42. Bus #1, #2 or #3 can drop you at the far end, in the original centre of town, where old houses in the traditional local style line Siske and Vázsonyi utca, and there's a touch of village atmosphere about the **market** off Arácsi út. During summer there may be **concerts** in the Calvinist church.

Practicalities

Balatonfüred's train and bus stations are both on Dobó István utca, midway between the old town north of the rail line and the newer resort area on the waterfront – a fifteen-minute walk in either direction. *Balatontourist* at Blaha Lujza utca 5 (June–Aug Mon–Sat 8.30am–6.30pm & Sun 8.30am–noon; Sept–May Mon–Fri 8.30am–4pm; ☎87/342-822) is the best source of **information**.

Accommodation

Private rooms (②–③), the cheapest of which are in the old town, can be booked through *Balatontourist* (address above); *Ibusz*, a few blocks from the station at Petőfi utca 4A (Mon–Fri 8am–4pm, plus Sat–Sun 9am–1pm in summer; ☎86/342-251); *Volántourist* at Petőfi utca 49 (☎87/342-259); and *Cooptourist* at Jókai utca 23 (May–Sept Mon–Fri 9am–6pm & Sat 9am–noon; ☎87/342-677). **College dormitory beds** (①) are sometimes available at the *Lóczy Lajos Gimnázium* in Ady Endre utca or the *Széchenyi Ferenc Kollégium* in Iskola utca. Beyond the *Hotel Marina* (bus #1 or #2) at Széchenyi utca 24 lies the huge *Füred* **campsite** offering tennis, watersports and bungalows on the lakefront (mid-April to mid-Oct; ☎86/343-823; ②–③). Other options include:

Horváth House, Gyógy tér. Quadruple rooms in this historic building are sometimes rented out to tourists. ⑤.

Hotel Blaha Lujza, Blaha Lujza utca 4 (☎86/342-603). The former villa of nineteenth-century actress-singer Lujza Blaha. Opposite *Balatontourist*, off Gyógy tér. Closed Jan & Feb. ⑤.

Hotel Marina, Széchenyi utca 26 (☎87/343-644). Classier and nearer the waterfront, with half-board over summer. Open April–Sept. ⑤.

Hotel Tagore, Deák Ferenc utca 56 (☎87/343-173). 36-room hotel on the lakefront. ⑤.

Hotel Uni, Széchenyi utca 10, 1km west of the centre (☎87/342-239). High-rise hotel with its own private beach, boat rental facilities and tennis courts. ⑥.

Korona Panzió, Vörösmarty utca 4 (☎87/343-278). A decent pension next to *Ibusz*, open year-round. ⑤.

Activities

Balatontourist has details of **horse riding** in the Koloska Valley outside town, where there is a riding school. You can hire **bicycles** outside the big hotels and campsite (300Ft per hour, 700Ft for three hours, plus 1000Ft deposit), and pedaloes and **windsurfing** boards at every *strand*. The *Gagarin*, moored alongside a small pier, rents out **yachts** (9am–8pm; closed Thurs) for 300Ft an hour, plus a fee for the skipper if you haven't got a licence. The only **waterskiing** on Lake Balaton is practised at *FICC Rally Camping*, using an electric-powered towing cable.

There are paying **beaches** (daily 8am–6pm; July–Aug till 7pm) either side of the harbour; the one by the *Hotel Marina* is best for swimming (though not for kids, as it drops away very quickly). On the eastern edge of town is a free *strand* where you can bathe at night – though this too may be turned into a paying beach soon.

Eating and drinking

The *Halászkert* on Széchenyi tér and the *Borcsa* on Tagor sétány are the best value **restaurants** downtown. To enjoy some fresh air and **music** with your meal, take a trip out to the *Tölgyfa Csárda* (daily 10am–10pm), a restaurant in the Koloska Valley (bus #3 or #4) specializing in game dishes.

Moving on

Moving on from Balatonfüred, the obvious **destinations** are Tihany (see below) or Nagyvázsony and Veszprém in the Bakony (covered later in this chapter) – all served by frequent buses. Ferries sail to Tihany and to Siófok on the far side of the Tihany peninsula: the rail line skips the peninsula as it forges eastwards.

Tihany

A rocky finger of land that was declared Hungary's first national park in 1952, **Tihany peninsula** is historically associated with the Benedictine order and a redoubtable castle (no longer in existence) that withstood 150 years of Turkish hostility. As one of the most beautiful regions of the Balaton, Tihany gets swamped with visitors over summer, though you can always escape the crowds by hiking into the interior. The coastal road from Balatonfüred passes through Dios (where Avar graves have been discovered) and Gödrös, entering **Tihany village** above the inner harbour (*Belső Kikötő*) where ferries from Balatonfüred and Siófok arrive. At the tip of the peninsula lies **Tihany-rév**, a modern resort dominated by the *Club Tihany* complex.

Around Tihany village

In contrast with Tihany-rév, **TIHANY** village remains a traditional-looking place, with many old houses built of grey basalt tufa with porticoed terraces, their windows and doors outlined in white. In days gone by, the village was dominated by a Benedictine abbey, established here in 1055 at the request of Andrew I and founded – true to the biblical injunction – upon a rocky promontory overlooking the Balaton. Andrew's body lies in the crypt of the **abbey church** – the only one of the Árpád line to remain where he was buried. The building itself is Baroque, the original having succumbed to wars and time. Inside are virtuoso **woodcarvings** by Sebestyén Stulhoff, who lived and worked in the abbey for 25 years after his fiancée died (her features are preserved in the face of an angel to the right of the altar) and grandiose **frescoes** by Lotz, Székely and Deák-Ebner. Recently restored, the church (open 10am–6pm, except during masses) provides a magnificent setting for **organ concerts** over summer. The abbey's foundation deed, held at Pannonhalma Monastery in Transdanubia (see p.198), is the earliest document to include Hungarian words among the Latin.

   The **Tihany Museum** (Tues–Sun 10am–6pm) is housed in the former priory (which four monks are currently trying to reclaim). It features an array of Balaton landscapes, costumes, implements and musical instruments gathered from far-

---

THE ORIGIN OF THE MAGYARS

When the **Magyars** swept into the Carpathian Basin and raided deep into western Europe (896–995 AD), they were identified with the invading **Huns** of the fifth century (hence the appellations "Hungarian", *Ungarn, Hongoris*, etc). This association persisted until linguistic and ethnographic investigations by János Sajnovics (1733–85), Antal Reguly and others traced their descent from the **Finno-Ugric peoples** of what is now Siberia. The language of the **Chuvash**, for example, has many similarities with old Hungarian, and their folk songs are based on the same pentatonic scale. More recently, however, the idea of a link between the early Magyars and the Huns has been revived following the decipherment of **inscriptions** on the "Treasure of Attila", which have much in common with ancient Magyar runes.

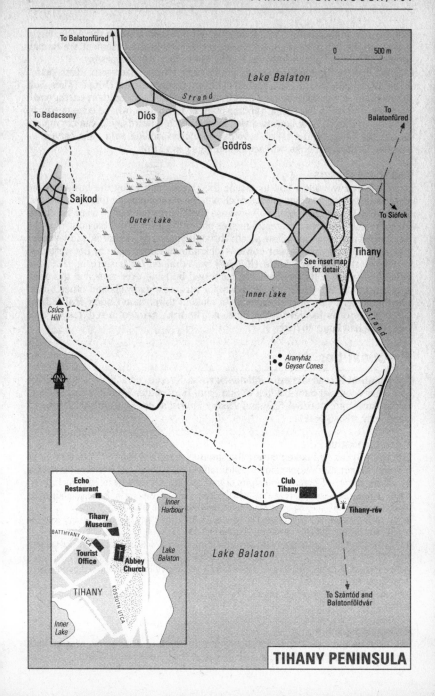

TIHANY PENINSULA

flung communities in the Ural Mountains and the *taiga* beneath the Arctic circle – whence the Magyars originated (see box above). In the basement are Roman altars and bits and pieces from the Paulite Monastery at Nagyvázsony.

Next door to the museum stands the **Pottery House** (Tues–Sun 10am–6pm). From here Pisky sétány leads past an old **Fishermen's Guild House** (Tues–Sun 10am–6pm) where folk dancing performances occur over summer, past a small *Skanzen*, and on to the scenic vantage point of **Echo Hill**, whose echo seems to have disappeared. By following a well-marked path onwards, you can circumambulate the **Óvár** (Old Castle), a volcanic outcrop riddled with cells carved by Russian Orthodox monks, whence hot springs gush forth.

Lakes and geysers

A trek inland will allow you to escape the crowds and enjoy the beauty of the peninsula, whose geology and micro-climate have produced an unusual flora and fauna. The **Inner Lake** (*Belső-tó*) – whose sunlit surface is visible from the abbey church – fills a volcanic crater 25 metres above the level of the Balaton. From its southern bank, you can follow a path through vineyards, orchards and lavender fields to the **Aranyház geyser cones** – rock funnels forced open by hot springs.

The northerly **Outer Lake** (*Külső-tó*) was drained for pasture in 1809, but refilled after 1975. Its reedbeds are harvested by hand over winter in the traditional manner, and provide a sanctuary for mallards, gadwalls and other **birds**. On the eastern side of the peninsula, a lookout tower atop **Csúcs Hill** (232m) offers a **panoramic view** of the Balaton. The trail, marked in red, takes about one and a half hours to hike.

Practicalities

Information is available from *Balatontourist* at Kossuth utca 20 in Tihany village (summer Mon–Sat 8am–6.30pm & Sun 8am–1pm; winter Mon–Fri 8am–4.30pm & Sat 8am–1pm; ☎86/348-519) and *Tihany Tourist* at no. 11 (April–Oct Mon–Sat 9am–7pm; ☎86/348-481).

Accommodation

Rooms (③) can be booked during the summer months through *Balatontourist* or *Tihany Tourist* (addresses above). Alternatively, if you simply wander the streets you'll see plenty of *Zimmer frei* signs dotted around. Other possibilities include:

Club Tihany, Tihany-rév (☎86/348-088). Holiday village run by a Hungarian-Austrian-Danish consortium, offering luxury bungalows and rooms with half-board. ⑦.

Park Hotel, Tihany-rév (☎86/348-611). Similar set-up to the *Club Tihany* with every conceivable sports facility, but only open from April to Oct. ⑦.

Erika Hotel, Batthyány utca 6 (☎86/348-010). Plush pension with 15 rooms and a swimming pool. ⑥.

Adler Panzió, Felső Kopasz hegy 1 (☎86/348-755). A decent enough pension but only open May–Sept. ④.

Kolostor Panzió, Kossuth Lajos utca 14 (☎86/348-408). A pleasant new pension with 7 rooms. ③.

Eating and drinking

While **bars** and snack stalls cluster round the dock at Tihany-rév, **restaurants** are concentrated in the village. Locals eat at the *Kecskeköröm Csárda*, Kossuth utca 19; the *Fogas Csárda* at no. 1 (11am–11pm); and the *Halásztanya* at Visszhang utca 11 (11am–9pm). The *Echo Restaurant* on Echo Hill is dearer, but offers a lovely view (Mon–Sat 10am–10pm).

Activities
Besides the paying **beaches** by *Club Tihany* and the Tihany docks, there are free *strand* along the reedier shores between Gödrös and Dios, and south of Sajkod on the other side of the peninsula.

Moving on
Tihany is connected to Balatonfüred by hourly **buses**, which stop on András tér below the abbey church and next to *Balatontourist* on Kossuth utca. **Ferries** from the inner harbour (*Belső Kikötő*) sail to Balatonfüred and Siófok, as well as Badacsony during the summer months. From April to November there are boats every half hour or so from Tihany-rév to Balatonföldvar and Szántód (the latter a car ferry) on the southern shore. Buses to Balatonudvari, Balatonszepezd or Badacsony are the best means of **heading west**.

West towards Keszthely

For thirty kilometres west of Tihany **the shoreline** is infested with holiday homes and nondescript resorts; perhaps worth stopping for if you hit upon a beach or campsite to your taste, but generally nothing special. **ASZÓFŐ**, where the peninsula road meets the highway, has a large **campsite**, *Diana Camping* (May–Sept; ☎86/345-013). At **ÖRVÉNYES**, 2km west, an eighteenth-century **watermill** is still operating (May–Sept daily 8am–5pm; Oct–April daily 8am–4pm) – one of the few that wasn't demolished in the Fifties to clear the way for state milling collectives. Nine kilometres further on, the cemetery in **BALATONUDVARI** features heart-shaped tombstones (also a popular motif in Austria and Germany during the eighteenth century).

BALATONAKALI, known for its *Akali muskotály* white wine, has four **campsites**. The huge *Holiday* (mid-May to mid-Sept; ☎86/344-093) and *Strand* (June to mid-Sept; ☎86/344-151) sites are by the lake on the eastern side of town, while *Privát Camping* at Kossuth utca 14 (May–Sept; ☎86/344-223) and *Pacsirta Camping* at Pacsirta utca 4 (mid-June to Aug; ☎86/344-281) are smaller and more central, but away from the lake. There are **private accommodation** bureaux at Kossuth utca 17, Petőfi utca 4, and outside the train station.

A fortress-like miners' rest home guards the road into **BALATONSZEPEZD**, where you can book **rooms** at Rózsa utca 122 (☎87/348-558; ②–③), and *Venusz Camping* (mid-May to Aug; ☎87/348-048) awaits visitors by the waterside, 1km east of the train station at Halász utca 1. Both are preferable to the overpriced *Napfény* site (mid-May to mid-Sept; ☎87/344-309) in neighbouring **RÉVFÜLÖP**, whence there are **ferries to Boglárlelle** on the southern shore. **ÁBRAHÁMHEGY**, 5km west, contains the Folly Aboretum of cedars and pines from all over the world, and a refreshingly unbuilt-up *strand*. Shortly afterwards comes **BADACSONYÖRS**, which has *Balaton Camping* (May–Sept; ☎87/331-253) and the *Szürkebárat Panzió* (③). The village is named after the massif that looms just around the coast.

The Badacsony

A coffin-shaped hulk with four villages prostrated at its feet, backed by dead volcanoes ranging across the Tapolca basin, **the Badacsony** is one of the Balaton's most striking features. When the land that was to become Hungary first surfaced, molten magma erupted from the seabed and cooled into a great semicircle of **basalt columns**, 210 metres high, which form the Badacsony's south-eastern face. The rich volcanic soil of the lower slopes has supported vineyards since the Age of Migrations, when the Avars buried grape seeds with their dead to ensure that the afterlife wouldn't be lacking in wine. Nowadays, the harvest is blended into *Badacsonyi Kéknyelü, Zöldszilváni, Szürkebarát* ("Grey Monk") or *Olaszrizling*, and there's a **harvest festival** during the second week in September.

Although trains and buses also call at Badacsonytomaj, Badacsony Lábdihegy and Balatontördemic, it is **BADACSONY** proper that gets all the tourists and ferries from Boglárlelle, Fonyód and Szigliget. If you don't fancy embarking on the **wine trail** immediately, pay a visit to the **Egry Museum**, just over the rail level crossing on Egri sétány (May–Sept Tues–Sun 10am–6pm). József Egry (1883–1951) was born into a poor local family and worked as a locksmith and roofer before winning a scholarship to the Academy of Fine Arts. His paintings capture the ever-changing moods and light of the Balaton.

Otherwise, hop into one of the jeep-taxis leaving from in front of the post office on Park utca – for 150Ft (Jul & Aug only) you'll be transported 3km uphill through the vineyards to the **Róza Szegedi House**. This charming residence is often called the **Kisfaludy House** after Róza's poet husband, Sándor Kisfaludy, who lauded the Balaton's beauties in verse. Just before the house is the **Róza Szegedi Museum** (Tues–Sun 10am–5pm).

Walking in the Badacsony

From Kisfaludy House you can follow a path up to the **Rose Rock** (*Rózsakő*), of which it's said that if a man and woman sit upon it with their backs to the Balaton and think about each other, they'll be married by the end of the year. The trail continues through the beechwoods to the **Kisfaludy lookout tower** (437m), about an hour's walk from Kisfaludy House, and on to the **Stone Gate** (*Kőkapu*), where sightseers ooh-aah at two massive basalt towers flanking a precipitous drop.

Longer hikes into the hills further north offer an escape from the crowds (ask for maps from the tourist office). A four-kilometre walk from the Stone Gate will bring you to **Gulács-hegy**, a perfectly conical hill (393m) near the Nemesgulács halt for trains en route to Tapolca. The **Szent György-hegy** (415m), on the far side of the tracks, boasts some impressive basalt **organ pipes** and the region's finest vineyards, where *Szürkebarát* is produced. A few kilometres to the east, 375-metre-high **Csobánc-hegy** is crowned by a **ruined castle** that was once defended against the Turks by women. Serious hikers might consider pushing on to Szentbékkálla and the beautiful **Seas of Stone**, created from layers of sand and pebbles deposited by the ancient Pannonian Sea.

The last three hikes will probably take the best part of a day and leave you closer to Tapolca than the Balaton. It's advisable to buy a 1:80,000-scale map of the region.

Transport and information

Badacsony's **train station** is in the centre of the village just north of the ferry pier. After Badacsony the rail line veers northwards up to Tapolca in the Bakony, so although you can switch trains there and ride back down to Keszthely, it's easier to continue along the shore **by bus**, changing at Balatonederics if necessary.

Maps and **information** are available from *Balatontourist*, in the *Capitano* shopping centre on Park utca (July–Aug Mon–Sat 8.30am–6.30pm & Sun 8.30am–noon; May, June & Sept Mon–Fri 8.30am–4.30pm & Sat 8.30am–noon; ☎87/331-249); *Ibusz*, also in the *Capitano* shopping centre (mid-May to Sept Mon–Sat 8.30am–5pm & Sun 8am–1pm; ☎87/331-292); *Miditourist* at Park utca 6 and 53 (June–Sept daily 8am–10pm; Sept–June Mon–Fri 9am–4pm; ☎87/331-028); and *Cooptourist* at Egri sétány 1 (April–Sept Mon–Sat 9am–6pm & Sun 9am–noon; ☎87/331-134).

Accommodation

All four tourist offices rent private **rooms** (②–③) and there are plenty of households advertising *Zimmer frei*, as well as a clutch of pensions including the *Harsfa Panzió* at Szegedi Róza út 1 (☎87/331-293; ③); the *Harsona Panzió* up the hill at Szegedi Róza út 37 (mid-May to Sept; ☎331-227); and the *Volán Panzió* further along at Római út 168 (☎87/331-013; ③–④). Badacsony's **campsite** is on the lake, fifteen minutes' walk west of the ferry pier (June–Sept; ☎87/331-091).

Eating and drinking

Of the various **restaurants** to choose from in Badacsony, the *Halászkert* at Park utca 5 is centrally located but crowded and pricey. The *Ludas Pince*, a good twenty-minute walk west of the centre along Római út, has a good reputation for its wines. The crowds thin out as you climb the hill and you are rewarded with the *Bormúzeum Pince* ("Wine Museum Cellar"), a restaurant housed in an eighteenth-century winepress house at Hegyalja út 6 (just west of Kisfaludy House). Best of the lot is the restaurant in the Kisfaludy House itself, which offers excellent food and service plus fabulous views of the lake.

Szigliget and beyond

The **Szigliget** peninsula beneath the Kamonkő cliffs looks most dramatic when viewed from a ferry, at which point you can imagine the Hungarian fleet moored under the protection of **Szigliget Castle**, as it was in Turkish times. Originally commissioned by Pannonhalma Monastery in the wake of the Mongol invasion, the now ruined stronghold can be reached by a path that starts behind the white church sited on the highest spot in the village (a 15-min walk). Below the ruins is a lush park containing over five hundred kinds of ornamental shrubs and trees, plus a former Esterházy mansion used as a holiday resort by the Writers' Union (non-members may stroll around the grounds with permission). On the main road just before you reach the turn-off for the church, the **Esterházy Wine Museum** at Kossuth utca 3 offers vinous tours round its beautifully decorated eighteenth-century cellars (June–Sept or by special arrangement in winter; ☎87/341-044). Next to the church itself you can enjoy a hearty meal at the *Vár Vendéglő*.

BALATONEDERICS, 5km further on, is notable only for the **hostel** at Kültelek 10 (mid-May to mid-Sept; ☎87/336-131; ②), and as a train station and junction for route 84 to Sümeg. Sticking to buses, you can carry on round the lake to **BALATONGYÖRÖK**, still partly a village of white-porticoed, thatched houses, with an expensive **campsite** right on the lake, on the Szigliget side of town, and *Carina Camping* in the town proper at Balaton utca 12 (April–Sept; ☎87/349-084). Its **Szépkilátó lookout** affords a vista encompassing the Szent György and Csobánc hills to the north, and the twin peaks behind Fonyód, across the lake.

After this comes **VONYARCVASHEGY**, where coach parties pack the outdoor *Fészek Vendéglő*. The lakeside *Zalatour Camping* is a popular spot among German tourists (May–Sept; ☎83/348-044); it offers bungalows (②), apartments and a restaurant, and is managed by *Zalatour* in Zalaegerszeg (p.224). There is another campsite (April–Oct) and a private accommodation bureau on Kossuth utca in **GYENESDIÁS**, which merges into the suburbs of Keszthely.

Keszthely and around

A tradition of free thinking that dates back to the eighteenth century gives **KESZTHELY** a sense of superiority over other resorts, and its university ensures that life isn't wholly taken over by tourism. The Belváros and *strand* somehow absorb thousands of visitors gracefully, without looking bleak and abandoned out of season. With the Festetics Palace to admire, and a thermal lake awaiting bathers at Hévíz nearby, Keszthely is the best hang-out on the Balaton.

The Town

Walking up from the train and bus stations, you'll pass the **Balaton Museum** (Tues–Sun 9am–5pm), which covers the region's zoology, ethnography and archeology, with artefacts dating back to the first century AD when road-building Romans disrupted the lifestyle of local Celtic tribes. Downtown Keszthely begins around **Fő tér** – an ambiguous square in the middle of which stands the **Trinity Statue**, erected in 1770 and now frequently enveloped in smog. Overlooking the square, the much-remodelled **Church of Our Lady of the Hungarians** was originally built in the fourteenth century, and still retains its Gothic rose window above the main portal. From here on, **Kossuth utca** is given over to cafés, buskers and strollers, with a **flea market** on Wednesday mornings.

Heading up towards the palace, you'll pass the **birthplace of Karl Goldmark** (1830–1915) on the corner of Fejér utca. The son of a poor Jewish cantor who enrolled him in Sopron's school of music, Goldmark went on to study at the Vienna Conservatory. Almost shot as a rebel for giving concerts in Győr during the 1848 Revolution, he survived to compose *Merlin*, *Zrínyi* and *The Queen of Sheba*. The **Marzipan Museum and Pastry Shop** at Katona József utca 19 (daily 9am–6pm) is just below the palace gates – well worth the detour for anyone with a sweet tooth.

The Keszthely telephone code is ☎83

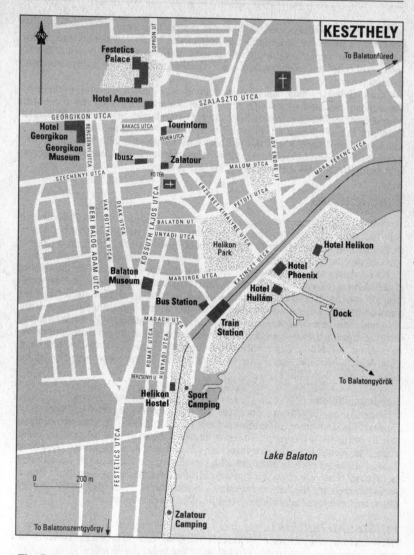

The Festetics Palace and Georgikon

The aristocratic Festetics family are chiefly remembered for Count György (1755–1819), founder of Keszthely's agricultural university and the Baroque **Festetics Palace** (April–Sept Tues–Sun 10am–6pm, midsummer till 7pm; Oct–March Tues–Sun 9am–4.30pm). During the early nineteenth century, the palace's salons attracted the leading lights of Magyar literature (now recalled by memorial trees) as Hungary's first public forum for criticism. The palace's highlights are its gilt, mirrored ballroom and the **Helikon Library**, a masterpiece of joinery by János Kerbl, containing 52,000 books in diverse languages. Chinese vases and tiled stoves jostle for space with portraits of the family racehorses and dachshunds (whose pedigrees are proudly noted), and the pelts and heads of tigers, bears and other animals shot by Count Windishgrätz. There are **concerts** here over summer.

Count György's most useful contribution was an agricultural college, or **Georgikon**, the first of its kind in Europe. Students attending the three-year course lived and worked together in a cluster of whitewashed buildings below the palace at Bercsényi utca 67, where dairy and viticulture equipment, cartwright's tools, old Ford tractors and the like are now displayed (daily 9am–6pm). The Georgikon was the forerunner of today's **Agrártudományi University**, a green and daffodil-yellow pile halfway along Széchenyi utca.

Practicalities

Arriving by ferry near the main *strand*, you can walk up Erzsébet királyné útja into the centre (10–15min). The train and intercity bus stations are further south, at the bottom end of Mártirok útja, but most buses entering town drop passengers on downtown Fő tér, sparing them a 600-metre trudge along Kossuth utca.

Half a dozen **tourist offices** cluster in the downtown area: by far the best is *Tourinform* at Kossuth utca 28 (May–June Mon–Fri 9am–5pm & Sat–Sun 9am–1pm; July–Aug Mon–Fri 9am–6pm & Sat–Sun 9am–1pm; Sept–April Mon–Fri 8am–4pm). The others include *Ibusz* at Széchenyi utca 1–3 (Mon–Sat 8am–6pm; also Sun 9am–1pm over summer; ☎314-320); *Zalatour* at Fő tér 1 (summer Mon–Fri 8am–5pm, Sat 8am–4pm & Sun 8am–noon; winter Mon–Fri 8am–5pm & Sat 8am–noon; ☎314-301); *Express* at Kossuth utca 22 (April–Oct Mon–Sat 8am–8pm; Nov–March Mon–Sat 8am–5pm; ☎312-032); and a few more agencies along Kossuth utca.

Accommodation

Private rooms (②–③) are bookable through any of the above companies or through *Volántourist* at Kossuth utca 43 (☎312-733); *Helikon* at Erzsébet királyné útja 1 (☎312-596); *Hongarije Tours* at Erzsébet királyné útja 26; and an *Ibusz* branch at Római út 2. The last three are all relatively near the station. *Non-Stop Tourist* at Bakacs utca 12 functions 24-hours during the high season, but charges more than other agencies. You can avoid their charges altogether by finding a room yourself: try the backstreets south of the station and tourist hostel or if all else fails, head for nearby Hévíz (bus #15). The alternatives are:

HOTELS AND PENSIONS

Hotel Amazon, Georgikon utca 1 (☎314-213). Run-down, eighteenth-century hotel near the palace. Singles (①–②) and doubles (③) with or without baths. Usually full.

Hotel Bacchus, Erzsébet királyné utca 18 (☎314-096). Modern hotel. ⑤.

Forras Panzió, Római út 1 (☎314-617). 39-room pension near the lake and a few blocks west of the station. ④.

Hotel Georgikon, Georgikon utca 20 (☎315-730). Renovated manor house four blocks west of the *Amazon*, and of a similar vintage. All rooms with baths. ⑤.

Hotel Helikon, Balaton-part 5 (☎315-944). Luxury high-rise eyesore with 232 rooms, sauna, pool and tennis courts. Open year-round. ⑦.

Hotel Hullám, Balaton-part 1 (☎312-644). Palatial nineteenth-century mansion on the waterfront, with use of the *Hotel Helikon*'s facilities. Closed Jan & Feb. ③–⑤.

Hotel Phoenix, Balaton-part 3 (☎314-225). A motel-style place just behind the *Hullám*. Open April–Oct. ③–④.

CAMPSITES AND HOSTELS

Castrum Camping, Móra F. utca 48 (☎312-120). Aimed at motorists, and far from the shore 1km north of the station. Very expensive. Open April–Oct.

Helikon Hostel, Honvéd utca 22 (☎311-424). Dormitory beds 10 minutes' walk south of the station. Reserve through *Express* or *Zalatour*. Open April to mid-Oct. ③.

Sport Camping, Csárda utca (☎312-842). A noisy and unappealing campsite with bungalows situated beside the rail tracks, behind the *Helikon Hostel*. Open mid-May to Sept.

Zalatour Camping, Balaton-part (☎312-782). 10 minutes' walk south of *Sport Camping*, a bigger and more attractively located site with tennis courts and bungalows for four people. Open May–Sept.

Eating and drinking

Keszthely is the best place on the Balaton for **eating and drinking**, but it's difficult to make specific recommendations – the scene is constantly changing as good spots turn bad, and as new places appear. As anywhere, restaurants frequented solely by tourists are likely to overcharge or give lousy service – the *Gösser* pub and restaurant on Fő tér being a case in point.

Better-value alternatives are the *Pizzeria Marcello* on Városház utca, a block north of Fő tér, and the slightly cheaper *American Pizzeria* across the road. The *Béke Vendéglő* at Kossuth utca 50 has a pleasant atmosphere and good ice cream next door, while the *Golf* restaurant across the road at no. 95 offers Hungarian food and lively music till midnight. For food with a Mediterranean flavour, try the moderately priced *Hellas Étterem* at Fő tér 2. A nameless outlet beside the *American Hamburger* does delicious ice cream, while the *Muskátali Cukrászda* at the upper end of Kossuth utca has fine cakes, coffee and a selection of newspapers to peruse. At Városház utca 9, the small and friendly *Piccolo Bar* is a local student hang-out.

Entertainment

Keszthely hosts a wide variety of festivals and cultural events every summer (for which *Tourinform* is the best source of information). These include the **Helikon Festival of Chamber and Orchestral Music**, held in the palace in May (even years); the **Balaton Festival** of music and folk dancing, also in May; and the **Balaton Film Festival** in June. In July and August philharmonic concerts are held at the palace every Monday, organ recitals at the Lutheran church on Wednesdays, folk dancing at the open-air stage (*Szabadtéri szinpád*) in Sörház utca on Thursdays, and live music on the lakefront *Zenepavilon* on Saturdays. The summer months are further enlivened by rock, folk and jazz concerts on Fő tér (as advertised), plus buskers and jugglers along Kossuth utca. If no discos appear to be advertised in Keszthely, neighbouring Hévíz can always provide some lurid **nightlife**.

Activities

Keszthely has two **beaches**: the *Városi strand* – with its own mole – near the ferry dock, and the *Helikon strand* between the two campsites further south (both open daily 8.30am–7pm). You can rent **windsurfing** gear at either, and play **tennis** or **mini-golf** by the waterfront hotels. Enquire at *Zalatour*, the *Hotel Helikon*, *Forrás Panzió* or *Sport Camping* about **horse riding** in Keszthely-Újmajor.

Moving on

Aside from Hévíz – which is best visited as an excursion (see below) – there are various possibilities for **moving on**. From June to mid-September, **ferries** sail twice daily (8am & 2pm) for the Badacsony and Tihany, continuing to Siófok in July and August. The **rail** around the lake's curve to Balatonszentgyörgy (change there for Nagykanizsa), is a continuation of the main line down from Tapolca and Sümeg – which provides the easiest means of reaching the Bakony. Over summer (late June–early Sept 9 Tues–Sun 11.45am) a wonderful old **steam train** runs up to Tapolca and down to Badacsonytomaj. Tickets cost only 300Ft, and there's a bar on board.

Buses leave from the bus stand on Fő tér for a range of destinations in Transdanubia, including Nagykanizsa, Szombathely, Zalaegerszeg, Győr and Sopron. The depot outside the train station is the point of departure for buses to Hévíz (every half-hour), Balatongyörök and overnight to Budapest.

Cyclists heading towards Zalaegerszeg, Szombathely or Sárvár might enjoy the tree-lined road that follows the River Zala through ZALASZENTGRÓT – which has a picturesque bridge and manor and a good restaurant, the ill-named *Grót Étterem*. On the road to VASAR, oxen and horse-drawn carts are more common than cars.

Hévíz

HÉVÍZ, 8km outside Keszthely, boasts the second largest **thermal lake** (*Gyógytó*) in the world (the biggest being in New Zealand). Indian waterlilies flourish on its surface, since the temperature rarely drops below 30°C even during winter, when steam billows from the lake and its thermal stream. Until recently, the lake was replenished by up to eighty million litres of warm water a day gushing up from springs a kilometre underground, so that it was completely flushed out every couple of days. However mining work in the area has caused water levels to fall drastically, prompting desperate measures to preserve this vital source.

Exploited since medieval times for curative purposes as well as for tanning leather, the lake was salubriously channelled into a bathhouse by Count György of Keszthely in 1795. By the end of the nineteenth century, Hévíz had become a grand **resort**, briefly favoured by crown princes and magnates like those other great spas of the Habsburg empire, Karlsbad and the Baths of Hercules. They'd be hard pressed to recognize it today, with high-rise hotels and tacky bars setting the tone.

Although the wooden terraces and catwalks surrounding the **baths** (*Tófürdő*) have a vaguely *fin-de-siècle* appearance, the general ambience is contemporary, with people sipping beer or reading newspapers while bobbing on the lake in rented inner tubes. Prolonged immersion isn't recommended on account of the slightly radioactive water, though mud from the lake is used to treat locomotive disorders. The baths are open year-round (daily 7am–4pm).

Accommodation

With half-hourly buses from Keszthely there's no need to linger in Hévíz, but plenty of **accommodation** is available should you decide to stay. Private rooms (③) can be booked through *Hévíz Tourist* at Rákoczi utca 4 (Mon–Fri 9am–4pm; ☎83/341-348); *Zalatour* at no. 8 (Mon–Fri 9am–4pm; ☎83/341-048); and

Valavolántourist at the bus station (Mon–Fri 8am–4pm; ☎83/314-954); otherwise Kossuth utca and Zrínyi utca are both teeming with *Zimmer frei* signs.

At the southern end of the lake, the four-star *Castrum Gyógycamping* rents plots for tents and trailers at exorbitant rates year-round (☎83/343-198). Marginally cheaper but still expensive is the *Solar György* campsite in neighbouring Alsópáhok (☎83/343-365), also open all year. Other possibilities include:

Aqua, Kossuth utca 13–15 (☎83/340-946). 230-room high-rise hotel at the southern end of the Parkerdő ("Park Forest"). ⑦.

Flavius, Rákoczi utca 11–13 (☎83/343-463). 125-room establishment offering some of the best deals in town. ③–④.

Park Hotel, Petőfi utca 26 (☎83/341-193). Elegant 30-room hotel near the lake – the classiest place in town. Rates include use of the *Thermál Hotel*'s indoor and outdoor pools and sauna. ⑦.

Hotel Thermál, Kossuth utca 9–11 (☎83/341-180). One of the most expensive hotels in town with the full range of facilities including indoor and outdoor pools, tennis courts, sauna and solarium. ⑦.

Nightlife

Hévíz's **nightlife** revolves around the *Bar Romantica* on Tavirózsa utca (Mon–Sat 6pm–4am) – with a disco, sex show and go-go dancers – and the even seedier *Autos* strip-bar near the marketplace. The alternative is to catch a bus (every 15min) to the neighbouring village of Alsópáhok, where the *Disco Sello* plays very loud Eurorock, and tourists hang out at the low-priced *Tranzit Büfe Kaffeeteria* – a café-bar with friendly English-speaking staff. Alsópáhok is actually a nicer, cheaper place to stay than Hévíz, with lots of private rooms to rent (②) – the British company *New Millennium Holidays* stashes its tourists here.

THE BAKONY

The Bakony range cuts a swathe across central Transdanubia, as if scooped from the ground to provide space for the lake, and piled as a natural embankment behind the lowlier Balaton hills. Abundant vineyards testify to the richness of the volcanic soil and, more recently, mineheads to the mineral wealth beneath it. With dense woods and narrow ravines, this was the Hungarian equivalent of Sherwood Forest during the centuries of warfare and turmoil, and the setting for a dozen castles, the finest of which stand at **Sümeg** and **Nagyvázsony**. The regional capital **Veszprém** boasts a wealth of historic architecture and serves as a base for trips to the highwaymen's inn at **Nemesvámos** and the **Herend** porcelain factory. Or you can get away from everything by walking in the hills around **Zirc** or **Bakonybél**. During autumn, pink crocuses spangle the meadows between Sümeg and the Balaton, and huge sunflower fields and red-podded trees abound nearer Sárvár.

Tapolca and Sümeg

From Szigliget on the Balaton, the rail line heads up to **TAPOLCA**, a blot on the landscape devoted to bauxite mining and aluminium processing. Until recently, Tapolca was slightly redeemed by the **Tavas Caves**, whose main grotto was used as a sanatorium for asthma and bronchitis sufferers, but mining operations caused its karstic spring to dry up and a cave-in has rendered the grotto unsafe. Now there is nothing to see except a **Museum of the Aluminium Industry** (Mon–Fri 9am–3pm) at Batsányi tér 2, which is every bit as dull as you'd imagine.

Although the *Gabriella Hotel* at Batsányi tér 7 (☎87/312-642; ③) and the *Aspa Panzió* at Kossuth utca 19 (☎87/311-695; ③–④) offer **accommodation**, it's best to stay on the train until Sümeg or head straight out on a local bus to Nagyvázsony and Nemesvámos (8 daily). There are also regular **buses** and trains down to Keszthely, including *nosztálgia* **steam trains** over summer (Tues–Sun at 4pm). *Balatontourist* at Deák utca 2 (☎87/311-179) has **information**.

Sümeg

SÜMEG, 14km north, is an altogether different proposition, with a dramatic-looking castle overshadowing a Belváros dating from the eighteenth century, when the town was the seat of the bishops of Veszprém. Now crumbling and overgrown, the **Bishop's Palace** (1753) stands on Kisfaludy tér in the centre of town – ask for keys from the Kisfaludy Museum director. Across the square at no. 2 is the **Kisfaludy Museum** (daily 10am–6pm), a memorial to the romantic poet of the Balaton, Sándor Kisfaludy (1772–1844). The former bishop's stables, at the bottom of Vak Bottyán utca, now house the **Museum of Saddlery** (daily 8–11.30am & 2–5pm) – **horse riding** in the surrounding countryside can be arranged through the museum or the *Lovasbolt* riding shop across the way.

Baroque mansions and parts of the medieval walls line Deák utca, leading to the **Church of the Ascension**. Outwardly unprepossessing, the church contains magnificent **frescoes** by Franz Anton Maulbertsch (1724–96) who, with a team of assistants, was able to cover the whole interior within eighteen months, mostly in biblical scenes. Exceptions are the rear wall, which depicts his patron Bishop Biró (the man kneeling before him has Maulbertsch's features, as does the shepherd in the Adoration scene), and the wall facing the choir, showing the churches Biró sponsored in Sümeg and Zalaegerszeg. Apropos of Biró, it was another Hungarian, László Biró, who invented the biro, or ballpoint pen.

Sümeg Castle

The most impressive sight around is **Sümeg Castle** (8am–sunset; ☎87/352-737), one of the best preserved fortifications in Transdanubia and worth visiting for the views alone. It dominates the town from a conical limestone massif, a unique Cretaceous outcropping among the basalt of the Bakony. Built during the thir-teenth century as a defence against marauding Mongols, the castle was rein-forced several times during the next few centuries. It proved impregnable against the Turks, but eventually fell to the Habsburgs in 1713.

A few years back the castle was rented out to a gentleman (calling himself the "Castle Captain") who agreed to carry out restoration work. Meanwhile, from June to August each year he organizes evenings of folk dancing, Gypsy music, jousting and the like (starts 6pm; May–Oct groups only; 1500Ft per person). Exhibits on the castle can be seen at the Kisfaludy Museum in the centre of town.

Practicalities

Sümeg's **bus station** is south of the centre on Flórián tér (a continuation of Kossuth utca); its **train station** is ten minutes' walk northwest at the end of Darnay Kálmán utca. Although the town has no tourist **information** office as yet, plans are afoot to install one in the Kisfaludy Museum – meanwhile, a list of private rooms is available from the museum. Hotel and pension **accommodation** includes the *Hotel Vár* at Vak Bottyán utca 2 (closed Jan; ☎87/352-414; ③); the *Király Fogadó* at Udvarbiró tér 5 (☎87/352-605; ③); the *Nelli Panzió* at Tapolcai utca 4 ☎87/352-511); and a small pension at Jókai utca 3 (☎87/351-287; ③). **Good places to eat** include the restaurant in the castle's cellar and the one by the car park below the castle.

Moving on

Travellers heading **into Transdanubia** by rail may have to change at UKK (for Zalaegerszeg) or Celldömölk (for Győr or Szombathely). Heading **towards Veszprém**, direct buses are quicker but less regular than trains (which entail changing at Boba). More frequent services **from Tapolca** pass through Nagyvázsony and Nemesvámos en route to Veszprém.

Nagyvázsony and Nemesvámos

Buses **along the Tapolca–Veszprém road** can drop you at two places redolent of the Bakony's history – Nagyvázsony (also accessible by bus from Balatonfüred) and an old highwaymen's inn near Nemesvámos (only 6km outside Veszprém).

NAGYVÁZSONY, 20km from Tapolca, harbours **Kinizsi Castle** (April–Oct 9am–dusk), given by King Mátyás to Pál Kinizsi, a local miller who made good as a commander. Formidably strong, he is said to have wielded a dead Turk as a bludgeon and danced a triumphal jig while holding three Turks, one of them between his teeth. During the sixteenth century, this was one of the border fortresses between Turkish and Habsburg-ruled Hungary. Its keep exhibits weapons and fetters, while the chapel across the way contains Kinizsi's red marble sarcophagus.

Towards the end of July, three or four days of **show-jumping and jousting** in the grounds enliven what is otherwise a sleepy market town. If you're planning to attend the festival, it's worth reserving a room (④) or bed (①) in the *Kastély* hotel and hostel, which occupy a former Zichy mansion at Kossuth utca 12 (☎80/364-109); or at the *Vázsonykő* at Sörház utca 2 (☎80/364-344; ③) where you can also get a good meal.

Approaching Veszprém, you can't miss the roadside *Vámosi Csárda* (or *Betyár Csárda*), an **eighteenth-century Bakony inn**. If you ignore the odd modern fixture and today's clientele, it's possible to imagine the inn's appearance in olden days: servants hurrying from the tap-room with its huge casks into the cellar, where swineherds, wayfarers and outlaws caroused, seated upon sections of tree trunk. Poor though most were, Bakony folk were proud of their masterless lives among the oak forests, esteeming the *kondás*, with his herd of pigs, and the highwaymen who robbed rich merchants. These latter called themselves *szegénylegények* – "poor lads" – and the most audacious, Jóska Savanyú, claimed the tavern as his home.

The village of **NEMESVÁMOS** lies 600m south of the inn. Nearby are the **ruins of a Roman villa** at **BALÁCAPUSZTA** (May–Sept Tues–Sun 10am–6pm). Its reconstructed frescoes and mosaics convey an impression of the lifestyle of wealthy Roman colonists in the early centuries of the Christian era. The Hungarian government asserts that the famous **Seveso Treasure** came from another such villa in the Balaton region – although its claim is disputed by Lebanon, Turkey and the former Yugoslavia, whose own claims to ownership are currently being judged in the courts.

Veszprém

VESZPRÉM spreads over five hills, cobbled together by a maze of streets twisting up towards its old quarter, on a precipitous crag overlooking the Bakony forest. Like Székesfehérvár, it became an episcopal see in the reign of Prince Géza (who converted to Christianity in 975). In 997, it was here that King Stephen crushed a pagan rebellion with the help of knights sent by Henry of Bavaria, father of his queen Gizella. During medieval times, Veszprém was the seat of the queen's household and the site of her coronation – hence its title the "Queen's Town". Utterly devastated during the sixteenth century and rebuilt after 1711, its Castle Hill and downtown parks are now juxtaposed with apartment buildings, a technical university and chemical factories.

Being only 20km from Lake Balaton, Veszprém could serve as a base for visiting the resorts without having to stay there, and for excursions to Nagyvázsony, Nemesvámos or Herend. **Motorists** coming in from the west will cross the 150-metre-long Valley Bridge over the River Séd, glimpsing Castle Hill en route to the centre.

Castle Hill

The Castle district is presaged by **Óváros tér**, a triangular plaza overlooked by Baroque and Rococo buildings painted in pinks, blues and the shade known as "Maria Theresa yellow" (which she ordained as the colour scheme for public buildings throughout the Habsburg empire). Behind nos. 7–8 rises the Baroque **Firetower** (*Tűztorony*), whose medieval base once formed part of the castle; a carillon in the dome plays a traditional recruiting tune every hour on the hour. You can climb the tower (daily 10am–6pm) for a fine view of Veszprém's urban sprawl – access is through the courtyard at Vár utca 17.

Nearby stands the **Heroes' Gate**, a neo-Romanesque portal commemorating the dead of World War I. Its right-hand gate-tower contains the **Castle Museum** (May–Sept daily except Wed 9am–6pm) which recalls various sieges of the *vár* and its final destruction by the Habsburgs in 1702, who replaced it with the mansions and churches that ennoble Castle Hill today. Following Vár utca uphill, you'll pass a **Piarist Church and Monastery** – now used for temporary exhibitions (May–Oct 9am–5pm) – whose facade bears three Greek letters, encapsulating the Piarist credo "Mary, Mother, God".

The **Bishop's Palace** on the main square is a typically massive Baroque pile by Jakab Fellner. During its construction in the 1760s workmen unearthed a vaulted chamber believed to be part of Queen Gizella's palace, which stood on the site until the fourteenth century. Dubbed the **Gizella Chapel** (May–Oct daily

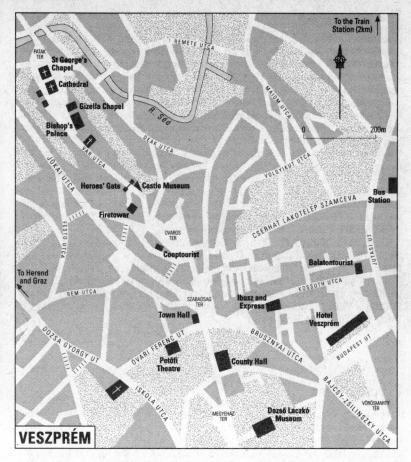

VESZPRÉM

9am–5pm), it contains Byzantine-style frescoes of the apostles from the thirteenth century. Across the square, at no. 35, you can view an **Ecclesiastical Collection** of votive statues, chasubles and such like to the sound of a taped Mass.

Beyond the Trinity Statue looms Veszprém **Cathedral**. Having been razed and resurrected half a dozen times since the eleventh century, its current neo-Romanesque incarnation (1907–10) has only a Gothic crypt to show for its origins. However, a glass dome behind the cathedral shelters the excavated remains of **Saint George's Chapel** (mid-April to mid-Oct Sun–Tues 10am–6pm), where Stephen's son Imre is said to have taken an oath of celibacy. His canonization – like that of Stephen and the latterday king László – cemented the Árpáds' adherence to Catholicism and gave the Hungarians their own saints with whom to identify.

Statues of Stephen and Gizella duly watch over the parapet at the far end of Vár utca, while a flight of steps round the side of the cathedral leads down to **Benedek Hill**, which commands a panoramic view of the Séd Valley and the Bakony forest. During summer, the Castle district is the setting for open-air **concerts**.

The lower town

Returning to Szabadság tér, head past the Baroque **Town Hall** (originally the mansion of the Kaposvári family) and right along Óvári Ferenc út to find the Art Nouveau **Petőfi Theatre**. The first large building in Hungary to be constructed from reinforced concrete (in 1908), it boasts a circular stained-glass window entitled *The Magic of Folk Art*, whose symbolic figures represent the attachment of Hungarians to their land. Its designer, Sándor Nagy, was one of the Gödöllő Pre-Raphaelites; his *Hunting of the Magic Deer* (a Magyar myth) decorates the rear of the building. Theatre tickets can be purchased at the *Petőfi Ticket Office* at Szabadság tér 7 (Mon–Fri 9am–5pm).

A short walk past the Eclectic-style **County Hall** brings you to Megyeház tér, flanked by Kálvária Hill and the **Dezső Laczkó Museum** at Erzsébet sétány 7 (April–Sept Tues–Sun 10am–6pm; Oct–March Tues–Sun 10am–2pm). The latter features an array of exhibits including Roman mosaics unearthed in the villa at Balácapuszta, regional folk costumes and material on the Bakony's *betyár* (high-waymen). Next door stands the **Bakony House** (same hours), a Thirties clone of a traditional homestead filled with peasant artefacts.

Three more sights lurk 700m west of the centre, off Kittenberger utca, which can be reached by walking from Dózsa György út, itself accessible by bus #5 or #10. First comes an antique **watermill** – one of many that once lined the banks of the Séd – followed by the **Kittenburg Zoo** (daily 9am–5pm) named after the nineteenth-century zoologist Kálmán Kittenberger. In the Fejes Valley 330m further south is a **Village Museum** of cottages and implements from the Bakony region (May–Oct Tues–Sun 10am–6pm).

> The Veszprém telephone code is ☎88

Practicalities

Arriving at the train station 2km out, catch bus #1, #11, #14V or #20 to the big *Áruház* store near downtown Szabadság tér; the intercity bus depot (which has a left-luggage office) is more conveniently situated near the town centre. From Szabadság tér, you can head north towards Castle Hill or strike out into the lower town.

Information is available from *Balatontourist* at Kossuth utca 21 (Mon–Fri 8am–4.30pm; plus Sat 8am–noon in summer; ☎329-630) or from *Ibusz* at Kossuth utca 6 (Mon–Fri 8am–3pm; ☎427-604).

Accommodation

Both *Balatontourist* and *Ibusz* can book private **rooms** (②), as can *Cooptourist* at Óváros tér 2 (Mon–Fri 8am–5pm; ☎322-313). *Express* (Mon–Fri 8.30am–4pm; ☎327-069), located above the *Ibusz* office, may be able to find **beds** (①) during the summer in one of the two *kollégium* in Stadion utca, or alternatively in the student hostel at Egyetem utca 12, beyond the Chemical Technical University 1km south of the centre (bus #2Y, #4, #8 or #14Y). Other options include:

Diana Panzió, József Attila utca 22 (☎327-897). 10-room pension in an attractive villa west of Calvary Hill. ③.

Élőgyöngy Panzió, József Attila utca 1. At the start of the Nagyvázsony road, 500m south-west of the Petőfi Theatre. ③.

Hotel Jutas, Jutasi utca 18/2 (☎326-666). 92-room hotel close to the train station; soon to become a student hostel. ③.

Hotel Veszprém, Budapest út 6 (☎324-876). Centrally located Seventies low-rise with 76 rooms – those at the back being considerably quieter. ④.

Eating and drinking

One of the best restaurants in town is the *Vadásztanya Étterem* at József Attila utca 22. Several upmarket **brasseries** cluster around Szabadság tér – for instance the *Tűztorony* and the elegant *Óváros Étterem*, where you can sit outside. Óváros tér is another place for trendy brasseries – the *Elefánt Étterem* on the corner of Óváros tér and Vár utca being one of the cheaper options. There's also the famous *Vámosi Csárda*, out along the Tapolca road (see p.179).

On from Veszprém

Leaving aside the places already covered in this chapter, you have a choice of destinations when it's time to move on. Heading northwest **towards Szombathely** (see the following chapter, p.213), it's easy to visit the famous porcelain factory at Herend, with the possibility of scenic detours for those with their own transport. The route more directly north **towards Győr** plunges through the heart of the Bakony, emerging on to the Little Plain to pass by Pannonhalma, with its famous monastery.

West towards Szombathely

HEREND, 12km west of Veszprém, makes an enjoyable excursion from town or an interesting stopover en route to Szombathely. The origins of its famous **Porcelain Factory** go back to 1826, when Vince Stingl founded a pottery in the village. Herend porcelain gained international renown at the Great Exhibition of 1851, when Queen Victoria ordered a Chinoiserie dinner service. Other famous purchasers have included Tsar Alexander II, Kaiser Wilhelm I, the Shah of Iran and the British royals Charles and Diana. The factory's **museum** (April–Oct Tues–Sun 8.30am–4.30pm; Nov–March Mon–Sat 8am–4pm) displays hand-painted dinner services, vases and statuettes – many of which go right over the top.

After Herend the scenery deteriorates around Ajka, but 6km beyond Devecser (where the rail line turns northwards towards Celldömölk) there's a great view of the Bakony from a lookout tower near **SOMLÓVÁSÁRHELY**. In clear weather Mount Kőris (see below) and even the Austrian Alps may be visible.

North towards Győr

Heading north towards Győr, both rail line and route 82 follow the River Cuha through the Bakony Hills. The only town en route is **ZIRC**, whose former Cistercian **Abbey Church** has altar paintings by Maulbertsch. The adjacent abbey now contains a **Natural History Museum** (April–Oct Tues–Sun 9am–5pm; Nov–March Tues–Sun 9am–1pm) and a **library** with Empire-style furnishings, named after Antal Reguly (1819–58), the pioneer of Finno-Urgic linguistic research who was born in Zirc. The *Erdőalja Panzió* has rooms and bungalows (mid-May to mid-Sept; ③).

If you fancy walking in the hills, **BAKONYBÉL**, 17km west and accessible by local buses from Zirc, is situated at the foot of **Mount Kőris**, the highest peak in the Bakony (713m). Several **hiking trails** emanate from the village, where you can stay at the *Bakony Panzió* at Fürdő út 57 (②). The main route continues northwards via **CSESZNEK**, where a **ruined castle** on a steep hill affords a fine view of the region. Although trains stop some distance away (at Porva-Csesznek), the rail journey is a scenic one, winding between cliffs, over bridges and through tunnels, along a line built in 1896. Most Győr-bound trains stop at Pannonhalma Monastery along the way; for details, see Chapter Four.

travel details

Trains

Budapest (Déli Station) to Balatonfüred (every 1–2hr; 2hr–2hr 30min); Siófok (8 daily; 1hr 30min); Székesfehérvár (every 60–90min; 1hr); Veszprém (5 daily; 2hr 15min–3hr).

Balatonfenyves to Csisztapuszta (Tues–Sun every 60–90min; 45min–1hr 30min).

Balatonfüred to Budapest (every 1–2hr; 2hr–2hr 30min).

Balatonszentgyörgy to Nagykanizsa (every 1–2hr; 45min).

Székesfehérvár to Balatonfüred (hourly; 30min–1hr); Budapest (every 60–90min; 1hr); Komárom (every 60–90min; 1hr 15min–1hr 45min); Siófok (hourly; 30min); Szombathely (7 daily; 2hr 30min–3hr 45min); Veszprém (hourly; 45min–1hr).

Tapolca to Celldömölk (every 60–90min; 1hr 15min); Sümeg (every 60–90min; 1hr 30min); Szombathely (4 daily; 1hr 30min).

Veszprém to Budapest (4 daily; 1hr 45min–2hr 15min); Győr (4 daily; 2hr 30min); Szombathely (4 daily; 1hr 15min).

Buses

Budapest (Erzsébet tér) to Balatonfüred (2 daily; 2hr 15min); Herend (2 daily; 2hr 45min); Hévíz (2 daily; 4hr); Keszthely (2 daily; 3hr 45min); Nagyvázsony (2 daily except Sun; 3hr); Siófok (3 daily; 1hr 45min–2hr 15min); Sümeg (2 daily; 4hr 30min); Székesfehérvár (every 40–60min; 1hr 15min); Veszprém (every 60–90min; 2hr 15min); Zirc (4 daily; 2hr 30min).

Badacsony to Keszthely (hourly; 1hr); Székesfehérvár (2 daily; 2hr 15min).

Bakonybél to Budapest (3 daily; 3hr 15min).

Balatonfüred to Győr (every 30–90min; 2hr); Nagyvázsony (every 1hr 30min; 45min); Sopron (1 daily; 4hr); Tapolca (1 daily except Sun; 1hr 30min); Tihany (hourly; 30min); Veszprém (every 30–90min; 30min).

Hévíz to Keszthely (every 30min; 15min); Pécs (2 daily; 4hr 15min); Zalaegerszeg (1 daily; 2hr).

Keszthely to Hévíz (every 30min; 15min); Pécs (2 daily; 3hr 45min); Sümeg (1 daily; 1hr); Szombathely (hourly; 2hr 30min); Zalaegerszeg (1 daily; 1hr).

Siófok to Győr (1 daily; 3hr); Mohács (1 daily; 3hr); Pécs (1 daily; 3hr); Szekszárd (1 daily; 1hr 45min); Veszprém (1 daily; 1hr).

Sümeg to Győr (3 daily; 2hr 15min); Keszthely (1 daily; 45min); Sárvár (2 daily; 1hr 15min); Sopron (2 daily; 2hr 15min).

Székesfehérvár to Badacsony (1 daily; 2hr 30min); Budapest (every 40–60min; 1hr); Kalocsa (1 weekly; 3hr); Pécs (1 daily; 4hr); Szekszárd (2 daily; 2hr); Veszprém (every 40–90min; 1hr); Zalaegerszeg (2 daily; 4hr 15min).

Tapolca to Balatonfüred (1 daily except Sun; 1hr 30min); Nagyvázsony (8 daily; 45min); Sümeg (hourly; 30min); Veszprém (every 2hr; 1hr).

Veszprém to Budapest (every 60–90min; 2hr 15min); Győr (4 daily; 2hr); Harkány (1 daily; 4hr); Herend (hourly; 30min); Nagyvázsony (7 daily; 25min); Nemesvámos (hourly; 25min) Siófok (1 daily; 1hr 30min); Székesfehérvár (every 60–90min; 1hr); Szekszárd (2 daily; 3hr 45min); Tapolca (7 daily; 1hr).

Zirc to Budapest (3 daily; 2hr 30min).

International trains

Balatonszentgyörgy to Zagreb (1 daily; 4hr).

Fonyód to Dresden (June–Sept 1 daily; 15hr); Leipzig (June–Sept 1 daily; 17hr); Zagreb (June–Sept 2 daily; 2hr).

Siófok to Dresden (June–Sept 1 daily; 14hr); Leipzig (June–Sept 1 daily; 16hr); Prague (June–Sept 1 daily; 10hr); Vienna (1 daily; 5hr); Zagreb (1–3 daily; 2hr 30min).

Székesfehérvár to Dresden (June–Sept 1 daily; 12hr); Leipzig (June–Sept 1 daily; 14hr); Prague (June–Sept 1 daily; 9hr); Vienna (1 daily; 5hr 45min); Zagreb (1–3 daily; 6hr).

International buses

Balatonboglár to Vienna (July–Aug 1 weekly; 5hr 15min).

Balatonföldvár to Banská Bystrica (July–Oct 1 weekly; 5hr 30min).

Balatonszeped to Vienna (July–Aug 1 weekly; 5hr 15min).

Hévíz to Vienna (July–Aug 1 daily; 6hr 30min).

Keszthely to Graz (June–Sept 1–2 daily; Oct–May 2 weekly; 4hr 30min).

Siófok to Amsterdam (June–Sept 1 weekly; 24hr); Bratislava (July–Aug 1 daily; 5hr 15min); Brno (July–Aug 1 daily; 7hr); Frankfurt (June–Sept 2 weekly; 18hr); Galanta (July–Aug 1 daily; 4hr 15min); Semmering (July–Aug 1 daily; 6hr); Trnava (July–Aug 1 weekly; 5hr 30min); Vienna (July–Aug 1 weekly; 5hr).

Veszprém to Nitra (1 daily; 4hr 30min); Vienna (3 weekly; 4hr 30min).

Zalakros to Vienna (1 daily; 4hr 45min).

Ferries

Unless specified otherwise, most of the following services run from mid-April until late August or mid-September. Bear in mind that schedules can change, so all departure times should be verified on the spot.

Badacsony to Balatonboglár (July–Aug 5 daily; 1hr); Balatonföldvár (July–Aug 1 daily; 2hr 45min); Fonyód (mid-April to mid-Oct 11 daily; 45min); Siófok (June–Aug 1 daily; 4hr 30min); Tihany (June–Aug 1 daily; 3hr).

Balatonboglár to Révfülöp (July–Aug 7 daily; 30min); Badacsony (July–Aug 11 daily; 30min).

Balatonföldvár to Balatonfüred (4 daily; 1hr); Keszthely (July–Aug 1 daily; 5hr); Siófok (4 daily; 2hr); Tihany (4 daily; 30min).

Balatonfüred to Balatonföldvár (4 daily; 1hr); Tihany (6 daily; 30min); Siófok (8 daily; 1hr).

Fonyód to Badacsony (mid-April to mid-Oct 10 daily; 30min).

Keszthely to Badacsony (July–Aug 5 daily; 45min); Balatonföldvár (1 daily; 5hr).

Révfülöp to Balatonboglár (July–Aug 7 daily; 30min).

Siófok to Badacsony (July–Aug 1 daily; 4hr 30min); Balatonföldvár (4 daily; 2hr); Balatonfüred (7 daily; 1hr); Tihany (6 daily; 1hr 15min).

Szántódrév to Tihany-rév (April–Nov every 40–60min; 10min).

Tihany to Badacsony (July–Aug 1 daily; 2hr 30min); Balatonföldvár (4 daily; 30min); Balatonfüred (4 daily; 30min); Siófok (4 daily; 1hr 15min).

Tihany-rév to Szántódrév (April–Nov every 40–60min; 10min).

CHAPTER FOUR

TRANSDANUBIA

ravelling between Budapest and Vienna it's easy to gain a poor impression of **Transdanubia** – the *Dunántúl* – from the monotonous Little Plain (*Kisalföld*) or the industrial gloom around Tatabánya. What you don't see in passing is lakeside Tata, Győr's antique waterfront, Sopron's cobbled streets, deer in the **Forest of Gemenc**, or the rolling **Mecsek Hills**. More than other regions in Hungary, Transdanubia is a patchwork land, an ethnic and social hybrid. Its valleys, hills, forests and mud flats have been a melting pot since Roman times, when the region was known as Pannonia. Settled since by Magyars, Serbs, Croats, Germans and Slovaks, it has been torn asunder and occupied by the Turks and the Habsburgs; and only within the last 150 years has it been raised from a state of near feudalism.

Though **Szombathely** has the most to show for its Roman origins with its Temple of Isis and other ruins, every main town has at its core a fortified castle – stark testimony to centuries of warfare. Constant upheavals decimated medieval culture, leaving only the **Pannonhalma Monastery** and a few superb churches such as those at **Ják** and **Velemér**. Around each weathered *vár* (castle*)* stands a *Belváros* (inner town), with rambling streets and squares overlooked by florid Baroque and the odd Gothic or Renaissance building. **Tata**, **Kőszeg** and **Győr** provide fine examples of the genre; so too does **Sopron**, the most archaic, and **Pécs**, which boasts a Turkish mosque and minaret.

While several towns host spring or summer **festivals** of classical music, drama, folk music and dancing, the most interesting event is the masked Busójárás Carnival at **Mohács** seven weeks before Easter. During summer, concerts are also held in two unique settings – the **Esterházy Palace** at **Fertőd** and the rock chambers of **Fertőrákos** – both close to Sopron and **Nagycenk**, where you can ride antique steam trains on the **Széchenyi Railway**. At the monthly **market** in Pécs, you'll sense the peasant roots underlying many

---

ACCOMMODATION PRICE CODES

All accommodation in this guide is graded according to the price bands given below. Note that all prices refer to the cheapest available double room in high season except where otherwise indicated. For more details, see p.26.

① Under 650Ft (under £4/$6/ DM10)

② 650–1500Ft (£4–8/$6–13/DM10– 20)

③ 1500–3000Ft (£8–17/$13–27/ DM20–40)

④ 3000–4500Ft (£17–25/$27–40/ DM40–60)

⑤ 4500–6500Ft (£25–36/$40–57/ DM60–85)

⑥ 6500–10,000Ft (£36–56/$57–88/ DM85–130)

⑦ Over 10,000Ft (over £56/$88/ DM130)

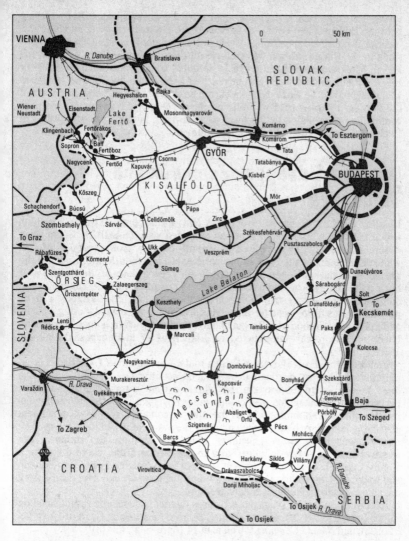

Transdanubian towns, whose sprawling *lakótelep* (apartment buildings) house recent immigrants from the countryside.

NORTHERN TRANSDANUBIA

Northern Transdanubia consists of the low-lying Kisalföld, bounded by the Vértes Hills and the Danube. Apart from the hills and the Szigetköz region bordering the river, its scenery is uninspiring, focusing one's attention on the towns. Lakeside **Tata** is delightful, and often overlooked by tourists travelling between Budapest and Győr – as is **Komárom**, the main crossing into Slovakia. Besides the intrinsic appeal of its lovely Belváros, **Győr** is an ideal base for excursions to the **Pannonhalma Monastery**. All these towns lie along the main rail line to **Mosonmagyaróvár**, served by frequent trains from Budapest's Déli or Keleti stations, and most can also be reached by bus from the Erzsébet tér depot. Motorists should be extra cautious on the stretch of the M1 between Győr and the border, a narrow road with an enormous volume of heavy traffic. Work is continuing on extending the highway to the border, but with the cancellation of Expo 1996 the urgency of the work has dimmed.

Out from Budapest: Zsámbék and Tatabánya

Heading out from Budapest, the Vértes Hills form a prelude to the Kisalföld, which is worth a brief detour if not an extended visit. **ZSÁMBÉK**, 33km west, deserves a mention for its **ruined thirteenth-century Romanesque church**, whose arches and walls look as romantic as a Piranesi drawing. Built for the Premonstratensians by the Ainard family (of French descent, they came over during the Angevin monarchy), the church later passed to the Pauline order, and was eventually destroyed by an earthquake in 1763. Zsámbék can be reached by bus from Széna tér (near Moszkva tér) in the capital – bring a picnic and make an afternoon of it. To get an idea of what the church once looked like, check out the replica constructed on Élmunkás tér in Budapest during the 1930s.

Following the direct Budapest–Vienna route, you can't miss **TATABÁNYA**, an ugly industrial town surrounded by ravaged countryside. Its only "sight", the giant bronze **Turul Statue**, can be glimpsed from a train carriage window, perched on a mountain top overlooking the grimy sprawl. Erected to commemorate the thousandth anniversary of the Magyar conquest, this great monument shows the legendary bird of prey clutching the sword of Árpád in its talons. The only reasons for a closer encounter with Tatabánya are the summer **Jazz Festival** and the chance to go **walking in the Vértes Hills**, where the **ruined Vitány Castle** broods on a crag 5km south of town (catch a bus to Vértessomló and walk up). Legend has it that the cowslips that grow around here during April are able to guide you towards hidden treasure.

Accommodation in Tatabánya's Újváros district includes the *Árpád Hotel* on Fő tér (☎34/310-299; ④); private rooms (②) from *Komturist* at Győri út 1A (☎34/311-936); and *Nomád Camping* at Tolnai út 14 (April–Sept; ☎34/310-753).

Tata

A small, sleepy town interlaced with canals and streams, **TATA** derives its charm from its lakes. Misty mornings enhance the romance of the central **Old Lake** (*Öreg-tó*), with its castle and pillared riding school, slender trees and spires. You can also rent boats here, or stroll across to the **Small Lake** (*Cseke-tó*), set in its own landscaped park a short distance to the east.

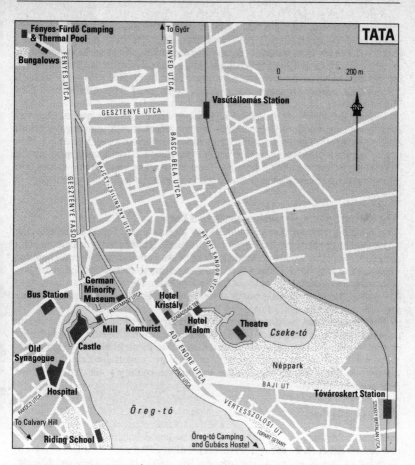

The Town

Following Tópart utca north along the lakefront to Alkotmány utca, you come to the beautifully restored **Nepomucenus Mill** (1758) at no. 1. Now home to the **German Minority Museum** (Tues–Sun 10am–6pm), it covers the history and lifestyles of the various German minority groups in the region – like Székesfehérvár and Pécs, Tata was almost entirely German-speaking for many centuries. Another ornate mill can be seen one street over at Bartók Béla utca 3. Beyond lies Tata's moated **Castle** (Tues–Sun 10am–6pm). Originally the hunting lodge of King Sigismund, it was badly damaged by both the Turks and the Habsburgs. Today it contains a museum of Roman miniatures and faience by local craftsman Domokos Kuny (1754–1822).

From here you can wander up Rákóczi utca into the old town, reconstructed under Jakab Fellner after the Turkish and Rákóczi wars. Tata's former synagogue is now the **Roman-Greek Statue Museum**, containing life-sized plaster casts of the Elgin Marbles, Hercules and Laocoön (May–Oct Tues–Sun 10am–6pm; Nov–April Tues–Fri 10am–2pm & Sat–Sun 10am–4pm). The mental **hospital** to the north of Hősök tere (Heroes' Square) occupies an old **Esterházy mansion** where the Habsburg King Francis took refuge from Napoleon in 1809. At the top of the hill, alleys lead off Kossuth tér towards **Calvary Hill** with its crucifixion monument, **nature reserve** and outdoor **Geological Museum** (Sat & Sun 10am–4pm).

Beyond the stretch of main highway dubbed Ady Endre utca, peace returns as you follow Szabadság tér into the 200-hectare **Néppark** surrounding the **Small Lake** (*Cseke-tó*). Laid out in 1780 and usually referred to as the Angol Park ("English Park"), this contains an outdoor **theatre** and **swimming pool**, and a fake ruined church cobbled together from Roman and Benedictine stonework. Hungary's Olympic team has its main training facility along the southern edge of the park.

The Riding School, Remetségpuszta and Kocs

Tata's **Riding School** (*Lovasiskola*) is over a century old, with a grandiose ring modelled on the Spanish Riding School in Vienna. It offers lessons, point-to-point races through the woods, extended riding tours and (in the autumn) hunting. *Komturist* or the *Hotel Kristály* (see below) can supply details, and also tell you about **fishing**. There is an outdoor **thermal pool** on the edge of town (bus #3 to the end of the line). Rowing **boats** (*csónakázás*) and pedal boats (*vízibicikli*) can be rented beside the Old Lake.

Remetségpuszta, south of town, is a **game park** with a hotel catering to wealthy hunters, a nice place to visit outside the hunting season (bus #4 to the end of the line). Lastly, it would be churlish not to mention **KOCS**, 11km southwest of Tata, where the **coach** (far lighter and more comfortable than the wagons used up to then) was invented in the seventeenth century – not that the village has anything much to show for it.

Practicalities

Arriving by **train**, you'll be deposited at the main Vasútallomás station 1km from the centre (bus #1), or at the Tóvároskert station, 600m east of Öreg-tó (bus #5). Arriving by **bus** is easier, as the intercity bus station is only a couple of blocks from the castle. **Information** is available from *Komturist* at Ady utca 9 (summer Mon–Fri 9am–5pm & Sat 8am–noon; winter Mon–Fri 8am–4pm; ☎34/381-805) and *Cooptourist* at Tópart-sétány 18 (☎34/381-602).

Trains are best for reaching Budapest, Győr or Sopron, but **buses** run more frequently to Tatabánya, Komárom and Esztergom. To reach Esztergom by rail entails changing at Almásfüzitő or Komárom.

Accommodation

Private rooms can be booked through *Komturist* or *Cooptourist* (addresses above), and there are also two **campsites** in the vicinity: *Fényes-Fürdő Camping* (April to mid-Oct; ☎34/381-591), by the thermal baths 2km north of the centre, where bus #3 terminates; and *Öreg-tó Camping* on Fáklya utca (April to mid-Oct; ☎34/383-496), which has bungalows (②–③) and tennis courts. The latter is between the lake and the highway – to get there from Tóvároskert station, follow Székely B. utca to the end, then Öveges J. utca. Other options include:

Hotel Kristály, Ady Endre utca 22 (☎34/383-577). Noisy location, but its 200-year-old dining room is appealing. Doubles and singles with showers or baths. ③–④.

Hotel Gottwald, Fekete út 1 (☎34/381-760). Beautiful hotel on the southwest shore of the lake with the best restaurant in town. ④.

Hotel Gubács/Youth Hostel, Fáklya út 4 (☎34/383-960). Single and double rooms, as well as dormitory rooms with 4–6 beds. ③.

Hotel Malom, Erzsébet tér 8 (☎34/383-530). A nice place near the park, but closed over winter. Shared bathrooms. ②.

Monika Panzió, Öregtó-part (☎34/383-208). About a 10-minute walk from the town centre around the lake to the south (before *Öreg-tó Camping*). ④.

Motel Patak, Fényesfasor (☎34/382-771). The latest name for a clutch of bungalows with tennis courts and a sauna, near the thermal baths (bus #3). ③–④.

Eating and drinking

Both the *Kristály* and *Gottwald* hotels have upmarket **restaurants**, the latter particularly recommended. Two lakeside restaurants worth trying are the *Halászcsárda*, which serves very fresh fish, and the *Tóvárosi Fogadó* next door. The *Bella Italia* at Andy Endre utca 33 specializes in Italian food (but beware of their arithmetic when it comes to paying the bill). For ice cream the *Gelato* stand at the *Hotel Kristály* is the place to go.

Komárom

KOMÁROM is the main crossing between Hungary and Slovakia, linked by a road and rail bridge to Komárno, across the Danube. The two towns formed a single municipality until 1920, and ethnic Magyars still predominate in Slovak Komárno, where shops and streets are signposted in both languages (though the Slovak parliament does occasionally threaten to remove the Hungarian signs, as ethnic friction worsens). Though neither town has much to offer in the way of sights, the easy crossing and good **connections** between Komárno and Bratislava make this a useful stepping stone en route to the Slovak capital.

From Komárom train station it's a five-minute walk to the **Hungarian side** of the 500-metre-long bridge, thronged by locals walking across the border. Since Roman times, the crossing has been secured by a fortress at the confluence of the Danube and the Váh. The existing **Csillag Fortress** was built by the Habsburgs, captured by the Hungarians in 1849, and occupied by Soviet troops until a few years ago. Despite its glamorous name ("Star Fortress"), it now serves as a mere storage place. More interesting is the **Monostori Fortress** (*erőd* in Hungarian) just west of the train station, or the **Igmundi Fortress**, a couple of kilometres south of the river down Igmundi utca. The town's **thermal bathing complex**, near the Csillag, is open year-round and much frequented by German visitors during the summer months (Tues–Sun 8am–6pm).

Should you cross over to **Slovak Komárno**, its bus and train stations are 2km northwest of the main street, Zahradnichka Slovanská. After crossing the bridge, turn right towards the recently done-up old town. On ulica Gábora Steiner (Sétány utca in Hungarian) is the small **Jókai Museum** which pays tribute to two local sons, **Franz Lehár** and **Mór Jókai** (Tues–Sun 10am–noon & 2–4pm). The former, the composer of the *Merry Widow*, was born here in 1870 and initially followed in his father's footsteps as bandmaster with the local garrison; Jókai was an extremely nationalistic Hungarian novelist who would not have approved of the town's modern-day split nationality. The museum stands next to a small **Orthodox church** built in the early eighteenth century by Serbian refugees who had fled from the Turks.

Practicalities

The best source of **information** is the *Tourinform* office at Mártirok útja 16 (☎37/341-790). *Ibusz* at Táncsics Mihály utca 38 (☎37/342-047) and *Komturist* at Mártirok útja 19 (☎37/341-767) can both help with money-changing and **accommodation**, most of which is clustered around the thermal baths. You'll find the *Thermal Hotel* at Táncsics Mihály utca 38 (☎37/342-447; ③ including entry to the baths), the marginally cheaper *Hotel Juno* across the road, and the year-round *Solaris Camping* (☎37/342-551) next door to the former. If you'd rather stay in **Komárno**, rooms in its three hotels can be booked through *ČEDOK* on Zahradnichka Slovanská.

For anyone wishing to savour the ambience of true Hungarian nightlife, there's *Lui's Disco* in the village of Szöny (5km east of Komárom along Road 10). Private buses will transport you back to Komárom at 2am and 4am.

Crossing the border

Crossing the border is quite straightforward, with both countries' passport controls at the Slovak end of the bridge. If you don't fancy walking, the information desks in Komárom and Komárno train stations can tell you the time of the next bus running from one to the other (every couple of hours). There are regular local trains from Komárno to **Bratislava** 110km away, eliminating the need to use international services (which cross the border here at night). If you're **entering Hungary**, there are fairly frequent trains and buses from Komárom to Budapest, Esztergom (for the Danube Bend) and Győr.

Győr

The industrial city of **GYŐR** (pronounced "Dyur") harbours a waterfront Belváros stuffed with Baroque mansions and churches, where streets bustle and restaurants vie for custom. With so much to enjoy around the centre, you can easily forget the high-rise apartments and factories that form the rest of Győr, whose Rába Engineering Works – producing trucks and rolling stock – is the third largest industrial complex in Hungary. The city also makes an excellent base for excursions to Pannonhalma Monastery.

Győr's **history** owes much to its location at the confluence of three rivers – the Rába, the Rábca and the Mosoni-Duna – in the centre of the Little Plain. The place was named Arrabona by the Romans, after a local Celtic tribe whom they subjugated, while its current name derives from *gyürü*, the Avar word for a circular fortress. During the Turkish occupation of Hungary, its castle was a Habsburg stronghold and the town was known as Raab (after the Rába River). After its military role diminished, Győr gained industrial muscle and a different kind of clout. In the 1956 Uprising, its town hall was occupied by a radical Provisional National Council that pressed the government to get Soviet troops out and to quit the Warsaw Pact immediately. More recently Győr hit the news when a neo-Nazi cell with links to Austrian and American fascists was unearthed in Győr.

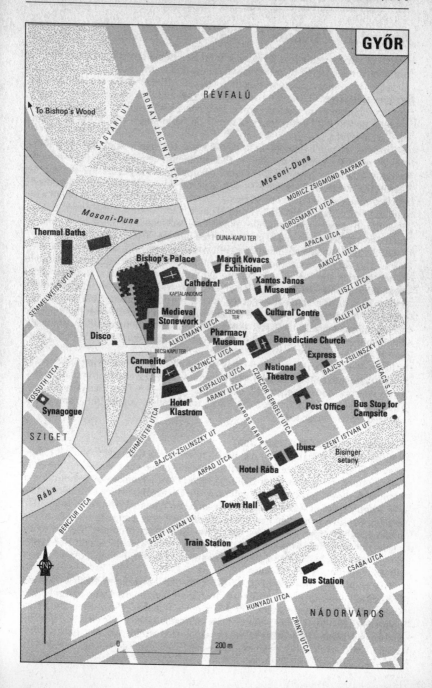

GYŐR

RÉVFALÚ

To Bishop's Wood

SAGVARI UT

RONAY JACINT UTCA

Mosoni-Duna

MORICZ ZSIGMOND RAKPART

VOROSMARTY UTCA

Mosoni-Duna

DUNA-KAPU TER

APACA UTCA

RAKOCZI UTCA

Thermal Baths

SEMMELWEISS UTCA

Bishop's Palace

Margit Kovacs Exhibition

Cathedral

Xantos Janos Museum

LISZT UTCA

KAPTALANDOMS

PALFFY UTCA

Medieval Stonework

SZECHENYI TER

Cultural Centre

Disco

ALKOTMANY UTCA

Pharmacy Museum

Benedictine Church

BECSI KAPU TER

KAZINCZY UTCA

Express

BAJCSY-ZSILINSZKY UT

Carmelite Church

National Theatre

LUKACS S.U.

KISFALUDY UTCA

KOSSUTH UTCA

ARANY UTCA

CZUCZOR GERGELY UTCA

Synagogue

Hotel Klastrom

Post Office

Bus Stop for Campsite

SZIGET

ZEHMEISTER UTCA

BAROSS GABOR UTCA

SZENT ISTVAN UT

BAJCSY-ZSILINSZKY UT

Ibusz

Bisinger setany

Rába

ARPAD UTCA

Hotel Rába

BENCZUR UTCA

Town Hall

SZENT ISTVAN UT

Train Station

CSABA UTCA

Bus Station

HUNYADI UTCA

NÁDORVÁROS

ZRINYI UTCA

0   200 m

Around the Belváros

A web of streets and alleys stretching from Széchenyi tér to Káptalandomb, the **old quarter** is covered by preservation orders and traffic restrictions, making it a pleasure to wander around. Heading up pedestrianized Baross Gábor utca, antique side streets beckon on your left, narrow and shadowy with overhanging timbered houses – the perfect setting for a conspiracy. Indeed, Communists met secretly during the Horthy years at no. 15 on Sárlo köz, a cobbled alley forking off Kazinczy utca.

Chances are you'll emerge on to **Bécsi kapu tér**, overlooking the River Rába, which reputedly escaped flooding in the eighteenth century thanks to a miracle-working statue of Mary of the Foam, occupying a chapel beside the former **Carmelite church**. Entering through a portal whose inscription proclaims "I worked zealously for the Lord of Hosts", you'll find a richly decorated high altar and other furnishings carved by Franz Richter, a lay brother in the order. Behind the church stands the erstwhile monastery, subsequently used as a refugee centre and military prison and now converted into the *Hotel Klastrom*.

On the eastern side of the square are two **mansions** with finely wrought iron-work. The Zichy Palace (no. 13), built in 1778–82, has a balconied Zopf-style facade bearing the coat of arms of the Ott family, who owned it at a later date. Next door stands the Altabek House (no. 12), with two corner oriel windows dating back to the sixteenth century, and a Baroque portico. Just around the corner at Alkotmány utca 4 is the so-called Napoleon House where the emperor stayed during a visit in 1809, and which now contains a **picture gallery** of mostly nineteenth-century works (April–Oct Tues–Sun 10am–6pm; Nov–March Tues–Sun 10am–5pm).

From Bécsi kapu tér you can carry on uphill past the surviving bastions of Győr's sixteenth-century **Castle**, where visitors can see a courtyard full of medie-val stonework and underground casements (April–Oct Tues–Sun 10am–6pm). The castle successfully resisted the Turks for decades – unlike the town, which was frequently devastated.

Káptalandomb and the waterfront

Káptalandomb (Chapter Hill) has been crowned by a **Cathedral** (daily 9.15am–noon & 2–6pm) ever since King Stephen made Győr an episcopal see in the elev-enth century, so the existing building incorporates Romanesque, Gothic and Baroque features. Just inside the entrance, the Gothic Hederváry Chapel contains a **reliquary bust of Saint László**, the canonized monarch who ruled from 1077 to 1095. Sensitively moulded and richly enamelled, it is a superb example of the goldsmith's art from the workshop of the Kolozsvári brothers. The frescoes inside the cathedral were painted by Maulbertsch, who decorated numerous Hungarian churches in the eighteenth century, while the Bishop's throne was a gift from Empress Maria Theresa.

The building to the southeast of the cathedral houses the **Miklós Borsos Collection** of paintings and sculptures by the self-taught artist who designed the Kilometre Zero monument on Clark Ádám tér in Budapest (April–Sept Tues–Sun 10am–6pm; Oct–March Tues–Sun 9.30am–4.30pm). In the other direction lies the **Bishop's Palace** (*Püspökvár*), a much remodelled edifice whose oldest section dates from the thirteenth century (April–Sept Tues–Sun 9am–6pm; Nov–March Tues–Sun 10am–5pm).

From here you can walk down Káptalandomb utca past the Zopf-style Provost House (no. 15) to reach the **Ark of the Covenant**, a splendid Baroque monument erected by Emperor Karl III by way of an apology for the Habsburg soldiers who knocked the monstrance from a priest's hands during a Corpus Christi procession in 1727. Just beyond lies **Duna-kapu tér**, a waterfront square alongside which Danube grain ships once moored, and where food **markets** are still held on Wednesdays and Saturdays. Notice the iron weathercock on top of the well, an allusion to the one that the Turks fixed above the town's gate, boasting that they would never leave Győr until it crowed.

Across the river

Should you want a change of scenery, cross the Mosoni-Duna River to the **Révfalu** district, where a fifteen-minute walk will bring you to the **Bishop's Wood** (*Püspök-erdő*), an attractive park with deer and other fauna. Alternatively, you can cross the Rába via a small island linked by bridge to Bécsi kapu tér and the **Sziget** district. At the northern tip of Sziget there's a **swimming pool** that's open during the summer and an outdoor **thermal bath** that's open year-round (Mon–Fri 6am–8pm & Sat–Sun 7am–6pm). Nearby at Kossuth utca 5 is a domed former **Synagogue** built in 1869 – worth a visit if you can get inside.

Around Széchenyi tér

There's more to see, however, behind Duna-kapu tér, starting with the **Margit Kovács Collection** at Apáca utca 1 (April–Sept Tues–Sun 10am–6pm; Oct–March Tues–Sun 10am–5pm). This is just as delightful as the museum of her work in Szentendre (p.122), but closer to home, as Kovács (1902–77) was born in Győr. On the other side of the road, Bread Alley (*Kenyér köz*) and Soap Alley (*Szappanos köz*) lead to **Széchenyi tér**, traditionally the main square, overlooked by eye-like attic windows from the steep roofs of surrounding buildings.

Notice the **Iron Stump House** (no. 4) on the northern side of the square, so-called after a wooden beam into which travelling journeymen hammered nails to mark their sojourn. The building now contains the **Imre Patkó Collection** of paintings and African art (April–Oct Tues–Sun 10am–6pm), which deserves a visit. Next door is the **Xantus János Museum** (April–Sept Tues–Sun 10am–6pm; Oct–March Tues–Sun 10am–5pm), named after a locally educated archeologist (1825–94) who emigrated to America and subsequently travelled in China. You can buy a leaflet in English describing the varied and fascinating artefacts relating to local history, while the collection of tiled stoves needs no explanation.

Further east, take a look into the Tuscan Renaissance-style courtyard of the erstwhile **Hospice** at Rákóczi utca 6; a second courtyard at the back contains a fountain embellished with statues of birds. Back on Széchenyi tér, with its ornate **Marian Column** commemorating the recapture of Buda Castle from the Turks, the Benedictine **Church of Saint Ignatius** was designed by the Italian Baccio del Bianco in the 1630s. A painting in the sanctuary by the Viennese artist Troger (1794) depicts the saint's apotheosis. Beside the adjacent monastery is the **Pharmacy Museum** (Mon, Tues, Thurs & Fri 9am–5pm; Wed & Sat 2–5pm; Sun 9am–1pm), a beautifully furnished seventeenth-century apothecary that still functions as a pharmacy.

Practicalities

On **arrival** at the bus or train station, you can either seek lodgings in the immediate vicinity, or head straight for the Belváros (inner city), a ten- to fifteen-minute walk which takes you across Szent István út – a veritable wind tunnel of an avenue serving as the main route to Vienna – and up Baross Gábor utca. Assuming you make it safely across Szent István út, *Ibusz* at no. 31 can help with **rooms** and **information** (Mon–Fri 8am–4pm; ☎314-135). The main **post office** is at Bajcsy-Zsilinszky út 46, while **police** headquarters are at Zrínyi utca 54, near the bus station. There are several **hospitals** along Felszabadulás útja, 1km further south. For anyone wishing to **rent a car**, *Hertz* is situated at Bartók utca 10 (☎313-013).

Accommodation

From mid-July to mid-August, the cheapest **accommodation** available is **dormitory beds** (①) in the Technical College at Ságvári Endre utca 3, on Révfalú. Bookings for college beds and private rooms around town can be made through *Express* at Bajcsy-Zsilinszky út 41 (Mon–Fri 8am–4pm; ☎328-833); *Ibusz* (address above); or *Cooptourist* at Jedlik Ányos utca 8 (Mon–Fri 8am–4pm & Sat 8am–noon; ☎320-801). Other options include:

HOTELS AND PENSIONS

Corvin Panzió, Csaba utca 22 (☎312-171). A small pension three blocks east of the bus station. ③.

Duna Panzió, Vörösmarty utca 5 (☎329-084). 14-room hotel with antique furniture and a good central location. ③–④.

Gróf Cziráky Panzió, Bécsi kapu tér 8 (☎310-688). An elegant and pricey pension smack in the centre of town. ④.

Hotel Klastrom, Zechmeister utca 1, just off Bécsi kapu tér (☎315-611). Very classy hotel occupying the 200-year-old priory behind the Carmelite church. Beautiful restaurant and inner courtyard, plus lovely views of the river. ⑤.

Hotel Raba, Árpád út 34 (☎315-533). A well-equipped Seventies establishment near the main street. ⑤.

Kuckó Panzió, Arany János utca 33 (☎316-260). A 7-room pension in an old townhouse, right in the centre of the old town. ③–④.

Pető Panzió, Kossuth Lajos utca 20 (☎313-412). On Sziget, accessible by bus #1 or #1Y from Aradi vértanúk útja. ③–④.

Szárnyaskerék Hotel, Révai Miklós utca 5 (☎314-629). The "Winged Wheel Hotel" (as its name translates) occupies the old hostel building across from the train station. ②–③.

Teátrum Panzió, Schweidel utca 7 (☎310-640). 10-room pension on a pedestrianized street. ②–③.

CAMPING

Győr's campsites are all situated some distance from the town centre.

Amstel Hattyú Camping, Híd utca 18 (☎313-586). Year-round campsite next to the River Rába. Accessible by bus #2 from the town hall.

Balázs Béla Camping, Vajcsuk L. utca 70 (☎329-033). Small private site near a housing estate in the Nádorváros district (bus #5 or #22 from the Baross Bridge). Open mid-June to late Aug.

Kiskuti Camping, Kiskút-liget (☎318-986). A big site with bungalows (②–③) near the stadium beyond the industrial district. To get there catch bus #8 from Szent István út, opposite Lukács Sándor utca. Open mid-April to mid-Oct.

Pihenő Camping, Szent Imre út 20 (☎315-304 or 317-678). Campsite in Szentivan, about 10km from the town centre (ask about buses at the bus station), with wooden bungalows (②) open all year and camping facilities when weather permits.

Eating

Győr has recently succeeded in entering the higher realms of international cuisine with the opening of *McDonald's* at Baross Gábor utca 21 and *Pizza Hut* on the same street at no. 1. Note that most **eating places** close early, around 10pm.

Chinese restaurant. A cheap place to eat above the *Jereván* bar on the island opposite Bécsi kapu tér.

Leto, corner of Aradi Vértanúk útja and Bajcsy Zsilinszky út. Pizzeria/gelateria serving the best ice cream in town.

Matróz Csárda, Duna-kapu tér 3. A less pricey option by the Bishop's Palace.

Sárkány Lyuk ("Dragon Hole"), Arany János utca 29. A local hang-out with good Hungarian food at reasonable prices.

Tejivó Salatbár, Kisfaludy utca 30. Specializes in salads and real fruit milkshakes.

Várkapu Étterem, Bécsi kapu tér 7. The place to go if you want to indulge yourself and money's no object.

Vaskakas, Bécsi kapu tér 2. Another upmarket restaurant built into the former castle walls near the river.

Drinking

Győr's **watering holes** include the *Szürkebarát Borozó* at Arany János utca 20 and the *Vár-borozó*, midway along Alkotmány utca. The *Jereván* on the island in the middle of the Rába is a cheaper late-night haunt than *Charly's Night Klub* at Nagy István utca 12, whose dance floor is almost deserted due to the 300Ft admission charge. Cocktails and spirits are also served in **patisseries** such as the *Rába Cukrászda* at Baross Gábor utca 30. Alternatively, catch a #4 bus out to the Nádorváros district to enjoy the old-fashioned ambience of the *Bergmann Cukrászda* at József Attila utca 29 (Wed–Sun 10am–6pm).

Entertainment

Express and *Ibusz* can give you a rundown of the **local entertainment** on offer. Culture vultures should look out for performances by the **Győr Ballet Company**, which achieved international renown under its founder Iván Márko, formerly the lead dancer of Maurice Béjarat's Twentieth Century Ballet Company. Although Márko has moved on and foreign critics now disparage the company, locals still cherish it, and performances always sell out at the brashly-tiled **National Theatre** on the corner of Bajcsy-Zsilinszky út and Czuczor Gergely utca (tickets at Kisfaludy utca 25). Foreign **films** are screened at the **Cultural Centre** at Czuczor Gergely utca 17, where other events are also held.

From mid-June to mid-July is Győr's **Summer Events**, a month-long festival of music, theatre and dance. Another source of pride is the city's **football** team, Győr ETO, which has in the past humbled such foreign clubs as Manchester United at their stadium in the eastern suburbs (bus #8).

Moving on

The obvious destination to the west of Győr is Sopron (see p.201), which is easily reached by train. Heading for Vienna or Bratislava instead, the only significant place en route is Mosonmagyaróvár (see p.199). Szombathely in western Transdanubia can be reached by trains routed through Papa, while another branch line runs south to Veszprém (see p.180) via Pannonhalma. Express trains and buses to Budapest take about two hours.

Pannonhalma Monastery

Twenty kilometres southeast of Győr the low-lying Kisalföld meets a spur of the Bakony, a glorious setting for the fortress-like **Pannonhalma Monastery** atop Saint Martin's Hill (282m). According to Anonymous, it was here that Árpád was "uplifted by the beauty of Pannonia" after the Magyar conquest, and Prince Géza invited the **Benedictine Order** to found an abbey in 969. The Order helped Géza's son Stephen weld the pagan Magyar tribes into a Christian state, and remained influential until its suppression in 1787 by Emperor Josef II. Re-established by his successor, the Benedictines thereafter confined themselves to prayer and pedagogy.

The monastery's imposing hillside buildings manifest a wide variety of styles and antiquity. Tourists are allowed to visit, but only on **guided tours** (Tues–Sun 9am–4pm, every hour on the hour except midday). The Gothic **cloisters** date from the first quarter of the thirteenth century, when Pannonhalma was remodelled under Abbot Oros, who later gave King Béla IV 220 kilos of silver to help him rebuild the country after the Mongol invasion. The wings are chiefly Romanesque, contrasting with the Baroque exterior of the **church** and a Neoclassical **tower**. Purists lament the church's neo-Romanesque interior, remodelled by Ferenc Storno in 1867. Notice the exquisitely carved portal and marble sepulchres containing the bones of two abbots and a princess.

Although Pannonhalma's most sacred **treasures** are displayed only on a couple of days around August 20, its medieval codices and ancient books are permanently on show in the Empire-style **library**. The 300,000-volume collection includes the foundation deed of Tihany Abbey. Dating from 1055, this is the earliest known document to include Hungarian words (55 of them) amongst the customary Latin. A one-room **art gallery** displays a portrait of King Stephen and paintings by Italian, Dutch and German artists of the sixteenth and seventeenth centuries.

Churchgoers have a choice of two **masses** on Sunday: with (9am) or without (10am) a sermon and organ music. Fully fledged **organ recitals** usually occur on Easter Monday, Whit Sunday, August 20, October 23 and December 26, drawing crowds of music lovers. Book at least a week in advance through *Pax Tourist* (address below).

Practicalities

The monastery can be reached from Győr by any bus or train heading for Veszprém (or vice versa), although the train station is 2km from the monastery. *Pax Tourist*, up by the entrance to the monastery at Vár utca 1 (Tues–Sat 9am–4pm & Sun noon–4pm; ☎96/470-191) can arrange private **accommodation** if you decide to stay overnight. The elegant *Pax Hotel* at Dózsa György utca 2 (☎96/470-006; ⑤) is an obvious option, though two cheaper establishments are the excellent *Pannon Panzió* at Hunyadi utca 7B (☎96/470-041; ④), and the small *Familia Panzió* at Béke út 61 (☎96/470-192; ③). *Panorama Camping* is beautifully sited on the side of a hill at Fenyvesalja utca 4A (signposted from the village or ask at *Pax Tourist*). Of the several **restaurants** in the village, the *Pannon Panzió* is particularly recommended for its good, cheap food.

Towards Mosonmagyaróvár

Driving to (or from) Vienna or Bratislava, you have the option of stopping over at Mosonmagyaróvár, or detouring off Route 1 to visit Lébénymiklós or the Szigetköz region. Since neither is accessible by bus or rail, travellers relying on public transport may reckon that it's not worth interrupting their journey for Mosonmagyaróvár alone.

Lébénymiklós and beyond

Detouring off the highway to **LÉBÉNYMIKLÓS** is only recommended if you're a fan of ecclesiastical architecture, since the village's sole attraction is a thirteenth-century **Benedictine church** that once came under the jurisdiction of Pannonhalma. Though touted as one of the oldest and finest examples of Romanesque architecture in Hungary, it was actually restored to its original style after receiving a Baroque face-lift from the Jesuits in the mid-seventeeth century. If this sounds enticing, you can reach Lébénymiklós by turning west off the highway at Öttevény, 16km from Győr.

On the other side of the highway lies the **Szigetköz** or "Island region", bounded by the meandering Mosoni-Duna and the "Old" or main branch of the Danube. This picturesque wetland abounds in rare flora, **birdlife** and fish, making it something of a paradise for hikers and naturalists alike. Unfortunately, the **Gabčikovo hydroelectric barrage** has reduced water levels sharply, thus posing a serious threat to the ecology and wildlife of the region. Amid much debate, the Győr *Reflex* environmental group (☎96/310-988) is pressing for the creation of a Trilateral National Park that would embrace the whole Danube region from Hainburg to Komárom, with Hungary responsible for the Szigetköz.

Meantime, you can traverse the Szigetköz by a minor road running between Győr and Mosonmagyaróvár, which is ideal for **cyclists**. The village of **LIPÓT**, 2km off the road, offers **accommodation** in the form of the *Holt-Duna Panzió* (☎96/316-196; ②) and a basic campsite (May–Sept).

Mosonmagyaróvár

MOSONMAGYARÓVÁR is a fusion of two settlements near the confluence of the Mosoni-Duna and Lajtha rivers. While **Moson** – one side of the highway – is utterly prosaic, **Magyaróvár** on the other is a pleasant old town with a picturesque castle and bridges. Both are visibly prosperous, since hordes of Austrians come here to shop or to receive inexpensive medical attention, while townsfolk travel to work in Austria in their Mercedes. If you have the choice, the best time to visit is late autumn, when the first pressing of grapes takes place at **vineyards** in the locality.

Entering town by the Győr road, you'll pass a couple of sights along Fő utca. The **Hanság Museum** at no. 135 is one of the oldest provincial collections in Hungary, covering local history since Roman times – but was closed for restoration when last heard. Once reopened, it is sure to include material on the event which made the town notorious in 1956 (see box below). Further up the road at no. 103 stands the Baroque Cselley House (April–Oct Tues–Sun 10am–6pm; Nov–March Tues–Sun 10am–5pm), hosting an **Exhibition of Fine and Applied Arts** from the seventeenth century onwards.

However the chief attraction is **Magyaróvár Castle**, just beyond Szent László tér (follow the signposts for Bratislava). Founded in the thirteenth century to guard the western gateway to Hungary, it gave the town its medieval name, Porta Hungarica. Much remodelled since then, it now houses a section of Keszthely's Agricultural University and a small exhibition on the fauna of the Hanság (Mon–Fri 10am–6pm), which enables you to gain access to the castle.

Information and accommodation

Both halves of town have their own **tourist office**. In Magyaróvár, *Ciklámen Tourist* is at Fő utca 8 (Mon–Thurs 8am–4.15pm, Fri 8am–noon & 12.30pm–3.15pm, Sat 8am–noon; ☎96/211-078), whilst in Moson you'll find their office at Szent István király út 108 (☎96/216-554).

Either tourist office can book **private rooms** (②–③), and there are plenty of *Zimmer frei* signs dotted around. **Campers** can choose from the *Magyar Autóklub* by the river at Gabona rakpart 6 (May to mid-Oct; ☎96/215-883), an unpleasantly overcrowded motorists' campsite with bungalows (③); or *Jóker Camping* (☎96/211-845), a smaller, private site on the corner of Alkotmány and Baratság utca, next to the Polish Market (bus #4).

For **hotel accommodation**, try any of the following:

Szent Flórian Hotel, Fő utca 127 (☎96/213-177). A comfortable three-star establishment with wheelchair access. ⑤.

Fekete Sas Hotel, Fő utca 93 (☎96/215-842). Smallish place near the centre. ③.

Solaris Hotel, Lucsony utca 19 (☎96/215-300). Well-equipped hotel just east of the castle. ④.

Lajtha Hotel, Palánk utca 3 (☎96/211-824). A one-star place with tennis facilities and wheelchair access. ③–④.

Minerva Hotel, Engels út 2 (☎96/211-367). Basic but relatively cheap. ③.

Eating and drinking

Aside from various cheap **restaurants** along Fő utca, you might investigate the *Széchenyi Étterem* at Városház utca 2 and the *Várpince Étterem* at Vár utca 2. The *Ambrozia Kávéház* on the corner of Szent László tér in downtown Magyaróvár serves delicious cappuccino and apple-poppyseed *retes*.

MASSACRE AT MOSONMAGYARÓVÁR

Three days after the Uprising began in Budapest, a quarter of Mosonmagyaróvár's population staged a peaceful march on the town hall, demanding an end to Stalinism. ÁVO guards opened fire on the crowd without warning, killing 100 people and wounding 250. An Italian journalist was present, and news of the massacre was flashed around the world.

While most of the perpetrators were lynched shortly afterwards, the officer in charge escaped to enjoy a peaceful retirement in the Kádár era. Following the demise of Communism, the popular wish that such crimes should be punished led Parliament to pass the **Zétényi–Takács Law** (named after the two MPs that drafted it) in November 1991. However, others feared that it could be used against anyone associated with the Communist regime, and argued that Hungary had already suffered enough from political witch-hunts. Among its critics were President Árpád Göncz and MPs Imre Mécs and László Rajk Jr, who had been gaoled under Communism. In March 1992, Hungary's Constitutional Court overturned the law on the grounds that "the ethical glory of punishing a villain is not worth risking the legal guarantees of our constitutional state".

THE AUSTRO-HUNGARIAN BORDER

The **Austro–Hungarian border** used to be wired and mined, with guards authorized to shoot would-be escapers. In the spring of 1989, the removal of life-threatening barriers encouraged thousands of East Germans to use Hungary as an escape route to the West, precipitating the dramatic events that led to the fall of the Berlin Wall. Hungarians gained the right to travel anywhere with the introduction of the so-called *Világ* (World) passport in 1988, but for citizens of Romania and the former Soviet Union the border was still a barrier unless they had a Western visa, which the average person had no chance of getting. Trains approaching the border crossing at Hegyeshalom were a notorious hideout for young Romanians attempting to 'sneak across. This is less the case nowadays, and you're less likely to come across stowaways, although the smuggling trade in goods is as strong as ever.

Border crossings

Mosonmagyaróvár is the last stop before two major border crossings. **Rajka**, 19km north, handles traffic bound for the Slovak capital of Bratislava (15km), while **Hegyeshalom** is the main road and rail crossing into Austria, whence it's 45km to Vienna.

WESTERN TRANSDANUBIA

Western Transdanubia, bordering Austria and Slovenia, has a sub-Alpine topography and climate, ideal for wine-growing and outdoor pursuits. Its Baroque towns and historic castles evince centuries of Habsburg influence and doughty resistance against the Turks. From the beautiful town of **Sopron**, you can visit the **Esterházy Palace** before heading south to **Kőszeg** and **Szombathely**, and thence to **Sárvár** or the picturesque **Őrség region**. This itinerary suits regional transport, since Sopron is easily accessible by express trains and buses from Budapest or Győr, whereas other places are easier to reach using local services. Starting from the Balaton, however, it's easier to work your way north via Szombathely or **Zalaegerszeg** (and in which case, backtrack through the following sections).

Sopron

With its 115 monuments and 240 listed buildings, **SOPRON** can justly claim to be "the most historic town in Hungary". Never having been ravaged by Mongols or Turks, the inner town retains its medieval layout, with a fusion of Gothic and Baroque architecture that rivals Castle Hill in Budapest. Sopron is also a major wine-producing centre and the base for excursions to Esterházy Palace, the vintage steam train at Nagycenk and other sites. The only drawback is its proximity to Vienna, which means that Austrians come here in droves to shop, eat out and get their teeth fixed, swamping the town over summer.

On **arriving** at the main train station south of the centre, head 500m up Mátyás király utca to reach Széchenyi tér and the Belváros (the old inner city). Coming in by intercity bus, a five-minute walk along Lackner Kristóf utca will bring you to Ógabona tér, on the edge of the old quarter. Once inside the horseshoe-shaped

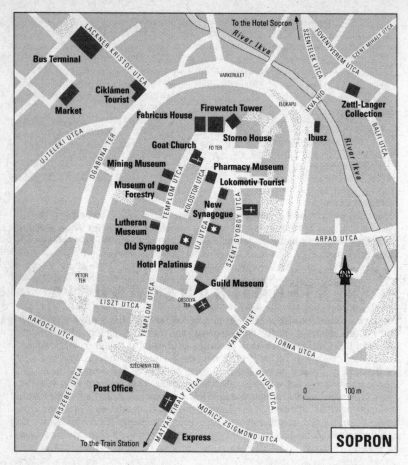

SOPRON

Belváros (old town), **orientation** is simple. The following account progresses northwards through the quarter.

Around the Belváros

Heading up Templom utca, turn right along Fegyvertár utca to reach **Orsolya tér**. This cobbled square gets its name from an Ursuline convent that once occupied the site of the **Church of the Virgin**, sandwiched between two neo-Gothic edifices dripping with loggias. The one on the left hosts an **Exhibition of Catholic Artefacts** (June–Sept Mon & Thurs 10am–6pm, Sat & Sun 11am–4pm), while the arcaded building at no. 5 contains a small **Guild Museum** where ceramics (both originals and replicas) are sold (summer Tues–Sun 9am–5pm; winter Tues–Sun 9am–1pm). In former times, animals were butchered under the arcades and the square was the site of the Salt Market.

Új utca (New street) runs off to the northwest and is actually one of Sopron's oldest thoroughfares. Its chunky cobblestoned pavements follow a gentle curve of arched dwellings painted in red, yellow and pink. During the Middle Ages it was called Zsidó (Jewish) utca and housed a flourishing community of Jewish merchants. As elsewhere, however, they were accused of conspiring with the Turks and expelled from Hungary in 1526, only returning to Sopron in the nineteenth century. At no. 22 on the left is a tiny medieval **Synagogue** with a ritual bath in the courtyard (April–Oct daily except Tues 9am–5pm).

When last heard, the northern end of Új utca was closed due to work on the water mains, compelling visitors to return to **Templom utca**. Heading up past the ornamental Töpler House (no. 22), you'll reach the **Lutheran History Museum** at no. 12 (April–Sept Mon, Thurs, Sat & Sun 10am–1pm). The adjacent **Lutheran church** dates from 1782, but only acquired its tower eighty years later, due to restrictions on the faith decreed by Emperor Josef II – as related in the museum.

The **Museum of Forestry** (*Erdészeti Múzeum*) at no. 4 (Mon–Fri 1–5pm & Sat–Sun 10am–6pm) features displays on forestry and environmental protection. Next door another exhibition can be found in the former Esterházy Mansion at no. 2, now a **Mining Museum** covering the industry's history (April–Oct daily except Wed 10am–6pm; Nov–March daily except Wed 10am–4pm). Directly across the street at no. 1 stands the **Chapterhouse**, whose beautiful vaulted interior dates from the fourteenth century, with allegorical images of the seven deadly sins decorating the capitals of its pillars and the bosses of its cross-vaulting. A full history and explanations of this excellently preserved building are provided in English and German (daily 10am–noon & 2–4pm). Beyond lies Sopron's historic main square.

Fő tér

The focal point of **Fő tér** is the cherubim-covered **Holy Trinity Statue**, which local protestants took as an affront when it was erected in 1700 by Cardinal Kollonich, who threatened: "First I will make the Hungarians slaves, then I will make them beggars, and then I will make them Catholics." Behind it stands the triple-aisled **Goat Church** built for the Franciscans in 1300, where three kings were later crowned and Parliament convened on seven occasions. Its curious name stems from the legend that the church's construction was financed by a goatherd whose flock unearthed a cache of loot – in gratitude for which an angel embraces a goat on one of the pillars of its Baroque interior.

Before crossing the square to visit the mansions on its northern side, check out the **Pharmacy Museum** at no. 2, which preserves the Angel apothecary founded by Tóbiás Marb in 1601. Though remodelled since then, its Biedermeier-style walnut furnishings and artefacts from the Dark Ages of pharmacology certainly deserve a look (April–Oct Tues–Sun 10am–6pm; Nov–March Tues–Sun 9am–5pm).

Directly opposite the church stands the **Fabricus House** at no. 6 (Tues–Sun 10am–6pm), which unites a Baroque mansion built upon Roman foundations with a patrician's house from the fifteenth century. A Renaissance stairway leads up to a small museum of archeological finds, also noted for its "whispering gallery", while the Gothic cellar contains three large Roman statues unearthed during the construction of the town hall. Next door at no. 7 is the **Lackner House**, named after the seventeenth-century mayor who bequeathed it to Sopron; his motto *Fiat Voluntas tua* (Let your will be) appears on the facade.

The Renaissance **Storno House** at no. 8 has the finest pedigree, however. King Mátyás stayed here in 1482–83, as did Franz Liszt in 1840 and 1881. It is still owned by descendants of Ferenc Storno, painter, architect and master chimney-sweep, who restored Pannonhalma and other medieval churches during the nine-teenth century. The family's private collection of Liszt memorabilia and Roman, Celtic and Avar relics are displayed in the **Sopron Museum** on the second floor of the house (group tours only; summer Tues–Sun 10am–6pm; winter Tues–Sun 10am–4.30pm).

The Firewatch Tower

North of the square rises Sopron's symbol, the **Firewatch Tower** (*Tűztorony*), founded upon the stones of a fortress built by the Romans, who established the town of *Scarbantia* here during the first century AD. As its name suggests, the tower was intended to give warning of a fire anywhere in town – while standing watch, the sentries blew trumpets to signal the hours. Ascending from its square, tenth-century base up through a cylindrical seventeenth-century mid-section, you emerge on to a Baroque balcony offering a stunning **view** of Fő tér and the inner town (April–Oct Tues–Sun 10am–6pm; Nov–March Tues–Sun 10am–4pm).

At the base of the tower is the **Gate of Loyalty**, erected in honour of the town-folks' decision to reject the offer of Austrian citizenship in 1921. The motif shows Hungaria surrounded by kneeling citizens and Sopron's coat of arms, which henceforth included the title *Civitas Fidelissima* (the most faithful town). Walking through it, you'll emerge on to **Előkapu** (Outer Gate) street, where the houses are staggered for defensive purposes; and "errant burghers" and "gossiping, nagging" wives were once pinioned in stocks for the righteous to pelt with rotten food.

At its junction with **Várkerület körút** you can cross the road to examine the colourfully tiled facade of the **Golden Lion Pharmacy** at no. 29, or head south along the boulevard to espy a section of the **medieval town walls** on the left.

Beyond the Belváros

Ikva híd (crossing a narrow stream which flooded noxiously in the nineteenth century) points towards a couple more sights. Off to the right at Balfi utca 11 is the private **Zettl-Langer Collection** (daily 10am–noon) of porcelain, earthenware and weaponry, assembled by a nineteenth-century businessman.

For a longer walk, follow Pozsonyi út uphill past the **House of the Two Moors** (so-called after the turbaned statues flanking its gate) to the partially Gothic **Church of Saint Michael**, whose gargoyles leer over a decaying thir-teenth-century Chapel of Saint Jacob. Nearby stand the cross-less tombstones of Soviet soldiers killed liberating Sopron from the Arrow Cross puppet-government, which massacred hundreds of hostages before fleeing with the Coronation Regalia in April 1945.

The Fool's Castle

In the western garden suburbs lurks a bizarre "**Fool's Castle**" (*Taródi-vár*), built by a local eccentric early this century and similar to Bory's Castle in Székesfehérvár. It is still inhabited by his descendants, who allow visitors to enter several rooms crammed with paintings and curios, and who have recently started taking paying guests. There are no set hours, but you can usually gain admission whenever someone's at home; the curator charges whatever she can get away with. The Fool's Castle is located at Csalogány köz 8 (square C5 on up-to-date town plans). Bus #1 from Széchenyi tér can drop you near the covered pool (*Fedett Uzsoda*) outside town – walk 50m back, turn left on to Tölgyfa sor, and then left again at the end.

The Lővérek Hills and the Bürgenland

South of town, the sub-Alpine **Lővérek Hills** are a standing invitation to hikers. Bus #1 or #2 will drop you at the *Hotel Lővér* near the start of the path up to the **Károly lookout tower** (April–Oct daily 9am–6pm; Nov–March daily 9am–4pm), which offers marvellous views of the surrounding countryside. Although several **hiking** trails continue into Austria, only locals may pass through the low-key checkpoints. Both sides of the border are inhabited by bilingual folk engaged in viticulture, following the division of the **Bürgenland** region between Hungary and Austria (which got the lion's share) after the collapse of the Habsburg empire – an amicable partition, it seems, since nobody complains about it today.

The Sopron telephone code is ☎99

Practicalities

Sopron's main train station (*Gysev pályaudvar*) is half a kilometre or so south of the centre, on Állomás utca, while its bus station is northwest of the Belváros on Lackner Kristóf utca. The best sources of **information** are *Lokomotiv Tourist* at Új utca 1 (Mon–Sat 9am–5pm; ☎311-111), *Ciklámen Tourist* at Ógabona tér 8 (Mon–Fri 8am–4.30pm & Sat 8am–noon; ☎312-040), and *Ibusz* at Várkerület 41 (Mon–Fri 8am–4pm & Sat 8am–noon; ☎312-455). *Express*, at Mátyás király út 7 (Mon–Fri 8am–noon & 1–3.30pm, Sat 8am–noon; ☎312-024), is strictly for booking college beds, while *Lokomotiv Tourist* can deal with tickets for the Széchenyi Railway (see Nagycenk on p.209).

Accommodation

During July and August cheap **dormitory beds** (①) might be available at Damjanich utca 9 (just off Lackner Kristóf utca) or the Jereván high school – *Express* can make bookings and point you in the right direction. Though **private rooms** (②–③) are scarce over summer, it's worth enquiring at *Lokomotiv Tourist*, *Ibusz* or *Ciklámen Tourist*, since most of the alternatives listed below are more expensive.

HOTELS AND PENSIONS

Brennbergi Panzió/Youth Hostel, Brennbergi utca (☎313-116). To the west of the city centre (bus #3 or #10 from the bus station). ① per bed. Open mid-April to mid-Oct.

Diane Panzió, Lővér körút 64 (☎329-013). 5-room pension in the Lővérek Hills, 4km south of the city centre. ③.

Hotel Sopron, Fövényverem utca 7 (☎314-254). Plush establishment up on Coronation Hill (north of the Belváros) with nightclub, sauna, solarium and tennis courts. ⑥.

Hotel Szieszta, Lővér körút 37 (☎314-260). Like the *Panoráma Hotel* (but easier to reach), this place was once reserved for trade unionists (bus #1). ⑤.

Jégverem Panzió, Jégverem utca 1 (☎312-004). Located just off Pozsony út, an eighteenth-century inn named after the old ice pit in the middle of its restaurant. ④.

Palatinus Hotel, Új utca 23 (☎311-395). 22-room hotel with an agreeable ambience in the heart of the Belváros. ⑥.

Panoráma Hotel, Panoráma út 38 (☎312-745). Formerly a trade union resort, now a fairly cheap bungalow complex. Situated about 2km from the town centre, and hard to reach by public transport. ③.

Patkó Fogadó, Somfalvi utca 24 (☎314-648). Country inn with horse riding facilities, double rooms (③) and a 5-bed dorm (① per bed). Accessible by taxi (5- or 6-min from the town centre), or by bus #1, #2, #10 or #12 to the end of the line, followed by a 10-minute walk.

Royal Panzió, Sas tér 13 (☎314-481). 6-room pension just around the corner from the *Jéverem Panzió* and slightly cheaper. ④.

CAMPING

Lővér Camping (☎311-715). Located 4km south of the centre and reached by bus #12 which runs hourly from Deák tér and the intercity bus station. Camping from mid-April to mid-Oct, with chalets (②–③) over summer. Reserve through *Ciklámen Tourist*.

Ózon Camping, Erdei Malom köz 3 (☎311-322). Smaller, private site with a few rooms (②), in the garden district 5km outside town, off the #10 bus route.

Eating, drinking and entertainment

There are **restaurants** attached to all the main hotels, but aside from the one in the *Hotel Palatinus* – which does excellent, inexpensive set meals in the evening – you'll eat better elsewhere. For traditional Hungarian fare, try the *Várkerület Söröző* at Várkerület 83, or the cheap and cheerful *Expresszó Ételbár* on Fő tér by the Storno House. Nearby, the *Corvinus Söröző* serves tasty pizza. Up on Fő vényverem utca at no. 15, the *Sopron Halászcsárda* is a charming fish restaurant with a garden (closes 9pm; ☎312-142) and opposite there's the reasonably priced *Fekete Bárány*, which serves Hungarian food.

Hearty red *Kékfrankos* and white, apple-flavoured *Tramini* are best sampled in **wine cellars** such as the *Gyógygödör Borozó* at Fő tér 4 (Tues–Sun 9am–9pm) and the *Poncichter Borozó* at Szentlélek utca 13. The *Cezár Pince* on the corner of Oroslya tér and Hátsókapu utca (9am–9.30pm) boasts vintage oak butts and leather-aproned waiters, but they can get a bit sniffy if you don't order a platter of *wurst* to go with your wine. For beer and disco-beat try the *Holsten Söröző* in the *Hotel Palatinus* (noon–10pm), or the *John Bull Pub*, a real English pub on Széchenyi tér with good food, draught *Guinness*, *John Bull* and *Double Diamond*. The *Stefánia Cukrászda* at Szent György utca 12 offers delicious cakes, as does the *Hoffer Cukrászda* at Várkerület 86.

Sopron is at its liveliest during the **Spring Days** (late March) and **Festival Weeks** (mid-June to mid-July), when all manner of concerts and plays are staged at the Petőfi Theatre on Petőfi tér and the Liszt Cultural Centre on Széchenyi tér – *Ciklámen Tourist* can supply details.

Moving on

Excursions to nearby atttractions aside (see below), the most obvious destinations are **Kőszeg** or **Szombathely**. With no trains to Kőszeg and three of the five daily buses leaving before 7am, you have to be sure to catch the 12.50pm or 3pm service. Szombathely is served by four trains (mostly in the afternoon) and five buses daily.

Other **buses** run to Bük, Sárvár, Veszprém, Komárom, Esztergom, Hevíz and Balatonfüred. Services to **Austria** cover a host of towns including Vienna (Mon–Sat 8am; also Mon, Thurs & Fri 9.20am), which is also served by train (arrive at the station one hour early to clear customs); and there is a daily bus to **Bratislava**.

Excursions from Sopron

To the east of Sopron lies the **Hanság region**, a once extensive swampland that has gradually been drained and brought under cultivation since the eighteenth century. Prone to thick fogs, the area is traditionally associated with tales of elves and water sprites, and with the dynastic seats of the Esterházy and Széchenyi families at Fertőd and Nagycenk. The most obvious feature on the map is the shallow, reedy expanse known to Hungarians as **Lake Fertő** and to Austrians as the Neuseidler See, which was out of bounds to prevent escapes until recently, but can now be reached by bus from Sopron (every 90min–2hr) and attracts naturalists and birdwatchers.

There are hourly buses to all of the following places from the depot in Sopron on Lackner Kristóf utca:

Fertőrákos Quarry

FERTŐRÁKOS, 8km north of town, presumably gets its name "cancerous slough" from the local **quarry** (May–Sept Tues–Fri 8am–7pm, Sat–Sun 9am–5pm), where limestone has been hewn since Roman times. Vienna's Saint Stephen's Church and Ringstrasse were built with stone from Fertőrákos, where quarrying only ceased in 1945. The result is a Cyclopean labyrinth of gigantic chambers and oddly skewed pillars, resembling the mythical cities imagined by H.P. Lovecraft: animal and plant fossils attest that the land was once submerged beneath a prehistoric sea. **Concerts** are staged in the quarry during the Sopron Festival Weeks (tickets are available in Sopron from the Festival Office at Széchenyi tér 17).

Fertőrákos itself boasts a former Bishop's Palace at Fő utca 153, containing a small **museum** of antique furniture (daily 10am–5pm for groups of 10 or more). Up the road at Fő utca 97 is the **Kristály Múzeum** or Crystal Museum (Tues–Sun 10am–5pm). Should you feel like **staying**, beds at the *Kastély Hotel* (☎99/355-040; ②) in the palace or the *Vízmalom Hostel* at Fő utca 41 (☎99/312-040; ②) can be reserved either directly or through *Lokomotiv Tourist* in Sopron. You'll also find the usual *Zimmer frei* signs both here and in neighbouring villages.

East to the Esterházy Palace

The Esterházy Palace at Fertőd lies 27km east of Sopron along a minor road that connects with the route to Fertőrákos at **BALF**, a bathing resort since Roman times. Its *fin-de-siècle* **spa** and gazebo are appealing, but not so much that you feel tempted to check into the *Kurhotel-Schloss Balf* (☎99/314-266; ⑤). Also worth noting in passing are the traditional cottages and barns in **FERTŐSZÉPLAK**, 5km before Fertőd.

FERTŐD itself began life as an appendage to the palace and was known as "Esterháza" until the family decamped in 1945. As you enter the village, post-war housing gives way to stately public buildings endowed by the Esterházys, presag-

THE ESTERHÁZY FAMILY

Originally of the minor nobility, the **Esterházy family** began its rise thanks to **Miklós I** (1583–1645), who married two rich widows and sided with the Habsburgs against Transylvania during the Counter-Reformation, for which he was rewarded with the title of Count. His son Paul was content to make his mark by publishing a songbook, *Harmonia Celestis*; but **Miklós II** "the Ostentatious" (1714–90) celebrated his inheritance of 600,000 acres and a dukedom by commissioning the palace in 1762. Boasting "anything the Kaiser can do, I can do better!", he spent 40,000 *gulden* a year on pomp and entertainment. Thereafter the family gradually declined, until under the Communists they were expropriated and "un-personed". Today, one descendant drives trams in Vienna, while two others (from a separate branch of the family) are respected figures back home: the writer **Péter Esterházy** and his cousin, **Marton Esterházy**, formerly centre forward on the national football team.

ing the palace at the eastern end. So long as you stay on the main street, it's impossible to miss.

The Esterházy Palace

Built on malarial swampland drained by hundreds of serfs, the **Esterházy Palace** was intended to rival Versailles and remove any *arriviste* stigma from the dynasty (see box). Gala balls and concerts, hunting parties and masquerades were held here even before it was completed in 1776, continuing without a let-up until the death of Prince Miklós "the Ostentatious" in 1790. Neglected by his successor, who dissolved the orchestra and moved his court back to Eisenstadt, the palace rapidly decayed. Its picture gallery, puppet theatre and Chinese pavilions disappeared, while its salons became storerooms and stables. Though basic repairs were made after World War II, restoration only began in earnest during the Fifties, and is still unfinished due to the prodigious cost.

Ornate Rococo wrought-iron gates lead into a vast horseshoe courtyard where Hussars once pranced to the music of Haydn, Esterházy's resident maestro. The U-shaped wings and ceremonial stairway sweep up to a three-storey Baroque facade, painted a rich ochre. **Guided tours** (May–Sept Tues–Sun 8am–noon & 1–5pm; Oct–April Tues–Sun 8am–noon & 1–4pm; 100Ft) cover only a fraction of the 126-room interior, which seems rather lifeless owing to a lack of furniture. The highlights of the ground floor are the panelled and gilded **Sala Terrena** and several blue and white **Chinoiserie salons**. On the ceiling of the **Banqueting Hall** upstairs is a splendid fresco by J.B. Grundemann, so contrived that Apollo's chariot seems to be careering towards you across the sky whatever angle you view it from.

An adjacent room displays **Haydn memorabilia** from the period following his appointment as the Esterházy *Kapellmeister* in 1761. Haydn subsequently took over the direction of palace orchestra, opera house and marionette theatre, and wrote six great masses for performance here between 1796 and 1802. The palace also witnessed the premiere of Beethoven's Mass in C, conducted by Ludwig in 1807. The tour over, you can wander around the **French Gardens** at the back, whose formal beds and hedges have grown wild through neglect.

Practicalities

The prospect of **staying at the palace** is almost irresistible. Rooms (②) with shared showers are available in the east wing year-round, and advanced booking is advisable (☎99/370-971). There are also dormitory beds on offer (①). Despite the somewhat oppressive mixture of socialist-realism and Crimplene carpeting, the place is still enchanting and the views are lovely. No food is served in the palace, so you must plan to eat elsewhere. From this latter point of view, though less romantic, it is handier to stay **in the village itself** – three pleasant establishments to choose from are the *Kastély Hotel* at Bartók utca 2 (☎99/345-971; ③); the *Udvaros Ház* ("Groom's House") at Fő utca 1 (☎99/345-921; ②); and the *Eszterházi Panzió* at Fő utca 20 (☎99/370-012; ③). For comestibles, try the *Grenadier House* opposite the palace gates (closed Mon), or the **restaurants** and supermarket in the village.

Ten kilometres west of Fertőd on the road to Sopron is the *Hegykő Termál* campsite (mid-May to mid-Sept; ☎99/376-818) with thermal baths (*Fürdő*) right next door. There's also a cycle path – along the shores of Lake Fertő for much of the way – from Fertőd to Sopron via Fertőrákos, with plenty of *Zimmer frei* signs in the small villages en route.

The Széchenyi Mansion and Steam Train at Nagycenk

Another feudal seat worth investigating lies 13km southeast of Sopron, near **NAGYCENK**. Buses from town can drop you at the **Széchenyi Mansion** (*kastély*), 1.5km from the village. As the family home of Count Széchenyi, "the greatest Hungarian" (see box), it has never been allowed to fall into ruin, and was declared a memorial museum in 1973. The museum (April–Oct Tues–Sun 10am–6pm; Nov–March Tues–Sun 10am–2pm) includes a fascinating reconstruction of his household – the first in Hungary to be lit by gas-lamps and to have flush toilets – and details his achievements, leading naturally into an exhibition on Hungarian industry since Széchenyi's day.

Across the road is a shining example of the heritage industry – the **Széchenyi Railway**. This outdoor museum of **vintage steam trains** comes alive every

---

COUNT SZÉCHENYI

Count István Széchenyi (1791–1860) was the outstanding figure of Hungary's Reform Era. As a young aide-de-camp he cut a dash at the Congress of Vienna and did the rounds of stately homes across Europe. The "odious Zoltán Karpathy" of Bernard Shaw's *Pygmalion* (and the musical *My Fair Lady*) was based on his exploits in England, where he steeplechased hell-for-leather, but found time to examine factories and steam trains. Back in Hungary, he pondered solutions to his homeland's backwardness and offered a year's income from his estates towards the establishment of a Hungarian Academy. In 1830 he published *Hitel* (Credit), a hard-headed critique of the nation's feudal society.

Though politically conservative, Széchenyi was obsessed with **modernization**. A passionate convert to steam power after riding on the Manchester–Liverpool express, he invited Britons to build rail lines and the Chain Bridge. He also imported steamships and dredgers, promoted horsebreeding and silk-making, and initiated the taming of the River Tisza and the blasting of a road through the Iron Gates of the Danube. Alas, his achievements were rewarded by a melancholy end. The 1848 Revolution and the triumph of Kossuth triggered a nervous breakdown, and although Széchenyi resumed writing after his health improved, he committed suicide during a relapse.

weekend from April to October, when 100-year-old engines run along a special line that terminates at Fertőboz, 4km away (though some turn back earlier). Advance details and tickets can be obtained from *Lokomotiv Tourist* in Sopron, or you can just turn up and hope for the best.

In the **village** stands the neo-Romanesque **Church of Saint Stephen** (designed by Ybl in 1864) whose portal bears the Széchenyi motto "If God is with us, who can be against us?" Across the road is a cemetery containing the **Széchenyi Mausoleum**, with a chapel decorated by István Dorfmeister, and a crypt including the graves of István and his wife Crescentia Seilern.

Practicalities

Accommodation is polarized between comfy rooms in the *Kastély Hotel* (☎99/360-061; ⑤–⑥) occupying the west wing of the mansion, and unheated chalets without bathrooms at the *Hársfa Panzió* behind the train station (☎99/360-015; ②). Similarly, you have the choice between the *Kastély*'s rather expensive dining room and the cheaper *Pálya Vendéglő* attached to the *Hársfa*. Should you travel to Fertőboz by steam train, bear in mind that this village is on the Sopron–Fertőd road, and has a tourist hostel at Fő utca 11 (☎99/312-040; ②). **Bus tours** and **horse riding** can be arranged at the 200-year-old Nagycenk Stud Farm (☎99/360-026).

Kőszeg

Nestled amidst the sub-Alpine hills along the Austrian border, the small town of **KŐSZEG** cherishes its status as the "Hungarian Thermopylae", and a Belváros of chocolate-box prettiness. While its castle recalls the medieval Magyar heroism that saved Vienna from the Turks, its Baroque houses and *bürgerlich* ambience reflect centuries of Austrian and German influence, when Kőszeg was known as Güns. Despite a summer blitzkrieg of tourists that briefly arouses avarice and excitement, this is basically a sleepy, old-fashioned town where folk are honest enough to leave fruit for sale (and the takings) lying unguarded in the streets.

The Town

From **Fő tér**, where the **Church of the Sacred Heart** stands aloof from two hotels and three tourist offices, Városház utca leads off to the **Heroes' Tower**. Erected to mark the 400th anniversary of the siege of Kőszeg, this fake medieval portal was one of several commemorative gates raised in the Twenties and Thirties, when Hungary was gripped by nostalgia for bygone glories and resentment towards the Successor States. You can go up the 27-metre edifice (Tues–Sun 10am–5pm) for a view of the square below and the storks' nests perched on top of each chimney. The same entrance leads to the former Baroque General's House, now the **Jurisics Museum** (Tues–Sun 10am–5pm), containing examples of bookbinding and other historic crafts.

Beyond the archway lies **Jurisics tér**, a cobbled square whose antique buildings are watched over by two churches and a statue of the Virgin. The most eye-catching facades are those of the **Town Hall** (embellished with oval portraits of worthies) and no. 7, on the eastern side of the square, where the pillory stood in medieval times. At no. 11, an eighteenth-century apothecary is preserved as a

Pharmacy Museum (Tues–Sun 10am–5pm). A day ticket will get you into all four of Kőszeg's museums.

Beyond the well and Virgin statue (where a brass band often plays on Sundays and holidays), the Baroque **Church of Saint Emerich** precedes the older **Church of Saint James**, a handsome Gothic edifice containing the tomb of Miklós Jurisics (see below) and frescoes dating back to 1403. From here you can follow Chernel or Rajnis utca off the square to find Kőszeg Castle.

The castle

The Turks swore that Kőszeg's **Castle** was "built at the foot of a mountain difficult to climb; its walls wider than the whole world, its bastions higher than the fish of the Zodiac in heaven, and so strong that it defies description". Since the castle is actually quite small, with not a mountain in sight, the hyperbole is probably explained by its heroic defence during the month-long **siege of 1532**, when Sultan Süleyman and 100,000 Turks were resisted by 400 soldiers under Captain Miklós Jurisics. After nineteen assaults the Sultan abandoned campaigning until the following year, by which time Vienna was properly defended. Weapons and other relics are displayed in the castle's **museum** (Tues–Sun 10am–5pm), while another hall off the courtyard serves as a bar-cum-disco.

Other sights

The former **Synagogue** at Várkör 36 resembles an outlying bastion of the castle, having two crenellated towers with slit windows. Built in 1859, the redbrick complex originally included a *yeshiva* and a ritual bath. Its dereliction is a sad reminder of the provincial Jewish communities that never recovered from the Holocaust, for – unlike the Budapest ghetto – their extermination was scheduled for the summer of 1944, when Eichmann's death-machine still ran at full throttle. Next door to the former synagogue, which can be viewed only from the street, is the **Lutheran belltower**. When the Lutheran church behind it was built in 1783, József II had decreed that non-Catholic churches could not have belltowers or steeples – this one was only built in 1930.

Where earlier editions left an ominous blank, recent maps of the **hills** around Kőszeg show the entire border region, with trails crossing the frontier via which locals may now leave the country. If you fancy hiking 6km, there is a well-signposted trail to the highest summit in the region (833m), where the **Írottkő lookout tower** straddles the border. Tourists with passports can ascend the tower (April to mid-Oct), but not cross over into Austria. Lastly, should you feel the need to cool off, there is a public **swimming pool** just across the river from the centre of town: follow Kiss János utca eastwards from the Várkör.

Practicalities

Arriving at Kőszeg's bus station on the corner of Liszt and Kossuth utca, walk 150m up the latter to reach the Belváros, which is encircled by a road (the Várkör) that follows the long-demolished medieval town walls. To get there from the train station in the south of town, catch a #1, #1A or #1Y bus as far as the junction of Fő tér and the Várkör. Maps and **information** are available from *Savaria Tourist* next to the post office at Várkör 57 (Mon–Fri 8am–4pm & Sat 8am–noon; ☎94/360-238), or *Ibusz* at Varosház utca 3, just off Fő tér towards the Heroes' Gate (Mon–Fri 8am–4pm & Sat 8am–noon; ☎94/360-376).

From Kőszeg, there are half a dozen buses a day to **Bükfürdő**, **Sopron** and **Szombathely** (mostly in the afternoon), plus ten trains daily to **Szombathely** (30min). Motorists can cross into **Austria** at Mannersdorf, 3km northwest of town.

Accommodation

Both *Savaria Tourist* and *Ibusz* can book private **accommodation**, while *Express* (Mon–Fri 8am–4pm & Sat 8am–noon; ☎94/360-247) next door to *Savaria Tourist* handles reservations at its own places outside town. There's also a **campsite** (May to late Sept; ☎94/360-981) on Strand sétány by the swimming pool.

Hotel Panoráma (aka *Napsugár Turistaszalló*). An *Express*-owned bungalow complex on Szabó-hegy (Tailor's Hill), southwest of town (bus #2 from the train station). ①–②.

Hotel Park, Park utca 2 (☎94/360-363). Quiet nineteenth-century pile at the western end of Hunyadi utca. Book through *Express*.; discount for IYHF members. ②–③.

Írottkő Hotel, Fő tér 4 (☎94/360-373). Pricey, but central and modern. ④.

Jurisics (Tourist) Hostel, Rajnis utca 9, opposite the castle (☎94/362-227). Dormitory beds (①) and a few double and triple rooms (②). Open April to mid-Oct.

Kóbor Macska Fogadó, Várkör 100 (☎94/360-490). Friendly 7-room pension with a restaurant, on the corner of Hunyadi utca. ③.

Strucc Hotel, Várkör 124 (☎94/360-323). A fine old hotel opposite *Savaria Tourist*. Doubles with showers. ③.

Várkör Panzió, Hunyádi János utca 19 (☎94/360-972). New 10-room pension. ③.

Eating, drinking and entertainment

Aside from hotel **restaurants**, the centre can offer the *Kulacs Étterem* at Várkör 12 (daily 6am–10pm) and the *Alpesi Vendéglő* opposite the bus station (Mon–Sat 9am–9pm). Two of the best eateries in Kőszeg are the *Betérő az Aranykoszorúhoz* at Temető utca 59 (closes at 9pm) and the *Szarvas Étterem* at Kossuth utca 6.

The large *Gesztenye Étterem* further down Kossuth utca often hosts **discos**, as do the castle and the *Park Hotel*. For **drinking**, try the *Bécsikapu Söröző* on Rajnis utca, opposite Saint James' Church, or the beer garden on the corner of Schneller utca at the northeastern edge of the Várkör (summer only). Wine-lovers are well catered for in Kőszeg, with a **Grape Festival** on April 24 (a tradition dating back to 1740), the **Summer Festival** in July and August (with theatre and opera in the castle's courtyard), and a **Wine Festival** in September. If you enjoy quaffing your wine in medieval surroundings, the vaulted ceiling and high Gothic windows of the *Old Cellar* at Rajnis utca 10 provide an ideal setting.

Bükfürdő

Sixteen kilometres east of Kőszeg, **BÜKFÜRDŐ** is a major new development designed to attract Western tourists (Austrian pensioners especially). Its **thermal spa** is one of the best equipped in Hungary, but the real selling point is the **Birdland Golf Club**, an 18-hole golf course and village run by a Swedish-Austro-Hungarian consortium. Though most foreigners can easily afford the daily fee (£10/$15), the course is effectively out of bounds to the average Magyar – and lodgings, too, are aimed at wealthy tourists, making this an expensive place for budget travellers. If you do decide to stay, the *Thermal and Sport Hotel* on Termál körút (☎94/368-500; ⑦) is an unmissable four-star hotel with sports and bathing facilities in the centre of Bükfürdő, while the *Hotel Bük* at no. 24 (☎94/358-028; ⑤) is its smaller, less palatial rival across the way. Further along at no. 12 is *Romantik Camping* (☎94/358-362), a well-equipped and costly camper-van haven.

Bük and Csepreg

A cheaper option is to stay 3km down the road in **BÜK**, which musters a few reasonably priced pensions and campsites. *Elizabeth Camping-Panzió* at Kossuth utca 72 (☎94/358-414) and *Sziszi Kemping* at no. 70 (☎94/358-280) are both open year-round, while **private rooms** (②–③) can be rented directly at Petőfi utca 22 (☎94/358-412); Kossuth utca 58 (☎94/358-623); Szabadság utca 7 (☎94/358-304); and Szabadság utca 13 (☎94/358-165).

Motorists intending to head for Austria might also consider staying at **CSEPREG**, 5km west of Bük. It is close to the border for an early start, with a nice family-run **campsite**, *Ottó Kemping*, at Bognár utca 1 (mid-March to mid-Oct; ☎94/365-393).

Szombathely and around

Commerce has been the lifeblood of **SZOMBATHELY** ("Saturday market") ever since the town was founded by Emperor Claudius in 43 AD to capitalize on the Amber Road from the Baltic to the Mediterranean. Savaria (as it was then called) soon became the capital of Pannonia, and a significant city in the Roman empire. It was here that Septimus Severus was proclaimed emperor (193 AD) and Saint Martin of Tours was born in 317. Under Frankish rule in the eighth century, the town – known as Steinamanger – prospered through trade with Germany. Nowadays, it is Austrians who boost the economy, flooding across to shop, get their hair done or seek medical treatment in the town which they have nicknamed "the discount store".

From a tourist's standpoint, the chief **attractions** are the outdoor Village Museum (*Skanzen*) and Roman ruins, a Belváros stuffed with Baroque and Neoclassical architecture, and the finest collection of Socialist art in Hungary. Szombathely is also the base for a side trip to the beautiful Romanesque church at Ják and, further out, to Sárvár Castle (see p.218 – where the "Blood Countess" Báthori acquired a taste for murder.

The heart of town

Exploring the Belváros doesn't take long unless you spend time in its museums and galleries. If your appetite for exhibitions is limited, it's best to make a beeline for the cathedral or the Temple of Isis, and conserve some enthusiasm for the Village Museum (see below). Otherwise, it's not a bad idea to begin with the **Savaria Museum** (Tues–Sun 10am–6pm) at Kisfaludy utca 9 (also accessible through the park from Széll Kálmán utca). This local archeology display starts with mammoth tusks and works through to Roman times, the latter represented by reliefs of mythical figures and other stonework.

Further west, the Belváros turns monumental around **Berszenyi Dániel tér**, dominated by the **County Hall** and a huge eighteenth-century **Bishop's Palace**

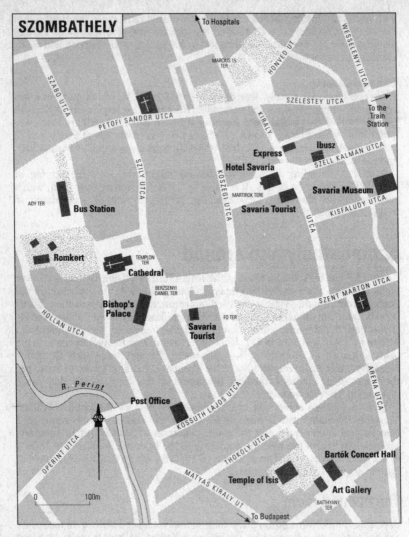

whose stuccoed facade is crowned by allegorical statues of Prudence, Justice, Fortitude and Temperance. The **Smidt Museum** (Tues–Fri 10am–6pm), which occupies one wing of the palace, represents the fruits of a life-long obsession. As a boy, Lajos Smidt scoured battlefields for souvenirs and collected advertisements and newspapers; after qualifying as a doctor he diversified into furniture and pictures. The destruction of many items during World War II only spurred him to redouble his efforts during retirement and, finally, he founded this museum to house his extraordinary collection.

The Cathedral and Romkert

Szombathely's **Cathedral** postdates the great fire that ravaged the town in the late eighteenth century, which explains why it is Neoclassical rather than Baroque or Gothic. Unfortunately, its exuberant frescoes by Maulbertsch were destroyed when US bombers attacked the town in the last months of World War II, and painstaking structural restoration has stopped short of recreating his work. Photos of the pope's visit here in 1991 now embellish the cathedral's interior.

Around the corner lies the **Romkert** or Garden of Ruins (April–Oct Tues–Sun 10am–6pm; Nov–March Tues–Sun 10am–4pm), comprising a crossroads and a mosaic floor from Roman Savaria. Recent archeological research would suggest this was either the site of the Basilica of Saint Quirinus – the largest church in Pannonia – or the Roman Governor's Palace. The majority opinion backs the latter theory.

The Temple of Isis

The most interesting relic of ancient Savaria only came to light in 1955, when construction work along Rákóczi utca uncovered the **Temple of Isis**, dating from the second century AD (April–Oct Tues–Sun 10am–6pm; Nov–March Tues–Sun 10am–4pm). One of three such *Iseum* extant in Europe, it is centred around a sacrificial altar which the rising sun illuminates, and decorated with a pantheon of deities. Reliefs depict Isis riding the dog Sothis, Victoria holding palm leaves, a glum-looking Fortuna-Abundantia and Mars-Harpokrates.

This mixed bag of deities reflects the eclectic religious life of the Roman empire in its waning era. The custom of daily Isis-worship at sunrise originated in Egypt, where the "Great Mother" was believed to have given birth to Horus, the divine avatar of the Pharaohs, and avenger of the murder of Osiris by his brother Seth, Lord of Chaos. Of all the cults that spread from the Middle East into Europe, it had the widest appeal; some argue that the Virgin Mary was Christianity's riposte to Isis in the battle for hearts and minds.

The *Iseum* in Szombathely was destroyed in an earthquake in 455. Since being partially restored in the 1960s, it has provided a setting for performances of the aria *Isis and Osiris,* from Mozart's opera *The Magic Flute*, during the annual Savaria Festival. Though the festival has temporarily bitten the dust, the temple still hosts events during the Spring Days.

The Szombathely Gallery and Bartók Concert Hall

Just south of the temple, the **Szombathely Gallery** contains a good collection of twentieth-century Hungarian art (Wed–Sun 11am–4pm). Unlike the hack painters and sculptors of the Rákósi era, radical artists of the Twenties and Thirties were inspired by genuine vision and commitment. **Gyula Derkovits** (1894–1934) was a member of the **Group of Eight** (*Nyolcak*) who "declared war on all those ideologies and styles of art that begin and end with the 'I' ". Living amongst the working class – his subject matter – Derkovits strove to rid his art of "every element of illusion", moving towards Cubism and studying at the Nyergesújfalu Free School during the heady days of the Republic of Councils. Its suppression left him desolate, as can be seen from *The Last Supper*, where Christ – with the artist's features – sits amidst a group of weary workmen.

The baton was taken up by another son of Szombathely, **István Dési Huber** (1895–1944), a goldsmith by trade. Abandoning Naturalism for Cubism to express his Marxist beliefs, he joined *Nyolcak* in the unequal struggle against the dominance of the "School of Rome" (modelled on Italian fascist art) during the Thirties and Forties. During the Communist era the group finally received due honour – but were simultaneously tarnished by association with the regime. Now, with political and cultural values turned upside down, they have become tragic – or kitsch – exemplars of the light that failed. Hopefully, the museum will continue to exhibit their work (Tues–Sun 10am–6pm).

Across the road stands Szombathely's former **Synagogue**, a lovely piece of neo-Byzantine architecture built in 1881, and now home to the **Bartók Concert Hall** and music college – another venue for performances during the Spring Days. Sadly, all that now remains of the town's Jewish presence is a meagre plaque recording that "4228 of our Jewish brothers and sisters were deported from this place to Auschwitz on 4 June, 1944".

Beyond the Belváros

Szombathely's northern suburbs harbour two more attractions which can be reached by bus #2 from Petőfi utca. The **Kámoni Arboretum** (Tues–Sun 8am–5pm) contains 2500 different kinds of trees, shrubs and flowers, with an especially varied assortment of roses. Just up the road is the grandly named **Gotthárd Astrophysics Observatory** (Mon–Fri 9am–4pm), with an interesting exhibition on cosmology.

Northwest of the centre lie **Lake Gondola** (*Csónakázótó*) and the **Anglers' Lake** (*Horgásztó*), two smallish ponds where locals fish and go boating near an outdoor **thermal bath**. Bus #7 from Operint utca takes you right to the **Village Museum** (*Skanzen*) by the Anglers' Lake (April–Oct Tues–Sun 10am–6pm). Reconstructed here are eighteenth- and nineteenth-century farmsteads culled from 27 villages in the Őrseg region, furnished with all the necessities and knick-knacks – an architectural progression from log cabins to timber-framed wattle-and-daub dwellings. Six Sundays a year there are demonstrations of traditional folk crafts and dances of the region.

The green-belt district south of the lakes includes a small **game park** (*Vadaszkert*) with deer, pheasants and other wildlife – nothing to get too excited about, but a nice place for a picnic. The park is situated off Középhegyi út, southwest of the *Hotel Liget*; alight from bus #7 on Jókai utca and walk from there.

> The Szombathely telephone code is ☎94

Practicalities

Arriving at the train station, you can walk west along Szell Kálmán utca into the centre (just under 1km), or catch a #2, #3, #5, #7, #7Y or #11 bus to Mártirok tere on Fő tér. The intercity bus station is next to the Romkert near the cathedral, so arriving there makes things even easier. As is often the case, the Belváros is compact enough to cover on foot with no risk of getting lost, but a town plan is useful for **orientation** once you venture outside the centre.

Information can be obtained from the helpful *Savaria Tourist* at Mártirok tere 1 (Mon–Fri 8am–5pm & Sat 8am–noon; ☎312-348); *Ibusz* at Széll utca 3 (☎314-

141); *Express* at Mátyás király út 12 (☎311-230); and *Cooptourist/Café*, next to *New York Pizza* on Savaria tér (Mon–Fri 8am–4pm & Sat 8am–noon; ☎314-765) – the latter also offers a car-rental service.

Accommodation

All four tourist offices can find dormitory beds (①) over summer and at weekends the rest of the year – probably in the *kollégium* facing the cathedral, or one of the colleges 50m west of the bus station. Northwest of the centre by the Anglers' Lake (a 10-min walk from the Village Museum), *Tópart Camping* (May–Sept; ☎314-766) at Kondics utca 4 offers huts sleeping two (②) or four (④). Hotel accommodation in the area includes:

Castle Hotel, in the village of Bozsok, 20km from Szombathely in the direction of Kőszeg (☎360-960). Seventeenth-century manor house set in a lovely park. Tennis court and sauna. ③.

Hotel Claudius, Bartók körút 39 (☎313-760). A modernistic pile where the ring road passes near Lake Gondola. Sauna, gym and restaurant. ⑥.

Hotel Savaria, Mártírok tere 4 (☎311-440). Centrally located, turn-of-the-century establishment with a ritzy restaurant. ⑥.

Hotel Liget, Szent István Park 15 (☎314-168). Motel-style lodgings further south on the ring road (bus #7 from the train station). ④.

Eating, drinking and entertainment

The best value **restaurants** in Szombathely are the *Gyöngyös Étterem* at Széll Kálmán utca 8 (closed Mon) and the *Tó Vendéglő* between the two lakes. The elegant restaurant in the *Hotel Savaria* doesn't deign to list prices on its menu, but they're high. The **beer garden** at Szent István Park 15, just south of the *Hotel Liget*, is something of a youth hang-out; or you can **drink** at the *Ferences Söröző*, near the Franciscan church on Savaria tér. *New York Pizza* on Savaria tér does the best pizza in town, while the *Saláta bár*, across from the Smidt Museum at Hollán Emő utca 3, serves cheap salads. Two kilometres south of the centre are a couple of more pricey restaurants: the *Halászcsárda* at Rumi út 18 serves good fish soup and has evening music, and across the road the American-style steakhouse, *California*, does good steak and salad.

The town has a strong musical tradition, with its own orchestra, the **Savaria Symphony**, and various cultural festivals including **Spring Days** in late March and the **Autumn Festival** in September. Lively **processions** in Szombathely and other towns in the region take place at Easter time. The international **Bartók Festival** in late July is another highlight, with seminars and concerts. At other times of the year, ask what's happening at the **Bartók Concert Hall** or the hideous 1960s **Cultural Centre** on Március 15 tér, or the one on Ady tér.

Moving on

Most **trains** from Szombathely head eastwards through Sárvár to Celldömölk (for Sümeg, Tapolca and the Balaton) or Pápa (for Győr), or south towards Zalaegerszeg and Nagykanizsa (for connections to southern Transdanubia, with an early morning express to Pécs). There are daily **buses** to Keszthely, Zalaegerszeg and Győr, and a weekly service to Vienna (Wed). However, most people travel to **Austria** by train to Graz, or drive across at Búcsú, 14km west of town. Train **information and tickets** are available from *MÁV Tours*, Thököly utca 39. Transport to **Ják**, **Szentgotthárd** and the **Őrség region** is detailed in the following sections (pp. 218, 220 and 221 respectively).

Ják

With hourly buses from Szombathely to **JÁK**, 10km southwest, you can easily pay a visit to Hungary's most outstanding **Romanesque abbey church** (April–Oct daily 8am–6pm; Nov–March daily 10am–2pm), far more impressive than the scaled-down replica you may already have seen in Budapest. The church is sited on a hilltop overlooking the feudal domain of its founder Márton Nagy (1220–56), who personally checked that his serfs attended Sunday services – and whipped any who failed to do so.

The church is similar in **plan** to its ruined contemporaries at Zsámbek and Lébény, and likewise influenced by the Scottish Benedictine church in Regensburg, the point from which Norman architecture spread into Central Europe. Its most striking feature is the magnificent **portal** on the western facade, where Christ and his apostles surmount an arch ribbed with complex patterns, guarded by whimsical lions. The twin towers and rose windows were restored in the 1890s by Frigyes Schulek, who performed a similar job on the Mátyás church in Budapest. For a small fee, you can turn on the light to view the **frescoes**, which the English-speaking priest may take the time to explain.

A tourist kiosk outside sells books on the surrounding area, but there's nothing much else to see in the village, so you might as well return to Szombathely or push on to Körmend (see p.220). If, however, you do decide to prolong your stay, there are several *Zimmer frei* signs around the village, or ask the locals for help.

Sárvár

SÁRVÁR, 27km east of Szombathely on the River Rába, is the most recently developed **spa centre** in Hungary following the discovery of hot springs 25 years ago. Located southeast of the castle in Vadkert utca, the thermal baths include both indoor and outdoor hot pools as well as special treatment facilities (ask at the *Sport* or *Thermal Hotel*). Equally therapeutic is to spend the day luxuriating in the baths and then to stroll round the lakes, accessible from the small path off Alkotmány utca. At the end of Vadkert utca there are **tennis courts** and a **riding school** offering lessons and pony-trekking.

Beer drinkers will enjoy the small **Kaltenberg Brewery**, where you can sample the product as you watch it being made. The brewery marks a renewal of ties between Sárvár and Bavaria, whose nineteenth-century monarchs owned the fortress that gives the town its name – Sárvár, meaning "Mud Castle".

Whilst this description might have been appropriate in the Dark Ages, it hardly applies to **Sárvár Castle** today (Tues–Sun 10am–6pm). Successively modified by many owners over the centuries, its pentagonal layout is credited to the **Nádasdy family**, particularly Tomás Nádasdy, who hired Italian architects and made this a centre of Renaissance humanism in the sixteenth century. It was here that the first Hungarian translation of the New Testament was printed in 1541. The **Festival Hall** is decorated with Dorfmeister frescoes of biblical episodes, allegories of art and science, and murals depicting the "Black Knight" Ferenc Nádasdy routing the Turks. Various collections of maps, weapons and uniforms can be admired in the castle's **museum**, as well as an assortment of Tomás and Ferenc memorabilia. Little reference is made to the latter's wife, the infamous Countess Báthori (see box).

COUNTESS ERZSÉBET BÁTHORI

Countess Erzsébet Báthori was possibly the first female serial killer in history. Born in 1560, the offspring of two branches of the noble Báthori family (whose intermarriage could explain several cases of lunacy in the dynasty), she was intelligent and well educated, but subject to fainting spells and fits of uncontrollable rage. A horrific experience in childhood (see Nagyescsed, p.335) and an illegitimate pregnancy that was hushed up so that she could marry Ferenc at the age of fifteen may have precipitated her psychosis.

While he was away at war, she began torturing serving women at Sárvár, cudgelling or sticking pins into them for any misdemeanour. A dozen maids were forced to lie naked in the snowy courtyard, doused with cold water, and froze to death as she watched. Though not averse to brutalizing servants himself, Ferenc balked at such extremes on his return, and it wasn't until after his death (1604) that she could give full rein to her lusts. With the assistance of two maids (one of whom was her lover), her son's wet-nurse and a male retainer, she tortured to death over 600 women and girls – sometimes biting chunks of flesh from their necks and breasts – the origin of legends which say that she bathed in the blood of virgins to keep her own skin white and translucent.

While *Die Blutgräffin* preyed exclusively on commoners – who could always be enticed into service at Sárvár and her later residences at Beckov and Čachtice (now in Slovakia), there was little risk that any accusations by the victims' relatives would be taken seriously. It was only after the demise of her lover Darvulia that she started killing aristocratic girls, making her **downfall** inevitable. In December 1610 sheriffs raided Castle Čachtice, catching her literally red-handed. Tried *in camera* to spare her family shame, she was walled up in one room of the castle and died there four years later. All mention of the case was prohibited, but after protests from relatives of her victims, her body was moved to the family vault at Nagyecsed.

Practicalities

Sárvár is accessible by hourly trains and irregular buses from Szombathely. To reach the castle, take bus #1 or #1Y from the train station, or walk east along Batthyány utca from the bus terminus. The thermal baths beyond the castle are well signposted. En route you'll see *Savaria Tourist* at Várkerület 33 (Mon–Fri 8am–5pm & Sat 8am–noon; Sárvár ☎578), which can supply **information**, change money and book accommodation.

Accommodation

Private accommodation (②–③) can be booked through *Savaria Tourist* (address above), or keep your eyes peeled for *Zimmer frei* signs advertising vacant rooms in Hunyadi and Rákóczi utcas. There's also the *Thermal* campsite near the baths at Vadkert utca 1 (Sárvár ☎292), open from mid-April to mid-October (250Ft per adult plus 220Ft tent fee; no bungalows) – take bus #1Y to the end of the line. Some of the alternatives listed below have no direct telephone connection, but can be contacted through the Sárvár operator.

Hotel Thermal, Rákóczi út 1 (☎96/316-088). The town's smartest hotel, with indoor and outdoor thermal pools, sauna, gym and curative facilities. ⑦.

Plátán Fogadó, Hunyadi utca 23 (Sárvár ☎623). A small pension en route to the castle. ③.

Sport Hotel, Rákóczi utca 46A (☎94/327-300). 20-room hotel with the full range of facilities including gym, sauna, free entrance to the thermal baths and discounts at the local riding school. ④.

Thermal Panzió, Temető utca 1A. A quiet, charming pension; price includes free entry to the thermal baths. ③.

Vadkert Fogadó, Vadkert utca vége (☎96/324-056). A rustic-style pension housed in a nineteenth-century hunting lodge on the "strip" between the castle and thermal baths. ④.

Wolf Panzió, Rákóczi/Temető utca (Sárvár ☎834). Small pension whose guests enjoy free entry to the thermal baths.

Eating and entertainment

The *Plátán* and *Vadkert Fogadó* both have good restaurants, the latter specializing in game dishes, while the *Matróz Vendéglő* on Árpád utca serves good fish dishes. Sárvár's annual **International Folklore Festival** is celebrated in mid-August in the castle's courtyard. "History Days" also take place every year, with concerts, traditional dancing and singing.

Körmend, Szentgotthárd and the Őrség

The hilly region to the **south of Szombathely** is defined by the River Rába, which flows from the Styrian Alps across the Little Plain to join the Danube at Győr. Its valley forms a natural route into Austria, straddled by two small towns with a sub-Alpine ambience and historic links with the now independent state of **Slovenia**. Though neither merits a special trip, Körmend and Szentgotthárd make pleasant stopovers en route to the border, and good jumping-off points for the Őrség region, further south. Both towns are accessible by train from Szombathely.

Körmend

KÖRMEND, 16km south of Ják, boasts a massive Baroque **Batthyány-Strattman Mansion**, incorporating four corner towers from a medieval castle. Located off Szabadság tér on the Várkör (Tues–Sun 9am–noon & 1–5pm), it houses a small local history collection and the **Shoe Museum** (*Cipő Múzeum*), whose exhibits include the footwear of various ethnic groups and a few distinguished Hungarian personalities. The park surrounding the mansion is a nature conservation area with many old trees and the finest magnolias in Hungary.

Should you care to stay overnight, *Savaria Tourist* at Rákoczi utca 11 (Mon–Fri 8.30am–5pm & Sat 8am–noon; ☎94/410-161) can supply **information**, change money and arrange **accommodation**. Two other places worth trying are the *Rába Hotel* at Bercsényi utca 24 (☎94/410-088; ④) and the *Halászcsárda Panzió* (Körmend ☎69; ③), by the river at Bajcsy-Zsilinszky utca 20. The latter also has an excellent fish restaurant.

Szentgotthárd

Twenty-nine kilometres west of Körmend and 5km off the main road to the Rábafüzes/Heilingenkreutz **border crossing**, **SZENTGOTTHÁRD** is a pleasant Baroque town that grew up around a twelfth-century Cistercian abbey. The influence of nearby Austria is manifest in its neat, tidy streets and ubiquitous recycling bins. The former presence of Slovenes here is evinced by a collection of their costumes in the **Pável Ágoston Museum** (Tues–Sun 10am–6pm) which, like the Dorfmeister fresco in Szentgotthárd's **Baroque church**, also commemorates the Battle of Mogersdorf (the town's German name) in 1664, when European mercenaries under General Montecuccoli repulsed a Turkish army. Tradition has it that one hundred Turks drowned in the River Lapincs, which joins the Rába at Szentgotthárd. A mere stream in summer, it becomes an icy torrent as the snow thaws in the Styrian Alps.

Practicalities

Szentgotthárd's **bus and train stations** are both east of the River Rába, which you cross as you walk towards the church steeple, and then continue up to the right to the town centre. *Savaria Tourist* at Kossuth út 2 (Mon–Fri 9am–4pm & Sat 9am–noon; ☎94/380-029) can help with money-changing, **information** and **accommodation**. Also worth trying are the *Hotel Alpokalja* on Füzesi út, on the northern edge of town (☎94/380-169; ②), and the *Rézi Panzió* on Mártirok útja (☎94/380-797; ② per person). Restaurants to investigate include the *Hármashatar Étterem* at Mártirok útja 1, the *Zöldfa Halászcsárda* at Széchenyi utca 18, and the *Makk Hetes Vendéglő* at Árpád utca 12. At Széll Kálmán tér 18, the *Café Picasso* pastry shop is a trendy hang-out among locals.

The Őrség

The forested **Őrség region** has guarded Hungary's southwestern marches since the time of the Árpáds, with hilltop watchtowers and isolated hamlets where every man was sworn to arms in lieu of paying tax. Moist winds from the Jura Mountains make this the rainiest, greenest part of Hungary; its heavy clay soil allows no form of agriculture except raising cattle, but provides ample raw material for the local pottery industry. Until well into this century, when the region declined as villagers migrated to Zalaegerszeg, houses were constructed of wooden beams plastered with clay. Whether tourism and the encouragement of crafts will revive the Őrség remains to be seen; meanwhile, its soft landscapes and folksy architecture are a powerful attraction.

There are several **approaches**, depending on your starting point. Trains from Szombathely to Szentgotthárd are met by buses to Őriszentpéter via Szalafő – two of the nicest villages. Alternatively, you could head for Zalalövo by train from Körmend or Zalaegerszeg (4 daily) and travel on to Őriszentpéter (14km) via Pankász, hitching or hiking if a bus doesn't materialize. Given the limited services and quiet roads, cycling is the best way of **getting around**. Bikes can be rented at several villages, but it's wise to bring a rainproof garment for those inevitable drizzles.

Őriszentpéter, Szalafő and Pityerszer

ŐRISZENTPÉTER is the obvious base, a charming village of thatched houses with bus connections to Szentgotthárd, Körmend and Zalalövo, and the best tourist facilities in the region. For local **information**, visit *Savaria Tourist* in the *Őrségi Fogadó* at Városszer 57 (Őriszentpéter ☎155) – private rooms (④) and camping facilities (May–Sept) opposite the church can also be booked through them. One kilometre from the centre, the *Dominó Motel* (Őriszentpéter ☎248) has expensive but excellently appointed self-contained units (⑤ for a double).

On the village's western outskirts stands a **Romanesque church** with traces of frescoes and fine carvings around the doorway, dating from the thirteenth century. The denomination of Őrség churches can be a contentious issue, since many of the Protestant ones built by German settlers (whose religious freedoms had been guaranteed as early as the eleventh century) were appropriated by the Catholics during the seventeenth-century Counter-Reformation.

Protestants whose ancestors had smuggled Lutheran Bibles in wine barrels claimed retrospective victory in the Eighties, when the church at **SZALAFŐ**, 6km up the road, was deemed to be of *Református* origin – the proof being newly discovered sixteenth-century murals depicting the duties of women! The village consists of eight hamlets, sited apart on high ground to reduce the risk of flooding.

At **PITYERSZER**, 3km west of Szalafő, is a mini-*Skanzen* (entrance free) comprising a group of heavy-timbered houses built around a central courtyard. Connecting porches allowed neighbours to chat and gossip undeterred by inclement weather. To reach the *Skanzen* take the bus to Szalafo-felso, the last stop, and continue walking in the same direction for a further kilometre. Nearby, you can rent similar houses **sleeping** five to ten people (① per head; minimum four persons) and **bicycles** – the best way to explore this area – for 160Ft per day.

If you happen to be in the area on May 1, look out for dancing and celebrations around branches of the May tree. The origins of this annual ritual have long been lost, but many pine trees in the Őrség region find themselves stripped of their lower branches for the purpose.'

Other villages in the region

Approaching the Őrség from Zalalövo, you can stop to admire the rustic **wooden belltower** at **PANKASZ**, 7km east of Őriszentpéter. **Bikes** and **rooms** can be rented at **HEGYHÁTSZENTJAKAB**, 3km north off the road between Zalalövo and Pankasz.

More appealing, though, are two villages along a minor road **south of Őriszentpéter**, well off the public transport routes. In the hills along the Slovenian border, 12km away, the tiny village of **MAGYARSZOMBATFA** (pop. 300) preserves the old tradition of **Habán pottery**, sold through the local *Fazekasház* (*fazekas* is the Hungarian for "potter"). The road continues 6km southeast to **VELEMÉR**, whose single-aisled Romanesque church contains beautiful frescoes from 1380. To view them, ask for a key at the signposted schoolhouse 400m before the church.

CROSSING INTO SLOVENIA

Midway between Őriszentpéter and Magyarszombatfa is a turn-off for Hodos/Salovci, Hungary's only border **crossing into Slovenia**.

Zalaegerszeg

The county capital **ZALAEGERSZEG** – familiarly known as Zala – began to metamorphose after the discovery of oil in 1937, and is now the most industrialized town in southwestern Hungary with a population of 70,000. Despite the futuristic television tower featured on tourist brochures, its main interest lies in the past, represented by vestiges of folk culture from the surrounding region, preserved in two museums and an annual festival.

The town itself consists chiefly of housing estates and landscaped plazas, with its **downtown** centring on three squares running into each other. Kazinczy tér is for local transport and information; Szabadság tér features a Baroque parish church, Trinity Statue and county hall; while Deák tér – named after the local politician (1803–76) who negotiated the historic Compromise with the Habsburg empire – is the site of a lively **market** selling Göcsej cheese and other local produce.

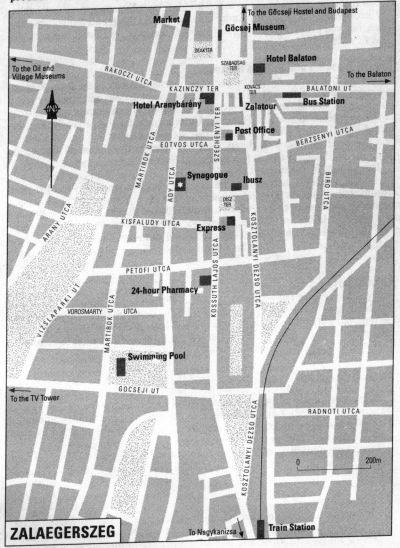

To the Göcseji Hostel and Budapest

Market

Göcsej Museum

DEÁKTÉR

To the Oil and Village Museums

RÁKOCZI UTCA

SZABADSÁG TÉR

Hotel Balaton

To the Balaton

KAZINCZY TÉR

KOVÁCS TÉR

BALATONI UT

Hotel Aranybárány

Zalatour

Bus Station

Post Office

EÖTVOS UTCA

SZÉCHENYI TÉR

BERZSENYI UTCA

MÁRTIROK UTCA

ADY UTCA

Synagogue

Ibusz

BIRO UTCA

DÍSZ TÉR

ARANY UTCA

KISFALUDY UTCA

Express

KOSSUTH LAJOS UTCA

KOSZTOLÁNYI DEZSO UTCA

PETOFI UTCA

24-hour Pharmacy

VÖRÖSMARTY UTCA

VÍSZLAPARKI UT

MÁRTIROK UTCA

Swimming Pool

GÖCSEJI UT

To the TV Tower

RADNOTI UTCA

KOSZTOLÁNYI DEZSO UTCA

0   200m

ZALAEGERSZEG

To Nagykanizsa

Train Station

In the old town hall at Batthyány utca 2, off Szabadság tér, the **Göcsej Museum** (Tues–Sun 10am–6pm) displays a rich haul of antique folk costumes from the region. Less colourful but more amusing are the **sculptures by Zsigmond Kisfaludi Strobl** (1884–1975). The son of a sculptor, he enjoyed early success with busts of British Royals and Hungarian aristocrats, then switched to producing glorified Workers (and the Liberation Monument in Budapest) under Communism, earning himself medals and the nickname "Step from Side to Side". Not far from the Göcsej Museum is the town's former **Synagogue**, an unmistakable, lilac-painted edifice at Ady Endre utca 14. Should there be a temporary exhibition on, you'll be able to see the interior, designed by József Stern in the Eclectic style in 1903.

The Oil Museum and Village Museum

On the northwestern outskirts of town near a dead tributary of the River Zala are two more museums (bus #1, #1Y or #8Y). Giant pumps, drills and other hardware dominate the **Oil Museum** (Tues–Sun 10am–6pm), which examines the history of the petroleum industry in Hungary. Unfortunately for the economy, exploratory drilling in the Fifties and Sixties discovered far more hot springs than oil, and the most promising field was found to straddle the Romanian border, so domestic production amounts to a fraction of Hungary's requirements.

The **Village Museum** next door (April–Oct Tues–Sun 10am–5pm) assembles traditional dwellings, barns and artefacts from the surrounding **Göcsej region**. Traditionally, this was so poor and squalid that no one would admit to being a part of it, and enquirers were always hastily assured that its boundaries began a few miles on, in the next village. Nowadays, Göcsej folk spend their weeks working and sleeping in hostels in Zala, returning home at weekends; some have bought apartments in town and are saving up to build a new holiday home in the hills.

Lake Gébárti

Just outside town is **Lake Gébárti** (a 20-min ride on bus #5 from the bus station to Ságod, then follow signs to the *Strand*) where boats, jet-skis and pedaloes can be rented. Lastly, there is the aforementioned **Television Tower**, on a hill to the southwest of town (bus #30 from Göcseji út), whose observation deck offers a panoramic vista of Zalaegerszeg (Tues–Sun 10am–4pm).

Practicalities

Zalaegerszeg's **train** station is situated south of the centre (bus #1, #7, #10 or #11), and its intercity **bus** depot is east of the main square. While trains run to Budapest and Pécs, Keszthely and neighbouring areas are best served by buses from Kovács tér, 100m west of the bus station.

Local **information** is available from *Zalatour* at Kovács tér 1 (Mon–Fri 8am–5pm & Sat 8am–noon; ☎92/311-389) and the *Ibusz* office at Dísz tér 4 (Mon–Fri 8am–5pm; ☎92/311-458).

Accommodation

Both *Zalatour* and *Ibusz* can arrange **private rooms** (②). Aside from the chance of **dormitory beds** (①) from *Express* at Dísz tér 3 (Mon–Fri 8am–4.30pm, plus July–Aug Sat 9am–12.30pm; ☎92/314-143), other **accommodation** includes:

Göcseji Hostel, Kaszahászi utca 2 (☎92/311-580). Beds in dorms (①) and quadruple rooms (②), 500m from centre (bus #3, #3Y or #5).

Hotel Aranybárány, Széchenyi tér 1 (☎92/314-100). The "Golden Lamb" is a fine old building in the centre. ④.

Hotel Balaton, Balatoni út 2A (☎92/314-400; telex 33-408). Not so attractive, but modern and likewise central. ④.

Hotel Zaév, Vizslaparki út 32 (☎92/311-561). Fairly basic rooms near the Youth Park, west of the synagogue. Apartments (④), doubles (②) and triples (③).

Eating and entertainment

Most of the downtown hotels have their own **restaurants** serving decent food. Alternatively, try the *Piccollo* at Petőfi Sándor utca 16 (about the best restaurant in town), the *Bella Pizzéria* on Rákóczi út, the *Göcseji Étterem* at Dózsa liget 1, or *McDonald's* at Széchenyi tér 1.

Local **entertainment** consists of whatever's on offer at the cultural centre off Ady Endre utca or at the Sportscsarnok a couple of blocks further east along Balatoni út. Though its future is uncertain, it's also worth asking about the **Göcsej Days**, a folklore festival previously held in August.

SOUTHERN TRANSDANUBIA

Heading for **southern Transdanubia** from Zala, Budapest or the Balaton, it's best to aim directly for **Pécs**, the region's attractive capital. Although the **Völgység**, the valley region between Lake Balaton and the **Mecsek Hills**, is pretty to drive through, none of the towns are really worth stopping for. Travelling from the Balaton by train, however, you might find it necessary to change at **Nagykanizsa** or **Kaposvár**. Express trains from Budapest to Pécs usually run via Dombóvár, while intercity buses are routed through Szekszárd.

Nagykanizsa

NAGYKANIZSA (pronounced "Nodge-konizha") is an old fortress town straddling the River Principális, 60km south of Zala. Together with Szigetvár and Siklós, it bore the brunt of Turkish assaults during the first decades of the occupation and, like them, ultimately succumbed. The fort has long since disappeared, its masonry used to build the **parish church** (*Alsóvárosi templom*) in Zárda utca. Mustafa Pasha, last Turkish overlord of Nagykanizsa, is buried here in a tomb into which baptismal fonts have been cut.

On the corner of Fő út and Ady Endre utca, the **Muncipal Art Gallery** (*Városi Képtár*) displays works of local artists (Mon–Tues 8am–5pm & Fri 8am–noon) in the eighteenth-century "Iron Man House". Behind Fő út 6 is another fine **Synagogue** in a wretched state of repair – like the one in Szombathely, it bears nothing more than a plaque commemorating the fate of the 3000 Jews marched off on April 26, 1944. Other downtown sights include two Baroque houses on Szechényi tér (nos. 5 & 7); Celtic and Roman artefacts and regional folk costumes in the **Thury György Museum** on Szabadság tér (Wed–Sun 10am–6pm); and modern **sculptures** in a pleasant municipal **park**. The local **brewery** produces *Gold Fassel* and *Dreher* beer – *Zalatour* (address below) can organize tours. If you happen to be visiting in early September, there's also a major beer festival known as the Kanizsai Days.

Practicalities

Nagykanizsa's **train station** is south of the centre, about a fifteen-minute walk along Ady Endre utca (or take bus #23 or #32); its **bus station** is just west of Erzsébet tér. Five **trains** depart daily to Pécs via Szigetvár. The nearest road **crossing into Croatia** is at Letenye, 26km west of town.

Zalatour at Fő út 13 (Mon–Fri 8am–5pm & Sat 8am–noon; ☎93/311-185) and *Express* at Deák tér 1 (Mon–Fri 8am–4.30pm & Sat 8am–noon; ☎93/314-375) are the best sources of local **information**. They will also change money and organize private **rooms** (②) or dormitory beds in the summer. Other places to stay include the *Hotel Central* at Erzsébet tér 23 (☎93/314-000; ⑤); the *Hotel Sport* by the sports centre on Kaán Károly utca (☎93/311-423; ①); the *Marika Panzió* at Cserfa utca 9 (☎93/319-186; ③); and the *Szőlőskert Fogadó* on Kaposvári ut, east of the centre by the entrance to Lake Csónakázó (☎93/310-639; ③). *Zalatour Camping* at Kemping utca 1 (May–Sept; ☎93/319-119) also rents bungalows.

As far as **eating places** go, the *Kis Kakas Étterem* on Múzeum tér is about the best restaurant in town, with a garden where you can sit outside in the summer. The *Ady Étterem* at Ady út 5 serves good food from 9am to 10pm, and there's a restaurant in the *Central Hotel* that's popular among the local denizens.

Kaposvár

Capital of Somogy county, the industrial town of **KAPOSVÁR** has an elegant centre with numerous Art Nouveau and classical buildings, making it a pleasant place to stroll around. However there's not much else to do in the town itself, so its main use is as a stepping stone for Szigetvár or Pécs. Arriving at the bus or train station, it's best to check travel connections before heading up Teleki or Dózsa György utca to investigate the sights – most of which can be found along or just off Fő utca, the main pedestrian street.

The **Somogy County Museum** at no. 12 (Tues–Sun 10am–6pm) contains the usual mix of ethnographic and historical material, as well as a gallery of contemporary art. It stands next door to the seventeenth-century **Golden Lion Pharmacy**, birthplace of József Rippl-Rónai (1861–1927), the "father of Hungarian Art Nouveau". Some of his paintings can be seen in the **Rippl-Rónai Museum** (Tues–Sun 10am–6pm), a nineteenth-century villa 3km southeast of the town centre on Lonkai utca, in the suburb of Rómahegy (bus #15). Other local artists are showcased in the **Kaposvári Gallery** (Tues–Sun 10am–6pm) at Rákóczi tér 4, just up from the train station. Directly opposite is the **Csiky Gergely Theatre**, one of Hungary's best theatres whose performances have gained kudos abroad (tickets from the *Színház Jegypéntzár*, Fő utca). There are concerts in the **Liszt Concert Hall** at Kossuth utca 21 during the **Spring Festival** in late March, and just nearby in Kossuth tér a proud sign proclaims how many kilometres you are from various metropolises around the world.

With time on your hands, you may want to head 9km south of Kaposvár to the small village of **SZENNA**. Here you'll find one of Hungary's smallest *Skanzen* (April–Oct 10am–6pm; Nov–March 10am–2pm), consisting of six farmhouses and a still functioning eighteenth-century Calvinist church, brought here from around the region. Buses run at least hourly from Kaposvár to Szenna; the *Skanzen* itself is opposite the main bus stop at Rákóczi utca 2.

Practicalities

Kaposvár's **bus and train stations** are sited one block apart on Nagy Budai Antal utca, half a kilometre south of Fő utca, the main pedestrianized street. **Buses** run to Pécs (every 1–2hr), Szigetvár (5 daily), Keszthely (daily), Siófok (daily) and Kecskemét (daily). You're required to have seat reservations on the express **train** to Pécs (3 to 4 daily); for these, and tickets, contact *MÁV Tours* on Csokonai utca (through the passageway from Május 1 utca 21).

    Information can be obtained from *Tourinform* at Fő utca 8 (Sept–June Mon–Fri 8am–5pm & Sat 8.00am–noon; July–Aug Mon–Fri 8.30am–5.30pm & Sat–Sun 8.30am–noon; ☎82/320-404). *Siotour*, in the eighteenth-century Dorottya ház at Fő utca 1 (summer Mon–Fri 8.30am–5.30pm; winter 8am–4.30pm; ☎82/320-537), and *Ibusz* at Teleki utca 3 (Mon–Fri 8am–4.30pm; ☎82/313-275) can also help with local information, money-changing and accommodation.

Accommodation

Accommodation in Kaposvár can be booked through *Ibusz* (address above), or simply by wandering the streets in search of *Zimmer frei* signs advertising vacant rooms. The nearest decent **campsite**, *Deseda Camping,* lies 6km northeast of town (bus #8 or #18 from the station, or get off at the Toponár stop on the Siófok–Kaposvár branch line).

Borostyán Panzió, Rákóczi tér 3 (☎82/320-735 or 321-746). Superb Art Nouveau building with 9 rooms near the train station. ⑤.

Csokonai Fogadó, next door to *Siotour* on Fő utca (☎82/312-011 or 316-716). The nicest hotel in town, occupying a renovated eighteenth-century building – often full. ②.

Hotel Dorottya, Széchenyi tér 8 (☎82/315-901). Refurbished 80-year-old hotel off Fő utca. ④.

Kapos Hotel, Kossuth tér (☎82/316-022). Ugly modern affair one block west of Fő utca. ③.

Pálma Panzió, Széchenyi tér 6 (☎82/320-227). Small pension on the same square as the Hotel Dorottya. ③.

Accommodation

The restaurant at the *Csokonai Fogadó* on Fő utca and the *Ipar Étterem* ("Industry Restaurant") at Teleki utca 8 both serve good, inexpensive Hungarian food. At Fő utca 46, the *Arany Szarvas Étterem* ("Golden Stag") specializes in game dishes, while the *Görög Taverna* on the corner of Fő utca and Irányi Dániel utca is a new cellar restaurant serving Greek food. The fanciest place in town is the dining room of the Art Nouveau *Borostyán Panzió* on Rákóczi tér.

Pécs and the Mecsek Hills

If there was ever a uranium mining town worth visiting, **PÉCS** (pronounced "Paych") is it. Tiled rooftops climb the vine-laden slopes of the Mecsek Hills, and the nearby mines of Újmecsekalja (aka "Uranium City") haven't contaminated Pécs's reputation for art and culture. As Transdanubia's leading centre of education, its population of 150,000 includes a high proportion of students, giving Pécs a youthful profile. The city boasts some fine examples of Islamic architecture,

To Hotel Hunyor

JURISICS UTCA

BALICSI UT

Idris Baba Mausoleum

NYAR UTCA

KODALY UTCA

Barbican Tower

KLIMO UTCA

Kollégium

ALKOTMANY UTCA

ALKOTMANY UTCA

IFJUSAG UTJA

Hospital

Jakovali Hassan Mosque

Medical University

SZIGETI UT

PETOFI SANDOR UTCA

JOZSEF ATTILA UTCA

KOLOZSVAR UTCA

TUZER UTCA

MEGYERI UTCA

0   200m

PÉCS

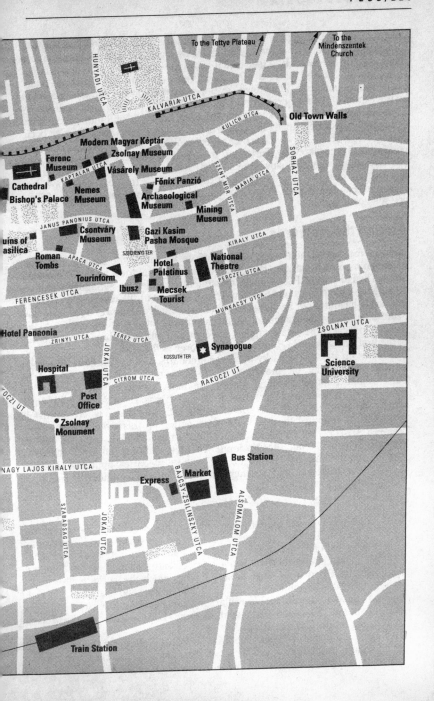

To the Tettye Plateau

To the Mindenszentek Church

HUNYADI UTCA

KALVARIA UTCA

KULICH UTCA

Old Town Walls

Modern Magyar Képtár

Zsolnay Museum

Ferenc Museum

KAPTALAN UTCA

Vásárely Museum

Cathedral

Bishop's Palace

Nemes Museum

Fönix Panzió

Archaeological Museum

SZENT MOR UTCA

MARIA UTCA

SORHAZ UTCA

Mining Museum

JANUS PANONIUS UTCA

Csontváry Museum

Gazi Kasim Pasha Mosque

KIRALY UTCA

uins of asilica

Roman Tombs

APACA UTCA

SZÉCHENYI TER

Hotel Palatinus

National Theatre

PERCZEL UTCA

Tourinform

Ibusz

Mecsek Tourist

FERENCSEK UTCA

MUNKACSY UTCA

Hotel Pannonia

ZRINYI UTCA

TEREZ UTCA

JOKAI UTCA

Synagogue

KOSSUTH TER

ZSOLNAY UTCA

Hospital

CITROM UTCA

RAKOCZI UT

Science University

OCZI UT

Post Office

Zsolnay Monument

NAGY LAJOS KIRALY UTCA

Express

Market

Bus Station

BAJCSY-ZSILINSZKY UTCA

ALSOMALOM UTCA

SZABADSAG UTCA

JOKAI UTCA

Train Station

several wonderful museums and galleries, and the biggest market in western Hungary. It is also a base for exploring Siklós, Szigetvár and Mohács, further south, and the **Mecsek Hills** (see p.235) above the city.

Settlements existed here in prehistoric times, but the city's **history** really began with Sopianae, a Celtic town developed by the Romans and later raised to be the capital of the new province of Pannonia Valeria. Made an epicospal see by King Stephen, the town – known as Quinqua Ecclesiae or Fünfkirchen (Five Churches) – became a university centre in the Middle Ages. Under Turkish occupation (1543–1686) its character changed radically, and its Magyar/German population was replaced by Turks and their Balkan subjects. Devastated during its "liberation", the city slowly recovered thanks to local viticulture and the discovery of coal in the mid-eighteenth century. While the coal mines now face closure due to bankruptcy, Pécs's uranium mines – dating from the early 1950s – are still going strong.

Around the Belváros

Most of the sights, hotels and tourist offices lie within the historic Belváros, encircled by a road marking the extent of the medieval town walls. On Kossuth tér you'll find one of Pécs's finest monuments, an elegant **Synagogue** built in 1865 (May–Oct daily except Sat 9am–1pm & 1.30–5pm). Its carved and stuccoed interior is beautiful but haunting, emptied by the murder of over 4000 Jews now listed in a *Book of Remembrance* – ten times the number that live in Pécs today. Thanks to local efforts, state support and contributions from abroad, this was one of the first synagogues in Hungary to be restored in the 1980s.

Further up Bajcsy-Zsilinszky utca, you'll come across the **Zsolnay Fountain** outside the church on the right. Local Zsolnay ceramics are typified by polychromatic, metallic-looking glazes; the bulls' heads on the fountain are modelled on a gold drinking vessel from the "Treasure of Attila". One block north, the road meets **Király utca**, traditionally the *korzó* where townsfolk **promenade**. Amongst the buildings worth noting on this street are the newly restored Art Nouveau **Hotel Palatinus**; the **Nendtvich House** (no. 8) with its ceramic ornamentation; the **National Theatre**, surmounted by a statue of Genius; and the **Vasváry House** (no. 19), with its allegorical figurines. However, there's more to see around Széchenyi tér, the city's main square at the top of Bajcsy-Zsilinszky utca.

Széchenyi tér

With its art galleries and tourist offices, modern-day **Széchenyi tér** is centuries removed from its Turkish predecessor, a dusty square crowded with "caravans of camels laden with merchandise from India and the Yemen". At its top end stands a Catholic church whose ornate window grilles and scalloped niches denote its origins as the **Mosque of Gazi Kasim Pasha**, which the Turks built from the stones of a medieval Gothic church. The vaulted interior and Islamic prayer niche (*mihrab*) decorated with Arabic calligraphy can be viewed during sightseeing hours (summer Mon–Sat 10am–4pm & Sun 11.30am–4pm; winter Mon–Sat 10am–noon & Sun 11.30am–2pm).

Contemporary artwork is exhibited in the **Pécsi Gallery** on the western side of the square (Mon–Fri noon–6pm & Sat 10am–6pm). It's worth a quick look in case there's anything remarkable, but with so many art collections in Pécs, it pays to be selective. On the northern side of the square, the **Archeological Museum** (April–Sept Tues–Sun 10am–6pm; Oct–March Tues–Sun 10am–2pm) covers the history of the region from prehistoric times to the Magyar conquest, but pales in comparison to the real Roman tombs a few streets over on Apáca utca (see below). Not far away at Mária utca 9 is the **Mining Museum,** another disappoint, for all the sparkle of its crystals (Tues–Sun 10am–6pm). At this point, you have the option of three routes to the cathedral – along Káptalan, Janus Pannonius or Apáca utca – via a clutch of museums.

Káptalan utca

Káptalan utca (Chapter Street) has no fewer than five museums virtually next to each other, all of them open Tuesday to Sunday from 10am to 6pm. The **Zsolnay Museum** at no. 2 is a must for its vases, plaques and figurines from the Zsolnay Ceramics Factory, founded in 1868 by Vilmos Zsolnay and the chemist Vince Wartrha, the inventor of eosin glaze. Some pieces are exquisite, others totally kitsch, but they deserve a look either way. In the basement are sculptures by Amerigo Tot (1909–84), whose *Erdély family* with its clamped grave-posts symbolizes the plight of the Magyars in Romania.

Across the road at no. 3, the **Vásárely Museum** exhibits Op-Art canvases by Viktor Vásárely, who was born in this house in 1908, but made his name in Paris and New York. The **Modern Magyar Képtár** next door to the Zsolnay Museum presents a *tour d'horizon* of Hungarian art since the School of Szentendre, with a large section devoted to Constructivist evocations of the proletarian struggle by Béla Uitz (1887–1972), who lived for fifty years in the Soviet Union. (Note that you can see the second installment of these paintings at the **Modern Magyar Képtár II** (April–Oct Tues–Sun 10am–6pm) at Magyar Szabadság utca 2.) The **Nemes Museum** at no. 5 honours the surrealist Endre Nemes (1909–85), who was born in nearby Pécsvárad but spent most of his life in Sweden. Diagonally across the street at no. 6, right by Dóm tér, the **Ferenc Museum** showcases work by Martyn Ferenc (1899–1986), an early exponent of non-figurative painting.

The Csontváry Museum

If you only visit one place in Pécs, make it the **Csontváry Museum** at Janus Pannonius utca 11–13 (Tues–Sun 10am–6pm). Kosztka Tivadar Csontváry (1853–1919) was born in the same year as Van Gogh, and his artistic career was similarly affected by madness and the pursuit of "the path of the sun". His fascination with Hebrew lore and the Holy Land was expressed in huge canvases – *Baalbek, Mary's Well at Nazareth* and *Pilgrimage* – while his hallucinatory vision of nature produced *Tatra, Storm on the Great Hortobágy* and *Solitary Cedar.*

After his death, these works came close to being sold as tarpaulin, but at the last moment were purchased by an architect. When Picasso later saw an exhibition of Csontváry's work in Paris, he asked to be left alone in the room for an hour and then remarked, "I did not know there was another great painter in our century besides me", and later told Chagall, "There you are, old master, I bet even you could not paint something like this".

Roman remains on Apáca utca

The necropolis of Sopianae lay more or less beneath Apáca utca (Nun street), where several **Roman tombs** decorated with scenes of the Gates of Paradise have been excavated in the courtyard of no. 9. After the Romans went home and waves of migrating tribes swept across Hungary, the tombs were used as refuges and modified accordingly. Across the road are the less impressive **remains of a chapel**, likewise dating from the third or fourth century AD. Opening hours for both sites are irregular, but the tombs are worth seeing if they're open. If not, another excavated ruin can be found nearby on Szent István tér.

Around Dóm tér and the Cathedral

Szent István tér, the lower, park-like extension of Cathedral Square, harbours a subterranean **ruined basilica** or **early Christian mausoleum** (there is doubt as to which it actually is). It houses a fourth-century AD chapel (Tues–Sun 10am–6pm), decorated with frescoes of the Fall and Daniel in the Lion's Den, and containing a white marble sarcophagus and skeletal remains.

Up the steps past the Szepesy statue, Dóm tér is dominated by a huge, four-towered **Cathedral** that has been endlessly rebuilt since a basilica was founded here in the eleventh century. Though a crypt and side chapels from eleventh- to fourteenth-century churches have been incorporated in the cathedral, its outward form is neo-Romanesque, the style chosen to replace Mihály Pollack's previous Baroque design. Its lavish blue and gold murals are by Lotz, Székely and other historicist painters of the 1890s.

The neo-Renaissance **Bishop's Palace** to the west is embellished with a modern statue of Liszt waving from the balcony, which might have amused Janus Pannonius (1434–72), the humanist poet and bishop of Pécs, or Bishop György Klimó, founder of its library, who told borrowers: "You don't have to pay for anything. Depart enriched. Return more frequently." Around the corner to the south, a circular **Barbican tower** punctuates the old town walls, giving access to Klimó György utca.

Around the periphery

From here, you can head uphill and on to Aradi Vértanuk útja to see a section of the **old town walls** – once a massive crenellated rampart 5500 paces long, buttressed by 87 bastions – erected after the Mongol invasion of the thirteenth century. Above the tunnel 300m along is a small garden with a decaying **Calvary Chapel**, offering a fine view of the Belváros.

Alternatively, head downhill around the peripheral boulevard – henceforth Rákóczi út – to find the inconspicuous **Jakovali Hassan Mosque** (daily except Wed 10am–1pm & 1.30–6pm). Unlike its counterparts at Szigetvár and Eger, this sixteenth-century mosque is still intact (though its minaret is closed) with friezes, a superbly carved *minbar* (pulpit) and Turkish carpets adorning its cool white interior. Around the corner on Sallai utca, you can see the ruins of a Turkish bath outside the *Minaret* restaurant.

A small **Ethnographic Museum** (Tues–Sun 10am–6pm) containing folk costumes from the Baranya region can be found at Rákóczi út 19. The nearby **Zsolnay Monument** gazes benevolently over the junction with Szabadság utca. Heading back towards the centre, notice the Romantic-style **Post Office** on Jókai utca.

Further out

Unless you're fascinated by Turkish death rites, it's not worth tracking down the *türbe* or **Mausoleum of Idris Baba** at Nyár utca 8 (off Kodály utca, 1km west of the centre), which is touted as a local attraction. Further out lies the Medical (*Orvostudományi*) faculty of **Pécs University**, Europe's fifth when it was founded in 1367. The Science (*Tudományi*) faculty is on the other side of the Belváros; buses #M14 and #30 run between the two campuses, which are still a couple of the liveliest parts of town.

For a fresh perspective on Pécs, catch bus #33 from Kossuth tér up to the **Tettye plateau**, where a ruined sixteenth-century palace – later used as a Dervish monastery – stands in a park. Higher up and further out, **Misina Hill** (534m) is crowned by a **Television Tower** with an observation platform (daily 9.30am–7pm), accessible by bus #35 from Kossuth tér or the train station. En route you'll pass a **Zoo** on Ángyán János utca, a prison-like place where the animals are kept in appalling conditions (daily 9am–6pm). Should you care to walk back from the plateau, Havihegyi út* offers a succession of views as it winds around the hillside, with several picturesque backstreets slinking down past the **Mindenszentek Church**, whose pastor supplements his income by selling poultry.

All kinds of livestock and farming paraphernalia appear at the monthly **Pécs Market**, a huge country fair held on the first Sunday of every month at a site 3km southwest of the Belváros – take bus #3 or #50 from outside the *Konzum* store on Rákóczi út and ask to be dropped off at the *Vásártér* on Megyeri út. On other Sundays, there's a lively flea market on the same site.

> The Pécs telephone code is ☎72

Practicalities

Arriving at the train station on Indóház tér, you can stash your luggage in a small building by platform one before catching a bus north into the centre. Any bus up Szabadság utca can drop you at the Zsolnay monument on Rákóczi út, while bus #30 follows Bajcsy-Zsilinszky utca as far as Széchenyi tér, the city's main square – this passes close to the intercity bus station on Zólyom utca, but from there you can easily walk to the centre in less than fifteen minutes.

In addition to various possible excursions from Pécs (see the following sections), the city has **bus connections** to Baja, Kecskemét and Szeged on the Great Plain; and Siófok, Hévíz and Székesfehérvár around Lake Balaton. Before the civil war in the former Yugoslavia, it was also the point of departure for buses to Osijek and Vukovar (now defunct, for obvious reasons) and trains to Osijek (still operating when last heard).

There are four tourist offices in town, all of which can help with **information** and accommodation: *Tourinform* at Széchenyi tér 9 (summer Mon–Fri 9am–7pm & Sat–Sun 9am–4pm; winter Mon–Fri 9am–7pm; ☎413-315); *Ibusz* at no. 8 (Mon–Fri 8am–4pm, plus in summer Sat 9am–noon; ☎412-148); *Mecsek Tourist* at no. 1 (Mon–Fri 8am–4pm; ☎413-300); and *Express* at Bajcsy-Zsilinszky utca 6.

Accommodation
Tourinform (address above) has a comprehensive list of hotels, dormitories and pensions in the area, though they won't book private rooms. *Ibusz* and *Mecsek*

---

*Old town plans show this as Mező Imre út, and Ángyán János utca as Beloiannisz utca. Other discarded street names include I. Ötéves terv utca – "First Five Year Plan street".

Tourist can also help with accommodation, while *Express* can help with dormitory beds. If the latter is closed, try one of the *kollégiums* (college hostels) listed below – Pécs is a big university town so there are plenty of them to choose from, some available during the summer months only (June to late Aug), others staying open at weekends during term time.

The *Família Privát Camping* at Gyöngyösi utca 6 (☎329-938) is the nearest official campsite. It's also possible to camp out at the site of the monthly market (see above), where Romanian and Polish traders sleep in their cars – facilities are minimal though and there's no security.

HOTELS AND PENSIONS

Fenyves Hotel, Szőlő utca 64 (☎315-996). 19 balconied rooms west of the Tettye plateau; accessible by bus #33 or a 5-minute walk from the *Toboz Panzió*. ④.

Hotel Főnix, Hunyadi út 2 (☎311-682). Small, modern place with a central location just off Széchenyi tér. Singles ③; doubles and triples ④.

Hotel Hunyor, Jurisics Miklós utca 16 (☎315-677). In the Mecsek hills northwest of town (bus #32), a 50-room hotel with a nice garden and restaurant plus lovely views of the city. Double rooms (④) and apartments (⑤–⑥).

Hotel Laterum/Youth Hostel, Hajnóczy utca 37 (☎315-829). New place open year-round. ①.

Hotel Palatinus, Király utca 5 (☎433-022). Recently restored *fin-de-siècle* pile with a magnificent lobby and modern rooms (no singles). ⑥.

Hotel Pannónia, Rákóczi út 3 (☎413-322). Ugly Seventies hotel off the ring road. Doubles ⑤–⑥; apartments ⑥.

Kertész Panzió, Sáfrány utca 42 (☎327-551). Small pension on a hill overlooking the river. ④.

Kikelet Hotel, Károlyi M. utca 1 (☎310-777). An old Art Deco resort hotel in the hills with superb views of the city. ③–④.

Mandulás Hotel/Panzió, Ángyán János utca 2 (☎315-981). Rooms with or without baths and motel doubles with showers on a **campsite** in the woods below the TV tower, near the penultimate stop on the #34 bus route. Open mid-April to mid-Oct. ④.

Mediterranean Hotel, Dömörkapu (☎315-987). Up in the hills, an ex-tourist hostel gone upmarket (bus #35 to the end of the line). ④.

Toboz Panzió, Fenyves sor 5 (☎325-232). A former trade union hostel now open to anyone. Take bus #34 or #35 to Károlyi utca, or walk uphill from the *Fenyves Hotel*. ④.

COLLEGE HOSTELS

Hunyadi Mátyás Fiúkollégium, Széchenyi tér (☎310-875 or ☎310-872). Boys hall of residence run by Cistercian monks. Open all summer and weekends during term time.

JPTE Kollégium, Damjanich utca 30 (☎310-055). Four-bed rooms at the university hall of residence. Open June–Aug. ① per bed.

Kollégium, Kodály utca 30. College hostel located 500m west of the cathedral.

Pollack Kollégium, Jókai utca 8 (☎315-846). College hostel on the same street as the main post office. Open all summer and weekends during term time.

Pollack Mihály Kollégium, Boszorkány út 2 (☎310-387). Two-bed rooms at 450Ft per person. Bus #30 to the end of the line.

Eating and drinking

The *Aranykacsa* eatery at Teréz utca 4 is excellent, while wholesome Hungarian food and tasty *pogácsa* (savoury scones) are the order of the day at the small *Dóm Étterem* at Király utca 3. Further up the hill (bus #33 from Kossuth tér), the *Tettye* is an upmarket restaurant with good music and enthusiastic accolades from the locals. The *Santa Maria* steakhouse on Klimó György utca is touristy and expensive while *Dairy Queen*, on the corner of Rákóczi utca and Bajcsy-Zsilinszky utca, lives up to its usual international reputation. *Főnix Pizza*, in the Hotel Főnix at Hunyadi út 2, does the best pizza around, and the *Elefánt Söröző* on Jókai tér is a trendy place to hang out in the centre of town.

Király utca has all the best **pubs** including the *Dóm* at no. 5 and the *Liceum* at no. 35. The *Gyár* (meaning "factory") at Czinderi utca 3–5 is Pécs's alternative rock club. **Live music** and rock 'n' roll dancing occasionally take place at the *Pepita Bar* in Balokány park, 400m beyond the Science University (bus #21).

Entertainment

Pécs's **opera** and **ballet** companies are very highly regarded, so it can be hard to obtain tickets for performances at the National Theatre on Király utca – ask about cancellations at the box office an hour before the show starts. *Tourinform* can give details of **concerts** and other events at local cultural centres, including the annual **Pécs Days** festival held in September. There's also a **puppet theatre** on the corner of Mária and Szent Mor utca.

The Mecsek Hills

The karstic **Mecsek Hills** north of Pécs offer panoramic views and trails fanning out from the television tower through groves of sweet chestnuts and almond trees. If you fancy some **hiking**, invest in a 1:40,000 map of the hills, available from most bookshops. Alternatively, you could catch a bus from the intercity depot out to Orfű or Abaliget, two popular resorts (a 40-min ride leaving every 60–90min).

ORFŰ features four artificial **lakes** surrounded by sports facilities, restaurants and accommodation, with a museum-piece **mill** to the east of the smallest lake. The town has private rooms for rent (②–③; look for the *Zimmer frei* signs) and several campsites on terraced slopes. *Orfű Camping* at Dollár utca 1 (mid-April to mid-Oct; ☎72/378-501) has plenty of tent space as well as bungalows with baths (③), and windsurfers and bicycles for rent. Other possibilities include the *Laterum Motel* at Dollár utca 10 (☎72/378-454), the *Cedrus Vendégház* at Hermann Otto utca 77 (☎72/336-134) and the *Molnár Panzió* at Széchenyi tér 18A (☎72/378-563). Near the latter is the *Muskátli*, Orfű's nicest restaurant.

A few kilometres further west is the larger settlement of **ABALIGET**, with an outdoor pool and a 640-metre-long **stalactite cave** inhabited by blind crabs beside one of its lakes. Should you wish to stay, there are plenty of private rooms for rent along Kossuth Lajos utca (the main street), as well as a couple of campsites. The lakefront *Abaliget Camping* has eighteen bungalows and a restaurant (72/378-530), or there's *Forrás Camping* near the thermal baths (72/390-777). **Accommodation** in both towns can also be booked through *Mecsek Tourist* in Pécs (see p.233).

Szigetvár

SZIGETVÁR, 33km west of Pécs, rivals Kőszeg for its heroic resistance to the Turkish invasion. Every Hungarian child is taught the story, which is enshrined in poetry and music. Even today the town has a military presence – nothing too heavy, but nonetheless a reminder of the lingering threat of war just across the border in Croatia. Though Szigetvár has recently acquired a striking **community centre** by the architect Imre Makovecz, and has an agreeable **thermal bath** 250m off the main square (head up Tinadi utca), it is the **castle** and **relics of the Turkish occupation** that are its main attractions.

The Town

Arriving at the train station, follow Rákóczi út 500m north to reach Zrínyi tér in the centre of town. Starting from the bus station, you have the option of a quick flit round the sixteenth-century **Turkish House** at Bástya utca 3, a small museum displaying objects of the Turkish settlement (May–Sept 10am–noon & 2–4pm). The ruined **Koran school** is nearby on Szecsadi Máté utca, and from here you can head up Rákóczi út to **Zrínyi tér**. The Baroque church on this central square has Turkish-style windows that betray its origins as the **Mosque of Ali Pasha**, built in 1596. Directly across the square, with its defiantly snarling lion statue, Vár utca leads off towards the castle. En route, the **Local History Museum** (*Várostörténeti kiállítás*) at Vár utca 1 (Tues–Sun 10am–4pm) displays eighteenth- and nineteenth-century shop signs, folk carvings, embroidery and the like; it also has a nice little café.

The Castle

As the town's name – **Island Castle** – suggests, this quadrilateral fortress (April–Sept daily 8am–6pm; Oct –March daily 8am–4pm) was once surrounded by lakes and marshes. Under local strong man Bálint Török it resisted siege by the Turks in 1541 and 1554, but its finest hour came in 1566, when 2400 soldiers under **Miklós Zrínyi**, governor of Croatia, resisted the onslaught of 100,000 Turks for 33 days. Enraged by the loss of 20,000 troops and the failure of his seventh attempt to march on Vienna, **Sultan Süleyman** died of apoplexy before the siege finally wore down the defenders. Spurning offers of surrender, Zrínyi donned his court dress before leading a final, suicidal sally when they could no longer hold out.

The sultan's followers buried his heart and innards 5km out of town in the village of Turbék, where his tent once stood (see below). His remains were later shipped back home by his son, Selim II. A commemorative **mosque** was also erected in the grounds of the castle – its minaret has long since disappeared, but the interior survives, complete with ornamental grilles, Koranic inscriptions, and frescoes depicting the deaths of Zrinyi and Süleyman.

In an adjacent **museum** (originally the summer house of Count Andrássy), coloured miniatures of Turkish life are counterpointed by praise for Magyar heroism (April–Sept 9am–4pm). Copies of the epic *Szózat* (Appeal) are on display, penned by Zrínyi's grandson, himself a general. A cry for liberty and a call for endurance, this seventeenth-century poem was adapted as a chorale by Kodály in 1956. Its single performance at the Budapest Academy turned into an emotional occasion for a symbolic protest against the Rákosi regime. Chanting crowds took up the refrain, "*Ne Bántsd a Magyart!*" ("Let the Magyars alone!"), thus causing government members present to walk out.

The Turkish-Hungarian Friendship Park

Five kilometres north of town in the village of **TURBÉK**, the **Turkish-Hungarian Friendship Park** (*Török-Magyar Barátság Emlékpark*) was opened in 1994 by the Turkish prime minister on the spot where Sultan Süleyman's tent once stood.

Practicalities

Szigetvár's **bus and train stations** are next to each other, about half a kilometre south of the town centre – follow Rákóczi utca north and you'll eventually emerge on to Zrínyi tér, from where Vár utca continues north to the castle.

Mecsek Tourist, in the lobby of the *Hotel Oroszlán* at Zrínyi tér 2 (Mon–Fri 8.30am–4pm; ☎73/310-116) can change money and find you private **rooms** (②). They can also make advance bookings at the *Kazamata Tourist Hostel* in the castle grounds (mid-April to mid-Oct; ☎73/310-116; ①) – advisable, since soldiers or school parties are often billeted there. Alternatively, there's the *Hotel Oroszlán* itself (☎73/310-116; ④), or the cozy *Kumilla Hotel* at Olaj Lajos utca 6 near the castle (☎73/310-150; ⑤). Six kilometres northwest of town in Zsibót, the *Domolos Kastély Hotel* is a nineteenth-century mansion on a small lake with fishing, horse riding and tennis facilities (☎73/311-222; ③).

Moving on

Szigetvár is accessible by regular **buses** from Pécs, and is a stopover for slow **trains** on the Nagykanizsa–Pécs line. **BARCS**, 31km southwest, has the nearest road **crossing into Croatia** (*Terezino Polje*); if you have to spend the night here, the *Határ* campsite and hotel at Nagyhíd utca 28 are both cheaper than the *Hotel Boróka* (Barcs ☎321) at Bajcsy-Zsilinszky utca 39.

South of Pécs

The area south of Pécs also has its attractions. Those in search of a therapeutic wallow in yet another thermal bath should visit Harkány, while nearby Siklós, Hungary's southernmost town, has a fifteenth-century castle. Villány is a must for the wine aficionado, with its extensive vineyards and cellars producing some of Hungary's best red wines.

Harkány

Thirty-four kilometres south of Pécs, **HARKÁNY** draws visitors thanks to its open-air **thermal pool** (June–Aug daily 8am–4pm & 5–11pm; Sept–May daily 9am–5pm), with a section for wallowing in **hot mud** that is therapeutically rich in sulphur and fluoride. Aside from this, however, there's not much else to visit aside from a small **market** near the bus station and an early nineteenth-century **Calvinist church** on Kossuth Lajos utca.

Should the mud baths tempt you into **staying**, *Mecsek Tourist* on Bajcsy-Zsilinszky utca (not to be confused with their other office at Kossuth Lajos utca 5 which handles tours only) can arrange cheap private rooms and car rentals, the latter costing from 2000Ft a day (Mon–Fri 8am–6pm, plus in summer Sat–Sun 8am–noon; ☎72/480-322). There's also the *Hotel Drava* at Bartók Béla utca 3 (☎72/480-434; ⑤), which has tennis courts; the *Baranya*, opposite the baths at Bajcsy-Zsilinszky utca 5 (☎72/480-160; ②); and, at the end of Bajcsy-Zsilinszky utca, a campsite with a motel (③) and bungalows (②), open from mid-April to mid-October.

Siklós

Most buses plough on a further 5km across the dusty plain to Siklós, another small town huddled around a castle. The birthplace of **George Mikes** (known for his humorous writings in the West), **SIKLÓS** is sleepier but more appealing than Szigetvár – in short, a nice one-horse town. The **castle**, visible from the bus station, has been continuously inhabited since its construction in the fifteenth century (castle open daily; castle museum: Tues–Sat 10am–4pm). Bastions and rondellas form an impressive girdle around the Baroque mansion at its heart, once occupied by the enlightened Casimir Batthyány, who freed his serfs in 1849. His tomb is in the Gothic chapel that is located (with no sense of incongruity according to medieval values) within whipping distance of a dungeon filled with instruments of torture and rank air. Below the castle on Batthyány Kázmér utca is the Malkocs bej djámi, a sixteenth-century **mosque** with occasional exhibitions of Turkish culture.

Private rooms in Siklós can be booked through *Mecsek Tourist* in Harkány or Pécs. The *Központi Fogadó* at Kossuth tér 5 (☎72/352-513; ① per person) is the only hotel in town, and is rumoured to have the best restaurant too. A cheaper, shabbier place to eat is the *Sport Vendéglő*, near the bus station at Felszabadulás utca 72.

Siklós has two **train stations**: the main one is at the end of Táncsics Mihály utca, northeast of Kossuth tér; the other is closer to the bus station, northwest of the centre. **Buses** depart every hour for Harkány and Pécs, and less frequently for Villány. The Drávaszabolcs/Donji Miholjac **border crossing** into Croatia lies 16km southwest of Siklós.

Villány

Fifteen kilometres east of Siklós, acres of vineyards lap the slopes of Mount Szársomlyo, producing red wine under the appellation **VILLÁNY**. The village's viticultural tradition goes back two thousand years. Its **Wine Museum** is housed in a 200-year-old cellar at Bem József utca 8, where a collection of wine-producing artefacts is displayed (Tues–Sun 9am–5pm). Wine-lovers can sample the local elixir at various places along the main road (Tolbuhin utca 46, 71 and 78) and at Diófas tér on Friday evenings in the summer. The more committed aficionado should head for the row of wine cellars at Villánykövesd, 2.5km northwest on the road to Pécs. House nos. 51–2 and 27A on Petőfi út are also recommended, as are nos. 5 and 15 on the small road above. Another local attraction is the **artists' summer camp**, whose presence is evidenced by bronze totems and concrete erections on the hillside. **Accommodation** in Villány is limited to the helpful *Gere Panzió* at Diófas utca 4 (Villány ☎195).

Székelyszabar and Himesháza

Travelling from Pécs to Villány you pass a range of hills to the northeast, where **SZÉKELYSZABAR** (Samar) and **HIMESHÁZA** (Nimmersch) were founded by Germans in the Middle Ages, but occupied after World War II by **Székely folk**

CROSSING INTO CROATIA OR SERBIA

Owing to the changing political situation in the states of the former Yugoslavia, it is advisable to check with local authorities or embassy officials before venturing across these borders.

from Romania, making them of interest to ethnographers. In Transylvania and Moldavia, where most of their kinsfolk live, the Székely are noted for erecting elaborately carved gateways outside their farms.

Mohács

The small town of **MOHÁCS**, hot and dusty beside the pounding Danube, is a synonym for defeat. As a consequence of a single **battle** here in 1526, Hungary was divided and war-torn for 150 years and lost its independence for centuries thereafter. The state was tottering before Mohács, however: its treasury depleted with an indecisive teenager on the throne. Only after Süleyman "the Magnificent" had taken Belgrade and was nearing the Drava did the Hungarians muster an army, which headed south without waiting for reinforcements from Transylvania, engaging the Turks on August 29.

Legend has it that an olive tree planted two hundred years earlier by Louis the Great suddenly became barren on the day, while the king's scribe records how Louis II gave orders for the care of his hounds before riding out to meet his fate. Attacking first, the Magyars broke ranks to loot the fallen and suffered a crushing counter-attack by Turkish janissaries and cavalry, which caused a rout. Louis was crushed to death by his horse when trying to ford a stream, and the 25,000 dead included many of Hungary's nobles and prelates, leaving the country unable to organize resistance as the Turks advanced on Buda.

The battlefield and town

The **memorial park** (*Emlékpark*) at the battle site in Sátorhely, 7km south of town, was opened in 1976 to mark the 450th anniversary of the battle. Amidst fields of corn and sunflowers and clumps of blue floss flowers, the horror of war is starkly portrayed in the statues of dying horses and agonized men. The wind tinkles the pendants adorning Süleyman's figure and adds a very poignant touch to the scene. The site (April–Oct 8am–5pm) can be reached along road 56 on buses bound for Nagynárád, Majs, Lippó, Bezedek or Magyarbóly.

Those unwilling to make the pilgrimage will have to content themselves with the small commemorative **museum** next to the Orthodox church at Szerb utca 2 (Tues–Sun 10am–5pm); the **Kanizsai Dorottya Museum** at Városház utca 1 (Tues–Sun 10am–5pm), with its displays of the various ethnic groups who repopulated Mohács in the seventeenth century; an ugly **votive church** on Széchenyi tér, erected in 1926 to mark the 400th anniversary of the battle; and a peep into the **Town Hall**, where the Sultan's calligraphic signature is engraved on one of the windows.

The Mohács Carnival

Aside from these, the River Danube rolling through town disconcertingly near street level is the only "sight" for 364 days of the year. The exception manifests itself each spring (exactly seven weeks before Easter), when the streets come alive with the annual **Busójárás Carnival**. With its procession of grotesquely masked figures waving flaming torches, the carnival assumes a macabre appearance at night. Originally, it was probably a spring ritual intended to appease the gods, but over time participants also began to practise ritualistic abomination of the Turks to magically draw the sting of reality. Similar carnivals are also traditional in Serbia and Croatia, whence come many of the revellers at Mohács.

Practicalities

Mecsek Tourist at Szentháromság tér 2 (Mon–Fri 8am–4.30pm & Sat 8am–noon; ☎69/311-961) can book private rooms (②) and supply information – including details of a **nudist campsite** located on an island a couple of kilometres north of the ferry terminal. The only time there's an **accommodation** shortage is during the carnival, so make reservations if you're planning to attend. The *Hotel Korona* at Jókai utca 2 (☎69/311-049; ③) costs less than the smarter *Hotel Csele* at Szent Mihály tér 6–7 (☎69/311-825; ④–⑤). On the island (*Mohács-sziget*), the *Laterum Hostel* at Porond utca 9 (☎72/315-495) is open from May to September.

There are daily **buses** to Szekszárd and Budapest (leaving around 7am & 2.40pm), and to Baja and Kecskemét or Szeged on the Great Plain (5–6 daily). Mohács is not on the rail line, but **trains** for Pécs, Szekszárd or Baja can be caught at Bátaszék, 28km to the north. Depending on the situation in Croatia, buses might run to Osijek, Novi Sad or Slavonski Brod via the **border crossing** at Udvar, 11km south of town.

Szekszárd and the Forest of Gemenc

The chance to sample red wine from vineyards dating from Roman times and to buy inexpensive black pottery makes **SZEKSZÁRD** the prime stopover between Pécs and Budapest. With its somnabulent air and pleasant architecture, the town itself is more restful than interesting, but the chance to visit the beautiful Gemenc Forest might tempt you to stay longer. Everything of interest in town lies along, or just off, Hunyadi út, the main street running up from the bus station. On the landscaped stretch designated Mártírok tere, you'll see a neo-Renaissance pile containing the **Béri Balogh Museum** (Tues–Sun 10am–6pm), with a rich collection of peasants' and nobles' artefacts.

After crossing Széchenyi utca, head uphill to Béla tér, where porticoed buildings tilt perceptibly around a statue marking the plague of 1730. The Neoclassical palace here stands on the site of an abbey church from the time of the Árpáds. Nearby, Babits utca runs off towards the **House of Mihály Babits** (Tues–Sun 9am–6pm), a homely residence exhibiting photos and manuscripts related to the journal *Nyugat* (West). This avant-garde publication was edited by Babits and included the Village Explorers' exposés of rural life in interwar Hungary, launching the literary careers of Endre Ady and Gyula Illyés. Alas for Attila József, the finest poet of that era, Babits hated him and refused to publish his work in *Nyugat*.

Practicalities

Information is available from *Tolna Tourist* (Mon–Fri 8am–4.30pm; plus in summer Sat 8am–4pm & Sun 8am–noon; ☎74/312-144) at Széchenyi utca 38, or *Ibusz* (☎74/312-766) at Augusz Imre utca 1–3, both of which can book private **accommodation** (②). The *Hotel Gemenc* at Mészáros Lázár utca 4 (☎74/311-722; ⑤), lies one block behind the Balogh Museum, while the *Alisca Hotel* (☎74/312-228; ④) is at the top of Kálvária utca, off to the right of Béla tér, with lovely views of the Sió Hills. There is a fairly grotty campsite about 5km north of the centre on the spur road between Szekszárd and route 6 (mid-March to mid-Nov; ☎74/312-458).

The *Hotel Gemenc* has a decent **restaurant**, or you have a choice between the *Kispipa Vendéglő* at Széchenyi utca 51 (9am–10pm), the *Halászcsárda* at Zrínyi utca 60 (for fish), or the *Krokodil* at Oseri J. utca 114. There are several cellars near Széchenyi utca where you can try **Szekszárd wine** – a heavy, dark red "ox-blood" exported as far afield as Britain, Holland and Turkey in the 1700s. Franz Liszt, Pope Pius IX and Emperor Haile Selassie all reportedly imbibed *Szekszárd Vörös*.

Visiting the Forest of Gemenc

The **Forest of Gemenc** is a remnant of the wilderness of woods, reeds and mudland that once covered the Danube's shifting, flood-prone banks. Only at the beginning of this century was the river tamed and shortened by 60km, ending the annual flooding of its backwaters and the *Sárköz* (Mud region). However, marshes and ponds remained to provide habitats for boar, wildcats, otters, deer, ospreys, falcons, bald eagles, black storks and other **wildlife**. Nowadays, the forest is a nature reserve of sorts (although the deer are fair game for Western hunters), with **boat trips** on its backwaters and a **miniature rail line** through the forest.

Unfortunately, its terminals at **BÁRÁNYFOK** (bus #7 from town) and **PÖRBÖLY** (on the main line between Bátaszék and Baja) are awkward to reach, and there are only three trains a day (leaving Bárányfok at 10am & 2pm; Pörböly at 7.30am). All in all, it's easier to sign up for a *Tolna Tourist* **excursion** which includes a visit to **DECS**. Traditionally, this Sárköz village was isolated yet *au courant*, as its menfolk worked as bargees, bringing home the latest news and fabrics. Their wives wore be-ribboned silk skirts and cambric blouses with lace inserts, and later acquired a taste for lime green and yellow metallic thread, making their **costumes** as lurid as rave attire. Nowadays, these are only worn at Decs's biennial **Marriage Festival**, a Sárköz folk bash.

Between Szekszárd and Budapest

The road and rail line between Szekszárd and Budapest pass through some dreary countryside which could be improved by removing the main towns along the way. If you're driving, consider a **scenic detour** along minor roads through the pretty villages of Högyész, Gyonk and Cece, before rejoining the trunk route at Dunaföldvár, which – aside from Baja – has the only bridge across the Danube. Irregular **car ferries** from Fadd-Dombori, Gerjen, Paks and Dunaújváros also enable motorists to cross over to the Great Plain (see Chapter Six).

Paks

PAKS, 52km north of Szekszárd, is the site of Hungary's first **nuclear power station**, a Soviet-designed VVER 440 which supplies about sixteen percent of the country's electricity. After Chernobyl, the public opposed plans to build another reactor, but the current minister asserts that Hungary must make a strategic choice between further nuclear- or coal-powered generating plants, and favours another reactor at Paks. However, the plant's director (who has been reappointed after resigning in disgust at how it was run in the old days) says that no new energy sources are needed until 2020, and consumption is actually falling. Another reactor would entail a huge increase in **radioactive waste**, which the industry wants to dump in the hills south of Bonyhád, as its present site at Puspökszilágy, outside Budapest, is almost full.

The reactor aside, Paks is notable for its **Railway Museum** (Tues–Sun 10am–6pm), where vintage steam trains are displayed in an old station, and for a new **Catholic church** designed by Imre Makovecz. Should you need them, private **rooms** are available through *Ibusz* at Táncsics utca 2, or directly from Kossuth utca 71A. The reputation of the 24-hour *Halászcsárda* (fish **restaurant**) at Dunaföldvár utca 5A hasn't suffered from the reactor, a mile downstream.

Dunaújváros

Forty kilometres upriver, **DUNAÚJVÁROS** (Danube New Town) is a monument to Stalinist economics, created around a vast steel mill which the Party saw as the lynchpin of its industrialization strategy for the 1950s. The construction of Sztálinváros (as the town was originally called*) was trumpeted as a feat by Stakhanovites, though much of the heavy work was performed by peasant women and "reformed" prostitutes living under appalling conditions. Nowadays, of course, the **steelworks** is regarded as an economic liability, and was recently forced to shut down its blast furnaces for 25 days because the local electricity supplier cut off its power for non-payment of bills.

travel details

Trains

Budapest (Déli or Keleti Station) to Győr (10 daily; 2hr 30min); Komárom (10 daily; 1hr 30min–2hr); Pécs (4 daily; 3hr); Sopron (5 daily; 3hr 30min); Székesfehérvár (every 60–90min; 1hr); Szekszárd (3 daily; 3hr); Tata (4 daily; 1hr 15min).

Dombóvár to Pécs (4 daily; 1hr–1hr 30min).

Fertőboz to Nagycenk (April–Oct 4 departures Sat & Sun; 30min).

Győr to Sopron (6 daily; 1hr); Veszprém (4 daily; 2hr 30min).

Körmend to Szentgotthárd (every 1–2hr; 30min); Szombathely (every 1–2hr; 30min); Zalalövő (6 daily; 30min).

Kőszeg to Szombathely (every 60–90min; 30min).

Mohács to Pécs (4 daily; 2hr 30min); Villány (every 1–2hr; 30min).

Nagycenk to Fertőboz (April–Oct 4 departures Sat & Sun; 30min).

Nagykanizsa to Balatonszentgyörgy (every 1–2hr; 45min); Budapest (every 1–2hr; 3–4hr); Pécs (5 daily; 1hr 30min–3hr).

Pécs to Dombóvár (every 60–90min; 1hr–1hr 30min); Mohács (3 daily; 1hr 30min); Nagykanizsa (5 daily; 1hr 30min–3hr); Szombathely (2 daily; 4hr 30min); Villány (5 daily; 1hr).

Sopron to Budapest (5 daily; 3hr); Győr (5 daily; 1hr); Szombathely (7 daily; 1hr 30min).

Szekszárd to Budapest (3 daily; 3hr).

*Since another industrial town created in the Fifties changed its named from Leninváros to Tiszújváros (Tisza New Town) in 1990, such names have vanished completely from the map of Hungary.

Szentgotthárd to Körmend (every 1–2hr; 30min); Szombathely (every 1–2hr; 1hr).

Szombathely to Körmend (every 1–2hr; 30min); Kőszeg (every 60–90min; 30min); Nagykanizsa (4 daily; 1hr 30min–2hr 30min); Pécs (2 daily; 4hr 30min); Sopron (8 daily; 1hr 30min); Székesfehérvár (6 daily; 2hr 15min–2hr 45min); Szentgotthárd (every 1–2hr; 1hr); Tapolca (4 daily; 1hr 45min).

Zalaegerszeg to Budapest (3 daily; 3hr 30min); Zalalövő (7 daily; 30min).

Zalalövő to Körmend (4 daily; 30min); Zalaegerszeg (7 daily; 30min).

Buses

Budapest (Erzsébet tér) to Dunaújváros (4 daily; 1hr 30min); Győr (every 40–60min; 1hr 15min–2hr); Harkány (1 daily; 4hr 30min); Mohács (2–3 daily; 4hr); Pécs (5 daily; 4hr); Siklós (1 daily; 5hr); Sopron (2 daily; 3hr 45min); Szekszárd (8 daily; 3hr 15min); Szombathely (2 daily; 4hr 15min); Zalaegerszeg (1 daily; 4hr 45min).

Bukfürdő to Budapest (1 daily; 5hr); Győr (1 daily; 2hr 15min); Szombathely (1 daily; 1hr).

Győr to Balatonfüred (every 30–90min; 2hr); Budapest (every 40–60min; 1hr 15min–2hr); Kalocsa (1 weekly; 5hr); Pannonhalma Monastery (every 30–90min; 30min); Siófok (1 daily; 3hr); Sümeg (5 daily; 2hr 15min); Székesfehérvár (1 daily; 2hr); Szombathely (3 daily; 2hr); Tapolca (1 daily except Sun; 4hr); Veszprém (1 daily; 2hr); Zalaegerszeg (2 daily; 4hr 30min).

Harkány to Budapest (1 daily; 4hr 15min); Pécs (3 daily; 35min); Siklós (hourly; 1hr); Szekszárd (3 daily; 2hr 15min).

Kaposvár to Hévíz (2 daily; 2hr 30min); Pécs (every 60–90min; 2hr); Siófok (1 daily; 2hr); Szekszárd (2 daily; 2hr 15min); Zalaegerszeg (1 daily; 3hr).

Komárom to Esztergom (3 daily; 1hr 30min); Sopron (2 daily; 1hr 45min).

Kőszeg to Budapest (2 daily; 4hr); Sopron (5 daily; 2hr); Szombathely (5 daily; 30min).

Mohács to Siófok (1 daily; 3hr); Szekszárd (1 daily; 1hr).

Pécs to Abaliget (hourly; 1hr); Békéscsaba (1 daily; 5hr 30min); Harkány 3 daily; 45min); Hévíz (1 daily; 4hr 30min); Kaposvár (every 60–90min; 2hr); Keszthely (4 daily; 4hr); Orfü (hourly; 1hr); Siklós (hourly; 1hr); Siófok (1 daily; 3hr); Székesfehérvár (1 daily; 4hr 30min); Szekszárd (every 1–2hr; 1hr 15min); Szigetvár (every 60–90min; 1hr); Zalaegerszeg (2 daily; 4hr 15min).

Sárvár to Sopron (2 daily; 1hr 15min); Sümeg (2 daily; 1hr); Szombathely (2 daily; 1hr).

Siklós to Budapest (1 daily; 5hr); Harkány (hourly; 1hr); Pécs (hourly; 1hr).

Sopron to Baja (1 daily; 9hr 30min); Balatonfüred (1 daily; 4hr); Budapest (3 daily; 3hr 45min); Esztergom (2 daily; 4hr); Fertőd (hourly; 1hr); Fertórákos (hourly; 1hr); Győr (3 daily; 2hr); Hévíz (3 daily; 3hr); Komárom (2 daily; 2hr 45min); Kőszeg (5 daily; 2hr); Sárvár (2 daily; 1hr 15min); Sümeg (3 daily; 2hr 15min); Szekszárd (1 daily; 8hr); Szombathely (1 daily; 1hr 45min); Zalaegerszeg (1 daily; 3hr).

Szekszárd to Baja (2 daily; 1hr); Budapest (3 daily; 2hr 30min); Mohács (1 daily; 1hr); Pécs (every 1–2hr; 1hr 15min); Siófok (1 daily; 2hr); Székesfehérvár (2 daily; 2hr); Veszprém (2 daily; 3hr 45min).

Szigetvár to Nagykanizsa (5 weekly; 2hr 30min); Pécs (every 60–90min; 1hr).

Szombathely to Budapest (2 daily; 3hr 45min); Bukfürdő (2 daily; 1hr); Ják (hourly; 30min); Keszthely (3 daily; 2hr 30min); Nagykanizsa (3 daily; 2hr 45min); Körmend (hourly; 1hr); Kőszeg (3 daily; 25min); Sárvár (2 daily; 1hr); Sopron (4 daily; 3hr 15min); Zalaegerszeg (6 daily; 1hr 30min).

Tata to Esztergom (every 60–90min; 1hr 30min); Komárom (hourly; 1hr); Tatabánya (every 20min; 15min).

Zalaegerszeg to Győr (2 daily; 4hr 30min); Kaposvár (1 daily; 3hr); Keszthely (hourly; 1hr); Körmend (1 daily; 1hr); Nagykanizsa (1 daily; 1hr); Pécs (2 daily; 4hr 30min); Sopron (1 daily; 3hr 15min); Szigetvár (2 daily; 3hr 45min); Székesfehérvár (2 daily; 4hr 15min); Szombathely (1 daily; 1hr 20min).

International trains

Győr to Berlin (2 daily; 13hr); Bratislava (3 daily; 5hr); Cologne (1 daily; 11hr 30min); Dresden (1 daily; 10hr); Frankfurt (1 daily; 9hr 45min); Gdansk (1 daily; 18hr); Munich (2 daily; 7hr 15min); Paris (1 daily; 16hr 30min); Prague (1 daily; 8hr); Vienna (8 daily; 1hr 45min); Warsaw (1 daily; 14hr).

Pécs to Osijek (2 daily; 4hr).

Nagykanizsa to Zagreb (June–Sept 2 daily; 3hr 30min).

Sopron to Vienna (1 daily; 1hr); Wiener Neustadt (4 daily; 1hr).

Szombathely to Graz (3 daily; 3hr).

Tatabánya to Bratislava (1 daily; 6hr); Gdansk (1 daily; 19hr); Warsaw (1 daily; 15hr).

International buses

Bükfürdő to Forchtenstein (2 weekly; 3hr); Graz (1 daily; 4hr); Schwarzenbach (1 daily; 4hr); Stegersbach (July–Aug 1 daily; 5hr); Vienna (July–Aug 1 daily; 4hr).

Dunaújváros to Komárno (1 daily; 4hr 30min); Vienna (2 weekly; 7hr).

Győr to Galanta (1 daily; 2hr 30min).

Kaposvár to Bratislava (June–Oct 2 weekly; 5hr).

Lenti to Ljubljana (1 daily; 5hr 30min).

Letenye to Prague (July–Aug 1 daily; 10hr).

Mohács to Novi Sad (1 daily; 5hr).

Mosonmagyaróvár to Bratislava (2 weekly; 1hr 30min); Vienna (4 weekly; 2hr).

Sárvár to Neunkirchen (July–Aug 1 daily; 4hr); Vienna (June–Sept 1 weekly; 3hr); Wiener Neustadt (1 daily; 5hr).

Sopron to Baden (1 daily; 3hr 30min); Bratislava (1 daily; 3hr); Forchenstein (2 weekly; 1hr 30min); Oberpullendorf (1 daily; 1hr 30min); Semmering (1 daily; 5hr); Vienna (1–2 daily except Sun; 1hr 45min).

Szombathely to Bratislava (1 daily; 3hr 30min); Oberpullendorf (1 daily; 2hr 45min); Oberwart (1–2 daily; 1hr 45min); Stergersbach (July–Aug 1 daily; 2hr 30min); Vienna (2 daily; 3hr).

CHAPTER FIVE

THE NORTHERN UPLANDS

Hungary's **Northern Uplands** (*Északi Felföld*) are generally hilly and forested. They encompass the famous **wine**-producing towns of **Eger** and **Tokaj**, as well as a succession of **castles** – some well-preserved (such as the one at Sárospatak), others clinging in picturesque decrepitude to the crags above the villages of Hollókő, Somoskő, Boldogkőváralja and Füzér. This part of Hungary was also the first to be industrialized, and the first to be affected by the collapse of the country's heavy industry. The idyllic woodlands of the **Bükk and Mátra mountains** lie cheek to cheek with drab, utilitarian **Miskolc** (at the heart of the so-called "Rust Belt"), the coal mines of the Borsod Basin and the despoiled Sajó Valley and, less than 50km further on, the amazing **Aggtelek stalactite caves**. Like the environment, lifestyles run the gamut between two extremes – at one end, skinheads prowling the housing estates of Ózd and Miskolc; at the other, horse-drawn carts clopping around tiny **Zemplén villages** where the siesta still reigns supreme.

Approaches to the Uplands

Although the westerly Cserhát mountains are adjacent to the Börzsöny Mountains (see *The Danube Bend*), and thus accessible from Vác and Balassagyarmat, the commonest **approaches** to the uplands are **from Budapest** or the Great Plain. Several trains daily leave the capital's Keleti station, passing through Hatvan and Füzesabony en route to Miskolc and Szerencs – all places from which to change on to **branch lines** heading further north. **Hatvan** is the link with the Mátra; trains from **Füzesabony** run to Eger; **Miskolc** is the starting point for journeys into the Bükk; while from **Szerencs** you can reach Tokaj, Sárospatak and many Zemplén villages. Balassagyarmat is accessible by train from Aszód, or by bus from Hatvan (where buses also depart for Hollókő).

ACCOMMODATION PRICE CODES

All accommodation in this guide is graded according to the price bands given below. Note that all prices refer to the cheapest available double room in high season except where otherwise indicated. For more details, see p.26.

① Under 650Ft (under £4/$6/ DM10)

② 650–1500Ft (£4–8/$6–13/DM10– 20)

③ 1500–3000Ft (£8–17/$13–27/ DM20–40)

④ 3000–4500Ft (£17–25/$27–40/ DM40–60)

⑤ 4500–6500Ft (£25–36/$40–57/ DM60–85)

⑥ 6500–10,000Ft (£36–56/$57–88/ DM85–130)

⑦ Over 10,000Ft (over £56/$88/ DM130)

Coming **from the Plain**, trains are again the easiest mode of transport. From Nyíregyháza, frequent services run through Tokaj to Szerencs, before branching off towards Miskolc or Sátoraljaújhely; while Karcag, Tiszafüred and Szolnok are linked by rail to Hatvan and Füzesabony.

FROM BUDAPEST TO MISKOLC

The only major east–west road connecting Budapest and Miskolc is the M3 (E71) via Gödöllő, Hatvan, Gyöngyös and Eger. Between Budapest and Eger the scen-

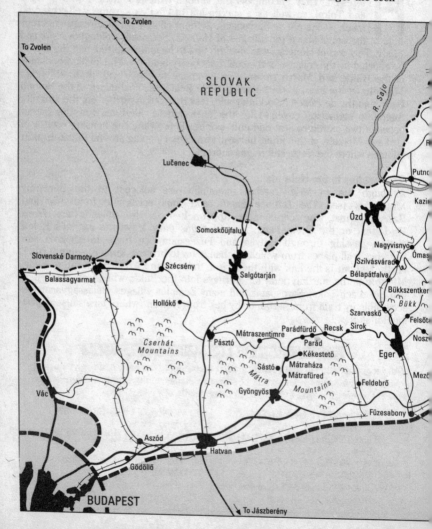

ery is unchanging, with extensive vineyards stretching as far as the eye can see. From Eger two routes lead to the industrial city of Miskolc: the E71 via Mezőkövesd, which is fast but dull; or the more picturesque northerly route, which wends its way through the Bükk mountains, offering some of the most beautiful scenery in the country.

Gödöllő

Most fast trains pass straight through, but if you're driving to Gyöngyös or Miskolc, it's worth considering a brief stopover at **GÖDÖLLŐ**, 30km east of

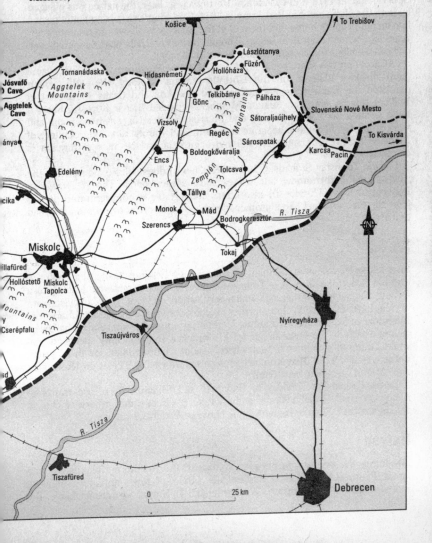

Budapest, which is also easily reached by HÉV train from the capital's Örs vezér tere station (50min). This small Baroque town used to be a summer residence of the Habsburgs, boasting a palace that rivalled the "Hungarian Versailles" at Esterháza.

The former **Grassalkovich Palace** dominates the south side of Szabadság tér, where the Budapest–Aszód and Vác–Isaszeg roads meet near the centre of town. Commissioned by Count Antal Grassalkovich, a confidante of Empress Maria Theresa, the palace was designed by András Mayerhoffer who introduced the Baroque style of mansion to Hungary in the 1740s. "Sissy", the wife of Emperor Franz Josef, preferred living here to Vienna. Commandeered by Béla Kun's General Staff in 1919, and by Admiral Horthy a year later, the palace was pillaged by both the Nazis and the Red Army in 1944. One wing was subsequently turned into an old people's home, but the rest of the palace was allowed to rot until a few years ago, when restoration began. Though it's not officially open to tourists yet, one can usually stroll around without being challenged.

At no. 5 on the same square, a **Local History Museum** (Tues–Sun 10am– 6pm) displays material on the **Gödöllő Artists' Colony** (1901–20), which emulated the English Pre-Raphaelites and the Arts and Crafts movement of William Morris and John Ruskin. Members included Aladár Körösfoi Kreisch (who wrote a book about Ruskin and Morris), Sándor Nagy (whose home and workshop may become a separate museum) and Károly Kós (the architect of Budapest's zoo). The museum will move into the palace once restoration is complete.

Gödöllő Tourist at Szabadság út 6 (☎28/320-685) doesn't have too much in the way of **local information**, but it does book private rooms. The *Tó Panzió* on Isaszegi út (☎28/320-345; ①) also offers comfortable **accommodation**. If you have the time and feel like a promenade, there's a lovely **aboretum** on the road to Isaszeg.

Aszód

Five kilometres beyond Gödöllő by car or bus, heading east along route 30 towards Aszód, you'll pass a Transylvanian-style wooden gateway leading to a former Capucl in church and monastery where several Grassalkovichs are buried. In **ASZÓD** itself, 10km further on, look out for the former **Podmaniczky Mansion** on Szabadság tér, another decrepit Baroque pile, whose main hall has a ceiling fresco by the Austrian painter J.L. Kracker. In the vicinity stands an erstwhile Lutheran grammar school where Sándor Petőfi studied for three years, hence a small **Petőfi Museum** on the premises (April–Oct Tues–Sun 10am–6pm; Nov–March Tues–Sun 9am–5pm).

Besides main-line services to Budapest and Miskolc, there are **trains** to Balassagyarmat (4 daily; 90min) and Vácrátót (2 direct trains; otherwise change at Galgamácsa). Regular **buses** shuttle between Aszód and Hatvan.

Hatvan

Straddling the crossroads between Budapest, the Northern Uplands and the Great Plain, **HATVAN** was traditionally a market town until its wholesale industrialization this century. While modern Új-Hatvan is unremarkable, the old centre retains another **Grassalkovich Mansion**, which has been used as a hospital since the last war. Its previous occupants were the Hatvany family, who owned the local sugar-beet factory and much of the surrounding countryside. The **Local History Museum** on Kossuth tér (Tues–Sun 2–6pm) is dedicated to Lajos Hatvany (1880–1961), local writer, critic and literary historian.

As befits a town whose name reflects its distance from Budapest (*hatvan* means "sixty" in Hungarian), **buses** fan out from here to the capital, Szolnok, Gyöngyös, the Mátra settlements, and as far afield as Eger. Moderately priced rooms can be found at the **hotels** *Park*, Kossuth tér 14 (☎38/312-870; ②); *Mini*, Hórvath utca 15 (☎38/312-469; ②); and *Strand*, Teleki út (☎38/311-200; ②).

The Cserhát Region

The Cserhát range, like its more impressive neighbours, the Mátra and the Börzsöny, was once continuous forest. Farming and rail lines in the Nógrád and Zagyva valleys have however made inroads and today there's little magic about the northern slopes or the monotonous flatlands around the Ipoly River, which marks the border with Slovakia. What colour there is is provided by the indigenous **Palóc ethnic group**, who sport fantastic costumes that have long since become museum pieces elsewhere – evidence of a backward agricultural economy or an eye for the tourist trade rather than any "separatist" feelings.

Balassagyarmat

After losing its medieval fortress and most of its inhabitants to the Turks, **BALASSAGYARMAT** (pronounced "Bolosho-dyurmot") was repopulated by a mixture of Germans, Slovaks and Czechs. It prospered during the eighteenth century, splashing out on several Baroque buildings – including a church decorated by the famous Maulbertsch – which were erected along its main street. Today however the town looks seedy and depressed, with little to show for its status as the "Palóc capital" except for a fine museum in the park off Bajcsy-Zsilinszky út.

Housed in an eclectic-style building, the **Palóc Ethnographical Museum** (Tues–Sun 9am–5pm) contains a fantastic collection of **costumes** from the Palóc community, which is thought to be of Slovak origin. For committed culture vultures, there are also two rooms devoted to local writers. **Imre Madách** (1823–64) began his career as a clerk in Balassagyarmat's County Hall, and went on to write *The Tragedy of Man* in 1860. Commonly held to be Hungary's greatest classical drama, performances of it were banned during the 1950s when its pessimistic portrayal of human nature was regarded as contrary to the lofty ideals required of "Socialist Realist" art. Conversely, the satirical short stories of **Kálmán Mikszáth** (1847–1910), exposing the shortcomings of the landed gentry, encountered no ideological difficulties. Another section is devoted to **Gyula Benczúr**, whose narrative paintings won him a teaching post at the Academy of Fine Arts, but were denounced as "reactionary art" during the short-lived Republic of Councils, when Benczúr was exiled here as a punishment.

Practicalities

With the closure of the *Hotel Ipoly* on Bajcsy-Zsilinszky út, **accommodation** is limited to a small campsite on the edge of town (run by the Sports Society) and whatever the **tourist office** in the *Képtár* gallery on Kösztársasag tér (☎35/312-186) can muster in the way of private rooms. Rákóczi utca has two **restaurants**: the *Palóc* at no. 23 and the *Balassa* at no. 34.

From the terminus on the main street, **buses** run to Szécsény, Hollókő, Pásztó and Salgótarján (see below), and once a day to Lučenec in Slovakia.

Szécsény

Less than an hour's bus ride from Balassagyarmat, the small town of **SZÉCSÉNY** is ennobled by **Forgách Castle**, a graceful eighteenth-century mansion occupying the site of a medieval fortress that was blown up by the Habsburgs during the War of Independence (1703–11). It was here that the Hungarian Diet elected Ferenc Rákóczi II ruling prince and commander in chief of the Magyar forces, and declared the union of Hungary and Transylvania in 1705.

The castle now serves as a **museum** (summer Tues–Sun 10am–6pm; winter Tues–Sun 9am–4pm) of hunting and local archeology and the caretaker's lodge contains a collection of religious artefacts collected by Sándor Csoma Körösi, who travelled widely in Asia and compiled the first Tibetan–English dictionary. Down the road, a **bastion** from the old fortress (ask one of the castle attendants to let you in) exhibits instruments of torture and engravings demonstrating their use – explanatory leaflets are available in English.

Tourinform has an **information** office at Ady Endre utca 12 (Mon–Fri 8am–4pm; plus May–Oct Sat & Sun 10am–6pm; ☎32/370-777), though they may be forced to close. If you're on the look out for **accommodation**, the local *Szakközépiskolai Kollégium* at Rákóczi utca 90 (☎32/370-131) can usually provide a bed for the night, or there's the *Panzió Paradisó* at Ady Endre utca 14 (☎32/370-427; ③–④). Time permitting, you may wish to travel 6km up the road to **BENZÚRFALVA**, where a six-metre statue of Lenin carved from a tree trunk still stands tall and proud.

Hollókő

From Szécsény you can catch another bus south to **HOLLÓKŐ** (Raven Rock), where a ruined **fortress** once owned by the Illés family overlooks a **museum village** on UNESCO's world cultural heritage list. Following a fire in 1907, Hollókő's whitewashed Palóc houses were rebuilt in traditional style with broad eaves and carved gables. Originally peasant dwellings, they are now largely owned by Budapest intellectuals who can better afford the upkeep – their original owners having long since installed themselves in modern boxes on the outskirts of the village. Hollókő's apotheosis comes on August 20, when local dance groups and international folk troupes in gorgeous costumes perform at the **Palóc Festival** (*Palóc szötés*).

At other times, traditional Palóc dress is chiefly worn by old ladies attending vespers at Hollókő's restored **church** – outwardly austere, but decorated inside with vibrant colours and flowers. Traditionally, however, each village had its own style of homespun attire: in nearby Örhalom, for example, the Hollókő-style cap was transformed into a bonnet by the insertion of a stiff cardboard lining. Fine examples from various Palóc localities are displayed in the **Folk Museum** at Kossuth utca no. 82 (April–Sept Wed–Sun 10am–4pm; Oct–March Thurs 10am–2pm, Fri noon–2pm, Sat & Sun 10am–4pm); the *Szövőház* or **Weaving House** at no. 94 (April–Oct Tues & Thurs–Sun 9am–5pm); and the **Tájvédelmi Kiállítás** at no. 99 (April–Oct Tues–Sun 10am–6pm), which also contains Palóc furniture.

Weaving, woodcarving and folk-dancing **courses** can all be booked through *Nógrád Tourist* in Salgótarján (☎32/316-940). They can also reserve **rooms** (③), some of them furnished with Palóc wardrobes and embroidered bolsters – a safer bet than relying on the local **tourist office** at Kossuth utca 68 (closed Mon & Tues; Hollókő ☎4). Alternatively there's the year-round *Panoráma* holiday complex 1km southeast of the centre on Orgona út (☎32/378-077), comprising a campground, bungalows (① per person) and a nine-room pension (③). The village has several places which serve **food**, and a couple of bars. **Buses** run regularly to Szécsény and Salgótarján (except between 9am and noon), and twice daily to Pásztó and Hatvan, the jumping-off point for the Mátras and trains back to Budapest.

Salgótarján and around

After folksy Szécsény and Hollókő, **SALGÓTARJÁN** whacks you with grim modernity. Scarred since the nineteenth century by industrial squalor and poverty, this mining town was extensively rebuilt during the Sixties – a tardy response to workers' demonstrations in 1956, when the ÁVO secret police shot dead 131 strikers in the aftermath of the Uprising. Court proceedings finally began against the alleged murderers in 1994, with only a couple of convictions to date. Many feel that those who were really responsible – those who gave the orders – will never be brought to justice. So the bitterness lingers on, but at the same time people's assessment of the past is changing. When the reformist Communists chose Salgótarján as the venue for their 1991 congress, massive protests compelled them to think again. However three years later in the 1994 elections the Socialists won the district and the diehard Communists performed well.

Aside from the huge statue of a partisan toting his machine gun on one of its central squares, Salgótarján's only "sights" are the **Glass Factory** at Huta út 1 (Mon–Fri 8–9.30am, 10am–noon & 1–3pm; 30-min guided tours in Hungarian) and the *Bányamúzeum* or **Mining Museum** (Tues–Sun 9am–5pm). The latter is buried in the inclined shafts of the now-defunct "József" pit and entered from Ady út, a block behind the outdoor market. Cramped and muddy, filled with props, tools and cables, the tunnels lack the dust, danger and noise of a working mine, but the explanatory leaflet still bids visitors "good luck", the traditional miners' greeting. On Fő tér stands a poignant sculpture by Imre Varga of the martyred poet, Miklós Radnóti, whose last works were found in his pocket in a mass grave after World War II.

Salgó Castle and Somoskő

In contrast with the grimness of the town, the surrounding countryside features volcanic rock formations and picturesque ruins. Regular buses from Salgótarján's terminal run 8km northwards to the village of **SALGÓ**, overlooked by a **ruined castle** which broods atop a 625-metre-high basalt cone. Constructed after the

Mongol invasion of the thirteenth century, it later belonged to Count István Werbőczy, author of the Tripartium law which bound the peasants to "perpetual serfdom" following the peasants' revolt of 1514. The castle was blown up during the Turkish occupation; however you can visit the ruins (Tues–Sun 9am–5pm) which still command superb views of the highlands further north. A little way past Salgó, on the same bus route, is the *Hotel Salgó* (☎32/310-588; ③), with tennis courts and skiing nearby.

Most buses carry on to **SOMOSKŐ**, a hamlet near the Slovak border. Just across the border, another **ruined castle** squats upon vast blocks of eroded stone. Founded during the fifteenth century, its five towers survey impressive **basalt formations** (*bazaltömlés*) resembling giant organ pipes. It used to be possible to visit both sites on organized tours, but this arrangement has now lapsed and they can only be reached from Slovakia. However, you can **stay** at the *Fogadó* (①) in the village (which is on Hungarian soil).

Practicalities

Salgótarján's **bus and train stations** (separated by rail tracks) lie just south of the town centre, close to the market and Mining Museum. For **information**, look up *Nógrád Tourist* at Erzsébet tér 3 (☎32/316-940), around the corner from the *Karancs Hotel* on Fő tér (☎32/310-088; ③). Cheaper **accommodation** is available in private rooms (②) from the tourist office, a bungalow at the *Cserfa Fogadó* on Rózsafa út (②), or chalets at *Tó-Strand Camping* (April to mid-Oct; ☎32/311-168; ①–②), at the end of the #6 bus route. There's also the option of staying in Salgó or Somoskő (see above).

In early May each year Salgótarján comes alive with an international **Dixieland Jazz Festival**.

Moving on

If you're dependent on public transport, **moving on** from Salgótarján amounts to heading northeast towards Ózd or south towards the Mátra region, assuming that you don't take the early morning **bus to Lučenec in Slovakia**, or the *Polonia Express* **train to Warsaw** (leaving around 1.25am).

Since the remote Aggtelek caves are the only reason for passing through Ózd, and bus connections are unreliable, **south** seems the obvious direction to take. Along the way to Hatvan (by bus or train), ore-buckets and slag hills disappear, giving way to vineyards and fields, and you can change buses at Pásztó and head **into the Mátra** by a scenic route. Services from Hatvan to Gyöngyös are likely to run more frequently, however.

Gyöngyös and the Mátra Mountains

Hungarians make the most of their highlands, and **the Mátra** – where Mount Kékestető just tops 1000 metres – is heavily geared to domestic tourism. Mount Kékestető itself is a popular place for winter sports, despite the relatively lacklustre resort facilities at Mátraháza and Mátraszentimre. In the summer families ramble the paths between picnic sites and beer gardens, ignoring the wild boar and deer that live deeper in the thickets of oak and beech. Few of the Mátra settlements have much of interest beyond their amenities, but the mountains and forests are, in any case, the main attraction.

Gyöngyös

Most visitors approach the Mátra via **GYÖNGYÖS** (pronounced "Dyurn-dyursh"), the centre of the Gyöngyös-Visonta **wine** region, where white *Muskotály* comes from. It's a pleasant enough town, but nothing to write home about. The town's bus station lies roughly midway between the two centres of interest, the main square – called just that, Fő tér – and the Mátra Museum.

Proceeding north from the bus station along Kossuth utca, you pass a parade of nineteenth-century buildings painted in garish reds and blues, presaging the grander edifices around **Fő tér**. At the northern end of the square stands **St Bartholomew's Church** (open mornings only), originally Gothic but heavily remodelled in the eighteenth century. Beyond the wine stalls outside the *Hotel Mátra*, a street leads off to Nemecz József tér, where a **Franciscan Church** endowed by the Báthori family displays their coat of arms in its chancel. To the west of Fő tér, across the Nagy-patak stream, a Baroque **County Hall** and a former **Synagogue** flank Vármegye tér. The latter, now a furniture store, was designed in 1816 by the celebrated architect Lipót Baumhorn.

Heading in the opposite direction from the bus terminus, Kossuth utca runs past the landscaped grounds of the former Orczy mansion, fronted by benevolent-looking stone lions. The mansion itself, at no. 40, houses the **Mátra Museum** (Tues–Sun 9am–5pm), where a reconstructed mammoth's skeleton is on show, along with a dazzling collection of butterflies and other dead Mátra wildlife.

A bit further on is the terminus of the *Mátravasút*, a **narrow-gauge rail line** up to Mátrafüred in the mountains (see below). Trains depart roughly every hour until nightfall.

Practicalities

Gyöngyös's train station is on Vasút utca near the eastern end of Kossuth utca, a twenty-minute walk into the centre of town. From the bus station on Koháry utca, it's a ten-minute walk north along Kossuth utca to Fő tér, the main square.

Accommodation and **information** on the Mátra region, including skiing during the winter, is available from *Mátra Tourist* in an ugly modern building at Szabadság tér 2 (Mon–Fri 8am–5.30pm & Sat 8am–1pm; ☎37/311-565). The staff here are more likely to speak English than at the rather sleepy *Ibusz* office on Kossuth utca. Just off Fő tér at Mátyás király utca 2 is the three-star *Hotel Mátra* (☎37/312-057; ④–⑤), while the fifteen-room *Vincellér Panzió* is a cheaper alternative at Erzsébet királyné utca 22 (☎37/311-691; ②). The Mátra resorts offer other possibilities (see below).

The Mátra Settlements

Several picturesque villages lie within striking distance of Gyöngyös at the foot of the Mátras. Frequent buses from Gyöngyös travel 5km west to **GYÖNGYÖSTARJÁN**, where a former *Jugendstil* hunting lodge, the *Vadászkastely*, is now a hotel. The nearby Fajzatpuszta Château, once the property of a French family, boasts a 542-metre-long wine cellar that was cut into the rock in the eighteenth century; wine tastings and a small exhibit on viticulture are held here. Northeastwards in the direction of Eger a minor road takes you past a hide-ous-looking power station to the village of **KISNÁNA**, which has a ruined fifteenth-century castle.

From Gyöngyös, there are also frequent services (every 60–90min) to Mátrafüred and Mátraháza, and four or five buses a day pass through Parád, Recsk and Sirok on their way to Eger. Recsk and Sirok are also accessible via the branch rail line down from Mátramindszent to **Kál-Kápolna** (the station before Füzesabony on the Budapest–Miskolc line). Anyone intending to visit Sirok or Feldebrő, or go walking in the mountains, should buy a large-scale **tourist map** (*A Mátra turistatérképe*) beforehand. But be warned that there's no tourist accommodation at either village.

Mátrafüred and Sás-tó

The *Mátravasút* is the fun way to get from Gyöngyös to **MÁTRAFÜRED**, and takes no longer than the bus. Passengers arrive at the lower end of this sloping, touristy settlement, a short walk from the local *Mátra Tourist* at Vörösmarty utca 4. Private **rooms** (②) can be arranged through the tourist office, otherwise there's the three-star *Hotel Avar* at Páradi út 5 (☎37/320-131) or the less expensive *Hegyalja Panzió*, a former trade union resort at Turista utca 7 (☎37/320-027). **Tennis** courts and **horse riding** can be organized through the *Hotel Avar*.

Four kilometres uphill from Mátrafüred lies **Sás-tó** (Sedge Lake), on the bus route between Gyöngyös and Mátraháza. More of a large pond than a lake, it's a friendly place full of Hungarians boating and fishing amid the usual *lángos* stands. If you feel like staying, *Sas-tó Camping* is a very attractive **campsite** complex (April to mid-Oct; ☎37/374-025) with the usual facilities plus a 28-room **motel** and **bungalows**. At 8pm the restaurant closes and action shifts down to the **disco** and bars in Mátrafüred. Heading on, you can easily walk from Sás-to to Mátraháza, on a footpath with **wild boars** reputedly lurking in the forests to the west.

Mátraháza and Mount Kékestető

Nine kilometres to the north, **MÁTRAHÁZA**, the next settlement, consists mainly of former trade union hostels converted into hotels, plus a few bars and plenty of walks in the vicinity. The chalet-style *Bérc Hotel* (☎37/374-095; ④) is a clean and pleasant place to stay, as is the friendly *Hotel Pagoda* (☎37/374-123) in the centre of the village. The latter consists of three buildings in good Socialist style, one of which houses the village's only restaurant.

From Mátraháza, you can easily make a quick return bus journey to **Mount Kékestető**, the highest point (1015m) in the Mátra range. Two **ski runs** (*sípálya*) descend from the summit, which is crowned by a nine-storey telecommunications **tower** offering an impressive view of the highlands (summer Tues–Sun 9.30am–4pm; winter Tues–Sun 9.30am–3pm). The *Hotel Hegycsúcs* at the top of the hill offers moderately priced accommodation (☎37/374-086; ④).

Parád and Parádfürdő

Roughly 10km to the northeast, a group of similarly named villages gathers around **PARÁD**, where Count Károlyi tried to set an example to other nobles in 1919 by distributing land to his serfs. The commune has an old **Palóc House** full of costumes and artefacts (Tues–Sun 9am–5pm), and an exhibition of **wood-carving**, signposted *Fafaragó Kiállítás* (daily 9am–7pm). Inexpensive **accommodation** is available at the *Palócz Fogadó* on Kossuth utca (☎36/364-008; ②), or at the lovely *Sanatorium* at no. 372 (☎36/364-004; ②).

A popular **thermal spa** where the sulphurous, fizzy water is said to benefit digestive complaints, **PARÁDFÜRDŐ** really deserves a visit for its **Coach**

Museum (April–Oct daily 9am–5pm; Nov–March Tues–Sun 10am–4pm). The *Kocsimúzeum*'s splendid collection includes vehicles for state occasions, hunting and for gallivanting around. For the record, the coach – which superseded the cumbersome wagon throughout Europe – was actually invented in a Hungarian village called – one might have guessed it – Kocs. Some beautiful horses can be seen in adjacent stables, which were designed for the Károlyi family by Miklós Ybl, the architect of Budapest's Opera House.

Follow the signposts from the main road to the far end of the commune to find cheap **rooms** (②) in the *Muflon Fogadó* at Peres utca 8 – which has a **restaurant** (daily except Tues 4–10pm) – or at no. 37 on the same street. The turn-of-the-century *Erzsébet Szalló* (②) next to the bus station is shabby and depressing, its only redeeming feature being a pleasant bar with a view of the park behind.

Recsk

Mention **RECSK**, a village 2km east of Parádfürdő, and many older Hungarians will share recollections of terror. During the late Forties and early Fifties, thousands of the tens of thousands of citizens arrested by the ÁVO were sentenced to labour in the quarries southwest of here. Half-starved and frequently beaten by their jailers, prisoners died of exhaustion or in rockfalls, but more usually while sleeping at night in muddy pits open to the sky.

Closed by Imre Nagy in 1953, **Recsk concentration camp** was effaced by a tree plantation during the Kádár years, and not until 1991 were its victims commemorated. A stone **monument** symbolizing repression and a bronze model of the camp stand near the still-working quarry, 4.5km up from the village (look for the *Kőbánya* signs).

Sirok and Feldebrő

SIROK, 8km further east, is worth visiting if you're wild about romantic views – the bus from Parádfürdő stops here en route to Eger. On a mountain top above the village, 1.5km northeast of the train station, there's a ruined thirteenth-century **castle** from which you can admire the mingled peaks of the Mátra, the Bükk and Slovakia. The village itself is also very picturesque with its old houses nestling among cliffs and crags.

A considerable detour – recommended only to antiquity buffs who have their own transport – takes you to **FELDEBRŐ**, a village with one of the oldest church crypts still extant in Hungary. Therein you'll find beautiful twelfth-century **frescoes** influenced by Byzantine art, and the **grave of King Aba** (1041–44), one of the ephemeral monarchs between the Árpád and Angevin dynasties. Keys for the crypt (Tues–Sat 10am–noon & 2–4pm; Sun & holidays 11am–noon & 3–4pm) are held at the *plébánia* (presbytery) behind the church. The local **linden leaf wine** (*Debrői hárslevelű*) is good for refreshing weary travellers.

Eger and around

Situated in its own sunny valley between the Mátra and the Bükk, **EGER** is famed for its wine, its minaret, and the heroic legend attached to its castle. Sadly though, for all its Baroqué glory, it also has the distinction of being one of the skinhead centres of the country, with an estimated 4000 of them committing

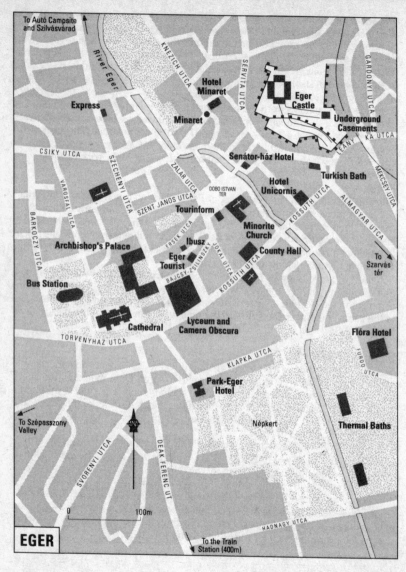

EGER

regular attacks on "undesirables", as well as desecrating the Jewish cemetery near Szépassonyvölgy in 1994.

From Eger, buses and local trains head to various villages bordering the Bükk national park, notably Szilvásvárad near the beautiful Szalajka Valley to the north, and Cserépvarálja to the northeast, just below the "rocking" stones in the Felső-szoros ravine. Thus you can enter the Bükk mountains from the west, or cut straight through on a bus to Miskolc, and re-enter them by train from Lillafüred (see "The Bükk Mountains" p.264) after you've finished with Eger.

The Town

With its colourful architecture suffused by sunshine, Eger seems a fitting place of origin for *Egri Bikavér*, the potent, throat-rasping red wine marketed as *Bull's Blood* abroad, which brings hordes of visitors to the town. A **Baroque Festival** is celebrated in July and early August, but the *Szüret* or **Harvest Festival** in September is when Eger is at its liveliest, with two weeks of numerous wine-related events around town, including folk dancing and a parade of floats. Despite occasional problems with accommodation, it's a fine place in which to hang out and wander around, not to mention all the opportunities for drinking.

The Cathedral and Lyceum

Occupying a site hallowed since the eleventh century, Eger **Cathedral** looms above a flight of steps flanked by statues of saints Stephen and László, Peter and Paul, by the Italian sculptor Casagrande. Constructed between 1831 and 1836, this ponderous Neoclassical edifice was architect József Hild's rehearsal for the still larger basilica at Esztergom. Its interior was largely decorated by J.L. Kracker, who spent his last years working in Eger. Particularly impressive is the frescoed cupola, where the City of God arises in triumph as evildoers flee the sword. Close by, facing Széchenyi utca, stands the **Archbishop's Palace**, a U-shaped Baroque pile with fancy wrought-iron gates. In the right wing of the palace you'll find the treasury and history of the bishopic of Eger (April–Oct Mon–Sat 9am–5pm; winter Mon–Sat 10am–2pm), while another wing now serves as the headquarters of *Egervin*, the local wine company.

The florid, Zopf-style **Lyceum**, opposite the Cathedral, was founded by two enlightened bishops whose proposal for a university was rejected by Maria Theresa. Now a teacher training college (named after Ho Chi Minh during the Communist era), the building is worth visiting for its **library** (Mon–Fri 9.30am–1pm & Sat–Sun 9.30am–noon), which has a huge ceiling fresco of the Council of Trent by Kracker and his son-in-law. The lightning bolt and book in one corner symbolize the Council's decision to establish an Index of forbidden books.

Even better, check out the **Observatory** (same hours as library) atop the tower in the east wing, where a nineteenth-century **camera obscura** projects a view of the entire town from a bird's-eye perspective. The camera's monocled curator gleefully points out lovers kissing in the backstreets, unaware of surveillance.

Kossuth utca and Dobó István tér

From the Lyceum and Provost House across the way, **Kossuth utca** leads past a Franciscan church (where a mosque stood in Turkish times) and the **County Hall**, whose magnificent gates were wrought by Henrik Fazola (notice the stork with a snake in its beak and a vine in its claws, on the county coat of arms). The same man who designed the gates was also responsible for the prison bars in the old Eger jail at Kossuth utca 9, now the home of a small **museum** on local history and artefacts (April–Oct Tues–Sun 9am–4pm). If your Hungarian is up to it, the friendly curator will give you an enthusiastic lecture on Eger's local swimming team and water polo club whose members formed the basis of the national

Olympic team. Otherwise, printed information is available in English detailing the exhibits of each room.

Continuing along Kossuth utca across the bridge you come to the "Buttler House" that featured in Mikszáth's novel *A Strange Marriage*. Alternatively, follow Bajcsy-Zsilinszky or Érsek utca into **Dobó István tér**, the starting point for further sightseeing. Along one side of the square stands the former **Minorite church**, a twin-towered Baroque edifice completed in 1771. The Latin inscription above its entrance asserts that "Nothing is Enough for God". Equally striking are the action-packed statues of warriors that commemorate the two sieges of Eger during the Turkish invasion – a tale of heroism known to every Hungarian. Next door to the church is a small Palóc folk art exhibition (April–Oct Tues–Sun 9am–5pm).

The first **siege of 1552**, described in Géza Gárdonyi's panegyrical novel *Egri csillagok* (Stars of Eger), was an unexpected victory for the Magyars. Ensconced in the castle under the command of **István Dobó**, two thousand soldiers and Eger's **women** (who hurled rocks, hot soup and fat) repulsed a Turkish force six times their number – shattering the impetus of the Ottoman advance until 1596. In their second attempt, however, the Turks triumphed. Eger's garrison of foreign mercenaries surrendered after a week and the Ottoman troops sacked the town, leaving only "blackened walls and buildings razed to the ground" and "the naked bodies of Christians baking in the sun, in some places four yards high".

A short distance from Dobó István tér are two relics of the Turkish occupation (which lasted until 1687). Eger's most photographed structure is a slender, fourteen-sided **minaret**, rising forty metres above Knezich utca. Despite looking rather forlorn since its mosque was demolished in 1841, the minaret offers fine views from its balcony (daily 9am–5pm) – if the door is locked, the reception desk of the adjacent *Hotel Minaret* will loan you a key. A passing glance suffices for the unimpressive remains of a **Turkish Bath**, en route to Eger Castle.

Eger Castle

With every approach covered by batteries of cannons, you can easily appreciate why **Eger Castle** was so formidable. Ascending from its lower gate past the Gergely Bastion, you enter the inner section of the castle through the Várkoch Bastion. On top of this lies the **tomb of Geza Gárdonyi**, on which is inscribed "Only his body lies here". Separate tickets for the Bishop's Palace and the underground *Kazamata* are sold at the ticket office straight ahead (daily 9am–5pm; Monday *Kazamata* and Hall of Heroes only). If you feel so inclined, you can also invest in an historical video (625Ft) and English-language cassette (120Ft) for a do-it-yourself tour.

One of the few Gothic structures left in northeastern Hungary, the **Bishop's Palace** harbours a **museum** containing tapestries, Turkish handicrafts and weaponry. On the ground floor are temporary exhibits and a "**Hall of Heroes**" (*Hősök terme*) where István Dobó is buried amid a bodyguard of siege heroes, the latter carved in best Stakhanovite style. The adjacent **art gallery** boasts several fine Munkácsys and three romantic Transylvanian landscapes by Antal Ligeti.

To the east of this complex lies a jumble of medieval foundations signposted as a *Romkert* or **Garden of Ruins**. Here stood Eger's Gothic cathedral, which was damaged by fire in 1506 and used as a gunpowder magazine during the first siege; the Turks used it as an arsenal "to spite the Christians". To the south, tour groups gather outside the concrete tunnel entrance to the *Kazamata* or **underground**

galleries, a labyrinth of sloping passages, gun emplacements, deep-cut observation shafts and mysterious chambers.

Wine and the Szépasszony Valley

Although the **Wine Museum** at Városfal utca 1 (Tues–Sat noon–10pm) offers a display of viticultural implements to whet your palate, it's more fun to go drinking in the **Szépasszony Valley**, just west of town (accessible by taxi). The "Valley of the Beautiful Women" is surrounded by dozens of vineyards producing four types of **wine** – *Muskotály* (Muscatel), *Bikavér* (the famous Bull's Blood), *Leányka* (medium dry white with a hint of herbs) and *Médoc Noir* (rich, dark red and sweet; coats your tongue black).

Finding the right **wine cellar** is a matter of luck and taste – some are dank and gloomy, and some have their own **musicians** (who appear only when tourist numbers have reached critical mass). Most cellars are open daily until 6–8pm or later, depending on custom. Particularly recommended are no. 31 whose proprietor Mr Szilagyi speaks English (try his excellent *Médoc Noir*); and no. 32 where János Birincsik stocks some fine old wines, including a vintage *Bikavér*.

Getting back into town is more of a challenge unless you've already arranged for a taxi to come and pick you up or you don't mind hoofing it (a 20-min walk). There's only one pay phone in the valley, just at the entrance before the row of *büfés* (snack bars); *City Taxi* can be reached on ☎412-111 and *Eger Taxi* on ☎311-222 (expect to pay around 300–400Ft).

> The Eger telephone code is ☎36

Practicalities

Travellers arriving at the **bus terminus** can easily stroll into the centre; coming from the **train station**, walk up the road to Deák Ferenc út, catch bus #10 or #12 and get off just before the cathedral.

The best source of **information** is *Tourinform* at Dobó István tér 2 (May–Oct daily 9am–6pm; winter Mon–Fri 9am–5pm & Sat 9am–2pm; ☎321-807) who do everything except book private rooms. Otherwise try *Eger Tourist* at Bajcsy-Zsilinszky utca 9 (summer 9am–7.30pm; winter 9am–5pm; ☎311-724) or *Ibusz* in the passage just behind (☎312-526).

Car rentals are available from *Welcome Tours* at Jókai utca 5 (Mon–Fri 8am–4pm & Sat 8–11.30am; ☎313-220) – about the cheapest vehicle on offer is a Lada at 1200Ft per day (plus tax and 12Ft per km). *Eger Tourist* rent better cars from between 2000Ft and 4500Ft per day plus tax (20 percent). **Bikes** can be rented from *Lajos Víg* at Maklári út 105 (☎317-134) for 800Ft a day or 400Ft for half a day.

Accommodation

As well as the booking services offered by *Eger Tourist* and *Ibusz*, Eger has two agencies that deal solely with accommodation: *Express* at Széchenyi utca 28 (Mon–Fri 9am–5pm & Sat 9am–1pm; ☎310-757) and the privately owned *Villa Tours* at Deák út 55 (April–Sept Mon–Fri 10am–8pm, Sat 10am–6pm & Sun 2–6pm; Oct–March Mon–Fri 10am–6pm; ☎317-803).

The cheapest lodgings are **student hostels** (*kollégiums*), bookable through *Express* or *Villa Tours* – multi-bed rooms can be found at Leányka utca 2, 100m east of the castle (late June to late August; ☎412-066; ①); Rákóczi utca 2 (April to mid-June weekends only; summer daily; ☎311-211; ①); Klapka György utca 10 (summer daily; winter weekends only; ☎313-943; ①); and Pozsonyi utca 4–6 (mid-June to Aug; ☎324-122; ①). **Private rooms** (②) can also be booked through *Eger Tourist, Ibusz* or *Villa Tours* (the latter charging a higher commission than the others).

HOTELS, MOTELS AND PENSIONS

Flóra Hotel, Fürdo utca 5 (☎320-211). Close to the entrance to the thermal baths. Only slightly cheaper than the *Park-Eger*. ⑤.

Fortuna Panzió, Kapás utca 35A (☎316-480). West of the first junction on Deák út as you come up from the train station. ②.

Hotel Park-Eger, Klapka György utca 8 (☎413-233). Three-star establishment with the full range of facilities and prices to match. ⑤.

MAV Turista Szállás, Allomás tér 2 (☎314-264). Plain but clean 4-bed rooms by the station. ① per person.

Minaret Hotel, Knezich utca 2 (☎410-020). Another well-situated two-star establishment, facing the minaret. ④.

Senátor-ház Hotel, Dobó István tér 11 (☎320-466). A lovely eighteenth-century inn near the castle. ⑤.

Tourist Motel, Mekcsey utca 2 (☎310-014). Just off Szarvas tér. Rooms sleeping 2–4 persons, with or without bathroom. ②.

Unicornis Hotel, Kossuth utca (☎312-886). One of the cheaper options in town. ②–③.

Villa Völgy, Tulipánkert utca 5, Szepasszonyvólgy (☎321-664). Comfortable place favoured by German bus groups. ③.

CAMPSITES

Autó Camping, 3km north of the centre by bus #10 or #11 (☎310-558). Two-person bungalows (②) and huts (①), tent space, a restaurant and snack bar. Open mid-April to mid-Oct.

Tulipán Camping (☎410-580), across the road from the riding centre at the entrance to the Szépasszony Valley. A newly opened, smaller site.

Eating and drinking

With a dozen restaurants and takeaways around the centre (especially on Almagyár utca), eating out in Eger is never a problem. The elegant *Dobos Cukrászda* at Széchenyi utca 6 and the outdoor *Pallas Presszó*, beneath the castle walls, are good for coffee and pastries. *Kopcsik Cukraszda* at Kossuth utca 28 is the best patisserie in town, with scrumptious parfaits and cakes decorated with marzipan icing to look like Palóc and Matyó embroidery.

Good, inexpensive and popular with locals are the *Vörös Rák* (Red Crab) at Szent János utca 11, with piano music at night, and the *Talizman* at Kossuth utca 19. About the cheapest **restaurant** in town is the *Várkapu Vendeglő*, further along Kossuth utca at no. 26, a self-service affair from 11am to 3pm with waiters later on (4–11pm). Somewhat dearer but still reasonable value are the *Mecset*, opposite the minaret with a nice garden and music (closed Mon); the *Dervis Halászkert* which offers fish specialities near the castle entrance; and the *Vadászkurt* at Érsek utca 4 (reservations advisable; ☎310-508). The *Fehér Szarvas* (White Stag), next to the *Park-Eger Hotel*, is also good but expensive (6.30pm–midnight). Recommended more as a sight than a potential eating place is the *Kazamata*, beneath the cathedral steps – a bizarre place resembling a set from *2001* crossed with the *Führerbunker*, all concrete, split levels and gloom.

For **drinking**, head out to the cellars of the **Szépasszony Valley** (see above) to sample the local wines. If you get hungry, you can eat there at the *Kulacs Csárda* or the *Ködmön Fogadó*. For those who prefer **beer**, there's the *HBH Söröző* on Dobó István tér, in town.

Eger activities

Contact *Eger Tourist* (address above) if you're interested in **horse riding** in the Szépasszony or Szalajka valleys, or **aeroplane tours** over town (May–Aug; 450Ft per person). Alternatively, head for the **thermal baths** and **swimming pool** (May–Sept daily 8.30am–7.30pm), where half the town comes to wallow and splash at weekends during summertime. Folk or rock **concerts** are sometimes held in the open-air theatre at the end of the Szépasszony Valley.

Moving on

There are five direct **trains** to Budapest daily; ten to Füzesabony on the Budapest–Miskolc line; five to Putnok (see "Stalactite Caves in the Aggtelek" on p.271); and one direct train to Szeged every week. **Buses** from the terminus on Pyrker tér cover a range of destinations including Budapest (last express service 5.45pm), Mátraháza, Kecskemét, Szeged and the Aggtelek Caves (8.50am daily); hourly buses also run to Szilvásvárad, calling at Bélapátfalva along the way. At weekends there are two buses **through the Bükk mountains to Miskolc** (leaving at 7am and 11.25am) via Felsőtarkány, one of several villages accessible by bus from where you can head into the mountains **on foot** (see below).

Up to Szilvásvárad and the Szalajka Valley

The road and rail line skirt the western foothills of the Bükk as they wiggle northwards towards Putnok, and 12km out from Eger the scenery is promisingly lush around **SZARVASKŐ** (Stag Rock), a pretty village with a ruined thirteenth-century castle and two hotels – the *Turistaszálló* (☎36/352-085) and the *Debmut* (☎36/352-057), both on Rózsa utca. Further on, quarries and an ugly cement factory spoil the view at **BÉLAPÁTFALVA**, where the sole reason to stop is a well-preserved Romanesque **abbey church** (Tues–Sun 9am–4pm) founded by French Cistercian monks in 1232. To get to the church, follow the signpost off the main road for 2km. On chilly days, the caretaker can be found at Rózsa utca 42 – look for the *"apátság gondnok"* sign on the right shortly after leaving the main road.

Szilvásvárad

Eight kilometres further north, **SZILVÁSVÁRAD** occupies a dell beside wooded mountains rising to the east. Once the private estate of the pro-fascist Pallavinici family, and then a workers' resort after 1945, nowadays it is chiefly known as a breeding centre for **Lippizaner horses** (see box below) and the site of Hungary's annual coach-driving championship, the **Bükk Trophy** (usually held the last weekend in Aug). Those who feel inspired to go **horse riding** themselves should head for the *Péter Kovács* stables, just out of town on the main highway to Eger (☎36/355-155; 700–800Ft per hour).

You don't have to be mad on horses to enjoy the **Horsebreeding Exhibition** (Tues–Sun 9am–5pm) at Park utca 8, which is reached via the Transylvanian-

---

LIPPIZANER HORSES

Descended from Spanish, Arabian and Berber stock, **Lippizaner horses** are bred at six European stud farms. The original stud was founded near Trieste in 1580 by the Habsburg archduke Karl, but when Napoleon's troops invaded Italy its horses were brought to Mezőhegyes in southern Hungary for safekeeping. Lippizaner horses are comparatively small in stature (14.3–15.2 hands tall), with a long back, a short, thick neck and a powerful build. They are usually white or grey. Like their counterparts at the famous Spanish Riding School in Vienna, Szilvásvárad's horses are trained to perform bows, provettes and other manoeuvres that delight dressage cognoscenti.

---

style wooden gate just beyond the *Hotel Lipicai*. The exhibition includes a collection of coaches and a stable of beautiful white Lippizaners. The totemic columns in the park around the stud farm are dedicated to the memory of the farm director's beloved mount, Zánka, who died in harness of a heart attack – evoking the time of the Magyar conquest, when favourite horses were buried in graves.

Except during the coach-driving championships, there shouldn't be any problem with **accommodation**. Along the road in from Eger you'll find the *Hotel Lipicai* (☎36/355-100; ②) and the slightly cheaper *Szalajka Fogadó* (☎36/355-257; ②). At Park utca 6 are the reasonably priced *Szilvás Kastély Hotel* and *Panzió* (☎36/355-211; ②), with tennis courts and other facilities. There's a campsite (open year-round) attached to the latter, and another one – *Hegyi Camping* (☎36/355-207) – at Egri út 36 (May to mid-Oct). **Private rooms** (①) are available from the branch of *Eger Tourist* at Egri út 22 (☎36/355-268), whilst *Express* in Eger can make bookings at the inexpensive *Pluto Szálló* (☎36/320-155; ②).

The Szalajka Valley

If you don't fancy walking a couple of kilometres, it's possible to travel by narrow-gauge train from Szilvásvárad into the **Szalajka Valley**, which really begins at *szikla-forrás*, a gushing rock cleft beyond the food stalls and captive **stags** that guard its approaches. Signposted just off the main path is an outdoor **Forestry Museum** (*Erdei Múzeum*) exhibiting weathered huts and tools (including an ingenious water-powered forge) once used by the charcoal-burners and foresters of the Bükk (April–Nov Tues–Sun 9am–4pm). Trout is on every restaurant's menu round here, freshly caught from the streams of the Szalajka Valley.

Higher up, the valley is boxed in by mountains, with paths snaking through the woods to the triangular **Istállóskői cave** (*barlang*) and the barefaced **Mount Istállóskő** – which at 959m is the highest in the Bükk range. The second highest, Bákvány, can be reached by footpath from Istállóskő (8km) or from Nagyvisnyó (9km), the next settlement after Szilvásvárad and on the same branch rail line.

The Bükk Mountains

Beech trees – *bükk* – cover the mountains between Eger and Miskolc, giving the region its name. Unlike most of the northern mountains, **the Bükk** were formed from sedimentary limestone, clay slate and dolomite and are riddled with sink-holes and caves that were home to the earliest tribes of *Homo sapiens*, hunters of mammoths and reindeer. As civilization developed elsewhere, the Bükk declined in importance – except as a source of timber – until the start of the nineteenth century, when Henrik Fazola built a blast furnace in the Garadna Valley, exploiting the iron ore which today feeds the metallurgical works in Miskolc. While industry continues to shape the grim towns of Miskolc, Ózd and Kazincbarcika, almost four hundred square kilometres of the Bükk have been declared a **national park and wildlife refuge**. This can be explored superficially by train and bus, or thoroughly if you're prepared to do some hiking.

If you are planning to **hike**, a *Bükk hegység* **map** is essential. Since paths are well marked and settlements are rarely more than 15km apart, it's hard to go far astray walking, but a few **preparations** are advisable. Food and supplies should be purchased beforehand, together with insect repellent/bite cream and a canteen. Drinking water (*ivóvíz*) isn't always available, though many of the springs are pure and delicious. To be sure of **accommodation**, make reservations through *Eger Tourist* in Eger or *Borsod Tourist* in Miskolc. If need be, you can also sleep in shelters (*esőház*) dotted around the mountains.

The Bükk is particularly lovely in autumn, when its foliage turns bright orange and yellow, contrasting with the silvery tree trunks. Among the mountain flora are violet blue monk's hood which blooms at the end of summer, yellow lady's slipper, an endangered species in Europe, and the Turk's cap lily. The undergrowth is home to badgers, beech martens, ermines and other animals, and you might encounter rock thrushes and other birds in abandoned quarries, or see an imperial eagle (*Aquila heliaca*) cruising overhead. The seldom-glimpsed "smooth" snake isn't poisonous.

Approaches from Eger

Starting **from Eger**, the most direct approach to the mountains is to take a bus, getting off somewhere along the route to Miskolc, or the rail branch line up to **FELSŐTÁRKÁNY** – an ideal starting point for walks and a lovely village in its own right with parks, ponds and vine-laden gardens. Paths also lead into the Bükk from Bélapátfalva, Szilvásvárad and Nagyvisnyó, north of the range (see above), and from villages to the south, accessible by bus from Eger. On the south side, arrowheads and other remains were found in the **Subalyuk Cave**, a Paleolithic dwelling 2km from **BÜKKZSÉRC** and **CSERÉPFALU** at the start of one of the footpaths. Further east "rocking stones" and hollowed-out pillars – used by medieval beekeepers and known as "hive rocks" – line the rocky **Felső-szoros ravine** north of **CSERÉPVÁRALJA**.

Accommodation is offered by two villages on this side of the mountains. Felsőtárkány has the *Park-Hotel Táltos*, Ifjúság utca 1 (Mar to late Nov; ☎36/320-760; ③), and the cheaper *Szikla Fogadó*, Fő utca 313 (open year-round; ☎36/320-904; ②). Noszvaj, 13km from Eger, features a Baroque mansion converted into the *De La Motte Kastély Hotel* at Dobó utca 10 (Noszvaj ☎2; ②), and two pensions – the *Bükk Panzió*, Béke út 73 (②), and the *Pepsi Panzió* at József utca 10 (☎36/363-094; ②) – all open year-round.

Approaches from Miskolc

The Bükk can also be visited **from Miskolc** (see p.265), which offers a number of approaches. From Újgyőri főtér in the western part of the city (bus #101 from Tiszai Station) a #68 bus will take you to **BÜKKSZENTLÁSZLÓ**. From here you can either walk or hitch via **BÜKKSZENTKERESZT** on to **HOLLÓSTETŐ** (6km further on) – the latter is on the Miskolc–Eger bus route, although services are infrequent. Bükkszentkereszt offers **private rooms** (☎46/350-694; ②), while Hollóstető features a **campsite** with **bungalows** (May to mid-Sept; ☎46/392-983; ①).

The easiest approach, however, is to aim for **Lillafüred** (see below), a small resort that's accessible by bus #5 or #105 from Majális Park in the western part of the city (bus #1 from Tiszai Station), or by narrow-gauge train from Miskolc's Killian Észak terminal (accessible by bus #101).

The train and buses #5 and #115 continue via Újmassa to Ómassa, further up the valley. The rail line also runs northwards from Miskolc along the Csanyik Valley, but this route is less suitable for entering the Bükk. All these places are marked on the "Environs of Miskolc" map on p.269.

Lillafüred and its caves

LILLAFÜRED ("Lilla Bath") was named after Lilla, the wife of Count András Bethlen who established the place as a resort in 1892. Despite its weekend popularity, Lillafüred can still be peaceful and romantic, with its lake and grand hotel set amidst wooded hills.

The village's principal attractions are three **stalactite caves** (*barlang*) that can be visited on guided tours, starting every hour or so from each cave entrance (mid-April to mid-Oct daily 9am–5pm; mid-Oct to mid-April daily 9am–4pm). Tucked away above the Miskolc road, the **Szeleta Cave** was found to contain Ice Age spearheads and tools. The **Anna Cave**, beside the road up to the hotel, has a long entrance passage and six chambers linked by stairs formed from limestone. If your appetite for stalactites is still unsatiated, walk 1km down the road towards Eger to find the **István Cave**, which is longer and less convoluted, with a "cupola hall" of stalactites, various pools and chambers.

Two hundred metres beyond this stands the wooden **house of Ottó Herman** (1835–1914), where the naturalist and ethnographer spent many years trapping and mounting local wildlife. Stuffed boars, birds and rodents, plus an extraordinary collection of giant beetles are the main attraction, but you can also see Ottó's top hat and butterfly nets, and a letter from Kossuth.

Lake Hámori, just north of Lillafüred, is used for **boating** during the summer and **ice skating** in winter.

Accommodation

Dominating the resort is the grand *Palota Hotel* (☎46/317-873; ③), a nostalgic creation built in 1927 in the style of a medieval hunting lodge – note the windows in its moderately priced restaurant, the *Mátyás Terem*, which represent towns from the former Hungarian territories lost in the Treaty of Trianon. Just around the bend from the *Palota*, the friendly *Szikla Turistaház* (☎46/354-469; ①) offers alternative lodgings in the form of an old army bunker built into the cliffs overlooking the lake. Though plain, the rooms are spotless and unbelievably cheap, with views of the lake to boot; the place also has a restaurant serving tasty home-cooked meals. Another possibility, albeit less memorable, is the *Lilla Panzió* at Erszébet sétány 7 (☎46/351-299; ②).

Újmassa and beyond

Open trains filled with shrieking children continue from Lillafüred up the Garadna Valley, which cleaves the Bükk plateau. At **ÚJMASSA**, the next stop, a

nineteenth-century foundry (Tues–Sun 9am–5pm) attests to the work of **Henrik Fazola**, a Bavarian-born Eger locksmith, and his son Frigyes, who first exploited the iron ore deposits of the Bükk. Nearby are the sooty camps of **charcoal burners**, who still live for part of the year in the forest.

ÓMASSA, further up the valley, is the last stop on the train and bus routes. From here it's a few hours' walk up a well-marked path to **Mount Bálvány**, south of which lies the "Great Meadow" (*Nagymező*) where wild horses graze. A ski chalet and the summits of **Nagy-Csipkés** (822m) and **Zsérci-Nagy-Dél** (875m) can be reached to the east, but more impressive crags lie to the south – **Tárkő** (950m) and **Istállóskő**. The land drops rapidly south of Tárkő, and water from the plateau descends through sinkholes, bursting forth in a spring at **Vörös-kő** (Red Rock). During winter, when the plateau is covered with snow, the entrances to these **sinkholes** are marked by rising steam.

MISKOLC AND THE AGGTELEK RANGE

To the north and east of Bükk National Park are the three cities that comprise Hungary's "Rust Belt", a region afflicted by the collapse of its heavy industry. **Miskolc**, straddling the road and rail network, is hard to avoid, but possibly deserves a visit if only for its gritty character and the "thrashing" cave baths in its resort suburb. **Ózd** and **Kazincbarcika** have no such redeeming features, except their transport links to more appealing destinations, including the wonderful **stalactite caves at Aggtelek** near the Slovak border.

Miskolc

Despite the fact that **MISKOLC** (pronounced "MISH-koltz") is Hungary's third largest city (recently surpassed by Debrecen), most residents express incredulity that any visitor might wish to spend time here. Tourist offices send you packing to the leafy mountain resort of Lillafüred or the lively cave baths at Miskolc-Tapolca, both of which offer attractive, moderately priced accommodation.

The city itself does have one or two attractions, though, including a medieval castle in its western suburbs and a summer festival featuring all kinds of performing arts. Its downside is high unemployment (currently running at 35 percent), industrial decline, boarded-up hotels and restaurants, and drab windswept housing estates. Sadly, the Gypsies have become the local scapegoats in all of this and "Gypsy-bashing" has become a problem in recent years. The council responded at one point by proposing that all Gypsies be moved to an outlying estate – a plan only dropped after a national outcry.

The City

The main downtown street is **Széchenyi út**, whose eclectic mix of boutiques and restaurants, interspersed with Baroque facades painted pea green and sky blue or in the last stages of decrepitude, gives the impression of a boom and slump

DOWNTOWN MISKOLC

Plank Church

0 200 m

PETOFI TER

JOKAI MOR UTCA

DOZSA GY. UTCA

Orthodox Ecclesiastical Museum

Greek Orthodox Church

BATTHYANY UTCA

Intercity Bus Station

ADY UTCA

BUZA TER

DEAK TER

PALOCZY UTCA

HOSOK TERE

Local Bus Station

To the Queen's Castle

KOSSUTH UTCA

DERYNE UTCA

KAZINCZY UTCA

Synagogue

REGIPOSTA UTCA

To Gömöri Train Station (700 m)

Ibusz

Hotel Pannónia

Express

BAJCSY-ZSILINSKY UT

KIRALY UTCA

SZECHENYI UT

Borsod Tourist

Baths

ERSZEBET TER

ARANY UTCA

VOROSMARTY UTCA

Cooptourist

Ottó Herman Museum

VOROSMARTY UTCA

To Tiszai Train Station (1 km)

Reformed Church

PAPSZER

To the TV Tower

GERGELY UTCA

KIS AVAS

CORVIN UTCA

Avas Hill

To Miskolc-Tapolca

Tourinform

MINDSZENT TER

To Népkert

happening simultaneously. In the backstreets to the north and south, nineteenth-century artisans' dwellings crouch in gardens, overshadowed by concrete high-rises. Such contrasts make the downtown area the most appealing part of Miskolc.

One block north of the main stretch, **Hősök tere** is flanked by two imposing buildings. The still-functioning **Synagogue** was designed by Ludwig Förster, the architect of the great synagogue in Budapest. Its magnificent but crumbling interior seems painfully empty on major feast days: only 250 Jews now live in Miskolc, whose pre-war Jewish population numbered 118,000 (of whom 114,000 were taken to the death camps). Ask at the office behind the synagogue for the keys. On the northern side of the square stands a former **Minorite Church** and monastery, dating from 1729–40.

Off to the right and round the corner, trees screen a **Greek Orthodox Church** founded by descendants of the Greeks who fled here from the Turks in the seventeenth century. Beside the entrance, at Deák tér 7, is an **Orthodox Ecclesiastical Museum** (April–Oct Tues–Sun 10am–6pm; Nov–March Tues–Sun 10am–4pm) containing religious art from all over Hungary. The church itself has a sixteen-metre-high iconostasis resembling a giant advent calendar, inset with the "Black Mary of Kazan" presented by Catherine the Great of Russia, and a jewelled cross from Mount Athos, both of which play a major part in Sunday services (liturgy at 10.30am). Due to lack of both funds and visitors, this is the only time that the church is actually open, though a key can be obtained from the caretaker at the museum. Until a few years ago, when their old homes were pulled down, the Greek quarter was situated around Búza tér.

Further north, beyond Petőfi tér, the spooky-looking **Plank Church** languishes like an unwanted import from Transylvania. Such Gothic-style wooden churches are rare in Hungary but common in northern Romania, where this kind of architecture reached its zenith in the eighteenth century. The interior is nothing special, however.

Avas Hill

To the south of Széchenyi út, a *fin-de-siècle* **bathhouse** (Tues–Sat 6–11am & 1–5pm, Sun 6am–noon) frames the view of **Avas Hill**. The Gothic **Reformed Church** at the bottom dates from 1560, although the pews – decorated with flower motifs – were added later. Its **wooden belfry** is separate from the church, as required by Counter-Reformation ordinances. From here, a maze of paths snakes upwards to the **Television Tower** and observation platform on the hill's summit. The right-hand paths climb through an extraordinary shantytown of miniature villas and rock-hewn wine cellars (some of them up to 50m deep), guarded by savage dogs. At the far end of Mendikás utca is an overgrown **Jewish Cemetery** with beautifully carved gravestones that date back to the eighteenth century.

The **Ottó Herman Museum**, at the bottom of the hill (Tues–Sun 10am–6pm), contains a dazzling collection of folk costumes, along with a section devoted to pottery. The pile of broken mugs is a result of the tradition of drinking and then smashing your mug at wakes.

The Queen's Castle

The oldest building in Miskolc is the **Queen's Castle** or *Diósgyőr vár* (April–Oct Tues–Sun 9am–6pm), located in the western suburb of Diósgyőr, beyond the steelworks. Built for King Louis between 1350 and 1375, the castle marked the introduction of the southern Italian type of fortress to Hungary. Though eminently defendable, it served chiefly as a royal holiday home and a residence for dowager queens. Blown up in the Rákóczi wars, it has been crudely restored with breeze blocks and poured concrete, but the views from its towers of Miskolc and the Bükk mountains are as splendid as ever. To get there, catch a #1 or #101 bus to the Ady Endre Cultural Centre and walk towards the four stone towers poking above the rooftops.

Miskolc-Tapolca

Given the drabness of Miskolc itself, it's hardly surprising that so many people head out to **MISKOLC-TAPOLCA**, a resort suburb twenty minutes' ride from Búza tér (bus #2 or #102). Crammed with holiday homes and school parties, its main attractions are an outdoor **pool** (late May to mid-Sept daily 8am–6pm), complete with rowing boats, water slides, electronic cars and rides; and the *barlang fürdő* or **cave baths** (daily 9am–1pm & 2–6pm), a series of dimly lit warm water grottoes, culminating in a "thrashing shower". Visitors who go **mushroom hunting** in the Bükk can have their fungi checked at the *Gomba Vizsgalat* hut (mid-May to mid-Nov daily 1–6pm) near the #2 bus terminal. There are snack stands aplenty and a **disco** in the *Hotel Juno*, as well as a wide range of hotels and private rooms (see "Accommodation" below).

> The telephone code for Miskolc and Miskolc-Tapolca is ☎46

Practicalities

Your likeliest point of **arrival** in Miskolc will be the **Tiszai train station**, one kilometre east of the centre, or the **intercity bus terminal** on Búza tér. From Tiszai Station you can catch a #1 or #101 bus to the castle or Majális Park (for Lillafüred: see p.264 and "The Bükk Mountains", p.262), or a #1 or #2 tram into the centre, getting off at Széchenyi út. From Búza tér you can either walk into the centre, or head straight for Miskolc-Tapolca by bus (#2 or #102). Should you arrive at the **Gömöri train station** instead, walk down to Zsolcai kapu, catch any bus heading west and alight near Ady utca.

For tourist **information**, the English-speaking staff at *Tourinform*, in the International Trade Centre at Mindzsent tér 1 (☎46/348-921), are extremely helpful and well informed – the only thing they won't do is book accommodation. Miskolc's other tourist offices include the remarkably unhelpful *Borsod Tourist* at Széchenyi út 35 (summer Mon–Fri 7am–5pm & Sat 9am–noon; winter Mon–Fri 7am–5pm; ☎350-666); *Ibusz* at Kossuth utca 2 (Mon–Fri 9am–5pm & Sat 9am–1pm; ☎324-411 or ☎353-465); *Express* and *Cooptourist*.

Accommodation

The closure of many hotels in Miskolc has narrowed the choice of accommodation. **Private rooms** can be booked through one of the tourist agencies listed above, but these tend to be inconveniently situated in housing estates on the edge of town. You're better off paying extra to stay in a **hotel** or **pension** in the centre. The *Gösser Udvar,* just off Széchenyi út at Déryné utca 7 (☎357-111; ③), has six rooms and a restaurant; or there's the plush and pricey *Hotel Pannónia* at Kossuth utca 2 (☎329-811; ⑤) with 34 rooms. At Kisavas 18, the *Korona Panzió* (☎358-400; ②) enjoys a picturesque location at the foot of Avas Hill.

As usual, student **hostels** are the cheapest option for solo travellers. The best is the *Teréz Kollégium* (①) at Győri kapu út 156 (bus #1 or tram), open full time from late June to late August, and at weekends throughout the year. The University Town (*Egyetemváros*) in the hills south of town (bus #12 from Hősök tere) is another possibility.

Private **rooms in Miskolc-Tapolca** can be arranged through *Borsod Tourist* at Károlyi Mihály utca 1 (☎368-917; ②), next to *Eden Camping*. There are numerous **hotels** along and just off the main road: try the *Mini Motel* at Branyiszkó utca 4 (☎368-104; ②–③); the *Hotel Lido* at Győri utca 4 (☎369-800; ②–③); the *Park Motel* at Bak utca 4 (☎360-811; ②–③); or the *Leányvárlak,* a new tourist hostel at Zója utca 124 (☎369-0421; ②). Dearer doubles are to be found along Martos utca, at the *Zenit Panzió* at no. 25 (☎366-811; ③) and the *Flóra Panzió* at no. 35 (☎368-

116; ③); or there's the three-star *Hotel Junó* at Csabai utca 2–4 (☎364-133; ④). **Bungalows** and tent space can be rented at two **campsites**: *Éden Camping* (mid-April to Oct; ☎368-421), a kind of manicured parking lot near the *Hotel Junó*; and *Autós Camping* (May to mid-Sept; ☎367-171), a leafier site popular with motorists, 2km up along Iglói út.

Eating and drinking

There's a **restaurant** attached to the *Hotel Pannónia* on Széchenyi út, and a few paces away the *Rori Cukrászda* is a good place for coffee and cakes – better than the smoky *Rác Kávéház* further along. For snacks, check out the **market** beside the local bus terminal. *Biggaton*, round the corner from *Ibusz*, serves decent pizza, and excellent pancakes can be had at the *Hagi Étterem* at Zsolcai kapu 5.

Miskolc's **drinking holes** include the flash *Spatzen Pince* beside the *Hotel Pannónia*; the *HBH Söröző* on Újgyőri főtér (off Győri kapu út); and the *Lokál Bar* on Budai József utca, south of the Népkert (park).

Entertainment

The city is at its liveliest during the **Miskolc Summer Festival** (June–Aug) when jazz, classical music and operas are performed at the Queen's Castle in Diósgyőr and in Miskolc-Tapolca. One of the festival's highlights is the interna-

ENVIRONS OF MISKOLC

tional **Kaláka Folklore Festival** in July, which attracts *Táncház* groups from all over Hungary and folkloric troupes from abroad. Events are advertised around town and tickets are available at Déryné utca 1 (☎344-711) – ask *Tourinform* or *Ibusz* for details.

Miskolc's **nightlife** boils down to **discos** at various cultural centres (as advertised on posters and at tourist agencies), and the "Bar Varíte" floor show at the *Tokaj* penthouse overlooking Győri kapu út (which also has a disco, and a beer hall downstairs).

For those into **football**, the DVTK stadium lies out along Győri kapu út, towards the castle. Also worthy of a mention is the **Kossuth Cinema** (next to *Ibusz*), which boasts a grand lobby and auditorium dating from the turn of the century.

Moving on

If you're not heading into the Bükk (see p.262), there are regular **trains** from Tiszai Station to the Zemplén, Szerencs, the Great Plain and the capital. The fastest services to Budapest are the non-stop *Borsod*, *Hámor*, *Sajó* and *Lillafüred* expresses (1hr 45min). Tornanádaska-bound slow trains from Gömöri Station can drop you at the *Jósvafő-Aggtelek vá*, for the caves of Aggtelek (see below). The latter is also accessible by bus (Mon–Fri 7.30am & Sat 9.30am) from Búza tér. Other long-distance **buses** – to Debrecen, Eger, Kecskemét, Szeged, Nyíregyháza and Salgótarján – also tend to leave early in the morning.

Volán **buses** run from Miskolc to the Slovakian towns of Rožňava and Košice, while express **trains** depart from Tiszai station for Kraków (*Cracovia*) in Poland, Warsaw (*Karpaty*) and Poprad-Tatry (*Rákóczi*), all calling at Košice along the way.

Kazincbarcika and Ózd

A planner's dream and a resident's nightmare, **KAZINCBARCIKA** was created in the Fifties for the purpose of manufacturing chemicals and energy from the coal deposits of the north. Laid out in a grid, its endless rows of numbingly identical *lakótelep* are ineffectually separated from the town's industrial zone by 500 metres of withered grass. Though decimated by state closures of its loss-making industries, the town still has the dubious distinction of being the only residential area in the world where a dangerous pesticide is manufactured.

Ózd

Of the three villages that originally stood here, only the **fifteenth-century churches** of Barcika and Sajókazinc and the **wooden belfry** of Berente remain. Though they're hardly worth staying the night for, the *Hotel Polimer* on Ifjúsági körtér lives in hope (☎48/311-911; ③).

ÓZD, which likewise contributes to the pollution of the River Sajó, has been harder hit by industrial decline than anywhere else in Hungary and its prospects remain grim despite endless rumours of German investment. While its southeastern suburb of lace-curtained brick houses with gardens is reminiscent of small towns in the Rhondda or Ohio Valley, Ózd's modernized centre is utterly depressing, and notorious for gang violence. It's there that you'll find the bus terminal – whose **services to Aggtelek** (daily around 8am, noon & 3pm) are the only reason to come here – and the *Hotel Kohász* at Ív út 9 (☎48/471-344; ③).

Stalactite Caves in the Aggtelek

Like the Bükk, the **Aggtelek range** bordering Slovakia displays typical **karstic** features such as gullies, sinkholes and caves, caused by a mixture of water and carbon dioxide dissolving the limestone. The **Baradla caves** between the villages of Aggtelek and Jósvafő, and the **Béke caves** to the southeast, constitute an amazing subterranean world with Stygian lakes and rivers, waterfalls, countless stalactites and 262 species of wildlife. Set in remote countryside that's ideal for walking, cycling, and birdwatching, the caves are deservedly popular with tourists.

Getting to the Aggtelek entails catching an early bus from Budapest, Miskolc or Eger; or travelling later in the day, starting from Ózd (see above) or from Putnok, where there are **buses** to Aggtelek and Jósvafő every hour and a half. Putnok (linked to Ózd, Eger, Miskolc and Kazincbarcika by rail) is the last outpost of *Ibusz* and banks. Alternatively, slow **trains** from Miskolc to Tornanádaska can drop you at the Jósvafő-Aggtelek station, 10km east of Jósvafő, whence regular buses run to both villages (infrequently on Sundays).

Jósvafő and Aggtelek

Aside from the fortified church with its picturesque cemetery in **JÓSVAFŐ**, and the algae-green lake outside **AGGTELEK**, both villages are fairly unremarkable. Shops are few and social life centres around the church and "drink shop" (active from 4pm). Jósvafő has a tourist house at Rákóczi utca 1 where you can stay the night or, a couple of kilometres outside the village, there's the *Tengerszem Hotel* at Tengerszem oldal 2 (✆48/343-159 or ✆350-006; ③), surrounded by forest and hiking trails. Accommodation in Aggtelek consists of the 70-room *Hotel Cseppkő* at Gyömrői út 2 (✆48/343-075; ④), picturesquely situated on a hill by the entrance to the caves; and the nearby *Baradla Tourist House* at Baradla oldal 1 (✆48/343-073; ②), which also has four-person bungalows. Both the *Tengerszem* and the *Cseppkő* have **restaurants** and display local **bus schedules** in their lobbies.

Visiting the caves

Both sets of caves are open daily from 8am to 5pm (Oct–April until 3pm), but hourly guided tours begin only once at least five people have assembled at one of the entrances (*bejárat*), the last one leaving an hour before closing.

The main **Baradla cave passage** twists underground for 22km, hence the option of one-hour, one-and-a-half-hour or three-hour **tours**. The **Aggtelek end** of the passage is more convoluted and thus more rewarding for shorter tours. Entering the caves from the **Jósvafő** end, the last medium (*kozep*) tour is at 4pm (1pm in winter) and the last short (*rovid*) tour at 5pm (winter 3pm). No description can do justice to the variety and profusion of **stalactites and stalagmites**, whose nicknames can only hint at the fantastic formations, glittering with calcite crystals or stained ochre by iron oxides. Among them is the world's tallest stalagmite, a full 25 metres high. In the "Concert Hall", boats sway on the "River Styx", and the guide activates a tape of Bach's *Toccata in D minor* to create a *Phantom of the Opera* type ambience.

Longer tours of the Baradla passage begin at the Vörös-tó entrance, situated in the Cool Valley (*Hideg völgy*) between the two villages, and require some stamina: three hours is a long time to clamber around dank, muddy caves, however beautiful they are.

Guided tours around the **Béke caves** are also fairly demanding. Although they contain a sanatorium, the underground air being judged beneficial to asthmatics, most of the caves are, in fact, untamed, even unexplored, and as recently as 1973 a new passage was found when cavers penetrated a thirty-metre waterfall. You'll need boots and warm, waterproof clothing, and visitors are issued with helmets. **Underground wildlife** – bats, rodents and bugs, mostly – keeps out of sight, and is easiest to view in the **Cave Museum** (Tues–Sun 10am–6pm) by the Aggtelek entrance, which also has photos and mementoes to gladden a speleologist's heart.

Excursions in the vicinity

The surrounding countryside is riddled with smaller caves and rock formations, clearly marked on the *Aggtelek és Jósvafő környékének* **map** sold at the Aggtelek cave entrance. This also shows the **border zone**, where armed guards still patrol with dogs, notwithstanding the demise of Communism. Always carry your passport when hiking. For those with a car or bike, lots of attractive **villages** are within reach in this part of the highlands, notably **RAGÁLY**, 11km back towards Putnok, and **RUDABÁNYA**, where the ten-million-year-old jawbone of *Rudapithecus hungaricus* – an ancient primate – can be seen at the mine where it was excavated.

THE ZEMPLÉN RANGE

The Zemplén range is the region to see in the north – largely unspoiled by industry and tourism, and richly textured by nature and history. Its volcanic soil and microclimates favour diverse wildlife (particularly snakes and birds of prey), whilst the architecture reflects a tradition of trade and cultural exchanges between the Great Plain and the Slovakian highlands. **Tokaj**, in the Tokaj-Hegyalja wine-making district, absorbs most of the region's tourists, surprisingly few of whom make it up to **Sárospatak**, site of the superb Rákóczi castle, or to little **Zemplén villages** such as Füzér or Lászlótanya, where Hungary's Stalinist dictator enjoyed hunting.

Approaches via Szerencs

Approaching Tokaj and the northern Zemplén from Miskolc* you're bound to pass through **SZERENCS**, a drab town with a reeking factory that's responsible for most of the chocolate produced in Hungary. If you've got time to kill between connections, pay a visit to the **fortified manor** at the far end of Rákóczi út, where István Bocskai (1557–1606) was elected Prince of Hungary. This event is recalled in the manor's **Zemplén Museum** (Mon–Fri 10am–noon), which also contains the world's third largest **collection of postcards** – 700,000 of them, donated by a local doctor.

Besides **trains** to Tokaj, Szerencs is the starting point for the branch line up to Hidasnémeti, via villages on the western side of the Zemplén; and for **buses** to Monok, Mád and Tállya in the Tokaj-Hegyalja (see below).

---

* The Miskolc–Szerencs–Sátoraljaújhely road bypasses all the villages en route, having been built to allow the Soviet Army rapid access to the plains in the event of war. During its construction house-building in the vicinity boomed, as contractors sold off materials on the quiet.

Tokaj and around

TOKAJ is to Hungary what Champagne is to France, and this small town has become a minor Mecca for wine snobs. Perched beside the confluence of the rivers Bodrog and Tisza, it's a place of sloping cobbled streets and faded ochre dwellings with wine cellars and nesting storks – all overlooked by lush vineyards climbing the hillside towards the "Bald Peak" and the inevitable television tower.

The Town

Coming from the train station, the first wine cellars (*bor pince*) in the old town centre pop up along the main street to Kossuth tér, interspersed with fried fish (*sült hal*) shops, and the rainbow-striped *Hotel Tokaj*. Further along are a couple of architectural "sights" – the old Town Hall and Rákóczi-Dessewffy mansion – but inevitably it's **wine** that attracts most people's attention (see box below).

Although lack of funds forces it to close over winter, the **Tokaj Museum** at Bethlen Gábor utca 7 (summer Tues–Sun 9am–5pm; closed in winter) puts on a brave face with displays of wine labels from Crimea, France and the Rhineland – where attempts to reproduce Tokaj all failed – and a huge antique wine press.

The former Greek Orthodox church at Bethlen utca 17 hosts periodic **exhibitions** of contemporary paintings and sculptures (April–Oct Tues–Sun). In a back-street around the corner stands a restored but empty synagogue with a storks' nest perched on its chimney. Other **architecture** worth a look includes the Zopf-style Town Hall at Rákóczi utca 44; the one-time Rákóczi-Dessewffy mansion at Bajcsy-Zsilinszky utca 15–17 (now a college); and Zopf and Baroque houses on Bethlen Gábor utca.

If you fancy a walk, follow the road behind Kossuth tér uphill to the summit of Tokaj's 516-metre-high "Bald Peak". The route takes you past dozens of vineyards, each carefully labelled with its owner's name. From the summit you can scan the distant Great Plain and the lush green Tokaj-Hegyalja – the hilly wine-producing region. Other **activities** in Tokaj include rowing, water-skiing, and swimming in the Tisza, or fending off inebriated conscripts at the campsite discos.

TOKAJ WINES

The three main **Tokaj wines** – *Aszú* (sweet), *Hárslevelű* (linden leaf) and *Furmint* (which is usually dry) – derive their character from the special soil, the prolonged sunlight and the wine-making techniques developed here. Heat is trapped by the volcanic loess soil, allowing a delayed **harvest** in October, when many overripe grapes have a sugar content approaching sixty percent. Their juice and pulp is added by the *puttony* (butt) to 136-litre barrels of ordinary grapes, the number of butts determining the qualities of the wine: rich and sweet or slightly "hot", with an oily consistency and ranging in colour from golden yellow to reddish brown.

Though some may find *Aszú* too sweet, Tokaj wine has collected some notable accolades since the late Middle Ages. Beethoven and Schubert dedicated songs to it; Louis XVI declared it "the wine of kings, the king of wines"; Goethe, Voltaire, Heine and Browning all praised it; and Sherlock Holmes used it to toast the downfall of von Bork, after troubling Watson to "open the window, for chloroform vapour does not help the palate". During the **Wine Festival** in October, the local vintners line the streets, giving out free samples.

Practicalities

From the **train station** (which is also the main **bus stop**) on Baross Gábor utca, it's a ten-minute walk north along Bajcsy-Zsilinszky utca to the old town centre. There's a handy **town plan** posted just outside the train station which is worth having a look at before setting off, especially as Tokaj no longer has a tourist information office.

Accommodation

Private rooms can be booked through *Nyír Tourist* in Nyíregyház. Or there are the usual *Zimmer frei* signs all over town, many of them leading to Ovar utca 6 where the landlady has her own wine cellar (whose contents she charges dearly for), and Bajcsy-Zsilinszky utca 19 (②). Rooms at Bethlen utca 49 (②) on the far (north) side of town come slightly cheaper because guests share a toilet – literally, as the loo has two doors, one from each room. Doubles with bathrooms (②) and quadruples without (②) can be found at the *Kollégium*, Bajcsy-Zsilinszky utca 15–17 (☎47/352-355), from June till late August, and possibly at weekends the rest of the year.

Among the other options, the *Makk Marci Panzió* is probably the most upmarket with singles (②) and doubles (③) just off Rákóczi utca at Liget köz 1 (☎41/352-366). The *Lux Panzió* has doubles (③) at Serház utca 14 (☎41/352-145); or there's the *Hotel Tokaj* at Rákóczi utca 5 (☎41/352-344), a rather drab affair but with a few balconied rooms facing the river.

Across the river are two **campsites**, one on either side of the road. *Tisza Camping* (mid-April to mid-Sept; ☎41/352-012) isn't overly clean but you can usually find space there; they also rent two-bed chalets (①) and canoes. *Camping Pelsöczi* charges slightly less for pitching a tent, and a faded notice in reception promises a free bottle of Tokaj to anyone booking two nights, which seems generous if true.

Eating and drinking

The venerable *Rákóczi* cellar at Kossuth tér 15 (May–Oct daily 10am–7pm), where 20,000 hectolitres of wine repose in 24 cobwebbed, chandelier-lit passages, is the most famous in Tokaj and a favourite place of pilgrimage. However, you'll get a more personal service if you drink in the small private **wine cellars** that line the hillside in the backstreets above the main street. The *Vajthó* cellar opposite the bridge is recommended – it also serves fish soup and a few other dishes.

The picture is otherwise pretty bleak for the gastronomer, at least in terms of the number of **eating places** available. By the bridge you have the *Halászcsárda* at Bajcsy-Zsilinszky utca 23 and the restaurant in the *Hotel Tokaj*. Down by the river is the *Kikötő Pihenő*, a bar that also serves food during the summer; and the stand-up buffet at *Tisza Camping*. Or you might consider tracking down the *Horgony Vendéglő* at Bodrogkerestur út 4, an unpretentious place frequented by locals (8am–midnight). It's fifteen minutes' walk north from the centre, just past the old Jewish Cemetery on the left.

Activities

Between mid-June and the end of August there are boat cruises along the Bodrog River to Sárospatak (journey time: 2.5hr).

The Tokaj-Hegyalja

The southern slopes of the Zemplén form the distinctive region known as the **Tokaj-Hegyalja**, which is largely devoted to producing wine. Most of its beautifully sited villages are accessible by bus from Tokaj or Szerencs (many are also served by the branch line from the latter to Hidasnémeti). Since few have any accommodation for tourists, you'll have to visit on day trips – you can stop off at one or two villages a day, depending on schedules.

TOLCSVA, 2km off the road to Sárospatak and around 30km north of Tokaj, can be reached by the hourly bus from Tokaj to Komlóska. Its erstwhile Rákóczi manor is now a **Wine Museum** (Tues, Fri, Sat & Sun 10am–noon, Thurs 2–4pm) containing the usual implements. The hillside is honeycombed with 2.5km of cellars, full of the local **linden leaf wine** (*Tolcsvai Hárslevelű*).

MÁD, midway between Tokaj and Szerencs, boasts a folk Baroque-style **Synagogue**, built in 1765. Just downhill stands the former **Rabbi's house** and **Yeshiva** (religious school), a whitewashed building with graceful arcades (the keys are held by the council at Rákóczi utca 50–52, Mon–Fri 8am–4pm; at weekends seek out András Novak at Danesics utca 22). The old **Jewish Cemetery** is on the northern edge of the village.

Nine kilometres up the road, **TÁLLYA** is the second largest wine producer after Tokaj, with hundreds of barrels maturing in seventeenth-century cellars near a former Rákóczi mansion. In the village church you can view the font where Kossuth (see box below) was baptized.

MONOK, 10km northwest of Szerencs, was actually the **birthplace of Kossuth**, whose childhood home is now a **museum** (Tues–Sun 10am–1pm & 3–6pm). Monok's other famous son is **Miklós Németh**, Hungary's prime minister during the transition from Communism to democracy in 1989.

Just up the road on the other side of the river lies the village of **SZABOLC**, once prominent enough to lend its name to the county. It has the only surviving earthworks fortress (*földvár*) in central Europe, dating from the ninth century.

LAJOS KOSSUTH

Born into landless gentry in 1802, **Lajos Kossuth** began his political career as a lawyer, representing absentee magnates in Parliament. His parliamentary reports, advocating greater liberalism than the Habsburgs would tolerate, were widely influential during the Reform Era. Whilst in jail for sedition, Kossuth taught himself English by reading Shakespeare. Released in 1840, he became editor of the radical *Pesti Hírlap*, was elected to parliament, and took the helm during the 1848 Revolution.

After Serbs, Croats and Romanians rebelled against Magyar rule, and the Habsburgs invaded Hungary, the Debrecen Parliament proclaimed a republic with Kossuth as *de facto* dictator. Having escaped to Turkey after the Hungarians surrendered in August 1849, he toured Britain and America, espousing liberty. So eloquent were his denunciations of Habsburg tyranny that London brewery workers attacked General Haynau, the "Butcher of Vienna", when he visited the city. Karl Marx loathed Kossuth as a bourgeois radical, and tried to undermine his reputation with articles published in the New York *Herald Tribune* and the London *Times*. As a friend of the Italian patriot Mazzini, Kossuth spent his last years in Turin, where he died in 1894.

Other sights include the eighteenth-century **Mudrány Mansion** at Petőfi utca 38 (Tues–Sun 10am–6pm), the **Torös Mansion**, and the fifteenth-century frescoes in the **Reformed Church**. The latter was originally built as a Catholic church in the eleventh century.

The western Zemplén

The western flank of the Zemplén is dotted with **villages** whose remote and sleepy existence today belies their historic significance. Unlike the other parts of Hungary with medieval churches and ruined castles, there's rarely another tourist in sight, while the **scenery** is great everywhere. In contrast to the rounded sedimentary hills on the western side of the valley, the volcanically formed Zemplén often resemble truncated cones (called *sátor* – "tent" – in Hungarian). If all of this appeals, and you don't mind the lack of bright lights and facilities, the region is well worth exploring.

Though private **transport** is definitely advantageous, most places are accessible by local buses or trains up the Szerencs–Hidasnémeti branch line. The scarcity of **accommodation** could be more of a problem unless you bring a tent, or encounter sympathetic locals. Try to buy a *Zemplén hegység* **map** showing all the villages mentioned below, even if you don't intend to go **hiking**.

The route described below approximately follows the **Hernád Valley** up towards the river's source in the Slovakian highlands, and the **border crossing** into Slovakia at Tornyosnémeti (by road) and Hidasnémeti (by rail).

Boldogkőváralja and Vizsoly

Best reached by road since the village lies 2.5km from its train stop, **BOLDOGKŐVÁRALJA** is dominated by a massive **castle** built upon a volcanic mound. Erected in the thirteenth century to discourage a return visit by the Mongols, its partial ruination mocks its name – "Happy stone castle on the hill". There are **guided tours** of this Gothic hulk (Tues–Sun 8am–4pm), and a tourist **hostel**, the *Tekerjes Fogadó*, in one wing (April to late Oct; ☎46/387-701; ①). Advance bookings should be made through *Borsod Tourist* in Miskolc (☎46/350-666).

At **VIZSOLY**, 2km from its train station (*Korlát-Vizsoly*), a thirteenth-century **church** harbours fantastic frescoes of Jesus's Ascension (leaving his footprints behind) and Saint George and the dragon. It also contains an original edition of the **Vizsoly Bible**, the Magyar equivalent of the King James Bible. As the first Hungarian-language translation, by Gáspár Károlyi in 1590, this played a formative role in the development of Hungarian as a written language. Keys to the church are at the *református lelkesz* at Szent János út 123, across the road.

Gönc

Accessible by buses from Hidasnémeti (7 daily) as well as by train, **GÖNC** is set in splendid countryside. This was once an important place, a thriving trade centre in the Middle Ages. The Vizsoly Bible was written here and Sárospatak's Calvinist College took refuge in the village during the Counter-Reformation. More recently, Gönc's fame has rested on the 136-litre oak **barrels** (*Gönci hordok*) used to store Tokaj wine – but even these are no longer made here.

The most concrete reminder of all this is the white **Hussite House** (Tues–Sun 10am–6pm) on Kossuth utca, where there's a weird bed that pulls out from a table and a Gönc barrel downstairs. Down in the cellar, the door to the left enabled the house's Calvinist inhabitants to escape into the maze of cellars beneath the village. If it's shut, the old woman at Rákóczi utca 80 (across the stream, and off to the right) can let you in: she was born in the Hussite House.

At weekends, visitors can rent **rooms** at the edge of the village (ask at Dózsa utca 39 or Kossuth utca 47). Some might enjoy a hard day's **hiking between Gönc and Regéc**, along an ill-marked path skirting the 787-metre-high Gergely-hegy (bring a compass, food and water). There are two buses a day to REGÉC from Encs (on the Miskolc–Hidasnémeti line), leaving around noon and 2pm.

Telkibánya, Abaújvár and Kéked

Buses from Hidasnémeti to Gönc carry on to **TELKIBÁNYA** (also served by two buses from Sátoraljaújhely, on the other side of the mountains), whose museum has a fine collection of colourful pottery, outsized carved heads and Zemplén crystals. During summer, the Children's Camp (*Gyermektábor*) offers self-catering **accommodation**. Beds can also be had out of season if you phone beforehand (Telkibánya ☎7). Jordán Istvánné is the woman to ask for.

A more northerly bus service (2 on weekdays only) from Hidasnémeti to Hollóháza (see p.284), via a new road unmarked on most maps, calls at **ABAÚJVÁR**, whose picturesque Reformed church incorporates some Gothic bits and battered frescoes dating back to 1332. Abaújvár can also be reached by a separate service to Gönc and Hidasnémeti (6 daily). **KÉKED**, on the Hollóháza bus route, has a **fortified manor** containing rustic knick-knacks and antiques (Tues–Sun 8am–4pm), and you could also stop off at an **outdoor bath** in the forest, fed by a cold-water spring (May–Aug).

Sárospatak

Half an hour's train journey from Szerencs, **SÁROSPATAK** (Muddy Stream) basks on the banks of the River Bodrog, a graceful, serene spot with almost unlimited expanses of green. It's a town that once enjoyed a significant role in Hungarian intellectual life, thanks to its **Calvinist College**: Magyars given to hyperbole used to describe Sárospatak as the "Athens on the Bodrog". In the last twenty years, some delightful examples of **Makovecz architecture** have drawn attention to the town, but Sárospatak's main claim to fame is rooted firmly in the past: its historic association with the **Rákóczi family**, whose **castle** is one of the main sights in town.

The Rákóczi family played a major role in Transylvania and Hungary during a turbulent era. Shortly after **György I Rákóczi** acquired Sárospatak Castle in 1616, his Transylvanian estates – and political influence – were augmented by marriage to the immensely wealthy **Zsuzsana Lorántffy**. In 1630 the nobility elected him Prince of Transylvania, hoping that György would restore the stability enjoyed under Gábor Bethlen – which he did.

György II, however, was as rash as his father was cautious, managing to antagonize both Poland and Vizier Mehmet, whose invasion of Transylvania forced the clan to flee to Habsburg-controlled Hungary in 1658. Here the Counter-Reformation was in full swing, and Magyar landlords and peasants reacted against Habsburg confiscations by sporadically staging ferocious revolts of "dissenters" (*kuruc*). Though the original revolt led by Imre Thököly was bloodily crushed, conspirators gathered around György's son **Ferenc I**.

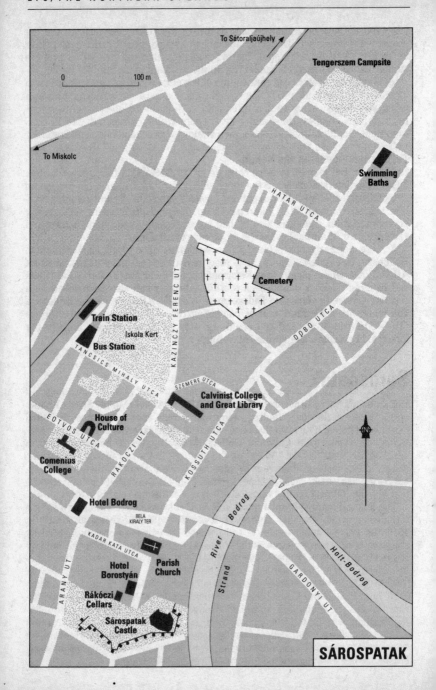

To Sátoraljaújhely

Tengerszem Campsite

0   100 m

To Miskolc

HATAR UTCA

Swimming
Baths

Cemetery

KAZINCZY FERENC UT

DOBO UTCA

Train Station

Iskola Kert

Bus Station

TANCSICS MINALY UTCA

SZEMERE UTCA

Calvinist College
and Great Library

EOTVOS UTCA

House of
Culture

RAKOCZI UT

KOSSUTH UTCA

Comenius
College

Hotel Bodrog

BELA
KIRALY TER

KADAR KATA UTCA

Bodrog

River

Strand

Holt-Bodrog

GARDONYI UT

Hotel
Borostyán

Parish
Church

ARANY UT

Rákóczi
Cellars

Sárospatak
Castle

SÁROSPATAK

By 1703, the insurgency had become a full-scale **War of Independence**, led by **Ferenc II**, whose irregular cavalry and peasant footsoldiers initially triumphed. But by 1711 the Magyars were exhausted and divided, abandoned by their half-hearted ally Louis XIV of France, and Ferenc fled abroad as his armies collapsed under the weight of Habsburg power, to die in exile (in Tekirdag, Turkey) in 1735.

The Town

As you walk from the train or bus station through the School Park (*Iskola Kert*), you'll pass statues of Sárospatak's famous alumni – testifying to the pedagogical prestige of the town's **Calvinist College** (Mon–Sat 9am–5pm, Sun & holidays 9am–1pm; closed Easter, Whitsun & Oct 31), just across the park. Founded in 1531, the college achieved renown under the rectorship (1650–54) of the great Czech humanist **Jan Comenius**, who published several textbooks with the support of György Rákóczi. During the Counter-Reformation, it was forced to move to Gönc, and then to Slovakia, before returning home in 1703. Illustrious graduates include Kossuth, Gárdonyi (see "Eger"), the writer Zsigmond Móricz and the language reformer Ferenc Kazinczy. Like the Calvinist College in Debrecen, it has long-standing ties with England and runs an international **summer language school**. Since regaining control in 1990, the church has been striving to make the college an educational powerhouse once again. Hour-long tours take in the Neoclassical **Great Library** (*Nagykönyvtár*) to the right of the main entrance and a **museum** of college history.

Sárospatak Castle

Sárospatak Castle (March–Oct Tues–Sun 10am–6pm; Nov–Feb Tues–Sun 10am–5pm) is a handsome melange of Gothic, Renaissance and Baroque architecture. Grouped around a courtyard in the Renaissance wings, the **Rákóczi Museum** (same hours) dotes upon the dynasty, even down to a series of watercolours depicting the stages of Ferenc II's exile. Heavy inlaid furniture, jewellery, monstrous stoves, and a banqueting hall complete with piped court music recreate domestic life, while other rooms contain life-size paintings of fearsome cavalry and the moustachioed portrait of Ferenc II that's reproduced on 50Ft banknotes.

A romantic loggia, like a prop from *Romeo and Juliet*, links the residential wings to the fifteenth-century keep, known as the "**Red Tower**". Guided tours (in Hungarian only) take you around the dungeons and underground wells, the labyrinth of galleries used by gunners and a series of impressive halls. The "Knights' Hall", remaining somehow austere despite its throne and stained-glass windows, hosted sessions of Parliament during the Independence War. Plots were hatched by Ferenc I in the adjoining circular balcony room, beneath a ceiling decorated with a stucco rose – the rose being a cryptic warning to guests to be discreet (hence the expression *sub rosa*, meaning conspiratorial).

The Parish Church and Rákóczi cellars

While in the vicinity of the castle, you can pay a visit to the **Parish Church** on Kádár Kata utca (Tues–Sun 10am–2pm). Though much remodelled since the fourteenth century, with painted-on rather than genuine vaulting, it remains one of the largest Gothic hall churches in eastern Hungary. Its huge Baroque altar was brought here from the Carmelite church in Buda Castle after their order was banned in 1784. Look out for posters advertising **organ recitals**.

On a more sybaritic note, the **Rákóczi cellars** behind the *Hotel Borostyán* offer tours and wine tasting for a price. The cellars are thickly coated in a black "noble mould", whose presence is considered so vital to the flavour of local **wine** that it's allowed to ferment in unsealed barrels. Although **tours** (Mon–Fri 7am–7.30pm) are only for groups of five or more, individuals can phone to find out if one is scheduled (☎41/311-902).

The Makovecz buildings

Since 1972, Sárospatak council has commissioned a succession of buildings by the visionary architect **Imre Makovecz**. His first project was the *Bodrog Arúház* on Rákóczi út/Bartók utca, a humdrum modernist supermarket by Western standards, but far removed from the then prevailing brutalist style. Next came the **House of Culture** on Eötvös utca, whose silvery, insectile facade masks an amazing wooden auditorium. The **apartment building** on the corner of Eötvös utca and Rákóczi út displays his passion for asymmetry and organic forms, rooted in a fascination with ancient Celtic and Magyar culture. Makovecz also designed the building in the courtyard of the Calvinist College, and the new **school** beyond the castle.

Practicalities

Orientation is fairly straightforward in Sárospatak, which is just as well as there are no longer any tourist **information** offices in town. The **bus and train stations** are virtually opposite each other at the end of Táncsics Mihály utca, just to the east of the School Park (*Iskola Kert*). A five-minute walk through the park and south along Rákóczi út will bring you to the town centre.

Accommodation

Express, 8km away in Sátoraljaújhely (Mon–Fri 8am–4.30pm; ☎47/322-563) can book accommodation – either **private rooms** (②) or, during the summer months, **beds** in the local *kollégium* (①). Rooms are also available direct at Szemere utca 5, near the Calvinist College, and at Katona utca 18, southeast of the castle. The next step up is the *Leskó Panzió* at Dórzsa György utca 30B (☎47/324-375; ③) or the *Aszú Panzió* at Kazinczy utca 27 (☎47/324-657; ③), while the best **hotel accommodation** in town is the *Hotel Borostyán* (☎47/324-611; ③), housed in a former Trinitarian monastery by the castle. The low-rise *Hotel Bodrog* on Rákóczi út (☎47/323-744; ④) has less ambience and costs more.

North of town near the swimming baths, *Tengerszem Camping* (April to mid-Oct; ☎47/324-753) has bungalows and good facilities, but rates are high and the staff are surly. Young Hungarians opt instead for the free **campsite** (*szabad kemping*) on the *strand* across the river – no facilities, though you can probably use the showers and toilets in the nearby boathouse.

Eating, drinking and entertainment

The *Borostyán*'s restaurant – occupying an old monastic chapel – is the nicest place **to eat** in town, but if cheapness is paramount you could join the locals at the unpretentious *Aszú Fogadó*, Kazinczy út 27, or the *Club Win* on Kádár Kata utca, which has a simple menu plus darts and billiards. The *Kávéhaz* in the House of Culture (2–10pm) is a hang-out for students and arty types, who also **drink** in the basement of the *Megyer Kisvendéglő*, opposite the *Hotel Bodrog*.

Ask at the House of Culture about concerts, plays and other events, especially during the **Music Days** or *Zenei Napok* (July–Aug). *Borsod Tourist* can arrange **horse riding** in the surrounding countryside, and have information on **fishing** in the Holt-Bodrog.

Moving on

There are five **trains** a day from Sárospatak to Szerencs and Miskolc – three of which continue on to Budapest (3hr 30min) – and a similar number run 8km up the line to Sátoraljaújhely, which is better served by buses. There are other **buses** up to Pálháza (2 daily) and across the river to Karcsa and Pácin (3 daily), plus **international services** to Trebišov (Wed, Fri, Sat & Sun) and Velké Kapušany (Wed–Sun) in Slovakia, leaving late afternoon or evening from outside the Calvinist College or further along Kazinczy út (bookings from the main terminal).

Sátoraljaújhely

Easier to reach than it is to pronounce ("SHAR-tor-all-yah-oowee-hay"), **SÁTORALJAÚJHELY** is the last Zemplén town before the border crossing to Slovenské Nové Mesto in Slovakia. Formerly a thriving county town, it was relegated to a backwater by the 1920 Treaty of Trianon and the provincial mergers which made Sárospatak the Zemplén "capital". Today, most people come here for buses to picturesque villages (see below) rather than for the town itself.

Walking up from the bus and train station, you'll pass several monuments that have known better days. On the left stands a wooden building resembling a church, now the offices of the *Tokaj* wine co-op, while further up you'll find a **Gothic Piarist Church** and a cluster of Baroque edifices around Kossuth tér, the main square. It was from the balcony of the **Town Hall** at no. 5 that Kossuth first demonstrated his talent for oratory, during the Zemplén cholera epidemic and riots of 1830. In the middle of the square stands an almost unrecognizable Soviet memorial covered with ivy. Dózsa utca, running off the main street, harbours a deserted **Synagogue** at no. 13, and the dull local history displays of the **Kazinczy Museum** (April–Oct Tues–Sun 9am–5pm; Nov–March Tues–Sun 9am–3pm).

If you fancy some walking, the wild ravines and forested slopes of **Mount Magas** (509m) loom just outside town. These heights saw bitter fighting between Magyars and Slovaks in 1919, and partisans and Nazis in 1944.

Practicalities

Sátoraljaújhely's **bus and train stations** are right next to each other, a couple of kilometres south of the centre. Follow Fasor utca north to Kossuth utca, and continue in a straight line until you reach Kossuth tér, where you'll find *Ibusz* (Mon–Fri 8am–4pm; ☎47/321-957) at no. 26 and *Express* at no. 22 (Mon–Fri 8am–4.30pm; ☎47/322-563).

Accommodation

Ibusz can help with local **accommodation** (which is pretty limited), while *Express* can make bookings throughout the Zemplén – it's also about the only place in town that will change money. Private rooms can be obtained directly at Bányácska utca 20 (☎47/312-763); otherwise there's the drab but clean *Hotel*

Zemplén at Széchenyi tér 5–7 (☎47/322-522; ②–③), or the slightly cheaper *Kovács Villa* on Uttörök útja (April–Oct; ☎47/321-064; ②).

Eating, drinking and entertainment

The dining room of the *Hotel Zemplén* has a reasonable menu, though the staff are a fairly surly bunch. On Kossuth tér there's a *Halászcsárda* serving good "Hungover" fish soup, while the *Zemplén Bisztró* at Dózsa György utca 2 serves simple, affordable dishes. Young people go drinking at the *Pipa* bar near the station, or at *Caffe Henriette* on Vásvari Pál utca.

If you're in Sátoraljaújhely in late summer, ask about the **International Folk Dancing Festival** – for children one year and adults the next (the next adults' one being in 1997).

Moving on

Besides services to Miskolc (5 daily) and Budapest (3 daily), there are four **trains** a day to Slovenské Nové Mesto in Slovakia, augmented between June and September by **international buses** to Trebišov (Wed, Fri & Sun 8pm) and Velke Kapušany (Wed–Sun afternoon or evening). However, it's the local buses that enable one to reach Zemplén villages such as Füzér (3 daily), Pálháza (8 daily), Hollóháza (6 daily), Karcsa and Pácin (hourly), or Telkibánya (twice daily on weekdays).

Into the Zemplén

The highlands **beyond Sátoraljaújhely** contain villages that are just as lovely as those on the western side of the Zemplén. With a car, you can visit half a dozen of them in a day and not feel cheated if a couple are less appealing than expected. Relying on local buses, you'll have to go for a simpler itinerary and be more selective. The following itineraries are basically structured around bus routes.

East to Karcsa and Pácin

Though easily reached from Sátoraljaújhely or Sárospatak, neither of these is officially a Zemplén village as they're located on the plain beyond the River Bodrog. They're not worth a journey in themselves, but merit a look if you're heading towards Kisvárda anyway (see *The Great Plain*).

On the edge of **KARCSA**, 20km from Sárospatak, stands a tenth-century **Romanesque church** with a Gothic nave and a freestanding belfry. The keys are next door, at the house with the *Belyegzes* sign. In **PÁCIN**, 4km further on, there's a fifteenth- to sixteenth-century **Renaissance manor** exhibiting peasant furniture (summer Tues–Sun 10am–6pm; winter Tues–Sun 9am–4pm – these, at any rate, are the official opening times). The kitchen cupboard carries a picture of a woman slaving over the stove, shouting "Hurry up, it's eleven o'clock!" to her husband who sits by the fire.

Towards Pálháza and Rostálló

This route can be a long excursion, or even a prelude to hiking over the Zemplén, depending on your inclinations. There are three buses daily from both

Sátoraljaújhely and Sárospatak via Szépmalom and Füzérradvány to Pálháza, from where you can reach Rostállo in the mountains.

The first place worth a mention, 5km from Sátoraljaújhely, is **SZÉPMALOM**, where a park beside the road contains a good restaurant and the **mausoleum of Ferenc Kazinczy** (Tues–Sun 10am–6pm). It was largely thanks to Kazinczy (1759–1831) that Hungarian was restored as a literary language in the nineteenth century rather than succumbing entirely to German, as the Habsburgs would have preferred.

At **FÜZÉRRADVÁNY**, 4km on, the **Castle Garden** (*Kastély Kert*) surrounding a derelict manor house has an arboretum of variegated oaks and pines which provides a haven for vipers and other wildlife. Buses stop by an avenue of pines that leads into the park (daily 9am–5pm). If the main gates are closed, follow the road round to the left and ask at the lodge. Füzérradvány village has a youth camp, the *Ifjúsági Tábor*, which sometimes lets **rooms** (① per person) from April to October (ask *Express* in Sátoraljaújhely; ☎47/322-563), or you can stay at the *Nagy-Tanya Fogadó* (Pálháza ☎59; ①–②) across the road. During summer it's wise to book through *Express* in Budapest or Sátoraljaújhely.

Another kilometre or so up the road lies **PÁLHÁZA**, the place to board the **narrow-gauge train** that runs 8km up to Rostállo, in the mountains. This *erdei vasut* (forest rail) runs three times daily between mid-April and mid-October, to coincide with buses for Sátoraljaújhely and Sárospatak. Its terminal is near the *Pálháza Ipartelep* stop; to reach this by car from the main road, follow the signs to Kőkapu and then Hidasnémeti. Kőkapu Kastely, up the line from Pálháza, is a nice spot for picnicking and also has a hotel.

ROSTÁLLO is the starting point for **hikes** in various directions – mostly ambitious ones for which you need proper equipment and a map. A good objective is **István kut** (Stephen's Well), a silver birch wood between Rostállo, Háromhuta and Regéc, noted for its special flora and diverse butterflies.

Füzér, Hollóháza and Lászlótanya

If one excursion is your limit, the village to aim for is **FÜZÉR**, a stopover for buses between Sátoraljaújhely and Hollóháza. From here you can walk to the hunting lodge at Lászlótanya where Party bigwigs once cavorted – and maybe even stay there yourself. Füzér itself is an idyllic village of vine-swathed cottages, dignified elders and wandering animals. It also has its own castle and *tájház*, a peasant house preserved in the traditional local style. Depending on the time of day, the village's social centre shifts from the tiny church to the *Italbolt* ("drink shop") and then the bus stop, for the last buses to Hollóháza (Mon–Fri 2.20pm; Sat, Sun & holidays 8.50pm) or Sátoraljaújhely (Mon–Fri 2.30pm; Sat, Sun & holidays 6.50pm).

The ruined **Perényi Castle** is almost directly overhead, although screened by trees and the precipitous angle of the hill. Erected in case the Mongols should return, it served as a repository for the Hungarian crown from 1301 to 1310, while foreign rivals squabbled over the throne. From the huge Gothic arches of its roofless chapel there's a magnificent view of the sleepy village below, the blue-green mountains along the border and the distant Plain beyond – the whole scene enlivened by flocks of swifts swooping and soaring on the powerful thermals. Due to the microclimate, the hillsides abound in **wildlife**, with special flora, vipers, birds of prey and – sometimes – wolves and wildcats.

Accommodation can be found at the school (②) on Kossuth utca (downhill from the bus stop; cross the bridge and turn right) where you should contact Bodnár Józsefné. With a bit of luck, however, you may be able to stay at Lászlótanya instead (see below).

The **porcelain factory** in the village of **HOLLÓHÁZA** was founded in 1831, and there's a **museum** relating its history (May–Sept Tues–Sun 9am–5pm; March–April & Oct–Nov Tues–Sun 10am–4pm) with a shop (Tues–Sat 10am–4pm) selling unbelievably lurid, flowery examples. When the factory and its shop are closed, an outlet selling seconds opens up around the corner. At the top end of the village is a small modern **church**, one wall bearing the stations of the cross (designed by the ceramicist Margit Kovács). However, the chief reason to come is to catch **buses** across the mountains to Kéked and Abaújvár (see p.277), leaving twice a day on weekdays; or to drive a few miles further north, up to Lászlótanya.

Accessible by road from Hollóháza, or a four-kilometre hike from Füzér, the tiny hamlet of **LÁSZLÓTANYA** gets its name from the former **hunting lodge** of László Károlyi, which stands only 400m from the Slovak border. During the Fifties, the lodge served as a holiday resort for top Communist officials – notably the then Party leader Mátyás Rákosi, the route being lined by ÁVO guards during his visits. It subsequently became a trade union resort, and more recently a hotel for tourists (②), complete with mock-Tudor decor and cedarwood-panelled bar (Hollóháza ☎8; or *Express* in Sátoraljaújhely can make reservations on ☎47/322-563). Should you feel like sleeping where the dictator once slept, **Rákosi's suite** is at the top of the stairs.

travel details

Trains

Budapest (Keleti station) to Eger (3 daily; 2hr); Miskolc (11 daily; 1hr 45min–2hr 15min).

Balassagyarmat to Diósjenő and Vác (5–6 daily; 1hr/2hr).

Eger to Budapest (3 daily; 2hr); Putnok (5 daily; 3hr).

Füzesabony to Debrecen (5 daily; 2hr); Eger (every 60–90min; 30min); Hortobágy (5 daily; 1hr); Tiszafüred (5 daily; 30min).

Gyöngyös to Mátrafüred (hourly; 1hr).

Hatvan to Salgótarján (every 60–90min; 1hr–1hr 30min).

Miskolc to Kazincbarcika (every 2hr; 30min); Putnok (every 2hr; 1hr); Nyíregyháza (every 60–90min; 2hr); Ózd (every 2hr; 2hr); Tornanádaska (8 daily; 2hr); Sártoraljaújhely (5 daily; 1hr–1hr 30min); Szerencs (hourly; 30min).

Szerencs Boldogkőváralja (4 daily; 1hr); Gönc (4 daily; 1hr 15min); Mád (8 daily; 15min); Tállya (8 daily; 30min); Tokaj (7 daily; 35min).

Buses

Budapest (Népstadion) to Aggtelek (1 daily; 5hr); Balassagyarmat (every 1–2hr; 2hr 30min); Eger (every 90min; 3hr); Lillafüred (1 daily; 3hr 30min); Mátraháza (4 daily; 2hr).

Aggtelek to Budapest (1 daily; 5hr); Eger (1 daily; 4hr).

Balassagyarmat to Budapest (every 1–2hr; 2hr 30min); Salgótarján (hourly; 1hr); Szécsény (hourly; 1hr).

Eger to Abádszálok (2 daily; 1hr 15min); Aggtelek (1 daily; 4hr); Békéscsaba (2 daily; 5hr); Budapest (every 90min; 3hr); Debrecen (1 daily; 2hr 45min); Gyöngyös (1 daily; 1hr 30min); Gyula (1 daily; 5hr 30min); Hajdúszoboszló (1 daily; 3hr 15min); Hortobágy (1 daily; 2hr 30min); Jászberény (1 daily; 2hr); Kecskemét (2 daily; 4hr); Mátraháza (1 daily; 2hr); Miskolc via the Bükk (2 weekly; 2hr 30min); Recsk (1 daily except Sun; 1hr 45min); Salgótarján (4 daily except Sun; 2hr); Sirok (1 daily except Sun; 1hr 30min); Szeged (1 daily; 5hr); Szilvásvárad (hourly; 1hr); Szolnok (1–3 daily; 2hr 30min); Tiszafüred (2 daily; 1hr 15min).

Füzesabony to Tiszafüred (hourly; 45min).

Gyöngyös to Abádszálok (1 daily; 2hr); Debrecen (1 daily; 4hr 30min); Eger (1 daily; 1hr 30min); Miskolc (1 daily; 3hr 15min); Mátrafüred (every 20min; 30min); Mátraháza (hourly; 45min).

Hatvan to Gyöngyös (hourly; 30min); Hollókő (3 daily; 1hr 30min).

Hollókő to Szécsény (3 daily; 45min); Hatvan (3 daily; 1hr 30min).

Mátraháza to Eger (1 daily; 2hr); Gyöngyös (1 daily; 45min); Miskolc (1 daily; 4hr).

Miskolc to Aggtelek (1 daily; 3hr); Békéscsaba (1 daily; 5hr); Bükkszentkereszt (1 weekly; 1hr); Bükkszentlászló (every 20min; 45min); Debrecen (1 daily; 2hr); Eger via the Bükk (2 weekly; 2hr 15min); Eger via Noszvaj (1 daily; 2hr 15min); Hajdúböszörmény (1 daily; 1hr 30min); Jászberény (1 daily; 5hr); Lillafüred (every 20min; 30min); Mátraháza (1 daily; 4hr); Miskolc–Tapolca (every 10min; 15min); Nyíregyháza (1 daily except Sun; 2hr); Ómassa (every 20min; 45min); Recsk (1 daily except Sun; 1hr); Sirok (1 daily except Sun; 1hr 15min).

Ózd to Aggtelek (1 daily; 1hr 30min); Debrecen (2 daily; 3hr 45min); Miskolc (2 daily; 3hr 30min).

Paradfürdő to Debrecen (1 daily; 4hr); Eger (1 daily; 1hr); Hajdúszoboszló (1 daily; 4hr 30min); Tiszafüred (1 daily; 2hr 45min).

Putnok to Aggtelek (5–6 daily; 30min).

Salgótarján to Eger (4 daily except Sun; 1hr 45min); Debrecen (1 daily; 2hr 15min); Gyula (1 daily; 5hr 15min); Hajdúböszörmény (every 30–

90min; 1hr 45min); Hajdúszoboszló (1–3 daily; 2hr 30min); Hódmezővásárhely (1 daily; 6hr); Szeged (1 daily; 6hr 30min); Szentes (1 daily; 5hr 15min).

Sárospatak to Sátoraljaújhely (hourly; 20min).

Sártoraljaújhely to Füzér (hourly; 45min).

Szécsény to Hollókő (1 daily; 45min).

International trains

Miskolc (Tiszai Station) to Bucharest (July–Sept 1 daily; 26hr 30min); Cluj (July–Sept 1 daily; 10hr 15min); Košice (5 daily; 2hr); Kraków (2–3 daily; 11hr 15min); Poprad Tatry (1 daily; 3hr 45min); Varna (July–Sept 1 daily; 26hr 30min); Warsaw (1–2 daily; 14hr).

Salgótarján to Częstochowa (1 daily; 10hr 15min); Katowice (1 daily; 9hr); Warsaw (1 daily; 13hr).

International buses

Balassagyarmat to Banská Bystrica (June–Sept 1 daily; 3hr); Lučenec (June–Sept 1 daily; 3hr 15min); Žilina (June–Sept 1 daily; 4hr 45min).

Eger to Banská Bystrica (June–Aug 1 daily; 4hr); Lučenec (daily except Sun; 3hr 30min).

Kazincbarcika to Moldava and Bodvou (5 weekly; 2hr 30min).

Miskolc to Košice (2–4 weekly; 2hr 30min); Rožňava (1–2 daily except Sun; 3hr); Uzhgorod (1 daily; 7hr); Velké Kapušany (July–Sept 2 weekly; 3hr); Zemplinska Širava (June–Sept 3 weekly; 3hr 30min).

Ózd to Rimavská Sobota (5 weekly; 1hr 30min); Uzhgorod (1 daily; 8hr 30min).

Salgótarján to Banská Bystrica (June–Aug 1 daily; 3hr); Lučenec (daily except Sun; 1hr 30min).

Sárospatak to Trebišov (1 daily; 1hr 45min); Velké Kapušany (July–Sept 2 weekly; 2hr).

Sátoraljaújhely to Trebišov (1 daily; 1hr 15min); Velké Kapušany (July–Sept 2 weekly; 1hr 30min).

CHAPTER SIX

THE GREAT PLAIN

Covering half of Hungary and awesome in its flatness, the **Great Plain**, or *puszta*, can shimmer like the mirages of Hortobágy, or be as drab as a farmworker's boots. Chance encounters and fleeting details are often more interesting than "sights" on the Plain – though vast herds no longer roam freely as in the nineteenth century, you'll still come across many villages that look virtually unchanged, their whitewashed farmsteads (*tanya*) characterized by rustic artesian wells, flocks of geese and strings of paprika hanging out to dry. One-street affairs with names prefixed *Nagy-* or *Kis-* (Big or Little), these communities are at their most archaic in Szabolcs-Szatmár county, where the majority of Hungarian Gypsies live.

Residents of **Debrecen** and **Szeged** disagree over which is the more sophisticated city – Szeged deserves the accolade if restaurants, architecture and festivals are the main criteria, but both have lots of students and a high cultural profile. The **towns** of Kecskemét, Baja, Hajdúszoboszló and Nyírbátor all offer some excuse for a visit, and a few more have at least one redeeming feature, yet the main attractions are possibly the **national parks**, preserving the wildlife and landscape of the old *puszta*. The **Kiskunság**, due south of Kecskemét, is rather overshadowed by the **Hortobágy**, a mirage-prone steppe where an equestrian Bridge Fair is held on August 19–20. This more or less coincides with **festivals** in Debrecen and Szeged: a Flower Carnival on St Stephen's Day, plus the climax to the Szeged Weeks of music and drama. The *Téka Tábor* festival at Nagykálló in late July will delight anyone interested in Magyar folk arts, whilst the pilgrimages to Máriapócs cast a fascinating light on religious life in Hungary.

The Puszta: a brief history

The word *puszta* is nowadays practically synonymous with the Great Plain (*Nagyalföld*), but it's actually a name that describes the transformation of this huge lowland. During medieval times **the Plain** was thickly forested, with

---

ACCOMMODATION PRICE CODES

All accommodation in this guide is graded according to the price bands given below. Note that all prices refer to the cheapest available double room in high season except where otherwise indicated. For more details, see p.26.

① Under 650Ft (under £4/$6/ DM10)

② 650–1500Ft (£4–8/$6–13/DM10– 20)

③ 1500–3000Ft (£8–17/$13–27/ DM20–40)

④ 3000–4500Ft (£17–25/$27–40/ DM40–60)

⑤ 4500–6500Ft (£25–36/$40–57/ DM60–85)

⑥ 6500–10,000Ft (£36–56/$57–88/ DM85–130)

⑦ Over 10,000Ft (over £56/$88/ DM130)

hundreds of villages living off agriculture and livestock rearing, and the mighty **River Tisza**, fed by its tributaries in Transylvania and Maramures, determined all. Each year it flooded, its hundreds of loops merging into a "sea of water in which the trees were sunk to their crowns", enriching the soil with volcanic silt from the uplands and isolating the villages for months on end. But the Turkish invasion of 1526 unleashed a scourge upon the land: 150 years of nearly unceasing warfare. The peasants that survived fled to the safer *khasse* (tribute-paying) towns like Szeged and Debrecen, leaving their villages to fall into ruin, while vast tracts of forest were felled to build military stockades, or burned simply to deny cover to the partisans (*Hajdúk*). Denuded of vegetation, the land became swampy and pestilent with mosquitoes, and later the abode of solitary swineherds, runaway serfs, outlaws (*betyár*) and wolves. People began calling it **the puszta**, meaning "abandoned, deserted, bleak", and something of its character is conveyed by other words and phrases with the same root; for example *pusztít* (to devastate), *pusztul* (perish, be ruined), and *pusztulj innen* (Clear out of here!). Not surprisingly, most folks shunned it, or ventured in solely out of dire necessity.

Yet another transformation began in the nineteenth century, as an unexpected consequence of Count Szechényi's flood-control work along the Tisza, when soil alkalinity increased the spread of **grassland**. Suitable only for pasturage, in time this became the "Hungarian Wild West", complete with rough-riding *csikósok* (cowboys), and wayside *csárda* where lawmen, Gypsies and outlaws shared the same tables, bound not to fight by the custom of the *puszta*. It was a man's world – women and children remained in the farmsteads close to town – and nineteenth-century romantics like Sándor Petőfi rhapsodized over it as the incarnation of Magyardom: "My world and home... the Alföld, the open sea."

By the 1920s reality had crushed romance. Irrigation enabled landowners to enclose common pasture for crops. Mechanization denied the evicted sharecroppers and herders even the chance of work on the big estates. Most of Hungary's landless peasants, or **"three million beggars"**, lived on the Plain. Their efforts to form Agrarian leagues were violently opposed by the gentry and gendarmerie, particularly around *Viharsarok* – the "Stormy centre" – today's Békés county.

True to their promises, the Communists distributed big estates amongst the peasantry and **nationalized land** "for those who till it" in 1947 but, following the dictates of Stalinism, forced them to join state-run co-operative farms two years later. Treated as socialist serfs, they unamimously dissolved "their" co-operatives in 1956 and reverted to subsistence production, vowing to prevent the landlords from returning. Bearing this in mind, the Party pursued a subtler **agricultural policy** from the Sixties onwards, investing in ever larger co-operative and state farms, whilst allowing peasants to sell the produce of their "household plots" (limited to 1.5 acres), which accounted for half the meat and 70 percent of the fruit and vegetables produced in Hungary. By Eastern European standards the co-operatives were successful, producing a grain surplus that earned one third of Hungary's hard currency income; but the urge to be master of their own land remained strong amongst the peasantry.

During the 1990 election, the **Smallholder's Party** pledged to dissolve the co-operatives and return the land to its pre-1947 owners, winning a majority of votes cast on the Plain. Following intensive negotiations with the Democratic Forum, a compromise was agreed whereby co-operative farm workers could claim 3.7 acres, while previous owners would be entitled to compensation. Many farmers

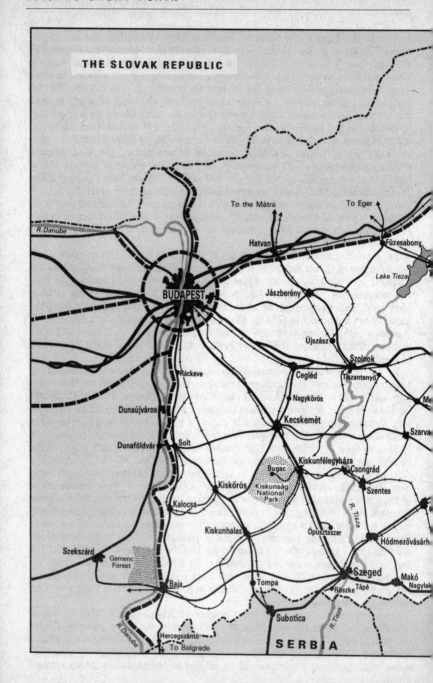

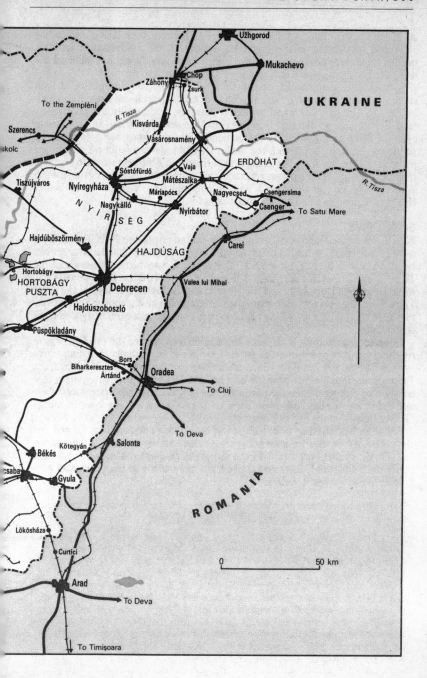

subsequently went into business on their own. However, their lack of capital has prevented investment in the high-tech equipment and cold storage facilities needed to produce food at competitive prices. Declining quality has followed the downward economic spiral in the country's agriculture.

Furthermore, many small farmers have abandoned the production of food staples in favour of produce currently fetching higher prices – as a result of which in 1994–95 Hungary even had to import potatoes, traditionally the poor man's food. Economists predict that Hungary could become locked into an unfortunate cycle of price and production fluctuations, with shortages one year causing surpluses the next. At present, the birth pangs of a new agricultural system are preventing Hungary from becoming one of the world's top producers in terms of price and quality. Though many farmers are joining forces once again to form Western-style co-operatives and limited companies, it will be years before Hungary regains its standing as a breadbasket.

Getting there

With its often monotonous vistas and widely spaced towns, the Plain is something most people cross as much as visit, and if you're pressed for time large areas can be skipped with a clear conscience. The region between the Danube and the Tisza is chiefly notable for Szeged, Kecskemét and Kiskunság National Park, while Debrecen, Hortobágy and the Nyírseg are the highlights beyond the River Tisza. Few other places merit more than an excursion or a stopover, though visitors keen on rural life or cycling might want to consider more off-the-beaten-track destinations.

Intercity buses from Budapest's Népstadion terminal are the quickest way of reaching virtually everywhere as far east as Szeged or Szolnok, including towns such as Kecskemét and Baja, which are awkward or impossible to reach by train. **Trains** come into their own for the long hauls to Debrecen and Nyíregyháza (see box), or for visiting the remote northeast (the only occasion when local *személyvonat* trains are useful). All these services from the capital are covered under "Travel Details" at the end of *Budapest*.

Although **hitchhiking** is feasible along the trunk routes to Baja, Szeged and Debrecen, it's not worth attempting it elsewhere unless there's no alternative. Conversely, **cyclists** are banned from major (single-digit) roads, but should find minor ones delightful. Carts and animals are more common than cars, and wild-flowers bloom along the verges.

THE BLACK TRAIN

Every Friday hundreds of migrant workers return to their homes in northeastern Hungary for the weekend, aboard the so-called **"black train"** (*fekete vonat*). The sobriquet actually applies to half a dozen trains leaving Budapest's Nyugati Station between 4pm and 7pm, bound for Debrecen and Nyíregyháza. Notorious for drunken passengers (home-brewed *pálinka* is sold in the toilets), gambling, theft and brawls, they are best avoided by women and the faint-hearted, but might appeal to adventurous types. As a foreigner you are likely to be accosted by Gypsies, whom the trains' barmen describe as "good company, but then they drink all their wages and want to fight". However, at least you needn't worry about outlaws holding the train up, which happened in the 1860s when the famous *betyár* Sándor Rózsa preyed on the first rail route across the Plain.

BETWEEN THE DANUBE AND THE TISZA

Approaching from the direction of Budapest or Transdanubia, your first experience of the Plain will be the region **between the Danube and the Tisza**. Its chief attractions lie along two main routes from Budapest: **Kalocsa** and **Baja**, on the road following the Danube southwards; and **Kecskemét** and **Szeged**, on the trunk road towards Romania. If you're short of time and want to see something of the *puszta* grasslands, the second itinerary has a lot more to offer. Other towns, such as **Cegléd** or **Jászberény**, can easily be visited en route or as day trips.

South to Kalocsa and Baja

The route south from Budapest should only be undertaken if you like the sound of laid-back **Baja**, on the lower reaches of the Danube. Although **Kalocsa** certainly deserves a look along the way, it's not worth a special trip. Whether you visit **Ráckeve**, closer to Budapest, depends on your means of transport: a convenient stopover by car, but not by bus, it is most easily reached by train from Budapest as a separate excursion.

Ráckeve

Situated on the east bank of Csepel Island, 50km outside Budapest, the little town of **RÁCKEVE** harbours two monuments of unexpected splendour. On Kossuth utca (a short walk south of the HÉV terminal) stands the **Savoy Mansion**, a grandiose fusion of Italian and French Baroque with a Neoclassical dome and other nineteenth-century additions. The original building overlooking the Danube was commissioned by Prince Eugene of Savoy, shortly after his armies drove the Turks from Hungary, and was constructed between 1702 and 1722 according to the designs of J.L. Hildebrandt. Restored in the 1970s after decades of neglect, it was turned into a plush hotel in 1982 (see below).

Ironically, Ráckeve was founded by Serbs (*Rác* in Hungarian) fleeing from the advancing Turks some two hundred years earlier. At the west end of the town centre, its magnificent **Serbian Orthodox Church** is the oldest in Hungary, dating from 1487. A Baroque iconostasis and frescoes by Tódor Gruntovich glow within its vaulted Gothic nave like gems against velvet.

Ráckeve is easily visited on a day trip from Budapest – to **get there** by car, turn off the main road just beyond Kiskunlacháza; alternatively, HÉV trains depart every twenty minutes from Budapest's Soroksári út terminal (bus #23 or #54 from Boráros tér), a journey of around an hour and a quarter. Should you decide **to stay** overnight, the classiest and most extravagant choice is Prince Eugene of Savoy's former mansion, the *Savoyai-Kastély* (☎24/385-253; ⑥). The *Keve Hotel* on Elnök tér (☎24/385-717; ③) is a slightly more modest alternative.

A couple of kilometres south of town in the village of **SZIGETBECSE** (accessible by bus or taxi) a small **museum** exhibits the work of the Hungarian-born photographer André Kertész, who spent his childhood here.

Kalocsa

Around 120km south of the capital, **KALOCSA** makes a pleasant and convenient stopover, with regular buses passing through en route to Baja further south. The town is promoted for its flowery **embroidery** and **"painting women"** (who made it their business to decorate everything in sight), and as Hungary's "**paprika capital**". If you happen to be here around September 8 (when the harvest season officially begins), head out to the surrounding countryside to see the paprika fields transformed into a sea of red.

Twenty minutes' walk from Kalocsa's bus station, the **Viski Károly Museum** at Szent István király út 25 (Tues–Sun 9am–5pm) has a dazzling collection of nine-teenth-century Magyar, Swabian (*Sváb*) and Slovak (*Tót*) folk costumes. The over-stuffed bolsters and quilts on display were mandatory for a bride's dowry, recalling the woman in a Panaït Istrati novel who rages "Why should I spend months sewing them, for some fat pig to muddy with his boots?" Further along the same street at no. 6, the **Paprika Museum** (May–Oct Tues–Sun 10am–noon & 1–5pm) lacks intelligible captions or the allure of paprika *alfresco*, but it's still worth a quick visit and you'll get the gist of the exhibits easily enough (see box below).

Carrying on into Szabadság tér, the old main square, you'll find Kalocsa's Baroque **Cathedral**, whose scruffy facade belies its delicate pink and gold inter-ior. The nearby **Archbishop's Palace** likewise dates from the eighteenth century, but its grandeur recalls the medieval heyday of Kalocsa's bishopric, when local prelates led armies and advised monarchs. Its 120,000-volume **library** contains a Bible signed by Luther, and impressive paintings by Maulbertsch.

Following Kossuth utca off to the right as far as the hospital, you'll see a sign-post for the thatched **Folk Art House** or *Népmüveszeti Szövetkezet* on Tompa utca (Tues–Sun 9am–5pm). Several of its rooms are decorated with exuberant floral murals, traditionally found in the *tiszta szoba* or "clean room" of peasant house-

---

PAPRIKA

More **paprika** is grown around Kalocsa and Szeged than anywhere else in Hungary. Revered as "red gold" (*piros arany*), no one really knows when this member of the Capsicum genus was first introduced – some theories ascribe its introduction to the Age of Migration via the Balkans, while others even credit Christopher Columbus via America. Its consumption received an important boost thanks to continental blockades in the Napoleonic Wars, which compelled Europeans to find a substitute for pepper.

The nineteenth-century preference for milder paprika spurred cross-fertilization and research, which led to the discovery of Capsaicin, produced by the plant in response to drought and sunlight and responsible for its piquancy. Inventions such as the Pálffy roller frame eased the laborious task of chopping and grinding, while the plant's nutritional qualities were investigated by **Dr Albert Szent-Györgyi** of Szeged University, who won the 1933 Nobel Prize for synthesizing vitamin C (paprika is also rich in vitamin A).

The paprika scandal of 1994 came close to being a national catastrophe, a tainted national symbol, when it was discovered that paprika powder was being sold laced with lead-cased paint – for that extra bright look. Firm action to remove all paprika from shop shelves dealt a temporary blow to the basic staple of the Hungarian kitchen.

holds, where guests were entertained. In Kalocsa, almost uniquely, these were painted by groups of women who were respected artisans. Also displayed is a host of Kalocsa embroidery, which has changed a lot since the 1920s. Whereas nineteenth-century embroiderers used only red, blue, white and black yarns to produce assured designs, the modern stuff is multicoloured and rather twee.

Finally, for something completely different, check out the 22-metre-high **Chronos 8 light tower** that beams over Kalocsa; or the smaller, kinetic works of Nicolas Schöffer, the locally born Parisian conceptual sculptor, in the **Nicolas Schöffer Museum** at Szent István király út 76 (Tues–Sun 10am–noon & 2–5pm).

Practicalities

Kalocsa's **train station** lies northeast of the town centre on Mártírok tere, about a fifteen-minute walk along Kossuth utca. Its **bus station** is at the southern end of Szent István király út, a 25-minute walk from the centre – often drivers will let you leap out on Kossuth utca, near Szentháromság tér (the main square).

For **information**, *Ibusz* is at Szent István király utca 28, halfway between the bus station and the main square (Mon 8.15am–5pm, Tues–Thurs 8.15am–4pm & Fri 8.15am–3pm). Virtually opposite, at no. 37, is the run-down *Hotel Piros Arany* (☎78/362-220; ③), while on Szabadság tér stands the beautifully restored *Kalocsa Hotel* (☎78/361-244; ⑤). There are **restaurants** in both hotels, and other places to eat and drink on Petőfi utca. Buses leave for Baja every thirty to ninety minutes.

Baja

BAJA, 76km further south, has an almost Mediterranean feel, with respectable citizens promenading up and down Eötvös utca, and young bloods revving their motorcycles around Szentháromság tér. The languid atmosphere and the shady banks of the Sugovica-Danube are the main attractions, for this is basically a town in which to rest. If that sounds too sleepy, come during the **Danube Folklore Festival** (every odd year; July 15–17) or the Baja **Summer Days** in the last week in May.

Just east of Szentháromság tér off Déak utca is the **Turr István Museum** (Tues–Sat 10am–4pm & Sun 2–6pm), containing an interesting exhibition on the Danube's history, as well as a picture gallery and a section covering various ethnic groups including the Magyars, southern Slavs and Gypsies. The museum is named after a Hungarian general who fought alongside Garibaldi in Italy, just as many Poles and Italians aided Hungary against the Habsburgs.

If it's open, icon buffs should try to visit the **Serbian Orthodox Church** on Táncsics utca, one of two ministering to locals of Serbian descent. There is also a German high school catering to a smaller community of Swabians, whom the Habsburgs encouraged to settle here after the Turks were evicted. From the church, a short walk down Telcs Ede utca brings you to Munkácsy Mihály utca and a fabulous Neoclassical **Synagogue** (now serving as a library) with a monument to the town's 5705 victims of fascism. Heading back towards Szentháromság tér, you pass the **István Nagy Gallery** (Tues–Sun 9am–5pm) on Arany János utca, where a collection of paintings by the Alföld School is displayed (Nagy himself being the group's best known proponent).

Across the river from the main square lies **Petőfi Island**, where Baja's festivals are held: a nice place to go boating, swimming or fishing. It was from here that the last Habsburg emperor was ignominiously deported (see box on p.294).

Arrival and information

Baja's **train station** is on the other side of Vonat kert ("Train Park") from the bus station, to the northeast of the town centre. From the **bus station** on Csermák Mihály tér it's a ten-minute signposted walk to **Szentháromság tér** (overlooking the Sugovica River), where *Pusztatourist* (Mon–Fri 8am–4pm & Sat 8am–noon; ☎79/321-237) and a couple of other tourist offices can help with local **information** and accommodation.

Buses depart regularly for Kecskemét (8 daily; 3hr) and Szeged (1 daily; 5hr) on the Plain; and Mohács (4 daily; 40min) and Pécs (4 daily; 2hr) in Transdanubia. However, **trains** are really only useful for reaching Kiskunhalas (7 daily; 1–2hr).

Accommodation

Across the square from *Pusztatourist*, where **private rooms** can be booked, is the old-fashioned *Hotel Duna* at no. 5 (☎79/323-224; ③) which, like the *Kolibri Panzió* at Batthyány utca 18 (☎79/321-628; ③), offers cheaper rooms than the pricey *Hotel Sugovica* (☎79/321-755; ④) on Petőfi Island. Just beyond the latter is the shady *Sugovica* **campsite** (May–Sept; ☎79/321-755) with huts and chalets, and pheasants strutting around at dawn. About the cheapest accommodation in town is at the *IYHF Youth Hostel* at the northern end of Petőfi Island (mid-June to late Aug; ☎79/324-022; doubles ③, dorm beds ①; 10 percent discount for IYHF card holders), and at the *József Eötvös College* at Szegedi út 2 (mid-June to August; ②).

Eating, drinking and entertainment

Several cafés spill out on to Szentháromság tér, where the *Belvárosi Cukrászda* sometimes features live music. Besides hotel-restaurants, Baja's **eating places** include the *Védió Étterem* on Petőfi Island and the *Csitanyica Vendéglő* at Szabadsag út 8; the lively *Laguna Pizzeria*, just south of the *Kolibri Panzió* on Babits Mihály utca, and the *Fondő Kert* on Kossuth utca – the last two offering a break from the usual Hungarian fare. **Discos** are a regular feature at the *Hotel Sugovica*, the *Black Out* on Árpád utca and *Let's Go* on Széchenyi utca.

THE LAST OF THE HABSBURGS?

Although the Habsburg Empire ended with the abdication of **Karl IV** and the establishment of republics in Austria and Hungary in 1918, the dynasty refused to die. In October 1921, Karl attempted to regain the Hungarian throne by flying into Baja, where a royalist force awaited him with trucks supplied by Major Lehár (cousin of Franz, composer of *The Merry Widow*). However, their advance on Budapest was swiftly halted by regular troops, and a British gunboat transported Karl into exile in Madeira. His widow **Zita** was barred from Austria until 1982 for refusing to renounce her claim, and only returned thereafter to be buried in Vienna.

Meanwhile, their son **Otto** had become a Euro MP and roving ambassador to the former Habsburg territories. An apocryphal story has it that when asked if he would be watching the Austria–Hungary football match, Otto replied, "Who are we playing?" Having retained Hungarian citizenship, he is also entitled to stand for parliament in Budapest, where nostalgia for the Dual Monarchy may yet restore a Habsburg to authority.

Jászberény

JÁSZBERÉNY, 50km east of Budapest, merits a passing mention for its historic links to the **Jász** (Jazygians), an Iranian-speaking people who migrated here from around the Caspian Sea at the beginning of the thirteenth century. Granted feudal privileges by Béla III, they prospered as cattle-breeders, tanners and furriers, each extended family owning several farms and a town house. A dozen settlements with names prefixed by "Jász-" denotes the extent of the Jászság region, which remained semi-autonomous until the 1890s, by which time they had become totally assimilated. As Patrick Leigh Fermor wrote, "this entire nation seems to have vanished like a will o' the wisp, and only these place-names mark the points of their evaporation".

Jász culture and history are explored in the **Jász Museum** (Tues–Sun 9am–5pm), which occupies the splendid old town hall on Lehel tér. The museum's star exhibit is the ivory **Lehel Horn**, intricately carved with hunting scenes. According to Jász tradition this belonged to a Magyar general, Lehel, whom the German emperor Otto I defeated near Augsburg in 955. Legend has it that Lehel begged to be allowed to blow his horn before being executed and, when the last notes had faded, suddenly stabbed Otto to death with it. Alas for legend, the horn is reckoned to be of eleventh- or twelfth-century Byzantine origin, and it was Lehel, not Otto, who perished at Augsburg.

The town's **Thermal Baths**, at Hatvani út 5, have an outdoor *strand*, sauna and indoor pool (May–Sept Tues–Sun 9am–6pm; ☎57/312-108).

Practicalities

Jászberény's **bus station** is just west of the Zagyva River on Petőfi tér, and the **train station** is at the western end of Rákóczi út. The town is served by regular buses from the capital, Cegléd and Szolnok, and from Hatvan in the northern uplands.

The best source of **information** on local events and accommodation is *Tourinform* at Lehel vezér utca 33 (☎57/311-976). *Ibusz* on Lehel tér can also book **private rooms** (☎57/312-143), or there's the *Hotel Touring* at Serház út 3 (☎57/312-051; ④), or the *Kakukkfészek Panzió* at Táncsics út 8 (☎57/312-345; ③ per person). For **food**, try the pub-like *Gösser* on Dózsa György út, the reasonably priced *Lehel Étterem* at Lehel tér 34, or the *Kolibri Salad Bar* on Táncsics Mihály utca 1, which also serves pizza and pasta.

In the first week of August, the Déryné Cultural Centre at Lehel vezér tér 33 (☎57/311-294) hosts the annual **Csángó Festival**, a celebration of the traditional folk music and crafts of the Csángós from eastern Transylvania.

Cegléd and Nagykőrös

CEGLÉD straddles two major rail lines across the Great Plain, linking Budapest with Debrecen to the east, and Kecskemét and Szeged to the south. With an hour or so to kill between connections, you can check out the **Kossuth Museum** (Tues–Sun 10am–6pm) on Rákóczi út, between the train station and the centre. A large oil painting in the foyer depicts the execution of György Dózsa, leader of the 1514 Peasants' Revolt, who was "crowned" upon a red-hot throne in Timișoara by the nobility. Some of his charred flesh was force-fed to his lieutenants, and the remainder impaled on the gates of five Hungarian cities as a warning. Three centuries later, the local peasantry responded enthusiastically to Kossuth's call for volunteers to defend the gains of the 1848 Revolution – principally the abolition of serfdom. The museum preserves the oak table on which he stood to speak, while a statue marks the site on Szabadság tér, near the bus terminal.

Another clue to the region's history is provided by **NAGYKŐRÖS**, further down the line towards Kecskemét. Like other settlements with names ending in "-kőrös", it recalls the so-called **Kőrös people** who raised sheep and tumuli on the Plain during the Neolithic era (5500–3400 BC). Near the bus terminal in the town centre is an **ornamental garden** (*Cifrakert*) containing the **Arany János Museum** (May–Sept Tues–Sun 10am–6pm) which commemorates the life and works of the poet, librettist and balladeer, János Arany (1817–82). Motorists might consider lunching at the *Csárda*, 500m outside town on the road in from Cegléd.

Kecskemét

Hungarians associate **KECSKEMÉT** with *barackpálinka* (the local apricot brandy) and the composer Kodály (who was born in what is now the train station), but its cultural significance doesn't end there. The town centre boasts some of the finest architecture on the Plain, while its film studio and festivals impart a metropolitan pizzazz. Given this sophistication, you would never imagine that its name derives from the Hungarian word for "goat" (*kecske*).

The Town

Although nothing remains of medieval Kecskemét, its size can be judged from the ring boulevard, which follows the old moat. Unlike most towns in the region, it was spared devastation by the Turks, as the Sultan took a liking to it. Waves of refugees settled here, and Kecskemét became the third largest town in Hungary. This fortunate history, underpinned by agricultural wealth, explains its air of confidence and the flamboyant, eclectic **architecture**, skilfully integrated with modern buildings by József Kerény.

Around Szabadság tér

Heading south into the town centre, on the northern side of Szabadság tér is the **Cifra Palace**, resembling a set from *Hansel and Gretel* on acid, ceramic mushrooms sprouting from psychedelic tiles above a gingerbread facade. Designed by Géza Markus in 1902, this wonderful example of Art Nouveau (termed the "Secessionist style" in Hungary) now houses the **Kecskemét Art Gallery** (Tues–Sun 11am–6pm).

The Transylvanian-Gothic hulk diagonally opposite the Cifra Palace is one of two buildings in Kecskemét in the style known as **National Romanticism**. Built between 1911 and 1913 as a Calvinist college, this one is a "mature" example of the genre that coincided with Hungary's millennial anniversary and campaigns to "Magyarize" ethnic minorities, reflecting the triumphalist yet paranoid *zeitgeist* of the 1890s and 1900s. Its steeply pitched roofs and intimidating tower hark back to the vernacular architecture of rural Hungary and Transylvania, regarded as pure wellsprings of Magyar culture. It now houses a **library** and

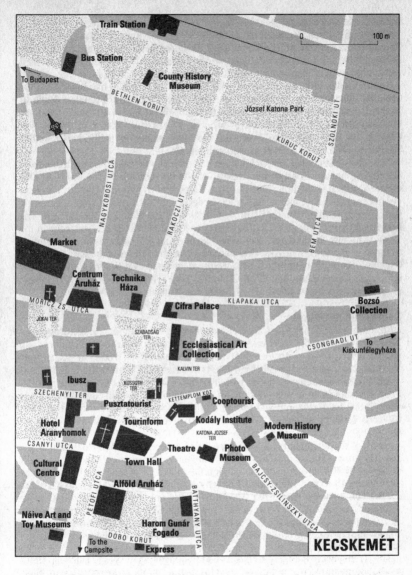

KECSKEMÉT

Collection of Ecclesiastical Art (Tues–Sun 10am–6pm); the entrance is on Villám utca.

Temporary exhibitions of a scientific nature allow you to see inside the white, onion-domed **Technika-háza**, a former synagogue on Moricz Zs. utca, at the north end of the square. Built between 1862 and 1871 in the Moorish style, it was sacked by the Nazis when they deported local Jews in 1944.

Kossuth tér and around

To the south, across Kossuth tér, is the building that started the whole National Romanticism movement: the **Town Hall** designed by Ödön Lechner and Gyula Pártos in 1893. Like Lechner's later works in Budapest, it is richly ornamented with Zsolnay tiles inspired by the decorative traditions of Magyar folk art and nomadic Turkic cultures. However, the building itself is a Renaissance-Baroque pastiche whose lack of "authentic form" was criticized by later National Romanticists such as Károly Kós. Its Grand Hall (Mon–Fri 10–11am) contains gilded murals by Bertalan Székely, who decorated the interior of the Mátyás Church in Budapest. The bells outside play snatches of Kódaly, Handel, Beethoven, Mozart and Erkel at regular intervals.

With five churches in the vicinity you can afford to be selective; the three most interesting are on Kossuth tér. Next to the town hall stands the so-called **Old Church**, which is Catholic and Baroque. Designed by Oswald Gáspár, an eighteenth-century Piarist father, its facade is decorated with reliefs commemorating the Seventh Wilhem Hussars and local heroes of the War of Independence. The **Calvinist Church**, behind *Pusztatourist*, was founded in 1683 and enlarged in the 1790s, when its "Red Tower" was added. Its meeting hall contains frescoes similar to those in the town hall. The **Franciscan Church** to the east is *really* the oldest one, but Baroque restoration has obscured its medieval features. Around the corner on Kéttemplom köz (Two Churches Lane) stands the former Franciscan monastery, which now houses the **Kodály Institute** (see box).

Kecskemét museums

Of the surprisingly large number of museums in Kecskemét, the **Photography Museum** is one of the most interesting, with a massive collection of cameras and photos and a room with excellent temporary exhibits (Wed–Sun 10am–5pm; ☎76/483-221). Situated just behind the grand Katona Theatre, the building was originally established as a dance hall, but was converted to a synagogue in 1918. Four decades later it was sold off by the decimated Jewish community, since when it has been restored and turned into a museum. On Bánk utca nearby, the **Modern History Museum** (Tues–Sun 10am–6pm) reveals how much the town has changed since the nineteenth century.

South of the main square, on the corner of Gáspár András and Hosszú utca, the **Toy Museum** (Tues–Sun 10am–6pm) occupies an airy wooden building, specially designed by Kerényi. It features a delightful collection of nineteenth- and twentieth-century toys, and the helpful English-speaking staff also do children's workshops. The adjacent **Naive Art Museum** (Tues–Sun 10am–6pm) exhibits naïve paintings from pre-World War I to the present day. Should you need an antidote to all this cuteness, wander round the corner to the **Medical Collection** (Tues–Sun 10am–6pm) at Kölcsey utca 3, which includes several gory exhibits.

Fans of Magyar folk art should head 500m south towards the junction of Petőfi utca and the ring boulevard (bus #1, #11 or #22). One block back, at Külső Szabadság út 19A, the **Museum of Hungarian Folk Craft** (Wed–Sun 9am–5pm) exhibits a wealth of textiles, pottery and embroidery from the 1950s onwards. Older artefacts, particularly furniture, are gathered in the **Bozsó Collection** (Fri–Sun 10am–6pm) at Klapka utca 34, 500m east of the Cifra Palace. About the same distance north of the palace in the József Katona Park, the **County History Museum** (Tues–Sun 10am–6pm) has little to offer and can easily be skipped with a clear conscience.

ZOLTÁN KODÁLY AND JÓZSEF KATONA

For a small town, Kecskemét has made a not inconsiderable contribution to national culture. The Spring Days festival, in particular (see "Entertainment" below) offers a good opportunity to catch the work of its two famous sons.

Through his researches into the folk roots of Hungarian music, **Zoltán Kodály** (1882–1967) was inspired to compositions that eschewed the Baroque and Western strains his colleague Bartók termed "New Style". He also revolutionized the teaching of music, inventing the "Kodály method" that is now applied throughout Hungary and around the world. Kodály's belief that music can only be understood by actively participating in it remains the guiding principle of Kecskemét's **Institute of Music Teaching** (*Zenepedagógiai Intézet*). Students on the **one-year course** are exhorted to approach music through the human voice, "the most easily accessible instrument for all", and build upon their national folk traditions when teaching children – a task Kodály considered supremely important. "No one is too great to write for the little ones," he said. "In fact one has to strive to be great enough." For those who want to know more, there's an exhibition in the institute itself, at Kéttemplom köz 1–3.

The town can also boast of **József Katona** (1791–1830), the "father" of Hungarian romantic drama, who was born and died in Kecskemét. His masterpiece, *Bánk Bán* (later made into an opera by Erkel), revolves around the murder of Gertrude, the German-born queen of King Andrew II, by his vassal Bánk. Katona himself expired of a heart attack outside the town hall, the spot now marked by a cloven block. The fallible organ was preserved in a jewelled casket, and his name was bestowed upon Kecskemét's playhouse. During the 1980s, the **Katona Theatre** was directed by filmmaker Miklós Jancsó, whose avant-garde productions scandalized many townsfolk.

The Pannónia Filmstudió

Kecskemét is also the home of the **Pannónia Filmstudió**, whose entire output consists of animated cartoons – short films, television series, advertisements and training films. The studio runs **guided tours** for groups of twenty or more by prior arrangement, so it's worth asking *Pusztatourist* if one is scheduled, or writing well beforehand to Dr Ferenc Miklós, Pannónia Filmstudió, Liszt Fő utca 21. Situated beyond the train station off Ceglédi út, the studio can be reached by bus #18 from Rákóczi út.

Practicalities

Kecskemét is accessible by **train** from Budapest's Nyugati Station or **bus** from the Népstadion terminal. There are equally regular services from Szeged, and less frequent buses from Baja and Cegléd.

Arriving at the bus or train station in the northern part of town, you are ten minutes' walk from the centre, a leafy conjunction of squares. Kossuth tér is where you'll find *Tourinform* (Mon–Fri 8am–6pm & Sat–Sun 9am–1pm; ☎76/481-065), the best source of **information**, and its less helpful competitor *Pusztatourist* (Mon–Thurs 7.30am–4.30pm & Fri 8am–4pm; plus May–Sept Sat 9am–1pm; ☎76/483-493). *Ibusz* (Mon–Fri 7.30am–4pm & Sat 7.30–11am; ☎76/322-955) is nearby on Széchenyi tér, *Cooptourist* (Mon–Fri 8.30–noon & 1–5pm; ☎76/481-472) is at Kéttemplom köz 9–11, and *Express* (Mon 10am–4.30pm, Tues–Fri 8am–4.30pm; ☎76/329-236) is slightly further out, on the first floor of block 11, Dobó körút.

Accommodation

During the summer holidays you may be able to get cheap **beds** in the colleges at Jókai tér 4 (☎76/486-977) or Izsáki utca 10 (☎76/321-916), bookable through *Express* or *Ibusz*. **Private rooms** (①) from *Pusztatourist* and other agencies are also good value, or there's the *Autós* **campsite** with chalets at Sport utca 5 (mid-April to mid-Oct; ☎76/329-398), midway between the *Szauna* and *Tó* hotels (accessible by bus #22). Alternatively, ask *Tourinform* about lodgings on one of the old thatched farms (*tanya*) in the countryside around Kecskemét (or ring ☎76/321-908).

Hotels and pensions in or near Kecskemét include:

Cassia Panzió, Gyenes M. tér 18 (☎76/481-685) An affordable, fairly central pension northwest of Széchenyi tér. Cassia is the patron saint of chess – the owner being an avid fan of the game. ③.

Colour Panzió, Jókai utca 26 (☎76/324-901). Located west of the *Cassia Panzió* along *Móricz utca* in the market district. ③.

Három Gunár Fogadó, Batthyány utca 1 (☎76/483-611). A smart and comfortable hotel with a restaurant off Katona tér. ④.

Hotel Aranyhomok, Széchenyi tér 2 (☎76/486-286). Named after the "golden sands" of the *puszta*, but not even vaguely romantic – its chief asset being its prime location. ④.

Szauna Hotel, Sport utca 3 (☎76/481-859). Well-equipped hotel with a sauna and gym, 1km south of the centre; bus #22 stops nearby. ④.

Szőlőfürt Fogadó, István király krt 23 (☎76/481-625). A motel-cum-inn, 4km out along the Békéscsaba road. ③.

Tó Hotel, Sport utca 7 (☎76/328-166). Near a boating lake, 400m beyond the *Szauna Hotel*. Also comfortable, but with fewer facilities. ④.

Eating and drinking

Apart from the **restaurants** of the ritziest hotels, there are several decent places to eat in the town centre. Near *Pusztatourist* you'll find the *Liberté Kávéház*, a plush establishment serving wonderful stuffed mushrooms. The *HBH* is a Bavarian-style place on Csányi utca, around the corner from the Old Church. For a Magyar nosh-up try the *Kisbugaci Csárda* at Munkácsy utca 10, beyond Széchenyi tér (daily noon–midnight). The *Görögudvar*, near the bus station on the corner of Hornyik János körút and Szabadság tér, specializes in Greek food and music, while across the road there's a restaurant serving *falafel*, and the *Italia Pizzeria* which does a quick pizza and pasta. For vegetarian food try the *Greenland Étterem* at Zöldfa (Green Tree) utca 12.

Most of the places described above are feasible **drinking** spots, while the bar opposite the *Három Gunár Fogadó* also serves food until late. Two **patisseries** worth a visit are the *Fodor Cukrászda* near the *Liberté Kávéház*, and the *Delicatesse Cukrászda* (7am–10pm) in an arcade on the corner of Kossuth and Széchenyi tér. The outdoor **market** is good for cheap snacks and fresh produce, while other purchases can be made in the *Centrum* department store on Móricz utca.

Entertainment

Kecskemét is at its liveliest during the **Spring Days** (in late March, coinciding with the festival in Budapest), with numerous concerts and theatre performances; and over the summer, when folk groups from several countries perform at the **Danube Folklore Festival** (July 15–17). In late August, **historical pageants** and **wine-tasting** sessions enliven Szabadság tér and Petőfi utca. *Tourinform* has details of all these events.

Look out for posters advertising **discos** in the *Hotel Aranyhomok,* or in the Cultural Centre and *Júlia Presszó* (above the *Univer* supermarket) on Petőfi utca – generally at weekends. On Thursdays *Club Robinson* has a nostalgia disco with Seventies and Eighties music.

Excursions

Kecskemét is surrounded by **horse riding country**, and *Tourinform* can point you in the direction of any number of riding schools on the Plain. The town also makes a good base for **excursions** to the Tisza resorts and the Kiskunság region (see p.302). Bus #2 from Széchenyi tér can drop you at the *Átrakó* terminal for narrow-gauge trains to Kiskunság National Park (see below).

International connections

The intercity bus terminal near the train station serves most destinations, including Eger in the northern uplands. It's from here that **buses to Romania** depart, bound for Miercurea Ciuc (Fri & Sun 6am), Oradea, Cluj and Tîrgu Mureş (Fri 6am). Note that these towns may be designated by their Hungarian names as Csíkszereda, Kolozsvár, Nagyvárad and Marosvásárhely. Depending on the political situation, there may also be services to Subotica in the Voivodina.

Lakitelek and Tiszakécske

Thirty kilometres east of Kecskemét are several low-key **resorts** where you can swim or wander beside the Tisza as it meanders through woodlands and meadows. Lakitelek and Tőserdő make for a relaxed excursion from Kecskemét or Kiskunfélegyháza, while Tiszakécske is more of a family holiday centre. **From Kecskemét**, five trains daily stop at Lakitelek en route to Kunszentmárton; to reach Tőserdő, you can take the same trains from Kecskemét, alighting at the Szikra station, or catch the bus. **From Kiskunfélegyháza**, the four daily Szolnok trains call at Lakitelek, Tiszakécske and Tőserdő.

The village of **LAKITELEK** is famous for hosting the **conference** that gave birth to the Hungarian Democratic Forum (*MDF*), which went on to win the 1990 elections. As the party tries to climb back after its big defeat in the 1994 elections, the "spirit of Lakitelek" is invoked by politicians who return to press the flesh at the local **festival** of folk music and dancing (*Lakitelek Falunapok*) on the first weekend in July. Another attraction is the lovely **Tőserdő**, a sylvan nature reserve located 4km away.

Accommodation is available at the *Tölgyfa Panzió* (☎76/342-037; ③), in rented cottages arranged by *Pusztatourist* in Kecskemét (④), and at two campsites. *Autóscamping* (May–Sept; ☎76/342-012) is on the main road near the *Tősfürdő* or **thermal baths** (May–Aug). From there, a path runs 1km to the Holtág, a dead branch of the river that's nicer for swimming, with cheap **restaurants** and the other campsite (mid-May to mid-Sept; ☎76/342-011).

TISZAKÉCSKE, further north, has more of a tourist industry by the river. There are several restaurants, a free camping place, horse-drawn carts and a **children's railway** (May–Sept). The **thermal baths** are open all year-round. Buses run here hourly from Tiszakécske station, passing *Pusztatourist* at Béke utca 142 (☎76/341-012), and various rooms for rent in the town centre.

The Kiskunság

The **Kiskunság** region, to the south of Kecskemét, is called "Little Cumania", after the Cumanian (*Kun*) tribes that settled here in the Middle Ages. This sandy tableland was unfit for anything but raising sheep until, in the nineteenth century, it was laboriously transformed by afforestation and soil husbandry to yield grapes and other fruit. While Magyars esteem this as "Petőfi country", where their national poet was born, its prime attractions for visitors are Kiskunság National Park and the exhibition complex at Ópusztaszer.

Kiskunfélegyháza

To Hungarian ears, **KISKUNFÉLEGYHÁZA** suggests people and paths converging on the "House of Cumania". The present town was actually created by Jazygian settlers in the 1740s, but the name is nevertheless appropriate as the Cumanian original was wiped out by the Turks. As regional capital, it is a rural foil to urbane Kecskemét – a town that lives by geese-breeding and market gardening, with storks' nests on the chimneys and draw-wells in the courtyards.

Entering town by bus from Kecskemét, you'll pass the **Kiskun Museum** (mid-March to late Nov Tues–Sun 10am–6pm), in an eighteenth-century manor house on the main street. Exhibits on the Cumanians and Jazygians and paintings of rural life by László Holló (1887–1976) pale before a section devoted to the **history of prisons**, in the very cell where the famous *betyár* Sándor Rózsa languished in 1860. The old **windmill** in the courtyard comes from the riverside village of Mindszent, where Cardinal Mindszenty was born.

Kiskunfélegyháza's main square strives to achieve the elegance of Kecskemét's, with a majolica-encrusted National Romantic **Town Hall** built by József Vass and Nándor Morbitzer in 1912. Diagonally opposite is the **Swan House** (*Hattyuház*), where Petőfi's father had a butcher's shop and the poet spent his childhood. His statue outside is decked with flowers and flags on March 15, the anniversary of the 1848 Revolution. At Petőfi utca 7, the new **Petőfi Ház** documents the life of the poet with newspaper articles, maps, old bills and the like. You can also visit the **birthplace of Ferenc Móra** (1879–1934), writer, journalist and antiquarian, at Móra utca 19 (Thurs, Fri & Sat 10am–2pm), or soak in the town's **thermal baths** (6am–7pm).

Practicalities

Coach parties **eat** at the *Halászcsárda* on Petőfi tér and the *Aranyhegyi Csárda* out towards Kecskemét, making the *Arany Piva Étterem* on Blaha Lujza tér a preferable option. With most visitors just passing through, there's usually **accommodation** to spare at the *Borostyán Panzió* at Szőlő utca 1 (☎76/362-573; ③) and the *Oázis Panzió* at Szegedi út 13 (☎76/361-427; ③).

More likely, though, you'll simply catch the first **bus** out to Bugac (every 60–90min) or Ópusztaszer (2–3 daily), the highlights of this region.

Kiskunság National Park

The 30,000 hectares of **Kiskunság National Park** consist of several tracts of land, the largest of which starts 3km beyond the village of **BUGAC**. Buses from Kiskunfélegyháza can drop you near the entrance to the park (April–Oct daily

10am–5pm). From here a sandy track runs 3.5km past flower-speckled meadows and lounging shepherds, to a **farm** where *csikósok* (cowboys) in white pantaloons stage equestrian displays, riding bareback and standing up with much cracking of whips.

Among the **animals** bred here are grey long-horned cattle, Merino sheep and Mangalica pigs (said to make the finest bacon). The surrounding reedy marshes support diverse birdlife and flora (including rare blue globe-thistles in August), and serve as baths for water buffalo, which plod back to their barns at sunset. In the wooden **Shepherds' Museum** (daily 10am–5pm) you can see felted cloaks and hand-carved pipes, and a grotesque tobacco pouch made from a ram's scrotum.

Practicalities

Apart from *Pusztatourist* excursions from Kecskemét, there are two ways of **getting to the park**. Buses from Kiskunfélegyháza drop you nearer to the entrance than the narrow-gauge trains from Kecskemét to the Bugac felső station (a 90-min walk from the farm), but the train ride is quicker and more fun. To catch the horse show you must get the first train (leaving 7.50am) or an early bus, since events are scheduled for groups, who then travel by buggy to a "typical" *csárda* (580Ft).

You can stay near Bugac at the *Bugaci Lovas Hotel* (☎76/372-522; ③), which also offers bungalows (mid-March to mid-Nov); or in **rooms** in the village, reserved through *Pusztatourist*.

Kiskőrös

Though hardly worth a special visit, **KISKŐRÖS** should be mentioned as the **birthplace of Sándor Petőfi**, who made Byron look tame (see box below). At Luther tér 2, the thatched **Petőfi House** sits incongruously in the town centre, preserved as a museum (Tues–Sun 9am–5pm) that won't do much to enlighten non-Hungarian speakers. Nearby stands the first Petőfi statue in a country where every town has at least one feature named after him. Such is the cult of Petőfi (which the Communists tried to appropriate, but which Hungarian youth reclaimed as a symbol of rebellion) that Kiskőrös was elevated to the rank of a city on the 150th anniversary of his birth, in 1972. On the edge of town is a small nature reserve, the **Szücs Moorland Wood**.

If you wish **to stay**, rooms are available from *Pusztatourist* (Mon–Fri 8am–4pm; ☎78/312-740) or the *Hotel Kiskőrös* (④), at Petőfi utca 112 on the southeast edge of town. **Meals** are served in the *Kurtakocsma Hotel* on József Attila utca, and the *Fürdővendéglő* by the **thermal baths** (whose temperature is a constant 58°C).

Kiskunhalas

Somewhat more appealing than Kiskőrös, especially if you're interested in lace, **KISKUNHALAS** can be reached by train from Baja or Kiskunfélegyháza. The town's medieval **lace-making** industry owed its revival in the 1890s to local school teacher Maria Markovits, who studied patterns and samples from before the Turkish occupation. Her statue stands outside the **Lace House** at Kossuth utca 37A (Tues–Sun 9am–5pm), a treasury of tablecloths, ruffs and petticoats, some composed of 56 different types of stitches.

Other sights in the centre of town include a handsome town hall and next to it, at Köztársaság utca 2, the **Thorma János Museum** (Tues–Fri 10am–6pm, Sat–Sun 10am–1pm & 2–6pm) which covers local history and the *oeuvre* of painter Tibor Csorba (1906–1985), who taught here before moving to Poland. The newly opened **House of Collections** (same hours) displays temporary exhibits at Bokanyi utca 4. Antiques and junk share stalls at the **flea market** (daily except Mon), while saddlemaker Balázs Tóth welcomes visitors to his workshop at Vas utca 1. At weekends, people make for the **thermal baths** (50°C) on the island in the river that flows through town, or go **fishing** north of town at Sóstó pond.

For **accommodation**, ask at *Pusztatourist* (☎77/321-984) or head straight for the *Hotel Csipke* (☎77/321-455; ④) on Semmelweiss tér, the *Malom Panzió* at Malom sor 4 (☎77/321-650; ②–③), or the *Sóstó Motel* (☎77/322-222; ③) and campsite (April–Oct). **Restaurants** include the *Akropolisz Étterem* at Szilády utca 6 and the *Tölgyfa Étterem* at Brinkus utca 1.

Ópusztaszer Historical Park

Ópusztaszer Historical Park (April–Oct Tues–Sun 9am–5pm), just outside the village of the same name, commemorates the conquest of the seven Magyar tribes who crossed the Carpathians and spread out across the Hungarian plains, each claiming a territory. The park supposedly marks the site of their first tribal "parliament" after the land-taking – in around 896 AD – although the only evidence for this comes from Anonymous, writing 300 years later. A huge memorial was erected here for the millennial anniversary celebrations of 1896, and in 1945 the Communists symbolically chose Ópusztaszer for the first distribution of land amongst the peasants.

SÁNDOR PETŐFI

Born on New Year's Eve 1822–23, of a Slovak mother and a Southern Slav butcher-innkeeper father, **Sándor Petőfi** was to become obsessed with acting and poetry, which he started to write at the age of fifteen. As a strolling player, soldier and labourer, he absorbed the language of working people, writing lyrical poetry in the vernacular, to the outrage of critics. Moving to Budapest in 1844, Petőfi fell in with the young radical intellectuals who met at the Pilvax Café.

From this time on, poetry and deeds were inseparable. His *Nemzeti Dal* (National Song) was declaimed from the steps of the National Museum on the first day of the 1848 Revolution ("Some noisy mob had their hurly-burly outside so I left for home," complained the director). Mindful of the thousands of landless peasants encamped outside the city, Parliament bowed to the demands of the radicals and voted for the abolition of serfdom.

During the War of Independence, Petőfi fought alongside General Bem in Transylvania, and disappeared at the battle of Segesvár in July 1849. Though he was most likely trampled beyond recognition by the Cossacks' horses (as foreseen in one of his poems), Petőfi was rumoured to have survived. In 1990, entrepreneur Ferenc Morvai announced that Petőfi had been carted off to Siberia by the Russians, married a peasant woman and later died there. The Hungarian Academy refused to support Morvai's expedition to uncover the putative grave, and it was subsequently reported that forensic analysis had proved the corpse to be that of a Jewish woman.

THE LEGEND OF ATTILA

The lower reaches of the Tisza are associated with the **legend of Attila the Hun**, who died in 453 AD of a nasal haemorrhage following a night of passion with his new bride, Kriemhild. The body of the Scourge of God was reputedly buried in a triple-layered coffin of gold, silver and lead, and then submerged in the Tisza at an unknown spot – unknown because the pallbearers were slain before the Huns departed. Archeologists have yet to find it, but the legend gains credence from the "treasure of Attila". Thought to have belonged to a Hun general, the treasure was discovered at Nagyszentmiklós (in what is now Romania) and is currently held by Vienna's Kunsthistorisches Museum.

Both themes are implicit in the diverse exhibits of the historical park. A **Village Museum** of households from southern Hungary is juxtaposed against combine harvesters, steam trains and aeroplanes. A ruined thirteenth-century monastery attests to Christian traditions, while the early freebooting, pagan Magyars are celebrated in the amazing **Cyclorama** by Árpád Feszty. This monumental canvas depicting Prince Árpád leading the tribes into the valley of Munkács was originally exhibited in Budapest's City Park. Damaged in the siege, it has only recently been restored and put back on show.

ÓPUSZTASZER itself lies 10km east of Kistelek on the Kecskemét–Szeged road. Direct **buses** to the village are scarce except on national holidays, but it's worth checking out the timetables in Kiskunfélegyháza or Szeged. Alternatively, you could try hitching from Kistelek, a stop for buses along the highway. On the way to the park on Árpád liget you'll find the *Szeri Csárda* restaurant and next door the basic *Szeri Camping* (☎62/375-123) with **horse riding** facilities across the way (same phone number; 400–600Ft per hour).

Szeged

SZEGED, as cosmopolitan a place as you'll find on the Plain, straddles the River Tisza like a provincial Budapest. Much of its friendly atmosphere is thanks to students from the university, while the old city's eclectic good looks have been saved by placing the ugly modern housing and industry over the river, in Újszeged. Though Kőrös folk settled here four to five thousand years ago, and the town flourished after 1225 because of its royal monopoly over the salt mines of Transylvania, Szeged's present layout dates from after the **great flood** of March 1879, which washed away all but 300 homes and compelled the population to start again from scratch. With aid from foreign capitals (after whom sections of the outer boulevard are named) the city bounced back, trumpeting its revival with huge buildings and squares where every type of architectural style made an appearance.

Around the Belváros

Heading southwest from Klauzál tér you'll emerge on to Dugonics tér, graced by a **Water Music Fountain** and dozens of students from the **University** who congregate here during their breaks. Overlooking the square, the university is

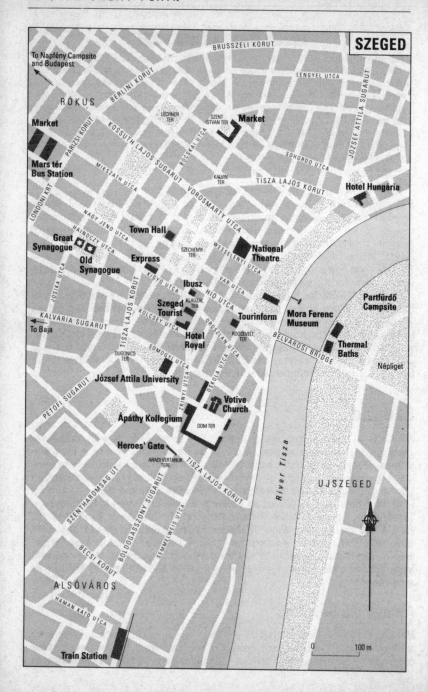

SZEGED

To Napfény Campsite
and Budapest

BRUSSZELI KORUT

LENGYEL UTCA

RÓKUS

BERLINI KORUT

JÓZSEF ATTILA SUGARUT

Market

LECHNER
TER

SZENT
ISTVAN TER

Market

PARIZSI KORUT

KOSSUTH LAJOS SUGARUT

BOCSKAI UTCA

SOHORDO UTCA

Mars tér
Bus Station

MIKSZATH UTCA

VOROSMARTY UTCA

KALVIN
TER

TISZA LAJOS KORUT

Hotel Hungária

LONDONI KRT

NAGY JENO UTCA

HAINOCZY UTCA

Town Hall

WESSELENYI UTCA

Great
Synagogue

Old
Synagogue

Express

SZECHENYI
TER

National
Theatre

JOSIKA UTCA

KIGYO UTCA

Ibusz

VAR UTCA

TISZA LAJOS KORUT

Szeged
Tourist

KLAUZAL
TER

HID UTCA

Partfürdő
Campsite

KALVARIA SUGARUT

To Baja

KOLCSEY UTCA

Tourinform

OROSZLAN UTCA

Mora Ferenc
Museum

Thermal
Baths

Hotel
Royal

ROOSEVELT
TER

BELVAROSI BRIDGE

Népliget

PETOFI SUGARUT

DUGONICS
TER

SOMOGYI UTCA

OSKOLA UTCA

József Attila University

ZRINYI UTCA

Votive
Church

Ápáthy Kollegium

DOM TER

River Tisza

Heroes' Gate

ARADI VERTANUK
TERE

TISZA LAJOS KORUT

UJSZEGED

SZENTHAROMSAG UT

BOLDOGASSZONY SUGARUT

SEMMELWEIS UTCA

BECSI KORUT

ALSÓVÁROS

HAMAN KATO UTCA

Train Station

0   100 m

named, by way of restitution, after the poet **Attila József** (1905–37) whom it expelled in 1924 for a poem which began "I have no father, I have no mother, I have no god and I have no country" and continued "with a pure heart, I'll burn and loot, and if I have to, even shoot". Attila's bitterness was rooted in childhood, when his mother – a poor washerwoman – died of starvation. Later he was expelled from the Communist Party for trying to reconcile Marx and Freudian pyschology and, living in dire poverty, he finally ended his days under the wheels of a train at Lake Balaton. Though unappreciated during his lifetime, Attila's poetry now finds widespread favour. Elderly Hungarians weep upon hearing his sentimental "Mama", while anarcho-punks relish lines such as "Culture drops off me, like the clothes off a happy lover".

Head on past the university, take a left turn, and you'll come to the so-called **Black House** on the corner of Somogyi and Kelemen utca. This Romantic-style edifice is actually painted brown and white, but the ironmonger who lived here in the nineteenth century always told peasants "You can find me in the Black House". After this brief detour, walk along Zrínyi utca and turn right to reach Dóm tér.

Dóm tér

Aside from the university, the main object of civic pride in Szeged is **Dóm tér**, flanked by arcades with twisted columns and busts of illustrious Hungarians. This 12,000-square-metre expanse was created in 1920 by demolishing a network of backstreets, to accommodate a gigantic **Votive Church** (Mon–Sat 9am–6pm, Sun 9.30–10am, 11–11.30am & 1–6pm) which the townsfolk had pledged to erect after the flood. Built of brown brick in the neo-Romanesque style, its portal is surmounted by a statue of the Virgin whose image recurs inside the church in peasant costume, wearing embroidered "butterfly slippers". Visitors are dwarfed by the white, blue and gold interior, where the organ, with its 10,180 pipes and five manuals, benefits from superb acoustics.

The eight-sided **Demetrius Tower** out in front dates from the eleventh century, but was largely rebuilt by Béla Rerrich, who designed the square. A chiming clock plays the folk song "Szeged, a famous town" at midday. On the northeastern corner of Dóm tér stands an eighteenth-century **Serbian Orthodox Church** with a magnificent iconostasis framed in pear-wood.

Banked opposite the Votive Church are rows of seats for Szeged's festival, where local operas are performed, some of them spectacularly melodramatic – for example one based on the life of Countess Báthori featured half-naked couples writhing in a vat of "blood". When performances (which start with everyone standing for the national anthem) finish, the crowds flood out towards the **Heroes' Gate** (*Hősök Kapuja*), which links Aradi Vértanúk tere with Boldogasszony sugárút. Though its origins are no longer publicized, the gate was raised to honour Horthy's henchmen, the "Whites". They gathered here in 1919, waiting for the Romanian army to defeat the Republic of Councils before they fanned out across Hungary to murder over 5000 Jews and "Reds" in the "White Terror". Fascist stone guardsmen still flank the archway, but Horthy's murals have been erased by dirt and time.

Around the waterfront and Széchenyi tér

By heading north past the Serbian church, you'll arrive at Roosevelt tér and the **Móra Ferenc Museum** (Tues–Sun 10am–6pm). Its Neoclassical facade of columns and decrepit statuary cloaks a typical mix of *objets d'art* and artefacts of local significance, notably a huge painting of the flood. More interesting is the display on the Avars, the people displaced by the arriving Magyars. Behind the museum you'll find another smaller **museum** featuring a geological display of the city (Tues–Sun 10am–2pm). The building is sited on the **remains of a castle** which in later times served as a prison for the outlaw Sándor Rózsa and for convicts who laboured on the river towpaths during the eighteenth century. As in Debrecen, this was a time of mass witch trials, when victims confessed to witchcraft under torture organized by the church elders.

From here you can walk up west past the **National Theatre** to spacious, verdant **Széchenyi tér**, Szeged's inner-city park. On the far (western) side stands a neo-Baroque **Town Hall**, likened by the poet Mihály Babits to "a lace-covered young woman dancing in the moonlight". The two allegorical **fountains** outside – known as "The Blessed and the Angry" – symbolize the benevolent and destructive aspects of the River Tisza. The town hall is linked to a neighbouring building by a charming "Bridge of Sighs", modelled on the one in Venice.

The Jewish quarter and beyond

Outside its inner boulevard, Tisza Lajos körút, Szeged is shabbier and more utilitarian, but not devoid of sights. One area worth checking out is the old **Jewish quarter**, south of Nagy Jenő utca. Dating from 1843, the **Old Synagogue** on Hajinóczy utca bears a plaque showing the height of the water during the flood – the building itself is only open during the summer festival, when it serves as a theatre. Around the block on Gutenberg utca is the Secession-style **New Synagogue** (Mon–Fri & Sun 9am–noon & 2–5pm), one of the largest in Europe and occasionally the venue for concerts of classical music. Its magnificent dome represents the world, with 24 columns for the hours of day and night, white flowers for faith, and blue stars for the infinity of the cosmos. The stained-glass windows illustrate texts from *The Flora and Minerals of the Jews*, by Rabbi Immanuel Löw, and scenes from Jewish life.

Around the outer boulevard (bus #11 or #21), to the south, parts of the **Alsóváros** or "lower town" resemble a village, with ochre-painted cottages and rutted streets. This quarter was traditionally inhabited by paprika-growers, and centres around the **Alsóvárosi Church** on Mátyás király tér, begun in the late fifteenth century. Its reworked Baroque interior contains the *Black Madonna*, a copy of the famous Madonna of Częstochowa, and the focus of attention during the reconsecration ceremonies at the annual melon harvest festival.

Two busy outdoor **markets**, on Mars tér in the Rókus quarter, and Szent István tér between the inner and outer boulevards, are well worth a visit. To the north of the centre (tram #3 from Dugonics tér) there's a **zoo** with a large collection of small monkeys and South American animals.

The Szeged telephone code is ☎62

Practicalities

Arriving at the train station or intercity bus terminal, both outside the Belváros, catch bus #83 to Tisza Lajos körút off Dugonics tér. A few minutes' walk from here you'll find the *Tourinform* **tourist office** at Viktor Hugo utca 1 (May–Sept Mon–Fri 8am–6pm & Sat–Sun 10am–2pm; Oct–April Mon–Fri 8am–4pm; ☎311-711) and *Szeged Tourist* on Klauzál tér (Mon–Fri 8.30am–5pm; plus May–Aug Sat 9am–1pm; ☎321-800), which handles private rooms and festival tickets. Both have English-speaking staff and are generally better than *Ibusz* across the way (Mon–Fri 8am–4pm & Sat 8am–noon; ☎326-533). Western **cars** can be rented from *Avis/Cooptourist* on Kiss utca, and cheaper Ladas from *Volántourist* at Fekete Sas utca 28.

Moving on from Szeged, express **trains** run daily to Kecskemét and Budapest; to Pécs; and to Békéscsaba. Other places are easier to reach by bus from Mars tér, with frequent services to Makó and Hódmezővásárhely, and more sporadic **buses** to Veszprém, Eger, Ópusztaszer, Siófok and Miskolc. **International services** run to Arad and Timişoara in Romania; and Subotica, Zenta, Zrenjanin and Novi Sad in the Voivodina region of Serbia.

Accommodation

Szeged Tourist or *Ibusz* can arrange **private rooms** (②) for considerably less than the cost of a hotel, but check first that the location is central. These are also better value than the dormitory rooms (③) available in vacant colleges during July and August – such as the one at Tisza Lajos körút 103 or the *Apáthy Kollégium* on Dom tér, bookable through *Express* at Kígyó utca 3 (Mon–Fri 8am–4pm; ☎322-522). It is also feasible to stay in Makó or Hódmezővásárhely (a 30-min bus ride from the city) or, 10km outside the city, there are **nudist camps** in Algyó and Kiskundorozsma. Local hotels, pensions and campsites are listed below.

HOTELS AND PENSIONS

Hotel Hungária, Maros utca 2 (☎480-580). A three-star pile to the north of the Belváros. ⑤.

Hotel Napfény, Dorozsmai út 4 (☎421-800). Near the campsite at the start of the Budapest highway (bus #78). ④.

Hotel Royal, Kölcsey utca 1 (☎475-275). As comfortable as the *Hungária*, and dead central. Romanian gymnast Nadia Comanesti briefly took refuge here after defecting in 1989. ⑤.

Fortuna Panzió, Pécskai utca 8 (☎431-585). In Újszeged, on the other side of the River Tisza from the city centre.

Marika Panzió, Nyíl utca 45 (☎313-861). A small place in the Alsóváros, south of the train station. ③–④.

Napfény Panzió, Dorozsmai út 4 (☎421-800). A bungalow-motel complex adjacent to the hotel of the same name. Triples ④.

CAMPSITES

Napfény Camping, Dorozsmai út 2 (☎421-800). Tent-space and huts next to the *Napfény Panzió*. Open May–Sept.

Partfürdő Camping, Középkikötő sor (☎353-811). A dearer site near the *strand* in Újszeged. Open May–Sept.

Eating and drinking

As a university town, Szeged enjoys a lively night scene with plenty of eating places and watering holes. The city is famous for its sausages and dishes such as *halászlé* (fish soup) and *halpaprikás* (fish in paprika sauce).

Alabárdos Étterem, Oskola utca 13. The smartest restaurant in town, specializing in fish and game dishes. Open Mon–Sat 2–10pm; reservations advisable. Expensive.

Bontond Étterem, Széchenyi tér 9. Good, reasonably priced Hungarian food in posh surroundings. Open daily 11am–11pm.

Doppelladler Étterem, Sóhordó utca 18, off Tisza Lajos körút (☎312-436). Elegant Austro-Hungarian cuisine. Expensive.

Faraó Étterem, Nagy Jenő utca 1. Dim in atmosphere but extensive Hungarian menu and soy dishes. Open 11am–midnight.

Hági Étterem, Keleman utca 3. Good Brno beer and Slovak food, but patchy service. Open 11am–midnight. Cheap *Bisztró* and beer hall next door.

Kiskörösi-Halászcsárda Smaller of two thatched restaurants out towards the fishing village of Tápé (bus #73 or #73Y), where the Prince of Wales (later Edward VIII) often came in the 1890s. Highly recommended.

Pagoda Étterem, Zrínyi utca 5. Unpretentious Chinese restaurant in the centre. Open noon–midnight.

Tisza Halászcsárda, Roosevelt tér 12. Also aimed at tourists, but fish-oriented and less pricey.

Virág Cukrászda, Klauzál tér. Delicious cakes and ice cream. There's more of the same at the cheaper, stand-up *Kisvirág* shop across the square.

Nightlife and entertainment

There are several places in Szeged that host **discos**. The *JATE Klub* is a typical student hang-out behind the university at Toldi utca 2, usually bopping on Friday and Saturday (8pm–4am;☎321-245). The *Mojo Club* plays alternative music near the university on Batthyány utca, and the *Sing-Sing Disco* is a popular spot near Mars tér and the bus station. At Vörosmarty utca 5–7, the *Juhász Gyula Művelődési Központ* has discos on Thursday and Friday and live music on Saturdays, while the *Tisza Gyöngye,* by the baths across the river, features a male striptease show and occasional dancing. If a game of **pool** sounds more appealing, look out for places advertising *biliárd*, such as the *Boss Klub* on Fekete Sas utca.

Other forms of **entertainment** are likeliest during the concert season (Sept–May) and the **Szeged Weeks** (roughly July 20–Aug 20), a huge festival of drama and music. Events are advertised around town, and **tickets** (100–500Ft) are available from the *Szabadtéri jegyiroda* ticket agency at Deák utca 28–30 (Mon–Fri 10am–5pm & Sat 10am–1pm).

Outdoor Activities

On hot summer weekends people flock to the **swimming pool** or the grassy *Partfürdő strand* in Újszeged across the river (undeterred by its less than clean reputation), while in winter wallowing in the outdoor **thermal baths** becomes the favoured pastime. A less crowded place to get some fresh air is the **botanical garden** (*Füvészkert*) at the end of the #70 bus line.

There are opportunities for **excursions** from the city, using buses leaving from Mars tér. With a few days' notice, *Szeged Tourist* can arrange **birdwatching** expeditions to the **Fehér-tó Nature Reserve**, a haven for 250 kinds of migratory **birds**, as well as **horse riding** trips and **archery courses** at Ópusztaszer.

CROSSING INTO SERBIA

Owing to the changing political situation in the states of the former Yugoslavia, it is advisable to check with local authorities or embassy officials before venturing across the border.

THE SOUTHERN PLAIN BEYOND THE TISZA

The **Southern Plain** beyond the Tisza is sunbaked and dusty, with small towns that bore the brunt of the Turkish occupation and often suffered from droughts, giving rise to such paranoia that "witches" were burned for "blowing the clouds away" or "selling the rain to the Turks". Resettled by diverse ethnic groups under Habsburg auspices, they later attracted dispossessed Magyars from Transylvania, who displaced the existing communities of Swabians, Serbs, Slovaks and Romanians. In the Fifties, geologists scoured the region for oil, but every bore hole struck thermal springs instead, hence the numerous spas in this region.

Many travellers miss this region altogether, and admittedly its attractions are rather low-key. **Approaches** are largely determined by where you cross the river. Crossing over at Szeged, the main trunk route heads towards Békéscsaba. Csongrád, further upriver, marks the start of a less clear-cut itinerary which might include Szarvas and Mezőtúr. The more northerly route from Szolnok to Debrecen is covered under the Northern Plain (see p.317).

Around Hódmezővásárhely and Makó

Heading on from Szeged (see p.305) there are two basic routes: northeast towards Békéscsaba via **Hódmezővásárhely**, or southeast through **Makó** to the Romanian border. While Makó could be a handy stop for motorists en route to Romania, neither is an essential stopover or an absolute "must". Counting the lovely park at nearby **Mártely**, Hódmezővásárhely is better endowed with sights than Makó, but the latter offers horse riding and trips to the famous stud farm at **Mezőhegyes**.

Hódmezővásárhely

HÓDMEZŐVÁSÁRHELY's tongue-twisting name can be translated as "marketplace of the badger's field", though it's disputed whether the *hód-* prefix really derives from the Magyar word for "badger". Either way, this long-established market town has diversified into leatherwork and pottery, consigning its rural past to the **Tanya Museum** (Tues–Sat 1–5pm), a converted former farmhouse and windmill you can find about 6km out along the Szeged road.

Downtown Kossuth tér is dignified by an eighteenth-century Calvinist church and an imposing town hall, across from which is the **Alföldi Gallery** (Tues–Sun 10am–6pm). On display here are scenes of *puszta* life by local artist János Tornyai (1869–1936), whose *oeuvre* was recently enhanced by the discovery of 700 canvases in a Budapest attic. The paintings of other artists who worked here around the turn of the century hang in the **Tornyai János Museum** (Tues–Sun 11am–5pm) at Szántó Kovács utca 16, whose basement contains the *Venus of Kökénydomb*, a 5000-year-old statue of a fertility goddess, and a recently expanded folk art collection. On the same street stands a fine Baroque **Greek Orthodox Church**, whose "Nahum iconostasis" from Mount Athos is named after an obscure seventh-century prophet. Another building worth a visit is the Secession-style **Synagogue** on Szent István tér.

Hódmezővásárhely is renowned for its black **pottery**, based on Turkish designs, which is fired in a manner dating back to Neolithic times. Examples are displayed in the **Csúcs Potter's House** (Tues–Sun 1–5pm) at Rákóczi utca 101, and alongside peasant costumes and furniture in the **Folk Culture House** at Árpád utca 21 (Tues–Fri 10am–5pm & Sat 10am–5pm). If you're interested in buying some pottery or seeing it being made you can visit János Szénasi at Eke utca 41 near the Csúcs House, or János Monus at Táncsics Mihály utca 27 near the synagogue.

Regular buses run 10km north to **MÁRTELY**, a gorgeous **park** beside a tributary of the Tisza, with boats for rent and hand-woven **baskets** for sale. Ideal for picnics and **horse riding**, it's also a nice spot in which to relax and unwind.

Practicalities

For **information**, contact *Szeged Tourist* at Szőnyi utca 1 (Mon–Fri 8am–5pm; plus mid-June to mid-Sept Sat 8am–noon; ☎62/341-325. Private **rooms** can be arranged through the tourist office; otherwise there's the *Fáma Hotel* at Szeremlei utca 7 (☎62/344-444; ③) and the *Vándorsólyom Fogadó*, a country inn at Tanya út 1447 (☎62/341-900; ③–④) with horses for cross-country riding and carriage driving. You can camp at *Thermál Kemping* at Ady utca 1 (June–Aug; ☎62/344-238), strategically placed for a plunge in the town's outdoor **thermal baths** next door (daily 7am–7.30pm); or there's the well-equipped *Tisza* **campsite** with chalets in Mártely 10km to the north (mid-May to late Sept; ☎62/342-753).

The best place for Hungarian **food** is the *Bagólyvár* at Nagy Imre utca 31, off the Szeged road (11am–11pm). The more expensive *Phoenix* offers Serb specialities, while the *Casino Söröző* at Hősők tere is cheap and has pool tables and a small bowling area.

In October each year Hodmezővásárhely hosts the **Autumn Art Festival**, featuring conferences and exhibitions of paintings by the Alföld School.

Makó and Mezőhegyes

The sleepy town of **MAKÓ** is the "onion capital" of Hungary, and notable for its therapeutic **baths in radioactive Maros mud**. Signposted off the main road is the **Attila József Museum** (Tues–Sun 10am–6pm), a typical collection of local paintings and artefacts, with a wagon-builder's workshop in the courtyard. The only other "sights" are an **Orthodox Synagogue** at Eötvös utca 15, and the **Attila Memorial House** at Kazinczy utca 8 (Tues–Sun 10am–6pm), where the poet lived all his life.

Aside from the *Hotel Korona* (☎65/411-384; ②), Makó has a couple of **campsites** beside the River Maros, 500m out towards Szeged, and another site 2km southeast of town along the road to the Romanian border (all three open May–Sept). There are also a few chalets and a grassy area for tents at **MAGYARCSANÁD**, a fuel stop 8km from the border crossing at **NAGYLAK**.

Enquire at *Szeged Tourist* about excursions to **MEZŐHEGYES**, 30km northeast of town, where a stud for breeding Lippizaner horses was founded in 1785. Today the **stud farm** breeds **Gidrán and Nonius horses**, the latter having been introduced from Normandy in 1810 to produce resilient cavalry chargers. There is a covered **riding school** offering horse or carriage rides, and the *Hotel Kozma* at Kozma utca 32 (☎68/381-045; ③).

Békéscsaba

Travelling between Szeged and Debrecen, **BÉKÉSCSABA** is practically unavoidable. While not perhaps deserving of a special pilgrimage, it is nevertheless a pleasant town with its fair share of history and worthy sights.

The Town

From Szent István tér, the town's main square, follow Széchenyi utca past the Catholic church to the Derkovits embankment to find the **Munkácsy Museum** at no. 9 (Tues–Sun 10am–6pm). Displayed alongside romantic canvases by Mihály Munkácsy (1844–1900) are oddments concerning the eighteenth-century Slovak settlers who revived Békéscsaba after a ruinous succession of earthquakes, invasions, plagues and fires. Next door, but still part of the same museum, is an ethnographic exhibition that traces the history of the Hungarian, German, Slovak and Romanian groups of the region. The recently opened **Mihály Munkácsy Memorial House**, at Gyulai út 5, has a collection of paintings and furniture dating from the time the Romantic painter lived here as a fourteen- to fifteen-year-old. A couple of blocks to the north, Slovak costumes and other artefacts are displayed in the ornate **Slovak House** (*Slovák Tájház*) at Garay utca 21 (Tues–Sun 10am–noon & 2–5pm).

From the Munkácsy Museum on the Derkovits embankment you can walk south along the **Promenade of Sculptures** beside the canal, or cross over the bridge to find the **István Malom**, another interesting (albeit unofficial) sight. This nineteenth-century flour mill, automated at the turn of the century, is crammed with wardrobe-sized shakers, rotating sieves and wooden chutes – objects of pride to the workers who may show you around. Alternatively, you could catch bus #4 or #9 out along Gulyai út and walk on a bit from the end of the line to find the **Corn Museum** (*Gabonamúzeum*) at no. 65, a brick windmill that was in use as recently as 1953. Beside it stands an old *tanya* (10am–6pm; closed Mon & Sat).

Practicalities

Arriving at the train station at the western end of Andrássy utca, catch bus #1, #1G, #2 or #7 to the start of the pedestrian precinct, and continue on foot towards the Körös canal. This route will take you past three **tourist offices**: *Express* at Andrássy utca 29–33 (Mon–Fri 8am–4pm); *Békéstourist* at no. 10 (Mon–Thurs 8am–4pm & Fri 8am–3.30pm; ☎66/323-448); and *Cooptourist* a few doors along (Mon–Fri 8am–4pm). Arriving by bus instead, it's a brief walk from the depot on Hunyadi tér to Szent István tér, the town's main square.

Accommodation

As usual, **private rooms** or **dormitory beds** (from *Békéstourist* or *Express*) are the cheapest form of accommodation. The beautifully restored *Fiume* on the corner of Szent István tér is Békéscsaba's top **hotel** (☎66/443-243; ⑤), the only downtown alternative being the run-down *Körös* on Széchenyi utca (☎66/441-741; ③). The *Fenyves Hotel* at Lencsési út 142 (☎66/456-126; ③) is on the József Attila housing estate, southeast of the centre (bus #17); and the *Trófea Hotel* (☎66/441-066; ④) is at Gyulai út 61, on the eastern side of town (bus #4 or #9). There's also a **campsite**, *Pósteleki Camping* (June to mid-Sept; ☎66/327-197), in the suburb of Békéscsaba-Póstelek.

Eating, drinking and entertainment

The *Fenyves Hotel* has a good restaurant and the *HBH Bayor* in the *Fiume Hotel* serves acceptable beer. Local youths go drinking across the square at the *Club Narancs* where live music is occasionally played; at the bar of the *Körös Hotel*; and at the late-night *Rózsafa Disco Bar* (10pm–4am) on the corner of Degre utca and Dr Becsei utca. The latter has **discos** at weekends and is near the **Árpád thermal baths** on the east bank of the canal (summer daily 6am–7pm; winter Tues–Sun 7am–7pm); bus #8 runs fairly close.

Moving on

From the intercity depot on Hunyadi tér there are **buses** to Debrecen (8 daily; 3–4hr); Eger (2 daily); Kecskemét (1 daily); Hajdúszoboszló (leaving around 8.45am); and Gyula (hourly); plus **international services** to Subotica (5am), Arad and Timişoara (5.45am).

Gyula

GYULA, 20km from Békéscsaba en route to the Romanian border, is probably the prettiest town in the Körös region, with the most to show for its history. Named after a tribal chieftain from the time of the Magyar conquest, it became a twin town after the Turkish withdrawal, with Hungarians living in *Magyargyula* and Romanians and Germans living in *Németgyula*.

Gyula's chief monument is a chunky **brick fortress** (Tues–Sun 10am–5pm) dating from the fourteenth century, the only one of its kind left in Hungary. Its Powder Tower is now a wine bar and the chapel a museum, while during July and August the castle (*vár*) provides a setting for the annual **Castle Plays**, which are mostly on historical themes. The fortress is situated in a park to the east of the centre, near a **Greek Orthodox Church** on Groza tér, and a complex of twelve **thermal pools** known as the *Várfürdő*. The temperature of these pools ranges from 46°C to 92°C – the latter can only be borne after you've acclimatized yourself, and then only for a very short time.

Running alongside Béke sugárút is a park containing "Erkel's Tree", named after the "father" of Hungarian opera and the composer of the national anthem who often worked in the tree's shade. The great man is commemorated in the **Erkel Museum** (Tues–Sun 9am–5pm) on Dürer utca, which also contains works by the rather more famous German painter Albrecht Dürer, whose ancestors lived in Gyula. Marginally more interesting is the **György Kohán Museum** (Tues–Sun 9am–5pm) in the park, containing some of the 3000 works that its namesake bequeathed to his home town – mostly bold depictions of horses, women and houses.

Practicalities

Gyula's **train station** is at the northern end of Béke sugárút (a 15-min walk from the centre), and its **bus station** is directly south of Eszperantó tér on Vásárhelyi Pál utca. **Information** is available from *Tourinform* at Kossuth utca 7 (summer Mon–Fri 9am–7pm & Sat 9am–1pm; winter Mon–Fri 9am–5pm; ☎66/463-421);

Békéstourist at Pálffy utca 1 (☎66/463-028); and *Gyulatourist* at Eszperantó tér 1 (Mon–Fri 8am–5pm; plus summer Sat 8am–noon; ☎66/361-192). For the benefit of travellers arriving late from Romania, there's also a **24-hour currency exchange** at Hétvezér utca 5.

Private rooms can be booked through either *Békéstourist* or *Gyulatourist*. Across from the latter is the *Hotel Aranykereszt* (☎66/463-163; ③) and, at Rábai Miklós út 2, the *Hotel Hőforras* (☎66/361-544; ③). There are two **campsites** with huts in the vicinity of the castle: *Thermál Camping* at Szélső utca 16, and the smaller *Mark Camping* at Vár utca 5.

The best place for cheap **meals** is the *Gulyáscsárda* near the junction of Városház and Kossuth utca. Other options include the *Park Vendéglő* at Part utca 15; the *Komló Étterem* in the hotel of the same name; and the *Budrió Vendéglő* at Béke sugarút 69. Don't miss the small *Százéves Cukrászda* at Jókai utca 1, which is the oldest patisserie in Hungary after *Ruszwurm's* in Budapest.

Csongrád, Szarvas and Mezőtúr

An alternative route across the Tisza is via Csongrád, east of Kiskunfélegyháza, whence you can visit Szarvas and Mezőtúr before joining the main route to Debrecen at Kiszújszallas. In many ways this region has even less to offer than places further south, but frequent **buses** mean that you needn't stay long in a town if it doesn't appeal. Unless you strike lucky or juggle timetables, **trains** are not much use here. However, the country roads are good for **cycling** – especially in the late summer, when the verges are awash with purple sea lavender.

Csongrád

The county town of **CSONGRÁD** retains a core of thatched **peasant houses** and a Secession-style high school that lends charm to Kossuth tér, but there's no trace of the "Black Castle" from which its name derives (called *Czernigrad* by the Bulgar princes who ruled it in the ninth century). Originally, the castle occupied a strategic position near the confluence of three tributaries of the Körös, which regularly flooded the low-lying region. During the nineteenth century these rivers were gradually tamed by embankments, thrown up by day-labourers who wandered from site to site with their barrows; their lives are commemorated by the **Kubikus Museum** on Iskola utca (Tues–Fri 1–5pm & Sat–Sun 9am–noon). At Györkér utca 1, the **Village Museum** (May–Oct Wed–Sun 1–5pm) occupies two typical thatched houses, with old household items and furniture displayed in its interior. Like most towns on the Plain, Csongrád also features a **thermal bath**.

Should you fancy staying, between May and September you can rent 200-year-old fishermen's cottages in the old town through *Szeged Tourist* at Fő utca 14 (Mon–Fri 9am–5pm; plus summer Sat 9am–noon; ☎63/381-069). More conventional **accommodation** is offered by the *Hotel Tisza* at Fő utca 23 (☎63/381-594; ③–④), the *Erzsébet Hotel* at Fő utca 3 (☎63/381-960; ②–③), and a pleasant **campsite** beside the river. **Restaurants** include the *Bökény* at Muskátli utca 1, *Csuka Csárda* at Szentesi út 1, and the *Halászcsárda* at Kossuth tér 17.

Travelling on by bus towards Szarvas, you will probably have to change services at SZENTES, across the river.

SUICIDES

Csongrád county has the unenviable distinction of the highest **suicide** rate in Hungary, which has long been the world's most suicide-prone nation, with an average of 50 suicides per 100,000 people. Nobody is really sure why, although theories are legion. Some blame the stresses of a society in rapid transition, but other countries experiencing the same are nowhere near as badly hit (and the rate in Hungary actually declined during the worst years of Stalinist terror). Others cite racial melancholy – there's an old saying that "the Magyar takes his pleasures sadly" – or blame the vast *puszta*. Another explanation is that the local custom of displaying corpses before burial encourages attention-seeking suicides. Whatever the cause, instances are all too common, the most famous examples being that of Attila József (whose death under the wheels of a train at Lake Balaton is emulated by several people every year), and seventeen-year-old Csilla Molnár, who killed herself shortly after becoming Miss Hungary in 1986. For one woman in Kaposvár, the final straw was when Bobby died in the Dallas series.

Szarvas

SZARVAS ("Stag") looks eerily empty, with a broad main street intersected by wide roads. The town was laid out like a chess board in the eighteenth century by the enlightened thinker Samuel Tessedik, and originally populated by Slovak settlers. Aside from a bronze statue of a stag in the centre, there is nothing much to see beyond the **Tessedik Samuel Museum** on Vajda Peter utca (Tues–Sun 10am–6pm), and an old **Slovak House** at Hoffmann utca 1 (Tues–Fri 1–4pm & Sat 10am–noon).

The town's principal attraction, however, is the **Arboretum** (mid-March to mid-Nov daily 8am–6pm; groups only the rest of the year), a few kilometres out along the road to Mezőtúr, beside a dead branch of the River Körös. This 84-hectare park contains 1700 different plants, laid out in emulation of the grounds of Schönbrunn Castle in Vienna by Count József Bolza, whose nickname – "Pepi" – gives the arboretum its sobriquet *Pepikert* (Pepi's Garden). You can also get there by rented boat, a nice little excursion – tickets can be arranged through the *Ciprus Restaurant* (☎66/311-700).

Should you feel like **staying**, private rooms can be booked through *Ibusz* at Szabadság út 6–10 (Mon–Thurs 8am–4pm & Fri 8am–3pm; ☎66/312-520), or there's the outwardly grand (but inwardly shabby) *Hotel Árpád* (☎66/312-120; ③) at Kossuth utca 64 in the centre, or the *Mohosz Üdülő* on Erzsébet liget, with doubles, triples and quads (☎66/312-702; ③).

Mezőtúr and Túrkeve

Heading north from Szarvas to Mezőtúr – a quaint old ferry takes you over the river – you cross a region known as the *Sárrét* (Swampland), nowadays largely drained but still rich in flora, frogs and insects. **MEZŐTÚR** itself has an exhibition of local **pottery** in the former synagogue at Damjanach utca 1 (a sight in its own right), and also serves as a base for trips to **TÚRKEVE**, 16km further north. Here you can see a big exhibition of sculptures by the Finta brothers at the **Finta Museum** on Attila út (Tues–Thurs 9am–5pm, Sat 9am–noon & Sun 9am–5pm). The brothers left Hungary in the 1920s in search of fame and fortune, Sándor

Finta moving to Paris and Gergely making it as far as New York. The most striking work displayed is Gergely's *Human Destiny*, a giant hand poised to absorb a
helpless figure.

Accommodation is available in both towns. In Mezőtúr there is the *Berettyó
Fogadó* (②) at Kossuth tér 8, while Túrkeve offers a choice between the *Kevi
Fogadó* (②) at Kenyérmezei út 27, or private rooms (①–②) at Petőfi tér 3–5,
Árpád utca 3A or Kenyérmezei út 8B.

Buses link both towns to Kisújszallas, along the main road and rail line
between Szolnok and Debrecen.

THE NORTHERN PLAIN BEYOND THE TISZA

The **Northern Plain** has more to offer than the south, with Hortobágy National
Park, the friendly city of Debrecen and picturesque villages around the headwa-
ters of the River Tisza. In July and August, you can catch colourful festivals at
Nagykálló, Hortobágy and Debrecen, while in September there's a carnival at
Nyíregyháza and a major religious festival at Máriapócs.

Most travellers head directly for Debrecen along the trunk route from
Budapest, which crosses the Tisza at Szolnok. Since the intervening towns have
little to offer, and most places are best reached from Debrecen, the following
sections have been structured accordingly.

Szolnok

Sited at the confluence of the Zagyva and Tisza rivers, **SZOLNOK** has never
been allowed to forget its importance as a bridgehead. Once the Mongols had
stormed its castle in the thirteenth century, there was nothing to stop them riding
on to Buda. Similarly in this century, the town's seizure by the Red Army foretold
its inexorable advance in 1944 and again in 1956, when it crushed the Uprising.
Given this history, it's not surprising that most of Szolnok consists of post-war
constructions, or that the population turned out to jeer the Soviets goodbye in
1990.

Such sights as there are can be found in the Tabán district beside the Zagyva,
which contains some old **gabled houses**. The local history **museum** at Kossuth
tér 4 (Tues–Sun 10am–6pm) bears the name of János Damjanich, who trounced
the Habsburg army in 1849. He is duly honoured inside along with members of
the **Szolnok Artists' Colony**, whose work can also be seen past the bridge
across the Zagyva. Another **art gallery** occupies an old synagogue on the corner
of Ságvári körút and Kolói utca. The latter street also boasts a handsome
Franciscan Church, where **organ concerts** are held in summer. Szolnok's **thermal baths** are to be found on the far side of the Tisza, in an ancient-looking (but
actually modern) building with a colonnade.

Practicalities

Szolnok's **bus station** is on Ady Endre utca, north of Kossuth tér, and its **train
station** is northwest of the city centre on Jubileumi tér (bus #24, #8, #7, #6 or

#15). The city is sited along the main road and rail line from Budapest to Debrecen. It serves as a terminus for **trains** to Kiskunfélegyháza via Lakitelek, and a nexus for **buses** to Jászberény, Cegléd, Tiszafüred and other towns on the Plain.

Information is available from *Tourinform*, across from the **bus station** at Ságvári utca 4 (Mon–Thurs 8am–4pm & Fri 8am–3pm; ☎56/424-803); *Ibusz* at Kossuth út 18 (Mon–Fri 8am–4pm & Sat 9am–noon; ☎56/423-602); and, also at no. 18, *Express* (Mon–Thurs 8am–4.30pm, Fri 8am–2pm & Sat 8am–noon; ☎56/424-010).

Apart from **private rooms** (bookable through all three tourist offices), **accommodation** in Szolnok does not come cheap. The *Tisza* at Verseghy park 2 (☎56/371-155; ④–⑤) is a pricey but wonderfully old-fashioned resort hotel with its own small thermal bath, a very pleasant patio overlooking the river and an ornate restaurant serving good food. The *Pelikán Hotel* at Jászkúrt út 1 (☎56/343-855; ⑤) and the *Touring Hotel* on Tiszaligeti sétány (☎56/379-805; ④) are two other possibilities; or there's the *Tiszaligeti Motel* (☎56/424-403; ③) at *Tiszaligeti Camping* near the baths, both of which are open from May to September.

Szolnok's **eating places** include a handful of hotel-restaurants in the centre, as well as the *Szolnok Étterem* at Jubileum tér 2, the *Gösser Söröző* at Kossuth út 9, the *Róza Étterem* at Petőfi utca 31, and the *Alexander Pizzeria* in Tisza Park. The *Irish Pub* at Szapáry utca 24 is a lively drinking place.

Karcag, Kenderes and Püspökladány

KARCAG, 85km east of Szolnok, was once a major settlement of the Cumanians, whose costumes and pottery are displayed in the **Győrffy István Museum** at Kálvin utca 4 (Tues–Sun 10am–noon & 2–6pm). Although much of the town's Cumanian identity has been lost, a couple of aspects still survive: there's a thriving local tradition of **pottery**, as a visit to the **Kántor Sándor Fazekas Tájház** (April–Oct Tues–Sun 10am–noon & 2–6pm) at Erkel utca 1 will confirm; and **food** based on traditional recipes – for instance *kunsági pandurleves*, a soup made of chicken or pigeon and seasoned with ginger, garlic, nutmeg and paprika – can still be enjoyed at such places as the *Kunsági Étterem* at Dózsa út 1, and the *Mészáros Vendéglő* at Madarasi út 63. Karcag is also the location of the largest rice-hulling mill in Europe, which processes the rice grown around Hortobágy. On the **accommodation** front, there's the *Fehér Holló* at Püspökladányi út 3 (☎50/313-555) and half a dozen tourist motels and a campsite in nearby **BEREKFÜRDŐ**, whose main attraction is its small and very popular **spa park** with three outdoor baths (8am–7pm).

Kenderes

About 15km east of Karsag lies the town of **KENDERES**, which hit the headlines in September 1994 when the body of Miklós Horthy, Hungary's leader during the interwar period, was brought here from Portugal to be reburied. The issue rekindled a long-time debate between Hungary's conservatives on the one hand, who were nostalgic for Horthy's nationalistic and anti-communist leadership, and the liberals on the other, who considered Horthy a dictator whose regime, which had allied itself with Hitler, precipitated the White Terror.

Püspökladány

A couple of kilometres further east, the industrial town of **PÜSPÖKLADÁNY** is nowadays notable only for its branch line down to Békéscsaba, also used by international services to Romania. Before the demise of Communism, however, it was a stronghold of the **Workers' Militia**, founded by the Party to break strikes in the aftermath of the Uprising. This, the *Munkásrendőrség*, remained the Party's private army until it was dissolved in 1989 as a prelude to free elections, by which time the Militia had grown middle-aged and pot-bellied, with conspicuously few recruits from the younger generation.

The spa town of Hajdúszoboszló, around 30km further along the route to Debrecen, is covered on p.328.

Debrecen

Once upon a time, **DEBRECEN** was the site of Hungary's greatest livestock fair, and foreigners tended to be snooty about "this vast town of unsightly buildings" with its thatched cottages and a main street that became "one liquid mass of mud" when it rained, "so that officers quartered on one side were obliged to mount their horses and ride across to have dinner on the other". Even so, no one can deny the significance of Debrecen (pronounced "DEB-retzen"), both economically and as the chief centre of Hungarian Calvinism. From the sixteenth century onwards there wasn't a generation of lawyers, doctors or theologians that didn't include graduates from Debrecen's Calvinist College (the city is still renowned for its university and teacher-training colleges); while in the crucial years of 1848–49 and 1944–45 it was here that Hungary's future was debated. During the late 1980s, local churches and employers helped to resettle thousands of refugees from Ceauşescu's Romania.

The City

Hungary's second largest city still follows the old, much maligned main street, which a few years ago reverted to its former name of **Piac utca** (Market Street)

WITCHCRAFT

The early Calvinists' hatred of popery was only exceeded by their animus towards pagan beliefs amongst the peasantry of the Plain, who regarded *táltos* (village wise men) with benevolence, while fearing *boszorkány*, their female counterparts. Until the eighteenth century, women accused of **witchcraft** were able to plead that they were beneficent *táltos* (for example Frau Bártha, who claimed to have learned *táltos* skills from her brother), but as the Calvinists' grip tightened this defence became untenable. Midwives were particularly vulnerable as it was popularly believed that the murder of a relative or newborn child was a prerequisite for acquiring their "magical" skills, but women in general suffered from the Calvinists' witch-hunting zeal, which also found scapegoats in herbalists, beggars and vagabonds.

Witch trials were finally banned by Maria Theresa in 1768 after the scandalous events in Szeged, when "witches" had confessions tortured out of them; and by the nineteenth century the bloody deeds of Debrecen's forefathers were buried beneath platitudes eulogizing the "Calvinist Rome".

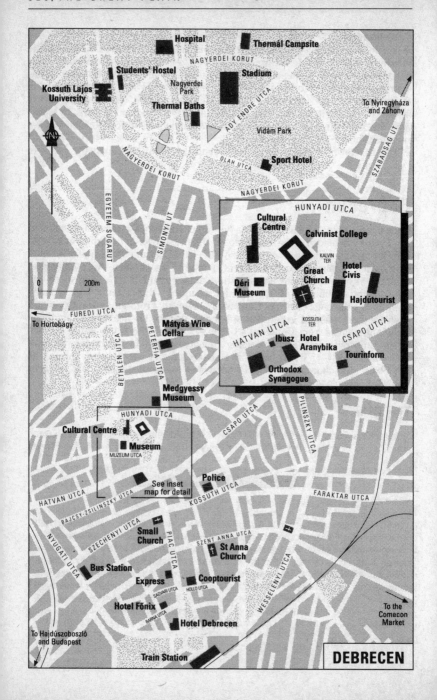

DEBRECEN

after forty years of being called Vörös Hadsereg útja in honour of the Red Army. Approaching from the direction of the train station you'll pass the former **County Hall** at no. 54, whose facade crawls with statues of Hajdúks made from Zsolnay pyrogranite. Further up, on the other side of the road, are the nineteenth-century **Csanak House** (no. 51), and the Romantic-style **Small Church**, whose bastion-like top replaced an onion dome that blew off during a storm in 1909. Facing the church is a Secessionist pile with a gilded doorway, originally a Savings Bank whose premises rivalled Budapest's Gresham Building for lavish ornamentation. A little further on the road widens into **Kossuth tér** and **Kálvin tér**, dominated by two monumental edifices.

The Great Church and Calvinist College

The **Great Church** (*Nagytemplom*) is an appropriately huge monument to the *Református* faith that swept through Hungary during the sixteenth century and still commands the allegiance of roughly one third of the population. Calvinism took root more strongly in Debrecen than elsewhere, as local Calvinists struck a deal with the Turks to ensure their security and forbade Catholics to settle here after 1552. In 1673, the Catholic Habsburgs deported 41 Calvinist priests (who ended up as galley slaves), but failed to shake the faith's hold on Debrecen. A reconciliation of sorts was achieved during the pope's visit in 1991, when he laid a wreath at their memorial.

The church itself (Mon–Sat 10am–1pm & Sun 11am–1pm) is a dignified Neoclassical building designed by Mihály Pollack. Its typically austere interior accommodated the Diet of 1849 that declared Hungary's secession from the Habsburg empire. The *Rákóczi-harang* – forged from cannons used in the Rákóczi War of Independence – is the largest bell in Hungary.

Around the back on Kálvin tér stands the **Calvinist College** (*Református Kollégium*), where students were compelled to rise at 3am and be in bed by 9pm until the end of the eighteenth century. The college motto, inscribed over the entrance, is *orando et laborando* ("praying and working"). Though venerable in appearance, this is not the original college founded in 1538, but an enlarged nineteenth-century version. It was here that the Provisional National Assembly of left-wing and centre parties met under Soviet auspices late in 1944, unwittingly conferring legitimacy on the Soviet occupation. Visitors can inspect a **Museum of College History** (Tues–Sat 9am–5pm & Sun 9am–1pm) whose exhibits include a meteorite which landed near town in 1857, as well as the **Oratory** and **Library** (upstairs).

Museums

A short walk west of the college is the excellent **Déri Museum** (April–Oct Tues–Sun 10am–6pm; Nov–March Tues–Sun 10am–4pm), fronted by allegorical statues by local sculptor Ferenc Medgyessy. The collection contains paintings and ethnographic material including the traditional shepherds' cloaks (*szűr*) which played a significant role in local courtship rituals. A herdsman would "forget" to remove his finest *szűr* from the porch when he left the house of the woman he was courting, and if it was taken inside within an hour then a formal proposal could be made. Otherwise, the cloak was hung prominently on the verandah – giving rise to the expression *kitették a szűrét* ("his cloak was put out"), meaning to get rid of an unwanted suitor.

A separate gallery contains **paintings** depicting romantic and patriotic themes by Viktor Madarász, Bertalan Székely and **Mihály Munkácsy** (1844–1900). Pride of place is given to the latter's vast canvas *Ecce Homo*, an allegorical representation of good and evil, truth and falsehood, which toured the world in the 1890s. Having viewed it in Dublin, James Joyce commented: "It is a mistake to limit drama to the stage; a drama can be painted as well as sung or acted, and *Ecce Homo* is a drama".

Although the small **Postal Museum** at Bethlen Gabor utca 1 is strictly of interest to philatelists (Wed, Sat & Sun 2–4pm), you might consider visiting the **Medgyessy Museum** at Péterfia utca 28 (Tues–Sun 10am–6pm), which honours the locally born sculptor Ferenc Medgyessy (1881–1958).

Synagogues and other churches

Given the focus on Calvinism, it's easy to overlook the existence of other faiths in Debrecen. A case in point is the pair of neglected synagogues in the backstreets west of Kálvin tér. On Pásti utca stands an eclectic-style **Orthodox Synagogue** dating from 1913 (now closed to the public), a block south from which you'll find the **Status Quo Synagogue** on Kápolna utca, built to serve the so-called Status Quo or middling-conservative Jews (☎415-861 for the key if door is locked).

If ecclesiastical architecture is your thing, consider tracking down **St Anna's Church**, a couple of blocks east of Piac utca, which is Catholic and Baroque and originally belonged to the Piarist order. Above the portal you can discern the coat of arms of its founder, Cardinal Csáky, while next door is the former Piarist grammar school, with an exhibition on their educational methods (mid-Sept to late May Mon–Fri 8am–2pm). The street on which it stands was previously called Béke útja (Peace Avenue), which raised a mordant chuckle amongst the townsfolk, since it leads to a slaughterhouse beyond the **Greek Orthodox Church** on Attila tér.

Nagyerdei Park and Kossuth Lajos University

North of Kálvin tér the city turns greener and quieter, with stylish residences lining the roads to **Nagyerdei Park** (formerly named after Lenin). In the western section you'll find the **thermal baths** (April–Oct daily 8am–8pm; Nov–March daily 8am–6pm), fed by springs of sulphurous "brown water" (*bárna-víz*) rising up from beneath the park. If it hasn't been removed by now, the plaque by the entrance reads: "Created with the support of the Workers' and Peasants' Revolutionary Party for the health of the workers."

Beyond the reedy lake and wooden footbridge rises the columned bulk of **Kossuth Lajos University**, fronted by fountains where newlyweds pose for photos. The university hosts a **Hungarian language summer course** (*Nyári-Egyetem*), usually in late July, which draws students from nations as diverse as Sweden and Vietnam – a good place to meet foreigners. Beyond the campus lies a **Botanical Garden**.

Markets

Though the great bi-monthly fairs "held here since time immemorial" no longer take place, Debrecen's **fruit and vegetable market** is a pungent, compulsive affair. The indoor *vásárcsarnok* (Mon–Sat 4am–3pm & Sun 4–11am), next to the supermarket on Csapó utca, is awash with kerchiefed grannies hawking pickles, meat, soft cheese and strange herbs; the air filled with smells and Magyar interrogatives ("*Hogy a... ?*" is slang for "how much is the... ?").

Until a few years ago, the wasteland at the back served as a "Polish Market", where traders from other Communist countries sold goods and exchanged currencies. Nowadays, the so-called **Comecon Market** (*KGST Piac*) is held in an industrial quarter of the city (daily except Wed 8am–noon or 1pm). Take a #30 bus from the train station and get off where everybody else does just past the cigarette factory (*Dohánygyár*). The market is across the road and through a portal, its 800-odd stalls selling clothes, tools, loads of junk and a few antiques. It is also a place to exchange forints or hard currency for Romanian lei, Czech crowns and other currencies – and get ripped off, if you're not careful.

> The Debrecen telephone code is ☎52

Practicalities

The **bus station**, from where there are frequent services to the Hajduság towns, is on Külső Vásártér, off Széchenyi utca; bus #31 runs from here to Szécseny utca (two stops), where any bus will take you one stop on to the train station. Outside the train station, in the southern part of town, you can board tram #1, which runs up Piac utca through the centre, continuing on to the University before looping back again – making sightseeing a doddle.

The most helpful place for **information** is *Tourinform* at Piac utca 20 (April–Oct 8am–8pm; Nov–March Mon–Fri 8.30am–4.30pm; ☎412-250 or ☎314-139), though you can also try *Hajdútourist* in the mall on the eastern side of Kálvin tér (Sept–May Mon–Fri 8am–4.30pm; June–Aug Mon–Fri 8am–5pm & Sat 8am–12.30pm; ☎415-588) or *Ibusz* at Piac utca 11–13 (Mon–Thurs 8am–4pm & Fri 8am–3pm; ☎315-555). *Cooptourist* at Holló utca 4 (☎310-770) and *Express* at Piac utca 77 (May–Sept Mon–Fri 8.30am–4.30pm & Sat 9am–1pm; Oct–April Mon–Fri 8.30am–4.30pm; ☎418-332) are really only useful for booking accommodation.

Accommodation

The cheapest accommodation is in **colleges**, which charge by the bed (①). According to *Express* there are vacancies on Friday and Saturday throughout the year, and daily throughout July and August. (However note that most places do in fact fill up during the annual festivals, many hotels being booked a whole year in advance for the August 20 Flower Festival.) Likely venues include the *kollégium* at Jerikó utca 17–21; Kollos utca 17 (near the terminal of the #31 bus in the north of town); and the annexe behind the university. The next cheapest deal are **private rooms** (②), bookable through *Hajdútourist*, *Cooptourist* or *Ibusz*. Other options are listed below.

HOTELS AND PENSIONS

Centrum Panzió, Péterfia utca 37A (☎416-193). Plain but comfortable pension near the Great Church. ③.

Cívis Hotel, Kálvin tér 4 (☎418-522). A flashy three-star establishment across from the Great Church. ⑤–⑥.

Hotel Aranybika, Piac utca 11–15, off Kossuth tér (☎416-777). Established in 1690, the 250-room *Aranybika* is reputedly the oldest hotel in Hungary, though most of what you see today dates from the early twentieth century. Its facilities include a wonderfully ornate restaurant, gym and sauna. Rooms range from ④ to ⑦.

Hotel Debrecen, Petőfi tér 9 (☎316-550). A Sixties pile directly opposite the train station – noisy and run down. ②–③.

Hotel Főnix, Barna utca 17 (☎413-355). 50-room hotel in a quiet side street off Petőfi tér, a couple of blocks from the train station. ③.

Hotel Sport, Oláh utca 5 (☎417-655). A well-equipped hotel in Nagyerdei Park. ③.

West Motel, Petöfi utca 12 (☎313-266). Noisy motel by the train station with doubles (②) and triples (②–③).

CAMPSITES

Termál Camping, Nagyerdei körút 102 (☎412-456). Tent-space and chalets northeast of Nagyerdei Park. Open May–Sept.

FICC Rally Camping (☎368-900), 6km south of town near Lake Dorcas (accessible by bus #26 from the bus terminal). Has huts and facilities for horse riding and angling. Open mid-April to Sept.

Eating

Although the **restaurant** of the *Hotel Aranybika* is fabulously ornate, the food is nothing special, and if you're going to spend that sort of money it's better to go for restaurants such as the *Gambrinus* (11am–11pm) at Piac utca 28B. The *Régiposta* (Old Post Office) at Széchenyi utca 6 occupies an arcaded building where Charles XII of Sweden stayed the night in 1714 – Hungarian Gypsy music is sometimes played here. More expensive but good is the *Csokonai* (Mon–Fri noon–11pm & Sat–Sun 4–11pm; booking advisable) opposite the theatre on Kossuth utca – at the end of the meal customers here roll three dice, and if the right symbols come up they don't have to pay anything.

For **cheaper meals**, try the excellent *Serpince a Fláskához* at Miklós utca 4 (☎414-582) which serves specialities of the region, or the *Halásztanya* at Piac utca 70 for fish and game. Otherwise there's the inevitable *McDonald's* on Piac utca, opposite the *Lordok Háza*, or *Gilbert Pizzas* (noon–10pm) in the shopping mall off Kálvin tér. Excellent ice cream can be found at the *Mandula Cukrászda* at Ember Pál utca 6, just off Simonyi út before Nagyerdei park.

Drinking and nightlife

For a university town, Debrecen has a real dearth of bars and clubs – aside from the *Hotel Aranybika* and a handful of restaurants in the centre, the best place for **drinking** is the northern part of the city. The *Mátyás* cellar (daily 11.30am–midnight) on Péterfia utca has a nice ambience and an enjoyable rigmarole of serving wine from glass spigots. In the backstreets nearby, at Marothy György utca 38, is the *Fácán Kakas*, with a great patio and dreadful music.

The liveliest (but hardly trendy) nightspot is the *Új Vigadó* **disco** in the eastern section of Nagyerdei Park, active most nights until after midnight. Drinks and admission to the more mellow rock'n'roll section downstairs are half the price of what you pay upstairs.

Festivals

Debrecen endeavours to dispel its austere image with three major festivals. In late March, the **Spring Days** (*Tavaszi Napok*) festival of music and drama is timed to coincide with events in Budapest, though Debrecen claims to have originated the custom – you'll find there's often something worth watching at the **Csokonai Theatre** on Kossuth utca, an exotic-looking Moorish structure named after the locally born poet Mihály Csokonai Vitez. The week-long **Bartók International Choir Competition**, held in early July of odd-numbered years, alternates with the biennial **International Military Bands** festival. In early September a big **Jazz Festival** (*Dzsessz Napok* or *Jazzfeszt*) attracts the best Hungarian performers and a sprinkling of foreign acts – details are posted around town and are available from *Hajdútourist*.

A more predictable event occurs on August 20, when the **Flower Carnival** trundles north along Egyetem sugarút: thirty floats laden with flowers, bands and operatically dressed soldiers. People hang from windows en route, cheer wildly when the band plays tunes from *István a király* ("Stephen the King", a patriotic rock opera) and surge behind the last float towards the stadium, where the show continues into the late afternoon. In the evening there's a **fireworks** display outside the Great Church.

Listings

Bookshops at Piac utca 47 and opposite the Small Church stock maps, books in foreign languages, records and cassettes.

Hospital Károlyi Gáspar ter, west of Hunyadi utca.

International calls can be made from direct-dialling kiosks on Piac utca.

Pharmacy 24-hour service on Csapó utca.

Police Kossuth utca 20.

Post office Hatvan utca 5–9.

Hortobágy National Park

Petőfi compared **the Hortobágy puszta** of the central Plain to "the sea, boundless and green". In his day, this "glorious steppe" resounded to the pounding hooves of countless horses and cattle being driven from well to water hole by mounted *csikósok* (cowboys), while Racka sheep grazed under the surveillance of Puli dogs. Medieval tales of cities in the clouds and nineteenth-century accounts of phantom woods, or the "extensive lake half enveloped in grey mist" which fooled John Paget, testify to the occurrence of **mirages** during the hot, dry Hortobágy summers. Caused by the diffusion of light when layers of humid air at differing temperatures meet, these *délibáb* sporadically appear at certain locations – north of Máta, south of Kónya, and along the road between Cserepes and the *Kis-Hortobágyi Csárda*.

Cumanian tribes raised burial mounds (*kunhalom*) here in the Middle Ages that were later taken for hills; one of them served as the site of a duel between Frau Bártha of Debrecen and two rival *táltos*. Nowadays, the grasslands have receded and mirages are the closest that Hortobágy gets to witchcraft, but the *puszta* can still pass for Big Sky country, its low horizons casting every copse and hillock into high relief. You should however be prepared for a relatively costly touristic experience – the *puszta* comes packaged at Hortobágy.

Around the Hortobágy

The 630-square-kilometre **Hortobágy National Park** is a living heritage museum, with state-employed cowboys demonstrating their skills, and beasts strategically placed along the way to the **nine-arched stone bridge** (depicted in a famous painting by Tivadar Csontváry) that lies just west of **HORTOBÁGY** village.

In the village, immediately to the south of Hortobágy train station, stands the much-restored **Great Inn** (*Nagycsárda*), a rambling thatched edifice dating from 1871 that's now a touristy restaurant. Across the road you'll find the *Pastormúzeum* or **Shepherds' Museum** (Tues–Sun 9am–5pm), whose embroidered *szűr*, carved powder horns and other objects were fashioned by plainsmen to while away solitary hours. Status had great significance within their world, and there was a distinct pecking order: horseherds outranked shepherds and cowherds, who, in turn, felt superior to the *kondás* or swineherd. Beneath the stars, however, all slept equally, only building crude huts (*kunyhó*) or sharing a reed *szárnyék* with their animals in bad weather. Attached to the museum is a **natural history section**, with a slide show on Hortobágy wildlife (May to mid-Oct daily 9am–6pm). There is also an **Art Gallery** of mostly *puszta*-inspired modern paintings (April–Sept Tues–Sun 9am–5pm; Oct–March Tues–Sun 9.30am–4pm).

Across the bridge and 2km to the north lies the **Máta Stud Farm**, the place to witness equestrian displays and go riding in horse-drawn carriages; tickets are sold from the stall by the Shepherds' Museum. The village of Máta is also the venue for an international **Horse Show** (*Nemzetközi Lovas Napok*) on the first Sunday of July and the preceding Friday and Saturday, as well as the annual **Bridge Fair** (Aug 19–20), a Magyar rodeo occasioning the sale of leatherwork, knives and roast beef.

Wildlife

Silvery grey cattle and corkscrew-horned Racka sheep can be seen just behind Máta, but most of Hortobágy's **wildlife** is dispersed over 100,000 hectares. The Hortobágyi-halastó lakes (6km west of Hortobágy village) are the haunt of storks, buzzards, mallards, cranes, terns and curlews, while the little ringed plover, the stone curlew and the pratincole favour dry sheep-runs. During spring and autumn millions of migratory **birds** pass through the national park. Red-footed falcons here behave unusually for their species, forming loose groups in the low foliage. Although there's not much to see at the bird reservation southwest of Nagyiván, a large colony of storks nest in the village of Tiszacsege till the end of August.

Mammals can be found in marshy thickets – boars near Kecskéses, otters at Árkus and ground squirrels near Kónya – while roe deer can be found in the reeds, meadows and copses between Óhat and Tiszaszőlős. Rather than making the long walk south from the *Kis-Hortobágyi Csárda* to the water buffalo reserve (which is pretty unrewarding unless you bring binoculars), hang around the two white barns only 300m from the *Csárda*, as this is where the beasts return in the evening.

Practicalities

A succession of small tourist inns gives advance notice of the park to drivers approaching via the Debrecen–Füzesabony road, but **getting there** by train offers a subtler transition from farmland to *puszta*. Services from Debrecen (towards Tiszafüred and Füzesabony) are better than trains from Nyíregyháza which leave you stranded at Óhat-Pusztakócsi, several miles west of Hortobágy village. During summer there might even be a "nostalgia" steam train from Debrecen. Buses – calling at Hortobágy en route between Eger and Hajdúszoboszló (or direct from the latter during high season) – are another option.

Some of the sites listed above are within walking distance of train stations along the Debrecen–Tiszafüred, Tiszafüred–Karcag and Nyíregyháza–Óhat–Pusztakócsi lines. However, if you can rent a bike from the campsite (see "Practicalities") or from a local, cycling is the best way of **getting around**.

Information and accommodation

Hajdútourist (☎52/369-039), near the Great Inn, can provide a **map** marking all the sites mentioned above, explain the various programmes on offer, help with **private rooms** and point you in the direction of *Puszta Camping* (May–Sept). Other **accommodation** in the vicinity includes the friendly *Hortobágy Fogadó* near the centre of the village at Kossuth utca 1 (☎52/369-137; ②), or the *Epona* resort hotel (☎52/369-092; ⑦) in the neighbouring village of Máta, with its own swimming pool, fitness centre and private riding school at Cinege János utca 1. Wooden houses sleeping four people (②) can also be rented in Máta, though these are usually fully booked in July and August – it's worth asking at no. 12, near the entrance to the village. Another option is to stay at one of the resorts around Lake Tisza, some 60km further west by rail.

Lake Tisza

Created by damming the upper reaches of the river, **Lake Tisza** has become a new centre for tourist developments – thankfully not yet so advanced as at Lake Balaton, but then much of it is marshy and not nearly so attractive. It's the only lake in Hungary where motorized boats are allowed, so rental places are everywhere – Tiszafüred, Abádszalok, Kisköre, Poroszló and Tiszacsege.

The resorts

TISZAFÜRED is the most developed of Lake Tisza's resorts, a junction linking the Plain and the Northern Uplands by road and rail. Its train station is at the western end of the main street, Somogyi út (a 10-min walk from the centre), while the bus terminus, *Tourinform* (Húszöles utca 21A; ☎59/353-000) and the town centre lie to the east. About the only "sight" in Tiszafüred is the **Kis Pál Museum**, which has a fishing and pottery display (Tues–Sun 10am–noon & 2–6pm). More enticing is the prospect of a **boat trip** on the lake (arrangeable through *Tourinform*), or **horse riding** in the countryside (☎59/351-828). Private rooms are legion here so you should have no problem finding **accommodation**; there's also the *Füzes Panzió*, with its own restaurant and disco a few doors down from *Tourinform* at no. 31B (☎59/351-584; ③), and *Thermal Camping* (May–Sept) near a dead and pestilent tributary of the River Tisza (no prizes for location).

Other places around the lake are fast gaining popularity. At **ABÁDSZALÓK** to the south, the noisy and crowded *Füzes* hotel and campsite at Feltáró utca 1 is near a beach that rents boats (☎59/355-408; hotel ③; campsite 160Ft per person plus 200Ft tent fee). A cheaper and more pleasant alternative is the small private campsite on the road in from Tiszafüred, marked by a small sign on a lamppost. Further along the shore it is possible to camp rough, though don't expect to have the place to yourself as you're bound to meet Hungarian holidaymakers cooking and fishing.

The Hajdúság

The **Hajdúság** region around Debrecen takes its name from the Hajdúk communities who occupied eight derelict villages here during the early seventeenth century. Originally cattle drovers and part-time bandits, their ranks were swollen by runaway serfs and homeless peasants, and they provided a fearsome army for István Bocskai's struggle against the Habsburgs. After Bocskai achieved his ambition to be Voivode of Transylvania, the Hajdúk were pensioned off with land to avert further disturbance. The result was a string of settlements with names prefixed *Hajdú-*, where the Hajdúk farmed, enjoyed the status of "nobles" (*natio*) and, if necessary, mustered to fight.

Hajdúszoboszló

The most attractive of the Hajdúság settlements is **HAJDÚSZOBOSZLÓ**, 24km from Debrecen, where many Hungarians, driven away from the Balaton by rising prices, now take their holidays. A **spa** has been operating here since 1927, the waters said to be good for arthritis and other muscular ills. These days Hajdúszoboszló gets about one and a half million visitors each year, and its **thermal baths** can be packed. Surveying the wallowing, guzzling crowds in the steaming brown waters (the consumption of beer and *lángos* is staggering), you might try the old Hajdúk war cry, *Huj, huj, hajrá!*, to clear some space before jumping in yourself. Away from the baths things are more relaxed, with **tennis courts** for rent in the park, and cafés and quaint old buildings around Bocskai and Hősök squares. Modern housing and supermarkets along the main street (called Szilvák alja or Debreceni út) nourish the illusion of a hedonistic urban environment.

Sixty feet of **fortress wall** – part of the fifteenth-century defences – lurk behind the inevitable Calvinist church, while a comically fierce statue of the Prince guards Bocskai tér. Around the corner at Bocskai utca 12, the **Bocskai Museum** (summer Tues–Sun 9am–1pm & 3–7pm; winter Tues–Sun 9am–1pm & 2–6pm) exhibits photos of nineteenth-century Hajdúk villagers, and assorted military relics – among them Bocskai's embroidered silk banner, given pride of place alongside the town's charter. Although Bocskai comes across as a benevolent leader, he didn't balk at betraying another group who fought for him: the Székely of Transylvania, who were butchered when they had outlived their usefulness during the so-called "Bloody Carnival". The room across the hall commemorates Hajdúszoboszló's spa, cultural achievements and the natural gas extraction plant.

On the edge of town, around the train station, the atmosphere is more rural. Chunky whitewashed cottages – their vegetable gardens fringed with sunflowers – shimmer in the heat, while errant cows, old women and wagon-loads of pigs move slowly in the dazzling sunlight.

Practicalities

Arriving at the **train station**, about 2km out, you'll find frequent buses into the centre (#1, #4 and #6), terminating at the **bus station** near the baths. **Information** is available from *Tourinform* at Szilfákalja út 2 (mid-June to Aug Mon–Fri 9am–6pm & Sat–Sun 9am–noon; Sept to mid-June Mon–Fri 9am–4.30pm & Sat 9am–noon; ☎52/361-612); *Cooptourist* around the corner at no. 44 (☎52/

362-041); and *Hajdútourist* at József Attila utca 2 (Mon–Fri 8am–5pm & Sat 8am–noon; ☎52/362-214).

All three tourist offices can book private **rooms** (②), and there's an enormous range of **hotels** including the *Mátyás Király* at Mátyás király sétány 17 (☎52/362-200; ③–④), which is about the most attractive and comfortable place to stay; the large *Barátság Gyógyszálló* next door at no. 19 (☎52/361-744; ⑤); the modern *Béké Gyógyhotel* (☎52/361-411; ⑤) attached to the thermal baths; and, just down the road, the *Mikro Hotel* (☎52/362-744; ⑥). The 47-room *Hotel Gambrinus* at József Attila utca 4 (☎52/362-054; ②–③) is very run down, but clean and relatively cheap. In the park beside Debreceni út, the noisy highway to Debrecen, the *Camping* hotel and campsite (☎52/362-427) has tent-space (May–Sept; ①) and several categories of rooms and bungalows. Of the various **eating places** in town, the *Arany Oroszlán* at Bessenyei utca 14 and the *Civis Venéglő* at Szifáklja utca 51 are both good value.

Nádudvar and Hajdúböszörmény

There are two other towns in the Hajdúság region that you might consider visiting. **NÁDUDVAR**, 18km west from Hajdúszoboszló by hourly bus, is particularly worthwhile if you're interested in **pottery**, as Lajos Fazekas continues a family tradition by producing black, unfired ceramics at his house and studio on the main street. Otherwise, this sleepy place offers two petite churches, a spanking new cultural centre and, sprawled around its outskirts, the **Nádudvar Co-operative farm**, where foreigners attending Debrecen's summer language course are sometimes taken for a glimpse of rural prosperity. In the past, some visits have culminated in a riotous *pálinka* binge, with students and workers riding pigs across moonlit fields.

Twenty kilometres north of Debrecen, the Hajdúság's military heritage is apparent in the layout of **HAJDÚBÖSZÖRMÉNY**. Old houses stand in concentric rings around a walled core that was once a Hajdúk fortress. Its pristine Bocskai tér is overlooked by a Calvinist church, Baroque town hall and, in the former Hajdú District Headquarters, the **Hajdúság Museum** (April–Sept daily 10am–6pm; Oct–March daily 10am–4pm). The latter exhibits items of local history including a 1659 engraving of "Giorgio Ragozzi" (better known as György Rákóczi), and relics from the communist era such as the red star that used to embellish the town hall. For enthusiasts of *puszta* paintings, the home of nineteenth-century artist Miklós Káplár, on Hortobagy utca, has a collection of his Great Plain scenes.

Should you feel like staying, **private rooms** are available from *Hajdútourist* on Kossuth utca (June–Aug Mon–Fri 8am–4.30pm & Sat 8am–1pm; Sept–May Mon–Fri 8am–4.30pm; ☎52/371-416), but far more memorable is the *Káplár* **campsite** off Highway 35 at Polgári út 92–100 (April–Oct; ☎52/371-388), a kilometre's walk from the town centre. The latter is actually a converted *Skanzen* of wattle-and-daub thatched houses dating from the early nineteenth century (③), complete with antique furnishings, indoor and outdoor cooking facilities and a restaurant playing Gypsy music. There's also plenty of room to pitch a tent and bikes can be rented for touring the surrounding countryside. Further along the same road (where it meets Highway 35) is one of the prettiest cemeteries around, overgrown with cornstalks, while another one across the way is full of boat-shaped wooden grave-posts typical of the region.

Szabolcs-Szatmár county

North of Debrecen, the Plain ripples with low ridges of wind-blown sand, anchored by birches, apple groves and tobacco fields. The soft landscape of the *Nyírség* (Birch Region) makes a pleasant introduction to **Szabolcs-Szatmár**, an area scorned by many Magyars as the "black country". More densely settled than other parts of the Plain, Szabolcs would be wholly agricultural if not for industrialized Nyíregyháza, straddling the main routes to the Northern Uplands, the Erdőhát villages and the Ukraine. Historically isolated by swamps, and then severed from Transylvania and Ruthenia in 1920, the region has remained poor and backward in comparison with the rest of Hungary.

If your interest in **rural life** is limited, stick to **Nyíregyháza** or **Nyírbátor**, whose Village Museum and striking churches convey something of the region's character. But for anyone seeking the challenge of remote areas, encounters with Gypsies on their own turf, or the folk customs and architecture of old Hungary, Szabolcs has much to offer, and there's the odd riding school and ruined castle to add focus to your wanderings.

Nyíregyháza

NYÍREGYHÁZA has grown into the Big Apple of Szabolcs county, thanks to the food processing industry developed to feed the Soviet market during the Sixties and Seventies. The collapse of this market has hit the region badly, though other businesses have sprung up in response to the flood of shoppers and traders from the former USSR. The town itself (pop. 121,000) has a core of old buildings girdled by factories and housing estates, with a garden suburb – **Sóstófürdő** – to the north. The best time to come is the first Saturday in September, when a **carnival** inaugurates the month-long **Nyírseg Autumn** arts festival.

A trawl of the downtown area yields several monuments that cast a bit more light on Nyíregyháza's history. Its confessional diversity is symbolized by three **churches** – Catholic on Kossuth tér, Lutheran on Luther tér, and Uniate on Bethlen utca – plus a former **synagogue** at the top of Síp utca. The latter has recently been restored and has some fantastic paintings inside (ask for the key next door or enquire at the shop two doors down). Ethnographic and archeological material appears in the **Jósa András Museum** (Tues–Sun 9.30am–5.30pm), a couple of blocks beyond pastel-hued Orszag Zászló tér, along with rooms devoted to the painter Gyula Benczúr (1844–1922) and the epicurean writer Gyula Krúdy (1878–1933), both of whom were born in Nyíregyháza.

However, the most cosmopolitan place in town is the **Comecon Market** on Tokaji út (not to be confused with the regular daily market on Búza tér nearer the centre), where Ukrainians, Magyars, Poles and Romanians barter and sell everything from fur hats to cars. The best times to go are weekend mornings and weekday afternoon (bus #1A from the centre), but check with the tourist office before setting out as timing and locale are both moveable feasts.

Sóstófürdő and the Village Museum

Nyíregyháza's chief attraction is the leafy resort of **Sóstófürdő**, or "Salty Lake Bath". Should you fancy a wallow, the **thermal baths** are on Blaha Lujza sétány, near the Igrice tourist complex and lake (where boats can be rented). The main

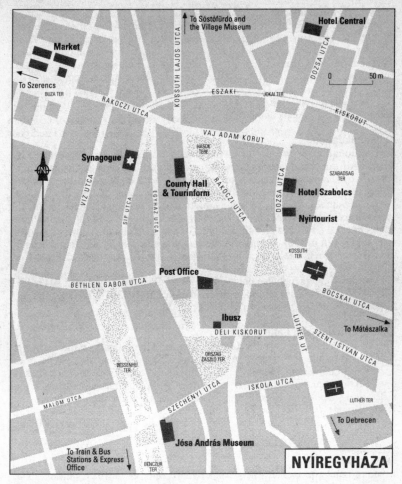

reason for coming here though is the outdoor **Village Museum** (April–Oct
Tues–Fri 8am–6pm & Sat–Sun 9am–3pm) on the other side of the main road
beyond the sports grounds. This *Skanzen* has an eerier feel to it than its counterparts in Szombathely and Szentendre. With clothes hanging on the washing-line,
tables laid and boots by the hearth, the farmsteads appear to have been abandoned by their occupants only yesterday, leaving mute testimony to their lives in
a nineteenth-century Szabolcs village. In this world, the size of the barns (*csűr*)
and stables (*istálló*) denoted a family's wealth, as did the presence of a Beam
Gate opening on to the street: "A gate on a hinge, the dog is big, the farmer is
great", runs an old proverb. Other clues to social standing are the knick-knacks
beloved of the "sandled nobility" or petty gentry, and the placing of a bench
between two windows in Orthodox households. A single communal bowl speaks
volumes about life in the poorest dwellings.

Arrival and information

Arriving at the **bus or train station** on Petőfi tér, 1km south of the centre, you can obtain a street map from *Express* at Arany utca 2 before catching bus #8 or #8A downtown, riding on to Sóstófürdő at the end of the line if you prefer. Most other buses leave from Jókai tér, in the centre. For **information**, contact *Tourinform* in the County Hall at Hősök tere 5 (Mon–Fri 8am–4pm; ☎42/312-606), *Nyírtourist* at Dózsa György utca 3 (Mon–Fri 7.30am–4.30pm; plus June & Aug Sat 7.30am–1pm; ☎42/409-344), or *Ibusz* at Ország Zászló tér 10 (Mon–Fri 7.30am–4pm, Sat 7.30am–noon; ☎42/312-695).

Accommodation

Accommodation is broadly divided between Sóstófürdő and the centre. In Sóstófürdő you'll find *Fenyves Camping* and its *hostel* (May to mid-Oct; ☎42/315-171; ①) by the Village Museum turn-off; and *Igrice Camping* and the *Summer Village* near the baths (same dates; ☎42/313-235), the latter offering flash bungalows (⑤), humbler chalets (①) and a *fogadó* (inn). Others options include the 26-room *Paradise Hotel* at Sótstói út 76 (☎42/314-822; ③–④), and the comfortable *Ózon Panzió* at Csalo köz 2 (☎42/311-084; ④) just off Sóstói út, halfway into town (bus #5, #7, #7A or #12). During the summer you may also be able to get beds in the *Tanárképző Fő iskola*, on the other side of the highway (ask at *Express* or *Ibusz*).

Downtown offers a choice between the *Hotel Central* on Nyár utca (☎42/341-167; ②–③), the *Palmero Panzió* at Széchenyi utca 16 (☎42/315-777; ②), and the *Hotel Szabolcs* on Dozsa utca (☎42/409-303; ②–③).

Eating, drinking and entertainment

The best **places to eat** are the *Ungvár Étterem* (11am–10pm) on the corner of Szent István utca and Luther út, and the *Kispipa* across the street from *Nyírtourist*. The *Korona Étterem* (11am–3pm), on the corner next to *Nyírtourist*, is a self-service joint. For **drinking** try the *Gosser Söröző* on Ország Zászló tér or the *HBH Bayer Söröző* on Hősök tere. Nyíregyháza's liveliest **nightspots** are the *White Orange Jazz Bar* on Pacsirta utca, where rock'n'roll music is played between 10pm and 4am, and the *Open Doors* at the cultural centre on Ország Zászló tér.

Moving on

If you're hoping to explore the Szabolcs hinterland, it's worth enquiring about buses from the intercity terminal on Petőfi tér before visiting the train station. **Buses** usually prove to be quicker than trains, and the timetable is certainly easier to understand than the cryptic indicator board in Nyíregyháza station (to give you an idea, *"Debrecen – 7 balra"* means that the Debrecen train leaves from the left-hand side of the seventh track from the main building).

That said, Nyíregyháza is a major rail junction, straddling the line between Miskolc and Debrecen, and branch lines into Szabolcs county. There are half a dozen daily expresses to Budapest (4hr) via Debrecen and Szolnok, and twice that number of slower, Szerencs-bound **trains** which call at Tokaj (20–30min). Szabolcs is served by three branch lines, with four or five slow trains along each (fewer on Sun). Trains bound for Zajtha can drop you off at Nagkálló, Nyírbátor or Mátészalka, while those for Vásárosnamény call at Vaja. Kisvárda is a stopover for slow trains to Záhony, but not for expresses originating in Budapest.

Nagykálló and Máriapócs

For those with private transport, it may be worth making a couple of stopovers on the way to Nyírbátor (see below). "Go to **NAGYKÁLLÓ!**" used to be a popular insult east of the Tisza, referring to the large mental asylum in this small town of converging houses painted a flaky ochre. Its sole attraction from a visitor's standpoint is the annual *Téka Tábor*, a workshop-cum-**festival of Hungarian folk arts** held a couple of kilometres from town in a weird "barn" shaped like a Viking's helmet, amid a cluster of Imre Makovecz buildings. The event takes place in late June and lasts about ten days – ask the Debrecen or Nyíregyháza tourist office for specific dates. The *Nagykálló Cultural Centre* (☎42/363-141) can supply further details; or write to *Téka Együttes*, PO Box 287, 1370 Budapest. Apart from the festival, the only things to see are a few Jewish monuments on Mártírok tere and Szarvas utca, among them the tomb of Rabbi Isaac Taub (an eighteenth- to nineteenth-century Hasidic leader known as "the miracle rabbi") which even today attracts many Jewish Hungarian pilgrims.

With the fall of Communism, a tiny village off the road between Nagykálló and Nyírbátor has resumed its role as a place of pilgrimage for the Orthodox and Catholic faithful. Now that old identities are reasserting themselves across the Carpathians, **MÁRIAPÓCS** has become a spiritual focus for ethnic Magyars and Uniate Christians in Romania, Slovakia, the Ukraine and the Voivodina. In August 1991, 200,000 worshippers attended an open-air papal mass at Máriapócs, whose **Orthodox Church** contains an icon of the Virgin that has been seen to shed tears since 1696, as well as crutches and other tokens of infirmity attesting to miraculous cures. **Pilgrimages** occur on August 15 (the Feast of the Assumption) and the Saturday closest to September 8 – the latter festival is especially holy to Gypsies.

Nyírbátor and around

The tangled history of Trans-Carpathia has also left its mark on **NYÍRBÁTOR**, an attractive small town whose name recalls the **Báthori family**, a Transylvanian dynasty which veered between psychopathic sadism and enlightened tolerance. Both attributes are subtly manifest in Nyírbátor's exquisite churches, which were equally funded by the Báthoris in an age when religious strife was the norm.

The Calvinist Church

The **Calvinist Church**, on a hill behind the main street, was originally founded as a Catholic place of worship in the 1480s, complete with a fourteen-seat pew now in the National Museum in Budapest. At the back of its web-vaulted Gothic nave lies the **tomb of István Báthori**, whose sleeping figure indicates that he died in bed, but reveals nothing of the character of this Transylvanian Voivode. Hungarian history judges him a shrewd ruler, forgiving his machinations against the Transylvanian Saxons, and the periodic bouts of orgiastic cruelty for which István atoned by endowing churches. Most likely these outbursts had a hereditary origin, for similar hysterical rages and sadism were also characteristic of "Crazy" Gábor Báthori, a short-lived successor, and István's cousin Erzsébet (see "Nagyecsed" below).

When the church turned *Református* in the late sixteenth century, it was obliged to erect a freestanding **wooden belltower**, since only Catholic churches were permitted stone belfries during the Counter-Reformation. From its wide-skirted base, the tower rises to a defiant height of thirty metres, with a spire like a wizard's hat sprouting four mini-towers known as *fiatorony* ("sons of the tower"), symbolizing a civic authority's right to execute criminals. Its hand-cut shingling and oak-pegged joists and beams can be inspected from the crooked stairway up to the balcony and bell chamber.

The Minorite Church and Báthori Museum

István Báthori's other legacy to Nyírbátor is situated on Károlyi utca, on the other side of the main street. Paid for by the spoils of war against the Turks (who, perhaps appropriately, gutted it in 1587), the **Minorite Church** contains fantastic Baroque wood carvings from Eperjes in Slovakia. The altars swarm with figures wearing disquieting expressions, suggestive of István's soul but actually commissioned by János Krucsay around 1730. To gain admission, ring at the side door marked *plebánia csengője*, which leads to an exhibition of photos of ancient Szabolcs churches.

Next door you'll find the **Báthori Museum** (Tues–Sun 10am–6pm), where various relics with unintelligible captions trace the history of the dynasty, whose estates included most of **Szatmár**. Though predominantly inhabited by Hungarians, this region was bisected as a result of the Treaty of Trianon, which allotted the provincial capital (nowadays called Satu Mare) and its surroundings to Romania. Relations have been awkward, if not hostile, ever since, which partly explains the small number of border crossings in these parts.

Practicalities

Rooms and tourist information are available through *Nyírtourist* on Szabadság tér (Mon–Fri 8am–4pm; ☎42/381-525), or you can try the *Mátyás Panzió* at Hunyadi utca 8 (☎42/381-657; ③); its flashy sister hotel next door, the *Bástya* (☎42/381-657; ④); or the classy *Hotel Hódi* at Báthory utca 11 (☎42/381-012; ④) – the latter conveniently situated by an "old-time" barbershop at no. 10. There's also the small *Holdfény Camping* on Széna tér (mid-June to late Aug; ☎42/381-494).

The *Hotel Hódi* has a decent **restaurant**, while the *Kakukk* on Szabadság tér offers good cheap **meals** and the occasional video-disco; for dessert try the *Csekő cukraszda* at Bajcsy-Zsilinszky út 62 which specializes in cakes and ice cream. Fruit and vegetables can be purchased at the local **market** on the corner of Váci and Fürst utcas.

Nyírbátor hosts **concerts** of choral and chamber music from mid-July to early September (details from *Nyírtourist*)

There are two **buses** (weekdays only) between Nyírbátor and Mátészalka, 21km away.

Mátészalka, Nagyecsed and Vaja

A shabby fusion of flaking estates and low yellow houses, **MÁTÉSZALKA**'s sole claim to fame is that it's the birthplace of Tony Curtis's parents, whose original family name was Kertes (Gardener). There are a couple of sights in the centre of town – the **Szatmár Museum** at Kossuth út 5 (Tues–Sun 10am–4pm & Sat–Sun 10am–3pm) with its collection of carts, ceramics and wood carvings; and the **Railway Museum** at Tompa M. utca 2–4 (☎44/312-756) featuring an exhibition of old steam engines. On Sundays the local population gravitates in homage to the Catholic and Orthodox churches and to enjoy a thermal bath.

Szátmar Tourist at Bajcsy-Zsilinszky út 3 (Mon–Fri 8am–4pm; ☎44/310-410) can arrange private **rooms** or point you in the direction of the *Liget* **campsite** (May to mid-Sept). More likely, though, you'll want **transport** to more interesting places. From the western end of Bajcsy-Zsilinszky út there are regular buses down to Nagyecsed and across to Vaja (see below), whilst both buses (10 daily; 2 at weekends) and trains (3–4 daily) travel to Csenger and Fehérgyarmat in the Erdőhát region. Other slow trains (5 daily) run up to Vásárosnamény and Záhony, and across the border to Carei in Romania.

The small town of **NAGYECSED**, 15km south of Mátészalka, deserves a passing mention as the **birthplace of the "Blood Countess" Erzsébet Báthori**, the most notorious of the Báthori clan, though her worst excesses took place at Sarvar (see p.219) and later in Transylvania. It was at the family château here that the young countess witnessed a Gypsy sewn into a horse's stomach and left to die – a formative experience which taught her that commoners could be killed with impunity, a practice she enjoyed in adult life. After Erszébet died a prisoner in her Slovakian castle and was buried nearby, the outraged parents of her victims protested until her body was transferred to the Báthori vault at Nagyecsed.

A less morbid attraction is the **fortified manor** (April–Oct Tues–Sun 9.30am–5.30pm; Nov–March Tues–Sun 8am–4pm) 14km northwest of Mátészalka in **VAJA**, the feudal seat of Ádám Vaj, an early supporter of Rákóczi's campaign against the Habsburgs. Within its thick stone walls, visitors in felt slippers shuffle across the parquet from room to room, gaping at painted furniture and the grand meeting hall, the *Rákóczi-terem*. The school next door can sometimes provide **accommodation**.

The Erdőhát

The **Erdőhát** is Hungary's most isolated region, a state imposed by nature and confirmed by history. Meandering and flooding over centuries, the headwaters of the Tisza and its tributaries carved out scores of enclaves beneath the flanks of the Subcarpathians, where dense oak forests provided acorns for pig-rearing and ample timber for building. Though invaders were generally deterred by Escedi Swamp and similar obstacles, scattered communities maintained contact with one another through their intricate knowledge of local tracks and waterways. When the borders came down like shutters in the twentieth century, people were suddenly restricted to three tightly controlled frontier crossings, which have been only partially relaxed since the demise of Communism.

Roads are poor and motor vehicles are rare in these parts, but if you're interested in rural customs and architecture that's almost extinct elsewhere in Hungary, the Erdőhát **villages** are worth the effort. Two small towns – Fehérgyarmat and Vásárosnamény – serve as jumping-off points for the region.

Fehérgyarmat and Vásárosnamény

Much of the southern Erdőhát is accessible from **FEHÉRGYARMAT**, a small town featuring a pleasant park entered via a Transylvanian-style portal; the *Hotel Szamos* at Móricz Zsigmond út 8 (☎44/362-211; ②); and the **Szatmár-Bereg National Conservation Museum** at Vörösmarty utca 1, with a collection of paintings and photos of the local flora and fauna. **Buses** fan out from here to

THE ERDŐHÁT

UKRAINE

Vámosatya

Csaroda

Tákos

Vásárosmanény

Tarpa

Gulács

Tiszacsécse

Uszka

Szatmárcseke

Sonkád

Tivadar

Túristvándi

Botpalád

To Vásárosnamény

Mánd

Vámosoroszi

Fehérgyarmat

Nemesborzova

Nagyszekeres

Mátészalka

River Szamos

Gyügye

Gacsály

Zajta

Csengersima

To Satu Mare

Nagyecsed

Petea

Csenger

ROMANIA

0   10 km

To Carei

River Tisza

Tivadar (hourly), Gyügye (less frequently), Csaroda (Mon–Sat 2 daily), Vásárosnamény and Csengersima (both Mon–Sat 5 daily; 1 on Sun), while **trains** to Zajta (2–3 daily) can drop you at Nagyszekres or Gacsály.

Villages in the northern Erdőhát are generally easier to reach by bus from **VÁSÁROSNAMÉNY**, an erstwhile trading post on the "salt road" from Transylvania, whose **Beregi Museum** at Rákóczi utca 13 displays local embroidery and cast-iron stoves from Munkachevo, with a room devoted to Erdőhát funerary customs. You'll have to see *Beregtourist* (Mon–Thurs 7.30am–4.30pm & Fri 7.30am–4pm) on the main square about private **rooms**, since the *Bereg Hotel* is closing for restoration. There's also a **campsite** (May to mid-Sept; ☎371-076) just across the Tisza in Gergelyiugornya (hourly buses June–Aug 25), a small resort whose holiday homes are raised on stilts to avoid flooding. **Buses** run from Vásárosnamény to Tákos, Csaroda and Vámosatya every couple of hours.

Around Szatmárcseke and Túristvándi

If you don't fancy staying in Fehérgyarmat, there's a small **campsite** in **TIVADAR**, 10km north of town and within walking distance of Tarpa (see below). The riverbank here has a *strand* whose water is cleaner than at Vásárosnamény downstream, where the Tisza joins the polluted Szamos. As far as sights go, however, there's more to recommend the villages on the other side of the river, further east.

The cemetery at **SZATMÁRCSEKE**, 20km northeast of Fehérgyarmat, contains a number of boat-shaped oaken **grave markers** (*kopjafa*), probably representing the ships that were supposed to transport the souls of the dead to the other world in ancient Finno-Ugric traditions. Next to the entrance is a world map indicating Hungarian populations around the world and, nearby, a pretty mausoleum commemorating **Ferenc Kölcsey**, the locally born poet (1790–1838) who penned the words to Hungary's national anthem. Between April and October, visitors can **stay** at the *Kölcsey Fogadó*, Honvéd utca 9 (Szatmárcseke ☎9; ①), which has a **restaurant** attached.

A few kilometres to the south, **TÚRISTVÁNDI** has a picturesque **wooden watermill** whose workings are demonstrated should a group of tourists materialize. The key to the mill is kept at the house on the corner, across the main road.

Other fine examples of wooden architecture used to grace Nemesborzova, Vámosoroszi and Botpálád, until they were removed to Szentendre's Village Museum in the Seventies. However, **TISZACSÉCSE** retains the thatched cottage where the novelist and critic **Zsigmond Móricz** (1879–1942) was born, and also affords fine views across the plain towards the Carpathian mountains.

Further south

The southern Erdőhát is notable for its beautiful churches, which are folksy adaptions of Gothic or Baroque architecture. Slow trains bound for Zajta can drop you off at **NAGYSZEKERES** or **GACSÁLY**, whose churches feature striking wooden **belltowers**. Even more appealing is the tiny **church** in **GYÜGYE**, its coffered ceiling decorated with astrological symbols (illuminated in turn by a sunbeam during the course of the year, so the priest says). Gyügye is easily reached by bus from Fehérgyarmat, or you can walk there in an hour from Nagyszekeres.

Committed church buffs might also visit **CSENGER**, where the **Catholic church** dates from the Middle Ages. Built of red and black brick, it similarly features a superb coffered ceiling with folk Baroque paintings. Csenger is the terminal of the branch line down from Mátészalka; the last train back leaves at 8pm.

Although **CSENGERSIMA**, a few miles north, has been designated a 24-hour **crossing into Romania** – it also happens to be one of the least crowded – the Romanian officials at Petea may refuse to admit travellers after dark. There are five **buses** daily (one on Sun) between Csengersima and Fehérgyarmat, but none across the border.

North of the Tisza

Another clutch of villages lies north of the Tisza, in the region known as *Bereg*. While some are only accessible from Vásárosnamény, others, such as Csaroda and Tákos, can also be reached from Fehérgyarmat.

TÁKOS harbours a wattle-and-daub Protestant **church** (called the "Peasants' Notre Dame"), with bold floral designs on its gallery and a coffered ceiling painted by Ferenc Asztalos in 1766. As in most village churches, the men sit up front and the women at the back. If the church is shut, track down the lady who has the key around the corner at Bajcsy-Zsilinszky utca 40; she might also be able to help with **accommodation**.

In **CSARODA**, 2km east, a thirteenth-century **Gothic church** with a shingled spire is the oldest in eastern Hungary. Originally built as a Catholic church in the eleventh century, it was decorated a couple of centuries later with frescoes of various saints including Helen, the "smiling saint" (who isn't smiling on this occasion). In 1552 the building was turned into a Calvinist church, and red and blue floral designs similar to those found on shepherds' cloaks were added. These were later painted over, remaining hidden from view until the 1960s when restorers brought them back to life by covering them overnight with raw minced meat. The church is normally open from 1 to 6pm daily, but the woman who lives opposite, at Kossuth utca 15, will open it for you if it's closed. Across the road, an old peasants' house has been turned into an exhibition of rural artefacts with a pub/restaurant attached. **Rooms** at the *Csarodai Panzió* (no telephone; ②) are best reserved through *Beregtourist* in Vásárosnamény, but you can try your luck by asking at József utca 20, en route to the church.

The restorers have also been at work in **TARPA**, to the southeast, where a large horizontal "dry" **mill** (*szaraz-malom*) with an intricate conical roof stands amongst the cottages. Another formidable-looking **wooden belltower** can be found in **VÁMOSATYA**, 18km northwest of Csaroda.

Around Kisvárda and Záhony

The fruit-growing area northeast of Nyíregyháza is called the *Rétköz* (Meadow Land) or *Tiszakanyár* (Tisza Bend). Though pretty to drive through, there is little to attract visitors beyond Kisvárda, midway along the road and rail line to Záhony, the only border crossing into the Ukraine.

Kisvárda

KISVÁRDA is a backwater **spa** with a **ruined castle** used for staging plays in the summer. Despite being undamaged in the war, a random selection of buildings along the main street have been replaced by ugly modern structures, spoiling the look of Fő utca, which leads to the main square. Just off Fő tér at Csillag utca 5 stands an old **synagogue** with an ornamental ceiling and stained-glass windows, housing the **Rétköz Museum** of local history (April–Oct Tues–Sun 9am–5pm). The **tourist office** in the nearby House of Culture can tell you about **horse riding** and book private **accommodation**. There's also a campsite and the *Strand Motel*, beside the castle ruins and thermal baths at Városmajor utca 37 (May to mid-Oct; ☎45/420-062; ②). Nearby, the *Amor* is a popular place to **eat**, or try the classy *Fekete-Black* across from the Rétköz Museum. Locals go **drinking** in the *Stilbar* at Fő utca 2, the *Várda* restaurant behind the town hall, or the seedy *Sport Falatózo* on Vár utca.

INTO THE UKRAINE

Since the spring of 1992 it has been possible to obtain **Ukrainian visas** on the spot. The **road crossing** is a narrow bridge, easily found by following the traffic. Be warned, however, that **customs** at CHOP on the Ukrainian side may be out to extort cash or confiscate desirable items from travellers.

The reason for this becomes apparent once you enter Trans-Carpathia, the mountainous region traditionally known as **Ruthenia**, control of which has passed from Hungary to Czechoslovakia to the USSR to the Ukraine within the last eighty years. This forgotten corner of central Europe is as poor and backward as Albania, with a tradition of emigration that took Andy Warhol and Robert Maxwell to their adoptive countries. Its ethnic mix includes Hungarians, Slovaks, Gypsies and Romanians, not to mention a large number of Ruthenians (*Rusyns*), who cling to their Uniate faith.

The main road and rail line run through **UZHGOROD** (also a border crossing into Slovakia), known as *Ungvár* to its Hungarian-speaking inhabitants. Another road heads east to **MUKACHEVO** (*Munkács*), the site of a last-ditch battle against the Habsburgs during the Kuruc War. From here, the road continues across the mountains towards the Ukrainian city of Lvov, via the **Verecke Pass** through which Árpád led the Magyar tribes into the Carpathian Basin.

Záhony and Zsurk

ZÁHONY is currently the "front line" between relatively prosperous, Westernized Hungary and the impoverished masses of the former Soviet Union. When travel restrictions were eased in 1990, people flooded in from the Ukraine and Russia to trade goods for foodstuffs at the **"free" market** on the edge of town, until controls were reimposed the following year. Since then, spivs and dealers from Hungary and Poland drive across the border to do business in Uzhgorod, using Záhony as a base. Unless you relish hobnobbing with such characters however, the only reason to come here is another picturesque **church** with a wooden belfry, in the nearby village of **ZSURK**.

Should either prospect appeal, it's possible to rent private **rooms** at Szamuely utca 22, or stay at the *Kemény Fogadó*, Zalka M. utca 1 (②), in Záhony. There are **trains** from here down to Nyíregyháza and Debrecen, but you are not allowed to board international expresses running in either direction.

travel details

Trains

Budapest (Keleti or Nyugati Station) to Békéscsaba (5 daily; 2hr 30min); Debrecen (11 daily; 2hr 30min–3hr 30min); Kecskemét (8 daily; 2hr 30min); Nyíregyháza (11 daily; 3hr–3hr 30 min); Szeged (8 daily; 2hr 30min).

Baja to Kiskunhalas (5 daily; 1hr 45min).

Békéscsaba to Budapest (4 daily; 2hr 30min); Szeged (7 daily; 2hr).

Debrecen to Budapest (10 daily; 2hr 30min–3hr 30min); Hortobágy (5 daily; 1hr); Mátészalka (6 daily; 1hr 30min); Nyírbátor (6 daily; 1hr); Nyíregyháza (every 30min; 30–45 min).

Kalocsa to Kiskőrös (5 daily; 1hr).

Kecskemét to Bugac (3 daily; 1hr); Szeged (7 daily; 1hr 15min–2hr).

Kiskőrös to Kalocsa (4 daily; 1hr).

Kiskunhalas to Baja (5 daily; 1hr 45min).

Mátészalka to Csenger (3 daily; 1hr); Vásárosnamény (4 daily; 30min); Záhony (4 daily; 1hr).

Nyíregyháza to Mátészalka (4 daily; 1hr 15min); Nagykálló (4 daily; 15min); Nyírbátor (4 daily; 45min).

Szeged to Békéscsaba (6 daily; 2hr); Budapest (6 daily; 2hr 30min); Keceskemét (6 daily; 1hr 15min).

Buses

Budapest (Népstadion) to Baja (every 1–2hr; 3hr 15min); Békéscsaba (3 daily; 4hr); Kalocsa (every 1–2hr; 2hr); Szeged (1 daily; 3hr 45min). Kecskemét (13 daily; 2hr 30min).

Baja to Budapest (every 1–2hr; 3hr 15min); Kalocsa (hourly; 1hr); Sopron (1 daily; 10hr); Szeged (8 daily; 2hr 15min); Szekszárd (1 daily; 1hr).

Békéscsaba to Abádszalók (2 daily; 3hr 15min); Békés (hourly; 30min); Budapest (3 daily; 4hr); Debrecen (8 daily; 3hr); Eger (2 daily; 5hr); Gyula (hourly; 1hr); Hajdúböszörmény (1 daily; 3hr 30min); Miskolc (1 daily; 5hr); Pécs (1 daily; 6hr 30min).

Csongrád to Szeged (1 daily; 1hr 15min).

Debrecen to Abádszalók (1 daily; 3hr 15min); Békéscsaba (6 daily; 3hr 30min); Eger (2 daily; 3hr); Gyöngyös (1 daily; 4hr 45min); Gyula (1 daily; 3hr); Hajdúböszörmény (every 30–90min; 30min); Hajdúszoboszló (hourly; 45min); Hortobágy (1 daily; 1hr); Jászberény (1 daily; 2hr 30min); Miskolc (every 30–90min; 2hr); Nyíregyháza (1 daily; 2hr); Szeged (2 daily; 5hr); Tiszafüred (2 daily; 1hr 45min).

Hajdúböszörmény to Debrecen (every 30–90min; 30min); Miskolc (every 30–90min; 1hr 45min).

Hajdúszoboszló to Debrecen (hourly; 45min); Eger (1 daily; 3hr 15min); Hajdúböszörmény (2 daily; 1hr); Hortobágy (1 daily; 1hr 15min); Miskolc (2 daily; 2hr 45min); Nádudvar (hourly; 30min).

Gyula to Abádszalók (1 daily; 3hr 45min); Debrecen (1 daily; 2hr); Eger (1 daily; 5hr 30min); Miskolc (1 daily; 5hr 15min).

Hortobágy to Debrecen (1 daily; 45min); Eger (1 daily; 2hr 15min); Hajdúszoboszló (1 daily; 1hr 15min); Tiszafüred (1 daily; 1hr).

Jászberény to Cegléd (3 daily; 1hr 15min); Debrecen (1 daily; 4hr 30min); Kecskemét (3 daily; 2hr); Miskolc (1 daily; 4hr 45min); Paradfürdő (1 daily; 2hr 15min).

Kalocsa to Baja (hourly; 1hr); Győr (1 weekly; 5hr); Székesfehérvár (1 weekly; 3hr).

Kecskemét to Cegléd (hourly; 30min); Eger (2 daily; 4hr); Gyöngyös (2 daily; 3hr); Jászberény (2 daily; 2hr); Kiskunfélegyháza (hourly; 45min).

Kiskunfélegyháza to Bugac (every 60–90min; 1hr); Kecskemét (hourly; 45min).

Nyíregyháza to Debrecen (1 daily; 2hr); Miskolc (daily except Sun; 2hr).

Szeged to Békéscsaba (4 daily; 2hr); Csongrád (1 daily; 1hr 15min); Debrecen (2 daily; 5hr); Hodmezővásárhely (1 daily; 1hr 30min); Miskolc (1 daily; 6hr 30min); Tiszafüred (1 daily; 5hr).

Szolnok to Eger (2–3 daily; 2hr 30min); Jászberény (1 daily; 1hr 15min).

Tiszafüred to Hodmezővásárhely (1 daily; 4hr 30min); Miskolc (2 daily except Sat & Sun; 1hr 30min); Szeged (1 daily; 5hr); Szentes (1 daily; 3hr 45min).

International trains

Békéscsaba to Arad (1 daily; 3hr); Bucharest (1 daily; 13hr).

Debrecen to Baia Mare (1 daily; 5hr 30min); Belgrade (1 daily; 7hr 45min); Braşov (July–Sept 1 daily; 12hr); Bucharest (July–Sept 1 daily; 15hr); Cluj (July–Sept 1 daily; 7hr 30min); Csop (1 daily; 4hr); Kiev (2 daily; 24hr); Moscow (2 daily; 38hr); Satu Mare (1 daily; 6hr); Valea lui Mihai (2 daily; 3hr); Varna (July–Sept 1 daily; 24hr); Warsaw (July–Sept 1 daily; 16hr).

Kecskemét to Belgrade (1 daily; 5hr 30min); Chop (1 daily; 6hr 45min); Kiev (1 daily; 23hr); Moscow (1 daily; 37hr).

Szeged to Chop (1 daily; 8hr).

Szolnok to Arad (4–5 daily; 4hr); Baia Mare (1 daily; 4hr 30min); Belgrade (1 daily; 6hr); Braşov (4 daily; 11hr); Bucharest (5 daily; 13hr 45min); Burgas (June–Sept 1 daily; 23hr); Cluj (1 daily; 8hr); Kiev (1 daily; 36hr); Košice (1 daily; 4hr 45min); Kraków (1 daily; 14hr 30min); Moscow (2 daily; 50hr); Satu Mare (2 daily; 7hr 45min); Sibiu (1 daily; 11hr 30min); Sighişoara (3 daily; 16hr); Sofia (1 daily; 25hr); Warsaw (1 daily; 17hr).

International buses

Services to Novi Sad, Subotica and Zrenjanin depend on the situation in Croatia and Serbia.

Baja to Subotica (1 daily; 2hr).

Békéscsaba to Arad (4 weekly; 4hr); Timişoara (1 daily; 5hr).

Debrecen to Košice (4 weekly; 4hr); Mukachevo (3 weekly; 7hr); Oradea (March–Sept 1 daily; 3hr 30min); Satu Mare (March–Sept 1 daily; 5hr); Uzhgorod (1 daily; 6hr).

Gyula to Subotica (1 daily; 5hr).

Hajdúszoboszló to Oradea (March–Sept 3 weekly; 4hr); Satu Mare (March–Sept 2 weekly; 5hr); Trebišov (June–Sept 2 weekly; 5hr).

Kecskemét to Subotica (1 daily except Sun; 3hr); Tatranská Lomnica (July–Aug 1 daily; 9hr).

Nyíregyháza to Košice (1 daily; 3hr); Satu Mare (1 daily; 4hr); Uzhgorod (1 daily; 5hr).

Szarvas to Arad (2 weekly; 5hr); Timişoara (2 weekly; 6hr).

Szeged to Arad (1 daily; 4hr); Novi Sad (1 daily except Sun; 4hr); Subotica (4–5 daily except Sun; 2hr); Timişoara (1 daily; 5hr); Zrenjanin (1 daily; 4hr).

Szolnok to Baia Mare (1 daily; 9hr); Oradea (1 daily; 4hr 30min); Satu Mare (1 daily; 7hr 30min).

PART THREE

THE

CONTEXTS

HISTORICAL FRAMEWORK

The region of the Carpathian basin known as Hungary (*Magyarország*) changed hands many times before the Magyars arrived here at the end of the ninth century, and its history is marked by migrations, invasions and drastic changes, as Asia and Europe have clashed and blended. Over the centuries borders have shifted considerably, so geographical limits as well as historical epochs are somewhat arbitrary. Transylvania, an integral part of Hungary for hundreds of years, was lost to Romania in 1920; the plight of its Magyar minority remains a contentious issue, while the situation of ethnic Hungarians in Serbia and Slovakia is also a cause for concern.

PREHISTORY

Although recorded history of the area now covered by Hungary begins with the arrival of the Romans, archeological evidence of **Stone Age** (3,000,000–8000 BC) humans has been found in the Istállóskő and Pilisszántó caves in northern Hungary, suggesting that the earliest inhabitants lived by gathering fruit and hunting reindeer and mammoths. The end of the Ice Age created favourable conditions for the development of agriculture and the domestication of animals, which spread up through the Balkans in the Neolithic era, and was characteristic of the **Kőrös culture** (5500–3400 BC):

clans herding sheep and goats and worshipping fertility goddesses, living alongside the River Tisza. As humans became more settled and spread into Transdanubia, evidence survives of mounds (*tell*) full of artefacts, apparently leading towards the rise of the **Lengyel culture** around Lake Balaton.

During the **Bronze Age** (2000–800 BC), warlike tribes arrived from the Balkans and steppes, introducing cattle and horses. Subsequent migrants brought new technology – iron came with the Cimmerians, and the Asiatic Scythians (500–250 BC) brought the potter's wheel and manufactured goods from Greek traders on the Black Sea coast – while the **Celts**, who superseded them in the early third century BC, introduced glassblowing and left mournful sculptures and superb jewellery (most notably the gold treasures of Szárazd-Regöly), before being subdued by the Romans.

THE ROMANS

The **Roman conquest** was initiated by Augustus at the beginning of the Christian era, primarily to create a buffer zone in **Pannonia** between the empire and the barbarians to the east. By the middle of the first century AD Roman rule extended throughout Transdanubia, from the Sava to the Danube, which was fortified with *castra* and formed the *limes* or military frontier. Trade, administration and culture grew up around the garrison towns and spread along the roads constructed to link the imperial heartland with the far-flung colonies in Dacia (Romania) and Dalmatia (Yugoslavia). Archeological finds at Pécs, Sopron, Szombathely and Buda show that these were originally Roman towns. The latter's amphitheatre and baths, the ruins of Gorsium and Szombathely's Temple of Isis are the best-preserved Roman remains.

During the fourth century the Romans began to withdraw from Pannonia, handing over its defence to the Vandals and Jazygians who lived beyond the Danube. In 430 they fell under the invading **Huns**, whose empire reached its zenith and then fragmented with the death of Attila (453). Other warring tribes – Ostrogoths, Gepidae and Langobards – occupied the region for the next 150 years, before being swept aside by the **Avars**, whose empire survived until the beginning of the eighth century, when the region once again came up for grabs for any determined invader.

THE MAGYARS

The **Magyars'** origins lie in the *Finno-Ugric* peoples who dwelt in the snowy forests between the Baltic and the middle Urals. Around the first century AD, some of these tribes migrated south across the Bashkiran steppes and fell under the influence of Turkic and Persian culture, gradually becoming tent-dwelling nomadic herders who lived on a diet of mare's milk, horse flesh, fish and berries. Some archeologists believe that they mingled with the ancient Bulgars north of the Caspian Sea (in a land known as "Magna Bulgaria"), before the majority fled from marauding Petchenegs (in about 750) and moved west-wards to settle on the far bank of the River Don in the so-called *Etelköz* region, around the year 830. Ties with the Huns and Avars have been postulated – including a common language – but there's more evidence to link the seven original Magyar tribes with three Kavar tribes; they were known collectively as the *Onogur*, or "Ten Arrows".

Overpopulation and Petcheneg attacks forced the Onogur to move westwards in 889, and tradition has it that the seven Magyar chieftains elected **Árpád** as their leader, pledging fealty to his heirs with a blood oath. Accompanied by smaller Kun (or Cuman) tribes, the Onogur entered the Carpathian basin in 896, and began the "**landtaking**" (*honfoglalás*) or conquest of the region. Six Magyar tribes settled west of the Danube and in the upper Tisza region; the seventh took the approaches to Transylvania, while the lower Tisza and the northern fringes of the Plain went to the Kuns and Kavars. For the next seventy years the Magyars remained raiders, striking terror as far afield as Constantinople and Orleans (where people thought them to be Huns), until a series of defeats persuaded them to settle for assimilating their gains.

Civilization developed gradually, after Árpád's great-grandson Prince **Géza** established links with Bavaria and invited Catholic missionaries to Hungary. His son **Stephen** (*István*) took the decisive step of applying to Pope Sylvester for recognition, and on Christmas Day in the year 1000 was crowned as a Christian king and began converting his pagan subjects with the help of Bishop Gellért. Royal authority was extended over the non-tribal lands by means of the *megye* (county) system, and defended by fortified *vár*; artisans and priests were imported to spread skills and the new religion; and tribal rebellions were crushed. Stephen was subsequently credited with the **foundation of Hungary** and canonized after his death in 1038. His mummified hand and the Crown of Saint Stephen have since been revered as both holy and national relics.

THE MIDDLE AGES

Succession struggles raged for decades follow-ing Stephen's death, and of the sixteen kings who preceded Andrew II (1205–35), only the humane László I (also canonized), Kálmán "the Booklover" and Béla III (1172–96) contributed anything significant to Hungary's development. Fortunately, invasions were few during the eleventh and twelfth centuries, and **German and Slovak immigrants** helped double the population to about two million by 1200. Parts of **Transylvania** were settled by the Magyars and Székely, perhaps before the second half of the eleventh century, when the "lands of Saint Stephen" were extended to include **Slavonia** (between the Sava and Drava rivers) and the unwillingly "associated" state of **Croatia**. The growth in royal power caused tribal leaders to rebel in 1222, when Andrew II was forced to recognise the "noble" status and rights of **the Natio** – landed freemen exempt from taxation – in the *Golden Bull*, a kind of Hungarian Magna Carta.

Andrew's son **Béla IV** was trying to restore royal authority when disaster struck from the east – the **Mongol invasion** of 1241, which devastated Hungary. Hundreds of towns and villages were sacked; refugees fled to the swamps and forests; crops were burned or left unharvested; and famine and plague followed. Population losses ranged from sixty to one hundred percent on the Plain to twenty percent in Transdanubia, and after the Mongol with-drawal a year later (prompted by the timely death of the Khan), Hungary faced a mammoth task of **reconstruction** – the chief achieve-ment of Béla's reign, to which foreign settlers made a large contribution. Renewed domestic feuding (complicated by foreign intervention and the arrival of more Cuman tribes) dogged the reign of Andrew III; and worsened when he died heirless in 1301, marking the **end of the Árpád dynasty**.

FOREIGN RULE

Foreign powers advanced their own claimants, and for a while there were three competing kings, all duly crowned. **Charles Robert** of the French Angevin (or Anjou) dynasty eventually triumphed in 1310, when his rivals went home in disgust; and despite colonial skirmishes with Venice, Serbia and Wallachia, Hungary itself enjoyed a period of peace, for the Mongols and other great powers were occupied elsewhere. Gold mines in Transylvania and northern Hungary – the richest in Europe – stabilized state finances and the currency. Charles's son **Louis the Great** reigned (1342–82) during a period of expansion, when the population rose to three million; and by war and dynastic aggrandizement crown territory grew to include Dalmatia, the Banat, Galicia and (in theory) Poland. Louis, however, sired only daughters, so that after his demise, another foreigner ascended the throne in 1395 – **Sigismund of Luxembourg**, Prince of Bohemia, whom the nobles despised as the "Czech swine". His extravagant follies and campaigns abroad were notorious, and while Sigismund recognized the growing threat of the Turks, he failed to prevent their advance up through the Balkans.

During the fourteenth century, the realm contained 49 boroughs, about 500 market towns and 26,000 villages. Everyone benefitted from peace and expanded trade, but the rewards weren't shared evenly, for the Angevins favoured towns and guilds, and most of all the top stratum of the Natio, on whom they depended for troops (*banderia*) when war posed a threat. The burden fell upon the **peasantry**, who lacked "free" status and were compelled to pay *porta* (gate tax) to the state, tithes to the church, and one ninth of their produce to the landlords – plus extra taxes and obligations during times of war, or to finance new royal palaces.

Sigismund died in 1447 leaving one daughter, Elizabeth, just as **the Turks** were poised to invade and succession struggles seemed inevitable. The Turks might have taken Hungary then, but for a series of stunning defeats inflicted upon them by **János Hunyadi**, a Transylvanian warlord of Vlach (Romanian)

origin. The lifting of the siege of Nándorfehérvár (Belgrade) in 1456 checked the Turkish advance and caused rejoicing throughout Christendom – the ringing of church bells at noon was decreed by the pope to mark this victory – while Hunyadi rose to be *Voivode* or Prince of Transylvania, and later regent for the boy king László. Following Hunyadi's death, László's early demise, and much skulduggery, Mihály Szilágyi staged a coup and put his nephew Mátyás (Matthias), Hunyadi's son, on the throne in 1458.

RENAISSANCE AND DECLINE

Mátyás Corvinus is remembered as the "**Renaissance King**" for his statecraft and multiple talents (including astrology), while his second wife **Beatrice** of Naples lured humanists and artists from Italy to add lustre to their palaces at Buda and Visegrád (of which some remains survive). Mátyás was an enlightened despot renowned for his fairness: "King Mátyás is dead, justice is departed", people mourned. By taxing the nobles (against every precedent) he raised a standing force of 30,000 mercenaries, called the Black Army, which secured the realm and made Hungary one of Central Europe's leading powers; but when he died in 1490, leaving no legitimate heir, the nobles looked for a king "whose plaits they could hold in their fists".

Such a man was Ulászló II (whose habit of assenting to any proposal earned him the nickname "King Okay"), under whom the Black Army and its tax base were whittled away by the Diet (which met to approve royal decrees and taxes), while the nobility filched common land and otherwise increased their exploitation of the peasantry. Impelled by poverty, many joined the crusade of 1514, which under the leadership of **György Dózsa** turned into an **uprising against the landlords**. Its savage repression (over 70,000 peasants were killed and Dózsa was roasted alive) was followed by the **Werbőczy Code** of 1517, binding the peasants to "perpetual **serfdom**" on their masters' land and 52 days of *robot* (unpaid labor) in the year.

Hungary's decline accelerated as corruption and incompetence bankrupted the treasury, forts along the border crumbled and the revived *banderia* system of mobilization turned makeshift. Ulászló's son Louis II was only nine when crowned, and by 1520 the Turks, under Sultan Süleyman "the Magnificent", had resumed their advance northwards, capturing the run-down forts in Serbia. In August 1526 the Turks crossed the Drava and Louis hastened south to confront them at the **battle of Mohács** – a catastrophic defeat for the Magyars, whose army was wiped out together with its monarch and commanders.

TURKISH CONQUEST: HUNGARY DIVIDED

After sacking Buda and the south, the Turks withdrew in 1526 to muster forces for their real objective, Vienna, the "Red Apple". To forestall this, Ferdinand of Habsburg proclaimed himself king and occupied western Hungary, while in Buda the nobility put **János Zápolyai** on the throne. Following Zápolyai's death in 1541 Ferdinand claimed full sovereignty, but the Sultan occupied Buda and central Hungary, and made Zápolyai's young son ruler of Transylvania. Thereafter Transylvania became a semi-autonomous principality, nominally loyal to the Sultan and jealously coveted by the Habsburgs. The tripartite **division of Hungary** was formally recognized in 1568. Despite various official or localized truces, warfare became a feature of everyday life for the next 150 years, and the national independence lost then was not to be recovered for centuries afterwards.

Royal Hungary – basically western Transdanubia and the north – served as a "human moat" against the Turkish forces that threatened to storm Austria and Western Europe, kept at bay by Hungarian sacrifices at Szigetvár, Kőszeg and other fortresses. Notwithstanding constitutional arrangements to safeguard the Natio's privileges, real power passed to the Habsburg chancellery and war council, where the liberation of Hungary took second place to Austria's defence and aggrandizement, and the subjugation of Transylvania.

Turkish-occupied Hungary – *Eyalet-i Budin* – was ruled by a Pasha in Buda, with much of the land either deeded to the Sultan's soldiers and officials, or run directly as a state fief (*khasse*). The peasants were brutally exploited, for many had to pay rent both to their absentee Magyar landlords and to the occupying Turks. Their plight is evident from a letter to a Hungarian lord by the villagers of

Batthyán: "Verily, it is better to be Your Lordship's slaves, bag and baggage, than those of an alien people". Peasants fled their villages on the Alföld to the safer fields around the expanding "agro-towns" of Debrecen and Szeged, the nexus of the cattle trade which gradually supplanted agriculture, while neglect and wanton tree-felling transformed the Plain into a swampy wasteland – the *puszta*.

The Voivodes of **Transylvania** endeavoured to provoke war between the Habsburgs and Turks, in order to increase their independence from both and satisfy the feudal **Nationes**. The latter, representing the élite of the region's Magyars, Saxons and Székely, combined to deny the indigenous Vlachs political power, while competing amongst themselves and extending the borders of Transylvania (then much bigger than today). István Bocskai's *Hajdúk* forces secured the Szatmár region; Gábor Bethlen promoted economic and social development; but Prince György Rákóczi II aimed too high and brought the wrath of the Sultan down on Transylvania.

Religion was an additional complicating factor. The Protestant Reformation gained many adherents in Hungary during the sixteenth century, and while religious toleration was decreed in Transylvania in 1572, in Royal Hungary the counter-reformation gathered force under Habsburg rule. The Turks, ironically, were indifferent to the issue and treated all their Christian subjects (*Rayah*) with equal disdain. After the expulsion of the Turks, Protestant landowners were dispossessed in favour of foreign servants of the crown – a major cause of subsequent anti-Habsburg revolts.

HABSBURG RULE

After heavy fighting between 1683 and 1699, a multinational army evicted the Ottomans, and the Turks relinquished all claims by signing the **Peace of Karlowitz**. Yet for many years peace remained a mirage, for the Hungarians now bitterly resented Habsburg policy and their plundering armies. The **Kuruc revolt** (1677–85) led by **Imre Thököly** was but a prelude to the full-scale **War of Independence** of 1703–11, when peasants and nobles banded together under **Ferenc Rákóczi II**, György's grandson, and initially routed the enemy. Ultimately, however, they were defeated by superior

Habsburg power and the desertion of their ally, Louis XIV of France, and peace born of utter exhaustion came at last to Hungary.

Habsburg rule combined force with paternalism, especially during the reign of Empress **Maria Theresa** (1740–80), who believed the Hungarians to be "fundamentally a good people, with whom one can do anything if one takes them the right way". The policy of *impopulatio* settled thousands of Swabians, Slovaks, Serbs and Romanians in the deserted regions of Hungary, so that in areas such as the "Military Border" along the Sava, **Magyars became a minority**. By the end of the eighteenth century they formed only 35 percent of the population of the huge kingdom. For the aristocrats it was an age of glory: the Esterházy, Grassalkovich and Batthyány families and their lesser imitators commissioned over 200 palaces, and Baroque town centres and orchestras flourished. Yet the masses were virtually serfs, using medieval methods that impoverished the soil, mired in isolated villages. Cattle, grain and wine – Hungary's main exports – went cheap to Austria, which tried to monopolize industry.

The **Germanization** of culture, education, and administration was another feature of Habsburg policy. Whilst the richest nobles and most of the urban bourgeoisie chose the Habsburg style, however, the petty gentry and peasantry clung stubbornly to their Magyar identity. The ideals of the **Enlightenment** found growing support among intellectuals, and the revival of the **Magyar language** became inseparable from nationalist politics. **Ferenc Kazinczy**, who refashioned Hungarian as a literary language and translated foreign classics, was associated with the seven **Jacobin conspirators,** executed for plotting treason against the Habsburgs in 1795.

THE NINETEENTH CENTURY: NATIONALISM AND REFORM

Magyar nationalism, espoused by sections of the Natio, became increasingly vocal during the early nineteenth century. Hungary's backwardness was a matter for patriotic shame and self-interested concern, especially after the occurrence of peasant riots in the impoverished, cholera-ridden Zempléni, and the publication of *Hitel* ("Credit"), which scathingly indicted the country's semi-feudal economy. However, most nobles were determined to preserve their privileges. One wrote that "God himself has differentiated between us, assigning to the peasant labour and need, to the lord, abundance and a merry life". Moreover, national liberation was seen in exclusively Magyar terms – the idea that non-Magyars within the multinational state might wish to assert their own identity was regarded as subversive.

The **Reform Era** (roughly 1825–48) saw many changes. Business, the arts and technology were in ferment, with Jews playing a major role in creating wealth and ideas (although they remained second-class citizens). The **Diet** became increasingly defiant in its dealings with Vienna over finances and laws, and parliamentarians like Ferenc Deák, Count Batthyány and Baron Eötvös acted in the shadow of the "giants" of the time, Széchenyi and Kossuth, who expounded rival programmes for change. Count **István Széchenyi**, the landowning, Anglophile author of *Hitel*, was a tireless practical innovator, introducing silkworms, steamboats and the Academy, as well as an unprecedented tax on the Natio to pay for the construction of his life's monument, the Chain Bridge linking Buda and Pest. His arch rival was **Lajos Kossuth**, smalltown lawyer turned Member of Parliament and editor of the radical *Pesti Hirlap*, which scandalized and delighted citizens. Kossuth detested the Habsburgs, revered "universal liberty", and demanded an end to serfdom and censorship; but Magyar chauvinism was his blind spot. The law of 1840, his greatest pre-revolutionary achievement, inflamed dormant nationalist feelings among Croats, Slovaks and Romanians by making Magyar the sole official language – an act for which his ambitions would later suffer.

REVOLUTION

The fall of the French monarchy precipitated a crisis within the Habsburg empire, which Kossuth exploited to bring about the **1848 Revolution** in Hungary. The emperor yielded to demands for a constitutional monarchy, universal taxation, widened voting rights and the union of Transylvania with Hungary; while in Budapest the nobles took fright and abolished serfdom when the poet **Sándor Petőfi** threatened them with thousands of peasants camped out in the suburbs. However, the slighted nationalities rallied against the Magyars in

Croatia and Transylvania, and the reassertion of Habsburg control over Italy and Czechoslovakia closed the noose. The new emperor Franz Josef declared that Hungary would be partitioned after its defeat, in reaction to which the Debrecen Diet declared **Hungarian independence** – a state crushed by August 1849, when Tsar Nicholas of Russia sent armies to support the Habsburgs, who instituted a reign of terror.

Gradually, brute force was replaced by a **policy of compromise**, by which Hungary was economically integrated with Austria and given a major shareholding in the Habsburg empire, henceforth known as the "Dual Monarchy". The compromise (*Ausgleich*) of 1867, engineered by **Ferenc Deák**, brought Hungary prosperity and status, but tied the country inextricably to the empire's fortunes. Simmering nationalist passions would henceforth be focused against Hungary as much as Austria, and diplomatic treaties between Austria and Germany would bind Hungary to them in the event of war. In 1896, however, such dangers seemed remote, and people celebrated **Hungary's millenary anniversary** with enthusiasm.

WORLD WAR AND ITS AFTERMATH

Dragged into **World War I** by its allegiance to the Central Powers, Hungary was facing defeat by the autumn of 1918. The Western or Entente powers decided to dismantle the Habsburg empire in favour of the "**Successor States**" – Romania, Czechoslovakia and Yugoslavia – which would acquire much of their territory at Hungary's expense. In Budapest, the October 30 "Michaelmas Daisy Revolution" put the Social Democratic government of **Mihály Károly** in power. But the government avoided the issue of land reform, attempted unsuccessfully to negotiate peace with the Entente, and finally resigned when France backed further demands by the Successor States.

On March 21, 1919, the Social Democrats agreed on co-operation with the **Communists**, who proclaimed a **Republic of Councils** (*Tanácsköztársaság*) led by **Béla Kun**, which ruled through local Soviets. Hoping for radical change and believing that "Russia will save us", many people initially supported the new regime, but enforced nationalization of land

and capital, and attacks on religion, soon alienated the majority. Beset by the Czech Legion in Slovakia and by internal unrest, the regime collapsed in August before the advancing Romanian army, which occupied Budapest.

THE RISE OF FASCISM

Then came the **White Terror**, as right-wing gangs spread out from Szeged, killing "Reds" and Jews, who were made scapegoats for the earlier Communist "Red Terror". **Admiral Miklós Horthy** appointed himself regent and ordered a return to "traditional values" with a vengeance. Meanwhile, at the Paris Conference, Hungary was obliged to sign the **Treaty of Trianon** (July 4, 1920), surrendering two thirds of its historic territory and three fifths of its total population (three million in all) to the Successor States. The bitterest loss was **Transylvania**, whose 103,093 square kilometres and 1.7 million Magyars went to Romania – a devastating blow to national pride, reflected in the popular slogan of the times, *Nem, Nem, soha!* (No, No, never!).

During **the Twenties and Thirties**, campaigning for the overturn of the Trianon *diktat* was the "acceptable" outlet for politics; while workers' unions were tightly controlled and peasants struggled to form associations against the landlords and the gendarmerie, who rigged ballots and gerrymandered as in the old days. Politics were dominated by the *Kormánypárt* (Government Party) led by Count Bethlen, representing the Catholic Church and the landed gentry, which resisted any changes that would threaten their power. Social hardships increased, particularly in the countryside where the **landless peasantry** constituted "three million beggars" whose misery concerned the **Village Explorers** (*Falukutató*), a movement of the literary intelligentsia ranging across the political spectrum. With the Social Democrats co-opted by conservatism and the Communist Party illegal, many workers and disgruntled petit bourgeois turned to the **radical right** to voice their grievances, and were easily turned against Jews and the "Trianon Powers".

Resentment against France, Britain and Romania predisposed many Hungarians to admire **Nazi Germany**'s defiance of the Versailles Treaty; a sentiment nurtured by the Reich's grant of credits for **industrialization**, and Nazi sympathizers within *Volksdeutsche* communities, commerce, the civil service and the officer corps. The rise of rampant nationalism and **anti-Semitism** gave power to politicians like **Gyula Gömbös**, and Hungary's belated industrial growth was partly due to the acquisition of territory from Czechoslovakia, following Germany's dismemberment of the latter. The annexation of Austria made the Reich militarily supreme in Central Europe, and Hungary's submission to German hegemony almost inevitable.

WORLD WAR II

With the outbreak of **World War II**, the government's pro-Nazi policy initially paid dividends. Romania was compelled to return **northern Transylvania** in July 1940, and Hungary gained additional territory from the invasion of Yugoslavia a year later. Hoping for more, Premier Bárdossy committed Hungary to the Nazi invasion of the USSR in June 1941 – an act condemned by the former Prime Minister, Teleki (who had engineered the recovery of Transylvania), as the "policy of vultures". The Hungarian Second Army perished covering the retreat from Stalingrad, while at home, Germany demanded ever more foodstuffs and forced labour. As Axis fortunes waned Horthy prepared to declare neutrality, but Hitler forestalled him with *Operation Margarethe* – the outright **Nazi occupation of Hungary** in March 1944.

Under Sztójay's puppet-government, Hungarian **Jews** were forced into ghettos to await their deportation to Auschwitz and Belsen, a fate hindered only by the heroism of the underground, a handful of people organized by the Swedish diplomat Raoul Wallenberg, and by the manoeuvring of some Horthyite politicians. Mindful of Romania's successful escape from the Axis in August, Horthy declared a surprise armistice on October 15, just as the Red Army crossed Hungary's eastern border. In response, Germany installed a government of the native **Arrow Cross fascists**, or *Nyilas*, led by the deranged Ferenc Szálasi, whose gangs roamed Budapest extorting valuables and murdering people on the frozen Danube, while the Nazis systematically plundered Hungary. They blew up the Danube bridges and compelled the Russians to take Budapest by storm – a siege that reduced much of Buda to ruins. Meanwhile in Debrecen, an assembly of anti-fascist parties met under Soviet auspices to nominate a **provisional government**, which took power after the Germans fled Hungary in April 1945.

THE RAKOSI ERA

In the November 1945 **elections** the Smallholders' Party won an outright majority, but the Soviet military insisted that the Communists and Social Democrats (with seventeen percent of the vote) remain in government. **Land reform** and limited **nationalization** were enacted, while the Communists tightened their grip over the Ministry of the Interior (which controlled the police) and elections became increasingly fraudulent. **Mátyás Rákosi**, Stalin's man in Hungary, gradually undermined and fragmented the "bourgeois" parties with what he called "salami tactics", and by 1948 – officially called the "**Year of Change**" – the Communists were strong enough to coerce the Social Democrats to join them in a single **Workers' Party**, and neutralize the Smallholders. Church schools were seized, Cardinal Mindszenty was jailed for "espionage" and the peasants were forced into collective farms. More than 500,000 Hungarians were imprisoned, tortured or shot in native concentration camps like Recsk, or as deportees in the Soviet Union, victims of the *ÁVO* secret police (renamed the *ÁVH* in 1949), who spread terror throughout society.

Soviet culture and the personality cults of Rákosi (known as "Baldhead" or "Asshole" to his subjects) and Stalin were stiflingly imposed. Hungarian classics like the *Tragedy of Man* were banned for failing to meet the standards of Socialist Realism. Under the 1949 **Five Year Plan**, heavy industry took absolute priority over agriculture and consumer production. To fill the new factories, peasants streamed into towns and women were dragooned into the labour force. Living standards plummeted, and the whole of society was subjected to the laws and dictates of the Party. "Class conscious" workers and peasants were raised to high positions and "class enemies" were discriminated against, while Party *funkcionáriusok* enjoyed luxuries unavailable to the public, who suffered hunger and squalor.

Although the Smallholders retained nominal positions in government, real power lay with

Rákosi's clique, known as the "Jewish Quartet". As elsewhere in Eastern Europe at this time, Hungary saw bitter **feuds within the Communist Party**. In October 1949, the "Muscovites" purged the more independently-minded "national" Communists on the pretext of "Titoism". The former Interior Minister **László Rajk** was executed; and his friend and successor (and, later, betrayer), **János Kádár**, was jailed and tortured with others during a second wave of purges. Two years later, following Stalin's death in March 1953, Kremlin power struggles resulted in a more moderate Soviet leadership and the abrupt replacement of Rákosi by **Imre Nagy**. His "**New Course**", announced in July, promised a more balanced industrial strategy and eased pressure on the peasants to collectivize, besides curbing the *ÁVO* terror. Nagy, however, had few allies within the Kremlin, and in 1955 Rákosi was able to strike back, expelling Nagy from the Party for "deviationism", and declaring a **return to Stalinist policies**. However, this brief interlude had encouraged murmurings of resistance.

1956: THE UPRISING

The first act of opposition came from the official Writers' Union, the *November Memorandum*, who objected to the rule of force. The Party clamped down, but also began to "rehabilitate" the Rajk purge victims. During June **1956** the intellectuals' **Petőfi circle** held increasingly outspoken public debates, and **Júlia Rajk** denounced "the men who have ruined this country, corrupted the Party, liquidated thousands and driven millions to despair". Moscow responded to the unrest by replacing Rákosi with **Ernő Gerő** – another hardliner – a move which merely stoked public resentment. The mood came to a head in October, when 200,000 people attended Rajk's reburial; Nagy was readmitted to the Party; and **students** in Szeged and Budapest organized to demand greater national independence and freedom.

In Poland, Gomulka's reform communists had just won concessions from the Kremlin, and Budapest students decided to march on October 23 to the General Bem statue, a symbol of Polish-Hungarian solidarity. About 50,000 assembled, patriotic feelings rose and the procession swelled as it approached

Parliament. A hesitant speech there by Nagy failed to satisfy them, and students besieged the Radio Building on Bródy utca, demanding to voice their grievances on the airwaves. The *ÁVH* guards opened fire, killing many. Almost immediately, this triggered a city-wide **uprising** against the *ÁVH*, which the regular police did little to control; and when Soviet tanks intervened, units of the Hungarian army began to side with the insurgents.

Over the next five days fighting spread throughout Hungary, despite Nagy's reinstatement as premier and pleas for order. **Revolutionary councils** sprang up in towns and factories and free newspapers appeared, demanding "*Ruszkik haza*" (Russians go home), free elections, civil liberties, industrial democracy and neutrality. Intellectuals who had led the first protests now found themselves left behind by uncontrollable dynamism on the streets. The Party leadership temporized, reshuffled the cabinet and struggled to stay in control, as all the "old" parties reappeared and the newly liberated Cardinal Mindszenty provided a focus for the resurgent Right.

The negotiated **Soviet withdrawal**, beginning on October 29, was a delaying tactic. The Russians regrouped in the countryside and brought in fresh troops from Romania and the USSR. On November 1, Nagy announced Hungary's withdrawal from the Warsaw Pact and asked the UN to support **Hungarian neutrality**; that night, Kádár and Ferenc Münnich slipped away from Parliament to join the Russians, who were preparing to crush the "counter-revolution". America downplayed Hungary in the United Nations while the Suez crisis preoccupied world attention, but the CIA-sponsored **Radio Free Europe** encouraged the Magyars to expect Western aid. Having surrounded Budapest and other centres with tanks under cover of a snowstorm, the **Soviet attack** began before dawn on November 4.

Armed resistance was crushed within days, but the workers occupied their factories and proclaimed a **general strike**, maintained for months despite **mass arrests**. Deprived of physical power, the people continued to make symbolic protests like the "Mothers' March" in December. Inexorably, however, the Party and *ÁVH* apparatus reasserted its control. Over 200,000 **refugees** fled to the West, while at home, thousands were jailed or executed, including Nagy and other leading "revisionists", shot in 1958 after a secret trial.

KADÁR'S HUNGARY

In the aftermath of the Uprising, the new Party leader **János Kádár** ruthlessly suppressed the last vestiges of opposition. After the mid-1960s, however, his name came to be associated with the **gradual reform** of Hungary's social and economic system from a totalitarian regime to one based, at least in part, on **compromise**. Kádár's famous phrase, "Whoever is not against us is with us" (a reversal of the Stalinist slogan) invited a tacit compact between Party and people. Both had been shaken by the events of 1956, and realized that bold changes – as happened in Czechoslovakia in 1967 and 1968 – only invited Soviet intervention, justified by the Brezhnev doctrine of "limited sovereignty".

Having stimulated the economy by cautious reforms in the structure of pricing and management, and overcome opposition within the Politburo, Kádár and Reszö Nyers announced the **New Economic Mechanism** (NEM) in 1968. Though its impact on centralized planning was slight, the NEM was accompanied by measures to promote "socialist legality" and make merit, rather than class background and Party standing, the criterion for promotion and higher education.

While generally welcomed by the populace, these reforms angered "New Left" supporters of either Dubček's "Socialism with a human face" in Czechoslovakia or of the Chinese Cultural Revolution, and also, more seriously, conservatives within the Party. With backing from Moscow, they watered down the NEM and ousted Nyers, its leading advocate, from the Politburo in 1973; expelling Hegedüs and other "revisionist sociologists" from the Party later.

Following a power struggle, Kádár was able to reverse the reactionary tide, and reduce constraints on the so-called "second economy". While structural reforms were extremely limited, consumerism, a private sector and even "forint millionaires" emerged during **the Seventies**, when Hungary became a byword for **affluence** within the Socialist bloc – the "happiest barracks in the camp", as the joke had it. Mechanics and other artisans with marketable skills were able to moonlight profitably, as demonstrated by the boom in private home-building; and workers and unions acquired some say in the management of their enterprises. This **"market socialism"** attracted the favours of Western politicians and bankers, and before *perestroika* the "Hungarian model" seemed to offer the best hope for reform within Eastern Europe.

In **the Eighties**, however, economic and social problems became increasingly obvious – ranging from thirty percent **inflation**, whose effect was felt hardest by the **"new poor"** living on low, fixed incomes, to Hungary's $14.7 billion **foreign debt** (per capita, the largest in Eastern Europe). Despite reformist rhetoric, vested interests successfully resisted the logic of the market, whose rigorous application would entail drastic lay offs and mass **unemployment** in towns dominated by the unprofitable mining and steel industries. Although frank analyses of Hungary's economic plight started appearing in the media during the mid-Eighties, other issues ran up against the limits of state tolerance. These included fears for **the environment** in the wake of Chernobyl and the decision to build a dam at Nagymaros (see Chapter Two); an unofficial **peace movement** that was quickly driven back underground; and any discussion of the Party's "leading role" or Hungary's alliance with the Soviet Union. Discussion of such topics could only be found in **samizdat** (underground) magazines like *Beszélő*, whose publishers were harassed as dissidents. Although in 1983 the Party announced that "independents" could contest elections, it proved unwilling to let them enter Parliament, as demonstrated by the gerrymandering used against László Rajk in 1986.

Yet the need for change was becoming evident even within the Party, where the caution of the "old guard" – Kádár, Horváth and Gáspár – caused increasing frustration among **reformists**, who believed that Hungarians would only accept income tax and economic austerity if greater liberalization seemed a realistic prospect. Happily, this coincided with the advent of **Gorbachev**, whose interest in the Hungarian model of socialism and desire to bring a new generation into power was an open secret.

THE END OF COMMUNISM

The **end of Communism in Hungary** was so orderly that it can hardly be termed a revolution, but it did set in motion the collapse of hardline regimes in East Germany and Czechoslovakia. Prefiguring the fate of Gorbachev, the politicians who created an opening for change hoped to preserve Communism by reforming it, but were swept away by the forces which they had unleashed.

At the **May 1988 Party Congress**, Kádár and seven colleagues were ousted from power by a coalition of radical reformers and conservative technocrats. The latter backed **Károly Grósz** as Kádár's successor, but his lacklustre performance as Party leader enabled the reformists to shunt him aside in July 1989, forcing conservatives and hardliners onto the defensive. As the ascendancy of **Imre Pozsgay, Rezsö Nyers, Miklós Németh** and **Gyula Horn** became apparent there was a "traffic jam on the road to Damascus" as lesser figures hastened to pledge support for reforms.

In mid-October 1989, the Communist Party formally reconstituted itself as the **Hungarian Socialist Party** (*MSzP*), dissolved its private militia and announced the **legalization of opposition parties** as a prelude to free elections. To symbolize this watershed, the People's Republic was renamed the **Republic of Hungary** in a ceremony broadcast live on national television, on the thirty-third anniversary of the Uprising.

Meanwhile, the iron curtain was unravelling with astonishing speed. Ever since May, when Hungary began dismantling the barbed wire and minefields along its **border** with Austria, thousands of **East Germans** had seized their chance to escape to the West, crossing over via Hungary at a rate of 200 every day. Despite protests from the Honecker regime, Hungary refused to close the border or deport would-be escapers back to the DDR, and allowed 20,000 refugees encamped in the West German embassy in Budapest to leave the country. After the DDR sealed its own borders, frustration spilled over on to the streets of Leipzig and Dresden, where mass demonstrations led to the **fall of the Berlin Wall** (November 9, 1989) and the ousting of Erich Honecker. A week later, the brutal repression of a pro-democracy demonstration in Prague's Wenceslas Square set in motion the "**Velvet Revolution**" in Czechoslovakia, which overturned forty years of Communist rule in ten days. The *annus mirabilis* of 1989

climaxed with the **overthrow of Ceauşescu** in Romania (December 22).

THE 1990 ELECTIONS AND BEYOND

After such events Hungary's first **free elections** since 1945 – in 1990 – seemed an anticlimax. During the first round of voting (March 6) Pozsgay and the Socialist Party were obliterated, while two parties emerged as front runners. The **Hungarian Democratic Forum** (*MDF*), founded at the Lakitelek Conference of 1987, articulated populist, conservative nationalism, encapsulated in the idea of "Hungarianness", whereas the rival **Alliance of Free Democrats** (*SzDSz*) espoused a neoliberal, internationalist outlook, similar to that of the **Federation of Young Democrats** (*FIDESz*). Two pre-war parties revived under octogenarian leaders also participated, namely the **Smallholders' Party** (under the slogan "God, Home, Family, Wine, Wheat and Independence") and the **Christian Democrats**.

Despite being diminished by voter apathy, the **1990 elections** unceremoniously swept the reformist Communists out of power. Their place was taken by a centre right coalition dominated by Hungarian Democratic Forum (MDF) and its Prime Minister Jozsef Antall, but with an important input from the smaller coalition partners, the Christian Democratic People's Party (KDNP) and the Smallholders' Party (FKgP). The coalition's fragile majority was held together by Antall's skilful leadership. A born politician with a schoolmasterly style, Antall relished the opportunity to take a role he had longed for but never expected to get during the Communist years. He dreamed of restoring Hungary to its pre-war state, restoring the traditions and the social hierarchies that had prevailed then. Very much a moderate, his policies rested on the belief that over forty years of Communism had destroyed the true values of Hungarian society. However, not everyone wanted the Catholic Church to return to the dominant social position it had enjoyed before the war, and his party's proud belief in restoring the Hungarian people to its former position sounded to some, including Hungary's neighbours, like a nationalist recipe for recovering the lost lands of Trianon – an interpretation that was strengthened by his failure to distance himself from the openly nationalist extreme right wing, in the form of István Csurka.

Antall died in 1993 after a prolonged illness, but his policies were continued by Peter Boross. However, the government's inability to bring an economic turn-round, as well as its unconciliatory style brought growing disillusionment among the voters, and the **1994 elections** saw the reformist Communists return to power, assisted by a very sympathetic media that presented the outgoing government as amateurish and arrogant. The Communists brought the Free Democrats into the government, to protect themselves against attacks on their past, but this has not been successful. The new Prime Minister, Gyula Horn, has shown himself a poor communicator, and his government has made little impact on the huge backlog of much-needed legislations. In early 1994, after Horn broke with his FInance Minister, the country was plunged into crisis, and the confidence of western investors was severely tested – not a good idea for a country so reliant on the co-operation of western banks in handling its massive debts. Meanwhile the Free Democrats have been totally ineffectual coalition partners, clinging on to power but without any grip on the levers themselves. The opposition parties remain disorganized and weak, and the great hope of the transition period, the Young Democrats, has declined into a right-of-centre party with few ideas. With the transition from Communism firmly over, Hungarian politics is settling down. However, where the transition has led, and how the country will cope with the pitfalls and opportunities of democratic politics, remains to be seen.

MONUMENTAL CHRONOLOGY

8000 BC	Palaeolithic cave-dwellers in the Bükk Mountains.	Remains found at Subalyuk, Szeleta and other caves.
400 BC	Celts enter Transdanubia.	Pottery, glassware; gold treasure of Szárazd-Regöly.
1st–4th c.	**Romans** occupy Pannónia, founding numerous towns.	Ruins at **Aquincum**, **Gorsium**, **Szombathely**, **Pécs**, etc.
896	Magyar conquest. The state and Christianity are established in Hungary by Stephen I during the eleventh century.	Ruins of the Székesfehérvár Basilica; eleventh-century crypts at Pécs and **Tihany** Abbey are virtually all that remain.
13th c.	Mongol invasion. Castles and new towns are founded during the reign of Béla IV.	**Romanesque churches** at **Ják**, **Zsámbék**, **Oskü**, and **Velemér** stand comparison with **Pannonhalma Monastery**. Ruined *vár* at **Esztergom**, **Füzér** and **Boldogkőváralja**, sited on precipitous crags.
14th–15th c.	Zenith of Hungarian power in Europe under the Angevin monarchs and then Mátyás Corvinus.	Remains of **Buda** and **Visegrád** where **Gothic and Renaissance architecture** attained great heights; **Diósgyőr** castle in Miskolc.
1526–1680s	After defeat at **Mohács**, Hungary is occupied for next 150 years by **Turks** and Habsburgs, and ravaged by warfare.	**Kőszeg**, **Sárospatak**, **Siklós** and other **castles** have remained largely intact; as have a few **Turkish** *türbe*, ex-*djami* and **minarets** at **Pécs** and **Eger**; most medieval towns were destroyed, although on the Plain, Szeged and Debrecen expanded vastly.
1703–11	Rákóczi War of Independence.	
17th–18th c.	Under **Habsburg rule**, many towns are wholly rebuilt around new centres; while Buda Palace and other monumental buildings are begun.	The **wooden belfrys**, pew-carvings and colourful coffered ceilings found at **Nyírbator**, **Zsurk**, **Csaroda** and other remote churches in eastern Hungary are part-Gothic, and partly the "folk" equivalent of the **Baroque style**. This characterized much of seventeenth- and eighteenth-century architecture, eg in the Belváros of **Győr**, **Veszprém**, **Székesfehérvár**, etc, and at the **Esterházy Palace** in Fertőd.
1830–1880s	After the Reform Era and the struggle for independence (1848–49), Hungary accepts the "Compromise" of 1868. Development of new centres of industry—Miskolc, Salgótarján, Csepel, etc.	The **Chain Bridge** presages a spate of construction in Budapest, where large houses are built alongside the new **boulevards**. **Szeged** rebuilt after 1879 flood. The rise of **Neoclassicism**—with Ybl and Hild's huge basilicas in Eger, Pest and Esztergom—but also **neo-Gothic**—the **Fishermen's Bastion** and **Vajdahunyad Castle** (in 1896, like the Metro)—plus Lechner's attempts to develop a uniquely "**Hungarian Style**" for the **Applied Arts Museum** and the public buildings in **Kecskemét**.
1896	1000th anniversary of the Magyar conquest.	

1918–1919	Habsburg empire collapses; Hungary briefly becomes a **"Republic of Councils."**

Paintings by the **Group of Eight** (Szombathely Gallery).

1920s & 1930s	Hungary loses two thirds of its territory to neighbouring states. Regency of **Admiral Horthy**.

Deliberate evocation of past national glories—the erection of "Heroes' Gates" in **Szeged**, **Kőszeg**, etc.

1944–45	**Nazis** occupy Hungary; massacre of Hungarian **Jews** and **Gypsies**. Heavy fighting with Soviet army.

Desecration of **synagogues**. Budapest and many towns incur massive damage. This is swiftly repaired.

1948–56	**"Rákosi era"** characterized by Five Year Plans, police terror and a propaganda blitz.

Dunaújváros and other new towns; crash urbanization and industrialization; the **Liberation Monument** and other Soviet-style projects exemplify this phase.

1956	**Hungarian Uprising**.

Widespread urban damage—Budapest is worst affected.

1960s & 1970s	Emergence of **"Kádárism"**—economic reforms to encourage greater public affluence. During this period, Hungary becomes a byword for **"consumer socialism"** in Eastern Europe.

The **Metro** is completed. **Modernistic** cultural centres at Győr and Sárospatak are notable examples of Sixties and Seventies **architecture**; while supermarkets, hotels and resorts around Balaton are more typical of the period.

1980s	Economic problems, made worse by energy shortfall after the Chernobyl disaster.

Go-ahead for construction of **Nagymaros dam** and more nuclear reactors at **Paks**. Closure of mines and other loss-making industries is proposed by the state.

1988	**Grósz** replaces Kadar as Party leader.

1989	Grósz replaced by **Nemeth** and **Pozsgay**. Revolutions in neighbouring Czechoslovakia and Romania.

Nagymaros dam project abandoned. Removal of border fortifications.

1990	**Free elections** result in **MDF** government.

1994	Elections sweep the former Communists to power.

BOOKS

Publishers are detailed below in the form of British publisher/American publisher, where both exist. Where books are published in one country only, UK or US follows the publisher's name. Hungarian out of print books are designated o/p. For a gentle introduction to current affairs and literature, look for the Budapest-published *The Hungarian Quarterly*.

TRAVEL BOOKS AND GENERAL ACCOUNTS

Gyula Antalffy, *A Thousand Years of Travel in Old Hungary* (Akademy Kiado, Budapest; o/p). Slightly stodgy in places, but with enough anecdotes and odd details to keep your attention as it surveys a millennium of Hungary through the eyes of foreign and native travellers.

Stephen Brook, *The Double Eagle: Vienna, Budapest and Prague* (Picador, UK/Morrow, US; both o/p). Taking their Habsburg traditions as a starting point, Brook's readable, personal exploration of three cities concludes that war and Stalinism have dissolved the bonds of common experience – a judgement which now rings less confidently than when this book was written in the late Eighties. Though more chapters are devoted to Vienna, it's the sections on Budapest, and above all Prague, that really shine.

Bob Dent, *Blue Guide Hungary* (A & C Black/ WW Norton). A left-wing slant distinguishes this from other *Blue Guides*, enlivening the typically thorough coverage of monuments. The skimpy treatment of Kőszeg and Szombathely and a general lack of practical information are major flaws, however.

Gyula Illyés, *People of the Puszta* (Corvina, UK; o/p). An unsentimental, sometimes horrifying immersion in the life of the landless peasantry of pre-war Hungary, mainly set in Transdanubia. Illyés – one of Hungary's greatest twentieth-century writers – was born into such a background, and the book breathes authenticity. Highly recommended.

Patrick Leigh Fermor, *A Time of Gifts* (Penguin, UK/US); *Between the Woods and the Water* (Penguin UK/US). In 1934 the young Leigh Fermor started walking from Holland to Turkey, and reached Hungary in the closing chapter of *A Time of Gifts*. The Gypsies and rusticated aristocrats of the Great Plain and Transylvania are superbly evoked in *Between the Woods and the Water* (a third volume, covering Moldavia and Bulgaria, is underway). Lyrical and erudite.

Claudio Magris, *Danube* (Collins, UK/ Farrar, Straus & Giroux). Highly praised account of the Danubian countries interweaves history and reportage in an ambitious attempt to illuminate their cultural and spiritual backgrounds. Lots of interesting stories and information, but rather intellectual.

George Mikes, *Any Souvenirs?* (Penguin, UK/ Harvard Common Press, US; both o/p). Born in Siklós in southern Hungary, Mikes fled the country in 1956 and made a new life in Britain as a humorist. This wry account relates his first visit home in fifteen years.

John Paget, *Hungary and Transylvania* (Ayer, US). Paget's massive book attempted to explain nineteenth-century Hungary to the English middle class, and, within its aristocratic limitations, succeeded. Occasionally found in second-hand bookshops.

Walter Starkie, *Raggle-Taggle* (John Murray, UK/Transatlantic Arts, US; both o/p). The wanderings of a Dublin professor with a fiddle, who bummed around Budapest and the Plain in search of Gypsy music in the 1920s. First published in 1933 and last issued in 1964 – a second-hand bookshop perennial.

András Török, *Budapest; A Critical Guide* (Zephyr Press, US). Just what its title proclaims, this witty, informative guide is written by a native of the city and fully revised every year. Available abroad and in Budapest itself. Highly recommended.

HISTORY AND POLITICS

John Bierman, *Righteous Gentile* (Penguin, UK; o/p/ADL, US). The best biography of Raoul

Wallenberg, the Swedish diplomat whose daring efforts partly frustrated Eichmann's attempt to exterminate the Jews of Hungary during 1944–45.

Miklós Haraszti, *A Worker in a Workers' State* (Penguin, UK; o/p/Universe, US). Factual, gritty investigation of "Piecework" (the book's Hungarian title) in Budapest's Red Star factory, which earned Haraszti a prison term for "defaming socialism" in the Seventies. *The Velvet Prison: Artists Under State Socialism* (I B Tauris/Farrar, Straus & Giroux) is a later, tediously ideological critique, less specific to Hungary than *Worker*.

György (George) Konrád, *Antipolitics* (Quartet/Harcourt Brace). Written in the mid-Eighties, when Konrád's strategy for the transformation of Hungarian society and East–West relations "from below" seemed highly optimistic, it now reads like a blueprint for the dissolution of Communism in Eastern Europe.

Paul Lendvai, *Hungary: The Art of Survival* (I B Tauris/St Martin's Press). This readable account of how and why Kádár was ousted by Károly Grósz was overtaken by events, as Grósz fell by the wayside before the book came out.

Bill Lomax, *Hungary 1956* (Allison & Busby, UK/St Martin's Press, US; both o/p). Probably the best – and shortest – book on the Uprising, by an acknowledged expert on modern Hungary. Lomax also edited *Eyewitness in Hungary* (Spokesman, UK), an anthology of accounts by foreign Communists (most of whom were sympathetic to the Uprising) that vividly depicts the elation, confusion and tragedy of the events of October 1956.

George Mikes, *A Study in Infamy* (Andre Deusch, UK; o/p). Better known in the West for his humourous writings, Mikes here exposes the activities of the secret police during the Rákosi era, using captured documents which explain their methods for surveillance of the population and use of terror as a political weapon.

George Schöpflin, *Politics in Eastern Europe 1945-92* (Blackwell UK/US). An excellent overview of the region in the last fifty years.

N M Nagy-Talavera, *Greenshirts and Others* (Hoover Institution Press, US; o/p). A well-written and researched study of the social dislocations, racism and paranoid nationalism which afflicted Hungary and Romania between the wars, giving rise to native fascist movements and bitter anti-Semitism.

Peter F. Sugar et al, *A History of Hungary* (I B Tauris/Indiana University Press). A scholarly but readable history from ancient times up until the late 1980s, with a postscript written just before the end of Communism. A revised edition deserves to be published in the future.

Nigel Swain, *Hungary: The Rise and Fall of Feasible Socialism* (Verso/Routledge Chapman & Hall). Analyses the "Hungarian model" of socialism in decline, and the prospects for a market economy in the Nineties. As throughout Eastern Europe, capitalism shows little sign of delivering prosperity *and* social justice.

ART, FOLK TRADITIONS, CINEMA AND COOKERY

The Hungarian publisher Corvina *publishes a number of books covering Hungary's folk traditions and artistic treasures, mostly translated into English or German. Some editions are available on import, and some of its British titles are available through US publishers of fiction and poetry, but they are cheapest to buy in the country itself – either in Bestsellers (V. Oktober 6. utca), which has a good range but is expensive, at bookshops in Vaci utca; in the Corvina discount shop on the second floor of the big modern building on Vörömarty tér; or in the Book Superstore on the corner of Báthory utca and Honvéd utca near the Parliament.*

Val Biro, *Hungarian Folk Tales* (Oxford University Press, UK/US). Merry tales of dragons and the like in a crisp, colloquial rendering close to original recountings, intended for children.

Susan Derecskey, *The Hungarian Cookbook* (HarperCollins US). A good, easy-to-follow selection of traditional and modern recipes.

Tekla Dömötör, *Hungarian Folk Beliefs* (Corvina, UK/Indiana University Press, US; both o/p). A superb collection of social history, folk beliefs and customs.

Tamás Hofer et al, *Hungarian Peasant Art* (Constable, UK/International Publications Service, US; both o/p). An excellently produced examination of Hungarian folk art, with lots of good photos.

George Lang, *The Cuisine of Hungary* (Penguin/Random House). A well-written and beautifully illustrated work, telling you everything you need to know about Hungarian cooking, its history and how to do it yourself.

Lesley Chamberlain, *The Food and Cooking of Eastern Europe* (Penguin, UK/US; o/p). A great compendium of recipes, nostrums and gastronomical history, guaranteed to have you experimenting in the kitchen.

Graham Petrie, *History Must Answer to Man: Hungarian Cinema Today* (Corvina/Zoetrope). Though you wouldn't guess so from the title, this is an unpretentious and very readable account of Hungarian cinema, surveying its history from the beginnings to the work of directors like Bacsó, Szabó, Jancsó, Makk and Kézdi-Kovács. Rather dated now, however, and very hard to find.

FICTION AND POETRY

Most **Hungarian classics in translation** are published by Corvina. Inside Hungary, you might find the swashbuckling romances of **Géza Gárdonyi**, novels by **Mór Jókai** and short stories by **Frigyes Karinthy**. Despite his stature, the romantic poems of **Sándor Petőfi** only appear in English thanks to the Hungarian Cultural Foundation in Buffalo, New York (1969; editor A. Nyerges). The same publisher and editor are responsible for the collected poems of **Attila József** and **Endre Ady** (1973).

The number of **modern authors** in translation has increased since the mid-Eighties, when only **Gyula Illyés** (see "Travel Books" above), **József Lengyel** and **György Konrád** were published abroad. You can now read émigré writers such as **Tamás Aczel**, contemporary standard-bearers of Hungarian literature like **Peter Esterházy**, and a host of other writers in anthologies.

ANTHOLOGIES

István Bart ed, *Present Continuous: Contemporary Hungarian Writing* (Corvina, UK; o/p). Short stories by twenty-five authors, many of them reportage in literary form, a genre that Hungarians term "sociography".

Loránt Czigány ed, *The Oxford History of Hungarian Literature from the Earliest Times to the Present* (Oxford University Press, UK/US). Probably the most comprehensive collection in print to date. Chronological structure; good coverage of political and social background.

Lajos Illés ed, *Nothing's Lost: Twenty-five Hungarian Short Stories* (Corvina). Another rich anthology of post-war writing, including real stunners by Endre Vészi, Ferenc Karinthy and Erzsébet Galgóczi.

Albert Tezlsa ed, *Ocean at the Window: Hungarian Prose and Poetry since 1945* (University of Minnesota Press, US; o/p). A good selection.

Éva Tóth ed, *MA Today* (Corvina). An anthology of stories, poems and essays from the literary and art review *MA*, which constitutes a *tour d'horizon* of cultural trends since 1916.

Miklós Vajda ed, *Modern Hungarian Poetry* (Columbia University Press, UK/US). A reasonable selection of post-war poetry.

Paul Varnai ed, *Hungarian Short Stories* (o/p). A fine collection of modern work ranging from the "magical realist" to astringent social commentary.

POETRY

Endre Ady, *Poems of Endre Ady* (University Press of America, UK/US). Regarded by many as the finest Hungarian poet of the twentieth century, Ady's allusive verses are notoriously difficult to translate. *Explosive Country* (Corvina) is a collection of essays about his homeland.

George Faludy, *Selected Poems, 1933–80* (McClelland & Stewart, UK; o/p/University of Georgia Press, US). Fiery, lyrical poetry by a victim of both Nazi and Russian repression. Themes of political defiance and the nobility of the human spirit, the struggle to preserve human values in the face of oppression. See also his cheerfully resigned biographical account of his journey through the Forties and Fifties and the prison camps of the period, *My Happy Days in Hell*.

Ágnes Nemes Nagy, *Selected Poems* (o/p). A major post-war poet, often speculating intellectually on knowledge and the role of poetry in trying to impose order on the world, despite the jarring and bitter realization that it can't.

Jónas Pilzinsky, *Selected Poems* (o/p). A major poet, with themes of humanity's suffering and sacrifice.

Miklós Radnóti, *Under Gemini: The Selected Poems of Miklós Radnóti with a Prose Memoir* (Ohio University Press, US). The best collection of Radnóti's sparse, anguished poetry. *The*

Complete Poetry (Ardis UK/US; o/p) is a fuller but poorly translated collection, ranging from exotic and erotic celebrations of nature to the agonies of repression and injustice. *Subway Stops: Fifty Poems* (Ardis, UK/US; o/p) has an over-scholarly introduction, but movingly contrasts love with the brutal surroundings of Radnóti's last years in a Nazi labour camp. His final poems before his murder appear in *Clouded Sky* (o/p).

Sándor Weöres and Ferenc Juhász, *Selected Poems* (Peter Smith, US; o/p). Two successful modern poets. Weöres is more preoccupied with primitive myth and mystical themes; Juhász, often quirkily, with folklore and rural culture and the folk oral poetic tradition.

FICTION

Tamás Aczel, *The Hunt* (Faber & Faber, UK/ Little, Brown, US; both o/p). A beautifully crafted allegorical novel of truth and falsehood, loyalty and betrayal, set on a remote rural estate in an unnamed country not unlike Hungary during the early Fifties.

Géza Csáth, *The Magician's Garden and Other Stories* (Penguin, UK/Columbia University Press, US; both o/p) *Opium and Other Stories* (Penguin, UK/US; o/p). Both of these volumes of stories are in a "magical realist" genre, questioning "reality". Csáth himself was tormented by insanity and opium addiction, and committed suicide in 1918.

Tibor Dery, *The Portuguese Princess* (Calder, UK/Northwestern University Press, US; both o/p). Short stories by a once-committed Communist, who was jailed for three years after the Uprising, and died in 1977.

Peter Esterházy, *Helping Verbs of the Heart* (Quartet/Grove). A moving account of a mother's death and her son's grief, interwoven with ironic *pensées* by Hungary's foremost novelist and essayist, a descendant of the famous aristocratic family. Another sprig of the dynasty has achieved fame as a Hollywood screenwriter – Joe Eszterhaze, who wrote the controversial *Basic Instinct*.

Tibor Fischer *Under the Frog, A Black Comedy* (Penguin/New Press). A fictional account of the 1956 revolution. Witty and enjoyable.

Agnes Hankiss, *A Hungarian Romance* (Readers International, UK/US). A lyrical first novel by "Hungary's new feminist voice", dealing with a woman's quest for self-identity during the sixteenth century, and the timeless conflict between personal and public interests.

Mór Jókai, *Tales from Jókai* (Ayer Co Publishers, US); *The Dark Diamonds* (Corvina, UK/ Arthur Vanous, US; both o/p); *Dr. Dumany's Wife: A Romance* (o/p). Colourful stories by the Magyar equivalent of Dickens. Jókai wrote over 100 novels during his lifetime (1825–1904).

György (George) Konrád, *The Case Worker* (Penguin, UK/US; o/p); *The City Builder* (Penguin, UK; o/p/Penguin, US); *The Loser* (Harcourt Brace Jovanovich, US). In contrast with his optimistic *Antipolitics* (see above), Konrád's novels are overwhelmingly bleak, dealing with misery, alienation, escapism, hypocrisy and madness. Despite the subject matter, his powers of insight and rich use of language are seductive and compelling.

József Lengyel, *Acta Sanctorum* (Peter Owen, UK); *Prenn Drifting* (Peter Owen, UK; o/p/ Beekman Publishers, US); *From Beginning to End/The Spell* (Peter Owen/Beekman Publications); *The Judge's Chair* (Peter Owen/ Beekman Publishers); *Confrontation* (Peter Owen/Carol Publishing). A dedicated Communist since his youth, Lengyel apparently kept his faith through several years in the Gulag, but later began to display doubts. His colourful semi-autobiographical novels concern morality under stress, ambition, and the question of ends versus means. *The Bridgebuilders* (Corvina, UK; o/p) is the least gripping, although Lengyel reportedly considered it one of his best.

Peter Lengyel, *Cobblestones* (Readers International, UK/US; o/p). An absorbing, multi-layered detective story spanning two centuries, where an ingenious theft and an unexplained murder are tied into the millennary celebrations of 1896, the Stalinist Fifties and the uncertainties of the Eighties.

László Nemeth, *Guilt* (Dufour, US). A Thirties novel of tragedy and its effect on a young couple.

Giorgio & Nicola Pressburger, *Homage to the Eighth District* (Readers International, UK/ US). Evocative tales of Jewish life in Budapest, before, during and after World War II, by twin brothers who fled Hungary in 1956.

Stephen Vizinczey, *In Praise of Older Women* (Hamish Hamilton, UK; o/p/ University of Chicago Press). The memoirs of a randy egocentric lad growing up in refugee camps and in Budapest during the Rákosi years. Soft porn mixed with social comment and supposedly profound insights into the nature of women, which made a splash when first published in the West in 1967.

FOREIGN WRITERS ON HUNGARY

Heinrich Böll, *And Where Were You, Adam* in *Adam and the Train* (Penguin, UK/ Northwestern University Press, US; both o/p). A superb short novel by one of the major post-war German novelists, consisting of loosely connected and semi-autobiographical short stories describing the panic-stricken retreat of Hitler's forces from the *puszta* before the Red Army in 1944. Told through both Hungarian and German eyes, these stories are a haunting evocation of the chaos, cruelty and horror of the retreat, but also of a rural culture that seems to resist everything thrown at it.

Franz Fühmann, *Twenty-two Days or Half a Lifetime* (Cape, UK; o/p). Disjointed metaphysical and literary ramblings interspersed with musings on Budapest and Hungary, by an East German writer (1922–84).

Hans Habe, *Black Earth* (NEL, UK; o/p). The story of a peasant's commitment to the Communist underground and his disillusionment with the Party in power; a good read, and by no means as crude as the artwork and blurb suggest.

Cecilia Holland, *Rakossy* (Hodder, UK; o/p/ Atheneum, US; o/p), *The Death of Attila* (Hodder, UK/Pocket Books, US; both o/p). *Rakossy* is a bodice-ripping tale of a shy Austrian princess wed to an uncouth Magyar baron, braving the Turkish hordes on the Hungarian marches; while the *Death of Attila* evokes the Huns, Romans and Goths of the Dark Ages, pillaging around the Danube. Two well-crafted historical romances.

MUSIC AND RECORDS

Hungarian music enshrines the trinity of Liszt, Bartók, and Kodály: Liszt was the founding father, Bartók one of the greatest composers of the twentieth century, and Kodály (himself no slouch at composition) created a widely imitated system of musical education. When you also take into account talented Hungarian soloists like Perényi, it's clear that this small nation has made an outstanding contribution to the world of music.

HUNGARIAN COMPOSERS

Franz Liszt (1811–1886), who described himself as a "mixture of Gypsy and Franciscan", cut a flamboyant figure in the salons of Europe as a virtuoso pianist and womanizer. The *Hungarian Rhapsodies* and similar pieces reflected the "Gypsy" side to his character and the rising nationalism of his era; while later work like the *Transcendental Études* (whose originality has only recently been recognized) invoked a visionary, "Franciscan" mood. Despite his patriotic stance, however, Liszt's first language was German (he never fully mastered Hungarian), and his expressed wish to roam the villages of Hungary with a knapsack on his back was a Romantic fantasy.

That was left to **Béla Bartók** (1881–1945) and **Zoltán Kodály** (1882–1967), who began exploring the remoter districts of Hungary and Transylvania in 1906, collecting peasant music.

Despite many hardships and local suspicion of their "monster" (a cutting stylus and phonograph cylinders), they managed to record and catalogue thousands of melodies, laying down high standards of musical ethnography still maintained in Hungary today, while discovering a rich source of inspiration for their own compositions. Bartók believed that a genuine peasant melody was "quite as much a masterpiece in miniature as a Bach fugue or a Mozart sonata . . . a classic example of the expression of a musical thought in its most conceivably concise form, with the avoidance of all that is superfluous".

Bartók created a personal but universal musical language by reworking the raw essence of Magyar and Finno-Ugric folk music in a modern context – in particular his six *String Quartets* – although Hungarian public opinion was originally hostile. Feeling misunderstood and out of step with his country's increasingly pro-Nazi policies, Bartók left Hungary in 1940, dying poor and embittered in the United States. Since then, however, his reputation has soared, and the return of his body in 1988 occasioned national celebrations, shrewdly sponsored by the state.

Kodály's music is more consciously national: Bartók called it "a real profession of faith in the Hungarian soul". His *Peacock Variations* are based on a typical Old Style pentatonic tune and the *Dances of Galanta* on the popular music played by Gypsy bands. Old Style tunes also form the core of Kodály's work in musical education: the "Kodály method" employs group singing to develop musical skill at an early age. His ideas have made Hungarian music teaching among the best in the world, and Kodály himself a paternal figure to generations of children.

For others Kodály was a voice of conscience during the Rákosi era, writing the *Hymn of Zrínyi* to a seventeenth-century text whose call to arms against the Turkish invasion – "I perceive a ghastly dragon, full of venom and fury, snatching the crown of Hungary. . ." – was tumultuously acclaimed as an anti-Stalinist allegory. Its first performance was closely followed by the Uprising, and the *Hymn* was not performed again for many years; nor were any recordings made available until 1982.

HUNGARIAN FOLK MUSIC

Until Bartók and Kodály's research, **Hungarian folk music** (*Magyar népzene*) was identified with Gypsy bands in cafés, whose popular songs were influenced by the stirring *verbunk* (recruiting tunes) of the Rákóczi wars; and Austrian music – the sort of thing that Brahms and Liszt made into Hungarian Dances, and is still heard in Budapest restaurants. Bartók and Kodály were more excited by what the former called "Old Style" music: simple pentatonic (5-note) tunes stretching back to the days when Magyar tribes roamed the banks of the Don and Volga, where similar music has been handed down and recorded by ethno-musicologists.

In Hungary today, folk music has little connection with rural communities, whose taste in music (as in other things) has been transformed by urban influences, television and radio. Folk music and village life are still closely linked **in Transylvania**, however, which was seen as a repository of Magyar traditions even in Bartók's day, particularly the Kalotoság and Mezőseg regions near the city of Cluj, and the Csángó districts of the eastern Carpathians. In Hungary, by contrast, Magyar folk music has enjoyed a revival in towns and cities thanks to the **Tánchás**. These dance houses are very popular with young people interested in traditional music and dances – mostly from Hungary and Transylvania, but also from the "South Slavs", Slovenia and Bulgaria.

RECORDINGS

Good quality **records and tapes** produced by *Hungaroton* retail for half or a third of what you'd pay abroad, which makes it well worth rooting through *zeneművesbolt* shops. After Western and Hungarian **pop**, the bulk of their stock consists of **classical music**. A full discography of the works of Liszt, Bartók and Kodály, directors like Dohnányi and Doráti, and contemporary Hungarian soloists and singers would fill a catalogue; and the following recordings (on tape or vinyl, sometimes in boxed sets with an English commentary) are merely an introduction to the equally wide field of Hungarian **folk music**.

VII. Magyarországi Tánchás Találkozó. A great mixture of dances, ballads and instrumental pieces from all over, recorded at the Seventh Dance House Festival in 1988. One of a series (MK 18152) – the Tenth Dance House Festival collection (MK 18190) is also especially good.

Magyar népzene 3. (Hungarian folk music). A 4-disc set of field recordings covering the whole range of folk music – Old and New Style songs, instrumental and occasional music – that's probably the best overall introduction. In the West, the discs are marketed as "Folk Music of Hungary Vol.1".

Magyar hangszeres népzene. (Hungarian Instrumental Folk Music). A very good 3-disc set of field recordings of village and Gypsy bands, including lots of solos (Hungaroton LPX 18045-47).

Muzsikás. Beautiful arrangements of traditional ballads by the Muzsikás group and Márta Sebestyén, Hungary's leading Tánchás singer. Highly recommended (Hannibal HNBL 1330).

The Prisoner's Song. More haunting songs by Márta and Muzsikás, released abroad on the Hannibal label (HNBL 1341).

Bonchidától Bonchidáig. The Kalamajka Ensemble, another Tánchás group, plays Transylvanian and Csángó ballads and dances (Hungaroton MK 18135).

Este a Gyimesbe Jártam. Music from the Csángó region performed by János Zerkula and Regina Fikó; sparser, sadder and more discordant than other Transylvanian music (Hungaroton MK 18130).

Tánchási muzsika (Music from the Tánchás). A double album of the Sebö Ensemble playing Tánchás music from various regions of Hungary. Wild and exciting rhythms (Hungaroton SPLX 18031-32).

Jánosi Együttes (Jánosi Ensemble). Another young group, performing "authentic" versions of some of the folk tunes that Bartók borrowed in his compositions. A record that makes a bridge between classical and folk music (Hungaroton SPLX 18103).

Serbian Music from South Hungary played by the Vujicsics Ensemble. More complex tunes than most Magyar folk music, with a distinct Balkan influence (Hannibal HNBL 1310).

LANGUAGE

Hungarian is a unique, complex and subtle tongue, classified as belonging to the Finno-Ugric linguistic group, which means that it's totally unlike any other language that you're likely to know. Its closest (though still distant) relatives are Finnish and the Siberian Chuvash language, although odd grammatical structures and words from Turkish have crept in, together with some German, English and (a few) Russian neologisms.

Consequently, foreigners aren't really expected to speak Hungarian, and natives are used to (but don't honestly appreciate) being addressed in **German**, the *lingua franca* of tourism. It's understood by older people – particularly in Transdanubia – and by many students and professional types, besides virtually everyone around the Balaton or in tourist offices. For a brief visit it's probably easier to brush up on some German for your means of communication, but a few basic Magyar phrases can make all the difference. However, **English** is gaining ground rapidly, particularly in schools and colleges, while French or **Italian** might also be understood in tourist areas or educated circles.

In addition to the following list of basic phrases, you'll find a detailed food glossary and a selection of basic words pertaining to transport in *Basics*. Berlitz's *Hungarian for Travellers* has an even wider range of phrases. If you're prepared to seriously study the language, *Colloquial Hungarian* (Routledge UK/US) is the best available book. As a supplement, invest in the handy little *Angol–Magyar/Magyar–Angol Kisszótár* dictionaries; available from bookshops in Hungary.

BASIC GRAMMAR AND PRONUNCIATION

Although its rules are fiendishly complicated, it's worth describing a few features of **Hungarian grammar**, albeit imperfectly. Hungarian is an agglutinating language – in other words, its vocabulary is built upon **root-words**, which are modified in various ways to express different ideas and nuances. Instead of prepositions – "to", "from", "in", etc – Hungarian uses **suffixes**, or tags added to the ends of genderless **nouns**. The change in suffix is largely determined by the noun's context: for example, (the) book = *könyv*, (give me the) book = *könyveket*, (in the) book = *könyvben*, (to the) book = *könyvnek*. It is also affected by complicated rules of vowel harmony (which you're bound to get wrong, so don't worry about them!). Most of the nouns in the vocabulary section below are in the subject form – that is, without suffixes. In Hungarian, **"the"** is *a* (before a word beginning with a consonant) or *az* (preceding a vowel); the word for **"a/an"** is *egy* (which also means "one").

Plurals are indicated by endings such as *-ek*, *-ok* or *–ak*, but *not* when qualified by a number: eg *emberek* means "men", but "two men" is *ket ember* (using the singular form of the noun).

Adjectives precede the noun (*a piros ház* = the red house), adopting suffixes to form the comparative (*jó* = good; *jobb* = better), plus the prefix *leg* to signify the superlative (*legjobb* = the best).

Negatives are usually formed by placing the word *nem* before the verb. *Ez* (this), *ezek* (these), *az* (that) and *azok* (those) are the **demonstratives**.

PRONUNCIATION

Achieving passably good **pronunciation**, rather than grammar, is the first priority (see the box on p.340 for general guidelines). **Stress** almost invariably falls on the first syllable of a word and all letters are spoken, although in sentences, the tendency is to slur words together. Vowel sounds are greatly affected by the bristling **accents** (that actually distinguish separate letters) which, together with the "double letters" *cs, gy, ly, ny, sz, ty,* and *zs*, give the Hungarian **alphabet** its formidable appearance.

HUNGARIAN WORDS AND PHRASES

BASICS

Do you speak . . .	*beszél . . .*	good day	*jó napot*
English	*angolul*	good evening	*jó estét*
German	*németül*	good night	*jó éjszakát*
French	*franciaul*	how are you?	*hogy vagy?*
yes – OK	*igen – jó*	how are you? (more formal)	*hogy van?*
no/not	*nem*	could you speak more	*elmondaná*
I (don't) understand	*(nem) értem*	slowly?	*lassabban?*
please–excuse me	*kérem—bocsánat*	what do you call this?	*mi a neve ennek?*
two beers, please	*két sört kérek*	please write it down	*kérem, írja ezt le*
thank you (very much)	*köszönöm (szépen)*	today – tomorrow	*ma – holnap*
you're welcome	*szívesen*	the day after tomorrow	*holnapután*
hello/goodbye (informal)	*szia*	yesterday	*tegnap*
goodbye	*viszontlátásra*	the day before yesterday	*tegnapelűtt*
see you later	*viszlát*	in the morning – in the	*reggel – este*
I wish you . . . (formally)	*. . . kívánok*	evening	
good morning	*jó reggelt*	at noon – at midnight	*délben – éjfélkor*

QUESTIONS AND REQUESTS

Legyen szíves (Would you be so kind") is the polite formula for attracting someone's attention. Hungarian has numerous interrogative modes whose subtleties elude foreigners, so it's best to use the simple *van?* ("is there?"/"is it?"), to which the reply might be *nincs* or *azok nincsenek* ("it isn't"/"there aren't any"). Waiters and shop assistants often rely upon the laconic *tessék?*, meaning "What do you want?," "go ahead" or "next." *Kaphatok . . . ?* ("Can I have . . . ?") is politer, but less widely used than *Szeretnék . . .* ("I'd like . . ."); in restaurants you can also order with *Kérem, hozzon . . .* ("Please bring me . . ."); *Kérem, adjon azt* ("Please give me that"); *Egy ilyet kérek* ("I'll have one of those"); or simply . . . *kérek* (". . . please").

I'd like/we'd like	*Szeretnék/szeretnénk*	It's too expensive	*Ez nagyon drága*
Where is/are . . . ?	*Hol van / vannak . . ?*	anything cheaper?	*van valami olcsóbb?*
Take me to . . .	*Vigyen kérem a . . .*	a student discount?	*van diák kedvezmény?*
Hurry up!	*Siessen!*	Is everything	*Ebben minden*
How much is it?	*Mennyibe kerül?*	included?	*szerepel?*
per night	*egy éjszakára*	I asked for . . .	*Én . . . -t rendeltem*
per week	*egy hétre*	The bill please	*Kérem a számlát*
a single room	*egyágyas szobát*	We're paying	*Külön-külön*
a double room	*kétágyas szobát*	separately	*kívanunk fizetni*
hot (cold) water	*meleg (hideg) víz*	what? – why?	*mi? – miert?*
a shower	*egy zuhany*	when? – who?	*mikor? – ki?*

SOME SIGNS

entrance – exit	*bejárat – kijárat*	room for rent	*szoba kiadó*
arrival	*érkezés*		(or *Zimmer frei*)
departure	*indulás*	hospital	*kórház*
open – closed	*nyitva – zárva*	pharmacy	*gyógyszertár*
free admission	*szabad belépés*	(local) police	*(kerületi) Rendőrség*
women's – men's	*női – férfi mosdó* (or *WC -*	caution/beware	*vigyázat!*
toilet	"Vait-say")	no smoking	*tilos a dohányzás*
shop – market	*bolt – piac*	no bathing	*tilos a fürdés*

DIRECTIONS

Where's the . . . ?	hol van a . . . ?	Do I have to change	át kell szállnom
campsite	kemping	for . . .?	. . .-be?
hotel	szálloda	towards	felé
railway station	vasútállomás	on the right (left)	jobbra (balra)
bus station	buszállomás	straight ahead	egyenesen előre
(bus or train) stop	megálló	(over) there – here	ott – itt
Is it near (far)?	közel (távol) van?	Where are you going?	Hova megy?
Which bus goes to . . . ?	Melyik busz megy . . .-ra/re	Is that on the way to . . .?	Az a . . . úton?
a one-way ticket to . . .	egy jegyet kérek . . .	I want to get out at . . .	le akarok szállni. . .
please	-ra/re egy útra	please stop here	itt álljon meg
a return ticket to . . .	egy retur jegyet . . .-ra/re	I'm lost	eltévedtem

DESCRIPTIONS AND REACTIONS

and	és	good	jó	quick	gyors	ugly	csúnya
or	vagy	bad	rossz	slow	lassú	Take your	ne fogdoss!
nothing	semmi	better	jobb	now	most	hands off me!	
perhaps	talán	big	nagy	later	később	Help!	Segitség!
very	nagyon	small	kicsi	beautiful	szép	I'm ill	beteg vagyok

TIME

Luckily, the 24-hour clock is used for timetables, but on cinema programmes you may see notations like $1/44$, $3/44$, etc. These derive from the spoken expression of time which, as in German, makes reference to the hour approaching completion. For example 3:30 is expressed as *fél negy* – "half (on the way to) four"; 3:45 – *háromnegyed negy* ("three quarters on the way to four"); 6:15 – *negyed hét* ("one quarter towards seven"), etc. However, ". . . o'clock" is . . . *óra*, rather than referring to the hour ahead. Duration is expressed by the suffixes *-tól* ("from") and *ig* ("to"); minutes are *perc;* to ask the time, say "*Hány óra?*"

NUMBERS AND DAYS

1	egy	20	húsz	900	kilencszáz
2	kettő	21	huszonegy	1000	egyezer
3	három	30	harminc	half	fél
4	négy	40	negyven	a quarter	negyed
5	öt	50	ötven	a dozen	egy tucat
6	hat	60	hatvan	each	darab
7	hét	70	hetven	Sunday	vasárnap
8	nyolc	80	nyolcvan	Monday	hétfő
9	kilenc	90	kilencven	Tuesday	kedd
10	tíz	100	száz	Wednesday	szerda
11	tizenegy	101	százegy	Thursday	csütörtök
12	tizenkettő	150	százötven	Friday	péntek
13	tizenhárom	200	kettőszáz	Saturday	szombat
14	tizennégy	300	háromszáz	on Monday	hetfőn
15	tizenöt	400	négyszáz	on Tuesday	kedden etc.
16	tizenhat	500	ötszáz	day	nap
17	tizenhét	600	hatszáz	week	hét
18	tizennyolc	700	hétszáz	month	hónap
19	tizenkilenc	800	nyolcszáz	year	év

PRONUNCIATION

A o as in hot
Á a as in father
B b as in best
C ts as in bats
CS ch as in church
D d as in dust
E e as in yet
É ay as in say
F f as in fed
G g as in go
GY di as in medium, or d as in due
H h as in hat
I ee as in feet
Í ee as in see, but longer
J y as in yes

K k as in sick
L l as in leap
LY y as in yes
M m as in mud
N n as in not
NY ni as in onion
O aw as in saw, but shorter
Ó aw as in awe, with the tongue kept high
Ö ur as in fur, but without any "r" sound
Ő ur as in fur, as above, but with the lips tightly rounded
P p as in sip
R r pronounced with the tip of the tongue

S sh as in shop
SZ s as in so
T t as in sit
TY tty as in prettier, said quickly
U u as in pull
Ú oo as in food
Ü u as in the German "unter"
Ű u as above, but longer and with the lips tightly rounded
V v as in vat
W v as in "Valkman," "vhiskey" or "WC' (vait-say)
Z z as in zero
ZS s as in measure

HUNGARIAN TERMS: A GLOSSARY

ABC national chain of supermarkets.

ALFÖLD plain; it usually means the Great Plain (*Nagyalföld*) rather than the Little Plain (*Kisalföld*) in northwestern Hungary.

ÁLLATKERT zoo.

ÁRUHÁZ department store.

AUTÓBUSZÁLLOMÁS bus station.

ÁVO the dreaded secret police of the Rákosi era, renamed the *ÁVH* in 1949.

BARLANG cave; the most impressive stalactite caves are in the Aggteleki karst region.

BELVÁROS inner town or city, typically characterized by Baroque or Neoclassical architecture.

BÜFÉ snack bar.

BOROZÓ wine bar.

CALVINISM the Reformed (*Református*) faith, which established itself in Hungary during the sixteenth century.

CASTRUM (Latin) a Roman fortification.

CIGÁNY Gypsy (in Hungarian); hence *Cigánytelep*, a Gypsy settlement; and *Cigányzene*, Gypsy music.

CSÁRDA inn; nowadays, a restaurant with rustic decor.

CSÁRDÁS traditional wild dance to violin music.

CSIKÓS (plural *csikósok*) *puszta* horse herdsman; a much romanticized figure of the nineteenth century.

DOMB hill; *Rózsadomb*, "Rose Hill" in Budapest.

DJAMI or **DZAMI** mosque.

DUNA the River Danube.

ERDÉLY Transylvania; for centuries a part of Hungary, its loss to Romania in 1920 still rankles.

ERDŐ forest, wood.

ÉTTEREM restaurant.

FALU village; **FALUKUTATÓ** "Village Explorers" who investigated rural life and pressed for reforms in the countryside during the 1930s.

FOGADÓ inn.

FORINT (*Ft*) Hungarian unit of currency.

FŐ UTCA main street.

FŐ TÉR main square.

FORRÁS natural spring.

FÜRDŐ public baths, often fed by thermal springs.

GYÓGYFÜRDŐ mineral baths with therapeutic properties.

HAJDÚK cattle-drovers turned outlaws, who later settled near Debrecen in the **HAJDÚSÁG** region.

HAJÓ boat.

HAJÓÁLLOMÁS boat landing stage.

HALÁSZCSÁRDA literally "Fisherman's Inn".

HALÁSZKERT literally "Fisherman's Garden".

HÉV commuter train to/from Budapest.

HÁZ house.

HEGY hill or low mountain (pl. **HEGYSÉG**).

HÍD bridge; *Lánchíd*, the "Chain Bridge" in Budapest.

HONVÉD Hungarian army.

IFJÚSÁGI SZÁLLÓ youth hostel.

ISKOLA school.

ITALBOLT "drink shop", or a village bar.

KÁPOLNA chapel.

KAPU gate.

KASTÉLY fortified manor or small castle.

KERT garden, park.

KERÜLET (*ker.*) district.

KÖRÚT literally ring, normally a boulevard around the city centre. Some cities have semi-circular "Great" and "Small" boulevards (**NAGYKÖRÚT** and **KISKÖRÚT**) surrounding their Belváros.

KÖRÚT (*krt.*) literally "ring", a boulevard around the city centre.

KÖZ alley, lane; also used to define geographical regions, eg. the "Mud land" (*Sárköz*) bordering the Danube.

KÚT well or fountain.

LAKÓTELEP high-rise apartment buildings.

LÁNGOS a popular snack made of deep-fried batter.

LÉPCSŐ alley with steps ascending a hillside.

LIGET park, grove or wood.

LIMES (Latin) fortifications along the Danube, marking the limit of Roman territory.

LOVARDA riding school.

MAGYAR Hungarian (pronounced "*Mod*-yor"). Also **MAGYARORSZÁG**, Hungary.

MALÉV Hungarian national airline.

MÁV Hungarian national rail.

MDF (*Magyar Demokrátia Forum*) Hungarian Democratic Forum; the right-of-centre party that currently governs Hungary.

MEGÁLLÓ a railway station or bus stop.

MEGYE county; originally established by King Stephen to extend his authority over the Magyar tribes.

MIHRAB prayer niche in a mosque, indicating the direction of Mecca.

MSzMP (*Magyar Szocialista Munkáspárt*) the Hungarian Communist Party.

MŰEMLÉK historic monument, protected building.

MŰVELŐDESI HÁZ community arts and social centre; literally, a "Cultural House".

NYILAS "Arrow Cross"; Hungarian fascist movement.

NYITVA open.

OTTOMANS founders of the Turkish empire, which included central Hungary during the sixteenth and seventeenth centuries.

PALOTA palace; *Püspök-palota*, a Bishop's residence.

PÁLYAUDVAR (*pu.*) rail terminus.

PANZIÓ pension.

PIAC outdoor market.

PINCE cellar; a **BOR-PINCE** contains and serves wine.

PUSZTA another name for the Great Plain, coined when the region was a wilderness.

RAKPART embankment or quay.

ROM ruined building; sometimes set in a garden with stonework finds, a **ROMKERT**.

SÉTÁNY "walk" or promenade.

SKANZEN outdoor ethnographic museum.

SÖRÖZŐ beer hall.

STRAND beach, or any area for sunbathing or swimming.

SZÁLLÓ or **SZÁLLODA** hotel.

SZENT saint.

SZIGET island.

SZOBA KIADÓ room to let.

TANÁCS council.

TANÁCSKÖZTARSASÁG, the "Republic of Councils" or Soviets, which ruled Hungary in 1919.

TÁNCHÁZ venue for Hungarian folk music and dance.

TEMETŐ cemetery.

TEMPLOM church.

TÉR square; **TERE** in the possessive case, as in *Hősök tere*, "Heroes' Square".

TEREM hall.

TÓ lake.

TORONY tower.

TÜRBE tomb or mausoleum of a Muslim dignitary.

UDVAR courtyard.

UTCA (*u.*) road or street.

ÚT avenue; in the possessive case, **ÚTJA** – eg *Mártírok útja*, "Martyrs' Avenue"

VÁR castle.

VÁROS town; may be divided into an inner Belváros, a lower-lying *Alsóváros* and a modern *Újváros* section. Also **VÁROSKÖZPONT**, the town centre.

VÁSÁRCSARNOK market hall.

VASÚTÁLLOMÁS train station.

VENDÉGLŐ a type of restaurant.

VÖLGY valley; *Hűvösvölgy*, "Cool Valley".

ZÁRVA closed.

ZSIDÓ Jew or Jewish.

ZSINAGÓGA synagogue.

INDEX

DIRECT ORDERS IN THE USA

Title	ISBN	Price
Amsterdam	1858280869	$13.59
Andalucia	185828094X	$14.95
Australia	1858280354	$18.95
Barcelona & Catalunya	1858281067	$17.99
Berlin	1858280338	$13.99
Brazil	1858281024	$15.95
Brittany & Normandy	1858281261	$14.95
Bulgaria	1858280478	$14.99
California	1858280907	$14.95
Canada	185828130X	$14.95
Classical Music on CD	185828113X	$19.95
Corsica	1858280893	$14.95
Crete	1858281326	$14.95
Cyprus	185828032X	$13.99
Czech & Slovak Republics	185828029X	$14.95
Egypt	1858280753	$17.95
England	1858280788	$16.95
Europe	185828077X	$18.95
Florida	1858280109	$14.95
France	1858281245	$16.95
Germany	1858281288	$17.95
Greece	1858281318	$16.95
Greek Islands	1858281636	$14.95
Guatemala & Belize	1858280451	$14.95
Holland, Belgium & Luxembourg	1858280877	$15.95
Hong Kong & Macau	1858280664	$13.95
Hungary	1858281237	$14.95
India	1858281040	$22.95
Ireland	1858280958	$16.95
Italy	1858280311	$17.95
Kenya	1858280435	$15.95
London	1858291172	$12.95
Mediterranean Wildlife	0747100993	$15.95
Malaysia, Singapore & Brunei	1858281032	$16.95
Morocco	1858280400	$16.95
Nepal	185828046X	$13.95
New York	1858280583	$13.95
Nothing Ventured	0747102082	$19.95
Pacific Northwest	1858280923	$14.95
Paris	1858281253	$12.95
Poland	1858280346	$16.95
Portugal	1858280842	$15.95
Prague	1858281229	$14.95
Provence & the Côte d'Azur	1858280230	$14.95
Pyrenees	1858280931	$15.95
St Petersburg	1858281334	$14.95
San Francisco	1858280826	$13.95
Scandinavia	1858280397	$16.99
Scotland	1858280834	$14.95
Sicily	1858280370	$14.99
Spain	1858280818	$16.95
Thailand	1858280168	$15.95
Tunisia	1858280656	$15.95
Turkey	1858280885	$16.95
Tuscany & Umbria	1858280915	$15.95
USA	185828080X	$18.95
Venice	1858280362	$13.99
Wales	1858280966	$14.95
West Africa	1858280141	$24.95
More Women Travel	1858280982	$14.95
World Music	1858280176	$19.95
Zimbabwe & Botswana	1858280419	$16.95

Rough Guide Phrasebooks

Czech	1858281482	$5.00
French	185828144X	$5.00
German	1858281466	$5.00
Greek	1858281458	$5.00
Italian	1858281431	$5.00
Spanish	1858281474	$5.00

Rough Guides are available from all good bookstores, but can be obtained directly in the USA and Worldwide (except the UK*) from Penguin:

Charge your order by Master Card or Visa (US$15.00 minimum order): call 1-800-253-6476; or send orders, with complete name, address and zip code, and list price, plus $2.00 shipping and handling per order to: Consumer Sales, Penguin USA, PO Box 999 – Dept #17109, Bergenfield, NJ 07621. No COD. Prepay foreign orders by international money order, a cheque drawn on a US bank, or US currency. No postage stamps are accepted. All orders are subject to stock availability at the time they are processed. Refunds will be made for books not available at that time. Please allow a minimum of four weeks for delivery.

The availability and published prices quoted are correct at the time of going to press but are subject to alteration without prior notice. Titles currently not available outside the UK will be available by July 1995. Call to check.

* For UK orders, see separate price list

DIRECT ORDERS IN THE UK

Title	ISBN	Price
Amsterdam	1858280869	£7.99
Andalucia	185828094X	£8.99
Australia	1858280354	£12.99
Barcelona & Catalunya	1858281067	£8.99
Berlin	1858280338	£8.99
Brazil	1858281024	£9.99
Brittany & Normandy	1858281261	£8.99
Bulgaria	1858280478	£8.99
California	1858280907	£9.99
Canada	185828130X	£10.99
Classical Music on CD	185828113X	£12.99
Corsica	1858280893	£8.99
Crete	1858281326	£8.99
Cyprus	185828032X	£8.99
Czech & Slovak Republics	185828029X	£8.99
Egypt	1858280753	£10.99
England	1858280788	£9.99
Europe	185828077X	£14.99
Florida	1858280109	£8.99
France	1858280508	£9.99
Germany	1858281288	£11.99
Greece	1858281318	£9.99
Greek Islands	1858281636	£8.99
Guatemala & Belize	1858280451	£9.99
Holland, Belgium & Luxembourg	1858280877	£9.99
Hong Kong & Macau	1858280664	£8.99
Hungary	1858281237	£8.99
India	1858281040	£13.99
Ireland	1858280958	£9.99
Italy	1858280311	£12.99
Kenya	1858280435	£9.99
London	1858291172	£8.99
Mediterranean Wildlife	0747100993	£7.95
Malaysia, Singapore & Brunei	1858281032	£9.99
Morocco	1858280400	£9.99
Nepal	185828046X	£8.99
New York	1858280583	£8.99
Nothing Ventured	0747102082	£7.99
Pacific Northwest	1858280923	£9.99
Paris	1858281253	£7.99
Poland	1858280346	£9.99
Portugal	1858280842	£9.99
Prague	185828015X	£7.99
Provence & the Côte d'Azur	1858280230	£8.99
Pyrenees	1858280931	£8.99
St Petersburg	1858281334	£8.99
San Francisco	1858280826	£8.99
Scandinavia	1858280397	£10.99
Scotland	1858280834	£8.99
Sicily	1858280370	£8.99
Spain	1858280818	£9.99
Thailand	1858280168	£8.99
Tunisia	1858280656	£8.99
Turkey	1858280885	£9.99
Tuscany & Umbria	1858280915	£8.99
USA	185828080X	£12.99
Venice	1858280362	£8.99
Wales	1858280966	£8.99
West Africa	1858280141	£12.99
More Women Travel	1858280982	£9.99
World Music	1858280176	£14.99
Zimbabwe & Botswana	1858280419	£10.99

Rough Guide Phrasebooks

Czech	1858281482	£3.50
French	185828144X	£3.50
German	1858281466	£3.50
Greek	1858281458	£3.50
Italian	1858281431	£3.50
Spanish	1858281474	£3.50

Rough Guides are available from all good bookstores, but can be obtained directly in the UK* from Penguin by contacting:

Penguin Direct, Penguin Books Ltd, Bath Road, Harmondsworth, West Drayton, Middlesex UB7 0DA; or telephone our credit line on 0181-899 4036 (9am–5pm) and ask for Penguin Direct. Visa, Access and Amex accepted. Delivery will normally be within 14 working days. Penguin Direct ordering facilities are only available in the UK.

The availability and published prices quoted are correct at the time of going to press but are subject to alteration without prior notice.

For USA and international orders, see separate price list

¿Qué pasa?

WHAT'S HAPPENING?
A NEW ROUGH GUIDES SERIES –
ROUGH GUIDE PHRASEBOOKS

Rough Guide Phrasebooks
represent a complete shakeup of
the phrasebook format. Handy
and pocket sized, they work like
a dictionary to get you straight to
the point. With clear guidelines
on pronunciation, dialogues for
typical situations, and tips on
cultural issues, they'll have you
speaking the language quicker
than any other phrasebook.

~ Now Available ~
Czech, French, German, Greek,
Italian, Spanish

~ Coming Soon ~
Mexican Spanish, Polish, Portuguese,
Thai, Turkish, Vietnamese

You **are**
A STUDENT

You **travel**
THE WORLD

You **want**
TO SAVE MONEY

Here's
how

The International
Student Identity Card

Available at Student Travel Offices Worldwide.

Entitles you to discounts and special services worldwide.